IRAN
THE CRISIS OF
DEMOCRACY

Fakhreddin Azimi is Professor of History at the University of Connecticut and an internationally recognized scholar of modern Iranian history. His most recent book is *The Quest for Democracy in Iran: a Century of Struggle against Authoritarian Rule* (2008).

Praise for *Iran: The Crisis of Democracy*

'It is a penetrating study of the political structure of Iran and an explanation of the reasons for which attempts to create a strong executive failed. The book is based on an exhaustive investigation of the available sources; it is a significant contribution not only to our knowledge of modern Iranian history but also to our understanding of political sociology.'   Albert H. Hourani

'Undoubtedly the most illuminating and outstanding work of research on developments in Iran between 1941 and 1953.'   Iraj Afshar, *Ayandeh*

'a wide-ranging, carefully documented analysis ... the thoroughness and detail of the research make this an indispensable introduction for every student of the period.'
Dr John Gurney, Emeritus Fellow of Wadham College,
Oxford University

'one of the best books written on Iranian political history'
Mark Lytle, *Middle East Journal*

'provides refreshing and valuable analysis ... essential reading for all those wishing to understand the crux of the Iranian revolution.'
A. Ehteshami, *International Affairs*

'A lucid account of an important period in the history of modern Iran which is based on solid scholarship and sound judgement.'
Said Amir Arjomand, Professor of Sociology,
State University of New York, Stony Brook

'Excellent ... an impressive piece of scholarship.'
James Piscatori, University Lecturer in Islamic Politics,
Oxford University

IRAN

THE CRISIS OF DEMOCRACY

From the Exile of Reza Shah
to the Fall of Musaddiq

Fakhreddin Azimi

I.B. TAURIS

LONDON · NEW YORK

New paperback edition published in 2009 by I.B.Tauris & Co Ltd
6 Salem Road, London W2 4BU
175 Fifth Avenue, New York NY 10010
www.ibtauris.com

Distributed in the United States and Canada Exclusively by Palgrave Macmillan
175 Fifth Avenue, New York NY 10010

First published in hardback in 1989 by I.B.Tauris & Co Ltd

ISBN: 978 1 86064 980 6

A full CIP record for this book is available from the British Library
A full CIP record is available from the Library of Congress

Library of Congress Catalog Card Number: available

Printed and bound in India by Rakesh Press

Contents

Preface to the Paperback Edition

Since this book was first published, more archival and primary sources on the period under study have become available and a considerable amount of secondary literature has appeared, providing additional details or shedding further light on certain issues upon which I have touched. For instance, the letter Ayatullah Kashani allegedly sent to Prime Minister Musaddiq on the eve of the overthrow of his government (referred to on page 332) can now with greater certainty be dismissed as a forgery or hoax. Otherwise, what has been written or has come to light since 1989 has not significantly affected the central arguments of the book and in many respects has complemented or confirmed them. Just to give one example: it was widely-maintained that Musaddiq's move to dissolve the 17th Majlis through a referendum was an avoidable mistake that precipitated his overthrow. In my view, however, he had essentially no real choice but to do so; the release in 2000 of the 'Secret History' of the coup of 1953, written by one of its architects, Donald Wilber, which reveals a detailed CIA–MI6 plan to bribe parliamentary deputies and to use the Majlis not only to engineer Musaddiq's overthrow but also to give the process a veneer of legitimacy, has vindicated my judgement. I have made use of this document, and other newly available sources, in a separate study of the domestic opposition to Musaddiq, which complements chapters 18 to 20 of the present book. (See supplementary bibliography). This later treatment of the subject has to some extent extenuated the need for a detailed revision of this book; I have corrected a number of factual or typographical errors and, whenever possible, imprecisions of statement.

Contrary to the assumptions of some readers, the title of the book does not imply that I considered the political arrangements in Iran during the period under study to have been in all respects an adequately functioning democracy. The title was meant to convey the problems and predicaments permeating the processes of governance and the political culture of the period. The prevailing sense of crisis reflected fundamental questions on how far Iranians as a nation were masters of their own destiny; to what extent they were a sovereign people able to rule themselves through constitutional representative institutions; how effective and meaningful such institutions were; how the imperatives of governmental effectiveness, the rule of law, and accountability could be successfully reconciled; and how viable *constitutional* monarchy was as a framework of rule.

I concentrated primarily on exploring why and how parliamentary institutions and constitutional structures in the period did not function adequately or smoothly. At the same time I attempted to convey some sense of the complexity, dynamism and richness of the evolving constitutional politics. I did not intend to write a comprehensive history of the period covering society, economy and culture. I was also constrained to forego any in-depth discussion of the dynamics of social, associational and civic life in this period, which I intended to explore in future studies.

Naturally, if I were to write this book now I would do so differently. The chronological narrative structure of the book should not, however, be taken to imply that I was unconcerned with thematic issues or questions. I tried to combine, albeit implicitly, the narrative account with an analytical problem-oriented approach, and sought to provide explanations that were both causal and interpretive. It should be borne in mind that this book, whatever its weaknesses, strengths, faults or merits, was the first detailed archival study of one of the most crucial periods in modern Iranian history – a period that warrants more work and more thorough exploration. I am gratified by the responses of many readers who have found this modest contribution helpful in making sense of the tangled politics of an era that continues to evoke nostalgia among many Iranians – those who lived through it, or have immersed themselves in its history, or who look to it as an era that demonstrated the potential for democratic politics in the country. I can also hope that my work remains of some assistance to other scholars who, in covering the same ground, will surely transcend its limitations. I would like to thank the editorial staff of I.B.Tauris, particularly Liz Friend-Smith, for their interest, support and cooperation while the paperback edition of this work was in process.

Fakhreddin Azimi
Storrs, Connecticut

Note on Transliteration

The system of transliteration used in this work is a modified version of that used by IJMES; the common spelling of names such as Reza and Tehran has been retained; diacritical marks have been omitted, with the exception of *ayn* and *hamza* (indicated by a prime) where they appear in the middle of the word.

Abbreviations

AIOC	Anglo-Iranian Oil Company
BBC	British Broadcasting Corporation
FO	The British Foreign Office
HMG	His/Her Majesty's Government
IJMES	International Journal of Middle Eastern Studies
IOR	India Office Records
MAIS	Military Attaché's Intelligence Summary
MEJ	Middle East Journal
MES	Middle Eastern Studies
NIOC	National Iranian Oil Company
NMF	National Movement Faction
UN	United Nations Organization
UWI	Union of Workers of Isfahan

Introduction

At the beginning of the twentieth century Iranian society bore few apparent signs of having emerged from the Middle Ages. A population of around 10 million, consisting primarily of peasants, herdsmen or nomadic tribesmen, inhabited a largely arid terrain. Only one-fifth of the inhabitants of the country lived in towns and cities, which were separated by vast distances and had no modern means of communication. A segmentary mode of life prevailed, which was imbued with deep-seated religio-traditional beliefs and sustained by entrenched primordial sentiments and sectional affiliations. A minimal government ruled virtually unchallenged, though it had few means of enforcing its dictates. The ruling Qajar dynasty intermittently introduced limited reforms but failed to create a state structure based on a standing army and having some degree of administrative competence.

Beneath the surface, however, the existing political arrangements had begun to prove incongruous with the steady process of social change. Increased contact with Europe and European ideas during the nineteenth century had begun to transform the traditional configuration of the Iranian polity. At the same time, repeated Anglo-Russian encroachments had continued to dislocate Iranian society and its economy. The challenge of the West had, above all, helped the emergence of a modern civic spirit. Those who had acquired some acquaintance with European culture gradually began to disseminate the ideas of scientific, social and economic progress, as necessary preconditions for overcoming vulnerability *vis-à-vis* foreign powers, and did not hesitate to criticize what they saw as the indigenous legacy of backwardness.

The government's limited reform measures, the arrival of the first outward manifestations of modernity – printing machines, the telegraph, telephone and electricity, and so on – as well as the establishment of modern educational institutions, although limited in scale, stimulated demands for further reforms, particularly in the political arena. Ideas critical of Qajar absolutism and advocating freedom and the rule of law were spread through a number of newspapers and pamphlets published abroad and smuggled into Iran, which were supplanted by many local 'nightly' newsletters (*shab-namih* – so named because they were distributed overnight). Various secret societies arose, with the aim of bringing about change, while a burgeoning nationalist consciousness began to capture the imagination of a growing number of the urban population. New literary trends emerged and the newly rediscovered pre-Islamic era of Iranian history served as a repository of nationalist mythology.

The accession of Fath Ali Shah Qajar (1797–1834) had marked the beginning of an era of significant territorial loss; henceforth, various international agreements detrimental to Iran were signed, concessions were awarded to foreign powers, and loans acquired from them which ensured the increasing dependency and vulnerability of the Iranian government. The continuing Anglo-Russian rivalry in Iran helped to intensify the fragility of the government without mitigating the arbitrary behaviour of the Shah and his subordinates. Lawlessness and insecurity in social, economic and political life gradually necessitated action aimed primarily at regulating the conduct of the government, setting limits to its authority and rendering it more accountable. Traditional strata, such as the guilds, and particularly the merchant class – who had strong ties with the *ulama* – had been adversely affected by the prevailing financial and economic strains and the general climate of lawlessness, and resented the protection and privileges accorded to their foreign rivals. The *ulama*, who acted as the mouthpiece of the merchants and were themselves alarmed at increasing foreign domination, began to voice their resentment and protests. Cumulative discontent paved the way for collective action aimed at bringing about change.

The initial intransigence of the government and its clumsy tactical errors emboldened the protestors; demands which were initially limited to calls for the establishment of a 'House of Justice' (*Adalat Khanih*) were broadened to include the setting up of a 'consultative assembly'. Inevitably, the essentially new vocabulary of political discourse deployed to articulate the demands for change was vague and subject to differing interpretations; this benefited the secular exponents of reform who were variously identified as constitutionalists (*mashrutih khahan*), liberals (*azadi khahan*) or nationalists (*milliyyun*). The changes demanded by them superseded the reforms initially advocated by the mullahs and religiously inclined merchants and guildsmen, without provoking immediate disagreement and disunity. The ailing Muzaffar ud-Din Shah submitted to pressure and on 5 August 1906 he issued a decree which heralded the new constitutional era in Iranian history. A National Consultative Assembly (*Majlis-i Shaura-yi Milli*) (hereafter referred to as the Majlis) was soon established and a Constitution promulgated.

From the outset Muzaffar ud-Din Shah's successor, Muhammad Ali Shah, was opposed to the Constitution; he was, however, forced to confirm formally that the government was constitutional (*mashrutih*), a fact previously only implicitly alluded to. He was also forced to sign the supplement to the Constitution, which together with the Constitution itself set out in detail the rights and duties of citizens, as well as those of the government and the Shah. Muhammad Ali Shah nevertheless continued with his efforts to undermine the fragile constitutional arrangements. The influential mullah Shaikh Fazlullah Nuri joined the ranks of the anti-constitutionalists, invoking Islam as the basis for his opposition to the Constitution, but met with the hostility of his own fellow *ulama*.

An assassination attempt on the Shah's life, however, gave the monarch the opportunity he had been seeking to launch a coup against the constitutionalists (June 1908). With the help of the Russians the Shah bombarded the Majlis and executed a number of leading constitutionalists. Eventually, growing widespread protests and the active resistance of regional constitutionalist forces brought about his overthrow. The re-established constitutional arrangements, however, encountered a number of domestic problems and external difficulties. In 1907, Britain and Russia signed an accord dividing Iran into two spheres of influence, thereby shaking the confidence of the constitutionalists. The continuing obstructive activities of the Russians and their refusal to evacuate the north-western areas of Iran, worsened the situation. Restoring order proved to be a major problem. There were few means of initiating urgently needed reforms. Money was in drastically short supply but the Majlis was adamantly opposed to seeking foreign loans.

The Majlis deputies were divided on many issues, but agreed on the absolute necessity of safeguarding Iranian sovereignty. The refusal of the Majlis to heed a Russian ultimatum to dismiss the American financial adviser, Morgan Shuster (1911) resulted in its suppression by the Bakhtiaris, who were then in control of the government. The efforts of the Russians and the British to engineer co-operative Cabinets were, however, consistently thwarted by the Majlis which, despite all its shortcomings, had become an effective forum for debating and defining the national interests of Iran and thus a means of nourishing the growing Iranian nationalist consciousness.

The outbreak of the First World War resulted in a further deterioration of the domestic political situation in Iran. The Russians and the British, on the one hand, and the Germans and the Ottomans, on the other, extended their conflict into Iran irrespective of its declared neutrality, and various regional movements challenged the enfeebled central government. The October Revolution of 1917 temporarily excluded the Russians from the Iranian political scene, and the British, now virtually unchallenged, tried by means of the Anglo-Persian Agreement of 1919 to transform Iran into a near protectorate. This attempt was thwarted by the Majlis. However, the inbuilt inefficiency of the Majlis and the inevitable fragility of the constitutional governments facilitated the bloodless coup of 1921 – led by the adventurous journalist-politician Sayyid Zia ud-Din Tabataba'i, and Reza Khan, an ambitious Cossack officer – and eventually paved the way for the abolition of the Qajar dynasty and the emergence of the authoritarian rule of Reza Shah Pahlavi (1925).

Reza Shah did not abolish the formal institutional and ceremonial framework of the parliamentary government, but his style of rule did not substantially differ from the traditional absolutist practice of the pre-constitutional era. During his rule, however, the structural prerequisites for the establishment of an effective form of government began to emerge. Irrespective of the manner in which most reforms were conceived or implemented, modernity assumed a degree of substance at this time: secular educational institutions were increasing in number, urbanization was rapidly spreading and a modern army and police ensured that order was established and the authority of the government recognized and feared. Roads, railways and other means of communication were constructed, industrial plants founded and the socio-cultural basis of Iranian nationalism consolidated.

Laying the foundations of a modern state was accomplished at the cost of suppressing political development and all manifestations of democratic aspirations. Modernization was perceived to be attainable only through autocratic measures and the suppression of representative institutions. Failure to broaden the socio-economic foundations of the government, to allow or encourage the formation of credible political parties, while relying on coercive means to ensure obedience and compliance and conduct the affairs of the state, was eventually bound to prove counterproductive. Reza Shah failed to create a credible impersonal state structure. His contemptuous and insensitive style of personal rule and his suspicion-ridden mind and crude political disposition effectively eliminated all those capable politicians he considered insufficiently servile. His rule did not bring about a political culture congenial with sustained democratic development. It obstructed the emergence of a body of able politicians possessing sufficient integrity, civic spirit and readiness to accept responsibility and be accountable for their actions. The incongruence between relatively rapid socio-economic change and the particular form of the prevailing autocratic political order had become increasingly evident. Such an anomaly was likely to result in a major crisis following the demise of the autocrat. The revived constitutional arrangements were likely to experience numerous problems in adjusting to the changing social circumstances.

The authoritarian rule of Reza Shah was terminated as a consequence of the Anglo-Soviet occupation of Iran in August–September 1941, and the political power which had previously been pre-empted by the Court was diffused. The political arrangements which replaced Reza Shah's regime were legitimized through the 'depersonalization' of the exercise of political power and constraints on its use arising largely from the re-establishment of parliamentary arrangements.[1] Although the perpetuation of the Pahlavi monarchy was not systematically challenged, the new regime tried to dissociate itself from the past both by invoking constitutionalism and by tolerating or even participating in criticisms of the past. From the moment that the fall of Reza Shah became certain many of those who had served him joined the ranks of his critics. The ruling elite quickly adapted itself to the new conditions, took up the cause of constitutionalism and, by holding Reza Shah responsible for dictatorship and everything condemnable in the past, managed to justify its own past and legitimize its new position.

The post-Reza Shah ruling elite was not, however, composed solely of his former servants. It also included men of influence who had previously been excluded from political activity. Such men now used their exclusion, non-collaboration or persecution in the past as proof of their integrity, genuine commitment to constitutionalism and consequent right to prominent positions in the new regime. Political power in the post-Reza Shah period was in the hands of a ruling elite which also included the new Shah, while the British, Russian and gradually the American embassies were also in a position to influence more effectively the outcome of events in Iran. Although the diffusion and depersonalization of political power was commonly taken to imply that the legislature, the executive and the judiciary were to be revitalized and were to assume their constitutionally defined authority, in practice there were many obstacles. In the case of the Majlis the problem arose from its underlying legal-procedural provisions as well as its place within the institutional-structural configuration of the body politic. In the case of both the monarchy and the executive, their formally defined authority was not commensurate with their actual share of power. The general political configuration of the ruling elite who administered, controlled or significantly influenced the operation of the state institutions was thus closely related to the form that the actual operation of parliamentary arrangements assumed and, ultimately, to the fate of constitutionalism. In order to elaborate these points, the main legal-procedural features and institutional-structural standing of the Majlis and the Cabinet will now be discussed, and the position of the monarchy *vis-à-vis* the parliamentary arrangements surveyed. Finally, the main characteristics of the ruling elite will be examined.

The Majlis: its main legal-procedural characteristics

The revitalization of the constitutional arrangements involved the effective but separate functioning of the legislature, the executive and the judiciary. According to the spirit of the Iranian Constitution, the Majlis was the cornerstone of constitutionalism. The Constitution, reflecting the anti-despotic spirit of the Constitutional Revolution as well as the influence of the Belgian and French constitutions on which it was based, had been drafted in such a way as legally to prevent the emergence of dictatorship.[2] This accounts for the lack of any practical provision or arrangemant in it for the dissolution of the Majlis, which was therefore in a very strong position. The fact that Shah simply bypassed the Constitution while preserving the façade of parliamentary arrangements left the legal potential of the Majlis intact. The disproportionately high degree of power constitutionally invested in the Majlis was originally intended to curb the excesses of the Crown, and to enable the Majlis not only to restrain the executive but also to control all governmental affairs. It was thought that a powerful Majlis would become a focus of national loyalty not easily susceptible to internal or external pressures. In practice, however, the power of the Majlis resulted in the impotence of the Cabinet.

Some leading constitutionalists had come to appreciate the intrinsic problems of the Iranian Constitution. Sayyid Hassan Taqizadih, for instance, had initially advocated the assumption by the Majlis of the role of an enlightened dictator as an ideal arrangement.[3] Having seen constitutional government in practice, however, he modified his views. Indeed he emphasized that the Constitution was defective without a provision for its revision; such a provision, according to him, had originally been envisaged but was not included in the text of the Constitution. He also pointed out the inability of the government to initiate a parliamentary recess, the absolute authority of the Majlis to reject or accept the credentials of deputies with or without reasonable argument, and above all, the role of the Majlis in the chronic instability of Cabinets. In Taqizadih's own words, 'no other factor indicating the chaotic condition of the country is as salient as the fact that in the course of 10 years between the establishment of parliamentarianism and now [1918] . . . 38 consecutive Cabinets have assumed office in Iran.'[4]

A further feature of the Majlis was its short life-span of two years. From the viewpoint of ensuring an effective government this was no doubt a liability, since it led to the even shorter life of Cabinets. A substantial part of the two-year term of each Majlis was spent on efforts by the deputies to reap the benefits of office and to procure their re-election. This was bound to have a disruptive impact on the opportunity of Cabinets. The provision of a short term for the Majlis was, however, understandable in terms of the spirit of the Constitution. The constitutionalists had hoped to impede the perpetuation of the political privileges of deputies. They had also tried to ensure that the deputies had frequent contact with the electorate and to prevent the inactivity and lethargy which might result from the assurance of a long period in office. The two-year term of each Majlis had also been left unchanged as it had not proved problematic during the reign of Reza Shah.

A number of other features characterizing the actual operation of the Majlis stemmed either from the Constitution or from the internal procedures of the Majlis. In view of their purely ceremonial nature in the time of Reza Shah, these had remained theoretically intact and thus could be easily revived. One such feature was the possibility of submitting frequent motions of interpellation, without any regard for the timetable of the Majlis. This could be done by one deputy or a group of deputies, against individual ministers, a number of ministers or the prime minister, who then had to attend the Majlis within a month, answer the interpellation and demand a vote of confidence, which if denied put an end to the life of the Cabinet. A deputy or a group of deputies who had put forward the motion of interpellation could spend many hours delivering speeches and elaborating the smallest points. Such prolonged speeches, which were publicized in the press, were generally radical in tone, and as such had a wide appeal. Through such speeches little-known deputies were transformed into national figures, adversaries were demoralized and an atmosphere created inside and outside the Majlis which did not encourage stable Cabinets.

Interpellation was a two-edged sword which could be used on the slightest pretext against any Cabinet. While ideally it was an instrument to prevent irregularities, put an end to ineffectiveness or mismanagement and stop dealings which bypassed the scrutiny of the Majlis, it was equally capable of preventing Cabinets from taking any major initiative, thus reducing their activities to mere tactics for survival.[5] The motion of interpellation was intended to protect the rights of opposition deputies, but in practice it was a strategic instrument in the hands of these deputies, the mere threat of which often debilitated even potentially effective Cabinets.

A further factor which had a significant impact on the operation of the Majlis was the principle of the quorum. A debate could only begin when, out of the deputies present in Tehran, at least two-thirds were in the Majlis. Three-quarters had to be present to enable a vote to be taken and a majority required more than half of those present to record votes of approval. This had been intended to prevent the approval of hasty and insufficiently backed bills and to provide the minority with the opportunity to hinder the imposition of Cabinets by the majority. In practice, however, it invariably impeded efficient legislation and the functioning of the Majlis. By withdrawing from the Majlis, a minority of one-quarter could easily paralyse it and delay important debates.

A number of further characteristics which effectively restricted the efficient operation of the Majlis arose from the position and functions of the Majlis committees and the procedures for handling draft laws submitted by the Cabinet. If a draft law was submitted to the Majlis without a procedure of urgency, it was immediately sent to a standing committee which would usually shelve it for a long time, if not forever. Procedures for the investigation of deputies' credentials occupied a substantial part of the life of each Majlis and enabled established members of the elite to exclude undesirable elements. Finally, although a measure of co-ordination, discipline and direction was provided by the Speaker of the Majlis, it remained to his discretion, as the British Ambassador Le Rougetel observed,

> [to] decide what question should be before the Chamber at any given moment, a tradition which itself gives further scope for lobbying and intrigue. It is therefore frequently impossible to foretell when any urgent measure which is theoretically before the Chamber will be debated.[6]

The Deputies: their characteristics and modes of behaviour

After the fall of Reza Shah, the 12th Majlis, which had served him for a period of over a year and a half, was not dissolved. This created a paradoxical situation since the Majlis, which was supposed to legitimize the new political arrangements, lacked a credible mandate since the deputies had been hand-picked on the orders of the ex-Shah. The same was true of the deputies of the succeeding Majlis, which could have no claim to be representative since its 'election' had been accomplished while Reza Shah was still in power.

A number of deputies tried to compensate for this situation by displaying – not necessarily insincerely – considerable concern for 'the public interest' and a desire to represent it. This involved criticizing and attacking both the past regime and the existing arrangements. Such deputies constituted the nucleus of a 'minority' which saw its task as resisting the 'majority' and exposing its activities to the public. While there was, as such, no harm in this, the problem was that both the 'majority' and the 'minority' were generally fluid, overlapping clusters of individual deputies, lacking any degree of genuine co-ordination based on a clear consensus on matters of principle and policy, and without any spirit of co-operation. The task of the 'majority' in the Iranian parliamentary division of labour was to form and maintain Cabinets, while the role of the 'minority' was to destabilize them – usually by mobilizing opposition inside the Majlis, among the dispirited members of the 'majority', and outside it. As long as the support of the 'majority' was somehow sustained, the Cabinets had no need to give up power. The 12th Majlis in its last few months, and its successors, displayed remarkably similar behaviour in the absence of overt coercion. When the ceremonial confirmation of government dictates was no longer considered to be the professional duty of a deputy rendered in exchange for the privilege and rewards of a seat in the Majlis, a wide range of other factors began to determine the actions of deputies, factors which were not conducive to sustaining parliamentary government. In the post-Reza Shah era, the deputies scarcely succeeded in living up to their self-proclaimed image as 'guardians of the nation's interests'. Intense factionalism and the parochial attitudes of the majority of deputies, as well as their inability adequately to understand their public duties and to put them before their private ends, were largely blamed for depriving the Iranian parliamentary arrangements of any meaningful content. The deputies, however, acted as they did because a number of internal, predominantly structural factors constrained their 'ability' to act differently. Furthermore, their 'opportunity' for acting differently was constrained by a wide range of structural factors external to the individuals themselves.[7]

Before determining his course of action, a deputy, like other members of the ruling elite, rationally calculated his own immediate and future interests as well as those of his family, friends, clients or affiliated groups, and the possible costs and benefits. More significantly, he was constrained by a number of structural factors such as ideology, beliefs and internalized value systems, which affected his behaviour. Only a small number of deputies held consistent ideological convictions, however, while the majority were staunch pragmatists whose rhetoric usually had little relevance to their actual behaviour. Most deputies, and indeed the bulk of the elite, were non-doctrinaire advocates of the existing pattern of stratification and modes of distribution of wealth and other privileges. Belief in the inviolability of private property, particularly the prevailing principles and practices of land ownership, and in the indispensability of the monarchy as the guardian of the traditional social and spiritual order of society, was shared by nearly all members of the elite. Such common concerns invariably conditioned their actions although they were not enough to provide the elite in general and the deputies in particular with any group cohesion, or to lead them towards identifying and promoting their broad collective interests.

The action – or inaction – of most deputies, and in fact of a large number of the ruling elite, was further constrained by other factors. Many deputies were men of 'weak' character, docile, indecisive, easily manipulated or susceptible to various temptations, as well as being incorrigible opportunists. On the whole, they lacked sufficient understanding of their civic responsibilities and the meaning of parliamentarianism. Many of them were unable to comprehend and identify national or public interests, or were incapable of distinguishing them from their own local or private concerns. Many of them were semi-literate men with neither a clear conception of their rights and duties, nor an adequate knowledge of the complexities of the economy or of socio-political problems. As Ali Dashti, a deputy in the 14th Majlis, put it:

> The majority of the present deputies are not versed in politics. They are mostly merchants and landowners who are not knowledgeable of political matters. It is therefore up to the government to have a policy and to have already decided the path it is to take.[8]

In addition to all these factors there existed significant structural constraints which were external to individual deputies. The opportunity of able men to act differently and, indeed, the very functioning of the entire parliamentary arrangements were constrained by a set of structural factors which ranged from international-political to geographical and economic, and from political to socio-cultural. Despite the Constitutional Revolution and the major achievements of the era of Reza Shah, the society had not undergone a fundamental break with the past. The population had remained predominantly rural, engaged in an archaic mode of agriculture, illiteracy was widespread, primordial loyalties persistent, and attitudes of resignation and passivity prevalent. The constitutional experiment had suffered many disruptions and there was very little experience of involvement in a steadily evolving parliamentary government. The structural prerequisites for a self-sustaining parliamentary system were undeveloped, if not lacking. Politics was basically an ongoing power struggle involving contradictory and conflicting interests, dominated by a disunited elite, and by the Court and the foreign powers. The Court, which had by no means been stripped of the substance of its power, and the foreign embassies, which had become more powerful, were in a position to constrain the opportunities of a large number of the elite, including all the deputies, and to restrict the chance of self-development of the Iranian parliamentary institutions.

A sizeable proportion of the elite constituted the Court entourage, and foreign embassies had their own clients-cum-friends among the elite. However, the Court entourage did not necessarily coincide with the client-friends of the British and the Americans, although such men were the objects of enmity of the client-friends of the Russian Embassy. Suspicion and distrust were not confined to relations between the various client groups; members of each group often suspected the nature and degree of each other's loyalty to their patrons. Such a situation increased factional behaviour and provided the possibility for one client group or a coalition of groups to constrain the opportunities of other groups and ultimately to contribute to the underlying crisis and vulnerability of the parliamentary institutions.

The power position of the Court and the foreign embassies constrained the opportunities of the deputies and other influential individuals, groups or institutions in a further and more fundamental sense. Those members of the elite who were neither attached to the Court nor too closely linked to foreigners could not nevertheless exceed certain limits in defiance of the preferences and interests of these powers. They could not afford to antagonize or ignore the Court or foreign powers and were normally forced to make certain calculations regarding likely reactions from these quarters before embarking on any course of action, and to modify their actions in the face of any opposition. On the whole, the power of the Court and the foreign embassies – particularly as there was often some measure of co-ordination between the former and at least one of the latter – was enough to thwart from the outset any course of action which they opposed.

Furthermore, in the absence of a rational-bureaucratic ethos and commonly recognized administrative norms and rules, any course of action was bound to create personal resentment on the part of one group or another. The group or groups whose interests were apparently harmed and whose desires were ignored usually considered that they had not been treated according to impartial and universally enforced laws and rules, but that they had been victimized by personal grudges and insidious designs. This tended to result in vindictiveness and a desire for vengeance. Without enjoying popular support, an effective organizational link or sustained foreign backing, a deputy could not – even if he wanted – consistently ignore the interests and demands of landowners, big merchants and the bazaar, tribal leaders, newspaper editors, the *ulama* or other influential groups and individuals, without seriously risking his position and chances of re-election. Nor could he alienate his clients, who expected favours of various kinds, and to whom he largely owed his position and fortunes.

The Cabinet

In the aftermath of Reza Shah's fall, the pattern of the diffusion and reallocation of political power, the legal-institutional standing of the Majlis *vis-à-vis* the Cabinet, as well as the power position of the Court and foreign embassies, rendered Cabinets vulnerable and ill-equipped to deal with the prevailing socio-political problems. The Iranian Constitution had not adequately clarified the position of the executive within the body politic, and the internal organization and procedures of the Cabinet, as well as its relations with other state bodies, had not been sufficiently defined. The Constitution had not elaborated a mechanism to reconcile the objectives of legality and institutional differentiation with the necessities of efficiency and institutional co-operation. The executive was thus provided with few, if any, effective mechanisms for the assertion of its authority in the face of the legislature. In fact, whatever subtle constitutional sanction could have been invoked in support of the executive, the Cabinet was in practice the virtual prisoner of the Majlis.

Following the Allied occupation of the country, for a number of years Cabinets were formed largely as a result of the tactical alliances of a few factions, and fell as the alliance disintegrated and as counter-alliances were formed. A prime minister entrusted to form a Cabinet by a coalition of factions had no choice but to allocate a number of ministerial portfolios to each faction and to promise further services of various kinds. A substantial part of a minister's time and energy was spent cultivating his own personal and sectional links, returning favours, providing his clients with a feeling of sharing the spoils of office and establishing a hold over the key positions in his ministry by appointing personal friends and clients. Ministers and prime ministers were therefore linked and cross-linked through patronage networks, debt-relations, various forms of exchange and other informal ties, with different sources of power and influence outside the Cabinet. This did not help to develop an atmosphere of trust or allow the prime minister to assert his formal authority over his colleagues. When possible, prime ministers would select their colleagues from their own clients or trusted friends, but they were often forced to work with other ministers whom they would not have chosen but for pressure from various circles. In addition, they were legally barred from dismissing one or a number of ministers without going through the ritual of resigning and forming a new Cabinet.

Cabinets largely lacked internal harmony and rarely enjoyed a spirit of co-operation. Many ministers did not enjoy the full confidence of the prime minister or were not sufficiently involved in the formation of policy. Collective responsibility was more a myth than a reality and the identity of the Cabinet was usually inseparable from the personality of the prime minister. In the words of Le Rougetel: 'In this country the Prime Minister is the Government; if he is strong the Government is strong and per contra.'[9]

The prevailing methods of allocating ministerial portfolios and other senior positions were bound to antagonize various groups and individuals inside and outside the Majlis. Those deputies who were excluded or had gained little from the process of distribution of spoils, as well as those who rejected the legitimacy of the prevailing arrangements of Cabinet-formation, voiced their opposition jointly or separately, and tried to undermine Cabinets and the coalitions on which they were based. The spectre of interpellation and motions of no-confidence haunted all Cabinets. It was rare for a Cabinet to be formed with any genuine confidence that it could adequately tackle even its short-term objectives, but this did not stop all Cabinets from paying lip-service to long-term strategies which invariably included references to grandiose fundamental reforms: the ending of corruption; the purging and reorganization of the administration; expansion of health services; elimination of illiteracy; and so on. The inclusion of ambitious reform programmes implied that Cabinets expected to remain in office long enough to fulfil their promises, although few entertained such illusions.

The constitutionally ambiguous position of the Cabinet and its institutional weakness, which contributed to the domineering position of the Majlis, also facilitated and encouraged the frequent encroachment of the Court in the sphere of authority of the executive. There were few Cabinets in which the Court was not represented directly or indirectly, and from 1948 onwards the Court increasingly initiated the formation of Cabinets and filled them largely with its own nominees. This was achieved by exploiting the disunity and inertia of the majority of deputies, exerting direct or indirect pressure, winning over the leaders of dominant factions, and circulating false or exaggerated stories of internal or external threats. Such tactics usually provoked a variety of reactions from opposition circles, and were seen as lending plausibility to widely held beliefs about the on-going collusion between the Court and the majority of deputies to undermine the parliamentary arrangements. The need to counter such assertions was one of the reasons why most deputies had eventually to abandon their support of Court-sponsored Cabinets.

When a Cabinet was primarily engineered by the Majlis and did not sufficiently represent the Court, even if it posed no threat to the Court, the Court would withdraw its support, knowing that it would not last long. The Court would not, however, normally oppose a Cabinet if it were mediocre and headed by a weak man. Mediocre Cabinets and weak prime ministers were favoured by the Crown; but if an assertive and able man was, by force of circumstances, entrusted to form a Cabinet, he would encounter intrigues, pressures and a variety of other manoeuvres instigated by the Court to force him into compliance or to hasten his downfall.

Moreover, Cabinets had to cope with the foreign embassies – the British, the Americans, and for a period the Russians – whose preferences and demands were often conflicting. In the absence of sustained internal sources of support, Cabinets were susceptible to these pressures. They frequently tried to gain the support of one embassy or another to compensate for the lack of sufficient internal backing. This was also expected to provide them with the support of that embassy's client-friends inside the country, and to immunize them, at least temporarily, against the intrigues and enmities of all those who had reservations about acting against a foreign power. Such tactics, however, were often counterproductive and no prime minister could ignore the need to pay lip-service to independence of action. Some prime ministers tried to play one embassy off against another and appear to ally themselves with all of them, treating them equally and positively in order to be dependent on none; or to ally with none and treat all equally but negatively in order to deter all and assert real independence.[10] The adoption of such policies, however, did not help to strengthen Cabinets and lengthen their lives. In the midst of relentless intrigues, press campaigns and rumours, and in the face of undeniable popular discontent, Cabinets fell one after the other. Given the prevailing political arrangements, even able prime ministers and ministers were helpless and, unless in an unusual situation, barely capable of surviving longer than a few months. Cabinets in Iran were not coalitions based on shared principles, specific objectives and defined policy preferences. They were normally composed of individuals who represented dominant elite sections and who owed their positions largely to complex networks of friendship, kin, and patronage ties connecting them to influential deputies and factions inside the Majlis and to sources of power and influence elsewhere. The very formation and composition of Cabinets usually reflected desperate attempts at compromise and represented clusters of interests which were often contradictory and even conflictive. A compromise prime minister tended to be a man of little ability, just as compromise Cabinets were uncoordinated and incohesive bodies incapable of presenting a credible face. If in a crisis situation a man of ability was assigned the task of forming a Cabinet, his survival depended on the length of the crisis; he was not immune to the active enmity of the Court, which was ready to orchestrate opposition in order to halt 'dictatorship' and save 'the Constitution'.

In the post-Reza Shah period opposing 'dictatorship' was the most common cry of all, but the meaning of dictatorship differed significantly according to who used it and in what context. For the Court, dictatorship meant any strong executive independent of the Crown, while for the Majlis it meant a Cabinet which did not accept total submission to the Majlis. In order to undermine a strong Cabinet, the Court and its allies inside and outside the Majlis would, among other things, provoke anti-dictatorial agitation and encourage press campaigns; thus substituting false issues and imaginary threats for real ones.

A prime minister with ability was normally denied the opportunity to fulfil his role effectively by a complex set of structural factors, while the very fact that a man was allowed the slightest opportunity implied that he lacked the ability to proceed with his tasks. The executive, which was constitutionally assigned the task of government, was without the necessary institutional strengths and structural preconditions to accomplish a great deal.[11] The frequency of the rise and fall of Cabinets as well as numerous reshuffles, brought about administrative disruption and seriously hampered the implementation of any long-term plan. This did not restrict the prospects of elite members, however, but allowed the continued and frequent exchange of ministerial portfolios and other senior governmental posts among themselves, often with scant regard for specialization or competence and involving a continuous traffic of personnel from one department to another. The position of prime minister and ministerial portfolios were exchanged or circulated among a limited number of men and the entire process was legitimized by exploiting the rituals of parliamentarianism. In the aftermath of Reza Shah's authoritarianism, arguments in favour of strong government were not attractive and invariably aroused suspicion. In this situation Cabinets were bound to encounter similar difficulties and suffer the same fate.

The monarchy

Muhammad Reza Shah Pahlavi replaced his father as Shah of Iran at the age of twenty-two. He had been brought up under the close supervision of his father at the Court and had spent four years in Switzerland. The milieu of his upbringing had a considerable impact on his character and outlook. In the words of Marvin Zonis the young Shah was 'filled with self-doubt and fears of his own weakness', which resulted from 'personal sickliness; enforced separation from his mother and father; a stern, powerful, and dominating father; and a milieu replete with sycophants'.[12] He himself claimed: 'The democratic Western environment moulded my character to an extent that was second only to my father's influence.'[13] His schooling in an insular private school abroad could not have included a serious acquaintance with Western democratic values. He did, however, appear to be genuinely interested in democracy; his succession to the throne was publicized as the dawn of a new era of parliamentary government and the strict enforcement of the Constitution. The young Shah was expected to respect his undertakings in regard to the Constitution and he frequently spoke publicly of his democratic convictions.

Although the definition of the constitutionally delineated boundaries of royal authority seemed problematic, the spirit of the Constitution had clearly confined the monarchical functions to the purely ceremonial. The Shah was charged formally to appoint prime ministers, customarily after they had been voted for by a majority in the Majlis; he was to sign decrees which were already signed by a minister; he could pardon criminals, send diplomatic delegations abroad and receive foreign emissaries; and he could hold ceremonial consultations with members of the government or the Majlis. He had numerous other tasks which ranged from the issuing of election decrees to the formal opening of the Majlis, and from frequent royal audiences on public occasions to the promotion of charitable activities. The fact that Cabinet sessions were often held in his presence entitled him to play more than a ceremonial role in political affairs. His most significant role which, constitutionally speaking, was no more than ceremonial, was his incumbency of the position of commander-in-chief of the armed forces. This, however, accounted for much of his influence.

It was not, however, the Constitution which effectively delimited monarchical prerogatives, but the 'institutional salience' of the monarchy within the Iranian body politic which determined the range of monarchical power and patterned its exercise.[14] In fact, the deep-seated practices of the past had transformed or reduced the entire state apparatus into the mere executive functionary of the Court. In the time of Reza Shah a symbiotic merger between the state and the Court on the one hand, and the army and the Court on the other, had taken root. It subsequently took twelve years to attempt to disentangle these two mergers, which eventually proved almost impossible.

Following the departure of Reza Shah the Court's power and its sphere of influence were considerably reduced, but it was not institutionally dislocated. Thus, the dominant mode of political activity remained largely confined to the contest for power, with the monarchy as the main contender. The institutional salience of the monarchy implied that it could significantly affect the life chances not only of its clients but of the entire ruling elite. Therefore the elite's calculation of its actions was considerably influenced by the Shah's likely reactions.[15]

The monarchy remained the foremost allocator of patronage and spoils. The Shah, along with his family and entourage, was structurally situated so as to enjoy unrivalled control over the flow of patronage, and maintained an overall, if negative, check over the distribution of scarce resources and positions of power and privilege. The privileged position of the Iranian monarch was anchored in his access to power and not in any historically rooted and culturally transmitted 'mystique' or symbolic system which generated legitimacy and ensured popular consensus.[16] The Iranian monarchy did not have any form of religious legitimation as had some Middle Eastern monarchies. The Shah was not the 'spiritual patriarch of a holy family' as the King of Morocco has been said to be.[17] Motivated by a nationalistic vision, Reza Shah had invoked traditions of ancient Iranian kingship and cultivated pre-Islamic myths which contravened the religious mechanisms of legitimation. This strengthened the ethos which, in varying degrees, had usually accompanied the Iranian monarchy and provided it with a 'secular' aura, while at the same time supplementing the intrinsic seeds of both its strength and its weakness.

The monarchy's predominantly non-religious character was, in a sense, a corollary to its institutional-structural strength, which was in turn inextricably linked to the military establishment. The Pahlavi monarchy and the army shared a deep interest in sustaining each other, the Iranian army having been created, nurtured and cherished by Reza Shah – himself an officer. In his era, senior officers enjoyed privileged positions, accumulated considerable wealth and appeared to recognize no object of loyalty but the throne.[18] The ignominious performance of the army confronting the Allies, however, resulted not only in its reduction to almost half its previous size because of disorganization and mass desertion, but also in the rapid erosion of its morale.[19] The army, or what was left of it, was in any case on the side of the monarchy, and the increasing criticism of it from various circles pushed it closer to the Court. The Shah – whose training was largely military and who had an unfailing enthusiasm for military matters – regarded himself as being far more than a ceremonial commander-in-chief of the armed forces. At a time when both the army and the monarchy were on the defensive, mutual insecurity made the resumption of close co-operation imperative, and thus the army willingly submitted to the command of the young Shah. The Shah did his utmost to rebuild and reorganize the army, to enhance its morale and its well-being. He was helped by the immediately-felt need for the restoration of order in a country which was fast succumbing to chaos and disorder.

In the time of Reza Shah, the War Ministry had been assigned a major role in co-ordinating the activities of the government with the wishes of the Court-army complex.[20] After his departure, the ministry lost its importance, although it remained a one-way channel which did not extend the authority of the government over the army, but transmitted the influence of the Court and the army over the Cabinet. The real centre of gravity in the army became the office of the Chief of General Staff, which was beyond effective governmental control. The War Ministry, which was formally in its charge, was either in harmony with the Court and the army or not equipped to bring the army into the domain of the government. The Chief of General Staff, along with all other senior officers, was installed or dismissed on the direct order or with the knowledge of the Shah, and all movement of personnel as well as promotions and demotions were carefully controlled and assessed by him.

In order to ensure his hold over the army and in view of emerging exigencies, the Shah resorted to the tactic of alternating the position of the Chief of General Staff between officers known for their deep mutual enmity. Generals Hasan Arfa and Hajji Ali Razmara, for instance, who frequently replaced each other as Chief of Staff, were both patrons of a sizeable number of client groups composed of army officers, politicians, officials and journalists. The ascent of one man entailed the fall of the other, as well as a considerable movement of personnel. In addition, a situation of tension normally existed between the Chief of General Staff and the War Minister. This was due both to the disproportionate access of the two officials to positions of command and the unequal power of the two offices. Tensions were not, however, alleviated but aggravated by the choice of personalities who occupied these positions. Such choices were the prerogative of the Crown, frequently in the case of the War Minister and almost always in the case of the Chief of General Staff. The exploitation of these divisions enabled the Shah to enhance his room for manoeuvre and to minimize the possibility of any co-ordinated action against monarchical interests.

Moreover, the function of the army was not simply to safeguard 'law and order'; nor was its vocation a purely military one. The army was a strategic instrument of considerable bargaining value in the hands of the monarchy in its attempt to outweigh its rivals and defeat and chastise its enemies. Riots and rebellions were promptly suppressed or prolonged according to the Court's desires.[21] Furthermore, matters were arranged in such a way that the Shah was credited with any successful performance of the army, while the government was blamed for its failures. The army was an indispensable instrument at election times, as it could influence the outcome of elections.[22] Therefore, the Shah had every reason to make the army his prime political concern and to maintain its expansion and morale. He rarely spoke to foreign representatives without obsessively referring to his objectives concerning the army and without asking for their assistance in achieving his goals. He cherished the idea of a strong and efficient army, not just as an instrument of internal control and national defence but as a major combative power of regional importance and scale, openly on the side of the West. The army could not have hoped for more than this and it could therefore not fail to identify itself with the monarchy.

The institutional salience of the monarchy, however, stemmed not only from the pattern of relations between the Court and the army, and the monarch and the military elite, but also from the privileged position of the monarch in relation to the entire ruling elite. The interactions between the Shah and the ruling elite constituted an asymmetrical relationship, since the Shah could affect the life prospects of elite members to a greater degree than they could affect his fortunes. Under the new arrangements, the power of the Court was considerably reduced, but remained sufficient to ensure the Shah's privileged position, particularly in view of inter-elite divisions. Nevertheless, the multiplicity of power centres and the much-publicized image of the young Shah as a politically detached sovereign intent upon reigning constitutionally, constrained his exercise of power. The new political arrangements and the prevailing milieu impelled the monarchy to assume a defensive appearance and, apart from its hold over the army, to confine itself to discreet, usually negative, manoeuvres. Thus, various tactics were employed to ensure that inter-elite divisions permitted no Court-independent elite faction to become so powerful as to outweigh its rivals and put itself in a position to challenge the throne. This usually involved concerted efforts to complicate the task of able governments and to undermine the coalitions on which they were based.

The disproportionate share of effective power held by the Shah as opposed to his constitutionally designated authority was largely due to the institutional salience of the monarchy, and became a major constraint on the functioning of parliamentary government. A government could only hope to achieve a degree of success and credibility if the monarch could be confined to the performance of his ceremonial functions. The active political involvement of the Shah, however, increased as the functioning of parliamentary government became more difficult, and in view of the growing appeal of radical ideologies and the threat they potentially posed to the existing socio-economic arrangements. In this situation an increasing number of the elite began to regard the Shah as the focal point of national consensus and the symbol of the country's internal cohesion and unity, and to identify loyalty to the Constitution with loyalty to the throne.

Open royal defiance of the existing parliamentary arrangements was, nevertheless, a matter of deep concern even to the vocal supporters of monarchical strength. The British and the Americans, who usually bypassed the government and communicated directly with the Court, contributed to its strength. For a long period, however, they advocated political restraint on the part of the Shah and socio-economic reform within the existing arrangements. The Shah lacked the self-confidence even to contemplate any initiative of far-reaching political consequence without their knowledge and tacit approval. In fact, social and ideological conflicts and movements which had surfaced since the 'fall of Reza Shah were potentially capable of challenging the monarchy, while the expansion of monarchical prerogatives without assured foreign backing was counterproductive and dangerous. Before the serious challenge of antimonarchical forces compelled them to change their strategy, the British and Americans saw the future of the monarchy as best assured if it discreetly exerted influence. The Shah was compelled by a combination of factors to play the role of constitutional monarch and await the day when the turn of events would convince his foreign and local supporters that he should take the lead. For many years, therefore, he did not publicly denounce democracy as an undesirable form of government, nor did he resort to any authoritarian rhetoric. He merely lamented the form that parliamentary government had assumed in Iran and blamed its inefficiency on the incompetence of the politicians and the corruption of self-seeking officials.

If the parliamentary arrangements barred the Shah from playing an active role in the process of decision-making, his strategic position allowed him to influence the process, to prevent undesirable decisions from being taken, and to suppress issues likely to harm monarchical interests. In this he was assisted by his vast clientele, who utilized the press, the expanding radio broadcasting service,[23] and other means of propaganda in order to publicize the importance of an active royal interest, if not involvement, in the political process. Since the preservation of royal power required the perpetuation of inter-elite divisions, various mechanisms designed to stimulate division were employed and inevitably encouraged fatalistic myths of doomed alliances, inevitable betrayals and ineradicable intrigues. In turn the inter-elite divisions served to give credibility to the publicized image of the Shah as an impartial arbiter seeking co-operation between the contesting factions in the interests of the nation. In reality the Shah was deeply involved in a power struggle which was eventually to win him the upper hand.

Given the domestic situation, as well as international political circumstances, the monarchy was in the best position to emerge as the eventual victor and to modify the existing arrangements in its own favour. Moreover, from the very outset following his accession to the throne, beneath the surface of the Shah's projected image as a ceremonial, detached sovereign, lay an increasingly obsessive desire to be a leader; to intiate reforms and supervise their execution; to be a guide and not just a symbol; to rule and not just to reign. The constraints of the parliamentary machinery, and the inefficiency and slowness of the legislative processes, led him to contemplate the modification of the Constitution and eventually to accomplish it. In view of the assumption that attempts to bypass the law were considered to be potentially counterproductive, as a first step towards his vision of leadership and the legitimization of his positive role in the process of government, he conceived it imperative to adapt the law to his designs. This would only be possible, however, if the Court did not have to share political power effectively with other state bodies, and if parliamentary government were reduced to a mere façade. There were preventive conditions which hindered the Shah's efforts to become the recognized and incontestable leader of the nation. For years to come he had to accept the less than glorious reality of being not the leader but the chief intriguer and leading manipulator of the ruling elite.

The ruling elite

The 'ruling elite' here refers to a cluster of individuals who, by virtue of their formal incumbency of leading positions of authority in various state institutions or their informal access to such institutions through mechanisms of patronage and their cognates, enjoyed a power position which enabled them to influence significantly the actions and thoughts of others who were excluded from enjoying similar positions. Elite members employed their power to engineer the adoption of certain policies and rejection of others, to suppress real issues and create false ones, often acting against the will and interests of subordinate groups or classes.[24] They acted collectively to preserve the social order and patterns of stratification which assured their strategic position, and individually or factionally to safeguard their power position and the material and symbolic benefits which stemmed from it.[25]

The ruling elite was composed of the Shah, members of the royal family, Court dignitaries, prime ministers, ministers, members of Parliament, the upper echelons of the officer corps, senior judges, deputy ministers, senior diplomats and other prominent officials, governor-generals, leading businessmen, eminent *ulama*, tribal leaders and local magnates. Members of the elite usually held formally defined positions of authority, but this did not necessarily equip them with effective powers; it was rather an individual's position within the vast network of patronage and other informal groupings which determined the amount of power accessible to him and enabled him to influence the allocation of authority positions. An adequate understanding of the ruling elite therefore requires a discussion of patronage and its cognates.

Following the fall of Reza Shah, the absence of a cohesive bureaucratic structure with rational and public criteria for the recruitment and dismissal of personnel, as well as impartial rules of conduct and mechanisms of accountability, became more widely felt. This contributed to the manifestation of previously suppressed or latent informal groupings, and to the overt revival of patron–client relations, which had always been a facet of Iranian public life.[26]

In a society with a widening intelligibility gap between the government and the mass of the governed, and in the absence of sufficient understanding of and common agreement over rights and duties, patronage and other informal relations were bound to become ubiquitous and provide channels for conducting any form of public business. All categories of people needed brokers to 'obtain benefit and to avoid persecution'.[27] With the disappearance of the binding power of the Court, conflicts over the distribution of resources and spoils were largely arranged within the context of informal group networks and systems of patronage. Like-minded men, friends, relatives and co-regionists were mobilized by a leader or clique of leaders and formed or revitalized their 'parties', factions, and societies.

These informal groupings were stylized social units, based usually on asymmetrical power relations but also on intimate personal links as well as on loyalties and recognized or assumed common interests and expectations. The mutual obligations of members of such groups were usually of a moral character and were neither explicitly contractual nor genuinely ideological. They aimed at facilitating the promotion of a set of interests or views as well as the realization of certain objectives. This implied working to undermine the activities of adversaries and preventing them from unduly increasing their advantages. Such groups were formed to reduce the unpredictability of political life and the political vulnerability or ineffectiveness of individuals and to provide them with a sense of belonging. They also served to combine political activity with leisure and were often not simply means for the realization of ends but ends in themselves.

In order to produce cohesive factions and alliances, threats of various kinds were often invoked. There were, however, no mechanisms for ensuring genuine mutual trust, even among members of the same group. Factions were, therefore, normally susceptible to internal tension and in a state of flux. Intra-factional alliances were also precarious, for group demarcations were blurred and dictated by circumstances. Actual friends were all too often suspected as potential enemies, and actual enemies were frequently considered to be potential allies.[28]

The nucleus of factions generally consisted of the personal following of a leader or a number of leaders. A faction leader in the Iranian Parliament was usually referred to pejoratively as a *mutavalli* (custodian of a shrine or administrator of an endowment). A *mutavalli* was usually wealthy and well-connected; he was distinguished by his dynamism, his gift for manipulation and his ability to influence others. He acted to ensure a greater share of political spoils for himself and his friends in the Majlis; he often worked to extend tangible rewards and services to his wider clients in his constituency, and to play the role of an intermediary between them and the government. He functioned as a political broker, and considerably influenced the ratification or rejection of bills in the Majlis, as well as the promotion of one set of issues or the demotion of others. He played a crucial role in orchestrating support for or opposition to policies and, most importantly, in bringing about and trying to maintain Cabinets, or conversely, paralysing and undermining them. Little business could, in fact, be conducted in the Majlis without the support or, at least, acquiescence of the *mutavallis*.

Political alignments were primarily articulated through factionalism, as formal, bureaucratically patterned large-scale organizations – i.e. political parties – were conceived by the elite to be unattainable and unworkable. Suspicion, envy and intrigue, inherent in the political subculture of the elite, were often conveniently invoked to rationalize factional behaviour and to refrain from any real efforts towards the creation of corporate organizations. Without committing themselves to any ideologically defined and organizationally patterned mode of behaviour, individuals resorted to forming factions primarily in order to attain what was individually unattainable. They aimed at increasing their access to material or symbolic advantage, in defiance of the formal-legal channels; in other words, factions functioned as vehicles for 'corruption', conceived here more heuristically than as a value-laden notion denoting moral indignation. Corruption has been defined as 'the breach of institutional rules for private material gain, usually working to the advantage of a privileged elite – a kleptocracy, in one telling neologism'.[29]

'Material gain' in the case of Iran as in the case of Senegal, and indeed many other societies, could 'assume different forms, from straightforward cash misappropriation to more complex advantages in terms of status hegemony or political power'. Corruption in this sense was closely intermingled with patronage and factionalism or with what has, in the case of contemporary Senegal, aptly been called 'clan politics'. In the words of Cruise O'Brien:

> The modern political clan is not defined by kinship, real or imagined, although kinship relations may exist and may help to reinforce political solidarity within a given clan group: there is no requirement for a common revered ancestor, real or imagined, no clanic name, no shared taboo, no role of exogamy. The clan is a political faction operating within the institutions of the state and the governing party: it exists above all to promote the interests of its members through political competition, and its first unifying principle is the prospect of the material reward of political success. Political office and the spoils of office are the very definition of success: loot is the clanic totem.[30]

The primary units of political activity in Iran were factions in a variety of forms; politics was conducted on the basis of personal or sectional interests and informal relations. A meaningful parliamentary polity, however, inevitably required viable institutional differentiation and co-ordination, civic disinterestedness and impersonal and formal modes of interaction. A functional and evolving parliamentary politics was of course not necessarily incompatible with clan politics; such a mode of politics could transform itself into a mechanism of political adaptation and even evolve into some form of functioning party politics. Yet the structural configuration of Iranian clan politics did not allow the development of sustained parliamentarianism: the semi-anomic nature of inter- and intra-elite relations generated a situation of political stalemate which was then subjected to incessant challenges, primarily from the Court. The picture was further confounded by diverse social and ideological factors which underpinned political threats to the prevailing kleptocratic mode of appropriation of wealth, power and prestige.

The essence of clan politics in Iran as elsewhere was the maximization of political gains and minimization of loss at the expense of other groups, as well as the arrangement of alliances in such a way as to undermine or destabilize the efforts of one group to gain the upper hand. This situation, together with the absence of institutional co-ordination, was responsible for the chronic stalemate of Iranian parliamentary politics. The prevailing stalemate was, however, of a dynamic nature, since dissatisfied and ambitious groups relentlessly challenged the distribution of political spoils. 'Change' was indeed all too prevalent, yet it usually had no positive large-scale social impact. Feuds were conducted in the name of the 'people' and the national interest, but the results were invariably adverse to both. The myth of change concealed the reality of directionless flux and stagnation, in which initiative and efficiency all too often fell victim to tensions and conflicts.

In spite of its internal tensions and rivalries, the ruling elite was nevertheless a socially integrated body. Kinship, affinity and friendship ties, as well as the exigencies of the political game which did not normally allow certain limits to be exceeded or rivals to be totally incapacitated, contributed to its 'social integration'.[31] However, the main factors which drew the elite together as a distinct socially integrated body were its common social origin, and interest in preserving the existing socio-economic arrangements. The ruling elite generally came from and constituted the apex of the 'upper class', which was a large and interrelated network of extended families – usually referred to as 'the one thousand families' (*hizar famil*) – composed of men and women of wealth, power and prestige who were engaged in land ownership and commerce and often had established familial connections with the administrative apparatus of the state – although they were not necessarily directly active in ruling the country.[32] These people constituted a class in view of a number of interrelated factors: their economic position, reward system, life chances, life experiences and particularly their guaranteed upward social mobility. Traditional mechanisms of socialization generated a deferential attitude toward this class and shaped common perceptions in such a way that the prevailing socio-economic arrangements were widely perceived as natural or inevitable. More significantly, strong bonds of ethnicity, language, religion, as well as tribal and regional affiliations impeded the intensification of class conflict, while the prevalence of patron–client relations which linked and cross-linked a large number of people from the subordinate classes to the upper class, contributed to this virtually uncontested perpetuation of class-based social divisions.[33]

A further factor contributing to the social integration of the elite also served to legitimize their position of privilege: high office was considered to be a just reward for educational qualifications, particularly from foreign universities, and titles such as 'doctor' and 'engineer' were important status symbols. Prominent lawyers, physicians, engineers, economists, military officers and so on, who constituted an important and prestigious minority within the ruling elite, self-righteously demanded respect and justified their careerism and actual or desired positions on the basis of their educational merits. Nevertheless, in view of the close links between wealth and educational opportunity, the criteria of ascent to elite positions were neither rational nor primarily meritocratic.

There were, however, cases where men of modest or low social origins worked their way up to the ranks of the ruling elite. However, whatever their ability and educational qualifications, this would not have been possible without access to connections and channels of patronage, and without connubial and personal relations with the upper class. They owed their upward social mobility to their co-optation and eventual dissolution into the upper class. They not only had to build and strengthen their connections with members of that class, but also to adopt its values and views in such a way that the impact of their social origins on their attitudes and political orientations were quickly concealed or eroded.

In order to gain acceptance and be successful, such men had to compensate for their humble social origins by becoming even more upper class than those born into that class. In a traditional culture deeply imbued with beliefs in the predestined character of hier-archical social divisions, rapid upward mobility or its legitimation was not easy. Humble origin was considered more a source of embarrassment than pride, and respect for men of lower origins who had climbed up the social ladder was far from automatic, as good lineage was an integral part of social prestige. In order to escape from these difficulties and be assimilated into the upper class it was necessary, for example, to provide frequent and ostentatious hospitality, feed the poor on religious occasions and help charities, above all it was necessary to respond unfailingly to the demands of an expanding clientele.

There were also cases of men of low or modest social origins who achieved positions of social prestige and political power by successfully utilizing popular support, through the favour of foreign embassies, or by achieving prominence as the result of specific circumstances. Such men, however, either did not retain their positions for long or became the object of suspicion and contempt, or were ostracized, by other elite members – particularly if they did not comply with the elite's rules of the game and codes of behaviour. The pattern of elite recruitment, therefore, was neither open nor totally closed, and the degree of its closedness or openness was socially determined and culturally patterned.

Although the ruling elite was socially integrated, it lacked 'moral' integration, that is its members did not share 'common ideas and a common moral ethos' and were not adequately 'conscious of an overall solidarity'.[34] This was a corollary of their fragmentation and sectionalist tendencies. An elite group or coalition of groups could dominate others if sponsored by the Court and blessed with the support or favour of foreign powers, through patiently nurtured clientele groups and careful exploitation of political needs at propitious moments, or the successful mobilization of popular support. This was bound to provoke counter-moves and the rearrangement of alliances either to prevent or abort such advances.

Such a situation was possible because the prevailing modes of power distribution and parliamentary arrangements did not normally allow the unchallenged dominance of a single faction. Among the contending groups, the Shah and his clientele enjoyed the most privileged access to effective power, and yet, in view of the constraints on their overt exercise of power, they were the least satisfied. What they desired was an assured position of hegemony and an uncontested opportunity for agenda-setting and leadership. Such a position demanded that the activities of unsubjugated elite members be confined to a sphere outside the expanding royal domain and interests. This was possible only if the spirit of constitutionalism could be effectively suppressed, and in fact several factors made this likely.

From the first moment of the much-acclaimed re-establishment of constitutional government in Iran, fragmentation of the elite reduced political life to a state of stalemate which became the hallmark of parliamentary government. The constitutionally sanctioned separation of powers contributed to inter-elite divisions, which in turn prevented intra- and inter-institutional co-ordination. The ensuing political stalemate was congenial with defensive moves and tactics for political survival rather than with positive initiatives and strategies.

This situation encouraged opportunism and a practical and relativistic morality rather than any genuine intellectual convictions. Traditionally rooted cynicism and a belief in the practical disadvantages of sincerity, trust, goodwill and attachment to noble principles,[35] were, moreover, intermingled with a deeply held belief in a conspiratorial theory of politics, which included the myth of foreign involvement in every aspect of Iranian public life. Such views were either genuinely held or, more often, used in order to explain shortcomings and failures by attributing them to foreigners and their agents.

The emergence of such reasoning and the mentality underlying it is understandable given the geographical location of Iran: the proximity to Russia and the British Empire – both of which had for long turned the country into a stage for their imperialistic designs and rivalries – lent plausibility to such views. They were, however, disseminated not only by malevolent intriguers but also by benign but simple-minded journalists and dilettante intellectuals, and had come to assume the function of magical beliefs and superstitions in previous ages, deeply affecting the political culture of the country. In such a political culture there was no place for the concept of the 'individual' as an autonomous being whose actions and thoughts were to a large extent the consequence of his own convictions and inner mental faculties. Individuals were considered to be motivated purely by factors external to themselves. On the other hand, conspiratorial thinking in such a culture often reached the boundaries of paranoia, and manifested itself in excessive suspicion of the intentions of others.

Such beliefs were widely used in order to explain phenomena which otherwise appeared unintelligible and baffling. They appealed to the ruling elite, and indeed the entire population, as they suited a style of life which was deeply affected by socio-political repression and marked by insecurity and conflict over the distribution of scarce resources. Pragmatism, cynicism, fatalism and a conspiratorial mentality were shared to varying degrees by all members of the elite,[36] yet such shared characteristics were not of a kind to endow the elite with 'moral integration'. In Iran, as in any other class-divided society,[37] the normative order was also class-differentiated, and the upper class more or less subscribed to a distinct 'meaning-system'.[38] However, this contributed more to the demarcation of intra-class boundaries than to inter-class cohesion. The ruling elite was fragmented, kleptocratic and parasitic, and was incapable of fulfilling its public duties in the interest of the effective functioning of parliamentary institutions. Even though its members were constrained by fundamental, predominantly structural factors, any meaningful attribution of power to them implies that it was in their power to act differently.[39] This contention does not allow responsibility to be dissolved in structural determination, and assumes thinking counter-factually to be, as John Dunn puts it, 'the central modality of political judgement, just as description in counter-factual depth is the core of social analysis'.[40]

PART I
Years of Contested Adjustment

1

The Government of Furughi:
AUGUST 1941–MARCH 1942

The German invasion of the Soviet Union was generally welcomed in Iranian political circles, and the possibility that the Russians would soon be defeated contributed greatly to the failure of Reza Shah and his Prime Minister, Ali Mansur, to respond to Anglo-Russian demands for the expulsion of German nationals from the country. British estimates put the number of Germans in Iran at around 2000;[1] according to Iranian sources there were no more than 690 – an insignificant number compared with the 2590 British nationals residing in the country at the time.[2] Yet the issue was used by the Allies to provide ostensible justification for an invasion of Iran in late August 1941, the primary aim of which was to safeguard British strategic and oil interests, both regional and local, forestall the possibility of a German takeover, and secure supply routes to the Soviet Union.[3]

As the Allies crossed the border and advanced towards the centre of the country, Reza Shah and the Government, discomfited and disoriented, were incapable of initiating any measure to cope with the escalating crisis. Deeply worried by the likelihood of the Allied occupation of Tehran, Reza Shah contemplated abdicating and moving to Isfahan and had to be constantly dissuaded by Cabinet Ministers. Since the British and Russian representatives indicated that they no longer had confidence in Mansur as Prime Minister some ministers recommended a change of government and the appointment of a prime minister who would initiate immediate negotiations with the invaders.[4] The change when it came, however, was confined to the replacement of Mansur by Muhammad Ali Furughi; the Cabinet, introduced to the Majlis on 28 August 1941, remained intact.

Furughi's name was put forward by a number of ministers and although Reza Shah was initially reluctant (apparently on account of Furughi's ill-health and old age) he eventually bowed to their view.[5]

The appointment was an expedient move. Furughi was an experienced and respected politician whose years of withdrawal from active politics, although involuntary, had increased his credibility and enabled him to distance himself from the unpopular policies of the final years of Reza Shah's reign. He was an able and skilful negotiator and a man of prudence, moderation and liberal manners. One politician described him as being 'enchanted by the Europeans' but otherwise wise, trustworthy and well intentioned. He was distinguished, in the words of one of his colleagues, by unparalleled 'bon sense'.[6] His qualities were justifiably deemed indispensable for the management of the prevailing crisis.

Furughi's first move was to announce that the Iranian army would not resist Allied troops. His most immediate problem, however, stemmed from the prospect of an Anglo-Russian occupation of Tehran which had caused paralysing panic. Sporadic bombing of the city, the speedy disintegration of the army which flooded its streets with 50,000 shabbily dressed and hungry conscripts, an acute shortage of petrol and insufficient supplies of grain all aggravated the looming sense of catastrophe. The royal family, along with many other prominent families, had already left for Isfahan and it was becoming increasingly difficult to persuade Reza Shah and the Crown Prince, Muhammad Reza, to stay. Despite his ill-health, Furughi none the less tried to establish a dialogue with the Allies and complied with their demand to expel the Axis nationals – a policy of appeasement rushed into by the panic-stricken Shah who seemed prepared to do anything to ward off the occupation of Tehran, and possibly to persuade the Russians to exclude his northern estates from their zone of occupation.

Although the British had initially believed that Reza Shah's 'remarkable hold over his people warranted his retention of the throne' so long as they 'could hope to secure his co-operation, or at least his real neutrality' they and their Russian allies had by this time developed a deep distrust of him. This change of attitude is reflected in a report compiled by the British Legation in Tehran:

His [Reza Shah's] obstinate refusal to get rid of Axis nationals with reasonable speed had already shaken our hopes when the Allied occupation showed that he was quite incapable of dealing with the problems of the moment. When his parade army collapsed he made no effort to prevent disintegration. Moreover he showed no consciousness of responsibility for the collapse of his pretentious military façade, or of recognition of the urgent need for reform: even after the occupation he one day beat the Minister of War and the Chief of Staff with his sword for putting up a scheme of which he disapproved, and then threw them into prison, and he would probably have had them executed if he had not had to abdicate.[7]

The Shah's continued authoritarian behaviour had also resulted in unease both in the Cabinet and the Majlis. Furughi had come to realize that essential reforms would not be achieved under Reza Shah, and the Majlis had convened several secret sessions to discuss the revival of constitutionalism. Domestic opponents of the old regime were particularly heartened by a series of broadcasts from the BBC which increasingly capitalized on the autocrat's mismanagement, greed and cruelty and seriously damaged his standing. Cabinet ministers, dismayed by his efforts to watch over them through the War Minister, had already asked Furughi to demand his abdication. This was finally precipitated by news of the advance of Allied troops towards Tehran. With his last glimmer of hope gone, Reza Shah handed his throne to the Crown Prince, immediately fled the capital, and soon afterwards left the country. Reza Shah's astonishing loss of nerve in the face of the Allied invasion of Iran can only be explained in terms of his complete lack of any popular power base. As Muhsin Sadr, his one-time Justice Minister and confidant, put it:

> In my view Reza Shah was forced out of the country neither by the threats of the Russians nor by the tricks of the British; it was his unbounded arrogance and the unbridgeable rift between him and the nation which resulted in his exile. His links with the nation had been severed to such an extent that when foreign troops took him away as a captive, the people not only showed no sorrow but rejoiced in his departure and congratulated each other, and in no way must this be taken as proof of the disloyalty of the Iranian people.[8]

The new Shah, Muhammad Reza, enjoyed neither the backing of the Allies nor any sustained domestic support. There was, however, no viable alternative. When the end of Reza Shah's rule proved imminent, 'speculation as to what form the future government should take was rife; there was talk of a republic and a revival of the Qajar Dynasty, but no new party with a clear-cut policy came forward'.[9] Furughi had refused a reported Allied offer of heading a new regime in Iran, opting instead to avoid complications and subscribe to the letter of the Constitution. This in effect meant supporting Muhammad Reza who, with the crucial aid of the new Prime Minister, took the ceremonial oath of accession in the Majlis on 17 September 1941.

Muhammad Ali Furughi (Zuka ul-Mulk) was born in 1875 into a wealthy merchant family disposed to culture and learning. His father was for some years in charge of the official translation bureau, which translated several classics of Western literature. Furughi was educated at the *Dar ul-Funun*, the first modern institution of learning established in Iran, where he first studied medicine but was subsequently attracted to the study of literature.[10] He was a man of considerable learning and diverse interests, well informed about world affairs and well versed in Western and Eastern philosophy, the traditional disciplines and literature. His translations into Persian were eloquent, as were his own philosophical and legal tracts; his erudite introductory exposition of the development of Western philosophy was the first systematic treatment of the subject in the Persian language. His editions of classical texts of Persian literature and his style of writing betray a refined mind, good taste and a sound aesthetic intuition.[11] With these qualities he not surprisingly appreciated the significance of cultural development in the consolidation of Iranian nationhood and played an important role in the formation of the Iranian Academy.[12]

Though as a young man he taught at the School of Political Science and tutored Ahmad Shah, after the Constitutional Revolution much of his time and energy were devoted to politics. He twice became deputy for Tehran, for a while presided over the Majlis, and in 1911 began his ministerial career, holding at various times the portfolios of Finance, Justice, Foreign Affairs, War and National Economy. On two occasions he served Reza Shah as Prime Minister, but his second term of office came to an abrupt end in 1935. In July of that year a group protesting in Mashhad against the removal of the veil and the enforced wearing of the European hat took sanctuary in the shrine of Imam Reza where they were violently dealt with by the army. One of the many casualties of this bloody incident was Muhammad Vali Asadi, the custodian of the shrine, who was subsequently executed on the order of the Shah. Furughi was forced to resign after trying to intercede on behalf of Asadi, whose son was married to Furughi's daughter. At the time it was widely believed that a letter had been discovered among Asadi's papers in which Furughi had described the Shah as 'a bloodsucking lion in whose clutches there is no choice but surrender or acquiescence'.[13]

This story, if authentic, sheds light upon the mentality of Furughi and his like-minded colleagues who justified their subservience to an autocratic ruler by perceiving themselves as men who desired to serve their country but were caught up in a situation which allowed no other positive course of action, and who thus held office until their services were no longer required. Furughi had welcomed and supported the assumption of power by Reza Khan in view of the chaotic socio-political conditions of the late Qajar era. As a member of the abortive Iranian delegation to the 1919 Paris Peace Conference, Furughi was doubly frustrated by the low standing of his country and asserted to one of his friends that Iran was a country with no nation; had there been an Iranian nation, the country would have been treated differently.[14] He might have hoped that Reza Khan would lay the foundation of the Iranian nation. Furughi's political style and experience, nevertheless, had a moderating effect on the dictates of the autocratic Reza Shah in whose shadow he performed administrative, consultative and other functions perhaps analogous to those of the grand viziers of medieval times.

In accepting the position of premier despite his failing health, Furughi, like any other politician, was motivated by a complex set of considerations, many of them personal. He seems also to have been motivated rather more than many of his colleagues by values and convictions arising from patriotism, a sense of civic duty as well as a belief in the preservation of the monarchy and the prevailing socio-economic structure of the country. Musaddiq believed Furughi to have been above corruption but not perhaps above subservience. 'Furughi was not a man to accept money [bribes]; he only wanted to remain in office and earn his salary by the month. He accepted whatever was dictated to him.'[15] Yet for all his positive qualities Furughi's political style and perceptions were not adequately suited to active involvement in the political situation of the post-Reza Shah period; nor was his less-than-dynamic character – a reality he was soon to discover.

Muhammad Reza Shah's accession provided Furughi with an opportunity to reshuffle his Cabinet and include seven new ministers. The new Cabinet was not, however, significantly different from its predecessors. Its ministers were all established members of the elite who had held a variety of senior posts under Reza Shah. The Prime Minister may not have been able to find a substantially different body of ministers acceptable to himself, the deputies and the Allies. He could perhaps justify his choice on the grounds that there were no suitable alternative candidates, and that there were other pressures on him. His tactic of introducing inter-Cabinet traffic and exchanges of portfolios with little regard for specialization and experience, as a substitute for more tangible change, was more difficult to justify. For example, the Minister of Education in his first Cabinet later became Minister of Health. On other occasions the Health portfolio was offered to a diplomat and to the Minister of Crafts and Arts. In his last Cabinet shuffle the Minister of Justice was offered the portfolio of Agriculture, while the Finance Minister of the first Cabinet became the Minister of Justice. However, this was a familiar pattern which would be repeated. The redistribution of portfolios had diverse and overlapping functions, being both a time-serving device and a mechanism for demotion and promotion. Any minister who was insufficiently co-operative was cut off, at least temporarily, from his clientele and web of relations in his ministry, thus forcing him to spend time and energy consolidating his new position rather than complicating the task of the Prime Minister.

Furughi and his colleagues saw their main task as the negotiation of a nationally beneficial and honourable understanding with the Allies, which would ensure the sovereignty and integrity of the country and the continuity of the monarchy. The Allies were satisfied with the Cabinet's co-operative attitude, particularly in expelling Axis nationals, and seemed unwilling to contest its objectives. The British Legation accepted Furughi as 'almost the only statesman who was trusted completely for his honesty'[16] and Sir Reader Bullard, the British Minister, described Furughi's Cabinet as 'good on the whole'. He believed that the majority of Ministers were pro-British, and Ali Suhaili, who later succeeded Furughi, had assured the British that any minister to whom they objected 'would be changed'.[17]

The Russians, of course, had little reason to welcome such a pro-British Cabinet. In a discussion with the British Foreign Secretary, Anthony Eden, the Russian Ambassador in London had clearly voiced his government's preferences: in his view Furughi and Suhaili represented the 'reactionary' section of opinion in Iran, 'composed of the landlords and the Army'. A second section, which was 'generally in favour of reform', was composed of 'merchants and intellectuals' and included Furughi's Minister of Finance, Hasan Nafisi (Musharraf). The third section was the Tudeh Party, consisting of 'the intellectuals who had been persecuted under the late regime' and who had 'championed the cause of the European democracies and favoured collaboration with the Allies'. In the view of the Russian Ambassador 'perhaps the best government of Persia would be a combination of the second and third sections'.[18] To Russian disappointment Furughi's Cabinet and its successors were confined to the first two 'sections'. However, as allies of the British, the Russians had no desire to rock the boat and openly contest the support for Furughi.

The programme of Furughi's Cabinet contained promises aimed at appeasing a wide range of social groups. The reduction of taxes and the suppression of 'unnecessary monopolies' were emphasized in order to win over the merchants, while legal reforms and respect for individual rights were underlined to appeal to the intellectuals.[19] Efforts were also made to satisfy civil servants, including military personnel, by putting forward a bill to increase their salaries. Although Furughi had reformist ambitions far beyond this limited programme, prevailing conditions did not allow even this to be implemented. Furughi and his colleagues had few illusions about the practicality of achieving reform, and their main aim was to ensure the formal integrity and sovereignty of the country by means of diplomatic negotiations and manoeuvres. These efforts secured the Allied evacuation of Tehran and finally resulted in the Tripartite Treaty of Alliance of January 1942, but only after considerable resistance and heated debates in the Majlis. The Treaty formalized the occupation of Iran, giving the Allies extensive rights to use Iranian transport facilities and keep as many soldiers in the country as they needed. On the other hand, it reaffirmed the sovereignty and territorial integrity of Iran and set a date for the eventual withdrawal of Allied troops.[20]

During the autumn and winter of 1941 the Cabinet had also to concentrate on restoring order and ensuring an adequate supply of food and other daily necessities. These tasks required the revival of government authority and the administrative machinery of the country. However, it was no easy task to reassert central authority in an occupied country whose autocratically maintained, centralized machinery of control and management had fallen into disarray. Furughi essentially faced three major interlinked problems.

First, he had to deal with insecurity and disorder in the tribal areas. Reza Shah had forcibly suppressed the tribes and tried to transform their way of life; he had eliminated, banished or imprisoned several of their leaders and confiscated their lands. In this way he had undermined their local political influence. Resentment at these policies had mounted, with the result that after the occupation and the fall of the Shah, and in the context of strong communal and local sentiments, they could no longer be contained.[21] Even before Reza Shah's abdication the Qashqa'i brothers had escaped from detention in Tehran to join their tribe.[22] Other tribal magnates in the south and the west also began to resume their power and influence, which was in effect an open challenge to the central government. The tribal problem was complicated by a set of traditionally rooted assumptions shared in varying degrees by almost all Iranian politicians. Paramount among these was the belief that tribal unrest was usually instigated by foreigners, particularly the British. This view had a certain credibility since some southern and western tribes saw the British as natural allies on many occasions, and for their part the British had always maintained close ties with certain tribes in order to exploit their potential for mobilization against the central government.

British tribal policy immediately after the occupation was either one of non-involvement or reconciliation and mediation between the tribes and the Government, while avoiding alienating either side. They believed such a policy was conducive to security and stability in Iran and would enhance their influence and bargaining power, both locally and nationally. The British Consul in Kirmanshah clearly stated his government's position:

> For the present, the most we can do is (1) give all possible assistance in re-organising the Persian Army and Police for security purposes, (2) do what we can to induce the Persian Government to be reasonable, without being weak, in their treatment of the tribes, and (3) make it clear to the tribes that the new Persian Government has our full support.[23]

In a context of mutual suspicion, however, the gap between the real or perceived demands of the tribes and what the Government was prepared to offer was wide. On the one hand, the tribes were equivocal about central authority and regarded it as easy to challenge; on the other hand, the Government lacked any clear understanding of the legitimate needs, rights and demands of the tribes and of the roots of their discontent. In the face of spreading tribal unrest, the central government opted for the threat of military operations, although during Furughi's term of office such threats were only implemented in Kurdistan. Army generals were dispatched to bring the situation under control, an opportunity which they were happy to exploit since it created a rationale for the speedy reorganization of the army and a means of recovering its morale. The 'solution' of the tribal problem was clearly beyond the life of one Cabinet, but it was a problem to which Furughi and many of his successors would have to attend.

The Cabinet's second major problem was the virtual disappearance of Iranian administrative authority from areas under Soviet occupation, particularly Azarbaijan. When the Russians crossed the border, Iranian military and governmental personnel ignominiously abandoned the province.[24] According to the British Consul, on their arrival the Russians 'armed a large number of Armenian riff-raff in order to maintain order among the Muslim population'.[25] The same official also reported that the confiscation of property and goods by the Russians led many factory owners and merchants to contemplate migrating to Tehran or Isfahan. Discontent was not confined to the rich and a German victory over the Russians was widely awaited. 'Every Persian without exception', wrote the Consul, 'expects and looks forward to the arrival of the Germans to the Caucasus and to this town and district within a matter of weeks, and most certainly within the next few months.'[26] There was a general feeling of insecurity and panic among the 'propertied and middle classes', and it was feared that the plundering of certain government premises such as the customs office, would be followed by the looting of the bazaar.[27] In some areas there was neither a Russian nor an Iranian government presence and the population was left to the mercy of rampaging tribesmen.[28] The Russian behaviour clearly puzzled the British:

> it is difficult to defend the Soviet policy of first disarming the gendarmerie and police and then refusing to assist in the maintenance of order on the grounds that this would be interference in the internal affairs of Persia.[29]

The most serious cause of concern for the Government, however, was the possibility that the Russians might exploit and mobilize local communal feelings. The British Consul perhaps referred to such feelings when he observed as early as September 1941 that 'the movement in favour of secession of Azarbaijan from the rest of Persia is still in being, even among the middle class and lawyer elements'.[30] Iranian politicians were well aware of these sentiments and deeply concerned about the potential for Russian manipulation of them and the possibility that the Russians would refuse to withdraw from Iran. With this in mind, it was imperative to re-establish Iranian administrative authority in Azarbaijan and other Russian-occupied areas. Once again, this would continue to pre-occupy several of Furughi's successors.

The third major problem confronting the Cabinet was the acute shortage of foodstuffs and other basic commodities, such as sugar, kerosene and particularly bread. The shortage of bread and its poor quality when available, as well as the scarcity and high prices of other basic commodities, had become a grim fact of life throughout the country which occasionally precipitated riots. In Kirmanshah, for example, the British Consul reported that food shortages along with general insecurity and increasing brigandage had created a situation completely opposite to 'the promises of drastic reforms in Persia and better times for the oppressed masses made by means of British Radio broadcasts'. As the population's raised hopes were dashed, anti-British feeling 'developed in strength'.[31] Similar situations arose in Mashhad, Shiraz, Tabriz, Hamadan and other places, with similar consequences. Anti-Allied feelings and pro-German sympathy were on the increase and this was not reassuring for the occupying powers.

The Allied invasion and concomitant breakdown of Iranian governmental authority had occurred at a moment when the 'last year's harvest operations were in full swing' in the main areas of production, and efforts to collect the requirements of the main cities were largely halted.[32] Allied needs and the economic and fiscal policies which they dictated to the Iranian Government aggravated the situation. For example the drastic devaluation of the Iranian currency (from 68 to 140 rials to the pound sterling), and the acute food shortages, encouraged panic buying and hoarding and a refusal on the part of the producers to sell. Another result of the situation was the emergence of scores of middlemen, hoarders, brokers, black marketeers and other parasitic elements.

The emergence of these elements coincided with the outbreak of political disorder and pillaging caused by the breakdown of the centralized administrative structure and the re-emergence of a multitude of competitive and sometimes conflicting forces in the political arena and various layers of the governmental hierarchy. The situation was greatly aggravated by the Allies' active political and military involvement in the affairs of their respective zones, and by the rebellious mood of local and regional magnates. Inevitably there was a marked increase in corruption in the various organs of the Government and this was intermingled with various forms of scheming in the non-governmental arena. The Government's efforts to contain hoarding and eliminate black marketeering invariably ended in failure since its agents were either easily bribed, had a vested interest in maintaining the situation or were forced to keep quiet. A number of factors contributed to the spread of corruption: rampant inflation (well above the salaries of civil servants), the highly remunerative nature of extra-legal enterprises and a decline in the efficiency of centralized mechanisms of investigation, inspection, accountability and punishment.

Although the spread of corruption among government officials was a major source of concern, corruption was not a new phenomenon. It was commonly used as a way of avoiding the cumbersome bureaucratic labyrinth and compensating for the chronic inefficiency of the formal administrative machinery. The elimination of corruption in an Iran just moving into the twentieth century, and faced with extraordinarily difficult political and economic conditions, was therefore impossible. Even to minimize it would have undermined the very basis of elite power. The kleptocratic nature of the ruling elite was nevertheless easily disguised, and governments concentrated on trying to depict corruption as a specific and legally ascertainable deviation, to restrict conspicuous excesses at lower governmental levels and to portray it as the crime of petty clerks, repugnant to the 'innocent souls' of high officials.

From the outset Furughi and his colleagues had to cope with and compensate for the disappearance of the autocratic, centralized mechanism of decision-making, by invoking the legitimacy generated by the establishment of parliamentary government. Furughi's task was made impossible by the consequences of the occupation. Shortages of food and primary goods certainly had a variety of complex economic, fiscal and other causes. Yet the lack of efficient management and co-ordination between various governmental agencies, and inadequate means of communication, were largely responsible. Since the erosion of administrative efficiency and the near-breakdown of the army and the gendarmerie were interrelated, so also their reorganization had to be a simultaneous process. It was imperative to ensure a measure of efficiency and co-ordination as well as a degree of law and order to facilitate a more even redistribution of scarce goods and the collection and transportation of surplus agricultural produce from one area to another. This task was often made more difficult by the obstructiveness of the occupying forces; hardly any of the surplus produce of northern Iran, for example, reached other areas due to Russian opposition. Moreover, according to a British report, the Russian-occupied zone which 'normally contributes about two-thirds of the total revenue of Persia, paid very little in tax after the occupation'.[33]

Had Furughi's Government enjoyed the sustained co-operation of the Parliament it might have been able to alleviate some of these difficulties. When he assumed the premiership the 12th Majlis had almost completed its term. Much of its remaining two months was spent recovering from the shock of the removal of Reza Shah and, occasionally, condemning his regime.[34] Furughi's Cabinet also came in for criticism,[35] although in a milder form. This period also saw the beginning of a campaign demanding the nullification of the 'elections' for the 13th Majlis, which were largely completed while Reza Shah was still in power and thus considered devoid of legitimacy and meaning. Although the elections clearly lacked credibility, Furughi and the bulk of the ruling elite felt that their nullification would not serve the country's interests.[36] In the prevailing turmoil they feared that new elections would invite intervention by the occupying powers and result in a Majlis which would be unmanageable and/or unwilling to resist foreign pressures. Furughi perhaps also hoped that by rejecting fresh elections he would win over a substantial number of the deputies already elected to the 13th Majlis. In any case, the demands were ill-defined and diffuse and Furughi had little difficulty rejecting the 'nullification of formally legal elections' on the grounds that it 'would create a bad precedent for future governments'.[37]

The 13th Majlis was officially opened on 4 December 1941. Furughi introduced his reshuffled Cabinet and his slightly modified programme, reminding the deputies that his colleagues were largely the same as before, and that the majority of the present deputies had also sat in the last Majlis, implying that he expected their support.[38] Although he was eventually offered the vote of confidence he sought and his programme was approved, he could not have entertained any illusion of lasting support from the Majlis. To those who had lived through a long period of imposed political silence – broken only by eulogies in praise of the Shah – the voicing of rejection, criticism and negation became appealing and fashionable. Many deputies were also swept along by the same wave which had overwhelmed other politically literate elements of the population. By publicly reiterating disdain for the past regime, irrespective of their previous or current position, they hoped to improve their reputation. Similarly, controversial debates and long speeches of opposition brought personal gratification. In addition, since their claim to be representative was weak, they hoped to compensate for this by representing and articulating popular demands, at least as they saw them.

The rebellious attitude and changing mood and loyalties of the deputies, moreover, were a manifestation of the re-emergence of factionalism. Political power previously monopolized by the autocratic monarch was now redistributed among institutions of the state which were, however, chronically fragile. Effective pressure groups and informed public opinion were, at the most, embryonic. Class consciousness was on the rise, but strong communal sentiments and sectional loyalties, as well as active, real or imagined foreign involvement all helped to bring about conspicuous and excessive factionalism. Such factors constituted the basis of clan politics with its underlying pluralistic ethos.

Furughi and his successors were faced with a situation in which the co-operation and support of the Majlis was not easily acquired or sustained. His Cabinet, which lasted only 184 days, was reshuffled three times. When it was first introduced to the Majlis it received 91 votes; the second reshuffle was approved by 77 votes; while the last was offered only 65 votes, leading Furughi to feel that he could not continue in office. His reshuffles, partly intended to buy support from the deputies, were ineffective. According to the British Legation, 'in an effort to placate [the deputies], the weary Prime Minister tried the novel expedient of selecting fourteen deputies by lot to advise him as to the formation of his Cabinet: that came to nothing'.[39] Furughi was not a skilful manipulator. He was not energetic enough to build up an extensive and effective clientele; nor capable enough to sustain the support of his friends, followers or sympathizers inside and outside the Majlis. He betrayed little ability or willingness to appreciate and adapt himself to the changing political milieu and mood of the country. He neglected, ignored or resisted many demands which it might have been politically possible and expedient to satisfy.

This was clearly discernible in his choice of colleagues – many were associated with the previous regime – who were thought incompetent, or simply lacked support in the Majlis. General Ahmad Nakhjavan, the War Minister, proved incapable of reorganizing the army and restoring order in the country. In his last reshuffled Cabinet Furughi himself assumed the position of War

Minister, which was no improvement. Ali Akbar Hakimi, his Minister of Agriculture, who had a vital task given the food shortages, was an ailing and incompetent person. Isma'il Mir'at, who initially held the portfolio for Education and later for Health, faced the strong disapproval of many deputies on account of his earlier radical views on the education of girls, and particularly their participation in sports. Those deputies who claimed to approve of Furughi personally, declined to vote for his last reshuffle on the grounds of such shortcomings. As Bullard put it:

> The general criticisms of the Firughi [sic] Cabinet was that it was inactive, having failed to solve the questions of security, food supplies, return of lands acquired forcibly by the late Shah, and so on. That it contained too many soldiers (the Ministers of War, Interior and Communication) and too many of its members had held office under the former regime and could be regarded as Reza Shah's men.[40]

Furughi was ill-equipped to cope with the prevailing crisis of authority and the emerging post-Reza Shah style of politics. 'Mr. Firughi', commented Bullard on the same occasion, 'was not made to deal with such a crisis. He is not good at lobbying; he believes in the power of reason, a commodity in small demand among the Deputies of the Majlis.' It is of course true that Furughi and his colleagues were facing an exceptionally difficult situation. Nevertheless the deputies were not satisfied and should logically have chosen successors who would succeed where he had failed. Yet even if the Majlis had been solely responsible for the appointment of prime ministers and even if more competent candidates had been available, the deputies would only have favoured candidates who shared their perception of parliamentarianism. Genuinely different behaviour would have violated the rules or even undermined the basis of clan politics. This mode of politics, however, was criticized both by those who suffered from it and those who were involved in it and benefited from it. Such criticisms were strongly expressed through the press.

Soon after taking up office, Furughi was faced with increasing criticism from the press. He initially resorted to admonition, repeatedly reminding the people of the value of the rule of law and the necessity of respect for it.[41] Such admonitions had little effect, and since the existing press law was inadequate, Furughi and his Justice Minister, Majid Ahi, tried, on the last day of the 12th Majlis, to pass through a bill to restrict the press. This was unsuccessful since the deputies argued that the people had only recently been rescued from dictatorship and that freedom should not be restricted.[42] To endorse such a bill would have substantiated press accusations of a new dictatorship, and in any case a growing number of deputies either financed or patronized newspapers and did not want to see them curbed. At the same time, cries of resistance against the restriction of 'liberty', however it was understood, had a powerful appeal and attracted wide attention. This meant that the Government could only deal with the excesses of the press by means of the martial law regulations, but these were essentially ineffective. The Government and its successors, therefore, had no means and were in no position to assure themselves of a responsible, law-abiding press.

During his period of office Furughi experienced no apparent problems in his relations with the Court. Muhammad Reza Shah, both personally and through Furughi, had promised to observe the law fully. Despite his youthfulness, he showed great talent in consolidating his position; he took into account the advice of the Court entourage and engaged in charitable activities. Only one week after his accession to the throne it was announced by the Speaker of the Majlis that the Shah had made fifteen donations for the provision of a large hospital, a hotel, an asylum, a public library and a university hostel in Tehran, medical schools in Tabriz, Shiraz and Mashhad, a hospital and high school in every town of more than 10,000 inhabitants, and other projects to help the poor.[43] Such activities not only enhanced his image but helped to remove some of the grievances arising from his father's confiscation of land.

The issue of these lands was frequently taken up by deputies and in one stormy session Bihbahani, Mu'ayyid-Ahmadi and Malik-Madani demanded that Reza Shah's right of ownership be nullified,[44] while others demanded that the lands be returned to their original owners without cumbersome legislation. A bill was passed in the Majlis but only a few people managed to recover their lands. The unrecovered lands, which were 'alleged to amount to between 1500 and 2000 villages and various other items of real estate',[45] remained under the administration of the Government until July 1949, when they were returned to the Shah. However, when the Shah placed his estates at the disposal of the Government at this point, to be used for the public benefit, it symbolically implied their return to the people. Moreover, in his occasional speeches the Shah frequently referred to the desirability of maintaining democracy in Iran and ensuring respect for constitutionalism, liberty and legality. He also often emphasized that the younger generation should assume a greater role in governing the country.

Apart from his persistent efforts to project a positive image, the Shah had given his full attention to the army. In his conversations with Bullard he often discussed the need for its speedy reorganization for the purposes of internal security and his 'cherished hope' of giving the army a combat role.[46] In his efforts to consolidate his position the Shah met no opposition from Furughi, but as yet he was not an important actor in the political arena. In the 'first days of his reign' the Shah had complained to Bullard that Furughi 'was keeping him in the dark', and that he (Furughi) 'hardly expected any son of Reza Shah to be a civilised human being'. Yet the Shah and Furughi were on good terms and enjoyed 'mutual confidence'.[47] Thus, when Furughi resigned as Prime Minister he was appointed Court Minister, a position which Bullard believed suited his 'education and personality'.

Furughi had assumed the responsibility of government at a critical moment in Iranian history. He performed a valuable task in reasserting the formal authority of the Iranian Government *vis-à-vis* the occupying forces, arranged for a smooth transfer of the throne and gave an air of credibility to the Government. However, he failed to consolidate his position with regard to the Majlis or develop effective means of mobilizing a parliamentary caucus in his favour. His political style, perceptions and skills did not conform with the emerging mode of clan politics, which suited men of a different calibre who possessed more dynamism, energy and flexibility.

2

The Government of Suhaili:
MARCH–JULY 1942

The resignation of Furughi precipitated considerable activity among the deputies as well as in the Court, the British Legation and the Russian Embassy. Various caucuses of the Majlis hurriedly tried to compromise and set aside their differences, and it was hoped that factional alignments and realignments would result in a co-ordinated effort on the part of the Majlis to put forward a candidate who commanded sufficient support. However, when the Majlis voted for its preferred candidates in a private session on 4 March 1942, it was clear that a consensus had not yet emerged. While there was little hope that Furughi would accept the premiership again, over 40 votes had been cast in his favour against 39 in favour of Ahmad Qavam.

Eventually Ali Suhaili, who had only received 4 votes, was summoned by the Shah and asked to assume office. When he introduced his Cabinet to the Majlis it received an unprecedented vote of confidence of 101 out of 104.[1] Suhaili's ability was initially doubted by the British. Bullard thought that 'by far the best possible successor' to Furughi was Sayyid Hasan Taqizadih[2] – the then Iranian Minister in London – a veteran constitutionalist and one-time Finance Minister of Reza Shah before he became *persona non grata*. The British also favoured Sayyid Zia ud-Din Tabataba'i (hereafter referred to as Sayyid Zia), who had co-engineered the coup of 1921 with Reza Khan, become Prime Minister for a short period and then found himself exiled first to Europe and then to Palestine. But Taqizadih had no 'wish to be at the mercy of the irresponsible Deputies' and Sayyid Zia showed no ambition to return to Iran at this stage.[3] Moreover, both the Court and the Russians disapproved of Sayyid Zia, whose links with the British made him suspect.

The British Legation was thus left with Suhaili, whose very success in gaining the premiership was enough to impress the British. Bullard had earlier doubted whether Suhaili could summon enough support or 'collect a body of Ministers that will be stable',[4] and he had found indications of his willingness 'to accept bribes'.[5] Later, however, Bullard changed his mind and decided that Suhaili was 'as good a Prime Minister as [we] could hope to get'.[6] At least he was 'active' and 'not afraid of the Deputies'.

Suhaili owed his appointment to the confidence and support of the Court, and his own readiness to employ all possible tactics to win over the deputies. He was a loyal monarchist, readily prepared to do whatever pleased the Shah. During the abdication crisis he had shown his enthusiasm for the continuity of the Pahlavi dynasty, betrayed no desire to question royal prerogatives, and strengthened his links with the young Shah. Moreover, he cultivated his relations with the deputies most effectively; winning the favour of some through his obsequious amiability, flexibility and courtesy;[7] the co-operation of others through inducement, cajoling or other forms of manipulation; and the compliance of the more recalcitrant by implied or open intimidation. For example, he exploited a widely aired rumour that the Allies were deeply dissatisfied with the attitudes and behaviour of the Majlis. He would often refer delicate matters to secret sessions of the Majlis, ostensibly to test attitudes in an atmosphere of confidentiality, but in fact to threaten and intimidate.[8] Moreover, uncooperative deputies would be reminded that their questionable legal status provided good grounds for dissolving the Majlis. The Court's backing of Suhaili was also used to secure votes; as Bullard reported, it was 'asserted with some credibility that the police canvassed Deputies' on Suhaili's behalf, saying that he was 'the Shah's candidate' and that 'they had better vote for him'.[9] Suhaili thus won the premiership not as a consequence of genuine consensus on the part of the majority, but rather through direct or indirect pressure combined with extensive time-serving promises and undertakings which could clearly not be fulfilled. Furthermore, his premiership was a clear indication of the Court's intention to resume an effective political role, in short a manifestation of the revived structural consolidation of the monarchy. Suhaili did not, however, rely on the Court alone. He also counted on the British, who were impressed not only by his tactics *vis-à-vis* the deputies, but also his willingness to consult them over the choice of some of his colleagues, notably the Foreign Minister, Muhammad Sa'id, whom they considered 'excellent'.[10] Suhaili also tried to co-operate over the three major issues which directly concerned the Allies, namely, the closing of the Japanese Legation, the arrest of Axis agents and 'currency questions, especially the supply of notes sufficient to tide over the increased demand caused by inflated prices and the Allies' war expenditure'.[11] In the words of a British Legation report:

> The device of a secret session was used to square the Majlis about the Japanese, vague promises were given us about the Axis agents, and the currency question was temporarily solved by the issue of 700 million new notes.[12]

Guarded optimism about the likelihood of Suhaili's success was premature. The mechanisms and tactics deployed to secure the deputies' compliance, combined with the invocation of royal support and British favour, could provide no more than a temporary and precarious base for any Cabinet. Yet given the prevailing institutionally fragile political arrangements, there was scarcely any other way of attaining the premiership. Suhaili's success also owed much to his character, mentality, style and objectives. A glance at his political career and personality traits provides an insight into the manner in which he and many politicians of Reza Shah's era successfully pushed their way upward through the governmental hierarchy, survived the removal of Reza Shah without any setback and even enhanced their privileges.

Born around 1890 into a humble family, Suhaili was a graduate of the School of Political Science who started his career as a junior clerk.[13] He entered the ranks of the elite through his association with various established politicians, including Taqizadih and Baqir Kazimi,[14] under whom he served during the reign of Reza Shah as under-secretary in the Ministry of Roads and Communications, and later the Ministry of Foreign Affairs. A change of Foreign Minister resulted in a posting to London, but after a year he was recalled and appointed Foreign Minister. In 1938 he was dismissed from this post along with the Minister of Education after incurring the wrath of Reza Shah over the dispatch of a telegram to the French Minister of Education at a time when a French newspaper had just published an article critical of the Shah. Aware of Reza Shah's temper Suhaili lived in self-imposed seclusion for eight months until he was appointed Governor of Kerman. Later he became Ambassador to Kabul and was recalled to be appointed Minister of the Interior in the Cabinet of Ali Mansur.[15] This position he retained until he became Minister of Foreign Affairs in Furughi's Cabinet.

Suhaili's political success was largely due to his ability to seek out and employ the patronage first of influential members of the elite, and eventually of Reza Shah himself. Ibrahim Khajih-Nuri, a pro-British politician-publicist who knew Suhaili well, portrays him as a man who from the outset had realized that political success is not ensured by integrity or a scrupulous sense of duty but by the 'favour of the superiors', and that in order to ensure such favour, 'speaking the truth, revealing one's intelligence and sincerity, preventing mistakes being made by the superior and guiding him' were 'not only totally useless, but even harmful'; as a man who simulated credulity when his superiors spoke and thus insinuated himself in their favour; and as a humble, cautious, unpretentious pragmatist whose 'elasticity of character' had enabled him to appease the fastidious Reza Shah. In the view of Khajih-Nuri, when Suhaili decided which course of action to embark on, he was motivated far less by the dictates of his conscience than the expectations of his superiors and the Shah.

Khajih-Nuri also asserts that Suhaili was a docile and obedient politician devoid of, or possibly capable of disguising, those qualities which aroused the envy of others. His ability to keep a low profile, to be prudent and defensive, to feign innocence and resignation, and to simulate loyalty were the essential ingredients of success in a society which fostered insecurity, and in which promotion was neither secured nor maintained through formal or rational procedures. A characteristic component of Reza Shah's autocratic rule was that politicians were either tame and obedient servants of the Shah or his staunch enemies, to be silenced, banished or even killed. Suhaili belonged to the first category.

In addition to soliciting patronage, Suhaili sought to build up his own clientele. This he tried to accomplish by lavish promises of potential gains rather than by the distribution of concrete spoils. He 'cautiously evaded decisively saying no to anyone', compensated for one unfulfilled promise by making two others and, as those remained unfulfilled, made yet further ones.[16] This behaviour was only temporarily effective, if at all. For it was essentially repugnant to the 'ethic' of patronage which involved reciprocity, a relatively sustained loyalty based on a mutually observed code of honour and a recognition on the part of clients not only of the power and influence of the patron but also of his prestige and credibility. Suhaili's unreliability, prevarications and spurious pledges were deeply damaging to his prestige and did not provide him with a reliable clientele. Suhaili thus remained primarily dependent on his own patrons, particularly Reza Shah himself and later his heir. The weakening of monarchical power, however, meant that Suhaili also needed to procure the favour of the Majlis deputies, which he did by employing the methods described.

Verbiage aside, Suhaili's Cabinet programme centred on the two interrelated problems of security and shortages. The security problem mainly involved the reassertion of the government's authority over the tribal areas, an objective equally valued by the British Legation. In his first interview with Suhaili as Prime Minister, Bullard asked him to issue a statement containing promises of concrete and specific reforms which would benefit the tribes and an unequivocal recognition of tribal grievances, to be promptly investigated by the Government.[17] To British disappointment, the statement Suhaili produced was too vague and general to attract any attention.[18] At that time, no less than any other, the tribal problem was tackled mainly by military operations, attempts to stimulate inter- and intra-tribal divisions, to exploit leadership rivalries and by bribery, co-optation and similar tactics.

Among the tribal leaders, Nasir Khan Qashqa'i was most successful in uniting his co-tribesmen and alarming both the central government and the British. The latter strongly suspected Nasir Khan of anti-British sentiments and feared that in the absence of the 'counter-balancing influence' of Ibrahim Qavam (Qavam ul-Mulk) he might even be able to secure the support of the Khamsih and Kuhgiluyih tribes. They therefore encouraged the return of Qavam ul-Mulk to Fars.[19] Born in 1888, Qavam ul-Mulk had inherited the headship of the Khamsih confederacy founded by his family. As governors of Fars, the Qavams were traditionally opposed to the Qashqa'is and were used by the central government and the British to counterbalance the influence of the Qashqa'is. Qavam was one of the wealthiest landowners in Iran and was described by the British as 'very pro-British in sentiment'.[20] Also, one of his sons was married to Ashraf Pahlavi.

In other areas the situation seemed less serious. In Kurdistan opposition to the Government did not enjoy 'combination and leadership', nor was there a strong anti-British tradition.[21] Moreover, Kurdish hopes in Hama Rashid, the initially acclaimed Kurdish leader, were receding. Hama Rashid, described by a British political adviser visiting the area as 'a brigand without any honour or principles', whose treatment of the Kurdish population had been 'worse than their treatment by the Persians', was, however, restraining the majority of the Kurds, 'who were ready to come to terms' with the central government.[22] Nevertheless, by the end of May 1942 it seemed clear that Hama Rashid had been defeated and violent Kurdish opposition to the central government had been at least temporarily suspended.[23]

The situation in the tense and disorderly Bakhtiari area had also caused some concern. In March 1942 a Bakhtiari leader, in conversation with the British Vice-Consul in Isfahan, had spoken of the unity of the Bakhtiaris and the formation of a government of their own. At the end of March, however, General Fazlullah Zahidi was appointed military governor of Isfahan. Zahidi managed to bring calm to the area, mostly by the use of manipulatory tactics and negotiations with various Bakhtiari leaders,[24] but in September 1942 he was kidnapped by the British and exiled to Palestine on charges of complicity with a pro-Axis organization. The complaints of the Bakhtiaris, shared by other tribes, stemmed from their mistrust of the central government, which in their view had little knowledge of tribal problems and no tribal policy, and from the feeling that the deputies of the Majlis were townspeople and therefore enemies of the tribes.[25]

A central complaint, however, concerned the confiscated lands. Although proper investigation and satisfaction of at least some of the tribal demands was not beyond the capacity of the central government, its tribal policy remained essentially coercive and manipulatory and devoid of any real understanding of the hardships and plight of the tribes. Nevertheless by the end of July 1942, when the end of Suhaili's Cabinet was imminent, the tribal problem seemed to pose a less serious threat. Although the Qashqa'i and Kuhgiluyih areas were not open to government troops and although the British were worried by the belief that the Qashqa'is were 'harbouring some German agents', at least Nasir Khan had made peace with the central government.[26]

The shortage of food and other necessities proved a more formidable problem and the Government was far less equipped to tackle it. The British arranged for the import of 70,000 tons of wheat, which amounted to only one-fifth of Iran's yearly requirement. Many people feared the prospect of famine on a scale similar to that experienced during the First World War, and, as a result, anti-Allied feeling gained further momentum. Bullar confessed that there were 'undoubtedly many Persians who would be glad to see the Germans come and put an end to the presence of Russian and British troops on Persian soil'. He attributed this feeling partly to 'not unreasonable nationalism' and partly to a widespread belief that the Allies were 'responsible for the short supplies of bread, sugar, piecegoods and other necessities, coupled with the very high prices'.[27] In the face of such feelings Bullard believed that the Allies could not do much by way of propaganda and pressure, but could only deploy 'moral influence' to induce the Iranian Government to show firmness and initiative in the alleviation of shortages.

The Government was intent on improving the food situation, which the British thought could only be done by a systematic campaign against hoarding. However, fearing the social consequences, the Government refused to endorse official price increases and confined itself to the coercion and prosecution of the hoarders, for which the Majlis had granted it full powers. But in the absence of an effective administrative machinery and trained, reliable personnel, matters seemed to get worse. By invoking the anti-hoarding bill, 'clever officials' could share the fortunes of the hoarders.[28] Rich hoarders with the proper connections lost no sleep over the Government's measures. The poor, however, continued to suffer and corruption proliferated. In practice, the Government's anti-hoarding measures were confined to a 'few local raids', particularly in the Khuzistan area.[29]

The critical stalemate in the food situation, with its consequent arousal of anti-Allied sentiments, inevitably worried British officials. They and the Russians were particularly concerned about the strength of pro-German feelings, as a network of organized pro-German groups, implicating a large number of senior Iranian governmental officials as well as military officers, was being uncovered by Allied intelligence. In such a situation, the alleviation of shortages was considered imperative. But neither the Allies nor the Iranian Government had the means to alter the food situation in any real way.

The Iranian governmental apparatus was clearly ill-equipped to deal with the consequences of the occupation and the impact of the war, and the Allies were obliged to help, or at least appear to help, both in the restoration of a degree of law and order and the alleviation of shortages. Of the two powers the British with their vital oil interests had a far greater stake in improving the bureaucracy's capacity to cope with both immediate problems and long-term reform. They therefore tried to exert their 'moral influence' to cope with the 'lethargy and corruption of Persian officialdom'[30] and soon began to involve themselves actively at various government levels, advising Iranian officials on all major issues and many minor matters. However, recognizing that this was unlikely to be either an effective or a popular strategy, they gradually turned to the idea of independent, legally sanctioned foreign advice. One British official expressed an outlook shared by many of his colleagues when he wrote:

> At the risk of hurting the feelings of Iranians (who wrongly believe that they can 'run their own show' properly without foreign advisers and inspectors), unless foreign officials are employed by the Iranian Government it is to be feared that corruption, tyranny and inefficiency will continue to flourish among all Iranian Government officials and that the tribal population will always be on the lookout for opportunities to avenge themselves for the wrongs and injustices suffered by them and be a potential menace to the peace of the country.[31]

Such ideas were current throughout the greater part of Suhaili's term of office and in one session of the Majlis the Prime Minister himself spoke frankly of his intentions to invite foreign advisers.[32] All this was eventually to culminate in the arrival of American financial and military missions. Before the Americans arrived, however, the British actively intervened in administrative affairs, and Suhaili often complied with their directives. For instance he acquiesced in a British demand that no visa for travel to Iran be granted without their prior consent; he agreed that specific and firm measures be adopted against Axis propaganda, and that the British be aided and given a free hand in arresting and prosecuting those suspected of pro-German activities.[33] Yet ironically, while actions of this kind brought Suhaili the alienation or enmity of a considerable number of people, it did not secure for him the sustained support of the British, who blamed him for mismanaging the distribution of scarce goods and held him responsible for the lack of improvement in the food situation. In the view of a Foreign Office official writing towards the end of Suhaili's term of office:

> No man who suddenly discovers that Tehran has less than one day's wheat supply really deserves any consideration from us and I do not think we need make any effort to keep Suhaily in power.[34]

On 28 July 1942 the Russian Ambassador sent Suhaili a letter of protest over his inability to deal with the food problem, communications and the German 'fifth column'. The very next day Suhaili was faced with an expression of British disappointment.[35] His suspicion that he had lost Allied confidence, and particularly British support, was thus confirmed. Bullard thought this was a 'deciding factor' in his resignation the next day, 30 July 1942, after 144 days in office. Suhaili's resignation, however, was not simply a consequence of Allied pressure; he had also faced considerable problems in his relations with increasingly critical deputies, as well as his own colleagues in the Cabinet.

Suhaili seemed solely concerned with the deflection of immediate troubles and myopically insensitive to the cumulative frustrations caused by his empty promises. Without giving up his usual style of appeasement, he threatened to dissolve the Majlis in order to prevent the obstructiveness of the deputies. The idea of dissolving parliament was also favourably entertained by the British (and ostensibly at least by the Russians and the Americans) as well as by the Shah.[36] The British Foreign Office did not rule out the possibility of 'communists' entering the next Majlis, but doubted that they could be as 'mischievous' as the 'present gang'. In any case, even if the next Majlis was not an improvement, its deputies could also be 'sent packing'.[37] Thus the Foreign Office endorsed not only the dissolution of the Majlis but also recommended that there be no hurry in starting the next elections or specifying any definite dates.[38] The Soviet Ambassador, however, finally came out in opposition, arguing that 'the moment was not opportune'.[39]

The growing criticism of Suhaili in the Majlis had also centred on his inability to tackle the problem of shortages and the distribution of food supplies, which had recently caused bread riots in towns such as Malayir and Burujird, where the harvest had been good and there was little justifiable ground for shortages.[40] Suhaili's failure on this score could not be attributed to the obstructiveness of the Majlis which had, on the contrary, given him special powers. Thus, it was difficult for Suhaili to justify the dissolution. Only an able Prime Minister who was clearly being restricted by the Majlis would have been in a position to implement the threat.

The deputies gradually realized that Suhaili could carry out neither his promises nor his threats. His indecisiveness, vacillation, prevarications and reputed dishonesty, which had earned him the sobriquet of 'liar number one',[41] eventually alienated most of his friends and supporters, and provoked the active enmity of others. For example, Musaddiq, who later steadily opposed him, described him as a man who even among foreigners was renowned for his 'untrustworthiness and corruption'.[42] Ali Dashti, the vocal Majlis deputy who had mobilized his friends and clients into the Justice Party, expended considerable energy in opposing Suhaili, concentrating on his unfulfilled promises. One such promise concerned Farajullah Bahrami, a one-time secretary and confidant of Reza Shah and a member of Dashti's party who had reportedly been assured the portfolio of the Interior but was eventually denied the position, which to everybody's surprise was offered to Sayyid Mihdi Farrukh, the then Governor-General of Kerman. Persistently pressed by the deputies for Kerman to recall Farrukh and unwilling to add him to his list of enemies, Suhaili had offered him the portfolio of the Interior.[43] Even so, Farrukh later became one of Suhaili's most uncompromising opponents. Other prominent deputies who joined in undermining Suhaili's position in the Majlis were Murtiza Quli Bayat (who later became Prime Minister) and Dr. Mihdi Malikzadih (an influential physician and landowner who had by then represented the southern city of Bam seven times in succession).

The erosion of Suhaili's prestige and parliamentary support, to which the activities of Qavam and Muhammad Tadayyun – both contenders for office – had contributed, helped bring the disagreements and frictions with his own colleagues to the surface. When Suhaili appointed Majid Ahi, his Minister of Justice, as Ambassador to Moscow, Ahi refused the offer and engaged in intrigues against him. This was a further important factor in undermining Suhaili's position and contributed to the public feeling that 'the Cabinet was on its last legs'.[44] Moreover, allegations about his dishonesty or, as Bullard put it, 'his financial and moral irregularities', increasingly became the subject of 'scandalous rumours'[45] and criticism in the press, which Suhaili tried in vain to curb. Like his predecessor, Suhaili had tried to restrict the press by legislation. The Majlis had of course refused to pass his bill and the Government continued to rely on ineffective martial law regulations to control the newspapers.

The major unresolved problems, the loss of support or acquiescence, and the dispersal of the tactical alignments which had constituted the basis of Suhaili's premiership, resulted in a fall in his own morale,[46] as well as a marked deterioration in the authority of the governmental apparatus, and left him with no choice but to resign.[47] He could not even turn to the Court, which had been instrumental in his appointment as Prime Minister. The Shah was not in a position to intervene on Suhaili's behalf, nor could he see much point in doing so. In speeches given on the occasion of the Iranian New Year, on 21 March 1942, both Suhaili and the Shah exhorted the people to 'unity', 'self-sacrifice' and the 'diminution of personal interests and concerns' in favour of 'public interests'.[48] The ruling elite, however, was clearly in greater need of such exhortations.

Civic virtues were sanctimoniously invoked along with constitutional rituals to provide legitimacy, but were essentially incongruent with the practical requirements of success in Iranian clan politics. Suhaili's lack of concern for the publicly valued qualities of statesmanship had in many ways facilitated his careerist aims. However, he had not observed the traditionally sanctioned 'ethic' of patronage: while he had feigned to be a loyal client, he had failed to act as a reliable patron. In the context of post-Reza Shah clan politics this was a liability which Suhaili endeavoured to convert into an asset. When he resigned, therefore, he was not disheartened; he immediately engaged in preparations for the moment when his qualities would again be required. In the event he did not have too long to wait.

Suhaili was able to assume the premiership as the result of political alignments, manoeuvres and tactics which were the by-products and, dialectically, the reproducers or reaffirmers of the structural configuration of Iranian clan politics. His premiership both demonstrated and contributed to the political stalemate which was built into elite-level political activity. The prevailing clan politics gave an opportunity to those men of ambition who strove to enjoy the benefits of office and brought in their friends and followers with promises of a share of the spoils, or at least a free hand to maintain or enlarge their own domains and patrimonies. Of course these men were also expected to pay attention to the needs and complaints of the mass of the people who did not even possess the basic necessities of life. Nevertheless the Iranian state was essentially a patrimony of the elite. Its main function was to legitimize and perpetuate domination by the elite, and to engineer consent, acquiescence or compliance. It provided the ruling elite with a framework for competition, a channel for ambitions, a vehicle for the preservation and enhancement of political gains and the distribution of rewards. The entire paraphernalia of the state primarily served the interests of the elite and, more generally, the upper class at the expense of the subordinate classes. Not surprisingly, its oppressive and exploitative functions were much more tangible than its public benefits.

The underlying and self-perpetuating stalemate of clan-monopolized politics defied any attempt to alter or modify the structural configuration of the state. Positions of authority were normally offered to and exchanged between men who had no greater ability than Suhaili. Although this was frequently denied or disguised, the experience of Ahmad Qavam's premiership provided a clear case in point.

3

The Government of Qavam:
AUGUST 1942–FEBRUARY 1943

Before Suhaili's resignation the usual moves had started to find a successor, and Ahmad Qavam (Qavam us-Sultanih) was considered a likely candidate. The experience with Suhaili had led the deputies to opt for a candidate of ability who would command respect. Although they knew he would refuse to take office, they unanimously voted for Husain Pirnia (Mu'tamin ul-Mulk), a highly respected retired politician. They did this to make a public show of goodwill and to deflect criticisms that the Majlis would only support unpopular and servile candidates. It was also a useful tactic to extract further concessions from the candidate who would eventually succeed. After Pirnia's publicized refusal of the offer, the six existing factions in the Majlis resumed their intensive bargaining, which eventually ended in a vote for Qavam.

The premiership of Qavam had been almost inevitable, despite the usual procrastinations of the deputies and long before their formal expression of approval. Qavam was quick to resume his political activities after Reza Shah's abdication. His exclusion from the politics of the Reza Shah era distinguished him from many of his rivals, facilitated publicity on his behalf as a man who stood for parliamentarianism, and legitimized his claim to be better qualified to lead a constitutional government than those who had served the previous regime. Qavam was in a position to win over an adequate number of deputies to support his candidature, having an active entourage and being less vulnerable to defamatory tactics than many of his rivals. As seen above, when Furughi resigned, Qavam had enjoyed far greater support in the Majlis than Suhaili. He later told one of his close friends that the Shah had at that time asked him to withdraw in favour of Suhaili and to advise the deputies to vote accordingly.[1]

It was not Qavam's political style simply to rely on his friends and clients inside the country, or on the actual or promised support of the deputies. He also considered the active support, or at least the acquiescence, of the Russians, the British and the Americans to be indispensable. Among the foreign powers the Russians favoured him because he was neither a Court favourite nor a known anglophile. In fact, he was suspected of being opposed by both, particularly the British. Moreover, his considerable estates were located primarily in the Russian-occupied zone, with the result that the Russians were in a better position to influence him. Enjoying the favour of the Russians also implied benefiting from the support of the Tudeh Party, some of whose leaders were in close contact with Qavam.[2] Qavam was also favoured by the Americans, since during his earlier political career he had consistently advocated the greater involvement of the Americans in Iranian politics as a counterbalancing force to the Russians and British.[3]

This view was part of a conventional wisdom shared by a large number of politicians and was based on an innocent but plausible assumption that imperialist encroachments and pressures stemmed primarily from geographical proximity and were rooted in traceable historical concerns. Thus, before and during the First World War and to some extent during the Second World War, Germany was welcomed and her victory widely hoped for. For the same reasons United States policy towards Iran was thought to be devoid of imperialist intentions, and the balancing effect of an expanding American influence in Iran was considered to be of more benefit than danger to the country, since the vested British and Russian interests prevented any third country assuming a unique position of dominance.

On resuming political activity, therefore, Qavam revived his contacts with the Americans and encouraged their active concern with Iranian political affairs. In this he was well received by them.[4] The British had initially suspected Qavam of being too inclined towards the Russians and they, along with his domestic supporters, either believed or were led to believe that this was still the British view.[5] In fact, after an interview with A. C. Trott of the British Legation, Qavam had been found to be independent of the Russians.[6] Thus, when on 29 July the Shah sent a message to Bullard that he was 'thinking of sending for Qavam', Bullard replied that he had 'no objection to him as Prime Minister'.[7]

In gaining the support of the Russian as well as the British and American representatives, Qavam had demonstrated considerable skill in appeasing all and alienating none, without being unduly servile. This was done in the knowledge that he would soon have to challenge the prevailing political stalemate and would thus provoke and encounter widespread enmity and opposition. He believed that such opposition could only be effective with the support of one embassy or another, and had therefore taken steps to prevent it. In reality Qavam's tactics were more in line with the perceptions of the elite than appeared at first sight. By providing himself with foreign support, or at least protecting himself from the intrigues and hostility of foreign powers, he hoped to be able to overcome any internal rivals and enemies. He later discovered that foreign influence was far more effective when negatively applied; the support of foreigners was not enough to replace an eroding internal base of support.

The Shah and a large number of deputies initially favoured or acquiesced in Qavam's premiership because the experience with Suhaili had clearly shown the need for a man of greater ability. Qavam was accepted not simply because he was the best-qualified person, but also because it was thought that to refuse him would provoke the Russians. In addition, it was feared that his refusal might lead him to participate in activities which would complicate the task of any government and eventually paralyse it. His supporters and enemies all shared a belief in his personability. His enemies, and those who distrusted his dealings with foreigners but did not yet actively oppose him, were all watching to see what course he would follow to satisfy all parties, within the constitutional conventions of prime-ministerial authority. Despite his personal qualities, however, neither Qavam nor any other prime minister could achieve much in unfavourable conditions, and his first attempt at premiership in the post-Reza Shah period was characterized by a struggle to increase his power and the concerted efforts of rival alliances to prevent it.

Ahmad Qavam, a brother of Hasan Vusuq (Vusuq ud-Daulih) – who was himself one of the most able but least popular prime ministers of the pre-Pahlavi era – was born in Tehran around 1877 into a wealthy land-owning family traditionally involved in the administration of the country. At seventeen years of age he was sent to France to study political science and on his return to Iran became Minister in a number of Cabinets. After the coup of February 1921 he was one of many influential politicians who were detained, and was in prison when asked by Ahmad Shah Qajar to form a Cabinet after the collapse of Sayyid Zia's short-lived Government (June 1921). From June 1922 to 1923 he again became Prime Minister, but later went into exile in Europe when Reza Khan suspected him of

complicity in a conspiracy against him. After some years he returned
to Iran to live in retirement until the fall of Reza Shah.[8]

Qavam was one of the most influential and prestigious members
of the Iranian elite of the pre- and post-Reza Shah eras. He was a
large landowner with vast tea plantations around the northern city of
Lahijan. His opulence, generosity and the weight of his personality
had attracted to him a motivated entourage and large clientele. His
reputed strength of character, courage, vigour and dignified manner,
his obstinacy and pride, which often reached the boundaries of
arrogance – particularly when in office – as well as his undisguised
self-esteem and love of respect, title and celebrity, evoked mixed
feelings of admiration and abhorrence.[9] Among Iranian statesmen
he was known for his 'natural authority and readiness to face
difficulties with self-confident cool-headedness and tranquillity of
mind'.[10] He was described as 'a sharp sabre indispensable for
battles'[11] by Sayyid Hasan Mudarris, a staunch parliamentarian later
eliminated by Reza Shah. With these actual or reputed qualities
Qavam could only hope for the opportunity to take office during a
time of crisis, and then only when his rivals had either failed or were
unlikely to succeed. The Shah, and also many deputies whose
excessive parliamentary privileges Qavam did not favour, or towards
whom he was not sufficiently obsequious, were of course bound to
oppose him sooner or later. Finally, his refusal to keep a low profile
clearly contrasted with Suhaili's style and was likely to expose him to
intense envy, endless intrigue and hostility.

Qavam agreed to form a Cabinet on condition that he would be
free to select his colleagues. Nevertheless his choice of ministers
showed his appreciation of the various interests which expected to be
represented. His colleagues were all established members of the elite,
and with one exception had all previously held ministerial portfolios.
In the hope of countering suspicions and affirming his allegiance both
to parliamentary government and to the monarch, he introduced an
oath of loyalty to the Shah and the Government, to be taken by all
members of his Cabinet.[12] Also, in order to deflect criticisms about
his 'despotic' manner and to reduce fears that he would act without
due consultation, he invited Sadiq Sadiq (Mustashar ud-Daulih) and
Ibrahim Hakimi, two respected elder politicians, to work with him
in an advisory capacity. As a further gesture to constitutionalism he
appointed Saham ud-Din Ghaffari Director of Press and Propaganda.
According to a British report Ghaffari 'was inclined to criticize the
Pahlavi regime, and to regret the disappearance of the Constitution

and liberty of speech' even while Reza Shah was in power.[13] In an effort to save time and prevent controversy, Qavam did not submit an extensive programme when he presented his Cabinet to the Majlis, but simply emphasized the improvement of security and food supplies as his main objective. He also gave a stern warning to hoarders and announced that his Government intended to make the best possible use of educated young people.[14] On 13 August 1942, the Cabinet was offered a vote of confidence of 109 out of 116, although the only characteristic which distinguished it from its predecessors was the personality of the Prime Minister himself.

As usual, this impressive vote of confidence was no guarantee of sustained support from the Majlis. The obstructiveness of the deputies was the subject of considerable concern to the British who now hoped that Qavam was the person who could accomplish the dissolution of the Majlis. Bullard was 'confident' that the Majlis represented a 'serious danger' and feared that if the Russians were defeated by the Germans the deputies 'might make nationalistic declarations and perhaps cancel their ratification of the treaty'.[15] In his exchanges with the Foreign Office Bullard provided elaborate justification for the dissolution of the existing Majlis and the need for a new one, and the Foreign Office categorically stated that 'the sooner the present Majlis is dissolved the better'.[16]

Obviously there were constitutional obstacles to the dissolution of the Majlis and the postponement of the next elections, but this did not impress Bullard who simply commented that 'attachment to the letter of the law' was 'not a feature of the Persian character, and when it came to the point ... a way of avoiding fresh elections would very probably be found'.[17] Similarly, the Foreign Office was not convinced that it was 'necessary to adduce specific constitutional arguments'. 'Indeed', it was argued, 'the Persians themselves, by failing to form the Senate in spite of the constitutional provisions, had not attached undue importance to the letter of their constitution.'[18] Bullard apparently had the agreement of his Russian counterpart in this matter, so they had only to wait for a suggestion from either the Shah or the Prime Minister.[19] On the other hand, if the Prime Minister was able to control the Majlis – as he did during his first two months of office – and if the Majlis did not create a 'nuisance' and hinder the task of the Government, then the British were prepared not to 'proceed for the moment'.[20]

Qavam experienced his first major crisis with the Majlis when he submitted his bill on military service. Although a very similar bill had been submitted by the previous Cabinet and extensively debated in the Majlis, the deputies expressed their intention of revising the bill, while Qavam demanded that it must either be passed as it stood or rejected altogether. The deputies jumped on this as an example of his authoritarian manner, while Ali Dashti delivered a spirited speech in defence of the 'sovereignty of the Majlis' which, he argued, was in fact the 'sovereignty of the nation' and reminded Qavam that 'we have recently been relieved of the burden of despotism and we will not submit to the despotism of Qavam us-Saltanih'.[21] Qavam was obliged to withdraw the bill for further study and was left in no doubt that he was as vulnerable *vis-à-vis* the Majlis as any other prime minister.

A few days after this first confrontation Qavam delivered a conciliatory speech to the Majlis repeating his genuine constitutional convictions as well as his respectful recognition of the authority of the legislature. In this way he hoped to improve his relations with the deputies, or at least prevent a further deterioration, but he did remind them of the immense difficulties facing the Cabinet and of his determination not to succumb to lethargy. He and his colleagues intended to exercise their full legal authority. Finally, he emphasized his reliance on all those who were concerned about the terrible consequences of governmental instability.[22] The majority of deputies interpreted this speech as a retreat on Qavam's part and publicized it as the Prime Minister's word of honour, which he could not afford to break. In fact there was growing apprehension (provoked by Qavam's recent suppression of a few newspapers) that he intended to eradicate existing political liberties and undermine the authority of the Majlis. The reported 'recent improvement in relations between the Prime Minister and the Shah' added to such fears.[23] Having received Qavam's reassurances, the deputies hoped that he would now proceed within the boundaries of the prevailing understanding of parliamentary government.

Qavam, however, had no illusions about the possibility of realizing his Cabinet programme without a freer hand and a greater measure of authority, and without immunity from continuous harassment by the Majlis. In a meeting with Qavam and his Minister of Foreign Affairs in early October 1942 Bullard found them 'very depressed'. However, after discussions he concluded that:

> The Prime Minister seems to be the most courageous of the Ministers in supporting our cause and the best way to help him and ourselves is

by agreeing to dissolve the Parliament even though we thereby furnish material for Axis propaganda.[24]

Apart from intractable constitutional difficulties, the dissolution of the Majlis on the grounds of manipulation of its elections would have undermined the legal status of the Tripartite Treaty of Alliance as well as those approved bills which had benefited the Allies. On the other hand, if the issue of the illegally conducted elections was not raised, what other pretext could be invoked to dissolve the Majlis? If extra-parliamentary methods were used, would it be possible to save the image of Iranian constitutional government? With these questions in mind the British were prepared to help dissolve the Majlis only in the unlikely event that the Iranians were themselves prepared to make the first move.[25] Qavam's willingness to dissolve the Majlis did not go further than a desire to impress the British, and a means of threatening the Majlis in order to extract concessions. It was highly unlikely that he or any other prime minister, on the basis of foreign support alone, would be prepared to step so far outside the essentially defensive and cautious mode of conduct of the Iranian political elite. Its positive consequences were at best unclear, while any negative outcome would inevitably include self-inflicted ostracization.

The Russians had by now changed their views on the dissolution and according to the Foreign Office were following a policy of procrastination. Finally, whatever the deputies' real motives and concerns, they did represent and articulate urgent public demands and grievances. It would be difficult in this situation to argue that the Majlis should be dissolved in order to protect the public interest. Bullard was quite clear that:

unfortunately the Majlis does represent the views of the Persian people on two questions which the people can now consider most important, viz. high prices and bread. The Majlis accuses the Allies of raising the prices by inflation of the currency, failure to supply goods and so on, and of exposing the country to famine by not bringing in food stuffs.[26]

Bullard confessed that the dissolution of the Majlis was probably more difficult now than it had been in the past. But Qavam needed to have either the support or the acquiescence of the Majlis if he hoped to respond to the demands of the Allies.

Abandoning all hope of winning sufficient support from the

deputies, Qavam attempted to free himself from their control or opposition by preparing a bill demanding the temporary granting of full powers to himself for a period of approximately nine months, ending in August 1943, primarily in order to tackle the problems of shortages, inflation, disorder and inadequate transportation.[27] If he was at all hopeful that such a bill would be approved, or even that its submission would result in an improvement in his situation, it was because he believed that the deputies might acquiesce in granting him full powers (or at least prove more prepared to bargain) in view of the danger to the very existence of the 13th Majlis. In the view of Bullard, 'if Qavam failed to secure the passage of the bill he would wish to dissolve the Majlis'.[28] Qavam received varied responses from his foreign supporters on this issue. The Russian Ambassador claimed not to have received any instructions; the Americans opposed the venture because of its 'bad political consequences for Iran and other Moslem countries'. The British, however, reassured Qavam on the eve of the submission of the bill that he had their 'full support in his efforts to secure full power'.[29]

The Allies' common objectives and concerns in their struggle against the Axis were not necessarily reflected in a co-ordinated policy towards Iran. According to one American official, the Russians appeared to view with suspicion 'every move made by the British and the Americans'. The Americans themselves, trying at least ostensibly to attune their policy to the spirit of the Atlantic Charter, disapproved of the 'blunt, uncompromising attitude' which charac-terized British policy in Iran, and felt it did not 'augur well for a future amicable adjustment of Anglo-Iranian relations'. This American official was far from reassured 'to recall the recent British proposal to arrogate to the Allies power to modify the Iranian Cabinet at will'.[30]

On previous occasions, including through a radio broadcast, Qavam had expressed his belief that 'the accomplishment of the Government's duties is not possible without authority'.[31] The introduction of the full powers bill to the Majlis in defiance of the very perceptual basis of the prevailing parliamentarianism, confirmed latent apprehensions about Qavam's 'despotic' tendencies. The generally anti-authoritarian milieu of the post-1941 era had made such non-constitutionalist moves unpopular and easy to exploit. Although he faced intense hostility Qavam did not resign, but circulated statements throughout Tehran publicizing and explaining his actions, particularly concentrating on the Allied support for his Government and their displeasure at the behaviour of the Majlis.[32]

The deputies realized that undue hostility towards Qavam would be interpreted as opposition to the Allies; under pressure from the British and Russians they agreed to the transfer of control of the note issue to the Currency Commission, an appendage to the Cabinet. This concession, and the toleration of Qavam after the date when he submitted the full powers bill, might suggest that his manoeuvres had been partially successful. Nevertheless Qavam owed his survival exclusively to Allied support and the threat they posed to the Majlis, which could scarcely be considered a dignified way of retaining office.

Whether intentional or not, Qavam's demand for full powers had coincided with the crisis arising from the Allies' increasing demands for rials and the Government's efforts to cope. Qavam appeared co-operative without wholeheartedly submitting to the Allies: the printing and issuing of money in response to their demands was bound to have grave inflationary consequences and aggravate other interrelated problems, namely high prices and shortages, particularly of wheat. The Allies' continuous demands were deeply resented by the deputies, especially since their co-operation was not acknowledged with help to alleviate the critical shortage of wheat. The American Minister, Louis Dreyfus, remarked that the British were reluctant to supply wheat since they maintained that there was 'sufficient wheat in hoarding to take care of Iran's needs'.[33] Dreyfus disagreed and believed that the Iranians were only 'one jump ahead of a bread shortage', which in Iran was 'tantamount to starvation'. It was therefore thought advisable for the American Government to provide as much wheat as it was able. This, Dreyfus thought, ran counter to the British policy, which he believed lacked 'comprehension and vision' and aimed at 'endeavouring to force out Qavam and obtain a more suitable Quisling'.[34] In fact, the British had no reason to dislodge Qavam, nor were they opposed to the extension of American aid to Iran, which soon materialized in the form of Lend-Lease aid.

The currency crisis resulted in the resignation of the Finance Minister who, according to one account, was also opposed to the full powers bill,[35] and 'feigned illness to avoid responsibility'.[36] The British anxiously tried to prevent a prolongation of the crisis and resorted to pressure and propaganda for this purpose, including arrangements for the publication in the Iranian press of a number of 'inspired articles'.[37] Having refused to comply with Qavam's demands for full powers, the Majlis was now left with no choice but to delegate to the Government its authority with regard to the issue of notes.

Although he was saved from the humiliation of complete defeat, Qavam was not satisfied. He summoned the British, American and Russian representatives and told them that 'either he must go or the Majlis'.[38] The Shah had always been suspicious of Qavam's convivial links with the Qajars and his antipathy to the Pahlavi dynasty. In addition, Qavam's personal retention of the War portfolio had now brought him into conflict with the Chief of the General Staff and the Shah himself. This was enough to persuade the Shah to enter the scene on the side of 'the Constitution'. He expressed his concern to Bullard about the 'possible effect of the dissolution on public opinion', but Bullard observed that his real fear was that if the Prime Minister were freed from the check provided by the Majlis he 'might try to reduce the power of the crown'.[39] Bullard, however, told him that there was no intention of changing the Constitution. The Shah pretended to be convinced and assured Bullard that they would soon get the required rials. With the Shah's dormant suspicion of him turned into active hostility, and faced with a hostile Court and an embittered Majlis, Qavam was pushed increasingly towards the Allies. On the other hand, this situation gave the deputies increased confidence and they became less reserved in their opposition to Qavam. Relations steadily deteriorated all round and three weeks later a new drama unfolded.

On 8 December a small gathering of students outside the Majlis protesting primarily at the shortage of bread, turned rapidly into a riotous crowd which for two days looted shops, sacked and set ablaze the Prime Minister's residence, and occupied the Majlis.[40] Throughout the worst moments of the unrest, the police and the military authorities did not effectively intervene, despite the fact that Qavam was nominally the War Minister.[41] It was only after the appointment of General Ahmadi as military governor of Tehran that order was eventually restored. The disturbances were instigated or manipulated by the Court's agents and followers among the deputies and journalists with the aim of harassing, demoralizing and eventually ousting the Prime Minister. An important role was played by Colonel Ibrahim Arfa, brother of the deputy Chief of Staff, and himself Commander of the Tehran Second Division and a known German sympathizer who had established close links with the Shah. The riots failed to give the appearance of an authentic expression of popular discontent. *Rahbar*, the official organ of the Tudeh Party, represented the views of many who doubted the constitutional concerns of the monarch and feared that such disturbances might provide the Government with a pretext to curb existing liberties. *Rahbar* later asserted that:

> A hired rabble, posing as freedom-lovers, gathered in Baharistan Square. While flagellating themselves, they attracted a handful of simple-minded folk, and in the name of seeking justice and desiring liberty incited the people and eventually burst upon the alley-ways and bazaars and started looting. . . . Nobody in the Majlis questioned the happenings . . . the events of 17th Azar were the first offensive of the reactionary forces.[42]

The events of 8 and 9 December resulted in considerable casualties and damage to property,[43] and were considered to be a 'riddle' by many people. The solution of the riddle was prevented by those who had instigated the riots: discussion was suppressed in the Majlis and investigations into them continued only as long as Qavam was in office. Although few observers doubted royal involvement, the agents of the Court (led by the Mas'udi brothers and in particular Abbas Mas'udi, the editor of *Ittila'at*, who was suspected of having been paid by the Court to instigate the riots) launched a campaign to attribute responsibility solely to Qavam. Some of Qavam's friends, on the other hand, blamed the British,[44] not so much because they subscribed to the prevailing stereotype of a British hand in everything, but in order to discredit Qavam's enemies by branding them as stooges of the British who could do little without foreign support. They also hoped in this way to deflect criticism of Qavam's reliance on the Allies. Underneath all these claims was a basic principle of the prevailing political culture that anyone who was or was believed to be opposed by the British must be a supporter of liberty and progress.

On the first day of the rioting the Shah, in an audience with some deputies, had complained 'several times that he had *no* authority' [original emphasis], stressed that 'unless something drastic was done there would be revolution from below' and suggested that 'a revolution from above would be better'.[45] He also emphasized that a government must come to power which would respect the principles of the Constitution.[46] The unrest of 8 and 9 December, however, was far from being a manifestation of 'revolution from below', nor would the emergence of a Court-sponsored government constitute an instance of 'revolution from above'. What was at stake was the Shah's determination to counter a Prime Minister who had dared to challenge the Court's patrimony and the royal prerogatives, by trying to curb the monarch's control over the military and by attempting to increase his own authority in defiance of the constitutional 'consensus'. The Court was against change unless it could be controlled to its own benefit, and it was only in this context that the idea of 'revolution from above' is comprehensible. The confrontation with Qavam was the Shah's main political test since his ascent to the throne, and a test also of the loyalty and reliability of the army. The Shah's determined opposition to Qavam was a warning to future contenders for power, as well as a defence of the royal domain and advantages. It was an exercise in royal self-assertion and a reconfirmation of the publicized image of the Shah as a protector of the Constitution.

In his efforts to oust Qavam the Shah enjoyed the support of the majority of the deputies. His influence and interest in politics had begun to increase soon after he assumed the throne. According to the British Legation, 'not only did he assume the powers and authority of an executive head of the army, but he cultivated relations with certain Deputies of the Majlis, subsidized certain newspapers and had done his best to secure the resignation of Qavam as-Saltaneh'.[47] In allying with the Shah to prevent the emergence of 'dictatorship', the deputies were not convinced of the monarch's democratic convictions. What they did hope was that his well-publicized constitutionalism would help to oust an unsuitable Prime Minister and to establish the limits and standards of royal behaviour. In their outcry against 'dictatorship' it was not that they were insincere, but rather they were blind to all but the exigencies of the moment. During the interval between Qavam's demand for full powers and the rioting in December, the deputies did little but deliver fiery speeches against him. The temporary closure of the Majlis following its occupation then confined the anti-Qavam battles to the Court.

As part of his efforts to force Qavam to resign, the Shah tried to persuade his foreign supporters to abandon him. Thus, in a meeting with Bullard, he suggested a change of government to satisfy 'public opinion' and declared that 'if the Majlis refused to co-operate he would dissolve it'. In this meeting the Shah proposed Muhammad Sa'id, who was Qavam's Minister of Foreign Affairs, as Prime Minister. Bullard, however, did not favour a change of government and it was agreed that Qavam should be retained while some of his colleagues were replaced. The Shah persisted and Bullard remarked that:

> The Shah's determined hostility to Qavam in the face of the advice of the British, Soviet and American representatives and the fact that the demonstrations were engineered and were allowed to reach such a dimension were disturbing factors of the situation.[48]

After consulting his Soviet and American counterparts, and much to the Shah's dismay, Bullard advised Qavam not to resign until further representations had been made, primarily because they were all satisfied with his responses to their demands. Qavam himself refused to be disheartened; in fact throughout the riots he had shown no sign of panic and had responded to the news of the burning of his house with 'extraordinary cool-headedness and stupendous courage and boldness'.[49]

At this point the Shah decided to concentrate on the reopening of the Majlis, complaining to Bullard that its closure was not only 'unconstitutional' but would have made him 'unable to impose any restraint on Qavam'. When the British reassured him that the Allies would not support Qavam if he 'ran amok or failed to co-operate', the Shah agreed to support him.[50] The War Ministry was now offered to General Ahmadi and the British appeared to have succeeded in reconciling the two parties. Meanwhile the Majlis was reopened after twelve days and the deputies appeared to be in a less hostile mood. Qavam delivered a conciliatory speech and stressed his respect for the Majlis; he did not raise the issue of full powers and no deputy was threatened with prosecution.[51]

On 22 January Qavam presented to the Majlis his new Cabinet, which had been reshuffled primarily to suit royal demands. Reconciliation between the Court and the Prime Minister now seemed to be a reality. However, he had not taken account of the deputies' expectations and his move to increase royal influence in the Cabinet was 'looked upon with some suspicion by many of the Majlis deputies'.[52] In addition, Qavam intended to establish a Ministry of Labour and National Economy and to appoint Nafisi, who had been Furughi's Finance Minister, to head it. This was strongly opposed by the deputies, since Nafisi was generally considered to be responsible for the inflation of the Iranian currency. Nafisi was not appointed, with the result that he became a fierce enemy of Qavam,[53] and the new ministry did not materialize.

In an attempt to win the deputies over to his new Cabinet, Qavam now introduced a bill designed to abrogate a restrictive law passed sixteen years earlier, thereby enabling deputies to assume ministerial posts without resigning their seat in the Majlis and waiting three months. According to Bullard, however, this 'merely succeeded in raising acute jealousy between rival deputies who longed for ministerial rank and the Bill was soon referred to a commission and shelved'.[54] The friction betwen the Shah and the Prime Minister also re-emerged as the result of a quarrel between Qavam and Fazlullah Bahrami, the new Minister of the Interior, over his direct and unauthorized approaches to the Shah. When asked to resign Bahrami replied 'very impertinently' and refused.[55] Qavam then threatened to resign himself but the Shah was well aware that Qavam's fall was imminent and therefore refused to accept any resignation. This left the Prime Minister with little choice but to concentrate his efforts on improving relations with the deputies.

In a conciliatory move he agreed to a Majlis bill designed to make the appointment of the head of the National Bank dependent upon the vote of the Majlis. Although this worried the British,[56] Qavam received a reprieve from the Majlis and was given a vote of confidence of 64 to 42.[57] In spite of this the precariousness of his Government was obvious and he continued his manoeuvres to strengthen his position in the Majlis. For example, he continued to press for the adoption of his bill enabling the deputies to assume ministerial portfolios without delay.[58] This was initially designed as a tactical gesture to show that the Prime Minister was prepared to share ministerial spoils with ambitious deputies. It would be a means of improving relations between the executive and the legislature by bringing into the Cabinet those deputies who were most vocal in criticizing its performance, and allowing them to experience the practical difficulties of government. Also, those influential deputies co-opted into the Cabinet would have a vested interest in prolonging its life, or at least would not continue to obstruct it. On the other hand, it could work negatively to produce new rivalries and factional alliances.

The deputies remained unenthusiastic, yet Qavam was optimistic about winning them over. To this end, he attempted to demonstrate his commitment to the broad range of the legislature's authority by arguing that it was the legislature's right to revise laws passed during the previous regime, and implying that it was even within its jurisdiction to revise the Constitution. In view of his recent attempts to extend his own power, this was unlikely to impress the deputies, while the Shah, according to Bullard, 'professed to detect the most sinister designs in his reference to the revision of the Constitution'.[59]

Qavam now faced a threat of interpellation but persisted in his efforts to strengthen his Cabinet. This was in fact beginning to disintegrate since his quarrels with the Court had disheartened royalist colleagues and resulted in their non-co-operation, if not enmity. Farrukh, Qavam's Minister of Food Supply, spoke not only for himself but for his royalist friends when he later referred to Qavam's efforts to restrict the Court as a 'disgusting plot' against the monarchy which, in his view, along with the Shi'ite religion, constituted the 'two pillars' of the nation.[60] Having failed to co-opt influential deputies Qavam now began to approach those politicians who were instrumental in orchestrating opposition to him, or whose influence and relations with the deputies could be used to prolong the life of the Cabinet. When this also failed Qavam attributed it to 'Court intrigue'.[61]

More isolated than ever, Qavam could no longer claim to enjoy any viable support inside the country, and even foreign backing was no longer effective. The Soviet Ambassador 'did his best to help' Qavam, but to no avail.[62] The British and Americans did not abandon him but saw little point in intervening on his behalf. In a meeting with Qavam on 12 February, Bullard found him 'perplexed and undecided', seeing himself as a 'victim of intrigue', and particularly angry about the intrigues of the Court and the Chief of the General Staff among the deputies.[63] On the very next day Qavam was informed by the Majlis that he no longer had the support of a majority. His Cabinet had spent most of its six months fighting for its own survival and had little energy left to tackle the urgent problems of high prices and shortages.

Qavam's initial desire to consolidate his position *vis-à-vis* the Majlis in order to deal with the most urgent problems, proved counterproductive. Exposed to hostility and faced with the contradictory demands, expectations and wishes of the deputies, the Court, the Allies and his own clientele, he turned and was increasingly pushed towards the Allies, who supported him in office in exchange for favourable responses to their demands and the promotion of their interests. Nevertheless Bullard found Qavam to be a 'vigorous, determined and sometimes obstinate old gentleman', confessed that the British Legation had 'very considerable difficulties' with him and admitted that they could not 'hope for complete subservience from any man with sufficient character'.[64]

If his approach to politics and diplomacy tended to conceal his nationalist concerns and constitutionalist beliefs, this did not mean that his relations with the foreign powers were determined simply by a lack of support within the country. He genuinely believed that Iran's national interests were best served by maintaining a foreign policy of positive equilibrium and by the emergence of a strong executive. Although his attempt to increase the power of the Prime Minister was motivated by personal as well as sectional interests and desires, it originated just as much from his appreciation of a situation in which the constraints on the authority of the Prime Minister allowed little opportunity for effective action. If his attempt to attain full powers was contrary to the existing consensus, his efforts to restrict the power of the Court and the monarch were generally conducive to a renewal of the spirit of constitutionalism. In fact, what he attempted to do was not very different from what Musaddiq hoped to accomplish later. In the end the effect of Qavam's challenge had been to strengthen rather than modify the existing stalemate. The preservation of equilibrium had proved to be the prime consideration of the ruling elite as well as the main outcome of their continuous manoeuvres, counter-manoeuvres and intrigues.

Qavam was no nobler than any other conventional politician. He did not refrain from unlawfully discriminating in favour of his supporters, and ceaselessly manoeuvred to sustain his friends, cultivate support and disarm the opposition. He departed from established practices, for example when he forbade government employees to break the fast publicly during Ramazan.[65] This he did to gain the support of the traditionally minded, as he enjoyed little support among the modernist intelligentsia. In fact his enemies were identified as 'journalists, lovers of freedom and the enemies of reaction'.[66] It is true that Qavam did not subscribe to the kind of freedom which the majority of journalists desired, and he succeeded in persuading the Majlis to modify the press law with the aim of bringing the press under greater government control.[67] In this he was only following the example of his two immediate predecessors and his treatment of the press was no harsher than theirs.

Qavam seemed to have believed that the Americans lagged behind the British and the Russians in their role in and concern with Iranian affairs, and that this was to the detriment of the country. It would thus be easy to attribute to Qavam all the blame or credit for the use of American financial advisers during his term of office.[68] However, it should not be forgotten that the idea of employing foreign advisers was very much in the air before Qavam became premier, and had been recommended to Suhaili by the British well before their arrival.[69]

In his preference for the Americans or his loyalty to the Allies Qavam was primarily motivated by pragmatic considerations. Since the outcome of the war was still unknown, he did not, therefore, entirely break with the Axis, as British officials discovered only later.[70] This was entirely consistent with a political style dictated by the demands of clan politics, whereby the possibility of contact or co-operation with those who are excluded from the circle of one's ostensible friends is never entirely eradicated. What distinguished Qavam from his rivals and enemies was not so much his unrivalled astuteness or cunning, as the fact that he was neither mediocre nor servile. In this he differed from almost all of those who had served and successfully survived the regime of Reza Shah.

4

The Government of Suhaili:
FEBRUARY 1943–MARCH 1944

Factional manoeuvres and negotiations to find a successor to Qavam and agree on the composition of the next Cabinet were already in full swing before he resigned. On the day he left office a number of deputies met the Shah and proposed Ali Suhaili as their candidate. The Shah's favoured nominee was Muhammad Sa'id, Foreign Minister in the last two Cabinets and a man who was more subservient to the Shah than was Suhaili. But the deputies refused to endorse Sa'id, even though the Shah had sent them away 'to think it over',[1] and on 17 February 1943 Suhaili's Cabinet received an overwhelming vote of confidence in the Majlis (89 out of 99).[2]

Suhaili's resumption of office, despite the inglorious record of his first term of premiership, was a result of the deputies' distasteful experience with Qavam. They were no longer prepared to accept any candidate likely to challenge their own perception of parliament-arianism. Yet it was not just passive observance of the 'rules of the game' that led to this choice. Elections for the 14th Majlis were in the offing and many deputies could only hope to secure re-election with the help of the Prime Minister. Although his promises may well have been spurious, Suhaili was the sole contender for the post who seemed ready to back his supporters or, at the very least, was unlikely actively to jeopardize the chances of success of men upon whom his position depended. His premiership aroused no enthusiasm in the Court or among the Allies, but there was no other candidate upon whom the interested parties could agree. Bullard, for instance considered Sa'id to be an 'honest' man willing to work with the Allies out of 'conviction', while Suhaili co-operated merely because he realized that the Allies would be victorious. Yet he objected to Sa'id on the grounds of his 'weakness' and thought that 'if he were Prime Minister, the country would probably be run, in fact, by the Shah and the Chief of the General Staff'.[3] This was not something the British desired at the time.

There was nothing distinctive about Suhaili's Cabinet. With three exceptions its members had served in previous governments, and its programme centred on the familiar problems of food shortages and high prices, though it also included a general reference to tackling 'fundamental problems' such as agriculture, health, education and so on.[4] For his part the Prime Minister was interested mainly in sustaining his base in the Majlis without alienating either the Court or the Allies. Nevertheless this period was marked by a new and significant underlying concern: namely the plurality of interests at work to influence the outcome of the impending elections. Apart from the foreign powers and the various alliances within the ruling elite which expected to be represented, whether directly or indirectly, there were now new forces contentiously at work to influence the outcome of the elections in their own favour and thus to the detriment of the ruling elite.

Chief among these was the Tudeh Party, the nucleus of which consisted of left-wing activists and intellectuals – and particularly the remnants of the group known as the 'fifty-three', who had been imprisoned in 1937 and released following the abdication of Reza Shah. The political relaxation which followed the fall of Reza Shah enabled the party to grow considerably, to enhance its appeal and influence, and to take advantage of, among other things, the deteriorating socio-economic conditions of Iran, as well as the marked inability of the ruling elite to tackle them.

In view of the wartime Anglo-Russian alliance and the preferences and guidelines of the Soviet Embassy, the party advocated a programme of socio-economic reform within the existing constitutional framework.[5] From the outset the moderate position of the party provoked the criticism of its radical elements; the leadership of the party was heterogeneous and there was no clear consensus on the nature of the party's relations with the Soviet Union.[6] Yet the public personality of the party was undisputedly pro-Soviet and the ultimate determinant of its collective posture was Soviet policy. The party had met with opposition from Furughi's Cabinet, but the lenient attitude of Suhaili's Government had allowed it to consolidate its position. Qavam had not reciprocated the help which some party leaders and the Soviet Embassy had given him, yet the party had continued to grow in size and organization. Its self-confidence as well as its open commitment to the Soviet Union were enhanced with the gradual triumph of the Red Army over the Germans, the Stalingrad victory of February 1943 constituting a turning point in the history of the party.[7] However, the party continued to emphasize its non-communist character, reiterating its commitment to constitutional-ism.[8] Yet the Tudeh Party's proclaimed reformist objectives and strategy in the context of its thinly disguised pro-Soviet stand, were far from comforting to the ruling elite. In view of its persistently denied commitment to communism, the elite's only weapon against the party was to advocate and work towards similar reforms.

However alarmed they were by this challenge, the propertied strata were not only structurally unable to implement such measures but were even incapable of seriously conceiving of them. British officials seemed far more preoccupied with the need for reform in Iran than many members of the elite. Soon after Suhaili's reappoint-ment Bullard advised him to adopt measures for the 'protection of industrial workers', the 'increase by law of the cultivator's share of the produce' and the 'limitation of estates to reasonable holdings'.[9] Within three weeks he underlined this advice in a letter to Suhaili containing an extensive and detailed programme of reform covering almost all aspects of Iran's economy and society.[10] On various other occasions similar advice was given to the Shah as well as the Prime Minister, both of whom seemed very much in agreement with the Legation's position. Once Bullard went so far as to propose some degree of decentralization, drawing a sympathetic response from both men who 'seemed to realize that a spontaneous grant of local councils to all the provinces might perhaps forestall a demand from Tabriz or the Kurdish areas for still wider concessions'.[11]

There was little difference between the reforms so persistently recommended by the British officials and those advocated by the Tudeh Party which, in Bullard's view, were 'mild in comparison with the conditions of the poor classes'. The Legation considered it in the British interest to favour, or at least not to impede the election of Tudeh candidates for the next Majlis. This policy was endorsed by the Foreign Office:

We doubt if our short or long term interests would be prejudiced if some of them [deputies] were from the Tudeh Party. Indeed, from a long term point of view does not the danger of a violent swing over increase the longer the present gang of corrupt and selfish landowners remain in control? To this extent the anxiety of wealthy classes about the activities of the Tudeh Party seems to us encouraging as evidence that they are beginning to realise their growing unpopularity.[12]

Ivor Pink of the Foreign Office Eastern Department, who had served in the British Legation in Tehran from 1938 to 1940, while stressing the necessity of such a policy and recalling the Foreign Office's view of the 13th Majlis and the fact that during the previous year they had sent five telegrams recommending its dissolution, contended that:

> The present internal situation is so serious that constitutional reform, whether imposed by the Shah from above or by some party from below, seems to be the only alternative to a social upheaval in a few years' time. I do not therefore see why we should strengthen the landowners who compose the majority of the Majlis and from whom we have nothing to hope, against the only party who have succeeded in frightening them to some extent.[13]

Hence The British Legation eventually decided to support, encourage, or at least not oppose the election of Tudeh and other reformist candidates.[14] They did so primarily because they thought the co-optation of such elements would both help to improve the country's administrative machinery and deflect inchoate extremist threats. In advocating reforms and the recruitment to the Majlis of members of a younger generation, British officials were, at the same time, consciously reacting against their increasing identification with reactionary forces.[15] It was, however, impossible to undermine the internalized and historically rooted belief of the majority of Iranians that the British pursued no interest but their own and inevitably impeded the march of real progress in Iran. Their reformist advice was thus suspect in the eyes of many members of the Iranian elite and often perceived as either spurious or confusingly paradoxical.

Of course successive Iranian Prime Ministers, in their Cabinet programmes, and the Shah on various occasions, had expressed a belief in the need for reform. In a meeting with a British official, the Shah, deeply fearful of communism, spoke of his future plans for 'breaking up the large estates and distributing them to the peasants on a co-operative basis'. He added that 'the hope of the country lay in the hands of the young in ideas and not necessarily only in age', and referred to what he called 'le type des jeunes' which he believed was growing and needed encouragement.[16] But however genuine the intention, the advocacy of similar ideas by British officials seemed to be counterproductive.

A more serious impediment to a significant elite-guided policy of reform and reconstruction was its essential incongruence with the prevailing mode of clan politics, the structural configuration of which allowed only tactical moves with short-term and limited objectives. The concern of the Shah and the British reflected their apprehension of 'the Soviet menace'[17] and of radical orientations and movements which, in the context of the great disparities of wealth and privilege in Iranian society, had a considerable chance of spreading rapidly. Unfortunately, in the absence of an adequate institutional framework, including an effective administrative machinery and a capable and motivated agency within the elite, the advice and recommendations of the reformists fell on deaf ears. The very idea of significant reforms to be realized by the ruling elite within the existing political arrangements was widely regarded as, at best, politically naive. It provided consolation for those who advocated it, but had no positive impact on those it was meant to benefit. Reformist rhetoric accompanied by little sustained action was counterproductive and self-defeating, and far from alleviating actually stimulated frustrations.

Having gained nothing from their somewhat abstract but ambitious recommendations, British officials now concentrated on more specific reformist measures. First, they induced the Iranian Government to support and co-operate with the American advisers. The British Legation had strongly backed the advisers and firmly believed that unless they could reform the Iranian administration and 'form a body of Persian officials able to carry on when they leave, the prospects for Persia [were] poor'. In their view, 'no Persian government unaided' could 'clear up the administration'.[18] Secondly, they encouraged the co-optation into the ranks of the elite of younger men who would work with and enjoy the support of foreign advisers.[19] Both these measures were also favoured by the American Legation and, being moderate in scope, were expected to bring about positive results. In addition, it was initially expected that the American advisers would be able to cope with the problems of shortages and high prices. But even this proved difficult.

By a law approved by the Majlis on 12 November 1942, Dr. Arthur Millspaugh was employed as the Director-General of Iranian finances for a period of five years with extensive authority to regulate finances, deal with the problems of food supply and shortages, stabilize and freeze prices, improve transportation and modify the budget. Millspaugh arrived in Iran in February 1943, but felt ill-equipped to tackle such problems and demanded that his authority be extended to include economic affairs as well. Bullard thought Suhaili initially showed 'unexpected courage and statesmanship' in persuading the deputies to comply with Millspaugh's demands,[20] but when they resisted he felt it was dangerous to press them. Two months after Suhaili resumed office, Bullard complained that:

This 'futility' Prime Minister utters fine words and makes fair promises but achieves nothing. In fact government business seems to have come to a standstill through lack of driving power and leadership. Important issues of inflation and high prices which Dr. Millspaugh is prepared to tackle are held up through delay of the Majlis even to debate grant of required powers. A programme of general reform has been proclaimed but no concrete proposals put forward.[21]

The merchants and shopkeepers expressed their opposition to the extension of Millspaugh's powers by closing the bazaars and shops and had to be forced to reopen by the military governor.[22] Nevertheless the Majlis eventually surrendered, and on 3 May Millspaugh was granted extensive authority to administer the Iranian economy with the aim of reducing and stabilizing prices.[23] Approximately three weeks later Millspaugh submitted an income tax bill to the Majlis. This aroused the opposition of the deputies and the propertied strata, and once again the bazaars were closed in Tehran and Tabriz.[24] A further reason for the closure of the bazaars was the arrest of Ayatullah Abulqasim Kashani who had been discovered by British Intelligence to be a prominent member of a pro-German organization in Iran. At this period the revival of political activity and the expression of resentment in the bazaar was intermingled with a revival of religion.

The revitalized and mutually beneficial ties between the merchants and the clergy were also evident on the occasion of the visit to Iran, in the summer of 1943, of Ayatullah Husain Qumi, who had resided in Iraq since the Mashhad events of 1935.[25] Qumi demanded, *inter alia*, that the ban on the wearing of the veil – imposed in 1936 – be lifted, that the management of theological schools and endowments be entrusted to the *mullahs*, that mixed schools be abandoned, and theological subjects be included in the school curricula.[26] He received a favourable response from the Government. Qumi's visit reportedly caused considerable popular excitement and he was 'everywhere greeted by large crowds'.[27] According to Bullard, the merchants showed particular enthusiasm in supporting Qumi and publicizing his visit; a number of the wealthiest merchants visited him, and 'the Chamber of Commerce, besides providing funds for his reception, published a pamphlet urging everyone to go out and meet him'.[28] By cultivating these clerical links, the propertied strata aimed at forestalling any distributive measure which threatened to question the sanctity of private property. Their alarm at the introduction of Millspaugh's income tax bill – which they saw as one such measure – was reflected in the strong opposition of the Majlis deputies to this bill.

After twenty-four weeks the income tax bill was approved in a modified form, and then only as a result of considerable pressure and an ultimatum from Millspaugh, who threatened to resign if the Majlis did not co-operate.[29] This bill in itself was progressive and commendable, yet in practice and in the context of the overall socio-political situation it was impractical. Even before its promulgation Bullard himself admitted that it would prove counterproductive, as it would have an adverse effect on the administrative apparatus of the country and disturb the existing informal mechanisms of transaction between the Government and local traders which were based on mutual confidence. In Bullard's view, although the income tax bill 'halved the rise in prices', it 'made the holders of goods inundate trade and frightened landowners who were at first willing to enter into contracts for the sale of wheat'.[30] Moreover, in the absence of proper administrative means for ascertaining personal incomes and effectively implementing the law, the income tax bill, as Musaddiq later forcefully argued, only contributed to the spread of corruption.[31]

The realization of Anglo-American-sponsored reform programmes, even in their modified and limited form, was constrained by a variety of predominantly structural factors. Foreign advisers were, for a number of reasons, opposed, disliked or suspected by those who were meant to co-operate with them, as well as by others. The Shah appeared at first to support Millspaugh, perhaps hoping to impress the British and American legations and substantiate his reformist claims. He summoned a group of some twenty deputies, and recommended they speed up the process of legislation and co-operate with Millspaugh. This, in Bullard's view, was an 'admirable and quite constitutional action [which] doubtless helped to secure the passage of the bill for the engagement of more Americans the next day'.[32] But the Shah and the military establishment gradually found themselves in conflict with the American advisers who opposed designs for the enlargement of the army; Millspaugh particularly disapproved of and refused to finance such plans.[33] In addition, the bulk of the elite, with the backing of the propertied strata, believed that the American advisers and their projected reforms were detrimental to their own vested interests.

Opposition to foreign advisers was also rooted in more pronounced beliefs and convictions. The leftists were initially ambivalent; in principle they disapproved of foreign advisers, but they supported measures such as Millspaugh's income tax bill.[34] With the beginnings of a 'cold war' in Iran, however, they uncompromisingly turned against all foreign (Western) advisers.[35] Moreover, the whole idea of foreign advice, carrying as it did the implicit assumption that Iranians were inherently unable to master their own destiny, fundamentally contravened the basic tenets of a mode of nationalism which at the time was gaining momentum and was to find its personification in Musaddiq. To summarize the argument of one exponent of the nationalist view, foreign advisers in a country which itself possessed a sufficient number of 'European-educated men' would attract the services not of 'noble patriots' but of 'vultures and sycophants', ready to exploit their unfamiliarity with local conditions and to dominate them. Foreign advisers would set up a cumbersome and costly apparatus of secretaries and interpreters and thus complicate the bureaucratic machinery. Most significantly, they would undermine Iran's 'national sovereignty'. This particular writer believed that no reforms could be accomplished 'except by the hand of our own people'.[36]

Such views were reflected in the dilemmas of precisely those younger politicians, favoured by the Americans, who were generally sensitive, nationalistic, far from docile and who often found it hard to co-operate with foreign advisers. One such was Allahyar Salih, Suhaili's Minister of Finance, who resigned his position because 'the American advisers had not treated him properly'.[37] The Americans and the British Legation were therefore left with little choice but to work with the 'old gang'. American advisers continued to work in the country but with few discernible results. Social discontent, rooted in poverty and aggravated by shortages and inflation, continued to grow, and found reflection in and was in turn incited by the press.

Qavam's press bill had not resulted in a reduction of the number of newspapers. In early March 1943 the British Legation estimated there were over forty dailies or weeklies in Tehran alone, with approximately the same number of requests for new permits.[38] The issue of goods in short supply, ranging from bread to kerosene, along with problems such as typhus epidemics or the misbehaviour of Allied soldiers, were widely discussed in the press and the Allies subjected to strong criticism. The real target of these attacks, however, was the British. The Russians were not only considered to be far less involved with the Iranian ruling elite, but anyone who ventured to criticize the Soviet Union was often stigmatized as siding with 'reactionaries' by the growing, ideologically motivated, but as yet discreet, pro-Soviet movement. Even the most anti-communist newspapers abstained from explicitly attacking the Soviet Union. Much to the resentment of the British Legation, the British had not been 'handsomely' thanked for the gift of a hospital specializing in the treatment of typhus. Yet a Soviet offer of 25,000 tons of wheat was acknowledged with gratitude by Suhaili, and the newspapers all produced articles full of praise and appreciation.[39]

Though not initially dominated by explicit pro-Soviet tendencies, the Freedom Front (Jibhih-yi Azadi), a newly formed union originally consisting of fifteen newspapers, gradually came to be utilized for propaganda purposes by the Tudeh Party. There was neither a comparable pro-British (or Western) movement, nor any publicly pronounced pro-British sentiment in the country. By this time the British had abandoned the idea of directly subsidizing newspapers; but in the hope of softening the tone of press criticism they tried to influence editors, who were frequently entertained by Legation staff seeking to cultivate their friendship. At the same time they tried to render the press less critical, negatively by partially controlling the supply of newsprint and positively through 'extra subscription' – an indirect form of subsidy.[40]

British officials did not of course confine themselves to such tactics. Despite a record of past failure and hostile public opinion they strongly urged the Prime Minister to silence the press. Some two months after Suhaili took office, the War Minister, General Ahmadi, was obliged to take personal charge of the military government of Tehran in order to control the press. His predecessor had failed and, as he informed the British, six officers had refused the position of military governor because they did not want to 'oppress the people'.[41] The newspapers' explanation of Iran's prevailing problems enjoyed widespread sympathy even among the elite, who were pleased to see the blame directed at foreigners. Moreover, by suppressing even vituperative newspapers, the Government exposed itself to the charge of violating the Constitution, so easing the task of its enemies in mobilizing support against it. None the less this was one of the few means whereby a government could demonstrate its goodwill towards foreigners. British officials were not prepared to act against Suhaili because of his marked inability to work towards even the minimum reforms they had proposed. The British, however, could be alienated by a failure to respond to their demands to silence the anti-British press. At the same time the Shah, whose improper actions unfailingly caught the newspapers' attention, was equally if not more persistent in calling for strong measures to silence them.

Although it was clear that the deputies could not remain indifferent to the inevitable social repercussions, Suhaili nevertheless embarked on a show of determination. On 17 June 1943 he submitted to the Majlis – under the procedure of double urgency – a bill to restrict the number of newspapers, until six months after the war's end, to seven in Tehran and three in other cities; and to empower the government to ban any newspapers which insulted either the foreign or Iranian authorities. Predictably this bill caused much agitation and resentment, resulted in the resignation of the Minister of Justice and the Director of the Department of Press and Propaganda, and, following heated debates, was eventually rejected by the Majlis.[42] The martial law authorities continued in their efforts to curb the press but remained ill-equipped and ineffective. It was standard practice among editors to keep stocks of unused licences. So a banned newspaper could appear with little or no delay under a different name, and if that was also suppressed, another name was used.

Soon after its formation Suhaili's Cabinet experienced considerable difficulty in its relations with the southern tribes, particularly the Qashqa'i, against whom military force was deployed. At the beginning of July, however, 900 government soldiers were overwhelmed and disarmed by Qashqa'i and Boir Ahmadi tribesmen in the southern town of Simirun. 'The Simirun disaster', as it came to be known, had widespread repercussions in the press as well as the Majlis. A motion of interpellation was tabled by the deputy Habibullah Naubakht accusing the Government of starting a 'civil war' in Fars province.[43] However, it had been discovered that Naubakht was one of the leading members of a pro-German organization and he was therefore wanted by the Allies. He fled to the south and was not present in the Majlis to pursue his motion. Many others doubted the claim that 'the Simirun disaster' was unavoidable and blamed the army, the increasingly high cost of which never seemed to produce commensurate benefit to the nation.

However, the blame and criticism were not solely directed at the army; some newspapers ventured to draw attention to the Shah's personal supervision of its command structure through the Chief of Staff, and alleged that the War Minister, General Ahmadi, had not been involved in or even informed of the Simirun venture in advance.[44] Incensed by such reports, the Shah ordered the War Minister to go before the Majlis, confess to having been fully informed of the situation and accept full responsibility for the entire débâcle. The War Minister told Bullard that the Shah had 'declared that he did not intend to relax his hold over the army or to refrain from interference in administrative matters, and would rather abdicate than be an Ahmad Shah'.[45] Furthermore, the Shah, demanding the suppression of those newspapers which were critical of the Court, presented Suhaili with an ultimatum 'to get on or get out'.[46] His behaviour was now a considerable cause for concern among British officials.

Bullard, whom the Shah met more than any other foreign official, disapproved of his indiscreet behaviour. He complained to the Foreign Office that the Shah ignored the Legation's 'good advice', particularly by interfering more than was wise in 'political and even administrative affairs and in not seeing members of missions other than the British'. He feared that the Shah's policy would bring him unpopularity, and were this to be expressed vocally there was a possibility that the British would be identified with him and accused of wanting to revive the 'military dictatorship' of the Reza Shah era. Still he found the Shah 'attractive' in his behaviour, knowledgeable about military affairs and seriously concerned about the welfare of his country. He also found him 'democratic' in sympathy, in the sense that he 'considered the rich too rich and the poor too poor'. On the other hand, he was 'young, inexperienced, and rather weak', a man who could easily be 'influenced by third rate confidants'. He did not, Bullard observed, limit the 'extravagance of himself and his family' and 'showed lack of understanding of the feelings of his own people in his blind admiration of his father and of the Persian Army'. Finally, he was as much anti-Russian as pro-British and of the opinion that American advisers had 'little to teach Persia'.[47]

Any fundamental disturbance in Iran would, in Bullard's view, be harmful to the Allies, and he believed that British interests would be best served by the Shah remaining on the throne. He therefore advised the Shah to resist the temptation of 'becoming a benevolent autocrat'; to confine himself to giving general advice and to refrain from active interference in political and administrative affairs; to consider Anglo-Soviet enmity as not in the interest of Iran; to support American advisers; and to try to 'base his throne on general popularity and support and not on the army alone'. He also urged him to visit various parts of the country, and to induce the Queen to take an interest in Iran and its welfare rather than spend all her time on 'new clothes'. Finally, it was thought best if the Shah's sisters, who did little but 'vie with the Queen in extravagance', lived away from the Court 'which in itself could be staffed by men of good character and status'. However, British officials dealing with Iran did not always agree among themselves and the Foreign Office was reluctant to endorse 'too rigid an attitude regarding the Shah's influence in political affairs', recommending instead that British policy be based on 'friendly guidance and constructive criticism'. It contended that a 'revolution resulting in a change of dynasty' was not in Britain's interest, 'therefore' they had to 'accept the Shah to keep some direct interest in the army'.[48] Bullard's commentaries shed considerable light on the Shah's character, his activities, and those of the Court at the time. Bullard was, of course, not noted for his liking for the Shah, yet the plausibility of his assessment was demonstrated by subsequent events. He was perhaps inclined to side with his colleagues at the Legation – A. C. Trott and General Fraser – who were opposed to the Shah, in contrast to counsellors Adrian Holman and William Iliff who favoured him, and Colonels Pybus and Macann who were neutral.[49] Whatever the division of opinion and attitude on the part of the staff of the British Legation, however, there was general agreement that the Shah should be kept on the right track, whether through direct or indirect advice.

British advice, even in the form approved by the Foreign Office, was never really heeded. The Shah continued with his restless manoeuvres to divide those whose collaboration was thought harmful to royal interests, or to hinder the rise of groups and individuals likely to challenge royal prerogatives. He tried, for example, to prevent co-operation between General Jahanbani, who was commander of the army division stationed in the south, and Qavam ul-Mulk, the Governor-General of Fars who was regarded with suspicion by the monarch.[50] Nor could he tolerate the prospect of collaboration between General Ahmadi, the War Minister, and General Riyazi, Chief of General Staff, both of whom were well disposed to the American advisers. So he appointed two other senior officers, Generals Razmara and Yazdanpanah, as chief of his 'military Cabinet' and his chief aide-de-camp, respectively, a strategy which inevitably aggravated existing disputes between the War

Ministry and the General Staff over their respective functions and spheres of authority. These two generals had different views from, and were rivals of, the War Minister and the Chief of Staff and were able in their new capacity to bypass and undermine the latters' authority. The Shah, commented Bullard with regret, had 'only one concept of the way to run an army, viz., to appoint intriguers to all posts so that they might counter-balance each other'.[51]

The Shah, moreover, aiming to isolate the Chief of Staff initiated changes without his knowledge and appointed to key positions officers who were his own or General Razmara's henchmen. He believed it essential that he should be free to allocate key military positions to those on whose personal loyalty and subservience he could rely; for he regarded the army as his political base and wanted to maintain it as his exclusive domain. The plans of American military advisers to create a small army solely designed for internal security were extremely distasteful to him and, confronted with their views, he persistently contended that 'Turkey has a large army; why should he not have one as large?'[52]

Naturally the Shah did not concentrate solely on the army at the expense of other concerns. He had inherited considerable wealth and had recently purchased large quantities of currency. In the second half of December the British learned, through a 'completely reliable source', that the Shah had $1 million in America and was looking for a 'safe investment for his money'. These were the funds on which, according to Bullard, 'he and presumably his father and the rest of the family' would have 'to live should he ever cease to be the Shah'.[53] He also persisted with his efforts to improve the monarchy's image and paid well-publicized visits to Isfahan and Mashhad. But most of his energy was spent on maintaining his privileged position and gradually increasing his prerogatives.

In the pursuit of these objectives the Shah met no opposition from Suhaili nor, despite attempts to exert pressure on him, did he receive much help from a Premier so dependent on the deputies. Suhaili had tried to control the press but at the expense of the policy of inactivity which largely accounted for the maintenance of his majority in the Majlis. The unenviable task of trying to appease the Shah – and the British – without undermining his basis of support in the Majlis was not, however, the only difficulty Suhaili faced during his term of office. Shortages and disorder were constant and intractable problems. At various times he had to deal with other difficulties: in early May 1943 the engineers went on strike, as a result of their resentment at their low salary and status. They enlisted the backing of university lecturers and lawyers, and the Tudeh Party supported them with the aim of increasing its appeal to the intelligentsia.[54] The strike ended in early June when the Government agreed to meet the engineers' demands. Suhaili was also involved in discord with some of his own colleagues which resulted, for instance, in the resignation of Ali Akbar Siyasi, the Minister of Education, in August 1943. He also witnessed the worrying growth of the Tudeh Party's influence, and feared the consequences for his own retention of office of Sayyid Zia's return.[55]

Yet Suhaili succeeded in maintaining a working majority primarily by behaving as the deputies desired. Colleagues were selected with an eye to satisfying them; in a show of goodwill seventeen deputies from various factions of the Majlis were invited to assist him in his tasks; and the portfolio of the Interior, a particularly important position in view of the impending elections, was offered to men acceptable to the majority. Furthermore, whenever he felt obliged to insist on a measure distasteful to the deputies, Suhaili would allude to the pressures to which he was subjected. The bill extending Millspaugh's powers, for instance, was imposed by him on the Majlis despite extensive opposition; yet the 'whole effect of this show of firmness', claimed the British Legation, 'was ruined by the Prime Minister declaring in secret session [of the Majlis] that such action had been forced on him by the British'.[56]

Of course there was some opposition to Suhaili, and three motions of interpellation were tabled against his Cabinet, including the one by Naubakht which was not debated. Another motion challenged, on constitutional grounds, the Government's appointment of deputies Ahmad I'tibar and Murtiza Quli Bayat as ministers, as well as the Government's right to delegate its authority under the martial law regulations to the War Ministry.[57] This motion, however, was defeated and the Prime Minister was offered an overwhelming vote of confidence (94 out of 102) without even being required to defend his position. The third interpellation, concerning the country's bread supply, also resulted in a vote of confidence for Suhaili. But despite the relentless intrigues of thirty deputies, who either opposed him on principle or saw no chance of their own re-election, Suhaili managed to maintain majority support.

His avowed reliance on the deputies was resented by both the Court and the British who could neither expect Suhaili to respond unquestioningly to their demands, nor claim that their support was indispensable to his survival. Both parties therefore tried on occasion to intimidate him by openly considering the chances of various alternative candidates for the premiership. Bullard, however, admitted that as long as the deputies favoured Suhaili there was little prospect of removing him. Moreover, British officials were only prepared to demand Suhaili's resignation if his policies became unduly 'injurious'. Suhaili's policies were not, as it happened, injurious either to the British or the Court – so neither party had much reason to turn its grievances into effective opposition. The Majlis, albeit in a different way, had its uses for the Shah as well as for Suhaili. In the words of a British Legation report:

> the Prime Minister had shown signs of using the Majlis as a smokescreen to cover up his failure to pass distasteful legislation, whilst the Shah no doubt felt that the Majlis had its uses in curbing the power of the Prime Minister.[58]

By the time the 13th Majlis ended its term on 22 November 1943, Suhaili had held office for over nine months.[59] He was to retain his position for a further four months; but with the deputies formally excluded from the scene during the parliamentary recess the Shah had more room for manoeuvre. This he used to press for a Cabinet reshuffle. The new Cabinet excluded men actively disliked by the Shah – including Tadayyun and General Ahmadi, who apparently lost royal favour following the Simirun incident; and it incorporated at least four royal nominees, two of them members of the Shah's entourage. According to the British Legation:

> it was generally thought that this was the Shah's first step in the experiment of governing the country through a subservient Cabinet as his father had done. [Ibrahim] Zand was the first civilian to be Minister of War for a long time, and the general opinion was that the Shah was determined to become commander-in-chief of the army in fact as well as in name, and to circumvent the weak civilian Minister by issuing orders through its Chief of Staff, despite the decree he had signed in the spring [1943] making the General Staff subordinate to the Minister of War.[60]

This Cabinet had little prospect of success with the 14th Majlis, the elections for which had been openly contested in a manner unprecedented in fifteen years. One Court-imposed minister, fearing confrontation with the new deputies, resigned even before the official opening on 26 February 1944.[61] Less than three weeks after the opening on 16 March 1944 Suhaili resigned, recognizing that a majority of deputies were determined to bring his term of office to a speedy end, even though no clear alternative to him had as yet emerged. He had owed his second term of office primarily to deputies who counted on his assistance to secure their re-election and along with Tadayyun, his Minister of the Interior, was later prosecuted on the grounds that he had illegally intervened on behalf of certain candidates. He was eventually acquitted of the charges against him. But the accusation resulted in his removal from the mainstream of Iranian politics: Suhaili was never again to appear among the ranks of viable contenders for the premiership.

PART II
Years of Uneasy Compromise

5

The Government of Sa'id:
MARCH–NOVEMBER 1944

Suhaili and his Cabinet were not alone in their attempt to influence the outcome of elections to the 14th Majlis. The Court, the army, the British and the Russians, as well as local magnates, all intervened in the proceedings in one way or another. Indeed the multifarious influences at play contributed to the intensity of factional behaviour and to the emergence of several factions in the new Majlis mobilized mainly around veteran *mutavallis*. An average of twenty deputies lead by Hadi Tahiri, Hashim Malik-Madani and Sayyid Zia formed the Fatherland (Mihan) faction; while Farrukh organized the Democrat (Dimukrat) faction which had less than ten members. The Democrats were joined by deputies from Azarbaijan and together the two groups were known as the Freedom (Azadi) faction incorporating some thirty members; the Freedom faction, however, later emerged independently. This coalition was countered by a merger between the National (Milli) faction, lead by Sayyid Muhammad Sadiq Tabataba'i, and the National Union (Ittihad-i Milli) faction, composed of deputies from Kerman. This alliance, which comprised about thirty deputies, retained the name 'National Union' and the leadership of Tabataba'i and in alliance with the Fatherland faction usually constituted the nucleus of the 'majority' in the Majlis. Ali Dashti also had his own Independent (Mustaqqil) faction, at one point numbering fifteen deputies. Those who were nominally ungrouped tended to follow Musaddiq, and along with the small Tudeh faction constituted the core of the 'minority'. The configuration of the 14th Majlis was clearly not conducive to the unproblematic formation of Cabinets.

Once the new Majlis was officially convened bargaining began to find a successor to Suhaili. On 18 March 1944, in response to a query by the Shah, a 'majority' of deputies, organized by the *mutavallis* and composed of elements from the Democrat, Fatherland, National Union and Iran factions, which then numbered twenty, nineteen, fourteen and nine members, respectively, as well as a number of individual deputies, opted for Muhammad Sa'id (Sa'id ul–Vizarih) to form a Cabinet.[1]

Sa'id was born around 1885 in Tiflis where his father, a *mullah*, had settled after leaving his home town of Maraghih in Azarbaijan.[2] Having studied law and politics in Russia and Switzerland, Sa'id entered the service of the Iranian Government, eventually becoming a professional diplomat. He was Iranian Ambassador in Moscow in 1942 when recalled by Suhaili to assume the portfolio of Foreign Affairs, a post he retained until his assumption of the premiership. This background had provided Sa'id with little experience of Iranian internal affairs; his knowledge of economics or finance was negligible,[3] and he spoke Russian better than Persian.[4] Although the British were less than enthusiastic about his appointment on the grounds of his 'weakness',[5] they nevertheless considered him a man 'always willing to help'[6] who was inclined towards them since he knew 'Russia and the Russians well', and entertained 'no illusion about others'.[7] The Russians, on the other hand, had little reason to welcome the turn of events, while the Court could hardly have expected a more acceptable development than the premiership of one of its most loyal protégés.

The choice of Sa'id, whose premiership the Shah had previously attempted to engineer, was not, however, simply inspired by a desire on the part of the deputies to make concessions to the Shah. The main consideration was to sustain the constitutive elements of the tacit consensus of Iranian clan politics. Sa'id was acceptable not because he possessed any exceptional qualities, whether strength of character, courage or statesmanship, nor because the deputies respected his reputed honesty and sincerity. Qasim Ghani's assessment of him as a 'very honest and truthful man'[8] was perhaps widely shared. Yet his appeal to the Shah, the Majlis *mutavallis* and, for that matter, the bulk of the ruling elite, emanated from his acquiescent character, moderation, discreetly reserved ambition, real or perceived humility, political piety and loyalty, and an innocence or simple-mindedness which gave rise to a host of anecdotes[9] but which, according to one account, was calculated and feigned.[10] Few other candidates could so readily be agreed upon, and among them Sa'id was least likely to provoke strong foreign or domestic opposition.

The consensus regarding Sa'id did not, however, extend to his proposed Ministers. His Cabinet, composed entirely of men who had previously held ministerial positions, received such an unfavourable reception in the Majlis that all its members were driven to resign. A considerable number of deputies apparently believed that the members of previous Cabinets had been imposed by the Court and should not be included in a new Cabinet.[11] Nevertheless, a few days later a Cabinet was presented which, with the exception of three members, was substantially the same in composition, although there were some changes in portfolio. Deputies from all factions promptly registered their names to speak against it, while only three were prepared to rally to its defence.[12] Sa'id, however, feared that any further concession to the deputies would both alienate the Court and the British, and result in a heterogeneous and incompatible body of ministers. He therefore informed the British Minister that if his reshuffled Cabinet were rejected he would prefer to resign.[13]

Opponents of the Cabinet fell into two groups: those who were dissatisfied with the distribution of ministerial positions; and those who contended that it would be unable to tackle the critical socio-economic problems of the country. The latter argued that its programme, limited to the establishment of security and the provision of sufficient supplies of food and other necessities, was inadequate.[14] Supporters contended that in the prevailing circumstances it would be impossible to find an alternative prime minister, and that in any case Sa'id himself had promised to resign should he fail to carry out his duties.[15] Fearing the effects of a continuation of the Cabinet crisis, which had already lasted over a month, the deputies eventually offered Sa'id's ministers a vote of confidence (64 out of 85, with the Tudeh faction voting against and the rest abstaining).[16]

The majority of deputies relented at this point not only because there was no better alternative but also because the elite was becoming increasingly aware of the power and appeal of the Tudeh Party, which was emerging as a potential countervailing force to a ruling elite weakened by incessant internal discord and rivalries. In addition to its effective party organization, its vocal faction in the new Majlis and its extensive propaganda machinery, the Tudeh Party had also worked systematically to organize industrial workers and now dominated the labour movement. This drive added greatly to the dismay of the rich and encountered the resistance of employers, often resulting in confrontations which had widespread political repercussions. The events in Isfahan in 1944 are a case in point.

In the spring of that year Taqi Fadakar, the leader of the Union of Workers of Isfahan (UWI), travelled to Tehran to take up his seat in the Majlis. His moderating role in the Union and his political skill in disarming the mill-owners of Isfahan and playing down the links between the UWI and the Tudeh Party had been a restraining factor in the industrial politics of the city. Once he left the situation quickly changed. On the one hand the Tudeh Party, which was becoming increasingly radical, tried to increase its influence over the workers, and on the other, the mill-owners threatened to lock workers out of the factories unless the Union severed its links with the Tudeh. When the owners began to carry out their threats, strikes were organized, clashes ensued and the workers opened the storage rooms of the mills and seized that part of their wages normally paid in goods. This was done with the authorities' knowledge;[17] yet the events were utilized both by the mill-owners and many deputies in Tehran as proof of the Tudeh Party's disrespect for the Constitution and private property.

The allegations were emphatically denied by the Tudeh deputies[18] (and some Tudeh leaders in fact argued against any strikes while the war against fascism continued). Yet the growing radicalization and ideological rigidity of the Tudeh Party, along with its suspected – and eventually verified – pro-Soviet stand, enabled the mill-owners to appeal to traditional customs and conventions as well as religious beliefs and to invoke patriotism in their own favour. The Tudeh Party's unqualified and contextually erroneous pronouncements on worker–capitalist contradictions did little to help the workers. On the contrary, they enabled the mill-owners to deny the legitimacy of the workers' needs and demands, alleging that they were under the direct or indirect influence and control of the Tudeh. In addition, the Government failed to adopt measures and provide regulations designed to give minimum protection to the workers. The eventual losers were, predictably, the workers, whose undeniable needs and legitimate demands were neglected. In Isfahan and elsewhere they remained exploited – economically by the mill-owners and politically by the Tudeh – and used by all the parties involved to promote or demote issues which were neither adequately comprehensible to them nor directly relevant to their immediate and real needs and aspirations. The crisis also weakened their union which subsequently split into two conflicting Tudeh-controlled and anti-Tudeh factions.[19]

Following the intensification of the crisis in Isfahan, the mill-owners succeeded in engineering the removal of Farajullah Bahrami, the Governor-General of Isfahan, who had not been fully co-operative. Alarmed by the events in Isfahan and by the combined power of the Tudeh Party and the UWI,[20] and encouraged by the approval of the British,[21] on 30 April 1944 Sa'id replaced Bahrami with the anti-Tudeh Reza Afshar who in 1936 had been permanently dismissed from government service on a charge of corruption and misconduct and was thus vulnerable to challenge. Afshar's appointment implied the Prime Minister's unequivocal support for the mill-owners and encouraged the Tudeh to utilize its propaganda machinery more openly against the Government. Objections also came from other sources. Ghulam Ali Farivar, a Tehran deputy whose ideas were close to those of Musaddiq, tabled a motion of interpellation against the Cabinet which it nevertheless survived,[22] since Sa'id's move was widely, if discreetly, endorsed. Afshar, however, had to be recalled a few weeks later as the High Court, to which the matter had been referred, did not vote in his favour. The whole affair was a setback for the Prime Minister and raised serious questions about the soundness of his judgement.

The growing strength and radicalism of the Tudeh Party alarmed its opponents enough to induce them into an attempt to bury their differences. Among the enemies of the Party, one man in particular came to be recognized as the personification of the reactionary forces – no less a figure than Sayyid Zia ud-Din Tabataba'i, who had returned from exile and re-entered the Iranian political scene in late September 1943. Sayyid Zia had been elected deputy for Yazd, but upon resuming his seat in the Majlis had been vigorously challenged by Musaddiq, the First Deputy of Tehran, who accused him of launching the 1921 coup with the collusion of the British.[23] If this charge had been sustained by the rejection of Sayyid Zia's credentials it would in principle have undermined the legitimacy of the Pahlavi dynasty. Naturally it was denied by Sayyid Zia, though his protestations did little to change the minds of those who believed the allegation.[24] No one ventured to speak in his defence, but eventually 58 out of 86 deputies voted in his favour.[25]

Sayyid Zia was looked upon with hope by many opponents of radical socio-economic reform. In the words of Bullard, 'wealthy friends from Yazd' had paid 'over £30,000 for premises for his political headquarters', and rich manufacturers of Isfahan who feared 'the violence of the Tudeh' looked on him as an ally.[26] He was, moreover, believed to enjoy a good deal of tribal backing, the favour of certain army officers and, last but not least, the full backing of the British.

Yet Sayyid Zia's unpopularity among leftists and liberal nationalists was far more deep-seated and politically significant than his

actual popularity among his supporters. The Tudeh Party prepared a
list of eight other parties and groups, as well as twenty-one
newspapers, which it claimed were busy campaigning against him.[27]
His real character, allegiances and socio-political disposition, as well
as the scale and objectives of the movement he was reputed to lead,
were often exaggerated by Tudeh propaganda which found in him a
tangible and convenient target. Replying to its critics, the Tudeh
Party argued that if Sayyid Zia were not supported by a 'great and
terrible power, the power of headstrong reaction', they would not
even bother to mention his name.[28]

Old-fashioned and possibly eccentric, Sayyid Zia was nevertheless a man of cunning, possessing skill and stamina. Although
essentially a pragmatist, he was known to have traditionalist views
and vague right-wing populist tendencies. Yet he appeared to be as
insistent as many of his opponents on reform, particularly where
agriculture and the condition of the tribes were concerned, and on
parliamentarianism and the need to limit royal prerogatives.[29]
Without necessarily endorsing the policy of alienating the Russians,
he believed in the inevitability, and even the necessity, of positive
Western influence, particularly that of the British, in Iranian politics.
Sayyid Zia and the British shared converging conceptions of Iranian
national interests and while he indefatigably tried to promote British
interests and objectives he in turn enjoyed active British support.

Sayyid Zia also had a growing clientele among government
employees and an effective network of friends among the elite. He
sponsored or was supported by a number of newspapers and
benefited from the services of 'parties' formed either by himself or his
friends. His relations with the Court were, however, far from cordial
for a number of reasons, including the prerequisites of a credible
propaganda strategy to counter Tudeh influence as well as the
composition and orientations of Sayyid Zia's following which
included anti-Court elements such as Muzaffar Firuz. Firuz, a Qajar
prince whose father had been killed in Reza Shah's prison, was the
licence-owner of *Ra'd-i Imruz*, the main pro-Sayyid Zia newspaper, and had in fact initiated his return to Iran. In early 1943
he travelled to Palestine, met Sayyid Zia and returned to publish
the text of a detailed interview with him which amounted to a
political manifesto.[30] Other factors accounting for discord
between the Shah and Sayyid Zia included his own personal
antipathy towards Reza Shah, who had brought about his exile;
his pronounced refusal to favour the enhancement of royal power;

and, by the same token, the Shah's distrust and ill-feeling towards him. The mutual animosity between the Shah and Sayyid Zia led the latter to suspect that the Shah was behind most of the press attacks against him,[31] while the Shah feared Sayyid Zia's intention to 'dethrone him',[32] since newspapers supporting him continually tried to undermine the Shah's image, for instance by posing questions regarding the 230 million rials which they claimed the Shah's father had 'stolen from the people' and which he, Muhammad Reza Shah, had inherited. This was a sum which, as Bullard put it, 'ought to have sufficed him [the Shah] for life, if spent at a rate suitable to the poverty of Persia, but unwise expenditure, especially on political intrigues' had 'wasted much of it'.[33] The Shah's political activities and the maintenance of his clientele seemed to require far more money than he possessed or was legally entitled to. Despite much press criticism, he was satisfied neither with his political nor his financial advantages. In one interview Bullard found him 'gloomy, dwelling particularly on, a) his power under the Constitution, b) his inadequate income'. It seemed to Bullard that the two were

> associated in his mind and that he felt that unless he could obtain more power, he would be at the mercy of the Majlis for lack of money. He compared his circumstances unfavourably with those of the king of Egypt whom he described as enjoying immense revenues, private and public, and a popularity which he had done nothing to deserve.[34]

In the face of the Tudeh's growing influence, the Shah and Sayyid Zia could not afford to live in a state of mutual animosity. The threat of the common enemy, the encouragement of the British and the continuous efforts of the Prime Minister eventually drew them together. As a result, differences were apparently set aside, mutual concessions were made, and to meet Sayyid Zia's demands the Shah went so far as to agree, among other things, to the 'numerical reduction of the army, strengthening of the gendarmerie and the retention of the Millspaugh Mission in exchange for a great increase in the Court budget'.[35] The inherent exigencies of clan politics, the personal and perceptual differences of the two sides and the unfeasibility of some of the Shah's undertakings meant that this agreement was basically tactical and ephemeral. Yet, the situation was serious enough to render imperative an attempt to observe it. On the basis of his conversation with Husain Ala, the Court Minister, Bullard reported that this development, apart from the 'more open advocacy of Sayyid Zia' by the British, was the result of the

> increasing conviction of the Shah and his advisers that the Tudeh can
> not be appeased and that the Russians are determined to create, before
> the convening of the Peace Conference, a state of general chaos which
> would offer pretext for intervention 'at popular request' in Azarbaijan
> for a start. The Court now appears to regard Sayyid Zia as the only
> hope of preventing this but without provoking the Russians to violent
> counter-measures.[36]

The *rapprochement* between the Shah and Sayyid Zia, however,
did not result in a noticeable unity of the forces of 'reaction', nor did
it in any way help to secure the Prime Minister's position, which had
inevitably deteriorated as a result of a few months in office. Sa'id had
only succeeded in disarming his unenthusiastic friends. Apart from
the numerous problems which Cabinets invariably faced, one major
issue had continued to occupy an increasingly significant place in the
Iranian political scene – the scope of authority of Dr. Millspaugh, the
American financial adviser. Millspaugh's supporters and opponents
were divided along factional and personal lines, and in their
ideological and pragmatic concerns. On the one hand, Musaddiq and
his followers,[37] as well as the Tudeh Party, vocally demanded the
termination of his contract. At a party conference in April 1944, Nur
ud-Din Kianuri, a prominent member of the Tudeh Party, had
opposed Millspaugh yet maintained that a 'disinterested and
knowledgeable financial mission with proportionate authority' and
guaranteed by the American Government 'will be useful for us'.[38] By
the summer of that year, however, at their first general conference,
the Tudeh resolved to oppose foreign advisers. Sayyid Zia, on the
other hand, actively supported Millspaugh, engaging in what Bullard
called a 'most spirited defence of him'.[39] In view of the recent
understanding between the Shah and Sayyid Zia which envisaged the
retention of Millspaugh, the general support of the British and
American diplomatic representatives for him, as well as the much-
propagated view that opposing Millspaugh implied opposing US
interests, Sa'id hesitated to embark upon any drastic action against
him. Yet in the face of growing criticism of Millspaugh and his
undeniable mismanagement of the Iranian economy and finances,
which Sa'id himself had publicly recognized,[40] inaction was equally
detrimental to his authority.

A face-saving alternative in which a majority of deputies

acquiesced was the restriction of Millspaugh's powers, which meant stripping him of his economic tasks and confining him to his original financial duties.[41] Sa'id tried to bring this about but Millspaugh, who was known for his intransigence, resigned and was soon installed with full authority.[42] This was another setback for Sa'id and the threat of a motion of interpellation against the Minister of Roads and Communications eventually resulted in the resignation of the Cabinet after a period of less than twenty-four weeks in office.[43] Sa'id, however, was again recalled to form a Cabinet, as the alliance of the Fatherland, National Union and Freedom factions could find no other acceptable candidate. In order to justify the reappointment of Sa'id the blame for the failure of his first Cabinet was laid on his colleagues whom the deputies had not themselves selected. As a result, in the hope of forestalling further dissatisfaction among his supporters, Sa'id complied with their wishes and chose all but two of his ministers from a list compiled by them.

Yet the alliance upon which the Cabinet was based was precarious from the outset, since not all members of the three factions had actually voted for Sa'id: the National Union faction had refused to involve itself in the compilation of a list of ministerial candidates; the Freedom faction was only prepared to commit itself to the initial vote for the reappointment of Sa'id;[44] and the Fatherland faction did not hesitate in turning against the Cabinet.[45] The Tudeh was hostile,[46] suspecting, according to Bullard, that the appointment of Ali Asghar Zarrinkafsh as Finance Minister was an indication of the Cabinet's intention to grant oil concessions to the West.[47]

The most sustained and vigorous criticism of the Cabinet and of Sa'id's lack of ability came from Musaddiq, who argued that if Sa'id's failure was to be blamed on his colleagues, they should not have been chosen in the first place. Criticizing the irresponsibility and unreliability of Sa'id's supporters, Musaddiq contended that if Sa'id was competent enough to form a Cabinet they should continue to support him. If not, they should not have opted for him at the outset.[48] Similar views were widely voiced by the press, and though valid in principle, in the context of the prevailing mode of clan politics, substantially different behaviour on the part of the elite would have been anomalous, if not inconceivable.

Sa'id's problems in coping with his friends and opponents, however, were soon overshadowed by one of the gravest crises ever to face the Iranian ruling elite. His Government had for some months been discreetly considering the offers of the American Standard

Vacuum, Sinclair Oil and British Shell companies which, with the active support of their embassies, were competing for oil concessions in south Iran.[49] It suddenly found itself faced with similar demands from the Russians when in mid-September 1944 Sergei Kavtaradze, the Soviet Assistant Commissar for Foreign Affairs, arrived in Tehran demanding a concession to explore and extract mainly oil but also other minerals in an area covering almost all the northern provinces of Iran. The Government acted promptly; stricken by panic, however, it treated the Russian demands in a manner which seemed entirely unfavourable in comparison to the treatment received by Western companies. Even some anti-communist deputies considered Sa'id's behaviour to have been discourteous.[50] Ala, however, explained to Bullard that in fact Sa'id had asked the Russians to put forward their terms for examination but they refused and wanted 'an acceptance in principle of their very wide demands'.[51] In any case, contrary to what was widely assumed, the Government's attitude to the British and American demands for oil concessions had also been one of deep suspicion and procrastination. As Bullard put it,

> It was inconceivable that that honest but timorous man, who had for months past been badgered by the Majlis and the press in regard to the British and American concession-seekers, should have committed himself immediately in regard to the far more disquieting demand from the Russians, whom he knew well from long years of service in the Soviet Union.[52]

Without referring the issue to the Majlis, the Cabinet decided to postpone all oil negotiations until the end of the war. This decision was not, however, taken in a vacuum. Sa'id would not have acted so swiftly had his intentions not been endorsed by almost the entire ruling elite. The Shah had, according to Ala, told Sa'id to postpone all negotiations concerning oil;[53] he had also told Bullard that 'the grant of any oil rights to the Soviet Government would mean the end of Persian authority in North Persia',[54] and in the Majlis only one deputy dared to speak in favour of the Russian request. But whoever was responsible for the decision the Russians were thwarted and humiliated, and Sa'id, whose undisguised pro-Western bias could not be mistaken for a credible nationalistic stand, became the personal target of a barrage of Russian and Tudeh propaganda. The Russians also exerted destabilizing pressures against the Government, while the Soviet wartime censor in Tehran prohibited the relaying abroad of press dispatches on the matter by any agency except Tass.[55]

The events surrounding the Russian oil demand constituted a turning point in the politics of the post-Reza Shah era. They provoked a crisis of conscience for the Iranian intelligentsia who agonized over the compatibility and relative merits of socialism and patriotism. They exposed the apologetic pro-Soviet stand of the Tudeh Party – which was to manifest itself more clearly after the cessation of hostilities in Europe – and marked the beginning of an incipient cold war in Iran. The Tudeh ideology, which had promised to be an articulation of spontaneous intellectual convictions, inspired by the iniquities of Iranian society and deeply sensitive to its specificities, was gradually transformed into a dogmatic and formalistic creed.[56] Basing itself on a claim to possess the exclusive ability to identify and represent the 'real interests' of the people, the Tudeh Party was prepared to use all possible means to stigmatize, suppress and outmanoeuvre its rivals, including renegades within its own ranks. Inevitably the Party's opponents adopted similar tactics and the net result was a gradual degeneration of civic political discourse and the strengthening of Manichaean cosmology in Iranian political culture. The behaviour of the Tudeh Party contributed to the further differentiation of ideological stands along left–right lines, and also served to lend substance to anti-leftist accusations and thus intensified right-wing tendencies. Yet at the same time it was to enhance, if inadvertently, the appeal of what Musaddiq and his followers stood for.

The demand for an oil concession by the Russians induced the Tudeh Party to abandon, without any real justification or concern for consistency, its earlier categorical rejection of foreign concessions. Whether concessions should or should not be granted was no longer the matter for debate in the Party: the real issue was how to grant them in return for optimal benefits for the country.[57] Ihsan Tabari, a Tudeh writer, went as far as to argue in favour of the renewal of negotiations to grant oil concessions not only to the Russians but also to the British and the Americans.[58] This view, based on a 'realism' rooted ironically in the Tudeh Party's disbelief in the capabilities of the Iranian people, was thereafter invoked to justify the Party's policies. Northern Iran was defined as the Soviet Union's 'security zone', a 'reality' which, according to Tabari, ought to be recognized for the first and last time. It was argued that, in view of the international political situation and the bankruptcy of Iran, the 'refusal to grant concessions to those who demanded them is a wrong and one-sided move, the objective of which is either to follow pernicious plans or to surrender to folly'.[59]

The Tudeh Party employed its entire propaganda machine, particularly the Freedom Front, in order to undermine Sa'id's position by increasing the momentum of the crisis, frightening others into submission and dissuading them from supporting the Prime Minister's stand. An attempt was made to render this propaganda more effective, and endow it with 'popular' legitimacy, by organizing, on 27 October 1944, large demonstrations with the assistance and in the presence of the Russian military police.[60] Sa'id was the prime target of these attacks and was described as the 'usurper of the rights of the Iranian nation',[61] a 'reactionary' and a 'fascist' who stood in the way of friendship between 'the Soviet Union and the Iranian people'.[62] Demonstrators demanded his death as well as that of Sayyid Zia who had, with British support, played a significant role in mobilizing opposition against the Russian demands for an oil concession.

However, the concentration on Sa'id was intended as a face-saving exercise on the part of the Russians to recover their prestige by bringing about his removal, and, according to Bullard, Sa'id was 'informed by the Russians through intermediaries, that if he resigned, Kavtaradze would depart and demand for an oil concession would be dropped'.[63] If the Russians had implicated others this would have hindered efforts at a *rapprochement* were Sa'id's Cabinet to collapse. The removal of Sa'id was not difficult, but it was unlikely to change the feelings about and repercussions resulting from the way in which the Russians had tried to enforce their demand.[64] The Russian demand had been clumsily made, aggressively pursued and when suddenly dropped, aroused great suspicion. The Russians had repeatedly contended, both publicly and in an audience with the Shah, that they wanted a concession mainly because it was in the interest of the Iranians themselves,[65] and because they wanted to assist Iran economically.[66] In abandoning, temporarily, their persistence, they were perhaps influenced by the 'representations which the British and American Ambassadors had made in Moscow'.[67] Their sole consolation was that although they themselves had achieved nothing, they had at least thwarted the West.

For their part, although relieved at the rejection of the Russian oil demand, the British and the Americans were inevitably disappointed at the frustration of their own demands. A few British officials thought it might be feasible to find 'some solution' which would meet 'the Russians' legitimate desire to obtain oil without giving them the dominating political position',[68] and they considered the possibility of negotiating an agreement between 'Persia, Great Britain, the USA and USSR on future oil concessions in Iran'.[69] Suggestions on much the same lines were also made by Gulbenkian and, apparently, Taqizadih.[70] The Foreign Office, however, opted to support Sa'id's strong stand and advocated that a similar policy be adopted by his successor.[71] Realistically there was little alternative. The Government's rejection of the Soviet demand had triggered Iranian national sentiments and raised public consciousness. Now any demand for an oil concession, whether by the West or the Soviet Union, was bound to meet with very strong resistance.

An additional blow to the embattled Sa'id was dealt by Millspaugh who had ventured, against the wishes of the Shah and the Prime Minister, to dismiss Abulhasan Ibtihaj, the Governor-General of the National Bank and a Court favourite.[72] The dismissal of Ibtihaj, who was reinstated after much pressure and the intervention of the Majlis, was overshadowed by the oil issue, but Sa'id's policy of patience and inaction towards Millspaugh had clearly failed. Although a majority of deputies supported Sa'id, in the face of Russian hostility and his own obvious inability, little could be done to prolong his term of office. Even the Shah believed that Sa'id's position was untenable, and having abandoned the idea of making Sayyid Zia premier – a move Sayyid Zia himself thought premature[73] – the Shah reconsidered Taqizadih as a candidate.[74]

Sa'id tried to rekindle Court support by pushing through the Majlis a bill to grant a credit of 150 million rials for the army, then 90,000 strong. The bill gave some deputies, notably Musaddiq and Amir Taymur Kalali, an opportunity to criticize the conduct of the office of the Chief of Staff, which acted independently of the War Ministry. Musaddiq in particular strongly warned the Shah against interfering in the affairs of the Government and the army, and expressed his alarm at the corrupting influence of the Shah's sycophantic retinue.[75] The bill was, however, passed, and little changed in the prevailing pattern of relations between the Shah, the Chief of Staff and the War Ministry. Previous efforts in this direction had proved unsuccessful and there was little reason to believe that they would succeed in the future. In September 1943, 'the Shah', in the words of the British Minister, 'under much pressure from the Government, very unwillingly signed a decree making the General Staff responsible and subservient to the Ministry for War, while reaffirming his own status as Commander-in-Chief'.[76] Yet the concentration of power in the office of the General Staff was essential if the Shah was to maintain his position as the effective commander-in-chief of the armed forces, and the army to play a significant role in Iranian politics. As a British official perceptively observed:

> As long as the present Shah remains on the throne, the Army will play an increasingly preponderant role in all the country's affairs, and will remain, as at present, the chief instrument of internal policy.[77]

Sa'id's efforts to regain the support of the Court did not bear fruit. The attacks on him increased and it soon became clear that the only way to diffuse Russian anger was to remove him. Thus, although still supported by the Majlis,[78] he felt he had little choice but to resign; according to Bullard, even the Shah encouraged him to do so.[79] Yet even had the oil crisis not precipitated the resignation of Sa'id, he would not have been able to retain his position much longer. He possessed all the characteristics which Iranian clan politics required to warrant his appointment to what was nominally the highest position of authority in the state, while he lacked the qualities needed to tackle successfully the socio-economic problems of Iranian society. Within the structural framework of the prevailing style of politics, the fall of Cabinets was as much an integral part of the political game as was their formation; it was neither unexpected nor necessarily a disgrace. Sa'id was perhaps saved from many of the repercussions of the usual desperate efforts to retain power by virtue of his resignation, primarily as a result of Russian pressure. Such pressure positively or negatively influenced the choice of future prime-ministerial candidates and increased the vulnerability of Sa'id's successors.

6

The Government of Bayat:
NOVEMBER 1944–APRIL 1945

After the fall of Sa'id's Cabinet, given the strained relations with Russia and the intensity of factional divisions in the Majlis, contenders or possible candidates for the premiership were not wholly enthusiastic about assuming the responsibility. Sayyid Zia, whose nomination had been considered by the Shah, told a British official that the Russians might try to engineer his election to office 'in order that he should have further to fall'.[1] Musaddiq, who was favoured by a number of deputies, made his acceptance of office conditional upon the right to resume his seat in the Majlis should he be relieved of his prime-ministerial duties.[2] However, this condition, intended to prevent his exclusion from parliamentary life, was not acceptable to the majority of deputies, who were, in all likelihood, prepared to acquiesce in his premiership precisely as a means of depriving him of his position in the Majlis.

On the other hand, the fall of Sa'id's Cabinet was followed by renewed factional disarray, realignments and compromises. After over two weeks of intense bargaining and brokerage between factional leaders or *mutavallis*, the National Union and Fatherland factions agreed to work together and support Husain Sami'i (Adib us-Saltanih) – an ex-Minister and Grand Master of Ceremonies in the Court of Reza Shah – on the condition that Murtiza Quli Bayat and a specified number of other deputies be included in any Cabinet he should form.[3] Sami'i, however, withdrew at the last moment,[4] and the two factions opted for Bayat who gained 50 votes. His closest rival, Sadiq Sadiq (Mustashar ud-Daulih), a respected elderly politician who had recently served in Qavam's Cabinet and was believed to enjoy Russian favour,[5] gained 45. Despite this narrow majority, Bayat agreed to form a Cabinet.

Murtiza Quli Bayat (Saham us-Sultan) was born in about 1887 into a prominent family. He was an influential politician and a large landowner who had represented his home town of Sultanabad (Arak) in the Majlis for ten consecutive terms. In a British account of personalities in Iran, he had been aptly described as 'a highly respectable and polite man, who will never set the world ablaze'.[6] In a characteristic précis Bullard described him as 'a nonentity'.[7] He was not distinguished for any particular administrative skill or quality, but was a moderate, practically minded politician whose membership of the Majlis during the entire period of Reza Shah's rule had not greatly affected his reputation for honesty and integrity.

The composition of Bayat's Cabinet reflected a wide range of interests and considerations. A significant number of his ministers had previously held ministerial portfolios and were identifiable with influential factions which had either supported Bayat or whose support he hoped to enlist.[8] At the same time the Cabinet appeared pro-Western and as sensitive to the expectations of the Court as its predecessors. Inevitably there was dissatisfaction; the Fatherland faction, for instance, was believed to be dissatisfied at having been allocated only one post in the Cabinet,[9] and other groups which could not identify with any minister were naturally disconcerted.

However, the performance and policies of a Cabinet were not dictated by its composition as much as by the personality of the Prime Minister himself, and change was therefore expected. Musaddiq, himself a relative of Bayat, had little faith in his ministers but was prepared to support him on condition of the cancellation of Millspaugh's contract;[10] the Tudeh faction unenthusiastically awaited clarification of the Cabinet's position vis-à-vis the Soviet Union,[11] and demanded the exact implementation of the Constitution, which implied restricting the involvement of the Court and the army in politics, as well as respecting the freedom of association and the press. Those who had brought about Bayat's premiership expected him to proceed with his tasks without making any real conciliatory gesture towards the Russians and the leftists.

Above all, the major test of Bayat's premiership was thought to be his oil policy; he would not have been appointed had he been suspected of wishing to pursue a policy different from that of Sa'id, which had the support of the entire Iranian ruling elite, as well as the British and the Americans.[12] Bayat had expressed his desire to find a way of settling issues with the Russians but at the same time had assured Bullard that 'there will be no change in policy on [the] oil question'.[13] He was, however, saved from having to tackle the oil issue when, on 2 December 1944, Musaddiq submitted a bill to the Majlis, under double-urgency procedures, banning governments from negotiating the granting of oil concessions to foreigners.[14]

This bill, which was approved unhesitatingly by all the deputies present – with the exception of the Tudeh faction – was an initiative on Musaddiq's part undertaken without the usual prior lobbying. It shocked many people, including Sayyid Zia, who confessed to having been taken by surprise;[15] it also exposed Musaddiq to increasing attacks from the Russians and the Tudeh, and inevitably to the accusation of collaboration with Sa'id and Sayyid Zia. Musaddiq's refusal to endorse Ghulam Husain Rahimian's bill concerning the cancellation of the British oil concession in the south, was exploited by the Tudeh Party. Khalil Maliki, for instance, accused Musaddiq of not living up to his claim of advocating a policy of negative equilibrium, but of endorsing a one-sided policy, and of pursuing an elite-approved method of maintaining the prevailing status quo to the detriment of the Russians.[16] Musaddiq, however, remained unshaken; his actions embodied a reassertion of Iranian national aspirations as well as a defiant response to pressure from the Russians and others.[17]

Bayat was undoubtedly relieved, since the Russians could no longer press their demands upon him, and soon after the approval of Musaddiq's bill Kavtaradze finally left Iran.[18] There was naturally general unease that indirect pressure would now be exerted and a few days after the approval of the bill there appeared widely publicized reports of large meetings of Azarbaijanis in many towns and villages demanding the usual Tudeh-inspired reforms, including provincial councils, good relations with the Soviet Union, the formulation of a 'real' coalition government, the improvement of the conditions of workers and peasants, as well as the trial of Sa'id and the exile of Sayyid Zia.[19] The Government responded by issuing a circular to all the provinces promising extensive constructive measures and administrative and social reforms, including the creation of provincial councils.[20]

At the same time the Government became more lenient towards the Tudeh Party and, hoping to appease the Russians, informed the Soviet Ambassador of its intention to set up an oil company as envisaged in Musaddiq's bill, to be manned by Iranians and personnel from neutral countries, in order eventually to exploit oil in northern Iran, offering the priority of purchase to the Russians. This failed to impress the Russians and, since Bayat had not informed the Majlis, provoked and alarmed many deputies who suspected him of promising the Russians that he would try to persuade the Majlis both to reconsider its oil policy and put an end to Millspaugh's service with the Iranian Government.[21] In fact Qavam later told Bullard how, on a visit to Moscow in early 1946, he learned that Bayat had proposed, without the knowledge of his ministers, to set up an arrangement for the exploitation of oil in northern Iran, in which the Iranians and the Russians would hold 51 per cent and 49 per cent of the shares, respectively.[22]

The removal of Millspaugh was a development for which Bayat was both credited and blamed. In the altered circumstances of post-Reza Shah Iran, Millspaugh's second mission, which began in 1943, some seventeen years after the end of his first, was not a success. It failed to reorganize finances, prevent price rises or secure general supplies. In addition, the various departments which he established, along with the salaries and allowances of his fifty colleagues, proved both costly and incommensurate with their achievements and performance.

Millspaugh's income tax bill not only provoked the enmity of the rich but also facilitated greater corruption (to the extent that it was later modified and in 1946 abandoned for all practical purposes). His scornful attitude towards the Iranian army and his procrastination in providing it with funds resulted in the souring of his relations with the Court. He was described by an Iranian politician who knew him well as 'intransigent and arrogant'. His condescending character, high-mindedness, insensitivity and obstinacy not only antagonized many Iranian officials but dismayed some of his own colleagues. His unreserved interference in Iranian politics, and his avowed pro-British and anti-Soviet bias adversely affected the attempted balance of Iranian foreign policy. His full use, with the aid of his domestic cronies, of the prevailing practices of intrigue, favouritism, bribery, the making of 'gifts' and the indirect subsidizing of particular newspapers, along with the incompetence, inefficiency or corruption of most of his colleagues, greatly discredited his mission. Even Bullard, a staunch supporter of Millspaugh, had considered only a dozen of his colleagues as competent and suitable for the tasks required of them.[23] He was also the target of increasing hostility from the liberal nationalists and the leftists. Millspaugh's standing with the American Government had also declined; as one report put it: 'responsible US officials, deprecating the anti-Soviet reputation acquired by Millspaugh, have withdrawn their support for him and would prefer to see him leave his post'.[24]

The retention of Millspaugh was thus no longer easily justifiable, and Bayat put his case before the Majlis which, on 8 January 1945, according to a bill presented by Musaddiq, voted to repeal Millspaugh's special economic powers.[25] Millspaugh did not readily surrender and threatened the Government with his own resignation if Ibtihaj was not dismissed or suspended.[26] The Government's refusal to meet his demands, however, eventually led to his resignation and departure from the country.[27] Some of the deputies who had helped to bring about Bayat's premiership regarded this action as prejudicial to good relations with the United States, which aggravated dissatisfaction with Bayat's efforts to give an appearance of neutrality. His efforts, regarded as 'surrender in the face of foreign demands',[28] resulted in a drastic change in the sources of his support in the Majlis.

The Fatherland faction turned against him; the National Union faction, the largest in the Majlis, to which Bayat himself was affiliated, split into opposing groups of supporters and opponents of the Prime Minister; and the Democrat faction,[29] followed gradually by the Independent faction, joined the ranks of his opponents.[30] These moves resulted in individual deputies, and gradually the Tudeh faction, uniting in support of Bayat. The position of the Cabinet became more difficult since Bayat's opponents now far exceeded his supporters in number, while the character and disposition of both Bayat and his colleagues were more in line with those of his previous supporters than his new ones.

Bayat's opponents were earnestly searching for a successor to him, and the spectre of Suhaili as a possible alternative began to haunt Bayat and his newly acquired supporters. Suhaili, however, along with Tadayyun, a minister in his second Cabinet, still faced charges of corruption and undue interference in the elections for the 14th Majlis. With the intention of attracting public attention and preventing the easy acquittal of politicians such as Suhaili, Musaddiq stormed out of the Majlis calling it a 'den of thieves'.[31] Two days later he returned accompanied by a group of university students, shopkeepers and merchants who had closed the bazaar in his support. Musaddiq's supporters clashed with the police and one person was killed as the result of shooting.[32]

Bayat's opponents suspected his personal complicity in the incident and their representatives approached the Shah, requesting him to ask Bayat to resign.[33] The Shah, however, did not seem ready or willing to intervene, and in any case Bayat's opponents were unable to agree on a successor. The Cabinet therefore continued its

precarious existence or, in Bullard's words, it seemed 'too inert even
to fall'.[34] The financial situation of the country and the distribution
of rationed goods deteriorated as no effective scheme had been
worked out to replace Millspaugh's economic organization. The
resignation of the Foreign Minister in early April 1945 and the trip
to Palestine of the War Minister 'for medical reasons' were regarded
as signs of the disintegration of the Cabinet,[35] while the election as
Speaker of the Majlis of Sayyid Muhammad Sadiq Tabataba'i – who
was believed to be a supporter of the Prime Minister – did not
positively affect Bayat's position.[36]

Bayat's Cabinet found little favour with the British, and Lascelles,
the British *chargé d'affaires* did not, for most purposes, see 'any
possibility of conducting business with it'.[37] The Russians, however,
seeing no prospect for the reappointment of Qavam, their favourite
candidate, appeared to regard Bayat as the least objectionable
alternative. The Shah, too, seemed unwilling to press the Government to resign: none of his prerogatives were being challenged or
under threat, and he had litle reason to provoke Bayat's followers by
hastening the fall of a Cabinet which was, in any case, soon to
collapse. Lascelles, however, provided a different account of the
motives behind the positions taken by the Russians and the Shah:

> Bayat appears to enjoy at least the qualified support of the Russians, to
> whom a state of administrative paralysis is not unwelcome, and of the
> Shah, who is widely said to be working for the exposure of the Majlis,
> as a prelude to some undefined derogation from constitutional
> regime.[38]

Bayat's opponents were now intent upon undermining his Cabinet
and induced him to attend the Majlis and ask for a vote of
confidence, which they apparently promised to give. His supporters,
particularly Musaddiq, argued that the Government should not ask
for such a vote unless a motion of interpellation were put against
it.[39] Bayat became infuriated with the conflicting demands of the
deputies: 'for a person who adheres to certain principles', he argued,
'taking into account the views of all gentlemen is very difficult,
indeed impossible, particularly if those views, God forbid, are
personal and not always consonant with the public interest'.[40]
Nevertheless he agreed to the vote of confidence which, not
surprisingly, went against him, with only 45 out of the 90 deputies
present voting for him and most of the rest abstaining. His Cabinet

was thus forced to resign after a period of less than five months in office.

Bayat's premiership witnessed an intensification of ideological or emotive tensions and confrontations, stimulated by the Russian demand for an oil concession. The Tudeh Party increasingly capitalized on the incompetence of the ruling elite, as well as the iniquities and defects of Iranian society, and advocated extensive reforms. Bayat's liberal style of government enabled the Tudeh to expand its organization, although it attributed this growth solely to its own 'invincible power' and gave no credit to the Government.[41] On the other hand, his attitude towards the left provoked the enmity of the right wing. Much later and with the benefit of hindsight, a Tudeh leader gave the following assessment of Bayat's Government:

> in the course of 53 years of Pahlavi's reign, with the exception of Musaddiq's Cabinet, the record of Bayat's Cabinet has been the most positive of all. He stepped forward courageously, accomplished a number of significant tasks, governed constitutionally, made a manly defence of himself, and fell. History will remember his Government palatably.[42]

Nevertheless, when the Tudeh Party had joined the ranks of his supporters towards the end of his term of office, they did not attempt to co-operate with him in his task.

The most immediately damaging manoeuvres against Bayat, however, came from Sayyid Zia who opposed his policies and his tolerance of the left. In early 1945 he and his followers, with the support of many of those whose privileges were threatened by the Tudeh Party, had succeeded in forming the National Will Party (Hizb-i Iradih-yi Milli). This party claimed a large following, was insistent on making wide-ranging reformist pledges, and aimed at constituting, both on ideological and organizational grounds, a countervailing force to the Tudeh Party.

The gross iniquities of Iranian society were undeniable. However, the incompetence of successive governments in tackling them, and the largely self-inflicted paralysis of the parliamentary system, ceaselessly exposed by the press, were bound to result in widespread discontent and frustration. This, in turn, provided a favourable ground for radicalism and sporadic instances of protest and rebellion, and for movements for autonomy, which were rumoured to be developing in Kurdistan and Azarbaijan. The ruling elite could not remain insensitive to such a situation, but its responses did not help to reduce its internal differences and bring about any positive action. Although clan politics was ostensibly concerned with the national interest, public issues and matters of policy, its primary aim was the achievement and allocation of tangible political spoils. The fate of Bayat's successors illustrated this point further.

7

The Abortive Government of Hakimi:
MAY–JUNE 1945

The search for a new prime minister began again, with the Shah anxious to form a government before the May Day celebrations.[1] However, it was not until 2 May 1945 that Hakimi received 64 votes in the Majlis and was entrusted to form a Cabinet. The fall of Bayat had precipitated the breakdown of the alliance between the Fatherland and Independent factions. The Fatherland faction, anxious not to remain in the minority, resorted to a compromise with the National faction, which advocated the choice of Hakimi and tried to enlist the support of as many members of other factions as possible.[2] As a result, a 'majority' was formed which opted for Hakimi – who provoked the least general opposition – on the basis of a tactical compromise conducive to little more than the relative disadvantage of all competing groups. As Bullard put it: 'Those who were unable to impose a candidate of their own persuasion . . . were able to block the election of any candidate of ability or character by their opponents. Hence the compromise on this non-entity.'[3]

Dr. Ibrahim Hakimi was born in 1880 into an Isfahani family residing in Tabriz. His father, uncle and elder brother had been traditional physicians in the Qajar Court. He himself, after studying medicine in Paris, joined the Court of Muzaffar ud-Din Shah, to become the Shah's private physician and, following the death of his uncle, assumed his title and came to be known as Hakim ul-Mulk. However, he soon abandoned the medical profession in favour of active involvement in politics.[4] Following his activities in the Constitutional Revolution, he was elected as a deputy for Tehran and Tabriz in the 1st, 2nd, 4th and 5th Majlis. Before the advent of Reza Shah he assumed, among other positions, several ministerial portfolios, notably that of Education. Throughout the reign of Reza Shah he lived in retirement, but following the abdication he resumed his political activities and held the post of Minister without Portfolio in Qavam's Cabinet.

Hakimi's prestige, credibility and reputation for integrity rested primarily on his withdrawal from the political scene during the entire period of Reza Shah's rule. He was in no way a charismatic or dynamic personality: he was deaf and suffered from a touch of amnesia, was rich but thrifty, and was an old-fashioned and intellectually uninspiring conservative.[5] Believed to be generally obstinate, he was certainly not well-disposed towards leftists or those who advocated a policy of appeasement towards the Russians, and probably not easily susceptible to the temptations or demands of *mutavallis*. However, he was incapable of upsetting the status quo, or of attempting to challenge the power and privileges of the deputies.

Musaddiq and his colleagues acquiesced in Hakimi's premiership because, in Musaddiq's view, he was one of those less active and usually honest statesmen who put the interests of the nation above their own private concerns, as opposed to the active politicians who usually embarked on decision-making without due reflection and calculation or concern for the public interest.[6] One characteristic of Hakimi which was not yet fully manifest was that he was 'a very staunch royalist', according to Mihdi Bamdad who knew him well and had worked with him.[7] He was not a servile or sycophantic courtier, but the British Ambassador was correct in commenting later that Hakimi was 'outstanding for his devotion to the throne and to the present Shah'.[8] This was shown in his choice of colleagues and deprived him of the support of an appreciable number of deputies.

In the selection of his ministers Hakimi did not pay enough attention to the views of the deputies, with the result that after debating his Cabinet programme for three weeks, the Tudeh deputies voted against him, 62 abstained and only 25 voted in his favour. His Cabinet thus ended before it had begun.[9] The deputies rejected the Cabinet not only for personal and sectional reasons, but also with an eye to the approaching elections for the 15th Majlis. Moreover, the majority of deputies preferred a Cabinet which would pursue a firm and determined policy, and at the same time follow their directions and be under their control. They could justify this on several grounds: the country was increasingly affected by ideological tensions and clashes of loyalty; Russian pressure and leftist activities were on the increase; disturbing news about the growth of a movement for independence in Kurdistan was in the air; and signs of anxiety about the promised evacuation of the country by foreign troops could already be felt. In fact one of the first meetings demanding the evacuation of the country and the release of Iranians interned by the Allies, organized by Ali Dashti's Adalat Party, was disrupted by a group probably inspired by the Tudeh Party, and two people were killed in the ensuing trouble.[10] Despite all this, on the whole the deputies were unable or unwilling to stop wasting time and effort in endless arguments, or to allow Cabinets a measure of autonomy and authority. The constitutional hegemony of a Majlis crippled by internal tensions was conducive only to a self-perpetuating crisis, the erosion of the shaky foundations of the prevailing parliamentary arrangements, and eventually a disillusionment with constitutional government.

Although it was only natural for the opponents of leftist radicalism to ally themselves with the Court, no solid royalist bloc had emerged. Sayyid Zia, whose National Will Party had grown in strength and power to mobilize anti-Tudeh elements and had a growing network of friends in the Majlis, was willing to improve his relations with the Shah, which had suffered as the result of incessant criticism of the Court by Muzaffar Firuz. Sayyid Zia even severed his relations with Firuz, as he believed the 'forces of resistance to Russian penetration should not be dissipated by attacks on the Crown'.[11] Yet the Majlis on the whole wanted to reduce the power of the Crown for its own advantage. Despite overt or covert threats against the internal security and integrity of the country, criticism by the press and some deputies of the Shah's hold over the army and its conduct was welcomed by many in the Majlis. In fact the speech of the Tudeh deputy, Abd us-Samad Kambakhsh, criticizing the Chief of Staff General Arfa, his political activities, his polarization of the army and the undue promotion of his friends, as well as the manner in which war ministers were chosen against the wishes of the Majlis, was reported to have received applause from the majority of deputies in an almost unprecedented manner.[12] However, the rejection of Hakimi's Cabinet was not an attempt by the Majlis to marginalize the Shah, but rather a sign of the deputies' determination to maintain the pattern of clan politics as the basis for the proportional distribution of political spoils.

8

The Government of Sadr:
JUNE–OCTOBER 1945

Immediately after the failure of Hakimi to muster sufficient backing among the deputies, members of the Fatherland, National Union, Independent and Democrat factions gathered in the Majlis with a few ungrouped deputies to select a prime minister. Of the sixty-eight members present, sixty opted for Muhsin Sadr. The Freedom faction, members of the National and Tudeh factions and the remaining ungrouped deputies in the Majlis were not present at this session.[1] The choice of Sadr was likely to provoke a strong reaction, in view of the political atmosphere following the oil concessions crisis, the increasingly ideological dimension of group differences and alliances, the contested manner of the fall of Bayat, the intrigues of prime-ministerial contenders, and the stillborn premiership of Hakimi. The unexpected success of Sadr in enlisting the support of sixty deputies was bound to look like collusion between him and the majority of deputies, and against the interests of all those who rejected the legitimacy or expediency of such deals or were excluded from them.

Soon after Sadr had formed his Cabinet, Musaddiq, who resented the manner in which the majority of deputies had treated the Government of Bayat, appeared to have succeeded in forming a stable minority when more than thirty deputies gathered around him to form a block against Sadr and his supporters in the Majlis. Throughout Sadr's term of office, they uncompromisingly used the parliamentary instrument of 'obstruction' in order to deprive the Cabinet of a quorum in the Majlis and thus to bring about its resignation. The 'minority', that is those deputies who gathered together largely due to Musaddiq's initiative and direction, consistently and implacably opposed the 'majority' on the basis of a number of objections usually put forward by Musaddiq.

The minority believed that the premiership of Sadr was the result of an undertaking on his part to conduct the elections for the 15th Majlis according to the wishes of the leaders of the majority.

Moreover, they regarded Sadr as senile and incompetent, out of touch with the problems of Iranian politics and society, a man with few principles, prepared to do what his supporters expected or demanded, unreserved in his services to the Court, whether Qajar or Pahlavi, and too easily identifiable with the British.

At a time when relations between Iran and Russia were at a very low ebb, and during the sensitive months following the end of the war when Allied troops were expected to be evacuated from Iran, Sadr's premiership was seen by the minority as a disaster which would aggravate Russian hostility.[2] With the support of many in the minority, Musaddiq persistently advocated the selection of premiers and ministers who were young and had not previously held ministerial positions, as well as those who would follow a policy of 'negative equilibrium' and attempt to deprive both the Russians and the British of undue privileges in Iran – in effect, men who would be identified with neither power.[3] Moreover, the minority regarded the premiership of Sadr, and the persistence of the majority in consolidating it, as a deliberate attempt to exclude them from the arena of positive political activity. Consequently they saw no choice but to continue with their policy of obstruction.

Faced with these allegations, the majority had great difficulty in producing any arguments in support of Sadr. In fact Ali Dashti, a *mutavalli* and leader of the Independent faction, confessed that the country was suffering from a lack of able statesmen (*rijal*).[4] Nevertheless, the leaders of the majority believed that Sadr was the only candidate who would act according to their wishes and was able to curb the growth of leftist radicalism. The majority of deputies seemed to believe that only closer relations with the West could protect Iran from Russian pressure.

The premiership of Sadr was a test for the policy of firm action against the excesses of the left, and perhaps a reaffirmation of goodwill towards the British. The majority contended that to abandon Sadr in the face of minority opposition would aggravate the problems which he had been assigned to tackle, and that the critical situation in the country would not allow a change of government. When the Shah advised the minority to cease their opposition, conditional upon Sadr's resignation, they reacted strongly on the grounds that: 'This would constitute a dangerous precedent for interference by the sovereign, and also for future obstructionist tactics by any minority which desired the removal of a Prime Minister.'[5] In the end, however, the choice of Sadr and the persistent support for him from the majority of deputies was counter-productive, since it led to a growth of leftist radicalism.

Sayyid Muhsin Sadr (Sadr ul-Ashraf), was born in 1871 in the provincial town of Mahallat into a religious family. His father was a *mullah* who owned land and exerted some local influence. Sadr studied theology and traditional subjects in his home town and in Tehran. He followed his uncle in entering the service of the Qajar Court as a teacher of one of Nasir ud-Din Shah's sons and as his assistant when the former was appointed Governor of Hamadan. In 1907 he joined the Justice Ministry and became increasingly prominent as a judge. According to his own account he did his utmost to secure the release of those constitutionalists who had been detained after the bombardment of the Majlis by Muhammad Ali Shah. Subsequently he served in various judicial capacities, played an important role in devising the Iranian civil code and in 1933 assumed the portfolio of Justice.[6]

Sadr was conservative, religious and had the appearance of a *mullah*, yet he had not been slow to adjust himself to the modernist ethos of Reza Shah's era. His apparent lack of resistance to the removal of the veil (*kashf-i hijab*) and to the wearing of the Pahlavi hat was taken by Musaddiq to be proof of his lack of principle. Sadr, however, contended in his own defence that he acquiesced to the wearing of the Pahlavi hat only after it had been enforced by a parliamentary law. His refusal as Minister of Justice to condone readily Reza Shah's arbitrary behaviour and onslaught against the principles of justice and legality resulted, according to his own account, in his dismissal in 1936.[7] He was, however, later allowed to represent his home town in the Majlis, a position which he retained until August 1943 when he was appointed Minister of Justice in Suhaili's second Cabinet.

Like Suhaili, Sadr rose from relatively humble origins to a position of prominence and influence through his energy and ability to enlist the patronage of the Court and established notables, and through his demonstration of loyalty and talent. For men like Sadr, pious withdrawal, intransigence or the rejection of assignments on the grounds of lofty principles were luxuries to be indulged in only by those who were in a secure position in the upper class. Access to upper-class privileges and entry into the ranks of the ruling elite depended entirely on the individual's public and private conduct. It is easy to dismiss the careers of such men as unprincipled and opportunistic, but this misses the sociological significance of the context in which upward social mobility was possible in Iran. Whatever the reasons for his behaviour, however, allegations that Sadr had helped to undermine the authority and independence of the judiciary, and that his respect for constitutionalist principles was not entirely sincere, made him ill-equipped to assume the premiership in an era of a revitalized constitutional ethos. Although he had ability and energy, his career record and his real or alleged political preferences made Sadr the wrong man to be premier in a situation in which even a rumour about the principles of a Prime Minister was enough to undermine his position.

His opponents continued to ensure that the necessary quorum was not achieved, and for a period of almost three and a half months Sadr was prevented from obtaining a vote of confidence. The deadlock in the Majlis, which denied the Government *de jure* authority, soon coincided with and to some extent provoked events which were directly or indirectly inspired by the Tudeh Party and which had nation-wide repercussions. In the Russian-occupied province of Azarbaijan unrest in the city prison of Tabriz and the attempted escape of a group of prisoners ended, according to a Tudeh account, with the death of seven inmates and the injury of eleven. In the same province in the city of Maraghih, the government offices were occupied,[8] and in the village of Liqavan clashes between Tudeh supporters and the influential landowner Hajji Ihtisham Liqvani resulted in his death, and aroused considerable alarm and publicity in Tehran. There was also unrest among industrial workers in Gilan and Mazandaran.

More significantly, in August 1945 some twenty-five officers and soldiers resorted to mutiny in the province of Khurasan, also under Russian occupation.[9] They had acted with the knowledge of the Tudeh Party's military section but apparently without the knowledge of the Party's central committee or the Russians. They aimed, however, to spark off a rebellion among the Turkomans, hoping that it would spread rapidly, attract domestic and Russian support and result in the assumption of power by the Tudeh Party. The Government of Sadr and its Chief of Staff, General Arfa, were, however, quick to act: the rebels were defeated a few days after their mutiny and the Russians and the Tudeh Party failed to act in their support. Sadr also resorted to measures to ward off any trouble in the capital and severely restricted the activities of the Tudeh Party.

The greatest alarm in Tehran was, however, caused by the growth of a movement for autonomy in Kurdistan and the formation of the

'Democratic Party of Azarbaijan'. Events of this kind occurred predominantly in the Russian-occupied zone, where Tudeh influence was widespread and the attempts of the Iranian Government to establish its authority were frustratingly foiled by the Russians. In September 1945 the Democratic Party of Azarbaijan issued a proclamation demanding autonomy for the province and proclaiming many aims distasteful to the Iranian ruling elite. The Soviet-backed radical propaganda and activities created a tense political atmosphere and provoked the continuing activities of Sayyid Zia and his followers in the National Will Party, while the Tudeh Party and its sympathizers came under attack from local notables in the southern areas. For instance, according to British reports Lutf-Ali Mu'addil, a deputy for Shiraz and a prominent landowner in the area, was 'suspected of implication' in the sacking and burning of the Tudeh Party's club in the sugar factory of the southern town of Marvdasht. Qavam ul-Mulk had also sent two *mullahs* to stir up anti-Tudeh feelings.[10] Sayyid Zia tried to stir up the peasants in the north,[11] but with little success. In Mashhad, for instance, the Tudeh Party with the help of the Russians successfully dispersed his supporters.[12]

In Tehran the martial law authorities banned all outdoor demonstrations, closed the Tudeh offices, and suppressed a few Tudeh papers; in this they were helped by the departure of the Soviet forces from Tehran, which deprived the Tudeh of a source of support.[13] The Tudeh Party thrived on the discontent resulting from the failure of the Government to initiate welfare measures and was likely to benefit from the rising unemployment following the end of the war. However, what most helped the growth of the party was the presence of the Russian forces, and consequently the issue of the evacuation of the country by foreign forces, due in March 1946 (six months after the end of the Second World War, as stipulated in the Tripartite Treaty of 1942), was of critical significance. Yet the prospect of evacuation by the Russians was bleak, as no positive gesture was made in this direction by the Conference of Foreign Secretaries held in London in September 1945. Soon after the end of the war in August 1945 most British and American soldiers left Iran. The Russians, however, gave no hint of intending to fulfil their undertaking to evacuate the country and this seriously threatened the Government of Sadr. Although staunchly anti-Tudeh, Sadr had tried unsuccessfully to reach an understanding with the Tudeh Party in order to mitigate Russian hostility. The Party's morale, however, was high following the end of the war which vindicated its consistent prophecy that the Soviet Union would emerge victorious. Moreover, the decisive Labour victory in the British general election raised the hopes of the Tudeh Party – and some other groups in Iran – that British policy towards Iran would change to the detriment of Sadr and his supporters. The party therefore saw little reason to modify its anti-Sadr position.

Although the events of summer 1945 had deeply impressed both the majority and the minority they were still not persuaded to reach a compromise, but blamed each other for the developments. The Government, at the mercy of the Majlis for its daily expenses and the payment of the salaries of its employees, had great difficulty in getting approval for its bills for the customary monthly or two-monthly budgets. The minority continued to ensure that the Majlis was inquorate and prevented the Cabinet from acquiring full legal status. When the deadlock finally ended it was because the minority changed its tactics.

In a meeting with the representatives of the minority, Sadr had reportedly stated that if the number of his opponents reached forty he would have little choice but to resign, and the minority took this to be an unequivocal undertaking on his part.[14] On 28 September 1945 the Cabinet repeated its demand for a vote of confidence and the minority deputies stayed to cast their 40 opposing votes; 70 votes were cast in Sadr's favour, with 4 abstentions.[15] Sadr, however, refused to resign and the minority, which had not been as effective as it hoped in achieving its objectives through obstruction, decided to change its tactics on the grounds that a relaxation of pressure by the minority would break the unity of Sadr's supporters. The minority hoped that this new manoeuvre would induce the pro-Government deputies to be more flexible with regard to the postponement of the elections, which Musaddiq opposed, and electoral reform, which he advocated. In any case, the dishonouring of promises was added to the list of charges against Sadr, and he had little prospect of surviving for long in the face of the vocal opposition of forty deputies.

In early October Sadr told the Shah that he could not continue in office in view of the opposition of Musaddiq and the minority, but was asked to stay 'a little longer'.[16] At this stage the Shah was only waiting for events to take their course, especially since it was likely that Hakimi would take Sadr's place.[17] In fact, from the outset of Sadr's premiership the Shah had shown him little favour. In Sadr's own words:

From the beginning of his reign, Muhammad Reza Shah had no genuine liking for me. In the course of my premiership too I not only experienced no backing from the Shah, but he even acted to weaken my position. The reason for this [behaviour] was that whenever it was not in the interests of the country or the real interests of the Shah himself, I refused to abide by or implement royal wishes.[18]

The British military attaché also reported that the Shah was known to be intriguing against Sadr and it was probably due to the Shah's influence that Amanullah Ardalan and Ahmad I'tibar, Sadr's Ministers of Justice and of Post, Telegraph and Telephone, respectively, had resigned soon after their appointment. According to the British military attaché, the Shah's opposition to Sadr was due 'mainly to pique, and a desire to get even with the majority of Deputies for having rejected Hakimi's Cabinet, which included some ministers of his own choice'.[19] This disregard for royal preferences and interests on the part of the deputies was not compensated for by Sadr's royalist credentials.

Less than a month after securing a vote of confidence the Cabinet of Sadr came to an end. In addition to the determined opposition of the minority, Russian hostility towards Sadr and disregard for the authority of the central government in the parts of Iran they occupied had continued to increase. Seven members of the 'Komala' (Kurdish Autonomy Party), led by Qazi Muhammad, paid a seven-day visit to Baku without the permission of the central government.[20] The Prime Minister's efforts to appoint Farrukh as Governor of Azarbaijan – although an inexpedient move – were thwarted by the Russians,[21] and the establishment of central government authority in Azarbaijan and Kurdistan was systematically obstructed. This provoked Sadr to protest to the Russians and make a bitter complaint to the Majlis.[22] On the other hand, even those who were expected to support the Government appeared to have turned against it. For example, Nasir Khan Qashqa'i, who had recently made peace with the Shah and the British and was according to one account the provincial leader of the National Will Party in Shiraz,[23] publicly criticized the 'reactionary' character of the Government, contending in a meeting of the minority deputies that it had been manipulated into re-establishing dictatorship.[24] Sadr had pursued a policy of firm action against the Tudeh Party, which in Tehran had to a large extent been 'rendered harmless'.[25] His suppression of the critical press, however, alienated some of his original supporters: Muzaffar

Firuz, for example, modified his earlier qualified support for the Government and attempted to bring together journalists opposed to such policies.[26] The displeasure of the journalists was particularly significant in view of the ever-present and easily mobilized fear of dictatorship and/or a military coup, which they ceaselessly brought up in their attacks against the Court and the Chief of Staff, General Arfa.

Although, as Bullard put it, Iran was perhaps the only country where 'the rich made hardly any contribution to the treasury',[27] the Government of Sadr was bent on appeasing the rich and, in particular, protecting the interests of the merchants. Thus, Mahmud Badr, the Finance Minister, promised the Chamber of Commerce to modify the income tax bill (although it was left to the next Cabinet to implement), the Cabinet abolished the cotton monopoly,[28] and Badr tried to transfer the capital's electricity power station from the ownership of the Tehran municipality into private hands, a move which provoked the strong opposition of Musaddiq and was thwarted.[29]

Sadr and his supporters did successfully postpone the elections for the 15th Majlis until after the evacuation of foreign troops, despite all the efforts of Musaddiq and others.[30] This measure was clearly aimed against the leftists and radical elements who would benefit from the Russian presence, but was beneficial to the established members of the elite. Musaddiq contended that the postponement was against the Constitution and the interests of the nation, and urged the approval of his electoral reform bill which would have restricted the ways in which local magnates could use their traditional ties and influences to determine the outcome of the elections. Not only did this fail to find favour with the majority, but even in a much diluted form failed to get the support of all members of the minority.[31]

Moreover, Sadr had succeeded in rendering a number of important services to the British; they 'owe[d] to him the conclusion of an agreement between the Ministry of Finance and the Imperial Bank of Persia' which 'was of great importance to British interests',[32] and he found 'the money for the purchase of British military telecommunications and the greater part of the American military assets', which had been installed in Iran for use by the Allies. He had shown himself to be 'aware of the pressing need for security in the AIOC's [Anglo-Iranian Oil Company] area and had undertaken to table a bill to provide the necessary credits' for that purpose.[33]

Mainly because of these efforts the British military attaché reported:

> In the face of the prevailing apathy in all government departments, the hostility of the Russians, the ceaseless opposition of the minority, and the obstruction of the Majlis as a whole, his record bears favourable comparison with that of his predecessors.

This was probably a fair assessment and if he had not encountered so much opposition he might have inspired far more enthusiasm on the part of the British. To his opponents, however, Sadr remained a reactionary conservative who had never acted in support of the Constitution and had always followed a one-sided, pro-British foreign policy. It was believed that he owed his premiership to these qualities.

But what did the minority achieve by its obstructive and other tactics, besides preventing the consolidation of Sadr's Cabinet? It certainly failed to find a common policy or a broad, collectively pursued objective. Musaddiq of course put forward a concrete programme and consistently demanded electoral reform, but these were primarily his own personal concerns rather than the collective goals of the minority. The minority did not attract enough public support to transform the amorphous wants and desires of those they claimed to represent into a coherent set of demands. They failed to persuade the ruling elite to recognize alternative policies or courses of action, and they did not succeed in changing the rules of the political game to the detriment of their rivals.

On the positive side they did succeed in re-establishing the existing rules of the game by challenging what they considered to be a violation of the formal or informal procedures necessary for the effective participation of the minority in the political process. This does not imply that political preferences were not important in demarcating the majority from the minority, but that the formation and persistence of the minority arose from a feeling of deliberate marginalization and exclusion from the process of the exercise of power and the allocation of political spoils. When on 6 October 1945 the Speaker and deputy speakers of the Majlis were all chosen from the majority, Musaddiq complained that the minority had been completely disregarded and that,

> we resorted to obstruction so that the majority would, to some extent, take the minority properly into account, and would involve the

minority in the public affairs of the country and political matters; for some time after we stayed away from the Majlis, the majority paid no attention to us and made no conciliatory gestures towards us. We therefore realised that if we stayed away, everything would eventually end to the benefit of the majority, and we would not gain any benefits. So we came back to the Majlis ... in order to co-operate with the majority ... [hoping] that such co-operation would result in an equilibrium in the politics of the Majlis ... but we realised that the majority refuses our offer of co-operation.[34]

Whatever the majority and minority gained or lost, much time was certainly wasted, and the Majlis was unable to perform its legislative function positively and efficiently. Well-reasoned parliamentary arguments and tempered discussions centring on matters of public interest or on contrasting interpretations of constitutional issues were often overshadowed by frequent outbursts of vituperation. Many deputies proved insensitive to the urgency and magnitude of the problems with which they were expected to deal.

However, all deputies were agreed that the Majlis, whatever its shortcomings, must be the centre of gravity of the body politic.[35] In this they could invoke the Constitution, and claim with some justification that they desired the prevention of authoritarianism. Yet the systematic incapacitation of the executive was potentially the most serious threat to the foundations of constitutional government. At the same time the inefficiency of the Majlis in tackling its legislative and other functions, combined with its internal squabbles and dissension, contributed to and was in turn affected by the institutional precariousness of the entire Iranian polity, and played into the hands of those who thought that Iran was not ready for democracy in any form. The performance of the Majlis induced the Shah to contemplate the revision of the Constitution in favour of royal authority. In an audience with the Shah Bullard found him to be:

sceptical about democracy as interpreted here as a method of government for Persia. The deputies appeared in the Majlis daily just long enough to collect salary [sic] and spent the rest of the time pressing the Ministers for jobs for relatives and friends. He believed that some change of constitution would have to be made when foreign troops had left; in particular, some means must be found to dissolve a Majlis which, like the present one, never passed any legislation at all.[36]

In the event the Shah only needed to exercise patience for, apart from short interludes, events were moving in his favour.

9

The Government of Hakimi:
OCTOBER 1945–JANUARY 1946

A compromise brought about by the urgent demands of the political situation and a tacit recognition of the inexpediency and cost of constant confrontation between the majority and the minority, resulted in the reappointment of Hakimi to form a Cabinet. Hakimi's second Cabinet was by all accounts a considerable improvement on his earlier attempt. He consulted the deputies in his choice of colleagues, and attempted to take into account the preferences of the minority, which, having lost its *raison d'être*, had begun to disintegrate.[1] Thus, on 6 November 1945, almost 100 deputies cast their vote of confidence for Hakimi, while only six Tudeh deputies voted against him.[2] This seemed a promising beginning for Hakimi to embark upon the formidable task of tackling the political crisis generated largely by events in Azarbaijan and Kurdistan.

Ja'far Pishihvari and Qazi Muhammad, leaders of the autonomy movements in Azarbaijan and Kurdistan respectively, had, along with their associates, exploited the near-absence of effective central government authority in their provinces, as well as the active or tacit support and encouragement of the Russian occupiers, to launch their own movements. Of the two, Pishihvari was the subject of greater attention and was better known in Tehran, not only as a veteran communist, a member of the old Adalat Party and an associate of Mirza Kuchik Khan Jangali, but also because following the fall of Reza Shah and his own release from prison, Pishihvari had established himself as a skilful journalist and editor of the newspaper *Azhir*.[3] He had not formally joined the Tudeh Party as he was not well-disposed towards most of its leaders. He was elected as a deputy for Tabriz in the 14th Majlis but his credentials were rejected and he could not take his seat. He returned to Tabriz and formed the Democratic Party of Azarbaijan to which the local branch of the Tudeh was affiliated, without the knowledge of the party authorities. As leader of the Democratic Party of Azarbaijan, Pishihvari betrayed considerable scorn towards the 'Persians' (*Fars-ha*), an attitude which two recent incidents had helped to aggravate. The general conference of the Tudeh Party held in August 1944 had rejected his credentials and thus prevented him from joining the conference as a representative for Azarbaijan; he had also been deprived of his parliamentary position.

The initial success of Pishihvari and Qazi Muhammad in enlisting popular support was largely due to their ability to mobilize the lurking feelings of discontent and deprivation which strengthened and were strengthened by strong communal sentiments and bonds. During Hakimi's second term of office these movements entered a new phase with the establishment of formal administrative frameworks. The proclaimed, essentially reformist objectives of the movements emphasized their respect for Iran's territorial integrity and stressed that the realization of provincial autonomy should be accompanied by the establishment of democratic arrangements throughout the country. They could thus appeal to large sections of the Iranian intelligentsia who were dismayed by the performance of the ruling elite and desired the extension of such measures to the entire country. These aspirations brought qualified outbursts of enthusiasm tinged with discreet sympathy and wishful optimism, but also unease and anxiety.[4] The oil crisis of the previous year had deeply troubled the consciences of the intellectuals, and the clash between patriotism and Western-inspired reforms, and between nationalism and Russian-style socialism, constituted central themes of the intellectual orientations in this period.[5]

The mixed feelings of this group of intellectuals towards the autonomy movements arose from the disturbing ambiguity of the very notion of autonomy (*mukhtariyyat-i milli*) and in particular the stress which the movements placed on the teaching and official use of Azari and Kurdish. The Iranian ruling elite, however, were deeply suspicious of the real aims of the movements, and regarded them as separatists in disguise, opposed to the sovereignty, territorial integrity and prevailing socio-political arrangements in Iran.[6] Since the conditions for growth of these movements arose largely from the presence and active involvement of the Russians, the ruling elite could cast doubts upon and even deny the authenticity and legitimacy of the aspirations and demands for improved living conditions which the movements claimed to originate from and to represent and articulate.

The ruling elite, and indeed many other Iranians, were deeply suspicious and fearful of the ultimate intentions of the Russians, who had systematically procrastinated in making any gesture of willingness to evacuate Iran. Such misgivings on the part of the Iranians can in fact be traced back to the beginning of the Anglo-Russian occupation of Iran. The attitude of the Russians and the autonomy movements was considered to be an orchestrated reaction against the rejection by the Iranian Government of the Soviet demand for an oil concession. The Russians were resented for having neither shown respect for Iranian sovereignty in the occupied zones, nor any appreciation of the vital role of Iran as the Allied supply route to Russia.[7] In the view of the Iranian Government much of the Russian-inspired propaganda about the oppressive measures of Iranian officials in Azarbaijan or Kurdistan was unfounded because the Russian occupation had virtually put an end to central government authority in these areas.

Yet, endowed with a mesmerizing ideological system, the Russians could induce even some moderately left-wing intellectuals to believe that the Soviet presence and behaviour in Iran was ultimately in the national interest, and brand those who doubted this as allies of Sayyid Zia, or reactionary advocates of imperialism. The vocabulary of radical political discourse, and thus an entire system of thinking and mode of argumentation, originated from Russia, mainly through the medium of the Tudeh Party, and was enthusiastically adopted in the vacuous and receptive intellectual milieu of post-Reza Shah Iran. This dominant vocabulary impeded the formulation of intellectually appealing objections to Russian actions or demands, and even hindered the perception of ulterior, non-humanitarian motives on their part. This mode of discourse persuasively explained and provided a ready remedy for the inbuilt incompetence of the Iranian governmental structure, but prevented the formulation of 'progressive' arguments in favour of patriotism (other than Russian patriotism), and in defence of Iranian sovereignty. The ruling elite's public position vis-à-vis the Soviet demands and refusal to evacuate Iran was essentially indolent primarily because of traditional fears of Russian aggression. Moreover, the advocates of Iranian independence, not to mention the 'reactionary forces' in the country, had extreme difficulty in producing intellectually persuasive counter-arguments to stop or resist the 'march of progress'.

On 12 December 1945 the National Government of Azarbaijan was formally established in Tabriz and, in the presence of the Russian Consul-General, a National Assembly was convened, to which Premier Pishihvari introduced his Cabinet, composed of ten ministers.[8] The programme of the National Government of Azarbaijan, approved by the National Assembly on the same day, included nineteen moderate, reformist articles. Not only was the elimination of conflict between peasants and landowners advocated, but private property in all spheres of life was recognized and respect for freedom of belief of all citizens emphasized.[9] The following day Bayat, the ex-Prime Minister who had arrived in Tabriz as Governor-General of Azarbaijan only sixteen days earlier with the hope of preventing 'such a development',[10] returned to Tehran; this marked the end of central government authority in Azarbaijan for the time being.[11]

The process was completed by the signing of a protocol between Pishihvari and General Darakhshani, the General Officer Commanding the Tabriz garrison, concerning the submission of his soldiers to the autonomous government of Azarbaijan.[12] The Democrats also impounded the central government's holding at the National Bank. They did not hide their intention of organizing a strong regular army,[13] and threatened that unless the central government provided them with funds to pay government employees, they would withhold taxes, and might even be forced to set up an entirely independent government.[14]

All these developments took place against a background of helplessness and frustration on the part of the central government, since troops and gendarmes dispatched from Tehran to Azarbaijan had been halted even before reaching Qazvin, less than 100 miles north-west of Tehran; and in response to an objection by the Iranian Government the Russians formally expressed their refusal to allow the arrival of central government forces in Azarbaijan.[15] The local tribes such as the Afsharis, Zulfaqaris and the Shahsavans, who regarded the Shah as their patron, had, like tribes throughout the country, benefited from a general amnesty which gave them the right to carry arms without a licence.[16] They had been prepared and were soon to be mobilized to counter the Democrats; yet the central government could effectively do little but seek a negotiated settlement through political and diplomatic channels.

Aiming to share his responsibility with the deputies and to involve them directly in the Government's policy towards Azarbaijan, Hakimi invited the Majlis to appoint sixteen deputies from all existing factions to form a committee to study the issues involved and to provide the Government with guidelines for action.[17]

Similarly, he had set up a 'National High Council' of which he himself, Qavam, Sadiq, Ali Reza Qaraguzlu and Ali Mansur were members.[18] These men were not reputed to harbour pro-British tendencies and were mostly looked upon with confidence by the Russians.

The composition of this Council was consistent with Hakimi's attempted policy of qualified appeasement towards the Tudeh Party and the Soviet Union. As further gestures in this direction he dismissed Ghulam Husain Ibtihaj, the mayor of Tehran who was disliked by the leftists and reputed to be pro-British,[19] and appointed Bayat, who as Governor-General of Azarbaijan had proved impartial or even favourably disposed towards the Soviet Union. Moreover, he eventually conceded the removal of Khalil Fahimi, the Minister of the Interior, whose appointment had disconcerted a number of deputies and whose suspected association with Sayyid Zia had provoked repeated criticisms from Musaddiq.[20] Fahimi was replaced by Allahyar Salih, the Minister without Portfolio who, along with Mahmud Nariman, the Minister of Post, Telegraph and Telephone was favoured by Musaddiq and his followers. Moreover, Salih, Nariman and Muhammad Husain Firuz, the Minister of Roads and Communications, were reputed to be in favour of a policy of appeasement towards the Soviet Union.[21]

Such moves were not sufficient to impress the Russians, nor did they please the British who were opposed to any direct Iran–Soviet negotiations from which they were to be excluded. Although he had on various occasions been described by Bullard as 'deaf and quite useless', 'futile and incapable of positive action',[22] and as 'old, tired and without ideas',[23] Hakimi did have British support since he was unmistakably oriented towards the West. His policy of appeasement towards the Russians was at best half-hearted, and was a response, as the British recognized, to a growing nervousness on the part of the Iranian ruling elite and disappointment with Western support. Since Hakimi had no chance of reaching a settlement with the Russians his main rival, Qavam, began to work towards resuming the premiership. In fact the spectre of Qavam was already haunting the Shah, who often spoke to Bullard of his 'deep suspicion' of Qavam, and of his efforts to support Hakimi.[24] Since the Russians would only negotiate with Qavam, who had already gained the support of many deputies, neither the Shah nor the British were in a position to prevent or even delay his return to office.

Concerned that the autonomy movements in the north-west of

Iran might spread southwards, Bullard had suggested to the Foreign
Office that they should attempt to persuade the Iranian Government
that a 'negative attitude to Azarbaijan is useless', and that instead
they should adopt positive measures to improve and implement the
law of provincial councils, following the evacuation of foreign troops
from Iran, and that reasonable appeasement of the minorities could
be achieved by allowing them to teach their own languages in
schools, while keeping Persian as the official language.[25] Initially the
Foreign Office did not receive this suggestion favourably,[26] but
Bullard warned that 'Persia is disintegrating because of over-
centralization', advocated 'local government' in all provinces as
opposed to autonomy, and asserted that any suggestion of the
uniqueness of Azarbaijan would constitute a step towards its
annexation by the Soviet Union.[27] The Foreign Office eventually
allowed Bullard to discuss privately with the Iranian authorities such
issues as the provincial councils.

Bullard's views seemed acceptable in principle to Hakimi, who
ordered the provincial governors to prepare for local elections; and
other Iranian officials (notably Salih, the Interior Minister) had
adopted the same views as Bullard and for the same reasons.[28] In
fact, according to Musaddiq, even the sixteen-man committee of
deputies recommended the establishment of such councils, but for
this very reason was suspended.[29] Opponents of the provincial and
district councils argued that, having postponed the Majlis elections
because of the presence of foreign troops, the Government could
hardly justify holding provincial elections. Hakimi was therefore
eventually obliged to announce that such elections should also be
postponed until the evacuation of the country. The future of the law
of provincial councils, as well as the survival of Hakimi's Cabinet,
began to look bleak after the events of early January 1946. The
Moscow Conference of late December 1945 had produced no
positive gestures concerning the problems of Iran; in fact it had not
even mentioned the country by name, which according to the British
military attaché drove the Iranians to 'despair, bordering on panic'.[30]
In early January 1946 the outline of an Anglo-American scheme for a
tripartite commission to 'advise' on the election of provincial
councils was submitted to the Hakimi Government which did not
reject the proposal, but demanded the inclusion of two Iranian
representatives, and the omission of references to minority languages.[31]
Neither was accepted by the sponsors of the scheme however, and
the Cabinet resolved to reconsider its position.

In the meantime the issue had come to public notice through a BBC announcement on 5 January 1946 that Britain, the United States and the Soviet Union would set up a tripartite commission to investigate the internal problems of Iran in general, and the situation in Azarbaijan in particular.[32] This revived the spectre of the 1907 *entente* and provoked such fear and hostility among Iranian politicians and journalists of all shades of opinion[33] that the Government was left with no alternative but formally to reject the scheme. Musaddiq and others described the scheme as far worse than the 1919 Agreement[34] signed by Hasan Vusuq (Vusuq ud-Daulih), Qavam's brother, which had offered the British very extensive concessions in Iran. Hakimi was severely criticized for having even considered it and, despite his insistence that the proposal had been promptly rejected,[35] was threatened with motions of interpellation. One such motion was tabled against him by Muhammad Reza Tehranchi, a deputy for Tehran, but withdrawn on Hakimi's promise to resign in due course.[36]

Although the substance of the Anglo-American scheme was not entirely disagreeable to many Iranians, as Bullard himself noted,[37] the proposal to form a tripartite commission was both insensitive and showed little understanding of the highly charged political milieu, the psychology of the politically literate Iranians, and the strength of nationalist sentiments. In its support for decentralization the proposal was widely and justifiably suspected in Iran of being a variation on the old theme of spheres of influence, which would benefit the Russians and the British in the north and the south of the country, respectively. It ran counter to the hopes and beliefs of those Iranians who perceived the independence of their country as emanating mainly from the discreet exploitation of the rivalries of the great powers, and as an outcome of a delicate balance between their competing influences. It was, moreover, regarded not only as an unjust and discourteous reward for Iran's contribution to the Allied victory, but also as a concerted move designed ultimately to undermine Iranian sovereignty.

The draft of the proposed scheme for the tripartite commission had been prepared by the British Foreign Secretary, Ernest Bevin, who also submitted it on 24 December 1945 to the Moscow Conference in the form of an urgent memorandum. Strongly in favour of an inter-Allied approach to problems in Iran, Bevin was not only opposed to direct Iran–Soviet negotiations, but also tried to prevent or postpone the Iranian appeal to the United Nations. Such an appeal, the Foreign Office believed, was 'likely to kill the Moscow proposal for the appointment of a tripartite commission',[38] and eliminate all chances of its acceptance by the Russians.[39] Bevin later tried in the House of Commons to justify his advocacy of the scheme for a tripartite commission as follows:

> While we accept Persian as a national language, the minority languages are very important from the point of view of unrest in these countries. . . . In addition, it is no use disguising the fact that amidst all these troubles, there were the very vital interests of the United States, ourselves and the Soviet Russia in regard to oil, with which so much of our defence was concerned.
>
> . . . One thing that must be done when a small country happens to possess a vital raw material is for allies to arrange their business so as not to make the small country the victim of controversy between the big Allies. I think that this is a sound policy; I tried to do it and failed.[40]

The Foreign Office also tried to encourage James Byrnes, the American Secretary of State, to dissuade the Iranians from taking their case to the UN,[41] but he did not react favourably[42] and the Iranians proceeded with the appeal.

Despite Stalin's initial inclination to accept it, the Russians eventually rejected the scheme.[43] Along with the leftist newspapers in Iran, they regarded Iran–Soviet disputes as a domestic issue calling for direct negotiations with a favourable Iranian government, and there were indications that these might be forthcoming. The Russian rejection of the scheme relieved many Iranians: Musaddiq thanked them for rejecting the proposal and contended that 'the day the three powers ally with each other, there would be no hope for us'.[44] The whole episode, however, adversely affected the British image and the credibility of their claims to respect and advocate the independence of Iran. It also persuaded many Iranians to regard decentralization with deep suspicion,[45] and marked the end of the Government of Hakimi and the policy of procrastination in the face of Russian demands.

Hakimi's position had also been undermined by other issues. He had not yet abandoned his policy of lenience towards the left and was even showing an interest in direct negotiations with the Russians, first offering to send his Foreign Minister and then volunteering to go to Moscow himself.[46] Such gestures did not appeal to pro-Russian Iranians or to the Russians themselves, but dismayed many of Hakimi's supporters. While publicly accusing the Russians of interference in Iran's internal affairs, he refused to yield to leftist pressure for the removal of the Chief of Staff, General Arfa, and proceeded to appeal to the UN.[47] Many of his supporters in the Majlis, however, believed that the problem of the autonomy movements and the evacuation of Russian forces would be resolved by a more active policy of seeking Western support.

As a concession to Musaddiq and his like-minded colleagues, Hakimi, as mentioned earlier, had appointed Salih as Interior Minister. But the retention of Hazhir as Finance Minister, as well as the Cabinet decrees abolishing sugar rationing and the monopoly of cotton cloth, became the subject of incessant criticism by Musaddiq.[48] Musaddiq strongly objected to the composition of the Cabinet,[49] while the efforts of Salih and Nariman to make the Cabinet more neutral or to conciliate the leftists served only to disaffect further Hakimi's original supporters.[50]

Although his failures were conspicuous, Hakimi did succeed in tackling two issues which Sadr had been unable to deal with. He passed through the Majlis a bill for the considerable expansion of the army and the increase of its budget,[51] and succeeded in modifying Millspaugh's income tax law.[52] Hakimi recognized the need to consult the deputies and seek the advice of senior politicians, but other factors led him, as the British military attaché put it, not to take the deputies 'sufficiently into his confidence';[53] factors such as the need for confidentiality in regard to the sensitive problems facing him, and the lack of trust and reliability which accounted for the near-solitary behaviour of most prime ministers. Hakimi was not noted for Cabinet consultation, but this was not unusual since Cabinet colleagues were always chosen in order to satisfy various and often contradictory interests. Yet, even had he been able to rely on a cohesive, collectively co-operative Cabinet and a supportive Majlis, Hakimi had no choice but to resign, in view of his unacceptability to the Russians as a negotiating partner.

On the eve of his resignation the Democrats were in control of Azarbaijan and Kurdistan. The Tudeh, the re-emerged Jangal Party and the Democrat sympathizers were believed to have joined in alliance in Mazandaran and Gilan, and there were rumours of an imminent uprising in these provinces. In addition the Tudeh Party was reported to be preparing a proclamation for an 'independent Tabaristan'.[54] The Iranian ruling elite was demoralized and this was further aggravated by frequent newspaper articles about the possibility of a military coup in the country. Any show of firmness on the part of the Government was portrayed by some newspapers as a first step towards the predicted coup, which invariably rendered it counterproductive. Overwhelmed by numerous difficulties and embattled by orchestrated ideological and psychological campaigns, the Government tendered its resignation to the Majlis on 21 January 1946 after a period of seventy-six days in office.

Hakimi's premiership in this period had been the result of an inevitable and uneasy compromise; yet, in defiance of the preferences of the bulk of the Iranian ruling elite and the exigencies of clan politics, the situation demanded a premier who would not only challenge the prevailing pattern of power distribution, but would also attempt to change or modify the aims and directions of government policies. Only such a prime minister – who was to be found in Ahmad Qavam – could hope to tackle successfully the prevailing crisis, primarily because he enjoyed the confidence of the Russians.

PART III

The Challenge of Qavam

10

The First Period:
JANUARY–DECEMBER 1946

From the time of his resignation in February 1943 Qavam lived in retirement but never relaxed his efforts to return to power. Without alienating his American supporters he had succeeded in enlisting the increasing favour and support of the Russians and, therefore, the backing of the Tudeh Party.[1] He had gradually acquired considerable support in the Majlis, and the new Islah (Reform) faction had been formed as the nucleus of a majority which was to bring about his second premiership in the post-1941 era.[2] As Qavam's return to power began to appear possible his clientele grew, and this in turn played a significant part in his return to office.

With all approaches to the Russians exhausted, Qavam was the only viable candidate for the premiership and his enemies were no longer in a position to block or even delay his return to office. Headed by Hadi Tahiri, an influential *mutavalli*, they resorted to a tactic which had been deployed during Qavam's previous term of office: while 53 deputies voted for Qavam, 51 cast their votes for Husain Pirnia,[3] who was, in view of his advanced years, neither capable of nor willing to assume office. While this did not please Qavam, he nevertheless had little to worry about. Although Tahiri furtively continued his activities against Qavam by trying to convince British officials that a Russian take-over of Iran was likely and that they must resort to counter-measures, the life of the 14th Majlis was nearing its end and Qavam's success seemed certain. His second term of office in the post-1941 period lasted over twenty-two months, which can be divided into two parts for the purpose of analysis: the first period, from late January until mid-December 1946 (the fall of the Democrats' regime in Tabriz) and the second from then until December 1947 (the fall of Qavam's Cabinet).

Qavam's major task in the first period was to tackle the crisis caused by the Russian refusal to evacuate northern Iran, and the establishment of the Russian-supported regimes in Azarbaijan and

Kurdistan. After forming his Cabinet, Qavam headed a delegation to Moscow to negotiate with the Russians but returned to Tehran on 10 March 1946 having failed to reach a settlement.[4] The Russians were faced with strong American pressure[5] and concerted efforts by the British to encourage the active involvement of the UN.[6] However, they preferred to negotiate a settlement with Qavam rather than any other Iranian politician and, therefore, soon after Qavam's return to Tehran, Sadchikov, the newly appointed Soviet Ambassador in Tehran, was ordered to renew negotiations. Eventually an agreement was concluded on 4 April which arranged for the Russian evacuation of Iran by mid-May and the formation of a joint Irano-Soviet oil company with an extendable fifty-year lease. The question of Azarbaijan was described as an internal Iranian matter, to be dealt with peacefully and in a spirit of goodwill towards the population of the province.[7]

Qavam was fully aware of his responsibilities and the implications of concluding this agreement. The most sensitive aspect was the proposed Irano-Soviet oil company, and Qavam left the ultimate decision to the discretion of the Majlis, specifying that any arrangement agreed to should be within the framework of the existing Iranian legal system. Although the full consequences and implications of the agreement were not clear at the time, it was generally welcomed by the left but considered by pro-Western politicians to be too high a price to pay. By reaching an agreement with the Russians independently, Qavam had increased his prestige with them and strengthened his ties with the Tudeh Party, but he had dismayed and provoked the British. In fact, from the beginning of his premiership he had been viewed with suspicion and disapproval by British officials in Tehran. The bulk of Qavam's ministers were at least as well qualified as their predecessors, and the number of pro-British, royalist and neutral ministers far exceeded those who were pro-Russian or advocated a policy of appeasement towards the Russians; yet Bullard went so far as to report that Qavam's Cabinet 'is the worst for ability and honesty that I have seen since the abdication of Reza Shah, and his chief henchmen are filling the key posts with Tudeh nominees, while Tudeh papers cover His Majesty's Government with abuse'.[8]

The first of the 'chief henchmen' referred to was Muzaffar Firuz, the Prime Minister's Political Under-Secretary and the Government's Director of Propaganda, and a driving force in the Cabinet. The other was Ahmad Ali Sipihr (Muvarrikh ud-Daulih), the Minister of

Commerce. Firuz and Sipihr were not reputed for trustworthiness or loyalty but their skill and dynamism had been crucial in mobilizing support for Qavam. However, in July 1946 Sipihr was exiled to Kashan for intriguing with the Court against the Prime Minister, and he admitted that his dealings with the Court had resulted in his exile. In addition he was unfavourable to the planned formation of Qavam's Democratic Party of Iran. Firuz, on the other hand, was adamant in his dislike of the Pahlavi dynasty and continued to support Qavam until his removal from office was forced on Qavam by the Shah.

In the early stages of Qavam's premiership, when Sipihr appeared to be as firmly behind Qavam as was Firuz, Bullard considered that they were both inclined to prevent co-operation between Qavam and the British Embassy.[9] The British were also alarmed by the removal of pro-British elements from the administration and by Qavam's detention of Sayyid Zia and other prominent opponents of the left, such as Ali Dashti, Tahiri, Jamal Imami and Sanandaji, as well as General Arfa, who was believed to have helped the armed campaigns of the Zulfaqari and Afshari tribes against the Democrats of Azarbaijan. These detentions disheartened the anti-Russian elements as much as they appealed to the leftists and the Russians. Some Foreign Office officials began to consider contingency plans, for example organizing an 'anti-Tudeh' party on a national scale, orchestrating an autonomy movement in the south-west of Iran or even occupying the area.[10] However, such measures were considered to be too dangerous, the Americans were not in favour of taking any action and the situation was not yet hopeless enough to warrant them.

A further factor which helped to restrain the British was the uneasy course of the negotiations between the central government and the Azarbaijani delegation, headed by Pishihvari, which had arrived in Tehran on 28 April 1946. Six days earlier the Cabinet had announced its decision to concede to the Azarbaijanis the establishment of a provincial council with extensive authority to appoint heads of local government departments, the recognition of the official use of the Azari language in addition to Persian, elementary education up to the fifth year in Azari, an increase in the representation for Azarbaijan in the Majlis, and the allocation of adequate funds for reform in the province. The Cabinet reserved the right to appoint the commanders of the provincial military forces and the gendarmerie, as well as the governor-general of the province, although it had conceded that it would take into account the views of the provincial council.[11]

The Azarbaijani delegation had arrived in Tehran to negotiate further concessions. It was accepted that the Majlis of Azarbaijan would become the provincial council and that the ministers would become the heads of local government departments; the issue of language was also agreed upon. The proposed method for the appointment of the governor-general and the heads of the military and the security forces was, however, contested, and the central government's demands for the evacuation of the Zanjan (Khamsih) area were ignored, while it was demanded that the central government endorse the redistribution of Crown and other confiscated land.[12] Despite the mediation of Sadchikov no more concessions were made and the fifteen days of negotiations proved inconclusive. Qavam had told the Russian Ambassador that he would have to resign if the negotiations failed, but he was urged not to. When the Azarbaijani delegation returned to Tabriz Pishihvari expressed his optimism, particularly regarding the Prime Minister.[13]

The gap between the two parties was wider than appeared and their opportunity to manoeuvre was restricted – in the case of Qavam by pressure from, as well as the actual or perceived reactions of, anti-leftist forces and their foreign supporters, and in the case of Pishihvari by revolutionary rhetoric, claims and promises. Moreover it was not always easy to understand Qavam's real objectives or to predict his future moves. A few days after the conclusion of the Qavam–Sadchikov agreement, Fazlullah Nabil, a senior official in the Ministry of Foreign Affairs, had told a British diplomat that the Government really intended to reoccupy Zanjan and encircle and undermine the Democratic regime in Azarbaijan. He believed that in order to secure a speedy evacuation of Iran it was necessary for the Government to give the impression of supporting autonomy and reform, and to bribe the Russians by detaining their known opponents in the country.[14]

Nabil's comments were undoubtedly intended to please the British, and as Qavam was in charge of the Foreign Ministry himself, it is probable that Nabil acted on his instructions. Similarly, Qavam had secretly expressed his support for Zulfaqari operations against the Democrats.[15] Through various emissaries he had also assured the British Embassy that his Government would not embark on any course of action detrimental to British interests.[16] On the other hand, however, he had not only assured the Russians of his goodwill but for a period seemed to be genuinely in favour or convinced of the inevitability of meeting Russian demands. Like other advocates of a policy of positive equilibrium, he regarded the Russians as at a disadvantage compared with the British who enjoyed an oil concession in the country, and the Americans who had a privileged position through various missions working with the Iranian Government. Firuz was also a firm believer in such a policy and did not doubt Qavam's willingness to allow the Russians access to oil in the north, with Iran an equal partner in the proposed company.[17] Following a conversation with Qavam in March 1946, Wallace Murray, the US Ambassador in Tehran, reported as follows:

> He considers that from the viewpoint of practical politics an understanding with USSR on northern Iranian oil is long overdue. He asserted that Soviet complaints that Iran had discriminated in favour of Britain by granting [the] AIOC concession were hard to meet in light of [the] fact [that] controlling interest in AIOC is held by [the] British Government. He believes that any future Majlis will approve concession to Soviets and that such concession is inevitable.[18]

Yet Qavam was skilful in the art of convincing people of his sincerity and disguising his real preferences and aims, which made it easier for him to change them as circumstances dictated. Having the expressed confidence of the Russians, he was apparently able to obtain the genuine co-operation of the leftists. On some occasions however, for example when the Azarbaijani delegation returned to Tabriz, he carried this role so far that British officials and Iranian politicians were equally in the dark about his future course of action. Nor was the Shah informed, according to Aramish, a member of Qavam's Cabinet, who was told by Qavam that he never informed the Shah of the secret aspects of his Azarbaijan policy, since he regarded the Shah as indiscreet and untrustworthy given his firm commitment to the British.[19]

The failure of the negotiations of course pleased the British, since it increased the likelihood of the active involvement of the UN. Although the Russian troops had been evacuated, Husain Ala, the Iranian Ambassador in Washington, persisted in his complaints to the Security Council that Russian intervention continued to prevent Iran from extending its authority over Azarbaijan.[20] Qavam felt obliged to confirm the evacuation of Iran but he did not restrain Ala, and nor did he demand the removal of Iran's complaint from the

Security Council's agenda.[21] At the same time he continued his policy of patient negotiations with the Azarbaijan regime.

On 11 June 1946 a government delegation headed by Firuz left for Tabriz, and two days later an agreement was signed which was an improved version of the Cabinet's decision of 22 April. The new agreement resolved most issues, including the appointment of the governor-general, who was to be chosen by the central government from a list provided by the provincial council; 75 per cent of the revenues collected in Azarbaijan were to be spent locally; the extension and improvement of roads and railways were promised; and it was agreed that an improved electoral bill, which would also provide for the extension of the franchise to women, would be submitted to the next Majlis. The distribution of Crown lands by the Democratic regime was endorsed on an *ad hoc* basis but the final decision was left to the Majlis. The command structure and fate of the Azarbaijan armed forces and the issue of confiscated lands remained to be studied by the representatives of the central government and the Azarbaijan provincial council.[22]

Both sides considered this to be a political success and the agreement was praised by the leftist and radical intelligentsia in Iran, although the outstanding issues gave Qavam an excuse for further negotiations and manoeuvres. His gradualist policy and 'wait and see' approach enabled him to observe developments and reactions over the entire political spectrum, and to change course accordingly. However, he continued with his calculated policy of appeasing the Russians and the leftists, lifting restrictions on leftist activities and reducing the number of rightist and moderate newspapers.

Determined to show his commitment to real reform, Qavam managed to ratify a comprehensive labour law[23] and other measures, such as a plan for the redistribution of Crown lands among the cultivators. In a public proclamation he also elaborated his land policy; this fell short of a real land reform but was significant at the time. He emphasized that he had no intention of undermining property rights, but desired to secure 'a correct and solid foundation' for the principles of land ownership in Iran, which would give rights only to those landowners who cultivated their land and thereby contributed to the improvement of the country.[24] These actions assisted Qavam's progressive image and he was personally given the credit for such reformist gestures. Firuz announced that such reforms should not be attributed to any party or minister but solely to the Prime Minister whose 'energy and perseverance' accounted for the 'reformist zeal' of the Cabinet.[25] This was repeated by Shams ud-Din Amir-Ala'i, Qavam's Minister of Agriculture.[26] It is probable that Qavam genuinely favoured a degree of social reform not only in order to improve his image with the leftists and deflate radical propaganda, but also to alleviate those social strains which adversely affected the task of government. This was the case with his labour law, whereas the reform of the principles of land ownership was in all probability 'window dressing designed to strengthen the Government against the attacks of Pishihvari and his supporters in Tabriz and Tehran', as Dr. Manuchihr Iqbal, Qavam's royalist Minister of Health, told the British Ambassador.[27]

In early June 1946 in a conversation with Le Rougetel (the new British Ambassador who had replaced Bullard in April that year), Qavam listened to the Ambassador's usual complaints about the Tudeh Party's activities against British interests in Iran, and revealed with a 'sly smile' that he intended to take 'one or two of them into the Government ... in the hope of sobering them with responsibility'.[28] The policy of co-opting elements from the Tudeh into the Cabinet, which materialized two months later, was intended to involve the Party actively in the difficulties which the Government faced, to help Qavam in his dealings with the Russians and the Democrats of Azarbaijan, to increase the Party's interest in the preservation of law and order, and to assist the Government in dealing with the frequent labour unrest in the south and in Isfahan. By implication it was also intended to vindicate the 'truly national and democratic' character of Qavam's Government, since it was only in such a government that the Tudeh had pledged to take part.[29] This latter point was bound to increase tensions within the Tudeh Party and, indeed, as one of Qavam's assistants later informed Le Rougetel, it had provoked 'marked dissension among the leaders of the party'.[30]

While this manoeuvre initially increased the importance and role of the Tudeh Party, it later weakened it, which was probably what Qavam had intended. The co-optation of Tudeh leaders into the Cabinet was undoubtedly beneficial to Qavam's mode of political activity, as well as to his short- and long-term objectives. The Tudeh Party had played a significant part in bringing him to office and saving him from the challenge posed by the 14th Majlis, in order, the party organ claimed, to save Iran 'from the danger of disintegration and civil war'.[31] While he was in Moscow his opponents among the deputies had engaged in manoeuvres to oust him,[32] but demonstrations and disruption by the Tudeh Party prevented the last few sessions of the Majlis from taking place,[33] and thus Qavam was saved from the constraint of any legislation covering the period of recess between the end of the 14th Majlis and the opening of the 15th. All this seemed to indicate that the increased co-operation of the Tudeh Party would give Qavam more scope to cope with the problems he encountered, including the growing power and influence of the Party itself.

The wisdom of the move was, however, rejected by the British and American Ambassadors, who saw it as further evidence of Qavam's increased leaning towards the Soviet Union and reliance on the leftists. He was saved from undue pressure since the British and American representatives in Tehran were unable to co-ordinate their policies or tactics. The American Ambassador considered that a 'joint US–UK approach to Qavam' was 'inadvisable', and 'United States action would lose its effectiveness if joined with British representations'.[34] Moreover, by promising to offer an oil concession in Baluchistan to the Americans,[35] and other friendly consultations and contacts, Qavam had hoped to prevent such joint action. In late June 1946, however, the State Department advised the US Ambassador in Tehran to co-operate with his British counterpart and to encourage Qavam to turn to countries other than the Soviet Union and to concentrate on reform. Qavam was also told that he 'would do well to support [the] formation of independent parties in Persia as alternative[s] to Tudeh. Such action could be a step in the direction of [a] democratic political system.'[36] This certainly encouraged Qavam in his long-cherished desire to create a political party, the formation of which was announced soon after, on 28 June 1946.[37] Although this was incongruent with Qavam's intention of co-opting Tudeh members, such a policy had not then materialized and the Americans therefore remained well-disposed.

In the formation of his party – ironically called the Democratic Party of Iran (Hizb-i Dimukrat-i Iran), in contrast to the Democratic Party of Azarbaijan – Qavam hoped to undermine the Tudeh Party's claim to be the sole champion and representative of the interests of the lower classes and the only party putting forward progressive ideas. The programme of his party was no less radical than that of the Tudeh Party,[38] and by advocating on a national scale what the Democrats of Azarbaijan advocated only for Azarbaijan it could claim to make the latter obsolete. The formation of the Democratic Party of Iran was also an attempt by Qavam, through the use of his position as Prime Minister, to organize his clientele and to ensure the presence, in the next Majlis, of a large and cohesive body of deputies who would adhere to the new Party and enable Qavam to retain his position. It can thus be seen as an attempt to institutionalize or maintain the ascendancy of Qavam's political clan to the detriment of other clans. The formation of the Democratic Party of Iran was, moreover, a pre-emptive move calculated to coincide with the formation of a coalition between the Tudeh and Iran Parties. This development resulted in the reserved criticism of the leftists,[39] and it was not welcomed by the Russians, although the Tudeh Party complied with Qavam's invitation to join the Government. The British did not try to conceal their pleasure and, according to Le Rougetel, Qavam became somewhat perturbed by the BBC publicity for his party.[40]

On 1 August 1946 a new Cabinet was formed which included four ministers belonging to the coalition of the Tudeh and Iran Parties; Iraj Iskandari, Murtiza Yazdi and Firaydun Kishavarz, three leaders of the Tudeh Party, held the portfolios of Commerce, Health and Education, respectively; while Allahyar Salih, the leader of the Iran Party, assumed the portfolio of Justice. The formation of this Cabinet was seen by the leftist and reformist groups as reconfirming Qavam's 'goodwill'.[41] In deference to the wishes of the Shah, the British and the Americans, three prominent royalist and pro-Western ministers were retained in the reshuffled Cabinet, despite their previous reluctance to co-operate fully with Qavam.[42] The Shah's dismay increased, however, since he had not been consulted and Firuz, his sworn enemy, had been promoted to a ministerial post. The American officials were told by Qavam that he intended to make 'one last attempt to conciliate the Russians', while Le Rougetel remained 'more than sceptical' about Qavam's belief that he '[could] "assimilate" the Tudeh'.[43]

Despite co-operation at a ministerial level, relations between Qavam's party and the Tudeh Party were contentious. Only a few days after the formation of the 'coalition Cabinet', a meeting of some 8000 adherents of the Democratic Party of Iran was addressed by Firuz, who maintained that the Party was the largest not only in the country but in the whole of Asia. When the meeting ended, according to Le Rougetel, members and followers of the Tudeh Party attacked the Democrats with 'knives and sticks'; the clash left six dead and many injured.[44] Such events and the mutual harassment of members of the Democratic and Tudeh Parties did not appear to weaken the coalition Cabinet. The Tudeh ministers had wasted no time in initiating considerable changes in the key positions of their ministries in the interest of their party.[45] In fact the Tudeh Party had annoyed Qavam by proclaiming that its reason for participating in the Cabinet was to bring about the 'true purging of the ruling apparatus' and bring it closer to the people.[46] On the one hand Qavam had succeeded, with the help of the Tudeh, in putting an end to the general strike of the workers in the AIOC in mid-July 1946,[47] but on the other the formation of the coalition Cabinet had dismayed both the British and the Americans. Indeed the American Ambassador was now prepared to side with the Shah to oust Qavam.[48] It had also provoked the southern tribes and raised their hopes of gaining British support.

Tribal activities against the Tudeh Party began soon after Qavam's return to power when Abbas Qubadian, the chief of the Kalhur tribe of Kirmanshah, had formed the 'tribal union of the west' to contain the influence of the Tudeh Party.[49] After the formation of the coalition Cabinet, however, tribal activities had been intensified and in late August 1946 the British Consul in Isfahan was informed of the formation of a 'defence pact' between the Qashqa'i and Bakhtiari tribal chiefs against the Tudeh Party with the intention of capturing Isfahan and Shiraz. The tribal leaders had asked the Consul whether they would be provided with arms.[50] The Government was aware of such developments and martial law was declared in Shiraz; upon his arrival in Isfahan in early September, Firuz arrested the Bakhtiari leaders involved. On the basis of confessions made and other evidence, Firuz declared that A. C. Trott, the British Consul in Ahvaz, had been involved in the affair.

Naturally the Foreign Office had considered exploiting tribal discontent and the threat of rebellion, in order to exert pressure on the Iranian Government to refrain from a pro-Soviet policy and to restrict Tudeh activities.[51] On the whole, however, the Foreign Office recommended a cautious policy which would neither alienate the discontented tribal leaders nor give the impression that the British Embassy was ready to encourage tribal rebellion. Should the Iranian Government act to their 'disfavour' in the future, the British would of course make the necessary 'arrangements' to protect their interests. In any case the Foreign Office argued that a tribal revolt at the time would not be in the best interests of the British, which would be better served by supporting the Iranian Prime Minister in the 'hope of securing political stability in Persia and a satisfactory attitude on the part of the Persian authorities in Khuzistan'.[52]

The Government persisted in its demand for Trott to be recalled, while the British Embassy insisted on his innocence.[53] Eventually the Iranians gave up the demand and the British made a statement confirming their non-involvement in the plot.[54] Meanwhile this dispute had been overshadowed by the continuation of disorder and agitation by the southern tribes, which the Iranian authorities, particularly the military, had been unwilling to curb. The British Consul in Shiraz observed that the 'movement' for autonomy in Fars, which was organized and led by the Qashqa'is, embraced 'all the tribal elements in Fars', including the Mamasanis, Dushmanziaris and Khamsih'is. In addition he reported that it had the support of the revived conservative, pro-German Democratic Party of Fars (formed during the First World War at the instigation of the German agent Wassmuss) and enjoyed the backing of the 'people of the province',[55] including the prominent provincial *ulama*.[56] The tribesmen demanded reforms along the lines promised to the Democrats of Azarbaijan, plus the dismissal of the Tudeh ministers and 'incompetent' army officers, and threatened to take action if their demands were not met.[57]

This tribal rebellion gave the Shah and the army the best possible lever against the Tudeh Party. And it provided them with a way to constrain Qavam's freedom of action and undermine his policy of conciliation towards the Democrats in Tabriz. The War Minister told the British military attaché that the help of the Qashqa'is was necessary to resist the Tudeh and added that Iran's 'only hope of salvation lay with the British'.[58] He stressed that he would even 'resort to direct action against the Prime Minister' in order to prevent the establishment of a communist-controlled government in Tehran.[59] General Zahidi, who had co-operated with the Qashqa'i chiefs in a pro-German organization during the war, was sent to Shiraz with a force of 2000 to restore order. But the army deliberately restrained from taking effective action. This demonstrated that the army had remained the exclusive patrimony of the Shah and outside Qavam's range of authority. Perhaps many leftists would have liked Qavam to use the Azarbaijan 'People's Army' against the tribes or to form a force of 'national guerrillas', but such measures would neither have appealed to him nor would they have been practical.

The reported dispatch of British warships to the Persian Gulf[60] and British soldiers to Basra,[61] the continued activities of Qubadian in Kirmanshah,[62] the news of the growth of an incipient autonomy 'movement' in Khuzistan and, in particular, the events in the south were all considered by Qavam to be reactions to his policies of appeasement towards the Tudeh Party, the Democrats of Azarbaijan and the Russians. Having no doubt that the British were involved in Fars he threatened to appeal against them to the Security Council,[63] but was discouraged by the US Ambassador. If the attempt to tackle one demand for autonomy was merely provoking similar demands in other areas, Qavam clearly had to question the success of his tactic. In early October he met the American Ambassador and indicated that he was considering a change of policy which would be to the detriment of the left, adding that he could do so if he had the financial and economic support of the United States.[64]

Although Qavam appeared to be shocked and dismayed by the growth of the 'national movement of Fars' and the capture of the southern towns of Bushihr and Kazirun by the rebels,[65] he took advantage of such events to justify his change of tactics and policies. One politician who was closely involved in the politics of the period goes so far as to assert that the Qashqa'is had acted with Qavam's tacit approval.[66] Qavam claimed to have had little choice but to order Zahidi to negotiate a settlement with the Qashqa'is. This was announced in mid-October and recognized 'the national movement of Fars'; it also promised the establishment of a provincial council, increased representation in the Majlis, the construction of a railway, the improvement and extension of roads in the province, and better educational and health facilities.

This was undoubtedly a major setback for the left and the Tudeh ministers ceased to attend Cabinet sessions from this date. Qavam's Chef de Cabinet, Azizullah Nikpay (I'zaz ud-Daulih) told Le Rougetel, however, that the reason for this was that they did not accept the appointment of new governors for Kirmanshah, Isfahan and particularly Tehran, where the ex-governor, Abbas Iskandari (an uncle of Iraj Iskandari, the Tudeh Minister of Commerce), had previously been a member of the Tudeh Party and was still regarded as a supporter.[67] The change of governors was important in view of the forthcoming Majlis elections and, despite the discouraging developments, the Tudeh still considered it vital to enter into an electoral coalition, or to form a 'common front against reactionary forces' with the Prime Minister's party.[68] Both the Tudeh and the Russians hoped that such a coalition would secure a large number of seats in the next Majlis, enabling the Party to influence the structure and policies of the Government and to push for the approval by the Majlis of the proposed Irano-Soviet oil company. This attempted coalition failed amidst mutual recriminations. The leftists blamed the failure on the 'sedition and ill-will' of some of the Democratic Party members,[69] while Nikpay alleged that the Tudeh Party had refused to allow the Prime Minister a majority greater than 51 per cent, and that Qavam had feared that an electoral coalition with the Tudeh Party would make it totally unmanageable.[70] Qavam was annoyed by mounting criticism from the leftist press of the composition, policies and tactics of his own party, and by the way the Tudeh ministers were promoting the interests of their own party instead of concerning themselves with ministerial responsibility.[71] Their refusal to attend Cabinet sessions provided Qavam with the opportunity to reshuffle his Cabinet and exclude the Tudeh ministers, despite the mediation of Salih, the Minister of Justice.[72]

Of course this new policy pleased the British and the Americans: Le Rougetel was quick to assure Qavam of full British support and described his Cabinet reshuffle as 'a sign that Persian national spirit is very much alive',[73] while the American Ambassador considered it 'a turning point in Iranian history'.[74] At the same time the Shah was delighted that the Tudeh ministers had been replaced and that Firuz had been dispatched to Moscow as Ambassador. However, fearing that Qavam's change of policy would bring him the support of the British and the Americans and that his own role in recent developments would be underrated, the Shah met the American Ambassador and claimed all the credit for the reshuffle. He asserted that 'despite Qavam's piteous warnings' he had 'forced him to reform his Cabinet, sack the Tudeh Ministers, and send abroad or sack Firuz'.[75] The British and Americans were prepared to give credit to both the Shah and Qavam but were also anxious actively to encourage and support Qavam. Fearing renewed royal activities and needing compensation for the diminished backing of the Russians and the left, Qavam increased his efforts to enlist the support and confidence of the British and the Americans. He therefore sought their financial and economic assistance for his reform projects,[76] renewed the contract of American advisers in the Iranian gendarmerie, and released General Arfa and, gradually, other detainees.[77]

The Russian Ambassador reacted angrily to these developments and accused Qavam of colluding with the British.[78] The leftists in general could barely hide their disappointment and discomfiture; the failure of the coalition Cabinet was the failure not only of a simple cost-benefit calculation but also of their theoretical arguments and assessments. By taking part in the Cabinet they had agreed to conform to the rules of clan politics. When the coalition collapsed they simply attributed the blame to 'imperialism' and the 'reactionary forces', and to Qavam for succumbing to them.[79] They expressed their resentment at the fact that their ministers had not been properly consulted by Qavam, and deplored the re-employment of officials whom they had sacked and the suppression of trade union and party activities by a government of which they themselves were members.[80] Since they claimed to have privileged access to the truth it is strange that they could justifiably expect that the situation could have been significantly different. Not surprisingly they claimed that they had been 'deceived' by Qavam into taking part in his Cabinet;[81] in that case it is surprising that they were so keen to enter into an electoral coalition with his party later.

In fact, whatever the Tudeh Party's rationalizations, Qavam invoked the confidence of the leftists and was able to manipulate them primarily because he had the support of the Soviet Union, whose policies the Iranian left apparently regarded as infallible. Even after the collapse of the coalition Cabinet, therefore, criticism of Qavam by the Russians and the Iranian left was muted, in the hope that he would arrange for the 15th Majlis to ratify the proposed Irano-Soviet oil company – which was the most important issue for the Soviets. The Tudeh Party's participation in the Cabinet was not, however, simply a tactical error, but a strategic miscalculation caused primarily by the very structure of the Party's ideological make-up; it became a fiasco which was bound to have an adverse effect on the Party's morale and intellectual orientations.

A more damaging development for the Tudeh Party was the fate of the Democrat's regime in Azarbaijan. The day after Qavam's Cabinet reshuffle the Azarbaijani delegation left for Tabriz after two months in Tehran negotiating with the Government. Qavam had previously told Le Rougetel that Salamullah Javid and Ali Shabistari, the Governor-General and the head of the provincial council of Azarbaijan, respectively, were 'disposed to be co-operative', but that Pishihvari had prevented them from giving any concessions.[82] Even if this were true the rising tide of anti-leftist forces and Qavam's own diminished enthusiasm for conciliation also contributed to the breakdown of negotiations.

One major issue in dispute between the Azarbaijanis and the Government remained that of the evacuation of the Zanjan area, which the Democrats of Azarbaijan had in principle agreed to, but had in practice obstructed. Around mid-November 1946 Qavam went to Gilan ostensibly to rest for a few days; his absence gave rise to various rumours, but his intentions remained unclear. While General Ahmadi seemed 'as much in the dark as anyone' about Qavam's plans, the American Ambassador learned from the Shah that the occupation of Zanjan was imminent.[83] On his return to Tehran Qavam endorsed the occupation after months of opposing it,[84] and on 23 November Zanjan, which had largely been evacuated by the Democrats, was recaptured in the first stage of an operation designed to dislodge the regime in Tabriz.

The few days away from Tehran had evidently helped Qavam to plan the second, or major, stage of the operations against the Democrats of Azarbaijan. In a meeting with Le Rougetel Qavam revealed his plan to announce his Government's desire to ensure the conduct of free elections for the 15th Majlis through the dispatch of armed forces 'to all constituencies', and stated that if the Democrats of Azarbaijan denied this right by refusing to accept the armed forces or restricting them, the authority of the central government would be openly challenged. The occupation of Azarbaijan would then probably become necessary, and it would be possible to appeal to the Security Council in the event of Russian involvement.[85] Le Rougetel encouraged an appeal to the Security Council, an action which was approved by the Foreign Office.[86] Qavam, however, was clearly prepared for more drastic measures.

The announcement of Qavam's plan on 22 November provoked a strong reaction from the Democrats, particularly Pishihvari, who threatened 'the reactionaries' with the extension of 'the freedom of Azarbaijan over the whole of Iran',[87] the destruction of 'the criminal and dilapidated' government in Tehran and its replacement with a 'national government'.[88] The Tudeh Party warned that the dispatch of troops could endanger the security of the southern border of the Soviet Union and, in view of the terms of the 1921 Agreement, result in the return of the Red Army to Iranian soil.[89] Firuz reportedly sent a private message to Qavam from Moscow warning that his intended action would be catastrophic,[90] and the Russian Ambassador, according to Nikpay, threatened that if Qavam persisted in the dispatch of troops the Soviet Government would have to 'revise their opinion of him personally'. Qavam is reported to have replied that if Azarbaijan was a part of Iran, the matter did not concern the Soviet Union, and if it was not, the 'sooner the position was made clear to the world the better'.[91] He was clearly determined not to give in to threats or to lose the initiative, and insisted that he would only stay in office as long as the interests of the country required.

The Shah, on the other hand, was extremely heartened by the collapse of the coalition Cabinet, the high morale of the army, the 'ability displayed by his Chief of Staff, General Razmara' and by what he described as 'the enthusiastic welcome' given to his troops by the population of Zanjan.[92] He was therefore willing to take the lead in actions against the Democrats. Combined with the outbreak of tribal unrest in the south this further restricted Qavam, but he was not prepared to concede the solution of the Azarbaijan problem to the Shah and the army. Deprived of unequivocal British support but assured of the vocal backing of the Americans, Qavam notified the Security Council and issued a stern warning to the 'rebels of Azarbaijan' who had broken their promises and failed to respect the authority of the central government,[93] which suggested that armed action was imminent. On 10 December 1946 the Iranian army, backed by the Shahsavan and Zulfaqari tribesmen, crossed the border of Azarbaijan and captured Tabriz two days later. This also brought to an end the Kurdish republic regime based in Mahabad, whose existence had been more or less consistently ignored not only by the Iranian Government but also by the left. This was probably due to its tribal nature, its distinct ethno-religious background (Kurdish Sunni) and its inability to invoke any local traditions of active involvement in the establishment or preservation of constitutionalism in Iran. Above all it was regarded as having open separatist aims, embodied in the establishment of a 'republic'.[94]

The fall of Pishihvari's regime coincided with the anniversary of its formal establishment and was not a glorious event. The Iranian army easily overcame the scattered resistance of the retreating Democrats and those who had not fled to Russia speedily surrendered. Despite their achievements in security, education and road construction, their popular base had been gradually eroded by persistent economic and financial problems, the imposition of harsh taxation, uncompromising conscription, often uncompensated expropriation of the peasants' share of the crops, as well as insufficient concern with local religio-cultural sentiments. Their problems had been exacerbated by the repercussions of some of their hastily imposed reforms, their subservience to the Soviet Union, the alienation of the propertied strata and the excesses of some of their protagonists, particularly the *Muhajirin*, who had emigrated from the Soviet Union and become the Democrats' 'political police'. In fact the

British military attaché reported that the inhabitants of Tabriz, Reza'iyyih and Khuy killed 421 *Muhajirin* before the arrival of the Iranian army.[95]

The conclusion of the Qavam–Sadchikov agreement marked the beginning of the abandonment of the Democrats by the Russians. They had used the Democrats to extract the concessions they desired from the Iranian Government and now they began to pressurize the Democrats to stop their radical pronouncements and 'to get in line' in their dealings with the central government.[96] Realizing that they really were going to be abandoned by the Soviet Union, the Democrats gave in to demoralization, paralysis and defeat. The collapse of the Pishihvari regime was also a severe blow to the Tudeh Party who had continued to support the Democrats despite tensions between them. The Tudeh had never realistically assessed the situation in Azarbaijan although they repeatedly warned the Government about the consequences of armed action against the regime. Its speedy collapse and the absence of any real Russian reaction thus humiliated and discredited the Tudeh Party, not only in the eyes of its enemies but even some of its own members.[97]

These events brought to the surface the latent doubts and bitterness over the behaviour of the Tudeh leadership in the face of the Russian oil demand and the experience of the coalition Cabinet. After the recapture of Tabriz the Party refused to participate in the elections for the 15th Majlis and issued a number of apologetic proclamations which stressed the Party's record in upholding the cause of liberty and preventing 'rebellions and revolutions', and asserted that the Party wanted to realize its modest reformist goals through parliamentary means and within the framework of constitutional monarchy. They went as far as to state that the Party was not opposed to private property, nor to capitalism and religion, and was not in favour of the dictatorship of the proletariat, or of workers' government, but was dedicated to national ideals and the homeland. In addition they confessed to the Party's 'mistakes', criticized the Democrats of Azarbaijan and promised a change of policy as well as a purge of all 'pernicious' elements.[98] This only served to aggravate internal dissent in the Party, particularly since there was little positive change in the structure and policies. A group of disgruntled members, which included some of the most dedicated, sensitive and capable party activists, led by Khalil Maliki, later defected.[99]

11

The Second Period:
DECEMBER 1946–DECEMBER 1947

In the second period Qavam was to discover that it was the very existence of such problems as the Russian occupation and the regimes in Azarbaijan and Kurdistan which had enabled him to assume power and to defy the constraints of clan politics. When these problems no longer existed his position became more difficult to maintain, although the issue of the Irano-Soviet oil company was yet to be tackled, and Qavam had not yet been fully exposed to the efforts of his rivals to dislodge him. There now began a gradual revival of clan politics, marked on the one hand by Qavam's attempts to confound his opponents, particularly the Shah, and to maintain his position mainly through fully exploiting the oil issue, and on the other, by the attempts of his opponents and rivals to use him to ward off or confront the Russians and to engineer his downfall following the solution of the oil problem.

Before embarking on the task of tackling the issue of the Soviet oil demand, Qavam had to hold the elections for the 15th Majlis. He had previously been urged by the Russians and the leftists to call the elections, but had been deterred by the anti-leftist forces, including merchants and prominent *ulama*,[1] who were opposed to the holding of elections as long as the regimes in Azarbaijan and Kurdistan, and the strength of the left, continued to flourish. Ayatullah Burujirdi was said to have threatened not only to boycott the elections but also to issue a *fatva* against the Government, and Ayatullah Bihbahani had threatened to wear a shroud and march in the streets if an election were called.[2]

As soon as the political situation had changed, therefore, there was no reason for Qavam to hesitate in calling the elections. Although he had frequently promised that his Government would not attempt to manipulate the elections, there were growing fears that he planned to consolidate his power by the exclusion of his rivals and opponents. Student demonstrations, political meetings, the publication of opposition manifestos,[3] and a number of open letters, written primarily by Musaddiq and addressed to Qavam, the Shah and the press,[4] failed to produce any guarantees from the Government.

Therefore, on 13 January 1947, a group of protesters of various dispositions, led by Musaddiq and his son-in-law, Dr. Ahmad Matin-Daftari, and including a number of prominent politicians, *mullahs* and journalists whose aim was to oppose Qavam's manipulations of the elections, took sanctuary (*bast*) in the royal palace.[5] They took to the palace because the traditional place of sanctuary – the Majlis – was in recess; moreover, by doing so they aimed not only to gain publicity but also to take advantage of the differences between Qavam and the Shah. Four days later they were forced to leave. The Shah later told George Allen, the American Ambassador, that Qavam had approached him with three options: to arrest those who had taken sanctuary; to call for the postponement of the elections; or to accept the Prime Minister's resignation. The Shah had rejected all these suggestions and stated that he saw no reason for Qavam's resignation.[6] Although he had recently expressed his satisfaction with, or even admiration of, Qavam's skill, competence and patriotism,[7] the Shah was undoubtedly on the side of the protesters. He was 'most apprehensive of a sweeping victory for Qavam at the polls'[8] but was as yet in no position to turn against him, and it was inexpedient and premature for him to do so.

Moreover, it was far from encouraging for the Shah to hear from Allen that he was 'making an unfortunate departure from the policy of his father' by 'allowing prominent mullahs to take "*bast*" in [the] royal palace'.[9] Although the idea of postponing the elections appealed to the Shah, he nevertheless feared the consequences and was uncertain what view the British would take. The sanctuary in the royal palace could have been a golden opportunity for the Shah to enhance his image, reassert himself as guardian of the Constitution, and jeopardize Qavam's control over the elections, but circumstances did not allow this. Some of the protesters reportedly tried to discover from Allen whether they could take sanctuary in the American Embassy, but received no encouragement.[10] This left Qavam's party in a position to determine the outcome of the elections virtually without any challenge.

The elections for the 15th Majlis were largely completed during the winter of 1947. Primarily through its control over the machinery of government, but also through its country-wide network, its links with local notables and its access to funds, Qavam's Democratic Party succeeded in manipulating the electoral process, excluding rival parties, groups and candidates, and winning an overwhelming number of seats in the Majlis. With the exception of Azarbaijan and Fars where elections had not yet taken place, the successful candidates of all provinces had been approved by the Prime Minister;[11] all the deputies for Tehran belonged to his party and the most prestigious parliamentary position was conferred upon him personally, when he was elected First Deputy for Tehran, a position which, as head of the executive, he could not take up. The stage appeared to be set for a long term of office for Qavam with a co-operative and docile Majlis. It seemed that he had consolidated the disproportionately privileged position of his clan to the detriment of his rivals, particularly the Court, and had thus modified the underlying structure of Iranian clan politics. Such a development was unlikely to be passively accepted by the Court.

Initially the Shah had felt obliged to acquiesce in Qavam's manipulation of the election, but he missed no opportunity to make the British and American representatives aware of his feelings of hostility to Qavam. In late February 1947, in a conversation with Allen, he openly criticized Qavam and the corruption of his government; Allen also learned from other sources that the Shah's relations with Qavam had recently 'undergone a change for the worse'. The Shah had been pressing for the purchase of American war materials valued at $40,000,000, and Qavam was opposed to such a deal, ostensibly because he preferred to spend money on more constructive ends, but in reality because the additional equipment would further strengthen the Shah.[12]

Qavam's intransigence on this matter and his increased power provoked the Court to contemplate his removal or the destabilization of his position, even before the Majlis was opened. The Court began to disseminate rumours that 'the British' intended to replace Qavam with Ali Mansur, the then Governor-General of Azarbaijan,[13] despite the fact that the British were now full of admiration for Qavam's skilful handling of the crisis he faced, and had no reason to welcome his removal from power.[14]

One major source of comfort for the Shah and Qavam's other enemies was the outbreak of tensions and discord within the Democratic Party even before the Majlis elections were completed. Following the departure of Firuz to Moscow, Ahmad Aramish, the Minister of Labour and Propaganda and a member of the Party's

Central Committee, had assumed the position of Secretary General of the Party and effective control of it.[15] Aramish had gathered around himself a group of younger members of the Party and had 'not wasted any time in filling the party coffers' and, it was generally believed, 'his own pockets' by 'the sale of import and export licences and by all kinds of other illegitimate means'.[16] The main opponent of Aramish was Ali Akbar Musavizadih, the Minister of Justice and a member of the Party's Central Committee. Musavizadih had established his name in the post-1941 period because of his vigorous prosecution of some prominent members of Reza Shah's notorious police; he was disdainful of Aramish and was supported by Nikpay, Qavam's chief assistant, and others. He had openly attacked Aramish for his corruption, but Le Rougetel suspected that the real reason was that Musavizadih disapproved of the 'social development policies' of Aramish and his followers.[17]

None of this was surprising since the Party's most salient feature was its kleptocratic structure. It was created and maintained through the abuse of prime-ministerial authority and the machinery of government, with the aim of extending the hold on power of Qavam's clan. Despite its corporate appearance, ideological pronouncements, workers', students' and women's sections, extensive provincial branches, large meetings, reportedly vast intelligence network and uniformed National Salvation Guard (*Gard-i Nijat-i Milli*) and its impressive headquarters, the Democratic Party of Iran was as organizationally fragile as it was ideologically amorphous. It effectively consisted of little more than a hastily organized and enlarged heterogeneous following of Qavam.

The Democratic Party was a mechanism for the distribution of electoral spoils, that is of seats in the Majlis and other positions of influence which embodied material or symbolic gains, among a clientele whose loyalty and pledges proved to be frustratingly short lived. The majority were opportunists who used their links with Qavam merely to secure a seat in the Majlis, and then abandoned him. Those who failed to get elected to the Majlis naturally joined his enemies, while those who were not given positions of power or authority within the party either lost their enthusiasm for party activities or engaged in rivalry with, or intrigue against their colleagues and even against Qavam. In the words of Rezazadih-Shafaq, a deputy in the 14th and 15th Majlis, who was a friend of Qavam and accompanied him on his journey to Moscow:

Qavam created a party in a few weeks with amazing speed. The first voice of dissent was aired among its leaders according to the spirit of individuality, contumacy and self-centredness which, one can say, is entrenched in our nature. The Democratic Party of Iran came with Qavam and went with him.[18]

Tensions within Qavam's party were also reflected in the Cabinet, where quarrelling ministers struggled to outmanoeuvre each other. The differences between Aramish and his colleagues in the Cabinet were further aggravated by a Government decree which deprived mill-owners of the right to dismiss workers without the prior approval of the Ministry of Labour and Propaganda. This decree, which caused much excitement in Isfahan, was turned by the opponents of Aramish into an issue of contention with the Prime Minister.[19] Musavizadih and his group also widened the campaign by attacking Habib Nafisi, the dynamic under-secretary at the Ministry of Labour and Propaganda, who was the 'driving force' behind the policies of his Ministry and a man whose integrity, in Le Rougetel's view, had 'never been suspected'. They advocated Nafisi's replacement by an under-secretary at the Foreign Ministry who was unfamiliar with labour affairs. Aramish and his supporters alleged that their opponents were acting as 'a mouthpiece of Isfahan employers', who were 'opposing at every turn the present policies and aims of the Ministry of Labour'.[20]

Such tensions within Qavam's party and in the Cabinet were, if not provoked, at least welcomed by his enemies, as were allegations of corruption against some of Qavam's friends. In early May 1947, Salman Asadi – an associate of Qavam whose father had been executed by Reza Shah and who was later to replace Aramish as the Minister of Labour and Propaganda and eventually to take a seat in the Majlis – informed Le Rougetel that in his last two meetings with the Shah he had found him critical of Qavam's waning authority and the corruption of his government and was 'toying with the idea' of dismissing him.[21] In response Le Rougetel asserted that the Shah should concern himself with the interests of his country and resist pressures for a 'premature and dubious use of his prerogatives'.[22]

In late May and early June 1947 the Shah paid a visit to Azarbaijan, Rasht and Qazvin in an attempt to enhance his popular image as the real champion of the 'liberation' of Azarbaijan. It proved a rewarding experience as he was accorded 'a very enthusiastic reception by huge crowds', and was warmly greeted by the Azarbaijanis,the 'spontaneity' of whose welcome Le Rougetel did not doubt.[23] Despite this boost to his morale the Shah was in no position to push for Qavam's removal without the approval or acquiescence of the British or the Americans. However, he began to manoeuvre more openly for concessions and a revival of his prerogatives. He strongly opposed the return of Firuz to his ambassadorial position in Moscow, which the latter had left in May for a visit to Europe. Initially Qavam had little choice but to encourage Firuz 'to take a leave' for a few months in Switzerland.[24] Over two months later, although Firuz had resumed his functions in Moscow, he was dismissed, upon the insistence of the Shah.[25] The presence of Firuz in Moscow had been of considerable advantage to Qavam in view of his dynamism and skill in dealing with the Russians and liaising between them and Qavam, especially when the oil issue was in its criticial stages. He was a man whose inclusion in Qavam's entourage had provoked resentment,[26] and with whom Qavam had not always agreed; yet he was a friend whose antipathy to the Pahlavis had appealed to Qavam. To protect him had symbolized the strength of Qavam's own position *vis-à-vis* the Shah, and to remove him clearly implied a weakening of Qavam's position and a victory for the Shah.

Hoping to eliminate tensions in his Cabinet, to dispel rumours of corruption among some of his colleagues, and to deprive the Court of the pretexts for many of its grievances, particularly before the opening of the Majlis, Qavam once again reshuffled the Cabinet on 22 June 1947.[27] Aramish and Nikpay, who had been increasingly suspected of financial irregularities, were relieved of their posts;[28] Musavizadih was retained as Minister without portfolio; a general was entrusted with the portfolio of the Interior, which the Prime Minister had previously retained, and Amir-Ala'i and Dr. Ali Shayigan, Ministers for Agriculture and Education, respectively, were replaced by men better disposed towards the Court. Moreover, the Ministry of Labour and Propaganda, despite earlier rumours, was not dissolved, while a new Ministry of National Economy was created in place of the Ministry of Crafts, Arts and Commerce. In Le Rougetel's view this Cabinet was distinctly better than its predecessors because, among other things, three of its Ministers, namely Issa Sadiq, Ali Asghar Hikmat and Salman Asadi, were 'good Moslems of character and ability' as well as 'old friends' of the British Embassy.[29] Similarly, the Shah could not reasonably claim to be dissatisfied. Later Qavam also announced the formation of five committees to investigate the charges of corrupt practices, dereliction of duty and incompetence brought against government officials, and to send the guilty to the Criminal Court for trial.[30]

Despite these conciliatory gestures the Shah, convinced that the full revival of his patrimony was not possible with Qavam as Prime Minister, was not prepared to relax his intrigues against him. In order to encourage the mounting opposition and abusive press criticism of Qavam and his party the Shah arranged for the suspension of martial law regulations in Tehran. This was followed, as expected, by the acceleration of Court-inspired press diatribes against the Prime Minister. When the offices of three anti-Qavam newspapers were attacked, his party denied involvement, but his enemies were provided with an added pretext for challenging him. Aware of the danger to which he was exposed, Qavam demanded the reimposition of martial law, but the Shah refused to comply.[31] A long Cabinet session resulted in a vote for reimposition, but General Ahmadi, the War Minister, subsequently withdrew his signature and insisted on the need to seek the prior approval of the Shah. When Ahmadi refused to comply or resign Qavam sought an immediate audience with the Shah, and obtained his approval for the reimposition of martial law, as well as an order for the dismissal of Ahmadi.[32] This was followed by the resignation of the Interior Minister, General Aqivli, as a gesture of support for his fellow general.[33]

Qavam had succeeded in reasserting his authority and obtaining these concessions because the Shah was as yet undecided about the extent and practical limits of his opposition to the Prime Minister. Qavam had given in to some of the Shah's demands and tried to counter his known desire to dismiss him by himself threatening to resign prior to the latest Cabinet reshuffle. Nikpay told Le Rougetel that Qavam was again 'seriously wondering' whether or not to resign before the opening of the 15th Majlis.[34] These tactics were intended as a statement of his dissatisfaction with his limited range of authority and his ostensible lack of interest in retaining office against the expressed desire of the Shah. Each refusal of his resignation was therefore taken as a reconfirmation of royal confidence, which the Shah could not easily contradict. On the other hand, each threat of Qavam's dismissal or resignation brought the disapproval of the British and American Ambassadors, the former arguing that such an action implied a lack of interest on the part of the Iranians to respect their undertakings in regard to their oil agreement with the Russians.[35]

When the Majlis was eventually opened on 17 July 1947 the long period of interregnum which had worked in Qavam's favour came to an end. Despite all his efforts, and although over seventy deputies had pledged their loyalty to the Prime Minister in writing,[36] when the Majlis opened forty of these deputies were already in rebellion against him.[37] Those who were in 'open revolt' against the Prime Minister were ready, as Le Rougetel put it, 'to follow the Shah against Qavam', but apparently the Shah 'was undecided what course to take'.[38]

The Shah had admitted that he had been 'reluctant to agree to the constitution of a Majlis in which the Prime Minister would have the support of a tame majority'.[39] In the event the feared 'tame majority' did not materialize; Nikpay confessed to Le Rougetel that the 'hard core of the party consisted of only 35 deputies',[40] while the opposition consisted not only of rebellious Democrats, but also those who had been elected without the support or approval of the party. In addition, the credentials of Qavam's most loyal supporters were disputed and rallying a quorum in the Majlis proved to be as difficult as it had previously been. Qavam had little doubt that the opposition inside and outside the Majlis was inspired by the Shah and his entourage and that the obstructive deputies were controlled by the Shah.[41] Similarly, Nikpay had 'no doubt that the Shah was busy fishing in troubled waters',[42] and Le Rougetel reported that 'intrigues of every kind' were 'afoot and the Prime Minister's enemies both within and outside the Majlis' were 'evidently straining every nerve to bring about his discomfiture'.[43]

Nevertheless the Shah and the opposition deputies had every interest in keeping Qavam in office until the country was extricated from the dilemma created by the Russian oil demand. The Majlis informed the Shah in late August 1947 that it was ready to assume its full functions;[44] and according to custom Qavam submitted his resignation, but received a majority vote of 78 out of 116 and was invited by the Shah to form a Cabinet.[45]

Qavam refused the offer and publicized his refusal, hoping to demonstrate his unwillingness to assume office under any condition, to obtain some real or symbolic assurances of support and to confirm the absence of any viable alternative candidate.[46] Eventually the Democratic Party declared that Qavam had decided to accept the premiership in deference to the demands of his party and a number of independent deputies,[47] and on 11 September 1947 he announced the formation of a new Cabinet. Since all prominent members of his party had been elected to the Majlis and probably in order not to provoke his opponents any further, Qavam included only one member of his party in the new Cabinet – Javad Bushihri, who held the portfolio of Post, Telegraph and Telephone. The Cabinet did not otherwise significantly differ from its predecessor and was unlikely to cause strong feelings either way. No Minister of Labour and Propaganda was appointed and the fate of this Ministry was left to be decided by the Majlis. Qavam also put forward a ten-point programme which made no mention of oil but included specific and crucial reform measures, such as bills for a seven-year plan, a labour law, a government monopoly of foreign trade and the protection of domestic industries, as well as for the establishment of provincial councils.[48] After lengthy debates, the opposition's threat of obstruction eventually forced Qavam's supporters to acquiesce in his receiving only a conditional vote of confidence; that is, his programme was approved but the conduct of his administration during the period of parliamentary recess was not. Moreover, the deputies passed a resolution demanding a detailed account of Qavam's term of office, and particularly of the oil issue, for examination and evaluation by the Majlis.[49]

There was little chance that the new Majlis, in which Qavam's followers formed a minority, would accept the terms of the Qavam–Sadchikov draft agreement. Qavam was under no illusion about this, and nor was he unhappy about it. The Russians frequently threatened Qavam that in the event of non-compliance with their oil demand, they would resort to retaliatory measures, which ranged from refusing to return over eleven tons of Iranian gold deposited in Moscow,[50] to putting an end to Iran's independence, a threat with which Molotov, the Russian Commissar for Foreign Affairs, had repeatedly intimidated Firuz.[51] Qavam had tried to persuade the Russians to modify their terms and accept alternative arrangements,[52] but they insisted that only the approval of a bill along the lines of the original oil agreement would convince them of Iran's interest in friendship with the Soviet Union.[53] The rejection of the oil agreement would prove, as Sadchikov allegedly warned Qavam, that the Iranian Government and people were the 'blood enemies' of the Soviet Government.[54]

Qavam knew that the mildness of the Russian reaction to the fall of the regimes in Tabriz and Mahabad was largely due to their expectation of success in regard to their oil demand, and was fearful of their reaction if this failed. He was, however, unable or unwilling to do more than minimize his own role and responsibility in the matter and to leave all decisions to the Majlis. He could plausibly plead that the erosion of his support in the Majlis prevented him from assuming an effective role in bringing about the acceptance of the Russian oil demands. But he was well aware that just as he had gained personal credit for a settlement with the Russians, he would equally become the prime target of their attacks in the event of failure. He knew that the Russians and the Iranian left would regard him as an imposter who had disguised his reactionary dispositions and pro-American leanings, enlisted the confidence of the Soviet Union, and gained considerable concessions in exchange for spurious undertakings, the final rejection of which he himself master-minded. The rejection of the Soviet oil demand was, in fact, described by one of the main Tudeh Party papers as a victory for US dollar imperialism and an event which Qavam could easily have prevented if he had so desired.[55]

To the great relief of his anti-leftist allies, this put an end to any hope Qavam might have had of gaining the support of the Russians or the left in the future. His only hope now was to improve his relations with the British and the Americans and assure himself of their support. When he had been faced with little choice but to pursue a policy of appeasement towards the Russians, he had been saved from co-ordinated Anglo-American pressure, largely because the British officials in Tehran had found it difficult to enlist the effective support of their American counterparts, and Qavam had proved skilful in exploiting such differences. Following Qavam's incipient break with the left and the fall of the coalition Cabinet, the Americans (whose foreign policy appeared to be based on their traditional political ideals and a barely disguised anti-Soviet attitude) had generously announced their support for Iran's independence and national sovereignty. The British, however, in their characteristically discreet and pragmatic style, followed an ambivalent policy unlikely to dispel American fears that they intended to revive their old policy of spheres of influence. It was even less likely to allay the suspicions and fears of the Iranians.

While the Americans had not hesitated to declare their support for the restoration of full Iranian authority in Azarbaijan long before the capture of Tabriz, the British expressed their support only after the Iranian forces had crossed the borders.[56] The Americans voiced both private and diplomatic disapproval and public opposition to the granting of an oil concession to the Russians.[57] The British, on the other hand, initially tried to convince Qavam that it would be 'most unwise' to deny the Russians 'legitimate access' to Iranian oil,[58] and later that he should deal with the Russians in a way which would not jeopardize the prospect of further negotiations.[59] The British were, of course, concerned that if the Soviet Union was deprived of a stake in Iranian oil, their own concession in the south of Iran would be threatened, and they even foresaw the possibility of a coup sponsored by the Russians or their occupation of Iran.[60] Fearing that the Iranians in their desire to mitigate Russian anger might be forced to advocate action against all foreign concessions, the British assured Stalin that they would encourage the Iranians to honour their agreement with the Russians.[61] Accordingly the Russians told Firuz that 'the Persian Government would be wiser to follow' the British lead rather than 'that of the Americans'.[62]

The British finally abandoned their efforts to reach an understanding with the Americans on the oil issue,[63] realizing that their position had caused suspicion and resentment among Iranians, which was expressed both privately by the Shah,[64] and in the press.[65] The British argued in their own defence that they had put no pressure on the Iranians.[66] They were also quite prepared to reconsider their attitudes in the light of changing circumstances,[67] and always claimed to be ready to support the Iranian Government.[68] Creswell, the British *chargé d'affaires*, was convinced that the Iranian 'mental attitude' was 'so precariously balanced between false courage and cowardice' that whatever advice the British gave was 'likely, if overdone, to push them off the balance one way or the other'; he asserted that 'given the basic chicken-heartedness of the Persian character, it is wise to err on the side of making them feel they have our full support'.[69] Despite their different attitudes to the oil issue, the British and Americans were agreed that until this was settled it was preferable for Qavam to stay in power. The British had often disconcerted the Shah by pointing out the negative international consequences of Qavam's premature removal. Qavam tried to enhance the extent of Anglo-American support for his Government and arrange for its frequent reconfirmation. However, when the Russian oil demand was eventually rejected neither the British nor the Americans could produce any argument in favour of keeping him in office.

On 21 October 1947 Qavam submitted a lengthy report to the Majlis listing his activities and achievements during his term of office.[70] In the same session the Majlis passed, by a vote of 102 to 2 abstentions, a resolution which rejected the Qavam–Sadchikov agreement but specified that should commercially viable amounts of oil be found in the north the Government could start negotiations for its sale to the Russians, keeping the Majlis informed of its activities. Without raising the controversial and much-discussed issue of the restoration of Iranian sovereignty over Bahrain, it assigned the Government the task of redeeming the impaired rights of the nation to the sources of its wealth, particularly the oil in the south.[71] The wording of the resolution and its reference to southern oil did little to appease the Russians and the leftists. Concerned at the growth of American influence in Iran and convinced that this was the result of a well-calculated policy, the Tudeh Party doubted or belittled Parliament's desire to restrict British advantages in the country.[72] The British considered that the substance of their advice had not been ignored since no 'blank negative' reply had been given to the Russians. They saw the reference to southern oil as primarily tactical, and were relieved that the issue of Bahrain had not been raised.[73] Neither they nor the Americans were yet ready to support the Shah's efforts to remove Qavam, whose position, despite continued Anglo-American support, became less secure than ever. He was ill and exhausted, and the target of attacks by the Russians and the leftist press, as well as a growing number of royalist and other anti-Qavam newspapers. His skilful handling of the oil issue had temporarily disarmed his opponents in the Majlis, but had inevitably increased the Shah's hostility towards him.[74]

The Shah seemed determined to increase his power on the basis of new orientations regarding foreign and domestic policies. In the area of foreign policy he claimed that neutrality for Iran was impossible, and had to be reminded by the British *chargé d'affaires* that it was in Iran's interest at least to 'keep up a façade of neutrality'.[75] Regarding internal politics he continued to be obsessed both by the expansion of the army and the extension of its role, and the revision of the Constitution to his own advantage.[76] He demanded recognition of his role in securing the rejection of the Russian oil demand and was outspoken in his determination to oust Qavam.[77] Encouraged by Princess Ashraf, his twin sister, who played a crucial role in orchestrating the Court's anti-Qavam activities, the Shah had even decided upon a successor to Qavam, namely Abdulhusain Hazhir, Qavam's Finance Minister. Hazhir's premiership was to follow a caretaker Cabinet, which would bring about the revision of the Constitution and which the Shah hoped would be headed by Reza Hikmat,[78] who was still the chairman of the Central Committee of

Qavam's party. According to information received by the British Embassy, the Shah had secured Hikmat's collaboration through the extension of substantial financial help which enabled him to settle his gambling debts.[79]

Qavam for his part resorted to his old tactic of asking the Shah either to support him or allow him to resign, but this was no longer effective and he was forced to resort to other measures. Among other things, he favourably raised in the Majlis the issue of the establishment of a Senate,[80] suggested the appointment of Taqizadih as Court Minister,[81] and according to the American Embassy in London he promised to support 'a bill asking permission to obtain arms from the United States on credit'.[82] Such efforts, however, produced few positive results, and the Shah intensified his intrigues and manoeuvres against Qavam. In the Majlis Qavam now suffered the rejection of the credentials of Hasan Arsanjani, his dynamic and resourceful confidant,[83] and faced moves to suspend martial law and thereby render him more exposed to the vitriolic press. Threats of interpellation and impeachment were incessantly made against him without appreciating his achievements or the difficulties he had faced; he was denied sufficient opportunity to defend himself in the Majlis, and his postponed budget bill remained unapproved. Faced with such a situation, in addition to betrayal by his erstwhile friends, Qavam became indignant and embittered.

At the same time his party suffered an internal coup when a provisional executive committee was elected in defiance of the one he had personally approved. In addition, the parliamentary basis of his Government, the Democratic faction, split into two opposing sections, one loyal to Qavam and led by Muhammad-Taqi Bahar, the other openly defiant and led by Reza Hikmat.[84] Hikmat also took with him some thirty 'independent' deputies, and thus led an anti-Qavam opposition of over sixty deputies.[85] On 4 December 1947, with the encouragement of the Court, most of Qavam's ministers handed in their resignations to the Shah, thereby destroying his last hope of remaining in power.[86] According to Le Rougetel, Qavam's broadcast of 1 December 1947, which the Shah had found offensive, as well as his intervention on behalf of Reza Rusta, the Tudeh labour organizer, which resulted in Rusta's release from prison, provided the Shah with additional pretexts to oppose Qavam. On these grounds, and heartened by the announcement of Hikmat and his followers that they were to join the opposition, 'His Majesty intimated to the Prime Minister's colleagues that he wished them to resign and they felt that they had no alternative but to obey'.[87] Qavam, however, refused to resign on the grounds that if he did so the country would be plunged into serious chaos.[88] Four days later he delivered an eloquent speech in the Majlis in which he defended his policies, complained of the betrayal and false pretensions of his friends, and underlined the dangers which threatened to end Iranian constitutionalism with a 'sorrowful tragedy'.[89] In the event he was denied a vote of confidence and his premiership came to an end.[90]

The main paradox of Qavam's premiership was that he could maintain his position only as long as the crisis which he had been appointed to solve prevailed. With the rejection of the Russian oil demand, therefore, the *raison d'être* of his premiership disappeared. As the American Ambassador put it, when Qavam 'had served his usefulness, the Shah gave the nod and the Majlis kicked him out'.[91] A few days before his downfall, in a last attempt to deny his opponents the pleasure of an honourable victory, Qavam turned against the British by advocating the restoration of Iran's full rights over the oil in the south and her inviolable sovereignty over Bahrain. This surprising move was intended to divert attention from his weakening position, to add to the problems of his successors, to reduce the antagonism of his pro-Russian enemies, and perhaps also to indicate his disgruntlement with the British, whom he suspected of failing to discourage the Shah from intrigues. Above all it was an attempt to deprive the Shah of the satisfaction of having ousted him. He turned against the British in order to attribute his removal from office to them; his main party newspaper took pains to stress that no factor accounted for Qavam's downfall more than his determination to recover Iranian rights over Bahrain and the southern oil.[92] Qavam tried to lend an air of dignity to his eventual failure by pronouncing it to be the consequence of nothing other than his struggle to reassert the rights of his country. He concomitantly hoped to embarrass, belittle and discredit his enemies by implying their complicity with, or manipulation by, the British. In the past the issue of Bahrain and its occupation by the British had frequently been raised by the left in order to divert attention from the Russian refusal to evacuate Iran, and from the events in Azarbaijan. In the 15th Majlis Abbas Iskandari, a controversial figure and an ex-member of the Tudeh Party, who was the deputy for Hamadan, championed an uncompromising irredentist stand on Bahrain, and demanded action to recover not only Iran's sovereignty over Bahrain but also control over the oil in the south.[93]

Qavam had resumed the premiership at one of the most critical moments in Iranian history. Although he may not have planned in every detail the recovery of Azarbaijan and Kurdistan, or the rejection of the Russian oil demand, he was undoubtedly the architect of the strategy by which they were attained. His remarkable skill, cunning and astuteness enabled him to tackle crises which had baffled and defeated almost all his rivals and had jeopardized Iran's sovereignty and territorial integrity. He also tried, by creating a political party, to modify the structural configuration of Iranian clan politics and make it less vulnerable to shifting personal loyalties and informal alliances. In this he failed, although he showed an awareness of the mechanisms which could potentially challenge the stalemate of conventional Iranian parliamentarianism and save it from self-destruction.

Many Iranian journalists branded Qavam as a reactionary with little interest in constitutionalism or reform,[94] and even the British *chargé d'affaires* seemed to believe that no real reform was possible while Qavam was still in power.[95] Qavam, naturally, did not endorse the prevailing perception of constitutionalism, but his activities, even if inadvertently, were more conducive to the ultimate consolidation of constitutionalism than were those of his royalist rivals. Although the creation of a ministry to deal with labour affairs and labour legislation, the attempt to set a minimum wage and ban the arbitrary dismissal of workers, the attempt to limit the powers of landowners, and the institution of reforms on the basis of a seven-year plan should not be credited solely to Qavam, nevertheless he played a significant part in these efforts. The failure of such efforts should be explained primarily in terms of the role of the opposition and in particular the absence of structural preconditions, rather than simply a lack of will on the part of Qavam.

Despite his frequent homage to the concept of collective Cabinet responsibility, Qavam often acted alone, working as he did in an atmosphere of mistrust and intrigues, with the result that few of his Cabinet colleagues were aware of his real objectives or could predict his moves. He showed enormous skill in exploiting differences between his rivals and enemies, and in invoking one threat in order to counter another – which was one of his main tactics in maintaining his foreign policy of reserved positive equilibrium.[96] His desire for respect and praise brought opportunists and sycophants in its train and his inflated self-image often led him to treat even his ministers in an imperious manner. Above all, in his persistent craving for power he had few scruples about his choice of means – but neither did many of his opponents.

Although the Soviet oil demand was the major problem which Qavam faced while in power, his real preoccupation was to confront the Court. Conflict between the Shah and Qavam was essentially a conflict over power and, by implication, a conflict of latent or discreetly expressed claims to leadership, to the detriment of rival clans. In a meeting with Le Rougetel in February 1947, the Shah had sardonically referred to Qavam as 'le père du peuple'.[97] This was a title which the Shah was keen to assume himself, and following the recapture of Tabriz some newspapers had added 'father of the nation' to his title of Commander-in-Chief of the Armed Forces. In April 1946 Michael Foot, who visited Iran as the representative of the British Labour Party, observed that the Shah's authority was 'shadowy and ill-defined' and that the Government was 'filled with the sons of his father's victims' and commented that 'if he chose now to exert his influence it might be the last act of a Shah of Persia'.[98] If this had been a plausible comment in 1946, it was entirely irrelevant in 1947.

The Shah's briefly eclipsed role in influencing the Iranian political process, whether by action or inaction, had been resumed even before the autumn of 1946. He was impatient to revive his full formal and informal prerogatives, which necessitated the removal of Qavam. The Shah's cumulative grip on power required the elimination of powerful rivals who relied upon various sources of support, whether a vast clientele, a popular base or even foreign powers. Both the Shah, through his desired revision of the Constitution, and Qavam, through his attempted use of party politics, hoped to modify the existing system of clan politics and undermine its equilibrium to the benefit of their own patrimonies. It could hardly be disputed that the existing parliamentary practices and attitudes were in need of genuine modification, but the increase of royal prerogatives was not the solution. Iranian parliamentarianism would be revived only by the establishment of a Court-independent executive with sufficient authority; and party politics, whatever the actual problems, was both an ideal and a method by which to pave the way for a viable mode of parliamentary government.

PART IV

The Attempted Royal Ascendancy

12
The Government of Hakimi:
DECEMBER 1947–JUNE 1948

The fall of Qavam precipitated the perennial problem of finding a successor. Although the Court's favourite candidate was Abdulhusain Hazhir, it was decided that it would be wiser to begin with an interim Cabinet, which Reza Hikmat was asked to form. Qavam's supporters in the Majlis had threatened that they would obstruct any Cabinet formed by Hikmat,[1] and he himself did not appear willing to sacrifice his safe position as the Speaker of the Majlis for the vulnerable premiership. Moreover Hikmat informed the Shah that before presenting his ministers at a royal audience he wished each of them to have been recommended by the deputies. This was clearly unacceptable to the Shah, and it was obvious that an alternative candidate was needed. In a secret session of the Majlis Musaddiq and Hakimi each gained 54 votes, but as Hikmat cast his vote in favour of Hakimi, the latter was called upon to assume office.[2]

Hakimi was always prepared to form a Cabinet, however narrow the majority on which it was based and regardless of the prospects for its duration or success. Although most of the problems which had forced him to resign in January 1946 – the Russian occupation of the north, the autonomy movements and the Russian oil demand – had been solved by Qavam, the task of governing the country still required far more energy and dynamism than Hakimi possessed. Indeed, there was an implicit, shared assumption that this was merely a stop-gap Cabinet. Nikpay informed Le Rougetel that supporters of the Shah had voted for Hakimi on condition that he included Hazhir in his Cabinet.[3] This he initially declined to do, but in any case his Cabinet contained enough royalist elements, including two generals. One of these was Murtiza Yazdanpanah, the Shah's Adjutant General since 1943, who had been a close friend of Reza Shah with whom he had collaborated in the coup of February 1921. As a Foreign Office official once observed, he was reputed to be 'intelligent, ambitious, incorruptible and xenophobic' but 'not to have a very high opinion' of Muhammad Reza Shah.[4] However, Yazdanpanah's presence in the Cabinet as War Minister was likely to increase royal control over it, and by March 1948 Hazhir was brought into the Cabinet as Minister without Portfolio. Hakimi's Cabinet programme was as unimpressive as the composition of the Cabinet: besides promising to reduce unnecessary expenditure and increase the participation of the provincial populace in the management of local affairs, it included little more than the usual platitudes.

When the new Cabinet was introduced to the Majlis it was attacked by Iskandari and Ghulam Husain Rahimian over the exclusion of the issues of southern oil and Bahrain from its programme.[5] These issues, particularly the oil question, which Qavam had formally put on the agenda of Iranian politics, were to haunt his successors. Hakimi was unwilling to commit himself in any way and if it had been possible he would have avoided or even suppressed these issues altogether. His Cabinet could not even inspire enthusiasm among his supporters, who had to fall back on the honesty and good faith of the Prime Minister and some of his colleagues in order to justify their qualified support for his Government.[6]

Taqizadih, an old and very close friend of Hakimi who had worked with him during the Constitutional Revolution, did defend him against his critics but he also expressed his disapproval of Cabinet plans to accept foreign loans and of the donation of public funds to the Imperial Organization for Social Services.[7] This was bound to displease the Shah who wanted foreign loans for military purposes and whose sister Ashraf was the patroness of the organization in question. The Shah's displeasure naturally affected the attitude of the royalist deputies towards Hakimi's Cabinet. Whatever the divisions among his supporters and opponents, however, most agreed that his Cabinet should be given the chance to prove itself and, accordingly, on 7 January 1948, of the 92 deputies present in the Majlis, 76 voted in his favour, 1 against and 15 abstained.[8]

Aware of the precarious position of his Cabinet and the strength of the opposition, Hakimi attempted to assert the authority of the Government and prove its reformist objectives. Thus, martial law which had been in force more or less continuously for seven years was terminated;[9] unpopular restrictions such as the rationing of tea and sugar were lifted;[10] and an attempt was made to reduce the extravagance of the government machinery. In addition, on the publication in January 1948 of a report prepared by Dr. Musharraf Nafisi, who had been commissioned by Qavam to devise a Seven-year Plan for economic and social development, Hakimi's Cabinet expressed its desire to implement the plan. However, Hakimi had no means of mobilizing steady support in the Majlis, to the extent that he was unable to fill all the portfolios in his Cabinet. Despite the enormous effort he put into gaining the favour of the Court and the royalist deputies in the Majlis, he achieved very little. The Shah was preoccupied with engineering the premiership of Hazhir and, most importantly, the revision of the Constitution. The Shah was hoping that the performance and fate of Hakimi's Cabinet would enable him to demonstrate further the inadequacy of the existing constitutional arrangements.

Although the Shah's dissatisfaction with his constitutional power was clearly discernible in the early years of his reign, it was in early 1948 that he became actively preoccupied with the issue of the Constitution which, he told Le Rougetel, was in its existing form 'beyond any shadow of a doubt ... quite unworkable'.[11] He concentrated on convincing the British and American Embassies of the wisdom of his objective, and on enlisting their support or approval, while very few Iranians were even aware of his plans. When these became known they would obviously provoke hostility, while the existing social strains – rooted in mass poverty, increasing unemployment and the growth of marginalized urban strata composed largely of peasants who had migrated to the cities in search of jobs created by the war and the occupation of the country – provided favourable grounds for protest and political agitation. In these circumstances, merely to mention the dangers of dictatorship was more than enough to rally a wide audience and mobilize the disaffected urban masses who longed for an outlet for their grievances.

The man best able to stimulate and mobilize popular sentiments and occasionally articulate public demands was Ayatullah Sayyid Abulqasim Kashani, a shrewd and ambitious patron-patriarch with a growing clientele among the traditionally minded urban strata. He was capable of combining extreme pragmatism with lofty principles and was a well-versed political actor, instinctively inclined towards parliamentary government but intellectually incapable of compre-hending its complexities or respecting its formal institutional arrangements.[12] In his manoeuvres to win an optimal share of political spoils for himself and his patrimony he was prepared to disregard formal administrative procedures and, more significantly, condoned the use of violence, intimidation and terror to further his political ends. Kashani collaborated with the Fida'iyan-i Islam, a group of xenophobic fundamentalist zealots recruited mainly from the ranks of small artisans which was bent on assassinating those public figures whom it regarded as acting against Islam and/or the national interest. The group had been founded by Sayyid Mujtaba Navvab-Safavi, a theological student who had recently arrived from Najaf in Iraq, in order to counter the influence of Ahmad Kasravi, a controversial and iconoclastic historian and essayist who was assassinated by a member of the Fida'iyan on 11 March 1946.[13]

Kashani was a versatile publicist and invoked Islam and the unity of Muslims as well as national independence and constitutionalism as sources of inspiration for political action. His deeply entrenched anglophobia, which had started in the First World War, had increased during the Second World War when he was interned by the British who discovered that he was a top member of a pro-German organization in Iran. On his release, he resumed his political activities and was for a period arrested by Qavam. By 1948 he was already a political figure to be reckoned with. Kashani was distinguished from other prominent *ulama* by his politico-religious activism, his populist style and his lack of strong social and kin relations with the senior *ulama*. The mode of his religio-traditionalist views and tactics, as well as the audience which he addressed, converged with those of Sayyid Zia, but the latter's devout anglophilia prevented any real co-operation.

Anti-dictatorial fears, which accounted for the direct or indirect alliance of Sayyid Zia with members of the Tudeh Party,[14] were encouraged by the suspension of martial law and further substantiated by an incident in February 1948: the mysterious murder of Muhammad Mas'ud, the talented and passionate journalist who had subjected the Court, the army, the bulk of the elite and the *mullahs* to incessant vitriolic attack. Although he was also capable of using his vituperative language in order to bribe and extract benefits to maintain or increase the readership of his newspaper, nevertheless his murder became a *cause célèbre* and was widely blamed on the Court, especially Princess Ashraf. Mas'ud's newspaper, however, accused Muslim fanatics, and attributed his murder to his opposition to the reintroduction of the veil (*chador*), which he had vigorously campaigned against.[15] Some former Tudeh Party members have, on the other hand, recently asserted that certain members of the Party's leadership arranged for Mas'ud's murder, presumably intending to implicate the royal family.[16]

According to one account at least 100,000 people accompanied Mas'ud's funeral procession.[17] A more imaginative or able politician would at least have feigned a genuine interest in investigating the murder and bringing the perpetrator to justice,[18] but Hakimi chose to concentrate his activities on cultivating his policy of royal appeasement. He succeeded, on 17 February, in passing through the Majlis a bill which provided for the purchase on credit of $10 million worth of arms from the USA, to be repaid in twelve annual instalments, beginning in January 1950.[19] His position in the Majlis, however, had greatly deteriorated; by late February he narrowly survived a motion of interpellation, inspired mainly by Mas'ud's murder, when only 55 deputies voted in his favour and 44 abstained. His resignation thus seemed imminent.

Hakimi did not, however, submit readily, but resorted to the well-tried tactic of reshuffling his Cabinet. He hoped to fill the vacant positions in his Cabinet and broaden his base, extend more concessions to the deputies or the *mutavallis*, and co-opt those who were, or were believed to be, involved in intrigue against him, or were regarded as contenders for the premiership. The last category included Suhaili – the former Prime Minister who had returned to the political scene following his acquittal on charges of illegal interference in the elections for the 14th Majlis – and Hazhir, both of whom were invited to join the Cabinet as Ministers without Portfolio. The inclusion of Hazhir, while aimed at satisfying the Court and the royalist deputies, was bound to provoke agitation by Kashani and, less explicitly, by Sayyid Zia. Kashani launched demonstrations against Hazhir, castigating him as a 'traitor' and a 'foreign hireling'; Sayyid Zia's followers were also opposed to him and, according to Le Rougetel, Sayyid Zia was 'said to have been expressing views which were disrespectful to the throne'.[20]

In addition to Hakimi's personal dislike of Hazhir, whose eventual premiership he was supposed to be facilitating, there was a strong likelihood of conflict between Hazhir and Najm, Hakimi's close friend and Minister of Finance, which would ultimately weaken the Cabinet. The presence of Hazhir in the Cabinet as Minister without Portfolio, rather than Finance Minister, a position which best suited Hazhir and usually held by him; the fact that Najm had continued to remove many of Hazhir's friends from the Finance Ministry; and differences of outlook and style – all created problems.

Another concession to the royalists was the appointment of the hard-liner General Ahmadi as Minister of the Interior, replacing General Aqivli who had been unpopular with the deputies. The appointment of Ahmadi was intended to deal with the problem of law and order which, in addition to political agitation, had resulted in an increase in instances of violence and theft in Tehran.

Hakimi's Cabinet reshuffle merely delayed its imminent downfall but was not enough to persuade the British to engage in any sustained dealings with it. Hakimi had lived up to his promise to turn 'a deaf ear to the agitation about Bahrain',[21] and, as Creswell remarked, neither this Government nor its successor, if led by Hazhir, was likely to 'do more than pay lip-service' to the task of recovering Iranian rights regarding her southern oil, which had been stipulated by the Law of 21 October 1947.[22] Hakimi's position according to Creswell and Seddon, the AIOC's chief representative in Tehran, was too uncertain to allow the return of N. A. Gass, the company's chief negotiator, to resume negotiations on the 'persian-ization' of the company's staff.[23] This was likely to weaken the Cabinet's image and self-confidence.

From the outset Hakimi's Cabinet had been subjected to pressures from the Russians, who regarded Hakimi as being 'very close' to the British and Americans, and 'notorious' for his enmity towards the Soviet Union.[24] They protested about the conclusion of an agreement between the Iranian and United States Governments to establish a military mission to work with the Iranian War Ministry and advise the Iranian army. The responsibility for the conclusion of this agreement, which was similar in substance to an unpublished agreement reached in late 1943, lay primarily with the Court. The agreement had been signed on 6 October 1947, towards the end of Qavam's last term of office, but Hakimi strongly supported it.

The agreement provided the American advisers with extensive privileges and prerogatives, and practically amounted to an entitle-ment to capitulatory rights.[25] The text of the agreement was published in Moscow,[26] and the Russians objected, among other things, to Article 24 which made the employment by the Iranian army of any foreign national conditional upon the consent of the Americans. Hakimi's Government rejected this protest and other objections and criticisms from within the country, and contemplated appealing to the UN.[27] Russian pressure was gradually relaxed, but the terms of the agreement remained unchanged.

An equally controversial issue which did not, however, attract similar attention was the renewal of the contract of the American mission in the Iranian gendarmerie due in October 1948. This contract, which had been concluded in November 1943, gave General Schwartzkopf, the head of the mission, 'actual command of the Gendarmerie', and the American Ambassador claimed to have 'from time to time shown attention to the incongruity of such an arrangement in peace time', and suggested that it 'be modified or terminated'.[28] He had reportedly invited the Iranian Government, both publicly and privately, to 'clarify its position' regarding the Schwartzkopf mission, and had emphasized that 'it must be an Iranian decision as to whether the contract should be continued as before, re-negotiated or terminated'.[29] Nevertheless he did not wholly refrain from discouraging any possible Iranian demand for the withdrawal of the American missions. He told Hakimi that any 'Iranian request for withdrawal of American missions would be interpreted by the American public as lack of interest by Iran in American assistance' Hakimi interrupted the Ambassador's statement several times to assure him that 'he strongly desired the retention of American advisers', and added that 'Iran could turn nowhere else for disinterested expert assistance'.[30]

Whatever the reasons, the Government did not opt to consider the termination or modification of its contract, which was renewed in September 1948.[31] American influence had been increasing since 1947 and was now consolidated. Hakimi had shown loyal friendship towards the Americans but could not claim to enjoy their active support.[32] The Americans favoured an effective administration capable of proceeding with reformist measures, particularly the Seven-year Plan.

Hakimi's precarious position in the Majlis arose mainly from his attitude to Qavam's followers, who were prepared to support the ratification of the Seven-year Plan Bill[33] but were likely to oppose Hakimi on any other issue. Far from attempting to appease the Iranian Democratic faction, Hakimi harassed Qavam's clients and expelled some of them from government departments. He also continued his efforts to dismantle the remnants of the Democratic Party of Iran, to invoke and amplify Qavam's corrupt practices and to resort to legal action in order to eliminate him from the political scene.[34]

Although Qavam's followers had failed to prevent the downfall of their patron, they were nevertheless highly capable of complicating the task of his successors. Faced with their opposition Hakimi needed to strengthen his relations with other factions. Yet he failed to enlist the steady support of the renegade ex-members of the Democratic Party of Iran; royalist deputies and other opponents of Qavam supported him only inconsistently and perfunctorily; and the National Union faction, consisting of a sizeable number of royalist deputies, was gradually turning towards the Iranian Democratic faction in order to work out a compromise on an alternative prime minister.[35]

Hoping to rally its supporters, the Cabinet now resorted to a policy of firmness and the enforcement of law and the order, which resulted, among other things, in the arrest and expulsion of Tudeh sympathizers from state factories on the Caspian littoral and elsewhere, and the arrest of some 500 people in the capital.[36] The Government also announced that martial law, only recently suspended, would be reimposed wherever deemed necessary. Such measures provoked journalists to hold large meetings in order to orchestrate counter-measures,[37] and were publicly used by opponents of the Government inside the Majlis to justify their opposition. The Cabinet was called upon to answer three motions of interpellation. In the event it was given a vote of confidence,[38] primarily because the choice of its successor or the timing of its fall had not yet been fully agreed upon.

On the basis of this unimpressive vote of confidence, the Cabinet proceeded to submit the Seven-year Plan Bill to the Majlis. In the hope of deflecting royal pressure for the revision of the Constitution, it also submitted a bill for the opening of the Senate.[39] It seemed that the Cabinet's self-confidence had increased, but in fact its position was soon damaged by a number of adverse developments. In early May Qavam returned from Europe after an absence of over four months.[40] Rumours were soon circulating that he had resumed his political activities, and that his relations with the Court and the deputies had improved, all of which encouraged his followers as much as it disheartened Hakimi.[41]

More immediately significant was the anticipated tension between Najm and Hazhir. Reacting to increased agitation about Bahrain, and more particularly the oil in the south, Najm contended in response to a Majlis question that Qavam's Government had done nothing about the oil issue and asserted that Hakimi's Government was prepared to deal with the issue within the framework of the concession which constituted the basis of the AIOC.[42] Hazhir, however, in response to an open letter by Iskandari, rejected Najm's assertion about the inaction of Qavam's Cabinet over the oil issue.[43] Najm's recognition of the despised and resented 1933 Oil Agreement annoyed most supporters of the Cabinet or gave them little option but to appear displeased.[44]

Even when the conflict between Najm and Hazhir was ostensibly settled,[45] it had shown that the Cabinet was far from co-ordinated on matters of policy and that it lacked one on oil. Disappointment with the Cabinet grew when some state employees went on strike, primarily over the removal of seniority rights granted by Qavam's Cabinet.[46] Dissatisfaction also spread to the wealthy strata who were not appeased by a bill to restrict to Iranian nationals the right to import foreign goods[47] and were apprehensive of the Cabinet's anti-corruption measures.[48] By early June the budget remained unapproved, expenditure continued to be financed on the basis of a monthly vote, the Seven-year Plan Bill was still being investigated by a Majlis committee, and factional manoeuvres to dislodge Hakimi were well under way.

On 8 June 1948 Hakimi attended the Majlis, gave an account of the achievements of his Cabinet and demanded a vote of confidence:[49] he received 38 votes, with 4 against and 43 abstentions. As was the usual practice, no reasons were provided for the shifting allegiances of the deputies and factions. Creswell, commenting on Hakimi's last days in office, reported 'The present spectacle is undignified in the extreme for the Government is not attacked on any specific measure nor even for its sins of omission; it is falling victim to backstairs intrigue by a number of Deputies.'[50] In the course of the twenty-three-week duration of Hakimi's Cabinet, disapproval and opposition were largely expressed through abstentions. It seemed that Iranian clan politics had exhausted itself to such an extent that enthusiasm was gradually giving way to cynicism and resignation in the face of royal rejection of politicians and prime-ministerial candidates whose differences were merely a matter of degree. The prevailing mode of politics could not allow anything other than an exhaustive stalemate, yet men who were at least potentially capable of arousing strong support and equally strong opposition were still to be brought to the fore by the force of circumstances.

13

The Government of Hazhir:
JUNE–NOVEMBER 1948

It had been assumed for some time that the new premier would be Hazhir, who was of course the Court's candidate but had also won over Qavam's followers, who expected him to be less hostile to their patron than would other potential candidates. Many royalist deputies and other opponents of Qavam now became less enthusiastic about Hazhir and, although Ashraf and her agents lobbied extensively in his favour,[1] on 13 June 1948 out of 120 deputies present in the Majlis, only 66 voted for him, while 43 cast their votes in favour of Sa'id, an alternative royal candidate.[2] Hazhir was called upon by the Shah to form a Cabinet, which he did against the background of several days of intensive campaigning, the closure of the bazaars and street demonstrations organized by Kashani and directed against the Prime Minister, which resulted in a considerable number of casualties.[3]

Born in Tehran in about 1895, Abdulhusain Hazhir became one of the youngest prime ministers of Iran. His father had been a servant of Muzaffar ud-Din Shah Qajar before joining the Ministry of Finance as a clerk.[4] Hazhir graduated from the School of Political Science, served in the Foreign Ministry and then joined the Russian Embassy as an interpreter. He subsequently re-entered the service of the Iranian Government, enlisting the favour of several politicians, including Mudarris, Taqizadih and especially Ali Akbar Davar, an influential politician of the Reza Shah era, who gave him 'various lucrative posts'.[5] Later he became the Head of the Industrial and Agricultural Bank, took up the portfolio of Commerce in Furughi's Cabinet in 1941, as well as other ministerial posts, particularly the portfolio of Finance, in later Cabinets.[6]

Hazhir was an intelligent, learned and hard-working man with a reputation for energy and resourcefulness, a keen interest in history and literature, and a good knowledge of Russian, English and French. He was, however, neither popular with the public at large, nor with older, more established politicians.[7] As a member of the younger generation of the Iranian ruling elite, a competent Finance Minister, an upholder of reformist ideas and, above all, a loyal and obedient royalist, he had appealed to the Court, where he in turn sought a secure base for the realization of his own ambitions.[8] In view of his general unpopularity, which was largely rooted in his suspected close links with the British, his premiership caused little joy among Iranians but great optimism among British officials. He was praised by Creswell for giving an impression of 'resolution and calmness' and 'an altogether un-Persian appreciation of the value of hard work'.[9]

Hazhir's Cabinet, which included four members of the previous Cabinet and four who were new to ministerial office, was on the whole more pro-British than its predecessors. The Cabinet programme included ambitious reform measures, promises and references to all major issues,[10] and was clearly intended to have widespread appeal. It was described by an ex-Prime Minister in the following way: 'Hazhir's programme is bulky and colourful; it has sufficient salt of reform, if the pepper of interpellation allows'.[11] Believing that the socio-economic situation of the country could not improve without adequate funds and foreign aid, Hazhir approached Creswell to enquire about the possibility of negotiating a credit of £10 million, to be spent on reducing inflation and executing the Seven-year Plan.[12] The British response was not positive,[13] nor was that of the Americans who had also been approached.[14] This was undoubtedly a source of disappointment for the Prime Minister and he did not pursue the issue further. By the end of June 1948 he seemed to have consolidated his position: his Cabinet programme had been approved and his Cabinet had received 88 votes out of 96.[15] The Cabinet was thus expected to proceed with some of its reformist and constructive objectives.

Optimism soon gave way to disillusionment, since from the beginning Hazhir showed an acute lack of resolution and self-confidence, a tendency to rely on others, especially the Court and the British, and a pathetic fear of his opponents. He frequently complained to the British Embassy about the machinations of Sayyid Zia, the activities of Kashani, whom he accused of being in contact with the Russians, and also about the manoeuvres of Qavam, whom he suspected of enjoying the favour of the Americans.[16] Creswell tried to encourage him and to 'dismiss from his mind any story of American interference' in Iranian politics. Hazhir's self-confidence, however, suffered a further blow when on 18 July the Shah left for Europe, including a trip to England.

Four days after the Shah's departure and some three weeks after Hazhir's Cabinet had been formally approved in the Majlis, Iskandari tabled a motion of interpellation against it.[17] This was soon followed by another motion tabled by Nasir Quli Ardalan, the deputy for Sanandaj, against the Government decree for exchange control.[18] Iskandari's eloquent and entertaining speeches against Hazhir, besides concentrating on Bahrain and southern oil, enumerated the many defects and problems of the country, and also listed the largest possible number of faults attributable to Hazhir and his Cabinet. Typically, he did not oppose Hazhir's Cabinet on any specific issue or policy, but rejected it in its entirety, consciously ignoring the fact that it had not as yet enjoyed any opportunity to assert itself, and disregarding the adverse consequences of Cabinet instability. In fact he stated that the frequent replacement of one Cabinet by another was characteristic of all parliamentary systems, and gave as an example the French Third Republic in which, according to him, the average life of Cabinets was seventy-five days.[19]

A few deputies did volunteer to speak, however feebly, for the Government, but even the speeches by Hazhir and his ministers lacked enthusiasm. A large number of deputies endorsed Iskandari's criticisms and few were prepared to dispute his emphasis on the issues of Bahrain and the southern oil. In view of the Shah's absence from the country for nearly six weeks (two weeks of which he spent in England pressing for military equipment, aid and even an alliance)[20] the Government was eventually given a 'silent' vote of confidence with no specific reference to the interpellation.[21] The Government had thus been effectively challenged before it had been allowed the chance to prove itself. Although the return of the Shah in late August helped to improve Hazhir's position in the Majlis, he showed no sign of realizing his reformist objectives or mustering a reliable majority among the deputies. As a former Finance Minister he was fully aware of the need for financial security to allow the Government to proceed with its tasks, and thus made the approval of the budget bill by the Majlis his main personal concern,[22] although the last full budget had been passed in 1943 and since then government expenditure had been met on the basis of monthly provisions. In other words the deputies had proved consistently unwilling to allow the Government any degree of real financial autonomy or security.

Hazhir, whose supporters in the Majlis were far fewer than

those of many of his predecessors, had thus in effect thwarted all his other objectives by starting with a measure which it was beyond his capacity to tackle. Against the well-argued speeches of Abulhasan Ha'irizadih and Taqizadih, who underlined numerous defects in the Cabinet's budget bill,[23] other deputies argued that a defective budget was better than no budget.[24] In the end, however, the budget bill remained unapproved, and Hazhir was prevented by his own actions from putting forward the Seven-year Plan and the labour bills.[25]

Hazhir was caught in the perennial dilemma of Iranian clan politics where inaction was normally more congenial to political survival and yet was inevitably regarded as a sign of weakness and incompetence. Positive action or firmness, on the other hand, would threaten the delicate balance of the competing clans and be considered a deviation from 'the law' or a move in the direction of 'dictatorship'. An ingenious, subtle combination of action and inaction had proved to be the optimal pragmatic response to such a mode of politics, but Hazhir lacked the imagination or experience for such an enterprise. He had been praised by Creswell as having 'a flair for the subtleties of political combinations on which the position of any Government' in Iran depended.[26] This assessment was subsequently proved to be unjustified.

On the last day of August 1948 the Cabinet decreed that government officials were no longer allowed to have direct commercial concern in or to own, edit or co-operate in the publication of newspapers.[27] The main aim of this move was to restrict the number of papers and to restrain the hostile tone of the press, in which a large number of government employees with access to confidential information were involved.[28] The move was seen as a blow against the free press while the Anglo-Iranian oil negotiations were in progress. Another motion of interpellation was brought against the Government by Abdulqadir Azad, the deputy for Sabzivar, to be debated following the conclusion of discussions on the budget bill.

In the hope of improving his relations with the deputies Hazhir reshuffled his Cabinet, bringing in three new ministers and personally assuming the portfolio of the Interior. This tactic was unsuccessful in convincing the disaffected deputies since the greatest source of tension and confrontation in the Majlis, and therefore the greatest problem for Hazhir, was the political future of Qavam. In July a Majlis committee set up especially to investigate the charges of corruption against Qavam voted in his favour,[29] and by the beginning of October the Justice Committee of the Majlis had almost unanimously voted for his acquittal.[30] Qavam's opponents, however, consisting of elements from most factions of the Majlis, led by the Mas'udi brothers and inspired and supported by the Court, continued to deploy every conceivable obstructive tactic to prevent his eventual acquittal by the Majlis. His supporters reacted by resorting to similar tactics against the Government for as long as the fate of their patron remained in abeyance. Hazhir was personally willing to compromise with Qavam, and there were even rumours that on Qavam's resumption of office he would serve as the latter's Finance Minister.[31] He also regretted the mutual estrangement of Qavam and the Shah, and seemed to believe that the Shah would eventually have no choice but to come to terms with Qavam.[32] Yet compromise with Qavam and aiding his acquittal would imply his formal return to the political scene and entail the alienation or enmity of the Court and the anti-Qavam deputies. Hazhir's only alternative was to acquiesce in a hopeless and debilitating parliamentary deadlock.

The 'spectre' of Qavam continued to haunt his opponents within the Majlis and outside it, as well as the feeble Government of Hazhir. Qavam's personality, his revitalized clan, his network of newspapers and the conspicuous incompetence or failure of his rivals all helped to re-establish him as the person most able to tackle the existing problems. Opponents of Hazhir and many who did not favour a Shah-sponsored, Court-dominated Cabinet had gathered around Qavam, and there were even reports that his former opponents, such as Taqizadih and Ali Mansur, an ex-Prime Minister and a prime-ministerial candidate, were in touch with him.[33] Similarly, the American State Department had also decided that 'there was little likelihood of any stability in Persia unless and until' Qavam returned.[34]

The Court, however, was not prepared to countenance Qavam's formal re-entry to the ranks of prime-ministerial candidates, and continued to prevent any settlement of the anti-Qavam charges in the Majlis. Since his return from Europe Qavam had had several lengthy meetings with the Shah,[35] but the gap between them remained unbridgeable. The Shah was as adamant as ever that neither Qavam nor any other prime minister independent of the Court was acceptable. In his view, effective government would be attained not by restraining the Court's interference in political and administrative matters, but by a formal increase in the range of the monarch's legal authority. Parliamentary stalemate was created as much by the Court's activities as by the constitutional premises or personal and sectional preoccupations of the deputies, but it was effectively used by the Shah to justify his insistence on the need to revise the Constitution.

The Shah seemed to be more concerned to gain the support or acquiescence of the British and American officials than of Iranian politicians, although the British, however sympathetic to the royal objective of administrative efficiency, did not condone his proposed means of realizing it, nor his timing of it. They hoped that reform measures such as the Seven-year Plan would improve the situation and diminish the need to change the Constitution.[36] Gradually, however, the position of the British and even the American Ambassador softened. By October 1948 Le Rougetel had concluded that 'no real progress' was likely to be made without constitutional changes of some kind.[37] In his view the attitude of the Majlis was 'not merely frivolous', it was 'criminal',[38] and 'the most dangerous course of all for the British to take', he asserted, was 'to perpetuate or even to acquiesce in the present sinister stalemate'.[39] The Foreign Office, however, recommended delaying consideration of the constitutional revision until the approval or rejection of the Seven-year Plan, and advised a cautious approach by the Shah following proper consultation with Iranian politicians.[40] The American State Department, on the other hand, did not believe that any radical revision of the Constitution was needed unless the stability of the country should be 'seriously endangered by subversive movements or any other event which made an increase in the Shah's constitutional powers essential'.[41]

None of this deterred the Shah, who told Le Rougetel that 'he absolutely refused to acquiesce any longer in the present deplorable state of the country'; that he was contemplating assigning Hazhir the task of informing the deputies to arrange for the revision of the Constitution; and that he would abdicate if they did not agree with his objective.[42] The Majlis was informed of the Shah's plans, but even had Hazhir been capable of effectuating the Shah's aims he did not consider the timing to be auspicious.[43]

Hazhir's position in the Majlis was precarious because the consideration of his budget bill was still in process and the interpellation by Azad had not been debated. Nikpay told Le Rougetel in late October that the Shah's patience was exhausted and if Hazhir did not soon succeed in pushing his budget bill through the Majlis he was to resign and probably be replaced by Sa'id, who would arrange for the convening of the Constituent Assembly.[44] Hazhir was thus under pressure from all sides. Not even the royalists in the Majlis gave him unconditional support, while his opponents dismissed him as a Court-imposed Prime Minister. In the elections for the Speaker of the Majlis a large number of deputies expressed their displeasure with the Shah's intended designs regarding the Constitution by not voting for the re-election of the Court-sponsored Reza Hikmat but for Taqizadih, who had adopted a critical attitude toward Hazhir and, by implication, toward royal behaviour.[45] Dissatisfaction with the Shah was more evident in the parliamentary paralysis in which Hazhir had become submerged: formally supported by a large majority, he lacked real majority support and received no respite from criticism and frequent interpellation.

One major issue which Hazhir could have used to good effect in order to gain support was the oil–Bahrain problem, but even if he had been willing he was neither capable of taking a firm stand nor did he consider it feasible. Alienation of the British was too high a price to pay for gaining support inside the country, and Hazhir did nothing apart from paying lip-service to the issue and occasionally airing privately some of the Iranian complaints about the AIOC.[46] On his assumption of office he had assured Creswell that he would favour the resumption of negotiations with the AIOC 'on the clear understanding that he in no way challenged or disputed the validity of the concession itself'[47] and he was even prepared to admit this publicly.[48] He took the precaution of conducting oil negotiations in an atmosphere of secrecy, but after the resignation in mid-October of his newly appointed Finance Minister, Muhammad Ali Varastih, who headed the Iranian negotiating committee, Hazhir had great difficulty convincing his opponents that his oil negotiations had not failed.[49]

Hazhir's failure to establish a credible image for himself lay primarily in the fact that he was a protégé of the Court and a loyal friend of the British. He himself suspected the Americans of regarding him as unduly pro-British. When General Schwartzkopf was withdrawn from the command of the gendarmerie and replaced by a colonel with 'purely advisory functions', and the head of the American military mission was changed, this was taken by some sectors of the American press as a sign of the pro-British attitudes of Hazhir's Government.[50] Hazhir complained to both the Americans and the British about the American attitude,[51] which he interpreted as a preference for Qavam and this aggravated his crisis of self-confidence.[52] Hazhir showed interest in resuming normal relations with the Russians, and in his meetings with Sadchikov exhibited a willingness to resume the Iran–Soviet trade talks, which had begun in May 1948 and continued intermittently.[53] He also met two leaders of the Tudeh Party who offered him a twelve-point programme for the restoration of 'internal political equilibrium and of friendly relations with the Soviet Union'.[54] In the end, however, he did not succeed in eliciting the friendship of the leftist intelligentsia, or even in reducing their enmity.

Nor did Hazhir's traditionalist or religiously inspired enemies relax their hostility towards him. By including opposition to the partition of Palestine in his Cabinet programme, enforcing the public observance of fasting with 'unusual severity', restricting the sale of food and alcohol during Ramazan, banning the sale of alcohol in Mashhad and Qum,[55] and attempting to facilitate the pilgrimage to Mecca,[56] Hazhir hoped to defuse religiously inspired agitation. Of course these measures were counterproductive since they were regarded as both hypocritical and signs of weakness.[57]

By early November it was obvious that Hazhir was in no position to push through the Majlis his budget bill or any other measure. Le Rougetel had learned from 'an excellent authority' that following the conclusion of debates on the motion of interpellation tabled by Azad, and irrespective of the result, Hazhir would resign and the Shah would recommend Sa'id as his successor.[58] On 4 November 1948 the debate on Azad's motion culminated in a vote of confidence for Hazhir's Government of 67 votes to 7, with 13 abstentions. This result, however, had been overshadowed by a BBC news broadcast of the previous day. Commenting on the private visit to London of Musa Nuri-Isfandiari, the Iranian Minister for Foreign Affairs, the BBC announced that he would be holding negotiations with Bevin on the 'proposed revision of the Iranian Constitution'.[59] Although repeatedly denied by the BBC and the Iranian Government, the report caused widespread agitation in the Iranian political arena and constituted an embarrassing setback for the Shah, who now had far more difficulty convincing Iranians that his plans for the Constitution were not entirely British inspired. The repercussions of the BBC broadcast proved to be the death blow for Hazhir's Cabinet.

The high hopes for Hazhir's premiership were reduced to enormous disappointment, and this only confirmed the inefficiency of the existing constitutional arrangements. Hazhir was not a skilful manipulator nor was he capable of perceptive initiatives. His paralysing fear of his adversaries and of the possible effects of his actions pushed him into self-defeating passivity. His indecisive character and susceptibility to self-doubt prevented him from counteracting the discomfiting flux of loyalties and intricate manoeuvres of his opponents and even his supporters. As a Court protégé he had no way of asserting himself as a credible patron, and was in any case devoid of those qualities which inspired loyalty, respect and a sustained clientele. Although he possessed those characteristics which clan politics favoured or allowed, he was constrained by the conflict between the clans of the Shah and Qavam, and the efforts of the former to legitimize royal hegemony and of the latter to remove the obstacles in the way of his own formal return to the political scene.

14

The Government of Sa'id:
NOVEMBER 1948–MARCH 1950

On 7 November 1948, the day after the resignation of Hazhir's Cabinet, on the recommendation of Le Rougetel, representatives of the various Majlis factions were called to the royal palace for consultation and the immediate selection of the next prime minister.[1] Subsequently, in defiance of the established practice, that is without a proper and formal 'vote of inclination' by the Majlis, Muhammad Sa'id was assigned to form a Cabinet. Following his resignation from the premiership in November 1944, Sa'id had turned to business before being elected as a deputy for Reza'iyyih (in Azarbaijan) in the 15th Majlis, and he was still a deputy when asked to form a Cabinet. Sa'id was to rely for support on the National Union faction, which contained a large number of royalist deputies and in which he himself had been a prominent figure. Nevertheless the way in which he had been appointed not only resulted in widespread press criticism,[2] but also dismayed most deputies who resented the gradual erosion of the legislature's authority.

In order to compensate for the manner of his appointment, Sa'id tried to select his colleagues in a way that would satisfy, or at least not provoke, most factions;[3] but when he attended the Majlis to introduce his Cabinet on 18 November, there was no quorum.[4] Since this was unprecedented in the history of Iranian constitutionalism, Sa'id's ministers handed in their resignations. These were not accepted and after three days of extensive lobbying and pressure Sa'id formally introduced his Cabinet to the Majlis.[5] Eventually on 8 December, after a well-argued though protracted criticism of Sa'id's Cabinet programme and his ability and competence by Deputy Ahmad Razavi – which provoked a vitriolic counter-attack[6] – he succeeded in gaining only 56 votes, with 37 abstentions and 2 against, while 30 deputies stayed away. The Shah immediately began consultations with Le Rougetel as to a successor,[7] but the absence of a viable alternative candidate gave Sa'id the chance to broaden the basis of support for his Cabinet in the Majlis and strengthen his own position.

The prolonged confrontation between Qavam's supporters and opponents in the Majlis, however, constrained Sa'id in the same way as it had Hazhir; and although it had enabled the Court to keep Qavam out of power this had been at the cost of legislative paralysis. For different reasons both Sa'id and the two contending groups wanted the problem resolved and eventually, on 22 December 1948, representatives of the two factions signed a formal agreement of understanding.[8] The most tangible result of this development was the ratification, with 90 votes, of the budget bill for the four remaining months of the Iranian year 1327 (March 1948–March 1949). This temporarily relieved the Government of dependence on the Majlis for the formal provision of its expenditure, and also removed a potential weapon to bring about its downfall.[9]

Of course these developments and Sa'id's role in them did not please the Shah, whose major preoccupation continued to be the revision of the Constitution. Yet, if Sa'id were to remain in office, he could not have feasibly followed an alternative course of action. The Shah, however, now believed that Sa'id was not unwilling but unable to arrange for the constitutional changes, and thus there was an urgent need for a 'strong government'. The Shah and Le Rougetel consulted together on all public matters and apparently had a cordial relationship. In one of their meetings the Shah discussed the idea of promoting the premiership of Ali Mansur, a former Prime Minister,[10] and, along with Le Rougetel, also seemed to favour the appointment of Taqizadih, at least as the Minister of the Interior.[11]

The Shah hoped to exploit Taqizadih's prestige as one of the architects of the Iranian Constitution, and to persuade him to join the Cabinet or assume the premiership and arrange for the constitutional revision.[12] The choice of Taqizadih, even as Interior Minister, was strongly opposed by some influential courtiers, and he himself advocated the retention of Sa'id.[13] However, he now seemed willing to co-operate with the Shah over the revision of the Constitution, but was not prepared to accept executive responsibility when such a plan was being realized.[14]

Officials at the British Foreign Office and the US State Department continued to give careful consideration to the issue of the revision of the Constitution. While the British had to some extent relaxed their attitudes, they still advocated restraint and caution. They saw the revision of the Constitution as a last resort, and tried to persuade the

Shah to limit his objectives initially to the convening of the Senate.[15] While accepting in principle the need to revise the Constitution, Le Rougetel stressed the importance of the right manner and timing and recommended concentrating on the Senate and consulting elder Iranian politicians. This was a line agreed by the Foreign Office, and Hazhir, who had now become one of the most trusted confidants of the Shah, shared similar views.

The Shah himself did not feel confident enough to proceed without at least tacit Anglo-American approval. He was therefore biding his time and was busy canvassing the approval and support of his advisers. The opportunity to proceed with the plan arose when, on 4 February 1949, the Shah narrowly escaped an assassination attempt while attending a ceremony at Tehran University. The Tudeh Party as a whole was implicated in the incident but, according to some members of the Party, only Kianuri among the leaders supported the attempt and he had acted without the knowledge of his colleagues.[16] The event created an atmosphere of urgency which the Shah was quick to exploit, and Le Rougetel now became convinced that failure on the part of the Shah to take decisive action would 'probably entail the overthrow of the present regime within the next few months'.[17] The Foreign Office and State Department were less convinced,[18] but Le Rougetel emphasized that the Shah was in no mood to take advice.[19] Primarily as a means of forcing his foreign and domestic advisers to provide him with full support the Shah invoked the threat of the dissolution of the Majlis. The issue now was not how to restrain the Shah from any action but how to prevent the dissolution of the Majlis, which the British and Americans both opposed.

Similarly, both Hakimi and Sayyid Muhammad Sadiq Tabataba'i – an ex-Speaker of the Majlis – who were among the main consultants of the Shah over the proposed revision of the Constitution and had been invited to form a Cabinet, refused to do so unless he dropped the idea of the dissolution of the Majlis.[20] A proposal made by Hazhir, by which the Shah would proceed with his plan for the Constitution but not the dissolution of the Majlis, proved acceptable to the Shah as well as to Le Rougetel and the American chargé d'affaires.[21] While emphasizing the need to consult elder statesmen, the Foreign Office endorsed the appointment of a 'strong government' which would proceed with the aim of convening the Constituent Assembly while trying to enlist the approval of the Majlis or to ensure its neutrality.[22]

The appointment of a 'strong government', which was a euphemism for a government loyal to the Shah and capable of realizing his objectives with regard to the Constitution, was bound to be regarded publicly as a move to undermine constitutionalism. The appointment of such a government did not appeal to the Americans, who were concerned about the internal and external repercussions, and advocated compliance with 'proper constitutional procedures'.[23] The Shah for his part was indecisive as to the choice of Sa'id's successor, and in any case there were not many volunteers capable of forming a strong government. On the other hand, the abortive attempt on the Shah's life had strengthened Sa'id's position and disheartened his opponents.

From the outset of his second term as Prime Minister Sa'id had been even more vulnerable than his predecessors with respect to the oil issue. Assertions made in an interview with Reuters, amounting to an unequivocal recognition of the increasingly disputed 1933 Oil Agreement,[24] resulted in the tabling of a motion of interpellation against the Cabinet by Iskandari, who threatened to leave the Majlis if Sa'id's position were consolidated by the deputies.[25] Iskandari's arguments and their impact on the deputies persuaded Taqizadih, who had been Finance Minister in 1933, to disclose in the Majlis the circumstances under which the Agreement had been concluded, revealing that he and others who had opposed the extension of the period of the concession had been reduced to acting as little more than helpless accomplices in the hands of Reza Shah, 'the almighty ruler of that time'.[26] This excited widespread attention and greatly weakened the prospects for the kind of settlement which the British desired.[27] It also strengthened the force of Iskandari's interpellation, which in any case had the agreement of many deputies.

From Sa'id's point of view the attempt on the Shah's life came at just the right time. It saved him from confrontation with an openly hostile Majlis, and enabled his Government to consolidate its position by resorting to firm measures against its opponents: martial law was reimposed, the Tudeh Party was proscribed,[28] journalists who had been disrespectful of the Court were arrested, trials were held, many politicians were detained, and Kashani was exiled abroad. The deputies were inevitably forced into retreat, Iskandari's motion was ruled out, another motion tabled by Rahimian was withdrawn, and the Government was offered an overwhelming vote of confidence. In addition the Seven-year Plan Bill was approved, the duration of deputies' speeches was restricted (a measure which the

Government had previously tried to push through the Majlis), and a new press bill was eventually ratified. Above all, the deputies felt unable to reject the Shah's projected convening of the Constituent Assembly, and even went as far as to endorse the plan in writing.[29] Sa'id thus emerged as evidently capable of combining readiness to comply with the Shah's objectives with a measure of decisiveness. He was able to overshadow those of his characteristics which had led the Shah to consider the appointment of another prime minister.

After strongly contested and sometimes scandalous elections conducted under martial law, a Constituent Assembly was eventually convened, and met from 21 April to 11 May 1949. It adopted a modified version of the views advocated by Taqizadih by attaching an article to the Constitution envisaging an arrangement for all future constitutional changes.[30] It also revised Article 48 of the Constitution and empowered the Shah to dissolve the Majlis. The task of revising those articles of the Constitution concerned with the internal procedural reform of the Majlis such as the quorum rule was, however, left to the two houses of the Parliament.[31]

It now seemed that the Shah had succeeded in ending that phase of Iranian constitutionalism which had been characterized by parliamentary chaos and inefficiency, and this was regarded as a positive or in any case inevitable development.[32] However, the revision of the Constitution did not mark the end of constitutional conflict between the Majlis and the Crown, particularly since modification of the regulations regarding the conduct of the deputies had yet to be accomplished. Prior to the opening of the Constituent Assembly, a number of deputies – notably Baqa'i, Makki and Ha'irizadih – had recovered from their shock at the assassination attempt and its repercussions and succeeded in using the widespread resentment over the way in which the elections for the Assembly had been conducted, as well as harassment of real or suspected opponents of the Government and the Court, in order to table motions of interpellation.[33] The target of attack was the Government, and in particular Iqbal, the Interior Minister and a self-confessed Court protégé, whose crusade against the Tudeh Party and insistence on dismissing teachers suspected of left-wing tendencies had disrupted the country's educational system; and General Razmara, the Chief of Staff, who had effectively used the attempt on the Shah's life to increase his own power and strengthen his links with the Court by manipulating the elections and suppressing opposition.

The deputies had clearly not overcome their fears and the

Government – without being able to disarm or convincingly answer its critics – won a vote of confidence of 90 out of 96 in late April 1949.[34] Two weeks later the Senate bill submitted by Hakimi a year earlier was also approved.[35] Now the Government appeared to be well established and the Majlis, which was soon to expire, posed no real threat. The main concern of the deputies was the elections for the 16th Majlis scheduled to start in early August. The deputies' pre-election concerns, notably their desire not to jeopardize their chances of re-election, provided an opportunity for the submission to the Majlis of bills which normally would have provoked controversy or widespread opposition. A number of deputies, notably Taqizadih and Matin-Daftari, tried to push through the Majlis a new electoral bill, similar in substance to that previously advocated by Musaddiq, and in effect excluding the illiterate from voting, which it was insisted should be direct and secret.[36] The reading of this bill proceeded smoothly, but the term of the 15th Majlis expired before its final approval.

Taking advantage of the deputies' desire to avoid controversy in the pre-election period, the Government tried to push through the Majlis the Gass-Gulsha'iyan Supplemental Agreement, which did not revise the 1933 Oil Agreement but simply increased royalties paid to the Iranian Government.[37] British officials had over-optimistically expected this to be approved, but soon discovered that even some members of the Government considered it inadequate, were actually opposed to it, or very reluctant to be seen supporting it.[38] After lengthy negotiations and pressure, however, and in view of the seeming inflexibility of the British, the Government felt that it had little choice but to submit the Agreement to the Majlis and try to gain its approval. With the support of Baqa'i, Ha'irizadih and Azad, however, Makki interpellated the Government.[39] His skilful fili-bustering, helped by the emotional performance of Dr. Abdullah Mu'azzami which moved several deputies to weep audibly,[40] prevented a vote being taken on the Agreement, which was talked out until the Majlis formally expired on 28 July 1949.[41]

This was a setback for the Government, and more so for the British, who nevertheless were soothed by the Shah's frequent assertions that, following the approval of its own procedural reform, the Majlis would pass the Oil Agreement. The Shah's optimism regarding the next Majlis was mainly rooted in his intention to prevent the election of 'candidates whose aims' were known to be 'subversive'.[42] Hazhir, who had been appointed Court Minister on

20 July 1949, tried his best on several occasions to enlist the approval of the British Embassy for this strategy and to draw the attention of Lawford, the British *chargé d'affaires*, to the importance for the British of a 'Majlis being elected which would be as favourable as possible to the ratification of the Oil Agreement'.[43] Hazhir even asked Lawford whether the British had 'any suggestion' as to what should be done about members of the former Majlis who had opposed the Oil Agreement. Lawford, however, was fully aware that despite the efforts of the Shah and Hazhir to exclude what they regarded as unsuitable elements from the Majlis, as far as the Oil Agreement was concerned the next Majlis was likely to be 'as intractable as the last'.[44] He recognized that even those Iranians regarded as pro-British, not only by their fellow countrymen but also by Le Rougetel, were demanding more 'sacrifices' by the AIOC.[45] The Foreign Office and the oil company, however, singularly failed to appreciate the symbolic and emotive significance of the oil issue and its crucial role in the revival of Iranian nationalism. They remained adamant in their resolve to continue with their 'firm' policy and to insist on an early discussion of the oil issue by the next Majlis.

The Government of Sa'id had no clear electoral policy, but its primary aim, championed by Iqbal and Hazhir, was to prevent the election of 'undesirable elements'. In early August the Shah entrusted Sayyid Muhammad Sadiq Tabataba'i with the task of arranging the elections for the Majlis and the Senate.[46] This provoked the deep resentment of Iqbal, who complained bitterly to a member of the British Embassy that Tabataba'i was a nepotist and an incompetent opium addict, and Reza Hikmat – who was to co-operate with Tabataba'i – a 'criminal'.[47] The appointment of Tabataba'i was intended to lend an air of credibility to the elections. The Government also gave repeated public assurances concerning electoral freedom.[48] Yet gross irregularities and manipulation by the governmental and military authorities provoked widespread complaints and growing protests.

The Government's patent inability to refute the charges of electoral misconduct provided Musaddiq with a rallying point. Accompanied by a group of nineteen politicians and journalists selected from a large number of people who had gathered in response to his call, he resorted to the tactic which he and some of his colleagues had used during the elections for the 15th Majlis. They expressed their intention to take sanctuary in the royal palace as a sign of protest and, if refused, in a mosque.[49] Musaddiq's popularity among the politically active elements in Tehran soon transformed the protesters into an effective pressure group which the Government was unable to suppress or ignore.

Hazhir tried in vain to enlist the support or approval of Lawford to deal with the protesters firmly, but was advised that the Government should not appear to be 'frightened of demagogues' and that the arrest of the protesters might turn them into martyrs.[50] Very reluctantly the Shah accepted them into the palace,[51] although he rejected their criticisms of the elections.[52] After four days the group left the palace, still expressing its deep alarm at the Government's intention to stage-manage the elections in order to reach an agreement with the AIOC.[53] Undeterred by the apparent lack of success the group attempted to formalize its structure, calling itself the Jibhih-yi Milli, or National Front,[54] and set itself the task of concentrating on crucial issues such as the freedom of elections, freedom of the press and the abolition of martial law.[55]

It may appear paradoxical that Musaddiq and his followers should have appealed to the Shah who, in their view, was guilty of open abuse of the principles of parliamentarianism by proceeding with the revision of the Constitution.[56] Yet in the absence of the Majlis they had no alternative; moreover, without entertaining any illusion about the Shah's democratic convictions, they resorted to this tactic as an effective method of publicly testing the Shah's professed attachment to democratic principles. The acceptance of the demands of Musaddiq and his co-protesters would have been a major setback for the Shah, while their rejection would constitute clear confirmation of the Court's identification with the worst aspects of the ruling elite. In the face of growing nationalist sentiments the Court was faced with a real dilemma; nor could it easily circumvent the mobilized public opinion to which it was increasingly exposed.

Musaddiq's appeal to the Shah was thus aimed at persuading him to endorse publicly his desired image as the guardian of constitutional principles and thereby leave him little choice but to comply, at least ostensibly, with his constitutionally prescribed role.[57] It was primarily inspired not by what the Shah actually represented but by what he ought to have represented: an impartial arbiter or supervisor of the correspondence between the actual practices of government institutions and the formal constitutional laws and premises. Although Musaddiq and his supporters were not immediately successful, resentment at the Government's electoral misconduct, particularly the activities of the General Staff in imposing candidates, continued to increase, along with calls for the replacement of Iqbal. Numerous petitions were made and the frequent outbreaks of violent clashes in the provinces were widely reported in the press.[58] City-dwellers were both unenthusiastic about participating in the elections and sceptical about the impact of their votes given the overt manipulation of village voters, who were transported to the polling stations in droves by the agents of the parliamentary candidates. Even less enthusiasm was shown in the first-stage elections for the Senate, which had begun in late August.[59]

While the Court, the Government and the army were not prepared to change their strategy, they were fully aware of the potential danger of the situation. Hazhir tried to rush through the opening of the Majlis before the departure of the Shah to the United States, scheduled for 14 November 1949, but the slowness of the electoral process prevented this. The Government remained incapable of dealing with the situation and, since it had no existence independent of the Court, the blame for its performance was largely attributed to the Shah, who had ignored the voices of protest and failed to dissociate himself from the Government's unpopular measures.

Resentment against the Court was not confined to those outside the conventional ruling elite. Jamal Imami, who had been Minister without Portfolio in the Cabinet, told a member of the British Embassy that Sa'id's Government was 'a travesty of Government', in which he and his colleagues were ministers 'in name only, without power or opportunity to achieve anything'.[60] Ali Asghar Hikmat, Foreign Minister and Acting Prime Minister in the absence of Sa'id who was on a two-week private visit to London (beginning on 11 October 1949), was even more explicit. He complained bitterly to Le Rougetel not only about the elections, but also that the Shah controlled everything with no pretence of consulting or informing him. Hikmat listed the causes of the Shah's unpopularity, including the return to the Shah's control of the lands confiscated by his father, the 'increasing dislike' inspired by the Shah's 'immediate entourage' and the appointment of a certain 'unpopular person' to an important position in the royal household.[61]

These comments were directed at the Ashraf clique and the appointment of Hazhir, one of its most prominent members, to the position of Court Minister. Princess Ashraf was notorious for her appetite for power and glamour and her penchant for intrigue, and was the patroness of a group of dynamic, ambitious but generally unprincipled young men which, besides Hazhir, included the highly unpopular Iqbal and Khusrau Hidayat, the organiser of the government-sponsored labour union (ISKI), as well as Abulhasan Ibtihaj, the Governor of the National Bank.[62] These men served Ashraf in exchange for protection and actual or potential favours. She was the focal point of a political clan which was able to manipulate the Shah and influence the politics of the Court in alliance with or against its other cliques; a clan which directly affected government policies and the allocation of political spoils. The incessant intrigues of Ashraf eventually resulted in the removal of the respected elderly Court Minister Mahmud Jam, who had to some extent restrained the excesses of the royal family.[63] Long before his formal appointment, Jam's successor, Hazhir, was already effectively acting as Court Minister.

Hazhir's life, however, was brought to an abrupt end by an assassin from the Fida'iyan-i Islam while he was attending a religious ceremony at one of the main mosques in Tehran.[64] Le Rougetel observed that at Hazhir's funeral government officials appeared deeply anxious, while the crowd were jubilant.[65] Hazhir's adherence to Islam was questioned, but he was hated more because of his ostentatious royalism, and his identification with the worst aspects of the Court and the Government. Moreover, he was so pro-British that he often appeared to be more concerned with British interests than the British Embassy itself. Hazhir was even disliked by many members of the ruling elite, including some of the most loyal advisers of the Shah. Hakimi told Le Rougetel that the death of Hazhir caused little regret because he was 'considered to have been inordinately ambitious and to have completely over-reached himself', and also because he was engaged in a 'feud' with the *mullahs*.[66] Hakimi also commented with regret on the influence of Ashraf and the fact that she refused to go abroad.

Hazhir's assassination was a severe blow to the Court, however, and particularly to the Shah who, as Le Rougetel put it, no longer had anyone 'to speak for him'. In the Ambassador's view, the Prime Minister was 'old, tired and in poor health'; his Government, with the exception of one or two ministers was 'incompetent even for Persia'; and the 'eminently competent' Chief of Staff, Razmara, was 'at daggers drawn with the Minister of War'.[67] The Government, however, took advantage of the death of Hazhir to reassert itself by a show of firmness: Razmara took military precautions to ward off any threat of disorder, opposition politicians were detained, Musaddiq was asked to move to his estate outside the capital, and the Tehran elections, in which Musaddiq and some of his followers were initially successful, were annulled.[68] This last move was presented as the Government's response to criticisms of election-rigging, while the real aim was to arrange for the election of some of its own candidates. By way of conciliatory moves, General Zahidi, who seemed sympathetic to the National Front, was appointed Chief of Police,[69] and the restrictions imposed on Musaddiq and some of his followers were removed.[70] In the event the Government failed to block their election.

Hazhir's assassination occurred only ten days before the scheduled royal trip to the United States and left the Shah uncertain about whether to depart. The monarch was still preoccupied with the idea of securing a strong government, either by replacing Sa'id and appointing him as a senator or, alternatively, by strengthening Sa'id's position by bringing in new ministers. To his dismay he could find no distinguished personality prepared to take part in the Government and was therefore uneasy about leaving the country.[71]

Le Rougetel had considered it unwise, even before Hazhir's death and more so after it, for the Shah to leave the country. He tried to persuade him that his visit should at least be as short as possible and to some extent even enlisted the agreement of the American Ambassador.[72] However, prevailing assumptions about the intense conflict of interest and rivalries between the Americans and the British in Iran,[73] to which the Shah also readily subscribed, meant that Le Rougetel's discouragement would be interpreted as an indication of British disapproval of royal efforts to get close to the Americans.[74] In the face of all these adversities, however, the Shah appointed a Regency Council and Hakimi as Court Minister, and went ahead with his trip, hoping perhaps that this would be taken as a reassurance that all was normal.[75]

Coming so soon after the attempt on the Shah's life, Hazhir's death and the popular response to it discouraged most politicians, including Sa'id and his colleagues, from adopting or endorsing policies which openly contravened popular demands and expectations. The need to show his commitment to legality, combined with his own moderate temperament, also prevented Sa'id from openly using coercive measures against the Government's opponents. The Government, although it had all too soon been relieved of the burden of the Majlis, had proved incapable of projecting an image of self-assertiveness, and simply relied on a strategy of avoidance. This was how it dealt with the charges of election rigging, and the threatened breakdown of the country's transport system. The Seven-year Plan had still to be implemented,[76] and most importantly the increasingly significant oil issue remained on the agenda after the Government's abortive attempt at a solution.

In other words the Government had not even impressed its own supporters. Hakimi confided to Le Rougetel that Sa'id lacked the necessary physical and moral energy, and that his Cabinet was a combination of nonentities, including men such as Iqbal who was as unpopular as Hazhir and might be the next head to roll.[77] Le Rougetel's own assessment of the Cabinet was much the same and, in fact, concurred with the Shah's views. Whatever his views, however, the Shah only paid lip-service to the necessity for strong government, while his strategy was to tolerate governments which differed little from that of Sa'id. Le Rougetel now regarded such a strategy as extremely dangerous given the existing socio-political problems, and demanded Foreign Office authorization to veto weak prime-ministerial candidates proposed by the Shah.[78] The Foreign Office agreed that there should be a strong government, and implicitly agreed to the Ambassador's demand by leaving it to his discretion as to how to handle the situation.[79]

Among the candidates for the premiership, the British favoured Sayyid Zia who was in close touch with Embassy officials. Although he was 'unfortunately' opposed to the Seven-year Plan,[80] this was not enough to make him less desirable as prime minister. Indeed Le Rougetel regarded him as 'one of the few, in fact the only, outstanding personality in public life who is both competent, honest and sincere'[81] – a modest appraisal in comparison with what many other British officials had said about him.[82] Le Rougetel missed no opportunity to promote him as prime minister or at least as a member of the Government. It is difficult to explain the remarkable unconcern on the part of the British about the popular response to the premiership of Sayyid Zia, which would certainly be hostile, regarding his appointment as an outright attempt to settle the oil issue to the benefit of the British. Following the attempt on the Shah's life, Sayyid Zia had improved his relations with the Court, but since he did not attempt to hide his disapproval of the Shah's increased power and undue intervention in governmental affairs, the Shah was not prepared to accept his premiership.[83]

The other main contender was of course Qavam who, following the suspension of charges brought against him in the Majlis, and despite old age and ill-health, which necessitated frequent journeys abroad, was one of the most dynamic and powerful candidates, with extensive contacts and a large following. But the Shah was adamantly against his premiership, and in this he was supported by the British.[84] The British were prepared to accept Ali Mansur who had been manoeuvring for the premiership for months and, despite some reservations, the Shah seemed reasonably well disposed towards him.

One of the main considerations in the selection of the premier was the oil question, and the Shah believed that Sa'id was perhaps the only person prepared to put the Oil Agreement before the Majlis.[85] The Shah used this argument in an attempt to convince Le Rougetel of the wisdom of retaining Sa'id; but not only was the latter generally incompetent, he was also anxious to resign, and simply awaited royal permission.[86] In line with his policy of favouring tame and loyal candidates the Shah presented Le Rougetel with a list of names but was told that 'none of them would be an improvement on Sa'id; indeed quite the contrary'. Le Rougetel reminded the Shah that this was no time for experimentation and stressed that a 'real leader' must be found.[87]

Mansur was high if not top of the list of candidates for the job. However, on his return from the United States the Shah announced a 'campaign against corruption', with 'work' and 'unity' as his main slogans; and insisted that Mansur's 'lack of integrity' ruled him out. Until the Majlis and the Senate were reconvened it was agreed to retain Sa'id and strengthen his Cabinet with the inclusion of young men recruited from outside the 'accepted ministerial clique'.[88] The reshuffled Cabinet was announced in mid-January 1950 and closely corresponded with the Shah's preferences; it included four new ministers and 'anti-corruption' formed a major feature of its programme. As a further conciliatory gesture to the opposition, Iqbal was demoted and appointed Minister of Roads and Communications. The Shah informed Lawford that he wished to allow Sa'id to submit the Oil Agreement to the new Majlis,[89] and again asked for some modifications by the British, but to no avail. While admitting that Sa'id was incapable of managing the Government, the Shah continued to assert that he was, nevertheless, perhaps the only prime minister prepared to take the Oil Agreement to the Majlis. His consistent support for Sa'id was rendered paradoxical or absurd by his admission of Sa'id's shortcomings. Yet the Shah could not get the co-operation of Le Rougetel in the selection of Court-favoured prime-ministerial candidates and was, therefore, trying his best to provide arguments for Sa'id's retention which would appeal to the British.

The 16th Majlis and the Senate were formally opened on 9 February 1950, and according to usual practice the Cabinet resigned, to await the verdict of the Majlis. The Shah, in a move to reaffirm his enhanced prerogatives, proceeded to invite Sa'id to form a Cabinet once again, without awaiting the 'vote of inclination' of the deputies.[90] Although the elections in Tehran had yet to be completed, and despite the fact that the sitting deputies predominantly owed their election to the Government, the manner of Sa'id's re-appointment unpalatably signified the Shah's intention to minimize the power of the legislature. This provoked strong criticism in both houses, as did the record of Sa'id's Government, particularly during the long period of parliamentary recess (28 July–9 February), as well as the slowness and irregularities of the elections, the incompetence of ministers and the irrelevence of the Cabinet programme.[91]

The aftermath of Hazhir's death had witnessed a cooling of the political temperature, particularly as Ashraf and the Queen Mother had expediently left the country.[92] Nevertheless the Government had failed to curb the growing underground activities of the Tudeh Party, while the banned party paper, *Mardum*, had secretly continued to be printed since 2 October 1949, reaching an estimated circulation of 4000 in Tehran and 2000 in the provinces.[93] In addition, the National Front had increased its popular appeal, continued its campaign against the rigging of the elections, and, despite the Government's efforts to thwart it, its success in Tehran seemed irreversible.

On the other hand, Sa'id's relatively long term of office and imminent replacement had stimulated inter- and intra-clan tensions and disagreements over the reallocation of spoils. Open disputes and rivalries among Cabinet ministers and high officials, the hostility of those who blamed the Government for their failure to get elected and the grudges of those who had been elected in the face of Government opposition, all worked against Sa'id's chances of remaining in office and his willingness to continue.

It was unlikely that Sa'id could get a vote of confidence in the Majlis or that the Supplemental Oil Agreement would be approved, since there was no one genuinely prepared to step forward in its defence. Even Sayyid Zia was unlikely to accept office if asked to sponsor the approval of the Oil Agreement.[94] The Shah, however, remained hopeful of solving the oil question, preferably through Sa'id, in order to procure funds which the Government desperately needed, and to reduce the increasingly active concern of the British over the choice of prime minister.

From the outset the 16th Majlis lost no time in expressing its disapproval of Sa'id who, despite his commitment to the Shah 'to see the Agreement through', was not willing to 'incur the odium' of submitting it to the deputies.[95] As expected, the deputies did not offer him a vote of confidence and his Cabinet came to an end on 18 March 1950 after a period of sixteen months in office. The relatively long period of Sa'id's term of office was the result of a series of helpful factors which marked this period, including the long parliamentary recess, Sa'id's co-operative disposition with regard to the oil question, the apparent absence of viable alternatives, and, most importantly, the consistent support of the Shah, or his lack of opposition to the Prime Minister and the Government.

In a report on the internal situation of Iran since the end of the war, written in January 1949, A. K. S. Lambton (press attaché at the British Legation in Tehran from 1939 to 1945, who was at the time Reader in Persian at the University of London) enumerated various factors which had given rise to widespread popular discontent 'against the ruling class in general, and the Shah, the Court and the Army in particular'. These factors included the general deterioration in the condition of the people, especially the lower-income groups; the absence of security and protection against the extortionate demands and misdemeanours of government officials and the military; the misuse of martial law; the disarming of some tribesmen without ensuring their protection from their armed neighbours; and the subjection of the peasants, particularly in Azarbaijan and Kurdistan, to undue pressure by both the landlords and the Government. All these contributed to the general disaffection of the population.[96]

The political milieu of the capital fostered cynicism and a readiness on the part of the population to believe most rumours disseminated against the elite, particularly the Shah and the royal family. The smallest incidents were 'seized upon by the discontented' and were used to 'fan the flames of discontent'. The extravagances of the royal family and the corruption of the army, which, along with institutions such as the National Railways and the Industrial Bank, were in effect 'outside the control of civil government', were widely criticized; 'large sums, such as the fantastic amount which appeared in the railway budget for "entertainment" ', were generally suspected of having been 'transferred to the Court and Princess Ashraf, in particular through the agency of Khusrau Hidayat, to be used for political ends'.

Allegations that the Industrial Bank 'was a centre of corruption and political intrigue', as well as suspicions that even the 'Imperial Institute of Social Services' was 'a cover, in some measure, for political intrigue', were widely subscribed to. As Lambton observed:

> The fact that these and similar topics are widely discussed and these allegations widely believed, whether justly or unjustly has . . . reduced the monarchy to a position where it is no longer regarded with respect, but with fear, contempt and disgust, and increased the almost universal hatred and pessimism with which the 'ruling class' is regarded.

The steadily deteriorating image of the monarchy, which was far more discernible in early 1950 than it had been a year earlier, was a development for which the royal family itself, and particularly the Shah, was largely, if not solely, responsible. The Shah's systematic rejection of strong Court-independent prime ministers, his imposition of ministers and his concerted efforts to restrict the authority not only of the Cabinet but also of the Majlis, contravened both the monarch's constitutional role and his publicly projected image. His disregard for constitutional principles was obvious in the appointment of Sa'id and the manoeuvres to retain him. Sa'id was a man who seemed content to be, and in fact proved to be, the Shah's loyal protégé and docile appointee. He willingly complied with his role as a mere figurehead relegated to the political background and with only ceremonial functions.

The Shah's increased power and reliance on the West had repercussions not only for the image of the monarchy but, more significantly, for the prospects of an autonomous polity. The Shah was more frequently in contact with the British and American Embassies than previously, and along with his prime minister and ministers, who enjoyed little real domestic support, turned increasingly to the embassy officials as confidants, consultants, arbiters and supporters.

Since the resignation of Qavam in 1947, the Shah had grown in experience, managed to expand his network of ties and his clientele, and increased the credibility of his image as a focal point for the preservation of a pro-Western political arrangement in Iran. In this way he had consolidated his power. At the same time his encroachments upon the parliamentary structure, which were increasingly justified with the full exploitation of legislative inefficiency, had become more direct and less discreet, eventually culminating in the revision of the Constitution. He gradually appeared to recognize no line of demarcation between his prerogatives and the authority of the executive. He was largely responsible for undermining the credibility of the Government and for its powerlessness, which he in turn invoked to justify royal dominance over the governmental machinery. In short, the optimal aim of the Shah was to ensure that no matter who was in office, he would be in power.

This contradicted both the Constitution and the institutional structure of existing parliamentarianism, and also contravened the basic tenets of clan politics and its fundamental pluralistic ethos. The steady attempt to undermine the balance of the existing political groups in his own favour was bound to be opposed, whether through the obstructionist behaviour of the deputies or the critical comments of the press, through street demonstrations or growing cynicism, through silent, but potentially dangerous, frustration or publicly acclaimed assassinations. In any event, the Shah's efforts did not help to achieve his proclaimed aim of political stability, governmental efficiency and socio-economic development. Le Rougetel, who had barely hidden his sympathy for the Shah's aims, reported in November 1949 that,

> a succession of weak governments selected and sponsored by the Shah has virtually paralysed this primitive economy. In recent months the cost of living has risen steadily and unemployment is still rising, while hoarding, smuggling and racketeering of every kind are rife, and the law has been brought into a degree of contempt that is remarkable even in Persia.[97]

Public opinion in the urban centres, sustained by the newly mobilized nationalist consciousness and repoliticized religious sentiments, was primarily directed against the Shah, the royal family, the Court clientele or the entire kleptocratic foundation of clan politics. It provided the main basis for small but influential groups such as the National Front, and accounted for this group's success in thwarting unpopular policies and preventing the settlement of the oil question in a manner contrary to perceived Iranian national interests. It also enabled the National Front to make full use of immensely emotive issues such as oil in order to minimize the Shah's opportunity to enjoy the fruits of his power and his formally increased prerogatives.

15

The Government of Mansur:
MARCH–JUNE 1950

Ali Mansur's efforts to resume the premiership can be traced back at least to the beginning of Sa'id's second term of office. The absence of viable rival candidates as well as growing anti-Sa'id opposition in the Majlis increased his chances. The Shah, however, had mixed feelings about Mansur whom he regarded as a politician of the old school not likely to be enthusiastic about the consolidation of royal hegemony. He therefore frequently referred to Mansur's suspect integrity of character as being the main factor preventing his appointment.

Le Rougetel, who was now determined to intervene in the choice of prime minister, had in late 1948 described Mansur as a 'man of character', 'remarkably intelligent' and with 'a reputation for being shrewd and determined'.[1] He also let the Shah know that he had a 'high opinion' of Mansur and believed that criticism of him was being put around by his enemies.[2] Over a year later Le Rougetel had modified his views: he reported that Mansur 'has certain definite weaknesses' and 'is reputed to take bribes in a big way', adding, however, that this was 'almost common for Persia' and otherwise crediting Mansur with possessing 'the necessary qualifications'.[3] On the other hand, a Foreign Office official remarked that Mansur's 'personal probity is, to say the least of it, in grave doubt', and hoped that the Ambassador would not find it necessary to do anything more than 'acquiesce' in his appointment.[4]

Since the Shah and the British could not agree on a candidate, the Shah reluctantly called on Mansur to form a Cabinet, a move approved by the British. Those 'necessary qualifications' which Le Rougetel had recognized earlier were of course the willingness to secure the oil agreement, and Sir Francis Shepherd, who succeeded Le Rougetel in March 1950, was optimistic about the prospects for this and less reserved than his predecessor about Mansur.[5] With the half-hearted approval of the Shah and the British, and as a result of his concerted efforts to recruit deputies to his side, Mansur therefore succeeded in assuming office.

No invitation for a formal parliamentary 'vote of inclination' was made before his appointment, at the cost of considerable criticism from both deputies and Senators. Moreover neither the composition of the new Cabinet – which was very similar to that of Sa'id – nor its programme appealed to the Parliament or the press. Nevertheless, on 10 April 1950, the Cabinet was approved unanimously by the Majlis,[6] and later with a majority of 40 out of 46, by the Senate.[7] Despite this vote the 16th Majlis was from the outset as jealously concerned as its immediate predecessors to reassert and preserve the pivotal role of the legislature in the body politic. Two weeks later the position of the Majlis was strengthened further when the deputies of the National Front, headed by Musaddiq, arrived in the Majlis to assume their seats.

Ali Mansur was born in about 1888 into a well-to-do family. Like many aspiring members of his generation, he was educated at the School of Political Science, before joining the Ministry of Foreign Affairs, where he was appointed an Under-Secretary in 1919. A year later he became Under-Secretary in the Ministry of the Interior, and served as Governor of Azarbaijan from 1926 to 1931, when he was appointed Minister of the Interior. In early 1933 he was offered the portfolio of Roads and Communications.[8] In January 1936 he was arrested on charges of 'misappropriation and incompetence',[9] but was acquitted in August of the same year. Two years later he was rehabilitated and appointed Minister of Industry and Mines. Although 'believed to have made money out of the sale of promotions while at the Ministry of the Interior',[10] he was offered the premiership in June 1940, but the Allied invasion forced his resignation. Subsequently he served as Governor-General of Khurasan and later Azarbaijan, before becoming head of the Seven-year Plan Organization. Mansur was a typical example of those politicians who built up their fortunes during and after the Reza Shah era, mainly through successful adaptation arising from sheer pragmatism; and in his case he was renowned only for his apparent cunning.

Following the nullification of the Tehran elections in mid-November 1949, and despite government efforts to exclude them, the National Front candidates had again succeeded in securing places at the top of the polls in Tehran. Musaddiq was already widely popular and was now re-elected as First Deputy for Tehran, while some of his friends had gained popularity through their performances in the 15th

Majlis. Their persecution following the attempt on the Shah's life and the death of Hazhir had also given them much favourable publicity which they had exploited to their advantage, and all governmental efforts against them had proved entirely counterproductive. For example, the trial of Baqa'i, who was accused of insulting the army,[11] ended in his triumphant acquittal and gave him a platform from which to increase his popularity by exposing the ineptitude and corruption of government officials.[12] Against all odds the National Front proved powerful enough to establish its claims concerning irregularities in the elections held in Lavasanat, a rural constituency close to Tehran. As a result, two friends of Musaddiq were elected, which increased the number of National Front deputies in the Majlis from five to seven.[13]

The parliamentary nucleus of the National Front was made up of the small 'Homeland faction' (Fraksiun-i Vatan), composed of the seven National Front deputies and Allahyar Salih, a deputy for Kashan. Yet this faction was qualitatively superior to all its rivals: none of its members was susceptible to charges of corruption, incompetence, allegiance to foreign powers or lack of moral integrity or courage, and no one could deny the authenticity of their election to Parliament or the strength of their social prestige and popularity. The National Front deputies enjoyed the sympathy of a number of their parliamentary colleagues, but the real source of their support and inspiration lay outside the Majlis, among various urban middle class strata: the intelligentsia, the politicized merchants, shopkeepers and artisans of the bazaar, and certain guilds in particular.

The National Front's ideology was broadly anti-authoritarian, with a strong nationalist component; its immediate policy was to oppose the Supplemental Oil Agreement in particular, and British influence in Iran in general. Its ultimate aim was the consolidation of parliamentary institutions and properly observed constitutional principles, as well as the establishment of real independence. Given its make-up, its social basis and its goals – which were popularized through a number of affiliated newspapers – the National Front was in a position to acquire a remarkable degree of moral and ideological hegemony in the Iranian political arena, or to achieve what Shepherd called 'moral ascendancy' over the Government and the Majlis.[14]

The National Front deputies had proved to be relatively well disposed towards Mansur and he, in turn, was keen not to alienate them. Soon after becoming Prime Minister, Mansur visited Musaddiq twice in the course of a short period,[15] and was reported to have offered him the portfolio of Finance, which he refused.[16] Musaddiq appreciated this gesture by the Prime Minister, but was intent on losing no time in promoting and realizing the objectives of the National Front. He insisted that the revision of the electoral and press laws be given priority over the constitutional reforms which the Constituent Assembly had envisaged would be completed by the Parliament prior to other matters.[17] Contrary to the Shah's expectations, Mansur asserted that his Government viewed the matter favourably.[18] The very next day, he submitted a new electoral bill,[19] followed by a new press bill,[20] both of which were acceptable in principle to the National Front.

On 25 May 1950 Musaddiq delivered a powerful speech to the Majlis strongly condemning the setting up of the Constituent Assembly which he described as illegitimate. He accused the Shah of acting in a dictatorial fashion, contrary to the national interest, and advised him to refrain from all unconstitutional behaviour and to abandon his insistence on acquiring the right to suspensory veto. He also condemned all intervention in governmental affairs by Ashraf and the Chief of Staff, and reasserted the National Front's determined opposition to dictatorship.[21] Musaddiq's speech was approved by the majority of deputies,[22] and Mansur's response, although non-committal, was fairly sympathetic.[23]

Musaddiq's uncompromising stand against the Shah's persistent attempts to enhance his constitutional authority and prerogatives, and Mansur's policy of non-provocation toward the National Front infuriated the Shah, but increasing parliamentary opposition to his objectives prevented him from resorting to any public or drastic action. Such opposition had led Shepherd to regard the postponement of debates in the Majlis on the Shah's desire to acquire the right of suspensory veto as being 'in itself no bad thing', because 'if a vote were taken and the proposal defeated, the blow to the Shah's prestige would be serious'.[24] The Shah's old enemy, Qavam – once described as the 'stormy petrel of Persian politics'[25] – had added to the animation of the Iranian political milieu by publishing a bold open letter to the Shah reproachfully advising him not to make encroachments upon the Constitution. The Court Minister, Hakimi, made a bitter and discourteous reply to the letter; on behalf of the Shah he withdrew the title of 'Excellency' conferred upon Qavam in July 1946, and accused him of treason, clearly reflecting the depth of the Shah's anger and anxiety.[26] Qavam's letter heartened the Shah's opponents, and Hakimi's reply did little to add to royal prestige. The

Shah now faced challenges from two established politicians, and a wide spectrum of determined opposition, but none of this weakened his self-righteous belief in the necessity of enhancing his formal prerogatives.

Although he recognized that he must project a public image of tolerance and disinterestedness, the Shah, dejected and frustrated, lost no opportunity to complain to the sympathetically attentive British Ambassador. A recurrent theme in the Shah's conversations with Shepherd was the harmful nature of the National Front. In one meeting, becoming 'quite animated' in condemning the Front, he described its policy of 'absolute neutralism' as 'absurd' and 'dangerous',[27] and in another he scornfully referred to Musaddiq several times as 'our Demosthenes'. He revealed that he regarded the National Front as more dangerous than the Tudeh Party, on account of its vague and negative attitude. He reiterated his conviction that 'the power of the government should derive from the Crown', insisting that kingship was 'ingrained' in the traditions of the people and inseparable from their 'thought'. He frankly admitted that he had intervened in the affairs of the Government and would continue to do so, and would not accept a strong prime minister unless he himself appointed him.[28]

Shepherd found the Shah 'somewhat contemptuous about the achievements of democracy in Iran hitherto, and the country's suitability at present for a democratic form of government'.[29] The Shah was quite unprepared to moderate his efforts to enhance his authority, and considered Mansur an inappropriate tool for his purposes. The political style and views of the Shah and the Prime Minister differed on many issues, including the much-publicized question of reform, to which they both paid lip-service.[30] The main cause of tension between them, however, was Mansur's efforts to placate the National Front, which had caused astonishment and regret on the part of both the Shah and Shepherd.[31] In fact Mansur had little choice but to try and work with both the deputies, particularly the Homeland faction, and the Court. Thus, while the Shah and the royalist deputies resented his subservience to the National Front, others such as Khajih-Nuri considered him to be 'a puppet for the Shah', regarding it as reprehensible for a statesman 'to sink his own personality and follow the wishes of the Shah to the extent that Ali Mansur was doing.'[32]

Faced with no viable alternative, however, Mansur tried to appease influential figures. He invited Kashani, who had been living in exile in Lebanon since early 1949, to return to Iran. Recently elected as one of the deputies for Tehran, Kashani returned triumphantly on 10 June 1950. The Prime Minister also dismissed Bahram Shahrukh, the unscrupulous and adventurous Director of the Propaganda Department, who had earned the enmity of the National Front but was close to the Shah. This provided the Shah with further cause to turn against the Prime Minister.[33] Mansur failed to prevent the removal of the Chief of Police, General Zahidi, who was opposed by Razmara but who favoured the National Front as a balancing force vis-à-vis the Chief of Staff.[34] However, in the eyes of the Shah, Mansur's pro-National Front disposition now completely outweighed his redeeming qualities.

Meanwhile the British were increasing the pressure for the submission to the Parliament of the Supplemental Oil Agreement. Shepherd insisted that it was 'favourable' to Iran,[35] and conveyed to the Shah that the AIOC had gone as far as it could in conceding to Iran.[36] Mansur had no desire to raise the issue, having made no mention of it in his Cabinet programme, but Shepherd reported that the Shah was insistent that Mansur submit the Agreement to the Majlis,[37] while the British expected Mansur to come out actively in support of it.

Mansur cautiously submitted the Agreement to the Majlis and invited a Majlis committee to study it, but despite the insistence of Musaddiq and his colleagues that he should clarify his own position he consistently refused to do so.[38] In the meantime the issue of the possible premiership of Razmara had come to preoccupy the Shah and the Americans, and the British gradually became less patient with Mansur. One Foreign Office official regarded the Government of Mansur as more 'spineless' than its predecessor, 'to the serious detriment of the British interests'.[39] Similarly the Shah was of the opinion that Mansur's qualities as an experienced politician and an 'intriguer' were not enough when 'leadership' was required. With this conclusion, Shepherd 'could not but agree'.[40]

Mansur's position had thus become highly unstable, and the British Oriental Counsellor was advised that the Shah only awaited British confirmation that 'nothing effective will be done by Mansur' in order to dispose of him.[41] In addition, it was widely believed that the Americans were unfavourable to him; in fact he himself had complained to the British to this effect.[42] Wiley, the US Ambassador, had told Shepherd that the State Department had instructed him 'to secure the dismissal of the Ali Mansur Government'.[43] Shepherd tried to restrain Wiley and commented: 'I was rather startled by the apparent willingness of the State Department to plunge into Cabinet-making in what appeared to be a clumsy and obvious manner'. Mansur was also opposed by some courtiers, particularly by Prince Abd ur-Reza, the honorary head of the Plan Organization.[44] He was obviously not capable of realizing the long-overdue 'reforms' and his 'dangerously complacent' position regarding the influence of the Tudeh Party among industrial workers had not been popular.[45] Fears of a communist resurgence had been reactivated following the assassination of Ahmad Dihqan, a Majlis deputy and a loyal protégé and mouthpiece of the Court.[46] In addition to all this, the Shah did not believe that Mansur's Government was capable of coping with the demonstrations and disorder which the return of Kashani was likely to inspire.[47]

On the other hand, despite a motion of interpellation which Reza Ashtianizadih had tabled against him,[48] the financial and economic difficulties which his Government faced, the resignation of some of his competent ministers, and the constant criticisms of Musaddiq and others, Mansur could still retain a hold in the Majlis and the Senate. In fact, a considerable number of deputies, particularly Musaddiq and his colleagues, as well as some Senators, were deeply apprehensive about the impending premiership of Razmara, which had been an open secret for weeks. These fears meant that several deputies, including Musaddiq and his colleagues, as well as some Senators, were prepared to tolerate Mansur's Cabinet and even actively to support it. Mansur was well aware of this situation and made use of it, for example by threatening to resign when he faced difficulty over the budget and needed to enlist further parliamentary support.[49] However, increased parliamentary support was not enough to save the Cabinet.

The news of his resignation on 26 June 1950 was received by some deputies with regret. Musaddiq castigated him for surrendering passively in order to ensure office in another capacity, and also for coming to an accommodation with the Court:[50] it was widely believed that in the face of pressure from the Shah to resign, Mansur had agreed, on condition that he should be appointed Ambassador to Rome.[51] On the other hand, Shepherd reported that the Prime Minister had been expected to resign earlier, but the Shah had impressed upon him that he would prevent him from doing so unless the Oil Agreement were submitted.[52]

From the outset of his premiership it was clear that Mansur was in an untenable position since he was not prepared to implement any drastic policies, but confined himself to traditional modes of action, resorting to a strategy of evasion and discreet inaction. This may have had some appeal for the deputies, but it was not acceptable to the Shah or the British and American Embassies. Mansur knew that what the British expected from him was active co-operation over the oil issue, while the Shah required submission. He was also aware that the deputies, particularly Musaddiq and his followers, were eagerly watching for a move on his part in support of the AIOC, or against their objectives, in order to pounce on him. In such a situation his room for manoeuvre was drastically restricted and he could not have hoped to retain his position for long.[53]

It is a matter of some interest as to what he − or other prime ministers in similar situations − had expected to gain by accepting office. Except in rare cases, where the candidates were motivated by a strong sense of civic responsibility, it would appear that most were simply seeking the advantages and material and symbolic rewards which came with the position. There was certainly no lack of contenders, however unsuitable, and if they were successful in gaining office they struggled to maintain it by manoeuvres and manipulations and seemingly unfailing efforts at the generous distribution of spoils. Although Mansur had hoped to cling to his position through the full use of the old rules of the game of clan politics − that is, by refraining from any inexpedient, provocative action − the Shah was determined to change these rules in his own favour, and the oil issue, the calls for reform, the fear of communism and the slowness of the parliamentary process all helped to move events in his favour.

16

The Government of Razmara:
JUNE 1950–MARCH 1951

Since the fall of Qavam in late 1947 there had been no effective Cabinets, and the Shah, as well as the Americans and the British, were gradually attracted by the idea of the premiership of General Razmara. Razmara was known to be strong and dynamic, claimed to hold reformist beliefs and had long awaited the fulfilment of his life's ambition to become prime minister. He had enlisted the patronage of Ashraf, the confidence and favour of the Shah and the support of a number of influential politicians, and had endeavoured with some success to convince the British and American Embassies of his sincere attachment to reformist ideals.[1]

When the US State Department began to show an interest in improving the economic situation in Iran and decided to dispatch Henry Grady, Ambassador in Greece, to replace Wiley in Tehran and lead an economic mission in the country, Razmara appeared to be the most appropriate and promising prime-ministerial candidate to ensure the success of the proposed mission. The State Department therefore informed the British that 'Razmara would be a distinct improvement on Mansur, and that he should be able to form a more stable and effective government'.[2]

As for the British, Shepherd was already on Razmara's side, reporting that 'from all accounts, Razmara should make an efficient, honest, and progressive Prime Minister'.[3] The Foreign Office was hopeful of a better prospect for the settlement of the oil question under Razmara, although one official feared that he might establish a military regime and would then be difficult to unseat.[4] The Foreign Office nevertheless informed the State Department that the appointment of Razmara might be the only chance of achieving that degree of 'resolution and efficiency' which the operation of the economic mission required. Although it was recognized that Razmara might be tempted 'to cut across the constitutional process', the Foreign Office estimated the situation in Iran to be such that a risk of this nature was 'well worth running'. Naturally it was hoped that Razmara could be restrained, in view of his dependence on the 'goodwill' of the British and the Americans,[5] and the Shah had instructed Shahrukh to give a 'categorical assurance' to the British Embassy that, as Prime Minister, Razmara would not be allowed any say in the affairs of the army; Razmara himself had given similar assurances.[6]

These assurances helped to convince the British and American Ambassadors, who approved the appointment of Razmara. Before leaving Iran on 18 June 1950 Wiley informed the Shah that Razmara should be appointed without further delay;[7] and Shepherd also informed him that 'HMG would be glad to see General Razmara as Prime Minister'.[8] Having at last gained the approval of the British and the Americans, the Shah promptly forced the resignation of Mansur on 26 June 1950. This was followed by the immediate appointment of Razmara, again without the prior approval of the Parliament.[9]

Born in 1901, Hajji Ali Razmara, whose father was also a military officer,[10] received his military education in Iran, joining the army before going to study in France at St. Cyr.[11] On his return to Iran in early 1927 he was made commander of the Kirmanshah mixed regiment, thus beginning his 'meteoric career'.[12] There followed a series of senior positions in the army, and in 1937 he was appointed brigadier-general. In 1942, although one of the youngest generals in the country, Razmara was nominated Chief of Staff. He lost this position after only forty-four days, but resumed it in April 1944.[13] In late 1944 pressure from Sayyid Zia and his followers contributed to the replacement of Razmara by his chief rival, General Arfa.[14] In 1946 Qavam was persuaded by Muzaffar Firuz, a relative of Razmara, to reappoint him as Chief of Staff,[15] a position which he held until his appointment as Prime Minister.

Razmara was one of the most controversial figures in post-1941 Iran. His rivalry with Arfa, which dominated the politics of the army's command structure, ended with Razmara's eventual victory. The opposition of other generals, such as Ahmadi, Yazdanpanah and Zahidi, failed to hinder his irresistible rise to power. Although he had regained the position of Chief of Staff through the offices of Firuz and Qavam, he succeeded in retaining it by his obsequiousness and success in convincing the Shah of his unswerving loyalty, as well as his skilful exploitation of any opportunity to ingratiate himself with the monarch.[16] The operation for the recapture of Azarbaijan was an example of this. In the words of the British military attaché:

> He pleased the Shah by following his advice in the formulation of
> military plans for the advance into Azarbaijan. He consulted him in
> matters of armament. He referred to him even the most trivial details
> of daily administration, thereby flattering him into thinking himself a
> commander in chief in more than name.[17]

The attempted assassination of the Shah and the elections for the
Constituent Assembly and the Parliament were other occasions on
which Razmara managed to strengthen his links with the Court and
consolidate his own power. He appeared to be a devout Court
protégé and a loyal monarchist genuinely in sympathy with the
Shah's reformist claims. He was also one of the least popular but
most powerful men in the country, surrounded by a coterie of
discredited opportunists, and his influence extended far beyond the
army. Over a year before Razmara became premier, Geoffrey
Wheeler, the British Oriental Counsellor, had described him as
'probably the most feared and disliked man in Persia today'; Wheeler
also quoted a report on personalities which described Razmara as 'an
able, energetic, but corrupt officer with a reputation as a disciplinarian
. . . very ambitious and a great intriguer, who trims his sails to any
wind. An unprincipled adventurer.' Wheeler observed that this
assessment probably reflected the beliefs of the majority of politically
literate people, but he added that Razmara lived 'a simple life', did
not 'engage in cheap personal publicity, like General Ahmadi' and
was 'an efficient and hard-working official'.[18] Opponents of
Razmara could not disagree with this and even Arfa confessed that
he was 'an extremely able man'.[19]

Razmara's Cabinet, which had been drawn up well before his
appointment[20] and in consultation with the British and American
Embassies,[21] was composed predominantly of under-secretaries and
other well-educated professional administrators in the hope of
substantiating its reformist intentions.[22] Razmara outlined his
Cabinet programme in a press interview, during which he also
stressed his respect for democracy and his reliance on the Shah and
the people.[23] The most salient point of his programme, which was
formally submitted to the Majlis on the occasion of the introduction
of his Cabinet, was the establishment of regional, provincial and
local councils. It also included the improvement of the economy
through the Seven-year Plan, a guarantee of the independence of the

judiciary, a reduction in the cost of living, and an improvement of living standards in general, and of health and education in particular, through the work of local councils.[24]

Razmara had hoped to obtain the acquiescence of the National Front deputies, since he enjoyed good relations with Ha'irizadih both before and after assuming office.[25] However, when he attended the Majlis they accused him of having won office solely through Anglo-American support, and of intending to establish a dictatorship.[26] To his dismay, his abandonment of military uniform and title, his stress on his civilian status, and the Shah's emphatic reference to him as 'Hajji Ali Razmara', not using his military title, did little to deflect the National Front's protests. Musaddiq warned that even the Shah's own position was threatened by dictatorship, attributed most of the misfortunes of the country to Razmara's machinations,[27] and condemned the aims of his Cabinet as being to oppress rather than to reform.[28] Baqa'i asserted that for two years the British had been intending to bring about a strong government, and had therefore imposed Razmara on the Shah.[29] Kashani was also unresponsive to efforts to win his co-operation,[30] and issued a proclamation strongly opposing Razmara.[31]

Razmara also encountered opposition in the Senate, where Matin-Daftari stressed the new Prime Minister's dictatorial intent, and asserted that he carried 'in his pocket the decree for the dissolution of the Parliament'.[32] His military background and foreign links made many Senators and deputies suspicious of him; they also resented the manner of his appointment and some were alarmed by aspects of his reform programme. Razmara's Cabinet programme was criticized exhaustively,[33] but in view of his royal backing he was given a vote of confidence in the Majlis of 95 votes to 8, with 3 abstentions;[34] in the Senate, 35 voted in his favour, 4 against and 10 abstained.[35]

The failure of the National Front to prevent Razmara's premiership signified, in Shepherd's view, the breaking of its 'moral ascendancy' and the regaining of the initiative by the Government, whose prospects he regarded as good if the Shah would continue in his support of Razmara. On a somewhat pessimistic note, however, Shepherd reported:

Unfortunately, His Majesty's character lacks precisely the degree of consistency for which the situation calls. Since his accession, it has been observed that after the appointment of any Prime Minister, the Shah tends to express dissatisfaction and to discuss possible alternatives.

The effects on such prime ministers' position in the Majlis has invariably been disastrous.[36]

Yet at the outset there was every indication that the Shah would support Razmara; assured of royal support, as well as the effective backing of the British and American representatives, Razmara concentrated on the most controversial part of his Cabinet programme – the issue of political decentralization and the establishment of local councils – which was submitted to the Majlis on 13 July 1950 as a single bill. This issue became the major cause of protracted contention between the Government and the Parliament.

The idea of provincial and local councils, although envisaged in the Constitution, provoked adverse reactions for a variety of reasons, and in particular because it was championed by Razmara, whose foreign links were used to cast doubt upon the sincerity of his intentions. Musaddiq, Kashani and their followers opposed the decentralization bill on the grounds that it would lead to the disintegration of Iran. Musaddiq recalled the aims of the proposed tripartite commission of 1946 in order to prove a link between the proposed decentralization scheme and foreign interests. He argued that if the Government genuinely desired reform, it would have concentrated its efforts on gaining parliamentary approval for a revised electoral bill.[37] Many other deputies and Senators also opposed the enterprise, and the more Razmara insisted on its approval the more suspicious they became, and the more Kashani denounced him.[38] Razmara resorted to threats,[39] but this proved counterproductive and his bill, described perhaps not entirely without justification as 'the most constructive bill to have been put forward in Persia for many years',[40] was virtually buried by the Majlis.[41] Undeterred, Razmara continued in his struggle with the Parliament over his decentralization bill until the issue of the purge of government officials had become so prominent that it overshadowed all other matters.

On 22 June 1949 the Majlis had passed a bill empowering the Government to investigate the country's administrative structure with a view to a possible purge. Some 1000 cases were examined and the purge committee produced a controversial report in August 1950 which classified officials using three categories. First, those whom it was considered vital to retain; secondly, those who were not directly required but were potentially employable in productive or educational sectors; and thirdly, those who were not considered to be fulfilling a vital function, or were incompetent and did not qualify for retirement, and were therefore to be dismissed.[42] The Government tried to keep this report secret, but the committee published it on its own initiative.[43]

The report revealed that seven members of the Government had been classified in the first category, five in the second and one under-secretary – Parviz Khansari, Under-Secretary in the Ministry of Labour and a protégé of Razmara – in the third. Moreover many influential politicians such as Reza Hikmat, the Speaker of the Majlis, and Qavam, as well as a number of Court protégés such as Iqbal and Khusrau Hidayat, also found themselves classified in the third category. The publication of the report caused the Government serious embarrassment: to accept and try to implement its recommendations would have been impossible and would have exposed the Government to bitter intrigues and enmities; on the other hand, to ignore it would damage the much-publicized anti-corruption and reformist claims of both the Shah and Razmara. Razmara was therefore faced with a baffling dilemma, while his opponents lost no time in turning the report into a crucial public issue and demanded its implementation.[44]

Confronted with an increase in inter-elite disagreements and changing factional alignments, in a face-saving effort Razmara submitted a bill to the Majlis which established two committees, one to hear the appeals of those who regarded themselves as having been wrongfully victimized by the report and another for the investigation of other employees.[45] This bill, which was referred to the Judicial Committee of the Majlis, was clearly aimed at obliterating the report of the purge committee. In view of the resounding pronouncements against corruption by various governments and the Shah over the last two years, the report virtually constituted a coup by the ruling elite against itself. Although tendentious, it was enough to confirm that the elite would suppress any internal purge. The moral and psychological implications of this were significant;[46] kleptocracy was exposed but virtually condoned. The Shah's attitude toward the report, whatever his justification,[47] revealed the emptiness of his claims and, most importantly, the entire episode undermined Razmara's reformist, anti-corruption pronouncements and weakened his self-confidence.

On the other hand many deputies felt emboldened by the episode, and Razmara was interpellated by Jamal Imami, a member of the 'majority', who decried the infighting among the deputies which was giving the Government a free hand. In this he reflected the traditional attitude of the majority of deputies toward the Government, asserting that: 'The Majlis ought to be calling the tune, but it is the Government which is making a clown of the Majlis.'[48] Razmara faced other interpellations and on attending the Majlis was told that by general consent he had no majority. He replied that he had come to seek reconciliation and promised to submit all matters to the Majlis for approval, including the establishment of his proposed local councils.[49] This was a major setback for him, since the issue of local councils was now abandoned for all practical purposes.[50] In the meantime Hikmat had managed, despite vociferous criticism by deputies such as Musaddiq, to persuade the Majlis to approve the report of its Judicial Committee (which nullified the report of the purge committee) with a majority of 50 out of 83 votes. All these developments meant that Razmara had lost the initiative vis-à-vis the Majlis.

Razmara had assumed office under the banner of strength, decisiveness and reform but, in the face of a recalcitrant Majlis in which a defiant minority aimed to challenge and counter the power of any government, he had proved as vulnerable as his predecessors. Despite the efforts of the *mutavallis*, such as Malik-Madani, Hikmat and particularly Tahiri, to ensure Razmara a majority in the Parliament, he was merely tolerated and no more. In December 1949 he complained to the British that 130 bills submitted by his Government had been held up by the Majlis.[51] He was evidently neither well equipped nor skilful enough to win over the deputies. Even Tahiri, who had contested the Speakership with the backing of Razmara but had lost to Hikmat, and who seemed more interested than others in mobilizing support for Razmara, often complained about him to Pyman, the British Oriental Counsellor. In Tahiri's view, Razmara did not indulge in enough lobbying or in sufficient consultation with the deputies, particularly before submitting his bills, and he believed that a reshuffle of the Cabinet was needed.[52] Pyman agreed and suggested the inclusion of elder 'respectable politicians' such as Khalil Fahimi in any reshuffled Cabinet.[53] Razmara for his part could claim to have shown deference to the wishes of his parliamentary opponents; in early August 1950 he had dismissed Shahrukh who had done much to prepare the ground for his premiership. Shahrukh complained bitterly of Razmara's 'meanness' which, he protested, had 'no limits', and tried to persuade the Shah that Razmara had been 'misleading him'.[54] Razmara now tried to increase his contacts with the deputies and abandoned his cavalier style in favour of a modest profile; he also reshuffled his Cabinet. None of this, however, convinced his opponents in the Majlis and the Senate (which included the Amiyyun group comprising prominent senators such as Taqizadih, Najm, Muhammad Sururi, Baqir Kazimi and Hakimi).

Razmara's supposed strength and reformism were bound to threaten the balance of clan politics, affect factional alignments and provoke counter-manoeuvres, but the Parliament sought not to unseat Razmara prematurely and continued with its tactic of minimal co-operation with him. This tactic had initially been adopted because of the implicit threat of parliamentary dissolution, which the Shah and Razmara had both dwelt on,[55] and which was hardly a secret.[56] As this threat gradually faded, the Majlis reasserted its authority and its role in articulating or channelling national ideals or popular demands. The deputies lost no time in enumerating the defects and mistakes of the increasingly vulnerable Government which, like its predecessors, remained dependent on the Majlis for the approval of its monthly budget.

The weakening position of the Government *vis-à-vis* the Parliament also forced Razmara to agree to nullify all the press laws save the original law of 1908,[57] and to revise the martial law regulations, which greatly increased the control of the Majlis over their use.[58] Despite his opponents' incessant attacks on his dictatorial character and his own statements of firm resolve, few prime ministers had ever made such concessions. Razmara's concessions and his diminishing insistence on the approval of his reform measures encouraged his opponents further, and insult was frequently added to the injury of harassment by the Majlis.[59] The dramatic escape from prison, in mid-December 1950, of ten Tudeh Party leaders was an added blow to his image, and it was later widely believed that they had enjoyed the connivance of Razmara. Shepherd, however, reported:

> Although it may be going too far to say that the Government connived at the escape of the Tudeh prisoners; there had been signs that the Government had not pursued Tudeh members with the zeal that it once showed.[60]

While Razmara had been forced to abandon his ambitious reformist objectives, such as the decentralization scheme or land reform plans, even such measures as his bill for an increase in the note issue were now aborted,[61] as well as bills dealing with an increase in judges' salaries, labour laws, teachers' social insurance and the organization of medical practice nation-wide. This time his opponents did not simply confine themselves to raising the spectre of dictatorship but attacked his inherent weakness.[62] Despite his military background Razmara was not apparently hostile to parliamentary principles and had proved deeply sensitive to allegations of dictatorship, to the extent that his resolve and self-confidence had been adversely affected. To make things worse, when he was spared these charges it was only to be accused of weakness. As always, clan politics allowed neither ostentatious action nor undisguised inaction: both could prove fatal to a prime minister's image and position.

The success of Razmara's foreign policy, which was in essence similar to that of Qavam, was more tangible: without the wholehearted support of the Shah he succeeded in concluding a commercial agreement with the Soviet Union and improving Iran–Soviet relations, which had been particularly strained since late 1947. Shepherd attributed the change in the attitude of the Russians 'to the strength of Razmara's Government',[63] and when Razmara was later assassinated *Pravda* insinuated American involvement in his death, asserting that, 'General Razmara's activity – to the obvious and more than once expressed displeasure of the US and British ruling circles – was actually directed at improving Soviet–Iranian relations.[64] These moves helped to counter his unduly pro-Western image, inspired parliamentary approval and admiration, and were even welcomed by the National Front.[65] Similar agreements were also concluded by the Government with France, Germany and Italy, although it failed to enlist the US financial aid on which Razmara had initially based his hope of success in his reformist plans. He had gone so far as to suggest that his premiership was the main prerequisite for the extension of US aid to Iran, and his disappointment in this regard was both a serious embarrassment and a real additional blow to his standing. Razmara inevitably remained primarily dependent on British support, and financial difficulties only made him more vulnerable to their pressures and demands. The British had confidence in him and did not deny him support, while he in turn tried to reciprocate: he had 'accepted a British security adviser' and had 'shown a clear tendency to take the Embassy into his confidence in important matters, including defence'.[66] Razmara's relations with Britain came into sharp focus in his efforts to tackle the oil issue.

This was undoubtedly the crucial problem facing him, since he had enlisted British support for his premiership by pledging to work for the approval of the Supplemental Oil Agreement. Both he and the Shah had hinted that without modification the Agreement had little chance of approval. The Shah regarded the following points as essential if the Agreement were to be ratified: adjustment of the method of calculating royalties, speedy Persianization and Iranian government auditing of the accounts.[67] But the British stuck to their position that the Agreement was fair and even generous, and that further concessions to the Iranians would only provoke additional demands.[68] The British were asking the Iranians to overcome what they considered to be greed and sentimental nationalism and to accept the Agreement as it stood, while Razmara was expected to justify and defend it. Having failed to clarify its position *vis-à-vis* the Agreement as demanded by the Musaddiq-led Oil Committee of the Majlis,[69] the Government was interpellated by the National Front deputies, who analysed the oil issue in detail, attributing most of the ills of Iranian society to the AIOC.[70] The Prime Minister had already spoken in favour of the Agreement in the Senate,[71] and now rejected the suggestions of a link between Iran's misfortune and the AIOC, and complained bitterly about time-consuming interpellations.[72] The interpellation in question was given a 'vote of silence', but the Oil Committee unanimously rejected the Supplemental Oil Agreement[73] and the National Front demanded nationalization, a call followed by demonstrations and backed by a number of *ulama*.[74]

In response to British pressure the Government did not abandon the Agreement, and Ghulam Husain Furuhar, the Finance Minister, ventured to defend it. Although he eventually withdrew the Agreement, Furuhar carried the distinction of being the first and last Iranian Cabinet minister to defend it publicly, asserting that nationalization would have undesirable consequences.[75] Furuhar's defence provoked strong reactions in the Majlis, and the deputies passed a resolution condemning his assertions and pronouncing them null and void.[76] The National Front deputies and thirty journalists who had taken sanctuary in the Majlis intensified their campaign against the Government. This aggravated tensions within the Cabinet, with some ministers adding their voices to the call for Furuhar's resignation with threats of their own resignation,[77] while others tried to recover the situation by dissociating themselves from the whole affair. For instance, Shams ud-Din Jazayiri, the Minister of

Education, asserted that Furuhar's statement resulted from 'stupidity', and swore that the Prime Minister had been totally unconnected with it.[78] This was a charge which Furuhar publicly rejected. The hostile reaction of the Majlis to the Government's attempted defence of the Agreement left little doubt that either the Parliament had to be dissolved or the Agreement changed. AIOC officials, however, were scarcely concerned with the awkward problems which Razmara had faced in trying to defend the Agreement.[79]

Geoffrey Furlonge, head of the Foreign Office Eastern Department, confessed that the Prime Minister had achieved little in regard to the reform projects which the British had suggested to him, although this was not for want of trying. Above all, Razmara had presented the Oil Agreement to the Majlis and had shown 'courage' and a 'grasp of Iran's fundamental need': 'funds for development'. In Furlonge's view the 'factors impeding progress' were 'lack of funds' and 'Majlis obstructions': funds could be obtained by ratification of the Agreement, were it not for these obstructions.

> This final difficulty with the Majlis has caused Razmara to consider advising the Shah to dissolve that body, impose martial law until tempers cool and then, in about three months time hold new elections. Razmara is understood to be taking a decision on this on the 4th January.[80]

Furlonge contended that such a move was warranted regardless of the risks and problems involved, and believed that 'in all events . . . he [Razmara] could hardly be worse off with a new Majlis' than he was with the present. Moreover,

> having regard to Persia's long acquaintance with dictatorship in one form or another, in the most recent of which the country undoubtedly made considerable progress, and having regard also to the fact that Razmara apparently does not intend any coup to lead to an established dictatorship, but merely constitutional elections following dissolution of the Majlis, it would seem advisable that he should carry out his plans. This opinion has already been expressed to Sir F. Shepherd . . . in short, firm action seems necessary and Razmara to be the man to take it.[81]

One major obstacle to the plan, however, was that while the Shah appeared to favour such a course of action,[82] he was in reality deeply averse to it. By dissolving the Parliament, and thereby removing most constraints on Razmara's exercise of power, the Shah would himself become increasingly vulnerable and insecure. In addition, the growing importance of the oil issue within the nationalist movement meant that the Shah's action against the Parliament would be portrayed as a traitorous undermining of Iranian constitutionalism in favour of a foreign company. Despite British pressures, therefore, the Shah could not meaningfully contemplate such a venture; and Razmara, irrespective of the backing of Shepherd, could not afford to aggravate the Shah's suspicions by pressing the dissolution. The Parliament, aware of such threats to its existence, restrained itself and the many motions of interpellation tabled against the Government received non-committal 'votes of silence' and, on occasion, even conciliatory votes of confidence were offered. The Shah, the Parliament and Razmara were all aware of the extreme sensitivity of the situation and the constraints on their freedom to act. Whether or not the British were, they had no choice but to be more flexible.

Nevertheless they still hesitated to make concessions, and explored various other ways of dealing with the situation. Following the failure of 'a good deal of lobbying' among Majlis deputies in favour of the Supplemental Oil Agreement, Keating of the AIOC had come to advocate the idea of a *rapprochement* with the National Front.[83] Yet this suggestion would have been 'violently' rejected by Shepherd, and also by Fry who argued that:

> it is often wise to make friends with one's adversaries and attempt to educate them, but I have no hope that we could accomplish that (apart, of course, from using substantial bribes with Musaddiq and his followers).[84]

The use of bribery would certainly not have resulted in the co-operation of Musaddiq and his followers, although there were some who asked for payment. For example, the veteran deputy Mir Sayyid Ali Bihbahani sent a message to Pyman 'to the effect that he was prepared to be reasonable about oil if "some help" were given to him'. He was informed that the Embassy was not in a position to help and that he would do better to contact Razmara: Razmara stated that he was aware of the 'problem of Bihbahani'.[85]

Shepherd also thought that parliamentary dissolution was possible if the oil issue could be 'relegated to some secondary position on the political stage', thereby giving the Shah and Razmara a chance to take decisive action.[86] The Majlis and particularly the National Front, however, aware of such a possibility, insisted on keeping the oil question firmly at the top of the Majlis agenda. British reluctance to make concessions had enabled the National Front to radicalize its attitudes and increase its public demands for nationalization. The British position proved increasingly indefensible when the Iranians learned, in the autumn of 1950, of negotiations between Aramco and the Saudi Government, which resulted in the conclusion of a 50:50 profit-sharing agreement in December 1950.[87] Razmara, however, while trying to prevent the Majlis Oil Committee from adopting the principle of nationalization, approached the AIOC representative, V. J. Northcroft, as late as 10 February 1951 enquiring about British readiness to consider an agreement on the basis of the 50:50 principle. He was told that 'the company would be willing to examine some similar arrangement':[88] Foreign Office and AIOC officials had for some time realized that such an arrangement was inevitable; but the realization came too late, since the call for nationalization had gained immense popularity and become difficult to oppose.[89]

Razmara was aware at least of the symbolic significance of the idea of nationalization and regarded it as impractical and yet irresistible. With the help of non-National Front members of the Oil Committee he therefore evolved two schemes, both of which envisaged nationalization as a desirable ultimate objective which, none the less, needed to be carefully studied after the conclusion of an interim agreement based on the equal sharing of the Company's profits.[90] Razmara told Shepherd that this meant paying lip-service to the idea of nationalization while, in effect, establishing a 50:50 arrangement. Although the British later offered this to Musaddiq in various forms, at this point any mention of nationalization was anathema to them. Shepherd discouraged the pursuit of such a plan by Razmara, regarding it as incompatible with the 1933 Agreement, which the British still regarded as the basis for any agreement with Iran but which the Iranians totally rejected.[91] Shepherd found Razmara's behaviour highly objectionable:

> I do not think that Razmara should be allowed to reap the benefit from this unhelpful conduct by means of any endorsement by us of the principle of nationalization. Persian oil and British industry are in fact in partnership and a 50:50 arrangement is perfectly reasonable.[92]

Similarly the Foreign Office pointed out that the British Government could not be expected to comment on any suggestion which referred to nationalization, although the AIOC was prepared to negotiate an equal share of profits on condition that the terms of the AIOC concession remained unaltered.[93] In the eyes of his Western supporters, however, Razmara's position did not seem to have been adversely affected by his ill-received suggestion regarding nationalization. In late January Fry had commented that 'HM Embassy, the Americans and Mr. Northcroft all agree that nothing better than Razmara could be found at the moment',[94] and this assessment still seemed to apply.

Discouraged by the attitude of the British, whom he could not afford to alienate, Razmara continued to spell out the difficulties and dangers of nationalization but without publicly disclosing the 50:50 offer. He was undoubtedly pessimistic about the acceptability of such an offer once the idea of nationalization had gained wide publicity. Perhaps he also intended to gain further concessions from the British which would, in some form, incorporate the idea of nationalization and enable him to settle or even resolve the oil problem in triumph.[95] His hopes in this regard anchored on the fact that no other prime minister had been more willing to risk his prestige by openly supporting the British.

By siding with the British against popular demands, however, Razmara had risked not only his prestige but also his life. On 4 March he reiterated his opposition to hasty nationalization at a meeting of the Oil Committee, which postponed voting until 7 March.[96] On that very day Razmara's life was brought to an untimely and tragic end by a member of the Fida'iyan-i Islam, while attending the funeral of an *ayatullah* in Tehran's Royal Mosque.[97] In all likelihood the Oil Committee would have recommended nationalization regardless of Razmara's fate; but his death removed all traces of doubt. It has been argued that had Razmara not concealed the 50:50 offer, his assassination and the nationalization crisis might have been averted.[98] However, discussions about such an arrangement had begun less than a month before the assassination, when nationalization was already a popular cause. Also, according to Razmara, at least the non-National Front members of the Oil Committee were aware of the offer, as was the Shah, and had they been hopeful about its acceptance they would have announced it.

On the surface Razmara's main problem seemed to have been confined to the oil issue and his uneasy relationship with the

Parliament. Yet his relationship with the Court, which was regarded as being his main source of support, was in fact deeply problematic. Influential Court officials such as General Yazdanpanah and Sayyid Hasan Muqaddam were averse to Razmara,[99] as, to a lesser extent, was Ernest Perron, the Shah's Swiss private secretary and long-time companion.[100] Sycophants, informers and professional gossips who milled around the Shah and Razmara played their part, but the underlying causes of variance between the Court and the Government were more complex. Prior to assuming office Razmara had complained to Pyman that the Shah saw 'all sorts of people' who, for their own 'private ends', persuaded him to intervene in politics, and recalled that as Chief of Staff he had asked the Shah to deal only with him and not to receive 'individual officers'.[101] Undoubtedly Razmara had tried to bar the Shah from undue interference in governmental affairs, but this was incongruent with the Shah's character and style and was not readily tolerated.

In order to cope successfully with the demanding task of government and realize his reformist objectives, which were also apparently shared by the Shah, it was imperative for Razmara to have both full royal support and effective freedom of manoeuvre. This, however, inevitably contravened the vague and ill-defined range of royal authority. Contrary to his own and British expectations, Razmara was left with little choice but to restrain his exercise of power, while the Shah supported him only as far as he needed to avoid the charge of openly opposing him. The Shah's tactic of creating different impressions of his position had led many deputies, or provided them with an excuse, not to support Razmara actively or consistently. The Shah's general pattern of behaviour toward any prime minister was to provide qualified, and usually passive, support for the inactive and docile, while actively opposing the recalcitrant and strong. In view of his putative strength, as well as his apparent docility and loyalty, Razmara did not easily fit either of these categories. The Shah's attitude towards him was, therefore, an equivocal mixture of qualified apparent support, covert non-co-operation and, above all, watchful control. The transitory predominance of any of these aspects of the Shah's attitude depended on Razmara's own behaviour. Aware of the royal attitude and strongly advised by friends such as Tahiri,[102] Razmara endeavoured not to provoke the Shah unnecessarily; upon assuming office he had, in fact, abandoned his position as Chief of Staff and severed his links with the military as a concession to the Shah. He had also refrained from actively pursuing his interest in forming a political party.

Given current concern with reform and progress, the elite were keen to show an interest in the formation of 'progressive' political parties. In July 1949, therefore, Hikmat had created the 'Socialist Party of Iran', which was socialist in name only and did not exist outside the mind of its founder. In the spring and summer of 1950 Reza Ashtianizadih, who was conducting a 'one man opposition of his own in the Majlis', claimed to have been asked by Razmara to create a 'Social Democratic Party',[103] and was trying to enlist British support since in his view no party could succeed without outside 'support'.[104] Sipihr, whom Razmara had reappointed as head of the Board of Directors of Caspian Fisheries, was also trying to persuade the British Embassy to support the creation of this party.[105] Sipihr and his colleagues – whom Razmara discreetly encouraged – were, however, 'afraid that the Shah might dislike the formation of such a party'.[106] Razmara himself told Pyman 'with a broad grin, that the Shah was afraid that he was going to build up a personal party' on the lines of Qavam's Democratic Party of Iran, and he felt compelled to assure him that 'he had no particular interest in the formation of a party'.[107]

Following such appeals the British Embassy tried to impress upon the Shah the benefit of political parties;[108] even though Razmara seemed to have lost his enthusiasm and was concentrating instead on 'economic development', which he believed 'would do more than any number of political parties to curb the spread of communism'.[109] Many pro-British politicians, including Sayyid Zia and Khajih-Nuri, had emphasized that any parties created in Iran were doomed to become 'personalist'.[110] Nevertheless the British Embassy was still prepared to help Razmara if he so desired. In the last month of his term of office Razmara reverted to the idea of forming a party, but the Shah's reaction was still his main concern; he had once told Shepherd that 'it would be necessary to speak to the Shah in order that his suspicions might be allayed'.[111]

He was only partially successful in reassuring the Shah, who was embittered by National Front opposition and because his efforts to increase his power through the Constituent Assembly had invariably provoked strong reactions.[112] Perceiving himself as perennially insecure and ineffective, the Shah interfered more and more in governmental affairs, involving himself in a growing Court-centred labyrinth of intrigues as a defence mechanism to outwit enemies and control friends. Of course the Shah was not satisfied with resorting primarily to negative actions; he frequently spoke to Shepherd of the 'unfitness' of Iran for 'democratic government', which he regarded as having reached an 'impasse'.[113] He was as adamant as ever to initiate a rearrangement in his favour. Yet the political situation was by no means congenial to any move in this direction. The growing gap between the Shah's ambitions and his achievements was bound to cause him even greater frustration and bitterness, and make him more susceptible to suspicions, often supplemented by naive credulity. The Shah even suspected that the British might actually help the National Front to gain power. To assume leadership was a compulsive desire for the Shah, an integral part of his character and mentality, but he evidently lacked the qualities necessary for the challenge.

The Shah's behaviour and attitude had alarmed even his friends. Alam, who was his close companion and adviser and had been appointed Minister of Labour by Razmara on 20 November 1950, had with 'regret and reluctance' come to the conclusion that the Shah was 'quite incapable of accomplishing what he had undertaken'.[114] He suggested to Pyman that a council of 'elder politicians' be established to 'guide the Shah',[115] but Pyman discouraged this since he believed it could lead to the formation of an alternative government.[116] Convinced that the Shah had to be kept 'on a consistent line', Alam pressed the British to provide the monarch with 'clear and firm' advice, and contemplated the appointment of a 'good' Court Minister to help him.[117] Among the Shah's friends Alam was neither the first to recommend the necessity of advising him, nor the last to complain of his undue interference in the affairs of state. Sayyid Zia had also repeatedly complained about direct royal activity which, in his view, had 'reached a stage dangerous to the dynasty itself'.[118] As usual, however, the Shah's reaction to such advice was negative, while Razmara felt his position constantly eroded.

Not long after becoming premier Razmara had threatened the British Embassy with resignation if two of his pressing problems, namely the 'lack of money' and the 'unsatisfactory attitude of the Shah', could not 'be put right'. The Shah frequently met Razmara's opponents,[119] and Razmara himself complained that 'in the matter of interference ... the Shah's conduct was not beyond reproach; he was not above sending for a minor official of a government department and telling him what to do'.[120] Many people, including Sayyid Zia, began to say that the Shah was not giving enough support to the Prime Minister, and Pyman asked Alam to elicit a show of support for Razmara from the Shah. Alam's reply revealed a great deal about the Shah's character, since he had been a close friend for some twelve years and knew 'how his mind works'. He would, said Alam, react to any suggestion of the sort with 'and who is Razmara that I should have to support him?' Pyman suggested that as long as Razmara enjoyed royal support the Shah should be obliged to arrange for a 'regular demonstration of support for him'. Alam expressed his full agreement, as he believed that 'without the Shah's support Razmara amounted to very little'.[121]

This assessment of the Shah's attitude and position was essentially valid: he had lived up to his promise to a group of deputies that he would 'not be an Ahmad Shah (Qajar), and nor Razmara become a Reza Shah'.[122] Contrary to the assumption of Baqa'i and others, the Shah was far more than 'an innocent deer, captive in the powerful claws of foreigners'.[123] In recent years all prime ministers had been his docile appointees, and Razmara was a royal candidate who had lost active royal backing after trying to reassert the authority of the executive. On the other hand the Shah and his entourage also had complaints about Razmara: in late September 1950 Alam had told Pyman that 'he was by no means confident that Razmara would be able to hold his position' when 'activity against the Shah was being carried on by Razmara, or at any rate by people in his confidence'.[124] Razmara had maintained good relations with Qavam, some of whose supporters had gathered around him (notably Ashtianizadih, Sipihr, Ghaffari, Iskandari and Arsanjani). Moreover his cancellation of all press laws except that of 1908, which contained no provision for firm action against those who insulted the royal family, was another serious blow to the Shah's prestige, according to Alam.[125] Confronted by the adverse attitude of the Shah, Razmara could not have remained entirely passive, but as a prime minister whose authority was constantly contested and who was faced with myriad problems, his opportunity for countering the Shah was severely limited.

Apart from the hostile attitude of the Shah, the royal family's political involvement also affected the position of the Government. Razmara had complained to Pyman that:

> There must be a proper chain of command if the Government were to function. It simply could not work if it were subjected to interference from members of the royal family; not to mention their respective entourages, who were by no means free from thought of financial gain.[126]

Sayyid Zia and Alam, among others, also complained about such interference: on one occasion Alam asserted that 'it was extremely undesirable that the Shah's family should be allowed to interfere in State affairs', and hinted that the British should advise the Shah on this matter.[127] However, previous experience had shown that the Shah was either unwilling to listen or had little control over his family. The Court was an arena in which various fluid cliques constantly manoeuvred to discomfit one another. The Shah's mother had her own retinue, composed of elder politicians, including at some point Qavam and Sayyid Zia, while Ashraf, with the help of Ali Reza, challenged Abd ur-Reza who seemed to have the support of Perron. Razmara was inevitably caught up in these webs of intrigue and counter-intrigue; he was opposed to Abd ur-Reza and appeared to support Ashraf and was believed to enjoy her favour, although Perron later told a member of the British Embassy that Razmara had secretly bribed the press to write articles against Ashraf.[128] In addition, Ashraf's husband, Ahmad Shafiq, was definitely *persona non grata* to the Prime Minister.[129] The activities of the royal family sometimes reached scandalous proportions: Ali Reza refused to pay customs duties on twenty tractors which he had imported,[130] and Ashraf was said by an official of the Opium Department to smuggle opium regularly in army lorries for sale in Tehran.[131] All of this obviously undermined the credibility of any Court-favoured government, or of any prime minister who was regarded, justifiably or otherwise, as being a Court protégé.

Razmara's relations with the Court had proved undeniably problematic; it is in this context that Alam's reported expression of relief while informing the Shah of Razmara's assassination – which he had witnessed – makes sense.[132] It is also in this context that the reported posthumous discovery of a republican coup which Razmara had apparently planned to launch, appears plausible. Ahmad Human, the Deputy Court Minister appointed on 4 March 1951, told Jackson that there was 'clear evidence' of Razmara's 'duplicity of character', adding that Razmara had planned to set up a 'strong left-wing republic' which 'would seek Soviet support'; he intended to become President, and in case of failure 'had plans already drawn up for an escape to South America'.[133]

Uncritically subscribing to the subculture of clan politics, Razmara had assumed that the active support of foreign powers was the main factor not only in the assumption of office, but also in its successful retention.[134] He had thus betrayed a singular lack of comprehension of and sensitivity towards the prevailing nationalist movement. He undoubtedly held reformist convictions and had the will and energy to implement them, but he was confronted with a situation which greatly hindered his likelihood of success. The fundamental constraints to which prime-ministerial authority was subjected, augmented by an unfavourable situation, had transformed Razmara from an enviably successful and strong Chief of Staff into an irredeemably enfeebled Prime Minister.

17

The Government of Ala:
MARCH–APRIL 1951

On the day of Razmara's assassination Alam rushed to Shepherd on behalf of the Shah to consult him about the next government: should it be strong, or 'inoffensive' as advocated by the Speaker of the Majlis?[1] Shepherd was of the opinion that 'a strong hand at the helm of the government was needed', but he 'strongly deprecated' the appointment of another military prime minister given the popular opposition to the late Razmara. Although Shepherd's favoured candidate was Sayyid Zia, in view of the existing difficulties he recommended the appointment of a 'caretaker government'. The Foreign Office not only favoured the appointment of 'as strong a personality as possible', but also the dissolution of the Majlis which it regarded as 'all the more desirable' if it were to be 'swayed by Kashani's views' into rejecting the increase of the note issue.[2] The Foreign Office also regarded Sayyid Zia as the 'most promising' candidate, but on the basis of recent experience was anxious that the position of Sayyid Zia or any other candidate, 'should not be prejudiced through unwise expression of support for him expressed in advance by the United States Embassy in Tehran, as we believe had been the case on previous occasions.'[3] On this the State Department agreed and considered it 'very undesirable that the prospective Prime Minister be regarded as an Anglo-American candidate'.[4]

Restraint on the part of the British and American Embassies left the Shah and his advisers with a greater responsibility in the choice of prime minister. However, in an atmosphere of thinly disguised disorientation, a non-provocative 'caretaker' Cabinet was the only real possibility: the Shah's advisers, including Taqizadih and Hikmat, were averse to firm action,[5] and in any case no candidate was prepared to take such action. Determined to ignore the Parliament in the choice of prime minister, the Shah asked Ala to form a Cabinet and, when he refused, turned to Khalil Fahimi, Minister without

Portfolio in Razmara's Cabinet. The Majlis was equally determined to recover its rights and refused to endorse Fahimi. According to Shepherd, the Shah then 'sounded' out Sayyid Zia, who was not yet ready to step forward; he therefore turned again to Ala and persuaded him to accept office.[6] No parliamentary 'vote of inclination' was sought by the Shah, so the National Front delegates (although they preferred Ala to the alternatives) refused to vote for him and left the Chamber after heated debates. The sensitivity of the situation and the lingering threat of dissolution meant of course that the Parliament had to acquiesce, and Ala was offered a vote of 71 to 28, while the Senate gave 36 votes in his favour out of a total of 40.[7]

Husain Ala was born in 1884 into a prominent family, educated at Westminster School and, like his father and brother, joined the diplomatic corps. By 1918 he had become Minister of Public Works; in 1919 he was appointed Minister in Madrid, and a year later in Washington. He returned to Iran in 1925 and assumed a seat as a deputy for Tehran in the 5th Majlis, where he defied Reza Khan and opposed the abolition of the Qajar dynasty, along with Musaddiq and three other deputies. In 1927 he was again briefly appointed Minister of Public Works, and following a number of other posts was appointed Minister in Paris in 1929. He was involved in the oil negotiations of 1933 and also held a prominent position in the National Bank of Iran. In July 1934 he was appointed Minister in London but recalled in mid-1936.[8] In September 1937 he was appointed Minister of Commerce, but, having lost Reza Shah's favour, he was removed from the post in April 1938, and thereby excluded from active politics. In the post-1941 period he acted as Court Minister before becoming Ambassador to Washington and to the United Nations in 1945. In late February 1950 he was briefly Foreign Minister in Sa'id's Cabinet and later in that of Mansur, and was reappointed Court Minister on 24 February 1951.

Ala was the son-in-law of Abulqasim Qaraguzlu (Nasir ul-Mulk), a one-time Regent, and his wife was 'one of the first of her generation to leave off the veil'.[9] In the British 'Report on Personalities 1940' he was described as:

A hard worker and a staunch patriot; intelligent and well-read; interested in the literature of many countries and quite a good pianist. He has a perfect command of English and speaks good French. In the past he has had a reputation for anti-British sentiments. In 1933 and 1934, however, his relations with the British Legation were excellent;

he seems a good deal more anti-Russian than anti-British, and is doubtless more pro-Persian than either.[10]

Ala was suspicious of British policy in Iran and was more oriented towards the Americans, believing along with many politicians of his generation that America was a countervailing force *vis-à-vis* the British and the Russians. He was a devout royalist,[11] but his insight into the strength of Iranian nationalism was unusual among politicians of his standing and was revealed clearly during the greater part of Musaddiq's premiership, when he acted as Court Minister. Musaddiq went out of his way to praise him publicly as 'an active, benevolent, humble and democratic man who takes seriously whatever job he is involved with, and who has not accepted office merely in order to earn his living and acquire elevated rank: a sincere and truthful man'[12]

Ala declined to form his Cabinet immediately; he proceeded with caution, refused to declare martial law, attempted to cultivate the friendship of the National Front and demanded an increase in the note issue of only 600 million rials – compared to the 2,200 million demanded by his predecessor[13] – and more importantly he refused to impede the process of oil nationalization. On 15 March 1951, following large demonstrations and public clamour, the Majlis unanimously endorsed the recent decision of the Majlis Oil Committee to approve the principle of nationalization, and asked the Oil Committee to study the best way of implementing it.[14] Both the British and the Shah had tried to dissuade the deputies from attending the Majlis session.[15] When this failed the British pinned their hopes on the Senate, but the Shah's efforts in this direction were also unsuccessful and the Senate unanimously endorsed the principle of nationalization.[16]

Now the British regarded the urgent dissolution of the Parliament as 'the best solution'[17] and the only chance of salvaging their oil concession. The Shah appeared 'anxious' to dissolve the Parliament, but not 'on the oil issue', and the Foreign Office was therefore 'inclined to doubt' if it would ever happen.[18] Shepherd, for his part, reported:

> If there is a change of Government within two or three months accompanied or followed immediately by the dissolution of the parliament, the existing [oil] commission will disappear, and it should be possible to strike a bargain with Qavam or Sayyid Zia, if either of

these is appointed. But it would be a hard bargain, especially with the former. In either case, the principle of nationalization would have to be conceded. Recent events have beaten the idea so deeply into the public mind that no Government could afford to ignore it.[19]

At long last Shepherd accepted that no government could be expected to oppose nationalization and began to advocate the course of action originally proposed by Razmara, namely to pay lip-service to the rubric of nationalization, but in effect to adopt a 50:50 arrangement. Ala was also apparently in favour of this, and was said to be 'thinking in terms of some kind of nationalization arrangement which would leave the management in the hands of the Anglo-Iranian Oil Company'.[20] Since the definition of nationalization and the manner of its implementation had yet to be clarified, he was given a breathing-space to consolidate his position and form a Cabinet.

Ala's declared aim in internal politics was to 'tranquillize matters' and he was opposed to the dissolution of the Majlis.[21] Following the assassination of Hamid Zanganih – the unpopular Education Minister in the Razmara Cabinet – he declared martial law and provoked the strong disapproval of the National Front.[22] On the other hand, he considered the preferences of the Front when forming his Cabinet, which included no members of the previous one. Ala's difficulties in forming a Cabinet without provoking or alienating the main parties was signified by the presence of five acting ministers in the Cabinet, but even Shepherd was impressed that he had formed a government at all.[23] His Cabinet programme was realistic and his position was strengthened by the fact that he had not pushed himself forward to be prime minister. His Cabinet was unanimously approved by the Senate and received 77 votes in the Majlis.[24] On 4 April he reshuffled his Cabinet and brought in Zahidi and Arfa, both of whom were close to Kashani. He also arranged for Ali Reza to be sent to Germany and Ashraf to take a long journey abroad. This had now become a standard way of dealing with resentment against the Court, and Shepherd believed that 'this camouflaged banishment should gratify public opinion'.[25] By now the Cabinet appeared to have gained sufficient parliamentary support, with even the National Front prepared to extend its qualified backing.[26]

In the aftermath of the Iranian New Year 1330 (22 March 1951), however, Ala's Government suddenly faced a serious problem in the form of a strike by southern oil-workers, sparked off by the oil company's removal of an allowance made to workers in Bandar Ma'shur. The strike began on 26 March and quickly spread to other places, particularly Abadan, and occasionally resulted in violence. The oil nationalization movement had raised workers' expectations, while the insensitivity of the Company further aggravated the situation.[27] Shepherd and Furlonge characteristically placed the entire responsibility for the strike on the communists,[28] and Shepherd and Grady both pressed Ala to act decisively.[29] Ala was fully aware of the gravity of the situation and declared martial law in the entire strike area for a period of two months, a move which was almost unanimously approved by the Majlis.[30] His determination to restore order was further justified when the unrest assumed serious proportions, spreading to Isfahan.[31] However, by late April the strike was over, the Government had succeeded in restoring order and the workers had prevailed over the Company, which agreed to resume the payment of the allowance.

Ala took prompt action because he was well aware that the British might use the situation as a pretext for military action, and in fact they had already dispatched gunboats to the Persian Gulf. They had failed, however, to enlist American co-operation for a 'common policy' towards the nationalization of oil in Iran through the Washington Conference of 9–19 April 1951,[32] and the Americans were averse to military action. George McGhee, the Assistant Secretary of State for Near Eastern Affairs, warned the British Ambassador in Washington of the danger of providing the Russians with a pretext for intervention, and added that the State Department 'earnestly hoped' that any measure towards the protection of British lives in southern Iran would be taken with Iranian consent and after consultation with the Americans.[33] Ala had also done his utmost to avert and forestall pretexts for British intervention in the south, warning Shepherd against provoking the Russians into intervening.[34] In an interview with *Le Monde*, Ala also expressed his fear that British action in the south might spark off a world war, and warned that strikes in Iran 'give no one the right to intervene in our internal affairs or infringe our independence'.[35] He also reacted strongly to a statement made by Morrison which failed to appreciate the efforts of his Government in restoring order in the south; even more so since Ala considered the strikes to have been caused by the 'Company's untimely and unwise action at Bandar Ma'shur and by their singular lack of comprehension of the psychology of the Persian people'.[36] Once the strike was over the danger of military intervention seemed to have receded, but the interim nature of Ala's Cabinet and the various rumours that the British were working to replace him with Sayyid Zia adversely affected his position and his readiness to continue in office.

After Razmara's death the British had been increasingly pre-occupied with the idea of Sayyid Zia's premiership. Shepherd and the Foreign Office considered him an ideal candidate, but realized that he would disagree with the Shah over the manner of his appointment or would demand the prior approval of the Parliament in some form.[37] They also recognized that he was not sufficiently experienced, that there would 'almost certainly' be 'friction between him and the Shah' and that he might not condone the dissolution of the Majlis, which they still felt to be desirable – although Shepherd had begun to be slightly pessimistic about its feasibility:

> It would, I believe, be good for the country if the Shah could seize this opportunity for teaching the Majlis a lesson and put in a period of sound government without it. I fear, however, that now that Razmara has gone, there is no one whom he could rely on to enable him to carry through anything of the kind.[38]

The one factor that the British attached no importance to was that Sayyid Zia had no popular support, and that his appointment was likely to provoke a strong public reaction, for he was widely regarded as a devout British protégé. Given the strength of the nationalist movement and the fate which Razmara had suffered as a result of being castigated as a British stooge, the British seemed to have learned very little. This surprising insensitivity to popular reaction can only be explained by the deeply held beliefs of Shepherd and his Foreign Office colleagues concerning the ultimate submis-siveness of the 'Persian character' in the face of a determined show of force. On the basis of this assumption, Sayyid Zia seemed the ideal person to overcome what he and his British supporters believed to be a temporary outburst of xenophobic and irrational sentiments.

A few days after Razmara's death, following consultation with the Shah, Sayyid Zia handed to Pyman a detailed plan for his assumption of office, which envisaged the dissolution of the Parliament by the Shah or the appointment of an interim prime minister, to be followed by his own appointment within two or three weeks. He undertook to resolve the oil problem on a 50:50 basis, restrain the royal family from intervening in politics, comply fully with royal views on 60 per cent of matters, while reserving 40 per cent to his own discretion, and to deal with the National Front with a combination of 'carrot and stick'. He demanded an economic adviser from the Embassy and asked them to contact the Shah, expressing their support for this plan. The Embassy welcomed the plan; Alam was asked to inform the Shah of it, and Sayyid Zia was told that the AIOC had already paid £5 million and was ready to make a monthly payment of £2 million for the rest of 1951 and to deposit £10 million in the Iranian National Bank in London.[39]

With the appointment of Ala as interim Prime Minister, the way seemed clear to appoint Sayyid Zia, who would proceed with the dissolution of the Parliament, if possible on the pretext of introducing reform. When he received the message from the British Embassy the Shah replied that Sayyid Zia would be appointed as prime minister within a month.[40] The dissolution of the Parliament, however, remained a major problem, and Sayyid Zia was shrewd enough not to feel confident about the Shah's intentions. He feared that once he became prime minister, 'the Shah might prefer to have the Majlis in being in order to have some means of working against him if necessary'.[41] Nevertheless Sayyid Zia demanded that the Embassy impress upon the Shah that his interests and those of his country would be best served with the premiership of Sayyid Zia, and this they were quite happy to do. With the full support of the British Embassy he now awaited the appropriate moment for his appointment to office.

However, there was another contender actively promoting his own appointment. This was Qavam, who had returned from Europe in October 1950, and was busy trying to improve his relations with the Court (which had suffered as a result of his 'open letters'). He was also attempting to enlist the support of the British Embassy through emissaries such as Nikpay, Asadi and others.[42] Qavam had some success in influencing the Embassy officials through Major Jackson,[43] and Ali Muqtadir-i Shafi'a worked on his behalf to win over the Foreign Office.[44] Shepherd, however, regarded him as *persona non grata*, opposed to reform, corrupt and untrustworthy, and believed that his appointment would be harmful to the Shah and the country.[45] Qavam's supporters, however, were so active on his behalf that Musaddiq subjected him to a strong attack in the Majlis in order to forestall his premiership.[46] His uneasy relations with the Court,[47] and his failure to win over the British Embassy, meant that Qavam had much less chance of success than Sayyid Zia.

One major obstacle to Sayyid Zia's chances was the attitude of the Americans, who regarded his relations with the Court as 'uncertain' and his identification with the British as weakening his position. They were 'impressed by the merits' of Suhaili,[48] but the Foreign Office had objections: his poor health, his connections with the land-owning classes and his association with Princess Ashraf.[49] Behind-the-scenes activities on behalf of Sayyid Zia, which entailed undermining the fragile position of Ala, alarmed the Americans. William Rountree, head of the office of Greek, Turkish and Persian Affairs at the State Department, expressed his 'serious concern' at British efforts to bring about Ala's downfall and arrange for the government of Sayyid Zia, whose intended dissolution of the Parliament and rule by decree would have 'incalculable consequences'. Rountree's concern that the successor to Ala should not attempt to govern by decree was reiterated by McGhee,[50] so that the British were left in little doubt about the American attitude.

The British Ambassador denied that they had been undermining Ala's position, and stated that they had themselves come to realize that the dissolution of the Parliament on the pretext of the intractable oil issue was 'most undesirable'.[51] Despite all the evidence to the contrary, the Foreign Office also denied that they wanted 'to appear to be influencing the Persians in their choice of Prime Minister'.[52] They expressed satisfaction with Ala's handling of the situation in Tehran and Abadan, and added that they would not like to 'see him go for the present', or 'to give a lead in this direction to the Majlis'.[53] Yet none of these claims disguised the fact that the British Embassy was anxiously trying to secure the speedy premier-ship of Sayyid Zia and had, therefore, not refrained from approving or encouraging anti-Ala opposition in the Majlis.[54] In the eyes of the British officials, the premiership of Sayyid Zia was the only hope of saving the AIOC and preventing the erosion of British interests and prestige in Iran, and Sayyid Zia himself seemed whole-heartedly prepared to oppose and suppress the oil nationalization movement. Aware of the insurmountable problems involved in attempting the dissolution of Parliament, including the attitude of the Americans, Sayyid Zia had changed his tactics. He claimed to be able, if assured of complete royal confidence, to muster a majority of between sixty and seventy deputies, to defeat Ala's Government and to assume office through the normal constitutional procedures – a move described by Shepherd as 'the best way out of the existing tangle'.[55] In this way Sayyid Zia could hope to avert many problems, disarm the Americans, make himself less open to the charge of being a British stooge and put himself in a better position to tackle the oil issue. He therefore concentrated his energies on cultivating support in the Majlis, with the Shah appearing to be genuinely on his side. These activities did not escape the notice of the National Front or the Government of Ala which, in any case, showed little enthusiasm for remaining in office.

On 25 April 1951, immediately following the termination of the strikes in the south, the Majlis Oil Committee unanimously approved a draft nine-point law, proposed by a subcommittee of seven, which provided a framework for the implementation of the oil national-ization principle. Shepherd reported that Ala had not been consulted and, in view of his 'unwillingness to support the resolution . . . and inability to oppose it successfully',[56] had immediately handed in his resignation after a period of forty-six days in office. Ala was both unwilling and unable to face what was to follow thereafter, and it was also known that the Shah no longer insisted on his retention.[57] He had accomplished his task as a caretaker prime minister with relative success, and could therefore return to the safety and security of his previous post, that of Court Minister, which was more suited to his character and temperament.

At this critical point in Iranian history a premier of a completely different calibre was required and the British remained confident that Sayyid Zia possessed the necessary qualities for the premiership and would soon be appointed. However, the Iranian political scene changed suddenly and dramatically, and it was not Sayyid Zia but his arch-opponent Musaddiq who became Prime Minister.

PART V

The Hegemony of the Nationalist Movement and the Eclipse of the Monarchy

18

The First Government of Musaddiq:
APRIL 1951–JULY 1952

On the eve of Ala's resignation it seemed certain that backstage activities had guaranteed Sayyid Zia the premiership. Sayyid Zia was in fact discussing the matter with the Shah and awaiting the approval of the Majlis and the royal decree for his appointment,[1] when, on the suggestion of Jamal Imami, Musaddiq caused surprise by accepting office. On previous occasions he had refused such offers, and only two weeks earlier he had stated: 'Some would say that I should form a government, but would the 50 year intervention of the AIOC allow me and persons like me to form a government and succeed?'[2] Imami and others, therefore, expected that Musaddiq would refuse again; but he and his followers considered that to have Sayyid Zia in office would be nothing short of a catastrophe and for this reason he accepted,[3] on condition that his nomination was formally approved by the Majlis. Accordingly the traditional parliamentary 'vote of inclination' was revived and 79 out of 90 deputies,[4] and 29 out of 43 senators cast their votes for Musaddiq.[5] This was followed by the royal decree for his appointment (29 April 1949).

Musaddiq's foreign and domestic opponents, including Imami himself, could now only console themselves with the hope that he would fail to solve the oil problem and be forced to quit the political scene. As Shepherd reported: 'Many politicians consider that Musaddiq will not last long and that his advent is a blessing in disguise because he will prove a failure in a very short time and will therefore become a non-entity.'[6] Sayyid Zia attributed Musaddiq's success to the lack of firm action by the Shah, the ignorance of the Majlis Speaker of what was being arranged in the Majlis and 'perhaps lack of activity on his own part', but believed that 'given a little rope Dr. Musaddiq would hang himself'.[7]

Musaddiq, however, was determined to tackle the oil question by implementing the nationalization law, and made his acceptance of office conditional upon the approval of the draft nine-point law, which the Majlis, irrespective of British threats, unanimously approved on 28 April 1951, after an emotionally tense five-hour session.[8] The nationalization law was also approved by the Senate the next day, despite the efforts of the Shah and the Court,[9] and was signed by the Shah immediately. The nationalization of oil and the premiership of Musaddiq were now inseparable and irreversible. Although Musaddiq had seemingly assumed office fortuitously or accidentally, his premiership was in fact more or less inevitable and only a matter of time in view of a number of interrelated factors: the hegemony of the National Front, the pivotal significance of the oil issue, the rising appeal of nationalism, as well as Musaddiq's own popularity.

Born in 1882 in Tehran, Musaddiq was still in his teens when charged with supervising the financial administration of Khurasan province and was twenty-five when elected to the Majlis as a deputy for Isfahan, a task he could not fulfil because of the Majlis age requirement. In 1909 he went to France to study finance and in 1913 gained a doctorate in law in Switzerland. He returned a year later to teach at the School of Political Science, and was eventually appointed as Under-Secretary at the Finance Ministry. Following a brief stay in Switzerland he returned to Iran to become Governor-General (Vali) of Fars, but resigned when Sayyid Zia became premier in 1921. He served as Finance Minister in Qavam's Cabinet from June 1921 to January 1922, became Governor-General of Azarbaijan and in 1923 assumed the portfolio of Foreign Affairs in the Cabinet of Mushir ud-Daulih.

Later in the same year he was elected a deputy to the 5th Majlis, where, along with a number of others, he opposed the transfer of the monarchy from the Qajars to the Pahlavis. He also displayed his continued scholarly interest in legal and financial matters by publishing a book and a number of articles. He was re-elected to the 6th Majlis (1925–7), subsequently barred from active politics by Reza Shah, and exiled to Birjand in June 1940. As a result of the intervention of the then Crown Prince Muhammad Reza, he returned to his estate in Ahmadabad in December of the same year and was only granted freedom of movement after the Allied invasion of the country. In the post-1941 period he was elected to the 14th and the 16th Majlis, and had been a deputy for a year before assuming the premiership in April 1951.[10]

Muhammad Musaddiq was born into a prominent upper-class family with Qajar links which was related by an extensive network to other established families. His behaviour and dispositions, however, cannot simply be explained by his class origins which he successfully transcended, displaying remarkable moral and intellectual autonomy.[11] Musaddiq owed his prestige and popularity to his championing of causes likely to benefit the entire nation, and particularly its middle and lower classes, and this, as well as other qualities of personality, distinguished him from the bulk of the Iranian ruling elite.

Having gained parliamentary approval for the oil nationalization law, Musaddiq presented his Cabinet to the Majlis. His Cabinet programme consisted of only two points: implementation of the oil nationalization law and the utilization of revenues for the improvement of the economy; and reform of the parliamentary and municipal electoral laws. His choice of colleagues was expedient and he sought the co-operation of a few established but respected members of the elite. According to *Bakhtar-i Imruz*:

> In the first meeting of the National Front, it was decided that a 'national coalition Cabinet' should govern so that various segments of the [state] apparatus would not be frightened and would not indulge in intrigue and obstruction. Had it not been for the oil issue, the Cabinet would have been differently constituted. It has been said that Dr. Musaddiq . . . has asserted that he has always believed in choosing his colleagues from the ranks of young people who have never assumed ministerial portfolios, so that their fresh ideas and capable minds should compensate for the existing misfortunes.[12]

Musaddiq's assumption of office had inevitably threatened the traditional configuration of clan politics and alarmed the Court and the pro-British elements. His non-provocative Cabinet and programme were therefore aimed at forestalling strong reactions, and this policy seemed effective: 99 out of 102 voted in the Cabinet's favour in the Majlis and 48 out of 51 in the Senate.[13] However, it alienated some of Musaddiq's own supporters who expected to be rewarded for their support: the deputy Azad, for instance, demanded that all parties and groups, including his own 'Independence' (*Istiqlal*) party, which had contributed to Musaddiq's assumption of office, be represented by two ministers in the Cabinet.[14]

Musaddiq seemed to have had little doubt that the enormity of his task could seriously jeopardize his life,[15] but was equally determined to accomplish his task regardless of the cost. Soon after taking up office, in a dramatic speech he claimed to have been inspired by a dream to proceed with his task regarding the oil issue, but added that his life was threatened by the Fida'iyan-i Islam and he would therefore remain in the Majlis until the fate of the oil issue was clarified.[16] This was hardly an auspicious start for a government intent on challenging the AIOC and the British Government, and Ashtianizadih quickly threatened Musaddiq with interpellation.[17] In fact, after a brief stay in the Majlis, he moved to his house and conducted all affairs of Government from there. Musaddiq's fears for his life were not exaggerated for the Fida'iyan had expectations which he could not possibly consider. Their specific demands were for the nation-wide compulsory wearing of the veil (hijab); the dismissal of women employees; a ban on alcohol; and compulsory public prayers for government employees.[18] They also demanded a complete break with the practices of previous governments, which implied granting them freedom of action and releasing their leaders. This Musaddiq was not inclined to do and after the arrest on 3 June 1951 of their leader Navvab-Safavi,[19] both Musaddiq and Kashani – who had also failed to fulfil Fida'iyan expectations – were subjected to direct pressure and intimidation.

For Musaddiq the nationalization of the oil industry in Iran represented not only the realization of Iranian national aspirations but the rebirth of the Iranian nation and its moral regeneration. The AIOC was viewed as an exploitative and iniquitous enclave with a revenue exceeding the earnings of the Iranian Government. In Musaddiq's view the Company had for fifty years been an insidious vehicle of British intervention in Iranian affairs, which had led to the moral decay of Iranian politicians, the corruption and dependency of their governments and the destitution of the people. Although he recognized the importance of oil revenues for welfare and economic development, he also believed that if necessary it was better for Iran to be poor and independent than to tolerate the survival of the AIOC and remain under British domination. This attitude has inevitably brought charges of naivety, unjustifiable optimism and ignorance of the real world of oil cartels and monopolies, as well as simplistic assumptions that Britain and the West needed Iranian oil more than Iran needed the revenues.[20] Such arguments, however, ignore the strength and importance of the desires and demands which Musaddiq articulated.

From the outset the movement for oil nationalization threatened to become the climax of an ongoing contradiction between a rising nationalism and a declining empire. Such a contradiction manifested itself not only in mutually discomfiting strife but also in a conflict of moral claims over such issues as entitlement. Sir Donald Fergusson, Permanent Secretary at the Ministry of Fuel and Power, for example, regarded as 'bunk' the claimed *moral* entitlement of the Iranians even to 50 per cent of the profits of 'enterprises to which they have made no contribution whatever'.[21] There was an inevitable lack of communication, and an absence of common idioms and shared criteria of judgement. It was in this context that Musaddiq's feelings and views about the AIOC and the British Government were fully reciprocated; he was implacably hated and described as a 'demagogue', a 'lunatic' and an 'irrational' man 'impervious to common sense argument', who had utilized an extremist emotional nationalism to jeopardize the civilizing mission of the AIOC; a man intent upon a course which would bring his country nothing but economic ruin, chaos and eventually communism.[22]

In this atmosphere of conflicting perceptions and claims the negotiations over nationalization began. The Musaddiq Government demanded the full acceptance of the nationalization law. The British, however, were only willing to accept nationalization of a kind which would enable them to preserve whatever they could of the arrangements existing prior to nationalization, and in particular to maintain their control over the process of production. Soon after Musaddiq's assumption of office, against a background of implicit British pressure and intimidation, a mission led by Basil Jackson of the AIOC began negotiations with him but failed to reach a conclusion.[23] Musaddiq was adamant that the nine-point nationalization law was irrevocable and in an effort to reconfirm his position resorted to the subsequently well-tried tactic of appealing to the Parliament. On the morning of 20 June 1951, however, Musaddiq's opponents, including the Shah and Sayyid Zia,[24] succeeded in breaking the quorum in the Majlis; but by the afternoon of the same day the Majlis had unanimously cast its vote of confidence in his favour, thereby affirming approval of his oil policy.[25]

In the wake of Jackson's departure, Averell Harriman arrived in Tehran to mediate on behalf of the US Government and to reconcile 'logic and feelings'.[26] His arrival coincided with large demonstrations in Tehran, launched to commemorate the strikes of five years earlier, and organized by various Tudeh-affiliated organizations, which regarded the nationalist movement as a rival and Musaddiq as a promoter of American imperialism in the country.[27] The clashes which occurred between Tudeh demonstrators and their opponents resulted in many deaths and injuries.[28] The Government claim to be fully in control of events was weakened and this created tension between Musaddiq and Zahidi, his Interior Minister, whose position made him directly responsible for what had taken place. These events also resulted in the removal of the Police Chief, General Baqa'i, and Musaddiq further discarded his own responsibility by stating that the appointment of the Chief of Police had been left to the Shah until 15 July (the day of the demonstrations).[29] The situation was, naturally, exploited by opponents in the Majlis.[30]

Nevertheless the prospects of continued negotiations disarmed Musaddiq's opponents. Harriman's journey raised hopes and paved the way for the mission led by Richard Stokes, the British Lord Privy Seal, which arrived in Iran in early August 1951. As the complex negotiations proceeded it became clear that the British were not prepared to offer more than a 50:50 split of the profits on operations in Iran, and the Americans supported them on this.[31] The negotiations broke down when Stokes demanded that there should be a British manager in charge of the entire oil production process, a point which clearly contravened the nationalization law.[32] On the eve of his return Stokes advised the Shah that the 'only solution' was a 'strong government under martial law and the bad boys in prison for two years or so'.[33] Although he refused to give way at that point, Stokes admitted that the British might eventually have no choice but to offer more and negotiate with Musaddiq.[34] The predominant view in British circles, however, was to offer no more and stand firm until Musaddiq fell.

After Musaddiq had submitted a full report on the negotiations to the Parliament,[35] he received a vote of confidence of 33 out of 36 in the Senate and 72 out of 81 in the Majlis.[36] His opponents were encouraged by the failure of the negotiations. Becoming increasingly restless in view of the imminent elections for the next Majlis, they intensified their manoeuvres aimed at bringing about the fall of the Government. In addition to anti-Government speeches and obstructive tactics in the Majlis, and articles in the press, they concentrated their efforts on persuading the British and Americans to refuse to negotiate with Musaddiq. Many British officials saw no prospect of achieving an oil agreement with Musaddiq, and Shepherd emphasized that they must not be seen to be willing to negotiate further with him:

I submit, it is not in our interest to take any action which might contribute to the survival, perhaps for a long time, of a Government which has shown its total indifference to economic needs of Persia and has already inflicted severe damage on the economic interests of the British people.[37]

The Foreign Office was prepared to make it clear that it had given up hope of being able to reach a settlement with Musaddiq, and the BBC was accordingly instructed.[38]

Opposition propaganda and pressure reinforced Musaddiq in his beliefs and on 5 September 1951 he delivered a speech in the Senate announcing that if he did not receive an acceptable offer from the British he would expel the Company's British personnel.[39] In response the Foreign Office announced the next day that the British Government considered negotiations to be 'no longer in suspense but broken off'.[40] A few days later Musaddiq repeated his Senate speech in the Majlis, but did not ask for a vote since he was aware of the extensive activities of his British-backed opponents.

He also proposed delivering an 'ultimatum' to the British Government, with Harriman as messenger, but failed to win the latter's co-operation. Musaddiq's opponents could credit themselves with having contributed to this refusal. The Shah, pressed by Shepherd to act decisively in order to bring about a change of government, tried unsuccessfully to persuade him to meet Musaddiq,[41] and Musaddiq's offer to accept a foreign national for the technical management of the Company's extracting and refining organizations was also rejected.[42] Shepherd informed the Foreign Office that the British position of no negotiation with Musaddiq had buttressed the opposition and advised that the BBC should maintain its line.[43] Meanwhile the implementation of the nationalization law proceeded steadily. Two bodies had completed the task of expropriating the old company: the Mixed Oil Committee (which included senators as well as deputies and had replaced the original Majlis Oil Committee) and the provisional directorate of the new NIOC (National Iranian Oil Company). The Iranians were more than willing to retain the Company's British personnel, but the latter refused to work under the new arrangements, and Musaddiq demanded their departure within a week of his announcement on 25 September 1951; on 2 October they were evicted.[44]

The British Government had always kept the military option in reserve, well aware of the impact that an Iranian victory would have on the prestige of the British Empire and its oil interests elsewhere. In addition, this was election year and the Labour Party was therefore attracted to the idea of teaching the Iranians a lesson, especially after the threat to expel British personnel. To capture the oil fields was virtually impossible, so a plan was adopted to capture Abadan ('Operation Buccaneer'). Despite the prospective adverse effects of inaction on the electoral prospects of the Labour Party, and the belligerent attitude of Herbert Morrison, the Foreign Secretary, Clement Attlee, the Prime Minister, was not in favour of military action and the Cabinet was on the whole inclined to restraint.[45]

The British had failed to enlist the co-operation of the Americans over military action, since there was no obvious communist threat. Many other factors contributed to the victory of restraint over jingoism: military action was bound to have adverse international repercussions, provoke the Russians, endanger the lives of British subjects in Iran, and was also for a variety of military, logistical and technical reasons unlikely to be successful. On the other hand confronting Iranian nationalism militarily would most likely have strengthened it, deepening its anti-British overtones and provoking strong resistance; in fact, even the Shah had asserted that the Iranians would have no choice but to resist military intervention.[46] Military action was therefore abandoned, but other pressures, such as economic restrictions or the prevention of the sale and purchase of Iranian oil, were increasingly deployed. The British were determined to thwart and undermine the nationalization movement, whatever measures they had to use.

Shortly after Musaddiq's assumption of office Robin Zaehner, a surprisingly ardent adventurer for an Oxford academic, was sent to Tehran to mobilize and co-ordinate anti-Musaddiq activities – on the suggestion of Ann Lambton, who was staunchly anti-Musaddiq and convinced that it was impossible 'to do business' with him.[47] Zaehner had been Assistant Press Attaché, then Press Attaché in Tehran from 1943 to 1947. He was a lecturer in Persian at Oxford University when dispatched to Tehran as acting Counsellor at the Embassy. He returned to Oxford in 1952 to become Spalding Professor of Eastern Religions and Ethics. Lambton described Zaehner as 'a man who knows almost everyone who matters in Tehran and a man of great subtlety' who had been 'apparently extremely successful in 1944 at the time that there was a serious threat that the Russians would take over Azarbaijan'. He had followed the 'line' of mobilizing 'public opinion from the bazaars upwards about the dangers of Russian penetration'.[48] Zaehner's brief was to indulge in any activity which would help to undermine Musaddiq's position, for which he was provided with considerable sums of money. After his arrival the communications network of the British Embassy was significantly extended and anti-Musaddiq activities gained a new momentum.[49] As the dissolution of the Parliament had not proved feasible, immediate destabilizing activities had to be concentrated mainly within the confines of the parliamentary arrangements, and the nucleus of a growing parliamentary opposition, which also enjoyed the backing of a few journalists, was increasingly cultivated.

The anti-Musaddiq opposition was composed primarily of a handful of conservative, unpopular and discredited elements who were directly or indirectly in contact with the British Embassy. Some of them were purely opportunist, but some conceived of the Iranian interests along the same lines as did the British. Their vested interests were seriously threatened by Musaddiq, whom they regarded as paving the way for Soviet penetration. They regarded it as extremely naive to believe that it was possible to prevail over Britain and establish full sovereignty over Iran's oil. They all shared with Musaddiq a belief in the ubiquitous British influence in the Iranian polity, but while Musaddiq wanted to eliminate such influence, his opponents regarded its diminution as both unthinkable and undesirable. In early July the deputy Husain Farhudi informed the British Embassy that a group of his colleagues intended to co-operate with a number of newspaper editors to oppose Musaddiq.[50] One of the latter, Amidi-Nuri the editor of *Dad*, soon became one of the most hostile opponents of Musaddiq, although he had initially been affiliated to the National Front. When he failed to get elected to the 16th Majlis he blamed the Front for lack of support and turned against it; in turn he was expelled.[51]

The effective leader of the opposition was Jamal Imami, who had been a member of the Majlis Oil Committee and had invited Musaddiq to assume office. Born into a prominent Azari religious family, Imami was a pro-Western conservative and an anti-communist admirer of Franco, who regarded the most effective means of countering communism to be not reform, as conventionally assumed, but repression.[52] He had a vast network of links, often frequented Ashraf's palace, and was discreetly in touch with the British Embassy through intermediaries such as Petrous Abkar and Abulqasim Fuladvand.[53] The Imami-led opposition, in addition to breaking the quorum, used a variety of pretexts to attack Musaddiq:

paradoxically either for refusing British offers or for being secretly in collusion with them; for coalescing with the Tudeh Party or for persecuting it.[54] After the departure of Stokes they resorted to the effective tactic of taking sanctuary in the Majlis on the grounds of lack of security.

The vocal parliamentary opposition to Musaddiq represented only a segment of a much wider body of opponents, composed largely of politicians who provided information for or advised the British Embassy on how to deal with Musaddiq. Tahiri, who acted against Musaddiq only furtively, frequently emphasized that Musaddiq must not be allowed to succeed in regard to oil; that his successor, preferably Sayyid Zia, be decided upon and helped to contend for office and organize the opposition;[55] that the Shah must clarify his opposition to Musaddiq and support for his successor; that Sayyid Zia revive his party and 'protect' his friends; and that the American Embassy be persuaded to press the Shah to act.[56]

Many other politicians, including Farhudi, Nikpay, Hasan Mukarram and I'tibar[57] as well as Suhaili, the Iranian Ambassador in London,[58] gave similar advice. Others, including Alam and Ali Dashti, as well as Senator Javad Imami (Zahir ul-Islam) and Dr. Hasan Imami (Imam Jum'ih) – Musaddiq's brother-in-law and his wife's nephew, respectively – reiterated the need for the Embassy to offer the Shah decisive advice and to press him to act.[59] Hikmat, the Speaker of the Majlis, despite his apparently neutral stance, claimed to have initiated the taking of sanctuary in the Majlis; he emphasized the necessity of a certain amount of bloodshed and even suggested the appointment of a few hundred assassins in order to overthrow Musaddiq.[60] It seems, however, that Hikmat and Tahiri were playing it both ways: Makki asserts that during the last months of the 16th Majlis Hikmat and Tahiri both co-operated with the National Front in countering the opposition, adding that 'in deference to public opinion, Hikmat furtively supported us'.[61]

The Iranian who had the greatest influence on the policy of the British Embassy was, nevertheless, probably Sayyid Zia, long regarded as the ideal prime-ministerial candidate, a committed friend and a sincere adviser. Encouraged by the Shah he revived his National Will Party in September 1951.[62] His aim was to alienate the traditional urban strata from the National Front and, with the help of people such as Qizilbash, a labour union leader, he tried to provide the 'protection' which Musaddiq's parliamentary opponents repeatedly requested.[63] While Sayyid Zia's best hope of becoming prime minister lay in the unconditional support of the British, this was also of course his greatest liability. Many of his own pro-British supporters recognized that he would not be 'digestible' immediately after Musaddiq. Senators such as Asadullah Yamini-Isfandiari,[64] and even Khajih-Nuri who had long worked for his premiership,[65] deputies such as Lutf Ali Mu'addil and the vocally anti-Musaddiq Manuchihr Taymurtash,[66] local notables such as Akbar Mas'ud (Sarim ud-Daulih),[67] influential courtiers such as Human,[68] and even Sayyid Zia's own brother were of this opinion.[69]

The British, however, regarded the advantages of Sayyid Zia's premiership as greater than any potential risk.[70] British disregard of the adversities involved was rooted in their belief in the artificiality, spuriousness and transitory nature of the movement which Musaddiq symbolized. This belief, although later slightly modified, was widely entertained in British diplomatic circles. Shepherd asserted that to conceive of Iranian nationalism as a 'coherent and positive movement of national regeneration' was 'false' and a 'mistaken' basis for policy formation.[71] Wheeler, the former Oriental Counsellor at Tehran who had rejoined the Embassy for a few months 'to advise on overt propaganda' believed that 'Dr. Musaddiq's venture does not appear either as a national movement or as a genuine outburst of public feeling'.[72] Another Foreign Office official stated that it had hitherto been the opinion of the British Embassy 'shared by the State Department', that Iranian nationalism,

> as exemplified by Musaddiq and his followers, was a spurious movement, artificially made to divert attention from the misdeeds and omissions of the ruling propertied class, without roots and command- ing no genuine popular support.[73]

However, at this time, he felt obliged to concede that 'for the time being at least' Iranian nationalism 'represents a force in Persia which must be reckoned with'.

The Shah at least fully realized the dangers of openly opposing Musaddiq and supporting Sayyid Zia. In this matter advisers such as Ala, General Yazdanpanah and Abulfath Diba (Hishmat ud-Daulih Valatabar) had proved to have more influence on him than lesser courtiers such as Perron and Human, who were both in regular liaison with Zaehner. Despite appearing to be favourable to his appointment, the Shah on one occasion said to Sayyid Zia that he could not tell the people that he had appointed him prime minister 'because London wanted it'.[74] The British insistence on Sayyid Zia, moreover, was bound to aggravate the Shah's suspicion of a man who not only enjoyed full British support, but had a record of dislike of the Pahlavi dynasty.[75]

The British none the less kept up their pressure on the Shah. Shepherd was authorized by the Foreign Office to contact the Shah in order to recommend Sayyid Zia. The Foreign Office wrote to Attlee: 'It has been our objective for some time to get Sayyid Zia appointed Prime Minister. We now have a chance of securing this objective and it should not be lost.'[76] Attlee approved the suggested action.[77] The Americans, on the other hand, remained opposed to such moves and regarded Sayyid Zia's chances as being 'virtually nil'.[78] The Foreign Office now instructed Shepherd to proceed with the 'representation' to the Shah without mentioning Sayyid Zia; he therefore told the Shah that 'it is now essential that steps should be taken to summon a more reasonable Government in the immediate future', and that the British Government 'deemed it necessary to take certain measures to protect their own economy against the effects of the present situation in Persia'.[79] The Shah was both anxious not to endorse unpopular measures and gravely doubtful of his ability to contend with Musaddiq. Unable to act decisively, he resorted more freely to compensatory manoeuvres and evasive tactics aimed at the creation of a variety of obfuscatory impressions of his position.

On some occasions he claimed to support Sayyid Zia, and on others to favour Qavam, but he was in fact inclined towards Ala as a successor to Musaddiq.[80] Sometimes he feigned ignorance of British intentions and preferences,[81] and on other occasions he implied that they were secretly in collusion with Musaddiq. Sometimes he tried to justify his inaction by claiming that he could not be sure of the collaboration of the deputies,[82] and on one occasion he told Hikmat that, 'the deputies were such a miserable lot that if he encouraged them to act against the Government they were quite capable of agreeing to do so and yet give Dr. Musaddiq a vote of confidence the very next day'.[83] Many deputies in turn complained to the Shah about the lack of a lead from the British Embassy, and at the same time used the absence of leadership from the Shah to explain to the Embassy their toleration of Musaddiq.[84]

The Shah and most of his advisers had no sympathy for Musaddiq or his ideals, but judged that a strategy of inaction, or close observance of constitutional principles, was the most certain means of preserving the throne, as well as being the safest of all choices. The

Shah was deeply troubled by the possibility of British military intervention which would involve action on his part as Commander-in-Chief of the armed forces. He therefore suggested other ways of undermining Musaddiq's position, such as the closure of the Abadan refinery.[85] As long as he was not directly involved he was prepared to condone any action, but his basic position, to which he more or less consistently adhered, was that Musaddiq could only be removed when his failure was clearly demonstrated. Despite being reduced almost to a 'spectator', the Shah's role in the political process, whether active or passive, was still crucial, and without his active support the anti-Musaddiq opposition could achieve little. This was a fact of which the British were resentfully aware.

The Shah's attitude and other adverse factors persuaded Sayyid Zia to withdraw from the list of Musaddiq's immediate successors.[86] This was a development in favour of Qavam who was not readily regarded as a British stooge and could credit himself with having provided the original impetus for the oil nationalization by sponsoring the Majlis resolution of October 1947. For this very reason – and many others – the British had turned against him; they believed that if he became premier he would not act according to their wishes, and neither were they reassured by the relentless efforts of Qavam himself and his clients such as Nikpur, Iskandari, Daliri, Arianpur, Muqtadir-i Shafi'a and others. With the withdrawal of Sayyid Zia, however, Qavam seemed the only viable alternative to Musaddiq and he seemed also to have succeeded in conciliating the Shah. In addition to providing moral support and encouragement, the Queen Mother contributed to his campaign funds,[87] and even his health seemed to improve along with his chances of resuming power. Accordingly the British abandoned their opposition to him.

Attempts were made by people such as deputy Ghulam Husain Ibtihaj to set up a coalition between Qavam and Sayyid Zia. However, Sayyid Zia disagreed with Qavam's ideas and methods, while Iskandari regarded such co-operation as harmful to Qavam, arguing that Sayyid Zia's candidature was a factor contributing to Musaddiq's continuation in power.[88] Qavam and his clientele therefore independently concentrated on cultivating the support of Musaddiq's parliamentary opponents and enlisting royal support.[89] They also tried to win over senior clerics such as Bihbahani and Burujirdi,[90] and gradually attracted politicians such as Tahiri who had previously been unfavourable. Nevertheless there was one major obstacle: despite his favourable promises the Shah remained non-committal, or was as opposed to Qavam as he was to Sayyid Zia.[91]

This situation heartened Sayyid Zia, who worked out a new plan according to which he would assume office following the appointment of Ala as an interim prime minister, on the condition that he, or rather the British Embassy, would nominate a number of ministers.[92] In the event more deputies favoured Qavam as a focus of opposition, and Sayyid Zia's hopes were dashed yet again. The British, despite assurances of goodwill given to Zaehner by Iskandari as well as Qavam himself, were still prevaricating over Qavam, and Sayyid Zia had strongly advised that some sort of commitment be elicited from Qavam 'before he became prime minister; he probably had not long to live and once in office might develop a desire to be an even greater anti-foreign hero than Musaddiq, which might mean an intransigent policy on the oil question'.[93] The Embassy accordingly asked to see Qavam's programme, and he submitted a signed letter containing the details of his policies, which included a promise to solve the oil issue on the basis of a 25:75 arrangement.[94] The British could expect no more direct undertaking of co-operation than this, and Middleton, the chargé d'affaires, informed the Foreign Office with some desperation that Qavam was the best available alternative to Musaddiq.[95]

Musaddiq's position, however, was by no means insecure; he skilfully exploited his popularity and with the help of Kashani and others countered his opponents in the Majlis by organizing demonstrations outside it. He had an aptitude for preparing the ground and choosing the right moment in order to explain his views and his efforts to defend the national interest, and then ask for a vote of confidence which the Majlis, fearful of the popular reaction, could not deny.[96] His tactic of frequently demanding a vote of confidence strengthened his position, since those who had voted in his favour could not, at least for some time, publicly turn against him; it also reaffirmed the shared responsibility of the Government and the Parliament, particularly regarding the oil policy. Musaddiq's reliance on public opinion frustrated his rival contenders for power. Indeed it had forced many of his opponents, such as Tahiri and Farhudi, to confine themselves to discreet and secret moves or had undermined the courage of others to speak their minds. Mustafa Misbahzadih, the editor of *Kayhan*, admitted to Shepherd that he was opposed to Musaddiq but was frightened to express his real opinions.[97]

After the failure of the Stokes mission the British appealed to the UN Security Council. This provided Musaddiq with an opportunity to defend the legitimacy of the Iranian case, expose it to world opinion, counter British propaganda and increase his familiarity with the complexities of the oil issue. Some of his opponents believed that the appeal to the Security Council was a grave blunder on the part of the British, as it would give Musaddiq an excellent opportunity to establish himself as the champion of Iranian national interests *vis-à-vis* a foreign power, thus rendering the task of publicly opposing him virtually impossible. Asadi complained that the Government was about to fall and was only saved by the British appeal to the UN.[98] Jamal Imami also accused the British of having helped Musaddiq, stating that 'the opposition had been finally hamstrung' by the referral of the oil question to the UN; a view with which Zaehner agreed, describing it as one of the 'bright ideas of Mr. Morrison'.[99] In fact, on the eve of Musaddiq's departure for the UN, his disheartened opponents felt obliged to announce that as long as the Prime Minister was defending the Iranian case at the UN they would refrain from opposing him.[100] On the other hand the absence of Musaddiq and some of his followers also provided the opposition with new opportunities.

Infighting had begun to develop among the ranks of Musaddiq's supporters, for instance in the bitter opposition of Baqa'i, Makki, Ha'irizadih and others to Senator Matin-Daftari, Musaddiq's son-in-law. Ha'irizadih accused him of being groomed by the British to succeed Musaddiq.[101] Matin-Daftari in turn described his opponents as mischief-makers provoked by foreigners.[102] By taking Matin-Daftari to America and leaving Makki, who regarded himself as the champion of the AIOC's expropriation, Musaddiq had aroused feelings of bitterness.[103] There were also allegations that Kashani was dissatisfied with Musaddiq and favoured Baqir Kazimi, the acting Prime Minister, as a successor.[104] The opposition naturally stimulated and exploited these disagreements, exaggerated their intensity and used events such as the disorder at Tehran University to make propaganda against the Government, emphasizing the danger of communism and the Government's role, inadvertent or otherwise, in spreading it.[105] Although they had promised to abstain from opposition while Musaddiq was abroad, they were deeply concerned about the approaching elections for the 17th Majlis and managed to secure the passage of a bill which postponed the start of the elections by a month. The opposition took it for granted that Musaddiq would return empty-handed from the UN and that this postponement would give them time to engineer his downfall.[106]

Musaddiq returned to Iran on 23 November 1951 after an absence of forty-nine days, paying a successful visit to Egypt on his way in order to forge a link between the anti-imperialist struggles of the Iranians and the Egyptians. The Security Council had postponed taking a decision on the oil dispute until The Hague Court, to which the matter had been referred by the British, gave its verdict. For Musaddiq and his followers this was nothing short of success, and he astutely linked the vote of confidence which his Government was to receive in the Majlis – on account of his activities at the UN – to the nullification of the election postponement bill.[107] In the face of this manoeuvre, the opposition failed to do anything other than feebly cast 16 votes of abstention, while 90 deputies voted in Musaddiq's favour;[108] the Senate unanimously voted for Musaddiq.[109]

One factor which helped Musaddiq to counter the opposition was the position of the Senate. Any opposition from the appointed senators would have automatically been attributed to the Shah, and it was too early for the elected senators to be concerned with their re-election prospects. In addition, some ambitious senators such as Farrukh challenged other contenders for the premiership in their own search for office.[110] More significantly, the influential Amiyyun group, and particularly Taqizadih, the President of the Senate, opposed both Sayyid Zia and Qavam and thus in effect supported Musaddiq. Taqizadih resisted the pressures of Hikmat and others to encourage an anti-Musaddiq opposition in the Senate, and also opposed efforts for the extension of the term of the 16th Majlis.[111] Similarly he resisted pressure to arrange for the approval by the Senate of the bill for electoral postponement.[112] Had this bill also been approved by the Senate, there would have been no possibility of nullifying it.

In contrast to many prominent members of the elite, Taqizadih favoured continued British negotiations with Musaddiq and had the moral courage and integrity to reject the legitimacy of the British Embassy's anti-Musaddiq interventions. In the face of efforts by Shepherd to enlist his co-operation in anti-Musaddiq efforts, he stated: 'No Persian Ambassador at the Court of St. James would recommend the King to change his Government.' Even Shepherd confessed to being impressed by his attitude, describing him as having 'far more statesmanship than most Persians' and crediting him with being 'logical and cogent in putting his points'.[113] With Shepherd's consent Taqizadih informed Musaddiq of the content of this conversation and Musaddiq in turn publicized it in a speech in the Parliament Square.[114] Taqizadih's position undoubtedly helped Musaddiq in his encounters with the opposition.

Musaddiq's recent success in the Majlis implied that he would face few obstacles in retaining office and conducting the Majlis elections. This was a disaster in the eyes of his opponents, which had to be averted by using all possible means available to secure his downfall. Convinced that Qavam was 'the only instrument at hand' with which to 'make a last effort before the election', Middleton demanded permission to tell the Shah that 'the responsibility must rest on the Shah alone if he persists in remaining a mere observer of political events in this country'.[115] The positive impact of such pressures on the Shah, however, continued to be limited.

At the same time the Shah faced increasing counter-pressure from the National Front to behave constitutionally and to restrain the Court. In mid-November 1951 Kashani – although suspected of being 'lukewarm' in his support for Musaddiq[116] – sent a message to the Shah threatening to expose the Court's support for Qavam. The Shah denied any such support and was compelled to reassure Kashani that Musaddiq continued to enjoy his support.[117] By late November Qavam had lost all hope of an imminent resumption of office and was about to leave for Switzerland to receive medical treatment; he had become convinced that he might even expect actual opposition from the Shah rather than any help.[118] Nor had he succeeded in winning over the Americans. The new Ambassador, Loy Henderson, who had succeeded Grady in September 1951, regarded him as 'too unpopular'.[119] and in any case the Americans were not prepared to recommend to the Shah a particular candidate to succeed Musaddiq. The Foreign Office could only instruct Middleton to tell the Shah that the British,

> considered that Dr. Musaddiq is leading the country to disorder, particularly owing to his continued leniency toward the Tudeh. His Majesty's Government therefore considers that a change is called for but that this is a decision that the Shah himself must make.[120]

Qavam's activities, which were reported to have included a detailed plan for overthrowing Musaddiq, as well as drawing up a list for a shadow Cabinet, raised many hopes but achieved little. Musaddiq's other opponents, however, did not miss any opportunity to weaken the Government.

One such opportunity arose on 6 December 1951, when students of Tehran University, protesting against the expulsion and detention of a number of fellow students, defied the police ban on demonstrations, broke the police cordon around the University and marched to Parliament Square. Large contingents of police and the army clashed with them and a considerable number of casualties resulted. Later on the same day there were largely right-wing counter-demonstrations with looting, ransacking and burning of the offices of the Tudeh and other anti-Government newspapers.[121] This riot, to which the police turned a blind eye, was led by a group of Baqa'i's followers who claimed to be supporting the Government. The group included professional thugs such as Sha'ban Ja'fari, who was later employed in activities against the Musaddiq Government. Throughout these events Amir-Taymur Kalali, Interior Minister and Chief of Police, and through him Musaddiq, had apparently been kept fully informed.[122]

This episode revealed that in an atmosphere of ideological strife, power struggles and relentless intrigues and conspiracies, when the boundaries between freedom and anarchy and criticism and abuse were blurred, the tactics of the Government's supporters and opponents were interchangeable. The Tudeh Party and affiliated organizations which had suffered at the hands of the Government's supporters naturally increased their attacks on Musaddiq. The Tudeh Party had scarcely relaxed in its anti-Government campaigns and its attitude regarding Musaddiq contained all the antinomies of Stalinist ideology.[123] It regarded Musaddiq as a prisoner of his class and an American stooge, but also expected him to adopt a position acceptable to the Party. Having followed a dubious strategy toward the oil nationalization it did not hesitate to denounce all of Musaddiq's efforts to reach a settlement with the British as outright compromise, and to radicalize political orientations against any oil settlement with the West and in favour of the Soviet Union. Regardless of the myriad adversities which Musaddiq faced, nothing short of a complete defiance of the West seemed acceptable to the Tudeh Party.[124] The Tudeh newspapers, along with the right-wing press, spared Musaddiq no abuse or accusation, and the Party continuously endeavoured to alienate the workers and the younger strata of the intelligentsia from the National Front and its affiliated groups.

Since the Tudeh Party had been declared illegal, Musaddiq should have had few problems suppressing it, but even assuming he had the means, his convictions and temperament would not allow suppression. He did, however, tactically invoke the danger of communism in order to enlist American backing. The Americans regarded Musaddiq and the movement which he represented as a bulwark against communism, while the British believed that his continuation in office would inevitably lead to a communist take-over. Musaddiq's policy toward the Tudeh continued to fluctuate between reluctant tolerance and intermittent firmness. The Tudeh Party exploited this situation in order to expand its organization, but continued in its disruptive opposition which relaxed or turned into qualified backing only when right-wing opponents of Musaddiq posed a serious threat. To the delight of the latter group, however, the Tudeh Party's opposition and support were both inevitably damaging to Musaddiq's position.

The events of 6 December not only brought Government–Tudeh relations into sharp focus[125] but greatly encouraged Musaddiq's parliamentary opponents. Two days later fifteen deputies again took sanctuary in the Majlis and were gradually joined by a group of fifty journalists. The opposition press intensified its diatribes against the Government,[126] and the Majlis was increasingly used as a platform for attacks against the Prime Minister.[127] Such tactics reached a turning-point on 11 December when Musaddiq was subjected to a barrage of abuse from the spectators' gallery in the Majlis, which had been filled with professional ruffians for this purpose. He proceeded to deliver his speech, listing various factors which in his view accounted for the failure of the oil negotiations, including British opposition to American mediation and the election of a Conservative government in Britain. He also stated that his Government did not approve of lawlessness and expressed his regret not for the student–police confrontation of 6 December but for the events of that afternoon, adding that he had ordered an inquiry into the matter.[128]

The behaviour of the Government's opponents in the Majlis inevitably provoked a National Front reaction, and on 13 December, with the help of Kashani, successful demonstrations were held to protest at the events of two days earlier.[129] The police also succeeded in forcibly expelling forty-five opposition-sponsored *mullahs* who had taken sanctuary in a mosque near the Majlis.[130] Aiming to limit the extent of Court-centred manoeuvres directed against his Government, Musaddiq attacked the continuous financial and moral support which the Shah's mother was giving to the opposition, and threatened to resign unless she left the country. Ala and the Shah both felt obliged to persuade him to remain in office.[131] It was also made public that Musaddiq had threatened that unless the Court gave up its anti-Government activities, he would resign and publicly state his reasons for doing so.[132]

The opponents of Musaddiq had never been united over policies or tactics and adding one frustration to another were now on the verge of disintegration. Some had even begun to adopt a conciliatory stand in the hope of neutralizing the Government on the eve of the election.[133] The behaviour of such deputies was directly attributed by many Government opponents, including Daliri, Amidi-Nuri and Jamal Imami, to the position of the British Embassy.[134] This significantly added to the confusion of opposition circles. The news of impending negotiations between the International Bank and Musaddiq, and Musaddiq's announcement that he would personally defend the Iranian case at The Hague, were further blows to the opposition.

When Makki gave up his efforts at mediation between the Government's supporters and opponents,[135] the opposition resorted to their last weapon: a motion of interpellation against the Government.[136] This could provide the opportunity for damaging anti-Government publicity, which was the primary intention. They could not hope to bring down the Government through such moves, and Qavam's departure for Europe in late September was an indication of despair in their camp. Alternatively, if the Government's supporters broke the Majlis quorum and prevented the motion being debated, the opposition hoped to be able to claim that the Government had no majority, to accuse it of defying the Constitution and thus make it vulnerable *vis-à-vis* the Senate, which was gradually assuming an active anti-Musaddiq stance.[137]

Musaddiq had two winning cards: one was his declared intention of going to The Hague, and the other the publicized closure of the British consulates in Iranian provincial capitals, which was done on 22 January 1952, the day that the motion of interpellation was to be debated.[138] The registration of a vote of no confidence against Musaddiq in this situation required more courage than most of his opponents were capable of displaying. On the other hand, it was a simple matter for Musaddiq's supporters to break the quorum in the Majlis since many had already left the capital to supervise their election campaigns. As expected, due to the absence of a quorum, the motion of interpellation was not debated, and the Majlis ceased to be effective a month before its formal date of expiry (19 February 1952). The sponsors of the interpellation motion appealed to the

Shah[139] but, having achieved nothing, tried to 'extricate themselves as best they could'[140] while the Government proceeded with the elections.

The conduct of the Majlis elections was a difficult and controversial task for any government and particularly for that of Musaddiq, who had long established himself as the champion of free elections. He had done his best to ensure electoral freedom by measures such as replacing governor-generals[141] and governors and ordering that members of supervisory councils be selected by the casting of lots among men of good reputation. Yet ensuring free and fair elections was not a readily attainable goal given the existing electoral laws, and Musaddiq was fully aware of this. Fearing the dangers of a parliamentary interregnum, however, he decided to proceed with the elections within the framework of existing electoral laws, with few illusions as to his ability to prevent improper interventions.[142]

Musaddiq could neither control the behaviour of the Court, the army and the local elite,[143] nor restrain some of his own followers, and the inevitable instances of electoral misconduct were capitalized upon by the Government's opponents, including unsuccessful candidates. Disputes and disagreements over the distribution of electoral spoils, on the other hand, aggravated tension within the National Front and contributed to the resignation of successive Interior Ministers Amir-Taymur Kalali and Salih, both close friends of Musaddiq. Kashani and Ha'irizadih both resented Musaddiq's lack of co-operation in the election of their favourite candidates,[144] and Musaddiq openly accused Kashani of being responsible for the 'confusion' of the elections.[145] Kashani's sons and entourage were widely engaged in influencing the electoral process to their own benefit, often causing dismay to other National Front candidates.[146] The personal conduct of Musaddiq and his immediate family remained beyond reproach; in order to allay any misgivings he even effected the resignation of his son Ahmad Musaddiq, who had been an under-secretary at the Ministry of Roads and Communications prior to his father's assumption of office.[147]

As expected, those who had failed to get elected came to regard their support for Musaddiq as unrewarded, and joined his opponents.[148] The Tudeh Party used the elections to gain more ammunition against Musaddiq. With no regard for the existing parliamentary arrangements the Party had participated in the election simply so that it could blame its failure on the Government and provide itself with further reasons to intensify its operations.[149] Eventually, the interventions of the Court, electoral irregularities and violent clashes in some areas resulted in the suspension of the elections until Musaddiq's return from The Hague. Despite all the allegations, the election of a sizeable number of its opponents finally revealed that the Government had not significantly interfered in the elections, and that when the 17th Majlis opened it would be far from co-operative.

When the 16th Majlis ceased to function effectively Musaddiq's opponents turned to the Senate, to which journalists seeking sanctuary had transferred themselves. Having gradually abandoned its earlier unobtrusive stand, the Senate had come to be regarded as the principal instrument for challenging Musaddiq,[150] and the main hope for getting rid of him.[151] Musaddiq's objectives, ideals and style had little appeal for most senators, who were greatly alarmed by his success in outmanoeuvring the Majlis opposition and feared that he could control the 17th Majlis more effectively. They also feared the growing radicalization of the National Front, which could seriously endanger the position of the established ruling elite and the very existence of the Senate. Nikpay, in fact, predicted that after the opening of the Majlis Musaddiq might move to dissolve the Senate.[152] The British continued to encourage the Senate in its oppositional stand, and in early January Pyman 'suggested' to Hikmat 'that he should get some of his friends in the Senate to interpellate the Government'.[153] Tahiri also regarded the Senate as a more appropriate means of countering Musaddiq as it did not have a quorum rule. He also believed that the withdrawal of Sayyid Zia and Qavam from the list of contenders for office had removed Taqizadih's main motive in supporting Musaddiq.[154]

At the beginning of March 1952, ninety representatives of Tehran guilds protesting about the Government's tax policy appealed to the Senate and threatened to take sanctuary if their complaints were not adequately dealt with.[155] This enabled the Senate to proclaim self-righteously that its task was the rectification of injustices and misdeeds perpetrated by the Government. Musaddiq remained defiant: when approached by three senators purporting to represent the Senate, who asked him to clarify his plan for coping with the existing problems, he reminded them that his plan had always been to extricate the country from colonialism and imperialism, and that the Senate must choose between freedom and independence or the restoration of the previous regime and the domination of the rapacious oil company.[156]

In late March 1952, following violent street clashes between the Tudeh youth and the Pan-Iranists (ultra-nationalists who were in general inclined to support Musaddiq), the Government for the first time since its inception declared martial law in Tehran. This required immediate approval by the Senate which could invoke Musaddiq's unfailing opposition to martial law in the past in order to oppose it. But the Senators themselves had often criticized the Government for its failure to maintain law and order. If they now voted against imposing martial law Musaddiq could accuse them of being disruptive, while if they voted for it, this would be taken as support for the Government. The Senate narrowly approved martial law, with 24 out of 47 votes in favour.[157] This was a setback for Musaddiq's opponents, who were nevertheless encouraged that so many senators had been willing to act against the Government.

Anti-Musaddiq activities continued in many different ways: press campaigns, Tudeh Party demonstrations, and intrigues between disaffected elite members and the British Embassy. The Fida'iyan-i Islam continued to threaten Musaddiq, who was virtually a prisoner in his own home, and Kashani, who could no longer restrain them.[158] The threats of the Fida'iyan had forced Amir-Ala'i to quit the Justice Ministry and become Minister without Portfolio; and on 12 February a youth belonging to the group, in an assassination attempt against Fatimi, wounded him and deprived Musaddiq of this loyal friend and competent adviser for many months. Ahmad Maliki, a one-time member of the National Front, has said that Fatimi was the driving-force in Musaddiq's entourage and that nothing positive was achieved in any session of the National Front at which he was not present.[159] The Fida'iyan were clearly in agreement with this assessment and believed that Fatimi's elimination would make Musaddiq more amenable to their demands.[160]

Among the ranks of Musaddiq's followers there were some mullahs, but many more were opposed to him. Mention has already been made of the forty-five anti-Government mullahs who had taken sanctuary. There were cases of religious families such as the Bihbahanis who were active in their opposition to Musaddiq,[161] and a few well-known preachers, represented by Muhammad Taqi Falsafi, who used the pulpit to speak against the Government. Other opponents tried to stimulate or mobilize resentments caused by economic and financial difficulties among some guilds and certain sectors of the bazaar traders and to recruit their support. This was also an attempt to counter support for the National Front among the traditional bazaar-centred strata, and the appeal to the Senate by ninety guild representatives was an indication of its success. Senator Nikpur, the pro-Qavam chairman of the Chamber of Commerce, also arranged for the expression of the top merchants' dissatisfaction with the Government, in the form of a critical and gloomy report which was read to the Shah on 22 April by the influential merchant Muhammad Reza Kharrazi on behalf of the Chamber of Commerce.[162]

At this point Musaddiq's popular support was undiminished, but the unity and enthusiasm of some of his followers was waning. The efforts of the National Front's opponents also had their effect. Encouraged by Middleton, Qavam's clients were trying to co-opt Makki,[163] and there were indications that Baqa'i had come to enjoy special royal favours.[164] Perron, crediting the 'astute policy' of the Shah for detaching Kashani, Makki and Baqa'i from Musaddiq, contended that 'thanks to the Shah the National Front had practically ceased to exist'. Zaehner agreed with this, but asserted that neither the Shah nor Ashraf 'deserved the slightest credit for anything'; the credit went only to him or his agents. In his view, disunity in the National Front 'was due to other factors, and these factors were created and directed by Brothers Rashidian'.[165] The three Rashidian brothers were pro-British political activists who were closely associated with Sayyid Zia and had helped him to create his National Will Party. During the mid-1940s, along with Sayyid Zia, they had co-operated with Zaehner in covert anti-communist activities. The Rashidians played a crucial role in orchestrating destabilizing activities against Musaddiq's Government. Despite their efforts, however, differences among Musaddiq's followers, were not yet as deep as their opponents claimed or hoped, and the National Front was still more united than the opposition.

Financial and economic problems were increasing, and in late 1951 Musaddiq turned to the people, through his national loan scheme which, as expected, was not well received by the rich.[166] When negotiations with the representatives of the International Bank failed – which Musaddiq blamed on their insistence on the return of British technicians, their refusal to operate the oil industry as the agent of the Iranian Government and their inflexibility on the issue of oil prices[167] – Musaddiq began to pursue his policy of an 'oil-less economy', despite objections from some of his own followers and opposition from the Shah.[168]

British obstacles to the sale of Iranian oil and relentless

accusations of having compromised with the British or submitted to the Americans had left Musaddiq with no real choice but to manage without oil and resort to austerity measures. The British continued with their policy of publicized non-negotiation with Musaddiq.[169] They were certain that Iran's cause would be defeated at The Hague and hoped that overt and covert activities, as well as financial and economic problems – whose effect they and their supporters exaggerated – would eventually force Musaddiq to surrender. Mustafa Fatih, a prominent pro-British ex-member of the AIOC and Sipihr's son-in-law, regularly sent his 'diaries' to the central offices of the Company in London enumerating various adversities which in his view rendered Musaddiq's downfall imminent. In the entry for 7 March 1952 he wrote: 'The prophecies of those who said "Give him enough rope and he will hang himself in due course" have come to be true.'[170]

However critical the situation may have been, Musaddiq was not ready to give up his ideals of national sovereignty and dignity and political neutrality, which were the guiding principles in his foreign policy. American financial aid, of which $23 million had been paid since November 1951 under the Point IV scheme, was desperately needed. However, Musaddiq and his followers resented the reference to 'backward countries' in the provision for the payment of such aid, and he said he was 'ashamed to hear it being said that backward nations must be helped'.[171] The aid was suspended in early January 1952 when Musaddiq refused to accept any commitment to defend the 'free world' in return for its continuation. There were implicit threats that this could result in the expulsion of American military advisers, a development which the Americans and the Shah needed to avert. Finally, on the insistence of the Shah,[172] Musaddiq agreed in late April 1952 to the continuation of American aid, but without accepting any specific conditions. This was as much a success for Musaddiq as it was a setback for his opponents, who relished any difficulty in US–Iranian relations.

Despite delaying manoeuvres, the 17th Majlis was eventually formally convened on 27 April 1952, and it soon became clear that it contained a sizeable number of actual or potential opponents. Two days later, against the advice of some of his followers,[173] Musaddiq sent a letter to the deputies already elected asking them to reject the credentials of those who had been fraudulently elected and had no 'local standing', and to ensure that the rest of the elections were properly conducted.[174] In his reference to persons of no local standing, Musaddiq had one person in mind above all: Imam Jum'ih, who had with royal support been 'elected' from the Kurdish-Sunni city of Mahabad, a place he had 'never set foot [in] in his life'.[175] The majority of deputies, however, not only accepted Imam Jum'ih's credentials, but were working for his election as Speaker of the Majlis, and Musaddiq's opponents, particularly Hikmat, the Chief of Staff General Garzan, Khajih-Nuri, Alam, Tahiri, as well as the British Embassy, were all behind him. At the same time, Sayyid Zia was preoccupied with organizing an attack on the credentials of the National Front-affiliated Tehran deputies, and appealing to the Shah to support Imam Jum'ih's speakership, as well as the approval in the Majlis of the credentials of the opposition deputies.[176]

The Shah was acting on both these issues through the Court officials Bihbudi and Human. The latter, in particular, worked against Musaddiq on the Shah's behalf like a 'beaver among the deputies'.[177] The Shah ordered Ala, who favoured Mu'azzami as Speaker, to support Imam Jum'ih instead. Moreover, far from yielding to Musaddiq's pressure to ask Imam Jum'ih to withdraw his candidature, the Shah actually encouraged him to remain a candidate.[178] In the first round of voting, Imam Jum'ih received 33 votes, while Dr. Ali Shayigan, the National Front's favoured candidate, and Mu'azzami, supported by independent deputies, gained 16 and 17 votes, respectively.[179] Shayigan withdrew in favour of Mu'azzami in the second round, but this did not prevent Imam Jum'ih from winning by 39 votes to 35.[180] In addition, the credentials of the opposition deputies were approved and Musaddiq and his followers suffered a severe setback.

Imam Jum'ih was a 48-year-old, turbaned, Swiss-educated lawyer and a Court protégé who had been partially paralysed in an assassination attempt some two years earlier (21 August 1950). Although related to Mussadiq he had no sympathy with his objectives and was in turn intensely disliked by him.[181] Imam Jum'ih was staunchly anglophile and repeatedly criticized the British for not interfering enough in Iranian affairs, for leaving Iran, which he described as a 'three year-old child', to its own devices, and for allowing the Americans to gain the upper hand.[182] He was a supporter of Qavam, and his religious links and role as the Friday Imam (prayer leader) of Tehran since 1945 were beneficial to the opposition, and it was hoped that he could attract the waverers and time-servers in the Majlis. Imam Jum'ih's success was largely owed to royal favours; the Shah's position concerning Musaddiq's successor as well as the manner and the timing of his replacement, had nevertheless continued to remain undecided.

Musaddiq's opponents had long stopped hoping for decisive action by the Shah. Amidi-Nuri believed that the Shah was in a state of 'complete collapse',[183] Nikpur contended that the Shah was not prepared to 'set his senators in motion against Musaddiq',[184] and Hikmat asserted that Musaddiq had reduced the Shah to 'virtual impotence'.[185] When he did make a move it was to ask Hikmat and Taqizadih to find a successor to Musaddiq.[186] In mid-March Perron informed Zaehner that the Shah intended to postpone anti-Musaddiq actions until the 17th Majlis had been opened. This was ridiculed by Zaehner as one of 'les folies imperiales'.[187] Zaehner and others advocated immediate action and the Shah accordingly sent a message stating that he had changed his view;[188] but he had not, as he still advocated that Musaddiq's reputation should be totally destroyed before his fall, and justified this by adding that the British also wanted to see him 'discredited' first.[189] In mid-May Perron informed Zaehner that the Shah was 'proud' of his own 'consistency', crediting himself with 'patience and foresight' in correctly resisting British pressures for 'precipitatory action',[190] and adhering to the view that Musaddiq should be removed by the Majlis whose election he had conducted, or by 'those very forces' which had 'brought him to power'.[191]

Several politicians, including Tahiri, Nikpur, Khajih-Nuri and Sipihr, now insisted on the need for a joint Anglo-American 'approach' to the Shah,[192] but this was unlikely to be effective. The Shah's strategy of evasion, however, had remained essentially unchanged and his predominant state of mind seemed still to be indecisiveness.[193] Much to the dismay of Zaehner, the Shah continued to repeat that the British actually wanted Musaddiq in office;[194] he was still apprehensive of openly opposing the National Front, and contrary to the general assumption his senior advisers still counselled restraint.[195]

In early July 1952 the Shah's self-confidence appeared to have increased, a development both signified and augmented by the return of Ashraf to the country, while developments such as the gloomy financial report of Muhammad Ali Varastih, the Finance Minister, provided some justification for royal action. Similarly, Musaddiq's departure for The Hague (28 May 1952) provided new opportunities for royal intrigues, of which the Prime Minister was fully aware.[196] When he returned the Shah retreated, but his support for Imam

Jum'ih indicated that he had finally come out against Musaddiq, although still undecided about his successor. In late December 1951 Qavam departed for Europe and the possibility of Hikmat's premiership was discussed for a while. Other candidates were Hakimi and Mansur, and the names of Ala and two of Musaddiq's ministers, Bushihri and Salih, were also mentioned as possible candidates. Apart from Salih, who showed little enthusiasm for the position and was not involved in any activity for his nomination, most of these candidates, including Bushihri, were in touch with the British Embassy directly or indirectly, but Middleton was not particularly impressed by any of them.[197]

The activities of all other contenders were overshadowed in any case by the return of Qavam in the second week of April. Full-scale campaigns in his favour started up again and efforts to ingratiate him further with the British and to win him American support were increased. Muqtadir-i Shafi'a, who was in contact with Julian Amery, a Conservative Member of Parliament and son-in-law of Harold Macmillan, had conveyed to the Shah messages in Qavam's favour from London,[198] and Amery was busy impressing Qavam's merits upon the Foreign Office. The Shah's mother, his brother, Abd ur-Reza,[199] and Ashraf all supported Qavam,[200] while Imam Jum'ih regarded him as the only hope for a settlement of the oil question.[201] Many others, including Sipihr, were working to arrange a meeting between Qavam and Henderson, and when this eventually took place in early June Henderson revised his opinion and decided that Qavam was the best successor to Musaddiq.[202] A few days later a meeting took place in Asadi's house between Qavam and Middleton; the latter was 'much impressed' by Qavam's 'physical and mental vigour'.[203] In short, the majority of Musaddiq's opponents seemed to favour Qavam; the Shah, however, did not.

In fact it seems that the Shah would have preferred any candidate to Qavam; when he heard of Qavam's meeting with Henderson, the Shah is reported to have told Sayyid Zia: 'I gather that he has managed to fool these idiotic Americans.'[204] The Shah clearly did not want himself to be 'fooled'. Aware of the Shah's attitude, Qavam was prepared to give any guarantee and seek royal advice in drawing up his list of ministers.[205] Similarly, seeing that the Shah was worried about how to dispose of Qavam once he was in power, Imam Jum'ih gave reassurances that whenever the Shah hinted at it, Qavam's removal would be promptly arranged. The Shah, however, was not ready to support Qavam actively, nor was he willing to oppose him.[206] Pressed by the British Embassy to concentrate on one candidate, Perron, on behalf of the Shah, contended that favouring one particular candidate before the fall of Musaddiq would lead to the disintegration of the opposition. Zaehner, having eventually realized the extent of British unpopularity, stated that 'I think it would be a tactical mistake to do any overt campaign on behalf of Qavam; we did this with Sayyid Zia and this did him no good.'[207] The policy now being advocated by Zaehner was similar to the Shah's much-criticized strategy: he believed that 'without creating an impression of supporting X and opposing Y, the Embassy should behave in such a way that any successful candidate would think he had gained office through its encouragement'.[208]

Nevertheless the hard core of the opposition, backed by the British and American Embassies, felt confident enough in early July 1952 to engage in full confrontation with Musaddiq and his followers. After his return from The Hague (24 June 1952) Musaddiq faced many disruptive manoeuvres which, *inter alia*, prevented the Majlis from formally starting its work. He therefore presented the Shah with a deadline: if the Majlis was not functioning by 8 July he would relinquish his prime-ministerial responsibility.[209] In compliance with traditional practice he also handed his ceremonial resignation to the Shah and broadcast a message to the nation in which he bitterly attacked his opponents:

> The Iranian nation witnesses that the moral decadence and disregard of all principles and standards has reached such an extent among this group that they are prepared to see Iranian national aspirations defeated so that they could cling for a few days longer to their privileged position and devilish arrangements. They must, however, know that the Iranian nation is wakeful and, whether this Government remains or falls, the previous situation will never be restored.[210]

In the meantime activities in favour of Qavam, particularly by Imam Jum'ih, had reached such a level that even Sayyid Zia was reported to be recommending him to the Shah.[211] The Shah eventually agreed to appoint him if the 'vote of inclination' of both houses could be obtained, but was not prepared to do more. Imam Jum'ih believed that this could be arranged but in the absence of an unequivocal royal lead 52 out of 63 deputies cast their 'votes of inclination' for Musaddiq on 6 July, while 10 abstained.[212] This was a considerable achievement for the National Front, but Musaddiq also needed the vote of the Senate, and it was here that the nucleus of a vocal opposition had long been formed, mainly through the activities of Senators Farrukh, Khajih-Nuri, Mas'udi and Nikpur, and several contingency plans had been drawn up in order to counter various manoeuvres by Musaddiq. The senators intended to deny Musaddiq a 'vote of inclination', and announced that they would not cast their votes unless they had first examined his programme.[213] Musaddiq for his part insisted that without the prior approval and support of both houses he would not resume office. Greatly alarmed by the possibility of a constitutional crisis, the Shah felt obliged to persuade the senators to vote for Musaddiq.[214] Although initially reluctant, out of the 36 Senators present, 14 voted for Musaddiq, while 19 abstained.[215] Sam Falle, the new Oriental Counsellor at the British Embassy, who had done his best to strengthen the resolve of Musaddiq's opponents in the Senate, despondently remarked that 'there are enough senators in the end who always do what the Shah orders'.[216] The position of the Senate did not reassure Musaddiq, but a delegation of senators persuaded him to accept office.[217] The next day (10 July 1952) he was formally reappointed Prime Minister by the Shah, and two days later the Senate went into summer recess.

It was expected by the opposition that the verdict of the International Court of Justice, which was due shortly, would go against Iran and thus help anti-Musaddiq moves. The Shah was still hopeful of procuring his removal through the Majlis, and sent a message through Bihbudi to Imam Jum'ih and Hikmat to the effect that they should tell the deputies not to give Musaddiq a vote of confidence until after the verdict was announced.[218] The implacable enemies of Musaddiq – particularly Imam Jum'ih, who had suffered a setback in his plans for Qavam's premiership – were, however, not only determined to intensify parliamentary moves against Musaddiq, but seemed prepared to use any means to bring about his downfall. Falle noted that:

The opposition, in particular the Imam Jum'ih, wants some money from us to form gangs and to make propaganda against the Government. My own reaction to this is that since all the wealthy and influential people in this country are opposed to Musaddiq, they should be prepared, if they have any guts or feeling of patriotism, to unite and find the money for this purpose. Unfortunately, few of the opposition seem prepared to make sacrifices to save their country.[219]

At the same time Musaddiq was considering the removal of Imam Jum'ih from the speakership of the Majlis.[220] He had moreover realized that with an obstreperous Parliament he would not only fail to tackle his intended reformist objectives, but would be chronically vulnerable. He therefore proceeded to demand plenary powers for himself for a period of six months. This move was made in the private Majlis session of 13 July 1952 and, although it was reported to have been endorsed there, it aroused hostility among most deputies.[221] Without awaiting the formal verdict of the Majlis on the plenary powers issue, he also introduced his Cabinet to the Shah, demanding the War Ministry for himself and the right to appoint the Chief of Staff and other army commanders. After a heated discussion the Shah refused to accept the terms,[222] and Musaddiq promptly submitted his resignation, shifting the blame on to the Shah and asserting that 'in the present situation, it is impossible victoriously to end the struggle which the Iranian nation has started'.[223] This time the Shah accepted the resignation regardless of the consequences and the first period of Musaddiq's premiership thus came to an end on 16 July 1952. His resignation was precipitated by his recognition of the fact that, in view of the determined hostility and stultifying machinations of his parliamentary and other opponents, his effective retention of office would have been impossible. A pre-emptive resignation, however, could at the very least save him from being reduced to virtual impotence, if not collapse, in the face of the Parliament, and at best return him to office with greatly increased power. It could also once again dramatically put his popularity and the public acceptability of his stand to the test.

19

Qavam's Débâcle and the July Uprising, 1952

Immediately after Musaddiq's resignation had been publicized, in a hastily convened and inquorate Majlis, 40 out of 42 deputies cast their 'vote of inclination' for Qavam, who was then formally appointed Prime Minister by the Shah, who also reconferred upon him the title of 'Excellency' withdrawn over two years earlier.

Qavam had long been convinced of the necessity of dissolving the Majlis, and Ghaffari and Sipihr, two of his clients, had told the British Embassy that Qavam would act like a 'dictator', arrest many of his opponents and dissolve the Majlis.[1] Since the Majlis contained a considerable number of deputies loyal to Musaddiq, he could not hope to achieve anything with the Majlis in session. Qavam hoped that the support of the British and American Embassies would be enough to persuade the Shah to dissolve the Majlis, particularly since a refusal would imply the return of Musaddiq and an unprecedented reduction of the monarch's prestige and power.

Qavam was fully aware that the Shah's attitude towards him was only reluctant acquiescence, and on the eve of his assumption of office confessed to having no confidence in the monarch, expecting his own activities among the deputies to provoke royal counteraction.[2] Whatever his feelings about Qavam, however, the Shah could not conceivably take the risk of dissolving the Majlis. Such a venture, at that critical juncture and in defiance of the popular mood and expectations, would have had incalculable consequences. It would have drastically intensified royal vulnerability and proved incongruent with the Shah's strategy for self-preservation, that is to play a minimal role within the confines of the Constitution. Qavam, nevertheless, unsure but not despondent, undeterred by his old age and delicate state of health and unable to resist the temptations of power, risked the acceptance of responsibility. Following formal assignment, Qavam's entire clan was galvanized into action and those who regarded him as the only man capable of countering

Musaddiq appeared to be optimistic about his chances. Some, notably Sipihr and Ghaffari, went to great lengths to stress that he was 'not as feeble as he looked' and Falle himself found him to be in excellent health,[3] although Arsanjani, his close friend, later stressed that his deteriorating health had reduced his 'power of resistance', he had become 'credulous' and was by no means the Qavam of 1946.[4]

Once in office and hoping to convey a reassuring image, Qavam displayed his characteristically stoic indifference, if not disdain,[5] and had an air of premature optimism and unjustified self-confidence which was reflected in the publication of his notorious declaration of 18 July. In this he solemnly pledged to solve the oil question, to restore order and to separate politics from religion; he condemned 'demagogy in politics' and 'hypocrisy in religion'; attacked those who had 'strengthened black reaction' under the pretext of 'fighting red extremists'; and he vowed to set up 'revolutionary tribunals' to try and punish 'criminals' of all classes.[6] The publication of this declaration was an unperceptive and imprudent move; it proved self-defeating and entirely damaging to Qavam's position, as his opponents could now convincingly denounce his dictatorial intentions, while Qavam, without unequivocal royal support and with the Majlis in session, could not hope to back his words with action.

The need to dissolve the Majlis had thus become more urgent, but the Shah remained non-committal and Imam Jum'ih and Hikmat echoed royal wishes in persuading Qavam to proceed without dissolving the Majlis.[7] Henderson and Middleton urged the Shah to support the Prime Minister and, pessimistic about the prospect for the dissolution of the Majlis, tried to persuade Qavam to concentrate on specific measures to consolidate his position. These measures concerned the inclusion in his Cabinet of men such as Hakimi and Mansur, who were trusted by the Shah, the appointment of a reliable general to mäintain order in Khuzistan, and the replacement of the 'unreliable' Chief of Police, General Kupal, with his own nominee.[8] Some of Qavam's friends also pressed him to form his Cabinet. With the Majlis in session, however, Qavam regarded his position as being virtually suspended and this aggravated the confusion and lack of co-ordinated activity among his entourage. He continued to no avail to impress upon the Shah that without the dissolution of the Majlis nothing could be accomplished, while at the same time reminding him of the repercussions of the alternative, that is the return of Musaddiq.[9] Regardless of this, he apparently claimed to have received a 'message' on 19 July giving royal assent.[10]

In the face of mounting opposition Qavam could not remain idle any longer. In an attempt to silence Kashani, who played a crucial role in stirring popular feelings against him, Qavam had already offered him the choice of six ministries in the Cabinet,[11] although there was no chance of a conciliation. Kashani's own earlier approach to Qavam had also produced no positive result.[12] On his own initiative and without the Shah's authorization, Qavam secretly ordered the arrest of Kashani; but in the event this was foiled when news of it was broadcast by the BBC on 19 July, well before the planned day of implementation. This report did considerable damage since it was taken 'as an expression of what HMG' would have 'liked Qavam to do', thus making it more difficult for Qavam to take any action against Kashani.[13]

While this failure led Qavam to despair, it emboldened Kashani to appeal to the army to disobey the Government,[14] and the National Front branded Qavam as a British stooge intent upon restoring reactionary arrangements and foreign domination.[15] The culmination of the activities of Musaddiq's supporters to unseat Qavam came on 21 July 1952, undoubtedly a turning-point in Iranian history. In response to an appeal by deputies loyal to Musaddiq the people came out on the streets. Strikes, demonstrations, riots and bloody confrontations with the police and army, which left heavy casualties, succeeded in overcoming the traditional elite and the coercive instruments of the state. Middleton and Henderson were sure that these events were organized by the Tudeh and that there was a 'formal understanding' between the National Front and the Tudeh Party.[16] The Tudeh Party was unfavourable to Musaddiq but deeply hostile to Qavam; by taking part in activities against him, it could reassert itself, and by helping to return Musaddiq to power it could enhance its political leverage. The Party, however, as its Central Committee later confessed, sided with Musaddiq after much hesitation and then only after some of its rank and file had entered the scene on their own initiative.[17]

The events of 21 July had strong anti-monarchist overtones and confirmed the deepest fears of the Shah as well as the views of some of his advisers that Musaddiq's removal would cause serious disorder. While the Shah had been kept fully informed of the details of these events, Qavam was almost completely ignorant.[18] Since 9.00 a.m. on 21 July Qavam had been awaiting a royal audience to finalize the issue of the dissolution of the Majlis, while the Shah was busy negotiating with the representatives of the National Front.[19]

When Qavam eventually saw the Shah at 5.00 p.m. his resignation had already been announced on the radio. Tehran was under the control of Musaddiq's supporters, the army had retreated to barracks and 'not even a single policeman was to be seen, even on traffic duty'.[20]

Middleton unequivocally placed the blame for Qavam's failure on the Shah and regarded it as 'poetic justice that his own position should as a result have been seriously weakened'. The Shah, in Middleton's view, had 'very nearly discouraged the opposition from voting for Qavam'. He also accused the Shah of withdrawing support from his troops and exposing 'their commanders to the risk of savage reprisal'; eventually 'the mob won only through the capitulation of the Shah'. To the Shah's 'lamentable record', his indecisiveness, fears and lack of 'moral courage', Middleton now added another dimension: 'I am now convinced we must see in him a deep-rooted dislike and distrust of the British.'[21] Undoubtedly the Shah failed to support Qavam; he would have done so only if Qavam had been able to consolidate his position and contain Musaddiq's followers. But there was no way he could do this without the prior and unequivocal support of the Shah.[22]

While the Shah was averse to the current wave of nationalism, he still remained aware of his responsibility as the sovereign of an independent country. His dilemma was to decide how far he should show deference to popular expectations and patriotic feelings, and how far he should go along with the wishes of a foreign power determined to restore its lost privileges by any means. The Shah's indecisiveness and inability to solve this dilemma undoubtedly contributed to the victory of the uprising of 21 July, but the main factor was the hegemony of the Musaddiq-led national movement and the remarkable devotion and perseverance of its followers.

Qavam's ignominious débâcle was a direct consequence of his own miscalculations and the inability of his foreign and domestic supporters to understand either the Shah's position or, more significantly, the gravity of the political situation and the strength of the movement which Musaddiq symbolized. The episode of 21 July humiliated the Shah and the royal family, discomfited all Musaddiq's opponents and put an undignified end to Qavam's political career. Qavam's sole strategy had been to assume and maintain office through the goodwill of at least one foreign embassy, resorting to an outward show of firmness and relying on his clientele in order to manipulate the intricate balance of clan politics in his own favour. In other words, he was well versed only to perform within the perceptual and practical confines of an essentially elite politics. His mode of political thinking and behaviour was disastrously inappropriate at a stage when politics had effectively transcended the boundaries of the elite and many critical issues were settled on the streets.

20

The Second Government of Musaddiq:
JULY 1952–AUGUST 1953

Throughout the period which culminated in the events of 21 July, Musaddiq confined himself to his house, was not in contact with his supporters[1] and made no public appeal or bid to return to power. He regarded the episode of 21 July, formally recognized by the Parliament as 'The National Uprising', as an authentic expression of a popular mandate for his resumption of the premiership, giving him a new source of legitimacy, authority and self-confidence, and reconfirming his ideals. His resumption of office, following a 'vote of inclination' of 62 out of 64 in the Majlis and 33 out of 42 in the Senate,[2] coincided happily with the announcement by the International Court of Justice of its verdict of no-competence in dealing with the Anglo-Iranian oil dispute.

Since many of Musaddiq's prominent friends had been elected to the Majlis, he had some difficulty finding suitable ministers; he did his best, however, to ensure that his colleagues were reputable as well as predominantly young and efficient. His Cabinet was unanimously approved by the Majlis, together with its nine-point programme of reforms which covered: reform of parliamentary and municipal electoral laws; financial reform and balancing of the budget through reduction of expenditure and direct and, if necessary, indirect taxation; economic reform through an increase in production, job creation and reform of the monetary and banking laws; utilization of the country's oil revenues; administrative reform and the reform of civil and judicial employment laws; establishment of rural councils; reform of the judicial laws; reform of the press laws; and reform of the education, health and communications services.[3] His plenary powers bill was approved by the Majlis, and with some difficulty by the Senate, and the authority of the Cabinet was thus consolidated. Musaddiq retained the portfolio of War (renamed Defence) for himself, and virtually for the first time in the history of Iranian constitutionalism, the army was put under the formal and effective jurisdiction of the Government. His success in regaining what he had so recently lost considerably damaged the prestige of the Shah and the Court, with the result that the Queen Mother, Ashraf and other members of the royal family had to leave the country. Other opponents also suffered: Qavam went into hiding, Imam Jum'ih resigned and Human, an actively anti-Musaddiq official in the Court, was suspended.

In the tense emotional atmosphere of 21 July and its aftermath there were many calls for retaliation. Baqa'i and a few of Kashani's followers obsessively pressed Musaddiq to take revenge, but he was more interested in using his new authority, and particularly his plenary powers, to bring about his programme of reform. To this end committees were set up to study and implement the proposed measures and no point in his programme was neglected as far as resources and circumstances allowed. One important point not included in the Cabinet programme was the Government's land reform policy which came later in the decrees of 6 and 19 October 1952.[4] The first concerned the deduction of 20 per cent from the landowners' share of the income from agricultural estates, of which 10 per cent was to go to the peasants who cultivated the land and 10 per cent to the development and co-operative funds, to be spent on rural development and administered by rural councils. The second decree prohibited the extraction of any dues or services from the peasants by the landlord over and above his legal entitlement. Musaddiq's measures for the improvement of rural life were not radically far-reaching, yet even if he had been willing and equipped with the resources and organization to do more, he could not have proposed further reforms at this time. To do so would have produced social divisions out of his control, alienated many of his supporters and enabled his opponents to appeal to the *ulama* and brand his regime as being in league with the communists.[5]

Musaddiq's Government also successfully initiated many other reforms; it promulgated a land tax bill and a bill for the revision of the income tax law of 20 July 1949. In addition it introduced legislation for the expansion and promotion of exports, the creation of a bank for this purpose, the formation of a customs police, regulation of the affairs of the Chamber of Commerce, an increase in the educational budget, a five-year plan for road construction, rent controls, the nationalization of telephone installations and the creation of a uniform bus service in Tehran.[6]

Perhaps the clearest indication of Musaddiq's reformist objectives was a comprehensive scheme for workers' social insurance introduced on 10 February 1952. The reform of the judiciary was also planned; laws for the employment of judges were revised,[7] special courts were abolished and the authority and competence of military courts were restricted to military issues.[8] The Court of Cassation was dissolved and reconstituted under the presidency of Muhammad Sururi, a respected politician and lawyer; similarly the Disciplinary Court was dissolved and reorganized.[9] The reform of the administration proved more difficult and was largely confined to the appointment or promotion of well-reputed officials, and the retirement of a number of corrupt employees.[10]

A comprehensive press bill ensuring reasonable freedom for the press, including trial by jury for offences committed by the press, was put to public scrutiny but provoked much criticism.[11] Aware of the dangers posed by an irresponsible and vituperative press, Musaddiq nevertheless proceeded to implement a modified version of the bill.[12] Electoral reform had always been an issue close to his heart and on 17 December he published the draft of his new electoral bill which, among other things, confined the period of voting to one day, increased the number of deputies from 136 to 172 and implicitly restricted the franchise to the literate. A municipal electoral bill signed by Musaddiq on 8 November had extended the franchise to women,[13] although the parliamentary electoral bill did not, and this aroused some controversy.[14] On the whole the bill caused widespread criticism and heated debates in the Majlis.

In the end the Government did not survive long enough to implement this or many of the other planned reforms, and much that had been accomplished was dismantled after Musaddiq's fall. Despite the lack of funds, the British oil blockade and other pressures, inadequate organization and personnel, inefficiency and corruption of the administrative machinery and stultifying oppositional moves embarked upon in the name of safeguarding freedom, Musaddiq and his colleagues indefatigably endeavoured to fulfil their reformist goals. They believed that the extreme inequities of Iranian society, which barred the establishment of meaningful parliamentary government, necessitated far-reaching reforms; they also shared the conventional wisdom of the age that reforms prevented communism.[15] The British, on the other hand, continued with their effective tactic of impressing upon the Americans that if Musaddiq remained in power there would eventually be a communist take-over, and behaved as if they genuinely believed in their frequently reiterated cataclysmic prognosis.[16] In the post-21 July period they were in no position to dictate their terms to Musaddiq, and came increasingly to regard a military *coup d'état* as the most effective means of achieving his downfall or, as Middleton put it, 'the only measure capable of preventing communism'.[17] In this they enjoyed at least the sympathy of Henderson.

The idea of an anti-Musaddiq coup can be traced back to the beginning of his premiership. In June 1951 Amir Amir-Kayvan, a labour union activist, had the distinction of becoming the first Iranian to provide the British authorities with a detailed plan for the overthrow of Musaddiq by means of a coup. The first officer whom he suggested for the task was General Zahidi, then the Minister of the Interior.[18] Shepherd had also considered the possibility of a coup. In his characteristic tone he wrote in September: 'It seems indeed to be a trait in the Persian political character to allow things to reach a state when a *coup d'état* becomes inevitable.'[19] By January 1952 Sayyid Zia feared 'that there might be no solution except a coup d'état'.[20] Falle also thought that a coup might be inevitable but had 'not yet worked out its practical details'.[21] However, it was not until the post-21 July period that the idea of a coup was seriously considered. By then the limits of manipulating parliamentary methods for the purpose of destabilizing the Government had been demonstrated, the extensive activities of Zaehner and others, and the considerable sums of money which had been spent had borne little fruit, and Zaehner had returned to England in a state of deep disillusionment about 'the plan which he had helped to launch'.[22]

The most promising candidate to lead a coup was Zahidi, who had resigned his post and furtively joined the opposition in July 1951. Even before the abortive premiership of Qavam the British had considered Zahidi as an alternative should the Shah refuse to accept Qavam.[23] Now his chances had dramatically increased; he was in close touch with disgruntled elements of the National Front, such as Makki, Baqa'i and Ha'irizadih, who often spoke to him of their dissatisfaction with Musaddiq.[24] He was also closely in touch with Kashani and claimed to have enlisted his support by offering him a 'say' in the composition of his Cabinet.[25] His strategy was to use them all in order to assume power and then to discard them. Among the old opposition, which looked to him with hope, he was in contact with some of the principal figures, such as Hikmat,[26] and his would-be Cabinet colleagues were virtually all engaged in activities on his behalf.

Zahidi naturally had rivals among the ranks of senior officers, and there were civilians, such as Mir-Ashrafi, Iskandari and Sayyid Zia who saw themselves as coup leaders.[27] None, however, possessed his qualities. A. H. Hamzavi, the former press attaché at the Iranian Embassy in London, met Ross of the Foreign Office in July 1952 and mentioned Zahidi, describing him as 'young and active, handsome, ruthless, and, best of all, a known *bête noire* of the English'.[28] His arrest by the British for pro-German activities provided an excellent cover which Falle also emphasized:

> I warned [Zahidi] against letting anyone know that he had any connection with us and I think he appreciated that at the moment his anti-British past is a greater asset to him than any promise of British support could be.[29]

His anti-communism, his close relations with the National Front and the support he had from the army were additional points in his favour, according to Falle. When the British military attaché was asked by the War Office to assess the chances of a coup, he replied that Zahidi may not have that much support in the army but he was 'probably more willing' to lead a coup than most other senior officers.[30] The Iranian agents of the British also placed more hope in him than in any of his rivals. One such agent was Asadullah Rashidian who, following Qavam's fall, only waited 'to be told what to do next' and who had an idea of his own: 'To form a party, and with the help of this, the army and the *mullahs*, to bring about a coup d'état in support of General Zahidi.'[31]

On the American side reactions differed. Charles Bohlen, a prominent member of the State Department, was 'greatly upset by the attitude of high-up people in London' who would 'rather see Persia go communist than make an unsatisfactory oil agreement' and 'very worried' to learn that the British 'were still thinking about the possibility of a military coup'.[32] Henderson, however, had a different attitude. He did not entirely share British optimism about Zahidi, but agreed with Middleton that the only way to topple Musaddiq was by a coup, to be launched in the Shah's name but without his knowledge.[33] On one point, however, there was agreement between the Americans and the British, as seen in this account of a conversation between Eden and the US Minister of State:

> Mr. Holmes said he wished there were a Neguib in the country. I said

there might be. Relations between Persia and Egypt in these days are often an imitative process. In any event I did not consider that we should give up hope that a local Neguib could be found.[34]

Zahidi was keen to become Iran's 'local Neguib'; he had intensified his efforts to win support and continued to impress upon the British and the Americans that any move on their part which might be construed as readiness to negotiate with Musaddiq would undermine his plans, a point also stressed by Sayyid Zia.[35] The activities of Zahidi had not escaped Mussadiq's attention, which meant that Kashani could not openly support Zahidi.[36] Nevertheless Zahidi was confident of Kashani's support, or at least of his opposition to Musaddiq who faced acute problems in controlling the army as well as the agitating pro-Zahidi retired officers. The temporary arrest of General Hijazi and the Rashidian brothers, whose conspiratorial relations with Zahidi and Khajih-Nuri, among others, were publicly hinted at, signalled an alarm to Zahidi. Making full use of his parliamentary immunity, however, Zahidi attacked Musaddiq in the Senate, where the former now had strong support, pleaded his innocence and issued a strongly worded statement against the Prime Minister.[37]

After the events of July the Senate had been forced to retreat and give votes of confidence to Musaddiq, although many senators were trying hard to revive its oppositional stand. On 3 August their chance came when the Majlis declared Qavam a 'perpetrator of corruption on the earth' (*mufsid fi-l arz*) and passed a bill for his prosecution and the confiscation of his property; four days later the Majlis approved a bill which amnestied Razmara's assassin, Khalil Tahmasibi.[38] The Senate refused to approve these bills, which were held up by its Justice Committee on the grounds that the amnesty was contrary to the constitutionally sanctioned separation of powers.[39] This provoked a strong reaction from followers of Kashani, who had much at stake sponsoring such bills.[40] Knowing that Zahidi drew much of his support from the Senate, and dissatisfied with its attitude towards the national movement, many pro-Musaddiq deputies also made speeches attacking it.[41]

In his memoirs Musaddiq denies any involvement in efforts to dissolve the Senate.[42] According to Middleton, however, Musaddiq tried to persuade the Shah to take such a step but the Shah refused, since 'in his own indirect way' he had 'been encouraging the Senate to oppose the Government',[43] and Hakimi warned him that by dissolving the Senate he would be signing the 'death warrant' of the monarchy.[44] Eventually, in a pre-emptive and defiant move, the Majlis reacted by introducing a bill which reinterpreted article 5 of the Constitution, reducing the term of the Senate to two years and thus effectively dissolving it.[45] Taqizadih repeated Hakimi's warning, and argued that the Majlis bill, which had not been referred to the Senate itself, was invalid. The Shah nevertheless felt compelled to sign the bill and the first Iranian Senate thus came to an abrupt end. This was not only a setback for Zahidi and his supporters, but also a further crucial step in restricting the Shah's authority.

On 22 October 1952, one day before the approval of the Majlis bill for the dissolution of the Senate, diplomatic relations with Britain were finally broken off. British consulates had already been closed in January that year, and the British Bank of the Middle East was effectively closed in July after many years of difficulties. Its position had become particularly difficult since September 1951 when it was deprived of the right of transacting foreign exchange.[46] In addition, Iran had refused to accept the appointment of Robert Hankey, the proposed successor to Shepherd, insisting that no diplomat sent to Iran should have served in the British colonies. The rupture of diplomatic relations – a turning point in the long history of Anglo-Iranian relations – was a direct consequence of the failure of Anglo-Iranian oil negotiations, which had resumed after the unsuccessful efforts of the International Bank. Musaddiq's attitude towards the oil settlement had naturally hardened when he returned to power with a popular mandate. His freedom of manoeuvre was also restricted in view of his broadened popular basis of authority and also as the result of the propaganda of his enemies and some of his nominal friends. In the view of Dean Acheson: 'Mosaddeq's self-defeating quality was that he never paused to see that the passions he excited to support him restricted his freedom of choice and left only extreme solutions possible.'[47] Musaddiq himself had played no direct role in 'exciting passions' during the events of July 1952 which returned him to power. He was, however, now subjected to more constraints, in view of which he hoped that the British would take the initiative. But they were determined that the first move must come from him. Ala's attempts at mediation were rejected and he was described by Middleton as 'a broken reed so far as we are concerned'.[48] In an earlier attempt to reach a settlement, Musaddiq had apparently offered to accept arbitration, but apprehensive of appearing lenient he withdrew his offer.[49]

Finally the British and the Americans moved on 20 August 1952, when the Truman–Churchill message was handed to Musaddiq demanding that the issue of compensation for the act of nationalization be put to arbitration.[50] Musaddiq and his advisers considered their offer to be a regression in comparison with previous ones and accused the British Government of resorting to evasive tactics and attempting to revive the 1933 Agreement and the AIOC. Musaddiq had realized that the gap between the two parties concerning the question of compensation – which had become the main issue of contention – was almost unbridgeable. According to his usual practice, Musaddiq informed both the Majlis and the Senate of these events, arguing that Iran could no longer remain silent in the face of British Government pressures and that his Government would only pay compensation for the AIOC's physical assets at the time of nationalization.[51] This was unanimously approved by both Chambers, which enabled Musaddiq to reject the Anglo-American offer and cut off diplomatic relations with Britain.[52] He was backed by public opinion which unanimously demanded the rejection of the offer. Middleton admitted this and remarked that 'a year ago, the joint Anglo-American proposal would have been greeted as a great victory for the Persians'.[53]

The severance of relations with Britain was bound to have an adverse effect on US–Iranian relations. The Truman–Churchill message had been a major blow to the wishful assumption of some Iranian nationalists that there still existed major policy differences between America and Britain over Iran. In fact the British had always tried to maintain a united Anglo-American front against Musaddiq, and Middleton echoed the views of all his colleagues when he stated that 'the greatest single blow to Musaddiq would be to break the idea of Anglo-American rift'.[54] Moreover, by demonstrating Musaddiq's failure to achieve positive results regarding the oil issue, not only with the British but also with the Americans, it was believed that 'his already uncertain position will be seriously shaken'. Musaddiq himself had long come to take Anglo-American collaboration for granted.

Musaddiq also strongly doubted that the British had any real intention of reaching an agreement with him. According to Acheson he was perfectly aware 'that the British wanted a fight to the finish and he took the declaration of a fight to the finish with dignity'.[55] As for the British Embassy, Musaddiq regarded it as beneficial only to his opponents, especially the plotters of a coup, which appeared even more likely after the Free Officers' coup in Egypt in July 1952. Also the gradual reduction of British diplomatic staff in Tehran had created the impression that the British might be about to take the initiative and break diplomatic relations themselves,[56] and Musaddiq could not afford to let this happen. To break relations with Britain was to his supporters the logical culmination of his consistent anti-imperialist stand. To the British, however, it was just one more step towards a communist take-over of Iran, and a further instance of Musaddiq's success in humiliating them, feelings clearly expressed by Middleton:

> I confess that for my part I shall be extremely sorry to go and bitterly disappointed to be kicked out in such circumstances. I suppose we took the wrong turning at some point; perhaps it was a mistake to fall in at all with the Americans that Musaddiq is 'negotiable'.[57]

The rupture in Anglo-Iranian relations was an inevitable result of mutual inflexibility over the oil issue. Non-compromise, besides its often exaggerated role in maintaining Musaddiq's popularity, was what his opponents had always tried to push him towards by attacking any flexibility on his part as outright compromise. For example, Zahidi accused him of having acquiesced in 'paying compensation on the basis of the invalid and nullified 1933 Agreement and the rejected Gass-Gulsha'iyan proposal'.[58] Some of Musaddiq's own supporters were also unprepared to accept anything less than total non-compromise. According to an American Embassy report of late October 1952: 'Members of the Government openly say that six weeks ago Mosaddeq was willing to accept terms to end the dispute which were comparatively favourable, but he was overridden by Kashani.'[59]

Similarly, a reliable account quoting Dr. Muhammad Ali Maliki, Musaddiq's Minister of Health, states that Musaddiq and his Cabinet had been prepared to accept the proposed scheme of the International Bank, but were prevented from doing so by some of Musaddiq's advisers.[60] The obstructive role of these advisers, notably Hasibi and Shayigan, also caused Fatimi to complain to the French Ambassador.[61] Nevertheless it was the activities of the opposition which most adversely affected the prospects for an oil settlement. Later, in the course of his trial, Musaddiq recalled that his Government had been ready to consider an American mediation effort, envisaging the payment of $800 million in compensation to

Britain over a period of twenty years. The opportunity to reach such a settlement had, however, been undermined in the Majlis by previous supporters who had now become his bitter enemies.[62]

The closure of the British Embassy in Tehran created mixed feelings among Musaddiq's opponents. On the one hand they lost the direct support of the Embassy; on the other, any settlement with Musaddiq had been shown to be impossible and the bogey of communism could more easily be invoked. The Shah was very perturbed by the breakdown in relations and there were rumours that he had threatened to abdicate. Middleton was 'reliably informed that the Shah's wife, Surayya, was urging him to do so,[63] while others were encouraging him to cling to the throne. In a conversation with Farrukh, while reiterating his belief in British support for Musaddiq, the Shah even alleged that the British themselves had engineered the rupture in diplomatic relations, otherwise, he contended, 'it could not happen'.[64] In any event, when it did happen the Shah had no choice but to accept.

The Shah's position in the post-21 July period, at least on the surface, was little more than unobtrusive acquiescence in the face of events. Musaddiq had reduced him to a position consistent with a non-royalist interpretation of the Constitution and in a meeting in late August Middleton found him 'most depressed, drawn and much aged', seeing no future for the monarchy in Iran, and himself reduced to a mere 'puppet king with no army and no following'. Middleton noted:

> I did my best to instil some courage into the Shah, who was full of reproaches for our position in deposing his father in 1941 and our alleged lack of support for the throne since then. His general theme was 'nobody loves me' and he refused to be comforted.
>
> It is abundantly clear that the Shah is likely to bow his head before any political storm, even though it means his abdication.[65]

The dissemination of the rumours of a royal abdication was in all likelihood a purely tactical measure, although some people believed that Musaddiq had personally prevented the Shah from taking such a step.[66] The Shah regarded himself as having surrendered virtually all his prerogatives to Musaddiq and with no choice but to praise him on public occasions.[67] He had felt compelled to acquiesce in the dissolution of the Senate, the release of Razmara's assassin, as well as the prosecution of Qavam and the confiscation of his property, measures which were even unfavourable to many of Musaddiq's Cabinet colleagues. In fact Henderson was told by Ala that most ministers agreed with the Shah in disapproving such measures but 'dared not stand up to Kashani'.[68]

If the Shah was 'mute' and 'helpless'[69] at this point, his predilection for intrigue and his cumulative bitterness and frustrations were, at least potentially, susceptible to exploitation by Zahidi and his followers. Middleton reported that the Shah might be persuaded to support Zahidi but that this would depend on 'which of his many fears' was 'uppermost at the time'. If he were 'seriously frightened of communism and anxious to keep his job' it was thought 'he might be panicked into doing the right thing'.[70] Despite his reduced prestige his support was vital to give legitimacy to any coup leader, and the symbolic use of his name could mobilize or stir the army, or at least significant parts of it.

Although he was formally in charge of the Defence Ministry, Musaddiq's efforts to control and reform the army were necessarily restrained: he avoided provoking the Shah and the army, or causing anxiety to the Americans who feared its weakening. He believed in maintaining an efficient army for the purposes of internal security, and had no desire to threaten the organizational interests of the military establishment. With this in mind he appointed as Defence Under-Secretary General Vusuq, who enjoyed royal confidence and was believed to be an able officer, made the royalist General Mahmud Baharmast Chief of Staff, and cut only a fraction of the army's budget. Vusuq's appointment was not, however, a success. It annoyed Kashani and a few other members of the National Front, apparently because in the events leading up to 21 July, when he was the chief of the gendarmerie, Vusuq had not adopted a pro-National Front position.[71] Musaddiq resisted pressure for Vusuq's removal and responded sharply to a threatening letter from Kashani to this effect, asserting that if there were to be any reforms, Kashani should for a while refrain from interfering in governmental affairs.[72] Eventually, however, Vusuq felt obliged to resign and Musaddiq 'agreed regretfully'.[73]

There would have been no point in Musaddiq taking on the Defence portfolio, however, if it had not resulted in changes in the top echelons of the military personnel, particularly a purge of the known enemies of the national movement, the old Reza Shah guard and the Tudeh infiltrators, as well as the promotion of officers sympathetic to the Government. Not surprisingly, any attempt to reorganize and reform the army met with resistance. According to his own account, Musaddiq had invited the Shah to appoint three officers in whom he had confidence to help with the running of the Defence Ministry, and they, along with the two under-secretaries, were assigned the task of studying a proposed retirement list of officers, compiled by elected committees of various military units. From the lengthy list, 136 officers (none of whom Musaddiq knew personally) were eventually retired.[74] These and other previously retired officers constituted a sizeable body and many of them became the most active members of the Zahidi-led Association of Retired Officers.[75] The activities of this group, combined with Musaddiq's inability to extend civilian authority over the military, were a source of great hope to the plotters.

Whatever Zahidi's optimism about the chances of a successful coup, the British and the Americans did not always share it. On his return to England Middleton, in an interesting report, contended that the National Front was divided into a 'right' and a 'left' wing. The 'right wing' was composed of the Kashani-led *mullahs*, as well as some rich landowners, 'professionals' and 'intellectuals', particularly from 'academic circles', who hoped that such a movement would forestall the danger of communism; the Fatimi-led 'left wing' included 'young turks', that is, men who were

> largely educated in France and Germany and [were] trained in one of the professions ... [were] dissatisfied with the existing regime, the inequities of wealth, the corruption and maladministration, and hope[d] to see a genuine national revival in their country.

Middleton predicted an imminent showdown between these two wings, adding that the 'only hope of success' for the West was to support the 'young turks', and that it was 'useless to expect any restoration of the old regime and we must be prepared to swim with the tide and not against it'.[76]

On another occasion Middleton repeated the need to use 'whatever opportunities ... to secure a change in [the] regime', and emphasized that as long as Musaddiq remained in power there would be no chance of a 'reasonable *modus vivendi*'. He added that the retirement of senior officers had resulted in the 'general break-up of the General Staff' and therefore the chance of a military coup 'was negligible'. On the other hand, he rated highly the chances of Makki, one of the 'young turks', assuming power:

[Makki] appeared to have the best chances of eventually being accepted as the national leader, with Fatimi as his chief lieutenant . . . [If Makki were to assume power he] would probably do so on the basis of a programme of national reform in contrast to the reactionary reforms proposed by Kashani and his fellow obscurantist mullahs.

Finally, Middleton believed that the British would 'find it possible to do business with' Makki.[77]

The idea of replacing Musaddiq with one of his own followers was not new: it had preoccupied the British both before and after the 21 July, and the State Department also apparently mentioned Makki and Matin-Daftari in this connection.[78] According to the same source, Sayyid Zia 'would not mind a National Front alternative to Musaddiq', and in this he probably echoed the views of many other opponents of Musaddiq. Unfortunately for the British, no follower of Musaddiq had his authority, charisma and popularity; none had his ability to keep together what was left of the National Front; and none, with the possible exception of Kashani, considered himself to be a credible rival. In any case, unless Musaddiq voluntarily withdrew there was no possibility of finding a viable successor from the ranks of his supporters.

Middleton's views were not shared by other Foreign Office officials, one of whom made the following assessment of Makki:

[he] is a clever, ruthless and ambitious man, whose chief talent is for fiery oratory. He probably has no strong principles; it has frequently been reported that he was willing to abandon the National Front if we would pay him. He has in the past allied himself to what he thought was the strong group. Now he is managing to get on both with Musaddiq and with Kashani . . . His complete lack of principle and scruple would make him a most unwelcome leader of Persia.[79]

In any case, Middleton's idea of supporting the 'young turks' proved to be irrelevant when the predicted showdown between the two wings of the National Front revealed that Makki was supporting the 'right wing'. Despite all constraints and intermittent doubts, many Foreign Office officials still believed that the most viable course was a military coup, and after the victory of the Republican Party in the US presidential elections in November 1952 the plan gained momentum with the development of an effectively co-ordinated Anglo-US policy to identify and counter 'communism'.

In view of the latent and manifest tensions in the National Front, predicting a 'showdown' between its various wings scarcely required any particular perceptiveness. The fundamental differences of political perceptions, character, style and the degree of adherence to principles between Musaddiq and Kashani were among the more salient manifestations of such tensions. Although the events of 21 July had temporarily suppressed these differences, they soon surfaced again. Musaddiq had always resented the unrestrained activities of Kashani's entourage who had, for example, set up an informal agency to issue letters of recommendation (tausiyih) which enabled the bearers to achieve their objectives regardless of the formal bureaucratic procedures. There were many other instances of disagreement which had manifested themselves earlier during the elections for the Majlis. Kashani regarded his role in the July events as crucial, and thereafter his self-esteem and expectations increased. He objected to some of Musaddiq's ministers and expected his preferences to be taken into account, but Musaddiq refused. This led to a deterioration in their relations when Kashani briefly left Tehran, ostensibly because of illness, but in fact in order to show his displeasure with Musaddiq, with whom 'he had had a row'.[80] After the resignation of Imam Jum'ih, Musaddiq's opponents rallied behind Kashani to secure his election as Speaker of the Majlis. Since Musaddiq's followers could not openly contest his candidature, Kashani was elected by 47 votes out of 62. This was not an auspicious development for Musaddiq,[81] since having Kashani at the head of the legislature, while Musaddiq was determined to reassert the authority of the executive, would not only serve to intensify the rivalry between the two leaders but would also aggravate intra-institutional discord. Musaddiq, however, refused to give in to any pressure or demands which he regarded as improper interference with the fulfilment of his duty; he resisted reshuffling his Cabinet which Kashani and his followers – unable to attack Musaddiq personally – often subjected to sharp criticism.[82] The gulf between the two leaders gradually reached such a point that opponents of Musaddiq optimistically looked to Kashani as their ally, if not their saviour.

Kashani's official position as the Speaker of the Majlis made some of his activities extremely embarrassing to the Government. For instance, he undermined the Government's attempts to create an impression of good relations with the Americans by openly attacking their policy in Iran. He sent representatives to the Vienna Peace

Conference against the expressed wish of Musaddiq, who regarded such a move as contrary to Iran's neutrality.[83] He sponsored demonstrations in support of the Iraqi nationalists, despite the critically delicate relations between Iran and Iraq.[84] Perhaps in order to threaten the Government he also gave the impression of favouring the Tudeh Party.

For his part, having maintained a close working relationship with Burujirdi, the most senior Ayatullah in the country, Musaddiq enhanced his ability to outwit Kashani. In April 1953 he made insult to Burujirdi a punishable offence, while Kashani enjoyed no particular immunity, a move deeply resented by Kashani who did not hide his bitterness.[85] Musaddiq, moreover, ordered that Kashani's letters of recommendation be ignored[86] and refused to help him in organizing an 'Islamic Conference', which for a variety of other reasons never took place.[87] He also appointed Brigadier-General Muhammad Daftari as Chief of the Customs Police, a move which led to more disagreements. Kashani had been treated discourteously by Daftari as long ago as 1949 (following the attempt on the Shah's life), and Baqa'i attacked the appointment as family favouritism, since Daftari was a relative of Musaddiq. Although Daftari had been unanimously recommended by the Committee for National Defence, which was composed of five generals, it was not until Kashani gave his unequivocal consent that the appointment went ahead.[88] An interesting episode in the history of Musaddiq–Kashani relations was the replacement of Abulfazl Tauliyat, the custodian of the Qum Shrine, by Sayyid Muhammad Mishkat, finalized in December 1952. According to the US Embassy in Tehran, Kashani had personally encouraged the dismissal of Tauliyat; he however

> bought off Kashani by making a contribution of some 100 thousand tomans to charities controlled by Kashani and his sons. He also agreed to make a public accounting of the Shrine's finances, whereupon Kashani informed Musaddiq that Tollat's [sic] dismissal would not really be necessary. Musaddiq allegedly advised Kashani that he had been so thoroughly convinced of Kashani's previous representations that he was unwilling to change his mind.[89]

The discord between Musaddiq and Kashani inevitably affected the configuration of political groups affiliated to the National Front. The Iran Party re-emerged after a long eclipse to become one of the main organizations behind the Government; the Maliki-led Third

Force Party, formed in October 1952 by the splinter group from the Toilers' Party of Baqa'i to become the largest pro-Government organization,[90] as well as the bulk of the pan-Iranists, were openly behind Musaddiq. Kashani could rely on the Association of Muslim Warriors (Majma'-i Musalmanan-i Mujahid), led by the notorious turbaned deputy Shams ud-Din Qanatabadi. Kashani could also hope to cultivate the Movement of the East (Nahzat-i Sharq), led by one of his sons, and Baqa'i's Toilers' Party, as well as his personal and traditional links and his followers in the Majlis. Open opposition to Musaddiq was, however, difficult even for Kashani. Disturbed by rumours that he was siding with the opposition, Kashani went out of his way to deny that there were any problems between him and Musaddiq and to reaffirm publicly his support. Musaddiq, on the other hand, made no mention of Kashani in his public pronouncements. This was in itself highly significant, but it did not reduce the impact of their contentious relations.

Conflict in the National Front was not of course confined to Musaddiq and Kashani. Makki, the First Deputy for Tehran, believed that he was the sole champion of the AIOC's expropriation and that his role had not been recognized; he consequently raised objections to the Cabinet and to Musaddiq's plenary powers.[91] Baqa'i, the professor of ethics who had few compunctions about using unethical means, was *inter alia* unhappy about the close relations between Musaddiq and the Iran Party, and about its electoral success.[92] He was still committed to the campaign for revenge on the instigators of the July events, and was becoming more forthright in his criticisms of the Government, as was Ha'irizadih. Yusuf Mushar, a deputy in the Majlis and an ex-Minister in the Cabinet of Musaddiq, left the ranks of his supporters while categorizing the deputies into two groups – *majzub* (enchanted) and *mar'ub* (frightened).[93] Besides succumbing to the effects of extraneous forces in stimulating their resentments, deputies such as Makki, Baqa'i and Ha'irizadih considered their rewards as wholly incommensurate with what they regarded as their decisive role in bringing Musaddiq to power, and regarded some 'newcomers' as having been given precedence over them. They were devoid of constructive ideas and plans, their political strategy consisting of sharp criticism of governments irrespective of the constraints and adversities faced, and, in the case of Musaddiq's Government, regardless of the alternative. Any move which threatened to upset the balance of political forces to the benefit of Musaddiq and against the Majlis and later the Court, was intolerable to them and contravened their mode of political thinking and action. The position of these people, as well as of Kashani *vis-à-vis* Musaddiq, found full expression in the arena of the Majlis.

Once Musaddiq had acquired plenary powers he was obviously in a much stronger position with respect to the Majlis, which was nevertheless still the main source of both support and trouble for the Government. Those deputies who had united in support of Musaddiq and in opposition to Qavam, formed the large National Movement Faction (NMF) (Fraksiun-i Nahzat-i Milli) consisting of thirty-four members and forming the parliamentary base of the Government.[94] However, even they were not all unconditional supporters of Musaddiq, while the remainder of the deputies, most of whom kept up an appearance of neutrality, were actually unfavourable to Musaddiq and awaiting a further outbreak of dissent among the ranks of his supporters.

The first difficulty in Government–Majlis relations arose over the extension of martial law, which had been declared in Tehran in March 1952 and was due to expire on 12 August 1952. The hostility of the deputies forced the Government to withdraw its bill for an extension, although it stated that if the necessity arose it would not hesitate to declare martial law and resubmit its bill to the Majlis.[95] Very soon afterwards a renewed outbreak of violent street clashes between the Tudeh Party on the one hand, and the pan-Iranists, Baqa'i's Toilers' Party and the small fascist party, Sumka, on the other, resulted in martial law being reimposed.[96] The Majlis and the Senate had little choice but to approve it. But the real test of Government–Majlis relations was yet to come.

During the period of the Majlis summer recess (11 August– 7 October 1952), which coincided with the Muharram ceremonies, the religious deputy Hasan Ali Rashid had begun criticizing the Government in the course of his sermons.[97] It was not criticism, however, which led the Government to resort to strong measures. Faced with the possibility of subversion or disruptive activities by the Tudeh Party, British agents and others in state organizations, industrial centres and factories, Musaddiq and his colleagues had become convinced of the need for increased law and order. They therefore drafted the nine-point 'public security law' (*Qanun-i Amniyyat-i Ijtima'i*) to be enforced for an experimental period of three months.[98] The new law, signed by Musaddiq on 23 October 1952, was aimed at improving security and curbing possibilities of incitement and provocation, and other activities detrimental to public order. It caused considerable press and parliamentary criticism; it was argued with some justification that the wide scope of this law and the imprecise manner in which it had been phrased rendered it too susceptible to abuse. Baqa'i went as far as describing it as worse than the Yasa of Genghis Khan.[99] But in one form or another such a law, and its rigorous implementation was urgently needed. Musaddiq went ahead regardless of all criticism and submitted his proposed law to the Majlis, insisting that it was a temporary experiment and must be approved because of the emergency situation.[100]

Not surprisingly his disgruntled supporters began to question his genuine love of liberty and were provided with an opportunity to justify their imminent desertion; but as yet none of them dared to attack Musaddiq directly. Instead they resorted to publicly appealing tactics such as invoking the issue of the evaded prosecution of those responsible for the July events. Baqa'i, for example, made a lengthy speech on this issue during which he rebuked and threatened the Government.[101] The tone and content of this speech dismayed the Government to such an extent that it announced it would no longer attend the Majlis.[102] In an attempt to avert a serious crisis thirty deputies signed a letter in support of Musaddiq. Nevertheless he demanded that those who had insulted the Ministers be dealt with according to the internal rules of the Majlis, insisting that criticism and guidance must be distinguished from insult.[103] Eventually Baqa'i was formally reprimanded by Kashani and a Majlis letter of apology sent to Musaddiq.[104]

Mutual resentment continued to simmer and was now further aggravated by the choice of the NIOC's board of directors. Ex-premier Bayat had been appointed General Manager and Reza Fallah, an old employee of the AIOC, was made head of the Abadan refinery. This gave rise to bitter criticism from Baqa'i, Qanatabadi and especially Makki who regarded Fallah as being devoutly pro-British. As a member of the High Council of National Iranian Oil, Makki was himself involved in the appointment of officials, but he did not accept the majority vote, resigned from the Council in protest and took the dispute to the Majlis.[105] According to the US Embassy, he now 'began in earnest to groom himself for the premiership'.[106]

Political differences were so deep by now that each new issue became a crisis. The next crisis arose over the Government's proposed new electoral law – published on 17 December 1952 – according to which the elections for the remaining seats in the 17th

Majlis were to be conducted. There were fears that the increase in the number of deputies which the law provided for and the consequent increase in the two-thirds quorum would virtually paralyse the Majlis for a period. In addition it would reduce the effect of a small vocal opposition. Apparently on the initiative of Ha'irizadih,[107] and with the support of Kashani,[108] sixteen deputies prepared a bill with triple emergency which barred the Government from invoking any bill to suspend the Majlis. They refused to accept the assurances of Shayigan and Dr. Ghulam Husain Sadiqi, the Interior Minister, that the new law would not be retroactive and that the Government had no intention of suspending the Majlis.[109] Musaddiq reacted immediately: in a radio broadcast he sharply and bitterly attacked the bill's signatories and appealed directly to the people.[110] This tactic was successful and the Majlis unanimously cast a vote of confidence for Musaddiq, with the exception of Ha'irizadih, who abstained.[111]

Immediately following this victory Musaddiq demanded the extension of his plenary powers for a further twelve months. Makki resigned his seat in protest, comparing Musaddiq with Hitler,[112] and other deputies voiced their strong opposition. In a meeting with members of the NMF Musaddiq justified his position on the grounds that it was the only way to deal with the oil problem and to facilitate speedy legislation which, he argued, the Iranian Parliament, not being organized along party principles, would otherwise not allow.[113] In any case, he asserted, the Majlis would not be stripped of its prerogatives as it could always express its dissatisfaction with the Government through a vote of no confidence. He accepted the suggestion of one of his supporters, Deputy Bahram Majdzadih, to submit his bills to the Majlis within three months of promulgation, and an absolute majority in the NMF then approved the extension of plenary powers. This did not, however, end the controversy.

Amidst acrimonious exchanges Baqa'i strongly opposed the move and, in line with a well-tried tactic, claimed to be in favour of Musaddiq but against the extension of his plenary powers.[114] Shayigan in turn accused Baqa'i of deceiving the people, and Karim Sanjabi denounced him as a 'hypocrite' (*munafiq*).[115] Qanatabadi turned against Sanjabi in defence of Baqa'i, who himself denounced 'sycophants' around Musaddiq. Despite the turmoil Musaddiq insisted that the Majlis approve the bill for the extension of his powers, announcing that this would amount to a vote of confidence.[116] It was obvious that the Majlis was in no position to deny him this vote. Having failed to sway much open support in their favour, and in an attempt to play down the divisions, Baqa'i and others exchanged apologies, and Makki, who had now returned to the Majlis, declared that the Iranian nation would back Musaddiq until its last breath.[117]

Despite these attempts at conciliation Ha'irizadih launched a strong personal attack on Musaddiq and denounced his entourage.[118] More significantly, Kashani, having vowed not to capitulate in the face of 'illogical' demands, expressed his unequivocal opposition to the plenary powers bill, which he described as 'absolutely contrary to the Constitution and in conflict with the interests of the country', asserting that 'as long as I am the Speaker of the Majlis I will not regard the consideration of such bills by the Majlis to be permissible'.[119] Kashani's intervention greatly complicated the whole issue and broadened confrontation.

On the other hand, popular gestures of support for Musaddiq were increasing; a large demonstration backed by Tehran's bazaar was organized and some members of the NMF decided to take sanctuary in the Majlis until the plenary powers bill was approved.[120] The Government applied pressure by announcing that the oil negotiations were at a critical stage. Baqa'i's objections were countered by Shayigan, and, following a heated debate, 59 out of 67 deputies voted in favour of the extension of Musaddiq's plenary powers despite Kashani's disapproval.[121] Kashani's immediate reaction was a conciliatory retreat, declaring that his move had been wrongly interpreted by 'some ignorant people' as a sign of disagreement with the Prime Minister. His sole aim, he claimed, had been to draw attention to the necessity for proper observance of the Constitution.[122] Musaddiq ignored Kashani and concentrated on explaining in general terms his demand for the extension of the plenary powers.[123] Of course the Musaddiq–Kashani disagreements were public knowledge, and a seven-man delegation was therefore appointed by the NMF to bring about a reconciliation of the two leaders. A meeting was successfully arranged and a joint declaration was issued reaffirming their continued co-operation.[124] Whatever hopes this may have raised, nothing had really been solved. Kashani continued more frequently to champion the inviolable sanctity of the 'Constitution' and less hesitantly to use such a weapon aginst the Government.

Musaddiq had initially co-operated with Kashani in order to counterbalance his opponents' exploitation of religious forces, and in the early stages of the nationalist movement this had proved rewarding. Now, however, Kashani and his followers invoked religiously loaded issues in order to extract concessions from and to put pressure on the Government itself.[125] Taking full advantage of the vulnerability of the Government *vis-à-vis* religious feelings, sixteen deputies submitted a bill for the implementation of a total ban on all alcoholic beverages within two months. A similar bill had been debated inconclusively in the Majlis in 1951, but in the present climate no one dared to oppose it. In addition the Government had been taken by surprise: Baqir Kazimi, the Finance Minister, argued that such a measure would deprive the Government of revenue of 250 million rials per annum and other difficulties were pointed out.[126] These statistics did not persuade deputies to change their minds and the bill was approved, although the Government was given a respite of six months instead of two, and the ban was extended to opium on the suggestion of Nariman.

Kashani's support for such measures appealed to groups such as the Fida'iyan-i Islam, whose pattern of allegiances had been affected by the Musuddiq–Kashani frictions and who were believed to be resuming their collaboration with Kashani.[127] Following the release of Razmara's assassin, Navvab-Safavi, the leader of the group, was also set free and Abdulhusain Vahidi, one of its prominent members who had been behind Mihdi Abd-i Khuda'i's plan to assassinate Fatimi,[128] was left undisturbed. This was not enough to dissuade the group from attacking the Government in its newspaper, or from rallying behind Kashani, particularly when the Government later decided to prosecute Safavi and Vahidi, as accomplices in the assassination of Razmara.[129]

The crisis in relations between Musaddiq and Kashani was now having repercussions across the entire political spectrum. In mid-February 1953, seventeen members defected from the Iran Party; in the view of Sanjabi, leader of the Party's Central Committee, Kashani was to blame for the defections, as his sympathizers in the Party attacked the Party leaders as stooges of the United States.[130] The split in the Toilers' Party and the open desertion of Makki, Baqa'i, Ha'irizadih and others from the NMF were also provoked by the conflict between Musaddiq and Kashani.[131] Most of those who had helped Musaddiq in the task of nationalizing the oil industry were now openly against him. The National Front had finally collapsed; its ideology had always been purposely vague, in order to appeal to a wide audience, but it was blatantly anti-authoritarian and thus contravened the seemingly authoritarian measures which Musaddiq deemed it necessary to adopt in order to cope with the existing difficulties. The National Front had proved to be appropriate for opposition but not for governing. The functions of the doomed National Front were taken over by the NMF, which was now purged of recalcitrant elements. In a conversation with a member of the US Embassy, Shayigan expressed doubts that Musaddiq's opponents could organize themselves in the Majlis, asserting that it was Musaddiq as a symbol who gave the Government its strength. Although he regretted Baqa'i's departure and believed that Makki was still trying to maintain a 'middle ground', Shayigan maintained that the faction was in a stronger position now that it was not hampered by deputies such as Ha'irizadih.[132] He was soon proved wrong in view of the formal emergence of various factions, and when factionalism was accelerated by a further deterioration of relations between Musaddiq and the Shah.

Musaddiq had always resented the intrigues of the Court, which was gradually re-establishing itself as a main source of inspiration and support for his opponents, and had long suspected that it gave financial support to anti-Government groups. He was also indignant that there was no governmental supervision over the expenditure of the Court's considerable revenues. This resentment now came to a head and he threatened that if the Shah did not abandon intrigues and improper activities he would resign and publicly explain his reasons. Ala was sent to see Musaddiq and was presented with a long list of complaints[133] as well as demands that the Shah desist from meeting opponents of the Government 'and give up control of Mashhad Shrine properties and the right to administer the distribution of the proceeds of the Shrine and other crown properties.'[134]

The Shah hoped to placate Musaddiq without taking any steps which would further weaken his own position. Thus, Ala told Musaddiq that the Shah was prepared to leave the country; Musaddiq, however, did not approve of such a move and the crisis continued. This development was welcomed by Musaddiq's opponents. In a meeting with Ala, Kashani 'seemed pleased' and told him that if Musaddiq were to attack the Shah in the Majlis, the Majlis would give the Shah its overwhelming support; he also mentioned Zahidi and Salih as successors.[135]

A number of deputies stepped in to mediate and the crisis was apparently contained. Ala informed Henderson with relief that a

'temporary composure of differences' had been achieved and
Musaddiq had been 'mollified not to press his grievances'.[136] It was
also suggested by these deputies that the Shah should take steps to
improve relations with the Prime Minister, for instance by encouraging the army to recognize Musaddiq as its commander, by refraining
from meeting the Government's opponents and by suspending the
distribution of Crown lands. The Shah resisted the last point, but did
show some readiness to negotiate with Musaddiq.[137] The possibility
of a *rapprochement* between the Shah and Musaddiq naturally
alarmed his opponents. According to Henderson: 'Ala said that
Kashani, Baqa'i and Makki were not pleased at these developments.
In fact Makki had telephoned Ala and urged him to try to persuade
the Shah not to seek a reconciliation with Musaddiq.'[138]

The 'reconciliation', however, proved illusive: neither Musaddiq's
long audience with the Shah on 24 February nor his subsequent
negotiations with Ala and Diba resulted in any tangible understanding. Encouraged by the attitude of Musaddiq's ex-supporters,
the Shah insisted on leaving the country for two months, and
Musaddiq eventually agreed to make the preliminary arrangements
for the trip. On 28 February Musaddiq went to the palace to
bid the Shah farewell, only to discover that he had been tricked.[139]
The Shah had asked Musaddiq to keep the proposed journey a secret,
but had himself arranged for its details to be leaked; Kashani had
consequently issued two letters publicly requesting the Shah to
abandon his trip and, together with Bihbahani, had appealed to the
people to prevent the royal departure.[140] Faced with pro-Shah
demonstrations, Musaddiq left the palace through a back entrance,
suspecting that there were plans for his own murder.[141] He returned
to his house, but was soon forced to escape from the mob, clad only
in his pyjamas.

The Association of Retired Officers played a crucial role in the
demonstrations of 28 February. Air force lorries were used to
transport peasants in from the suburbs of Tehran where the Crown
lands had been distributed, and uniformed officers, including a few
generals, did their best to excite emotions, haranguing the crowds
that Musaddiq had pressed the Shah to leave the country with the
intention of removing him from the throne.[142] The small, staunchly
royalist Arya Party, which was financed by the Court, led the
demonstrators, who included right-wing groups and hired professional thugs. The activities of the Rashidian brothers and the sums of
money which they had spent on behalf of the British were beginning

to pay off. The Americans and the British did not deny that the demonstrations were staged.[143] The Foreign Office informed Eden that:

> it would seem that Kashani, seizing upon the emotions surrounding the departure of the Shah, cleverly managed to couple popular clamour for the Shah remaining, with attacks on Musaddiq. The popular clamour itself was certainly organized by Kashani and was not a spontaneous expression of a loyalty deep-seated or significant enough to stiffen the Shah.[144]

Musaddiq's pressure on the Shah had provided Kashani with a 'heaven-sent opportunity' to recover lost ground.[145] In all probability Musaddiq had not fully appreciated the extent of Kashani's readiness to exploit the situation and to side openly with the Court. He had also perhaps underrated the cumulative effect of opposition activities on his increasingly vulnerable Government. In fact the royalist demonstrations on 28 February were a proto-coup aimed at toppling the Government. A few days earlier Ardishir Zahidi had informed the American Embassy that his father, General Zahidi, might soon become Prime Minister and 'had already allocated portfolios in his Cabinet'.[146] Whether Musaddiq was informed about this plan or concerned about Zahidi's involvement in the rebellion of the Bakhtiari chief, Abulqasim Bakhtiari, he now ordered his arrest.[147] Musaddiq's supporters, in the meantime, had succeeded in prevailing upon the royalist demonstrators and the Government was able to reassert its authority.

Deeply shaken by his forced departure from his house, Musaddiq had gone first to the Chief of Staff's headquarters and then to the Majlis where, in a state of indignation and anger, he recounted what had happened, giving a 48-hour ultimatum to the deputies to find a new prime minister. He threatened to inform the nation of all the facts, asserting that 'I am the Prime Minister not of the Majlis or the Shah but of the nation.' He also intimated that he might call for a referendum. However, he failed to sway all the deputies; Ha'irizadih denounced him as a 'rebel' and this encouraged other opponents.[148] Sensing the mood of the Majlis and encouraged by some deputies, Musaddiq returned home and did not insist on a vote of confidence. Both his supporters and opponents then initiated new formulas which reaffirmed the last vote of confidence cast in favour of the Government on 6 January 1953, and the

Government spokesman announced that these were acceptable.[149]

The crisis seemed to have subsided. The Government's opponents temporarily retreated, and although Musaddiq also showed some restraint he resorted to a number of measures to strengthen his position. He appointed General Taqi Riyahi, who was affiliated to the Iran Party, as the new Chief of Staff and ordered the arrest of some of the main culprits of the events of 28 February. It soon became very clear, however, that Musaddiq's parliamentary opponents, particularly Kashani, would do everything possible to prevent his consolidation of power,[150] and these relentless challenges became the main problem facing the Government.

In the immediate aftermath of the February crisis, the embarrassed Kashani had once again felt obliged to declare publicly his support for Mussadiq, and deny any links with the Court.[151] Making fuller use of his formal position as the Speaker of the Majlis, however, Kashani began to intensify his moves against the Goverment. Open friction developed over two issues: first, the rotation in succession of the two deputy speakers of the Majlis. Kashani had not taken up his seat in the Majlis and according to customary practice the Majlis sessions were presided over by the two deputy speakers, Muhammad Zulfaqari and Ahmad Razavi. Kashani suspended this practice, instructing only Zulfaqari to preside; in protest the NMF, led by Razavi, announced that it would not attend the Majlis until the rotation system was restored.[152]

Equally disruptive was the struggle over the replacement of the commander of the Majlis guard, Colonel Zahidi, whose well-demonstrated anti-Government bias had led Razavi to call for his replacement. Zahidi's successor, Major Mahmud Sakha'i, was strongly opposed by opponents of the Government, particularly Kashani who contended that the Government had no right to initiate such a change. As a sign of protest Kashani ordered that no Majlis session should be held.[153] This infuriated Musaddiq who again threatened to resort to a referendum.[154] Renewed mediation efforts eventually produced a committee of eight deputies, including supporters and opponents of the Government, who were assigned the task of settling the outstanding issues between the Government and the Majlis (or its Speaker), as well as those between the Prime Minister and the Shah.[155] Ha'irizadih soon announced that the differences between Musaddiq and Kashani had been resolved,[156] and it was also agreed that the system of rotating the deputy speakers would be resumed, and that the commander of the Majlis guard would be appointed by the Majlis from a list of five officers suggested by the Chief of Staff.

After several meetings with the Shah and Musaddiq, the eight-man committee prepared a report which was read in the Majlis session of 12 March 1953. This report unequivocally reaffirmed Musaddiq's understanding of the Constitution, emphasizing that the Shah was required only to reign, while the Government was empowered to rule.[157] For this very reason the report provoked bitter opposition from the outset,[158] and became the most significant issue of contention between supporters and opponents of the Government. Musaddiq's supporters demanded its approval by the Majlis in order to strengthen the position of the Government and reconfirm the legitimacy of its position *vis-à-vis* the Court. Ha'irizadih (who had, ironically, dictated the report himself),[159] together with Baqa'i and, less explicitly, Makki, who had also signed it, insisted that the report be approved by the Majlis only when Mussadiq discarded his plenary powers.[160] Many other deputies regarded the approval of such a report as an unforgivable betrayal of the Constitution.[161] In their eyes, it implied depriving the Shah of his cherished incumbency of the position of Commander-in-Chief of the armed forces, and of his remaining power and prerogatives; it was also viewed as likely ultimately to jeopardize the foundations of the monarchy, and to make opposition to Musaddiq increasingly difficult.

It was by now fully apparent that the intrinsic inconsistencies and ambiguities in the Constitution would not allow any clear demarcation of the boundaries and nature of the authority of the Shah, the Parliament and the Cabinet. All groups proclaimed the sanctity of the Constitution, despite the fact that it contained no clear-cut mechanism to help solve conflicts between the various institutions of the state, but actually contributed to these conflicts. What Musaddiq and his followers were demanding, therefore, was a formal clarification of these ambiguities which were the basis of most of the problems faced by governments independent of the Court. Opponents, on the other hand, regarded such a step as fatal to the monarchy, the monarch and themselves.

Opposition to the report of the eight-man committee was encouraged by the Shah, who was in touch with the Government's opponents.[162] Instead of capitulating on the issues of command of the armed forces and control of the Crown lands, he repeated his threat to leave the country.[163] Assured of the loyalty of the bulk of the army and encouraged by recent developments, he began to show a growing readiness to work against the Prime Minister, although, true to character, he was still inclined to delay action and await the prophesied destruction of the Musaddiq myth.

Even Ala was now trying to encourage the Shah 'to take some definite step' before Musaddiq deprived him of all his power and sources of revenue. In Ala's view, the only candidate with the 'necessary energy and backing' to succeed Musaddiq was Zahidi, who 'had agreed to present his undated resignation to the Shah in advance so that, should the Shah be displeased with him, he could dismiss him at any time'. Ala was confident that Zahidi was backed by Kashani, Ha'irizadih and other ex-supporters of Musaddiq, by 'influential political leaders not connected with the movement' and by 'many mullahs', and therefore recommended speedy action in his favour.[164] According to this report the Shah 'seemed impressed' by the merits of Zahidi but had not yet summoned up enough courage to do more than 'wait-and-see'. Moreover he could claim that his policy was the right one since so many of Musaddiq's original supporters were now trying to unseat him.

Aware of the extent of activities aimed at the violent overthrow or the resignation of his Government, Musaddiq reacted by announcing on the eve of the Iranian New Year (21 March 1953) that he regarded resignation as treason and that a majority in the Majlis of a half plus one would be sufficient mandate for him to stay in office.[165] He revealed the extent of his resentment against the Shah by refusing to pay him the customary New Year visit[166] and broadcast a frank account of the circumstances leading to the events of late February.[167]

Musaddiq's supporters continued their efforts to procure the approval of the report of the eight-man committee which the opposition uncompromisingly tried to obstruct. Their task was greatly facilitated by the internal regulations of the Majlis, which enabled a small group constantly to frustrate the majority by breaking the quorum. The Government had no means of preventing the obstructive tactics masterminded by its vociferous ex-supporters, whose enmity had vitiated the Government's capacity to lead or control. The Majlis had ceased to be divided into the Government's self-confident supporters and its cautiously unobtrusive opponents. It had given way to manifest factionalism patterned mainly on the basis of attitude toward the Government.

In early March Baqa'i, his henchman Ali Zuhari, Qanatabadi and Karimi formed the Salvation of the Movement faction (Fraksiun-i Nijat-i Nahzat), and in mid-March Ha'irizadih with a group of notorious right-wing royalist opponents of the Government, created the Freedom faction (Fraksiun-i Azadi), consisting of some ten deputies. These two factions constituted the core of the anti-Government opposition in the Majlis, with Hari'izadih assuming a role similar to that of Jamal Imami in the previous Majlis.[168] These two factions encouraged the formation of two more named Union (Ittihad) and Country (Kishvar) which, along with some ungrouped deputies, adopted a more or less middle position.[169] They behaved in such a way as to ensure that they were on the winning side, and some tried to play the role of 'disinterested' mediators while ingratiating themselves with both sides. Although Musaddiq's supporters were still in a majority in the Majlis, his opponents could easily paralyse it.

For example, the Freedom faction moved to Qum in order to disrupt the functioning of the Majlis and extend its anti-Government publicity. When a group of deputies tried to mediate, Hai'irizadih insisted that he would not return to the Majlis unless the right to appoint the chiefs of police, the gendarmerie and the general staff was transferred to the Majlis for a period of five years.[170] Knowing that the real bone of contention was the report of the eight-man committee, Musaddiq called his opponents' bluff by stating that he would continue in office whatever the fate of the report, and that its approval would merely be helpful to his Government. Nevertheless he wanted the report debated in a public session of the Majlis and his opponents were equally determined to prevent it.

Efforts to destabilize the Government were not confined to disruptive quasi-parliamentary activities. In April 1953 the Government's newly appointed energetic Police Chief, Brigadier Mahmud Afshartus, was kidnapped and brutally murdered. The abduction of Afshartus, masterminded by a number of pro-Zahidi activists – including one politician who later became a close confidant of the Shah – as well as by British secret agents, was apparently intended to be followed by a series of subversive activities. The intention was primarily to extract information from Afshartus and to demoralize the Government. His defiant attitude towards his torturers and his abuse of the Shah, however, pushed the kidnappers to murder him.[171]

General Zahidi, who had been released after a brief period of detention in relation to the February events, was summoned to the Military Governor's office after the murder but escaped arrest by taking sanctuary in the Majlis, while Kashani personally ordered that he should be properly looked after.[172] Many of those arrested in connection with the murder of Afshartus were closely linked to

Baqa'i and had implicated him.[173] Baqa'i, however, could not be arrested as he enjoyed parliamentary immunity. Although the murder of Afshartus had been a serious blow to the Government, the huge popular attendance at his funeral procession[174] was a clear indictment of his murderers and a sign of continued public support for Musaddiq.

The alleged complicity of Baqa'i in the murder made the possibility of a reconciliation even more remote. Baqa'i had been elected as a deputy both for Tehran and his native city of Kerman, and contrary to the usual practice had retained both seats. The Government now decided to restrict him to his Tehran seat and arrange for the pro-Government Ali Ruhi to be deputy for Kerman, since he had come second in the election there. Baqa'i promptly resigned his Tehran seat and demanded that his credentials for the deputyship for Kerman be investigated.[175] The affair resulted in a bitter dispute, and even fisticuffs in the Majlis, where Ruhi himself was assaulted.[176] When the Majlis committee of investigation voted overwhelmingly against Ruhi,[177] the NMF abandoned him.

The Minister of Justice had, in the meantime, formally demanded that the Majlis strip Baqa'i of parliamentary immunity so that he could be put on trial in connection with the murder of Afshartus. There was a further escalation of hostilities in the Majlis which a reconciliation committee of eighteen deputies was helpless to deal with. In the event, the ease with which the Majlis could be paralysed eventually led the Government and its supporters to accept all the demands of the opposition deputies on the condition that they would allow a full Majlis session to deal with the report of the eight-man committee.[178] This session was held on 19 May but became an occasion for yet more anti-Government attacks; Baqa'i accused the Government of torturing those arrested in connection with the Afshartus murder in order to extract confessions; Qanatabadi accused the Government of intending to eliminate Baqa'i, while Mir-Ashrafi dismissed the Government and the Prime Minister as 'illicit'.[179] Two days later these accusations were forcefully repudiated by Sanjabi.[180] Whatever the rights and wrongs, this was a dangerous situation where the only dialogue between the Government and the opposition was a series of accusations and counter-accusations.

About a week later the opposition was outmanoeuvred into agreeing to attend a few sessions of the Majlis; Government supporters succeeded in pushing through the Majlis a motion on the triple emergency status of the report of the eight-man committee, which they then submitted as a bill.[181] It was of course unlikely to receive final approval since the opposition was determined to prevent it and, for that matter, any other measures put forward by the Government. Baqa'i had begun a new campaign, accusing the Government of colluding with the Tudeh Party and intending to abolish the monarchy.[182]

In the Majlis session of 28 May, Mu'azzami, one of Musaddiq's supporters, emphatically denied these accusations and expressed his regret that in its first year the 17th Majlis had accomplished nothing beyond empty verbosity, mutual accusations and abuse.[183] This could not be disputed and, if anything, parliamentary standards were declining, often to the level of undignified scuffles in the Chamber. On 7 June Deputy Speaker Razavi was subjected to an unrestrained barrage of abuse by Makki, on the pretext of deviation from the agenda, and several deputies were physically assaulted in the general uproar which followed.[184] The Government's supporters demanded that Makki should either apologize or be reprimanded according to the regulations of the Majlis, failing which they would refuse to attend. This new dispute now overshadowed all others and reconciliation attempts were no more successful than those which had gone before.[185]

Again Musaddiq's supporters appealed to the people by organizing a meeting in Parliament Square. This alarmed their opponents, who could not themselves enlist public support for their anti-Government struggles. Kashani declared that this proved the Government had no majority support and was worried about its position in the Parliament. He characteristically contended that the opposition only demanded the proper implementation of the Constitution and this was not incompatible with reform.[186] Although the meeting was not as large as pro-Government newspapers claimed, it did boost the morale of Musaddiq's followers whose policies and tactics were approved by the meeting.[187] However, the mid-term election for the Speaker of the Majlis was soon due and it was therefore necessary for the Majlis to recover its quorum.

Kashani, who was the opposition candidate for Speaker, had so far shown no willingness to settle the outstanding disputes. On the contrary, he had allowed himself to become a source of inspiration for the opposition and his activities had reached a point where the British and Americans did not discount the possibility that he might become premier.[188] Since the election for Speaker required a full session of the Majlis, Kashani did eventually bring about a reconciliation between Razavi and Makki on 23 June.

Kashani argued that the country would be 'lost' if the prevailing situation were allowed to continue, and his remedy was the correct implementation of the 'Constitution'.[189] This amounted to little more than perpetuating the chronic vulnerability of the Government *vis-à-vis* the Majlis. Musaddiq agreed that the country was in a dangerous situation and also advocated constitutionalism, but his conception was fundamentally different. In a meeting with representatives of the Union and Country factions he declared that wherever parliamentarianism had existed so had these types of problems. Evolution could only be gradual and he maintained that the existing achievements should not be sacrificed in the hope of electing a perfect Majlis, because without the Majlis even fifty years of preparation would achieve nothing.

> Yet the Majlis must be capable of initiating beneficial outcomes ... it must have a stable majority and minority, one supporting the government and the other guiding it ... [if] the government is compelled to spend all its time on countering the disruptive activities of the opposition, it would by no means be able to accomplish reforms ... I must say with utmost regret that this Government, which is responsible to the people for the affairs of the country, has no choice but to appeal to the people themselves for the solution of this difficulty, and somehow put an end to this unacceptable state of affairs.[190]

In the past Musaddiq had set a standard of oppositional behaviour which his opponents could now use against him. When they resorted to parliamentary obstruction, they recalled Musaddiq's own use of the weapon against the Government of Sadr, and denounced him as the inventor of this tactic.[191] They also frequently referred to Musaddiq's own earlier opposition to martial law, plenary powers and the weakening of the Majlis, and made full use of the quorum rule, the modification of which Musaddiq had always opposed. The task of holding office in the face of all adversities, however, had awakened Musaddiq to the dangers of the inordinate power of the Majlis, or a handful of opponents within it, in contrast to the constant vulnerability of the executive. By demanding plenary powers, Musaddiq had put forward an *ad hoc* remedy, but this had deeply threatened the structural configuration of clan politics, without protecting him from the obstructiveness of the Majlis.

No one in the past had championed the power of the Majlis as vigorously as Musaddiq, but he now believed that a referendum was the only answer. His supporters hoped that this could be averted by securing the election of Mu'azzami as Speaker, while the opposition were confident of Kashani's victory. Both groups therefore agreed to allow a full session of the Majlis to take place in order to elect a Speaker. The election took place on 1 July and Mu'azzami was successful with 41 votes, compared to Kashani's 31.[192] In order to detract from this Government victory, Baqa'i's protégé, Ali Zuhari, immediately tabled a motion of interpellation against the Government, accusing it of having tortured the alleged participants in the murder of Afshartus.[193]

This was the second motion of its kind to be tabled against Musaddiq's Government and was a move likely to exacerbate the existing conflicts. Efforts to prevent the ultimate approval of the report of the eight-man committee also continued, with the opposition deputies formally proposing twelve diversionary amendments.[194] They also succeeded in countering the Government's control of the Majlis secretariat by dominating several important parliamentary committees. There was every indication that the Government's relations with the Majlis were to become more tense and strained. The Deputy Prime Minister and the Minister of the Interior, Sadiqi, nevertheless announced that the Government was ready to answer the motion of interpellation, and set a date for this purpose.

On the same day as this was announced (9 July) the Majlis elected Makki and one other deputy, by a majority of over 40, to supervise the note reserve of the Government.[195] This created a real problem for Musaddiq. In order to meet governmental needs and as recommended by the economic missions of Schacht and Gutt (September–October 1952),[196] Musaddiq had ordered a note issue of 3,100 million rials, but had kept this secret in order to curb inflation and because it would certainly have aroused the hostility of the deputies. When Razmara had demanded an issue of a lesser amount of notes in 1951, there had been strong opposition from many deputies, including Musaddiq himself. With Makki in charge of the note reserve, the matter of the note issue would become public knowledge, and this would defeat the Government's purpose, aggravate its financial and economic difficulties and provide its opponents with a decisive weapon. In fact, Musaddiq confessed that this was a crucial factor in convincing him of the need for a referendum.[197]

Since the demonstrations in February, anti-Government challenges had increasingly been launched in the name of the Shah, and it was with royal backing that the approval of the eight-man committee had been thwarted. Nevertheless Musaddiq had succeeded in excluding the Shah and his family from direct involvement in the political process. Many members of the royal family were abroad, while the Shah spent most of his time on the Caspian shore unable to receive foreign diplomats or travel without Musaddiq's consent. In defiance of increasingly obtrusive royalists as well as his previous supporters who had joined the royalist camp in depicting the Shah as a much-maligned, innocent and law-abiding monarch, Musaddiq was still capable of hindering the resuscitation of the Court as the centre of gravity of the body politic.

Ala's resignation on 25 April 1953 and the appointment of Abulqasim Amini as the acting Court Minister was a further development beneficial to Musaddiq. His relations with Ala had been uneasy since the latter had announced that the idea of a royal journey in February had initially been proposed by three members of the NMF, a charge which provoked strong denials.[198] Ala had also been in frequent contact with the US Embassy and encouraged the Shah to support Zahidi. For these reasons Musaddiq would have welcomed his replacement and it has been claimed that he offered to make him the Deputy Prime Minister.[199] When he did resign, Amini seemed a suitable successor – an ex-Majlis deputy who had recently served as Governor-General of Isfahan – who might mediate between the Court and the Government.[200] Following his appointment, Amini actively tried to maintain a dialogue between the Court and the Government but was naturally kept in the dark by the Shah about many aspects of his activities.

Musaddiq achieved a much-needed victory on 9 May when the Shah was compelled to return to the state those Crown lands which had been conferred on him by the law of 11 July 1949. In exchange the Government agreed to give an annual 60 million rials to the Imperial Organization for Social Services, to be spent on welfare services with governmental supervision.[201] Although this was a significant defeat for the Shah he was likely to regard it as purely temporary, being much encouraged by the activities of the opposition and the financial and economic problems of the Government.

Musaddiq's most notable failure, which was considered most likely to bring about his downfall, was that there was still no settlement with the British. In early April Makki had told a member of the US Embassy that 'barring some act of God' Musaddiq could not stay in power for more than two months, as he needed to sell 5–8 million tons of oil in order to meet his 'financial commitments'.[202] This may have been only wishful thinking, but it was a fact that no tangible solution for the oil problem seemed to be in sight. Musaddiq still insisted on compensation on his terms, while the British demanded compensation for breach of contract and refused to indicate the extent of their claims in advance.[203] Any sign of compromise by Musaddiq would, as always, have been attacked by Kashani, Ha'irizadih and others who were adamant that the British were not entitled to receive any compensation from Iran.[204] Nobody had any suggestions, however, as to how the dispute might be resolved.

Although there was a British blockade, the Government was of course able to sell oil to some countries such as Italy and Japan. The British appealed to the courts of Venice and Tokyo, but these ruled in Iran's favour.[205] Although this was an important breakthrough, its effect was reduced by the 50 per cent discount at which the oil was sold and the opposition continued to decry and denounce it.[206] Musaddiq's policy was to persevere until the British made a concession or to reverse the very strategy which they themselves deployed against him. In order to do this he needed a secure power-base – which had proved impossible to maintain. During his first period of office the opposition had helped to harden British attitudes towards him, now they were weakening him and raising British hopes that if they could hold on they would reach a settlement with Musaddiq's successor.

All hope of reaching an oil settlement was abandoned on 29 June 1953 when Eisenhower informed Musaddiq that unless a settlement was reached Iran could expect no significant US financial aid, no US purchase of Iranian oil and no increase in military and technical aid. He also emphasized that settlement should not be 'based on the payment of compensation merely for loss of the physical assets' of the company, implying support for the British demand concerning compensation for the premature termination of contract.[207] The publication of this letter finally dispelled the myth of continued American support for Musaddiq and this encouraged many of his opponents. However, it also showed that Musaddiq had been denied financial aid because he had refused to compromise, contrary to the frequent accusations of the opposition.

The American position aggravated the financial and economic problems of the Government, but these problems were not critical enough or sufficient to bring the Government down. Despite all the difficulties, the Government had in fact managed to tackle some of these problems, mainly in the area of foreign trade. Exports had been increased, bringing much-needed foreign exchange, and in January 1953 the Government had felt able to repeal the provision of 18 June 1948 which had barred foreign merchants from importing goods to Iran; it also began issuing foreign trading licenses to encourage exports.[208] To compensate for the loss of oil revenues the Government concentrated on developing the tobacco and textile industries, and continued its efforts to stabilize the rate of exchange.[209] Restrictions on imports and the devaluation of the rial, despite the inflationary consequences, helped to stimulate domestic industries to such an extent that the period has been referred to as one of 'industrial recovery'.[210] Until this time Musaddiq, like his predecessors, had remained at the mercy of the Majlis for the budget; using his plenary powers, however, he proceeded to approve a full budget bill for the year 1332 (March 1953–March 1954).[211]

Since the Second World War the Russians had owed Iran 11 tons of gold and other sums of money – primarily in return for the use of Iranian transport facilities and currency during the war. If the Government could have recovered it, some of its problems may have been solved, but the Russians continued to procrastinate. Consistent with his policy of negative equilibrium, Musaddiq had nationalized the Caspian Fisheries in January 1953 when the Irano-Soviet Fishery Agreement of 1927 expired. Although the Russians demanded its renewal,[212] there was no tangible deterioration in the already cool relations between the two countries. Towards the end of Musaddiq's premiership, negotiations continued with Ambassador Sadchikov to improve bilateral relations and expand trade, particularly barter trade, but nothing concrete was achieved. Although the economic and financial problems were serious, even the American Embassy believed as late as the eve of the coup of August 1953 that the Government could use remedial measures and 'avert an acute financial crisis for an indeterminate period'.[213]

By comparison, problems of law and order at first seemed far easier to tackle. Since early 1953 the Government had resorted to measures such as the establishment of a 'security council'[214] for the co-ordination of decisions on matters of security, as well as an increase in the number of pro-Government officers in the command positions of the security forces. It had also removed tribal affairs from the control of the military and put them under the jurisdiction of the Interior Ministry,[215] with the aim of reducing the political exploitation and oppression of the tribes by the army, and redirecting tribal loyalties against the Shah and in favour of the Government. It had also been successful in scaling down royal contributions to opposition groups and parties, but had not detected the full extent of activities such as those of the Rashidians.

The Government, in fact, experienced serious difficulties in maintaining law and order. Treatment of anti-Government offenders was surprisingly lenient and most of those arrested in connection with the February events had soon been released. One reason for this was the enormous pressure put on the Government by the opposition to release such offenders,[216] often stipulating that it was a precondition for any debate on the report of the eight-man committee. In addition, the Government was highly sensitive to the charges of dictatorship which, somewhat ironically, were incessantly levelled against it in the vast network of the opposition press and were even reproduced in pro-Government newspapers.[217] More significantly, by adhering strictly to legal and civic standards the Government had in fact left matters to be dealt with by the existing legal processes which were inefficient, susceptible to pressure, often corrupt, and had resulted in the release of some serious political offenders. The Government had neither a proper intelligence system, nor any efficient means of law enforcement; it was not fully in control of the state apparatus or the army, and any moves to assert its authority simply provoked its opponents. Nevertheless, armed with Musaddiq's plenary powers, the public security law and the continuation of martial law since March 1952, the Government should have been capable of exhibiting more resolution and decisiveness in dealing with conspirators and lawbreakers. Instead it was so lenient that those accused of murdering Afshartus not only felt no need to defend themselves, but continued to abuse the Government and even tabled a motion of interpellation against it.

One of the main tactics of Musaddiq's opponents was to focus on his attitude towards the Tudeh Party, which they believed to be very lenient compared with the allegedly harsh treatment they themselves received. The Tudeh Party had not significantly changed its views on the nature of the Government,[218] or its efforts to stir labour unrest,[219] but would half-heartedly side with the Government whenever it faced a serious threat. Musaddiq, for his part, had not entirely abandoned his earlier tactic of using the Tudeh Party as a countervailing force against his other opponents, or as the French military attaché put it, 'apparently to play the Tudeh and the extreme Right off against each other'.[220] To suppress the Tudeh Party was against his democratic convictions, and he also realized that he could not afford to alienate it totally in the face of growing right-wing opposition. This was, however, a far cry from the 'coalition' with the communists of which the Government was constantly accused. The Government was not helped, and was possibly greatly harmed, by the decision of a Tehran magistrate that the Tudeh leaders could not be prosecuted on the false charge of harbouring communist and anti-monarchist ideas. This attracted much attention in the press and was interpreted as a confirmation of the Government's lenient policy towards the Tudeh Party.[221] Although the Government promptly repudiated the decision it has been regarded as contributing to Musaddiq's downfall.[222] On the occasion of the first anniversary of the uprising of 21 July the Government instructed its supporters to hold demonstrations separate from those of the Tudeh Party, but Tudeh demonstrators outnumbered the supporters of the Government.[223] This provided the right-ring opposition and its Anglo-American supporters with an ideal propaganda tool and proof of the impending communist take-over.

Although the Tudeh had been successful in enlisting a number of officers,[224] the military authorities were not unaware of this. Moreover, in the prevailing international conditions, even if capable of doing so, the seizure of power by means of a coup was not a part of Tudeh strategy, and it was also unlikely that the Russians, greatly disorientated following the death of Stalin, would endorse such a move. In any case, the state, no matter how fragile, and the army, no matter how demoralized,[225] not to mention the religious establishment, were still capable of countering a Tudeh coup. Nor was Musaddiq as powerless vis-à-vis the Tudeh Party as it was assumed or propagated; it was not a Tudeh take-over that he feared, but rather a right-wing royalist coup,[226] which the Tudeh Party was also predicting. As the Majlis had become the main hope of his enemies, Musaddiq determined to bring about its dissolution.[227]

Musaddiq's concern with a referendum can be traced back at least to early 1953 and the beginning of serious difficulties with the Majlis; in a conversation with Henderson on 23 February he had even mentioned the details of its implementation.[228] Resorting to a referendum, initially intended to be a warning, was regarded by some as a bluff, but gradually began to become inevitable as Government–Majlis relations deteriorated further. Most deputies were against it, and not only the Union and Country factions[229] but also several of his own followers tried their best to dissuade Musaddiq.[230] When it was clear that he would not be moved, members of the NMF submitted their resignation and were followed by others, so that by 28 July fifty-six deputies had already resigned.[231] Since the Majlis could no longer function it was hoped that the need for a referendum had been averted. However, the Government's opponents still enjoyed parliamentary immunity and could therefore continue with their activities, Makki could still demand to supervise the note reserve, and consequently Musaddiq was determined to dissolve the Majlis and seek legitimacy by a popular mandate.

Contrary to the claims of some newspapers,[232] Musaddiq did not and could not appeal to the Shah to dissolve the Majlis, since this would have implied accepting the legitimacy of the Constituent Assembly of 1949. In an effort to prevent the referendum, the opposition took sanctuary in the Majlis and tried unsuccessfully to get an anti-referendum *fatva* from Burujirdi and Bihbahani.[233] Kashani's house had now become a meeting place for open anti-Government activities, and he issued strong denunciations,[234] as did Bihbahani.[235] Baqa'i, who had become increasingly violent in his anti-Musaddiq language, declared that he and Zuhari would resign their seats and go to prison if Musaddiq refrained from holding a referendum.[236] Above all, the opposition tried to stimulate fears of communism, but despite all their efforts the referendum was held. Its conduct was highly controversial and inconsistent with normal democratic procedures: voting was confined to the cities, where supporters and opponents of the Government voted in separate polling stations and separate ballot boxes. Altogether over 2,400,000 votes were cast in favour of the dissolution of the Majlis with only a negligible number against.[237] For Musaddiq and his supporters, the referendum constituted an overwhelming vote of confidence and a clear denunciation of anti-Government groups; for those who sought a violent overthrow of the Government, particularly the Anglo-American agents, however, the referendum created an opportunity which they had long awaited.

The holding of the referendum, which was portrayed as an anti-constitutional move, more than any other factor enabled the Shah to step forward in the name of safeguarding the 'Constitution'. He had become less diffident and indecisive, yet it was only the categorical assurance of Anglo-American support which eventually led him to approve drastic action. The mysterious return to Tehran of Ashraf was to reconfirm such support and to reassure him that what the Rashidian brothers and other agents were doing was fully approved by the British and the Americans. This was also one of the main aims of General Schwarzkopf's trip to Tehran. [238]

The Shah apparently agreed to sign two decrees for the dismissal of Musaddiq and the appointment of Zahidi. He preferred, however, to be in a position to leave the country promptly in case the coup was unsuccessful. When an attempt by a few military units, and particularly the Royal Guard, failed on 16 August, the Shah hastily fled the country. At this point some State Department officials began to doubt whether it was possible to defeat Musaddiq. For example, the US Under-Secretary of State, General Walter Bedell-Smith, told the British Ambassador in Washington that 'the latest developments made it necessary for the administration to take a new look at policy towards Persia . . . [and] to cultivate good relations with Musaddiq'.[239] The British, however, did not favour any positive gesture[240] since neither they nor the US Embassy in Tehran were pessimistic: Zahidi was given a safe refuge and paid and unpaid mobs were mobilized by local agents and by certain *mullahs*. Full advantage was taken of the tense atmosphere and royalist sentiments caused by the Shah's flight and aggravated by the much-stimulated fears of communism and republicanism. *Agents provocateurs* planted by the Rashidians actively took part in activities such as demolishing statues of the Shah and his father, all of which was blamed on the Tudeh Party and the extremist supporters of Musaddiq.[241] Three days later, on 19 August 1953, with the decisive help of the army, the abortive coup was turned into a victory.

The fact that a coup was in the offing was well known to Musaddiq and others; in fact the Tudeh newspapers had published near-accurate accounts on 9 August, and the Tudeh leader Kianuri claimed to have learned details of the coup through the party's military network and passed these on to Musaddiq.[242] It had therefore been possible to foil the initial coup, but there were no means of preventing a recurrence: no organization existed to mobilize the masses and co-ordinate counter-measures. Musaddiq had strengthened the defences of his own house after 28 February but had done little else, since the Chief of Staff had assured him that he was in full control.[243] After the failure of the first coup Musaddiq considered a second attempt very likely and needed no warning. On the eve of Zahidi's coup, however, he apparently received a personal letter from Kashani informing him of its imminent occurrence. Assuming that the letter was authentic, it indicates that Kashani was in the grip of some misgivings about the fall of Musaddiq through a military coup; in this case it might have been more appropriate for him to issue a public announcement calling on the people to resist such moves. The main aim of Kashani's letter, however, was to hedge his bets and enable him to dissociate himself from the conspirators in the event of the coup failing. On the other hand, the letter contained no revelations; Musaddiq knew about the coup and had done his best to prevent it, including offering a reward for the arrest of Zahidi. He regarded Kashani as guilty of contributing to the formation of the coup and the incapacity of the Government to counter it. His reply to Kashani that 'I am relying on the support of the Iranian nation' contained a telling irony.[244]

Kashani's opposition to Musaddiq had in fact reached such an extent that the CIA deemed it appropriate to seek his active support in mobilizing a violent anti-Musaddiq mob. According to one account, in response to the request of Kermit Roosevelt, the head of CIA operations in Iran, to contact Kashani, the Rashidians directed him to Ahmad Aramish. Bill Herman and Fred Zimmerman, two CIA agents, met Aramish on the morning of 19 August. They gave him $10,000, which was apparently passed on to Kashani, to be used for mobilizing an anti-Musaddiq crowd. The use of this money resulted in a sharp fall in the black market exchange rate.[245]

The structural fragility of the Government, the cumulative effects of extensive destabilizing measures to which it was subjected, the unreliability of the army and the suspect loyalty of even those commanders whom Musaddiq trusted,[246] rendered the Prime Minister unable to prevent or suppress the coup. The initial coup resulted in the disorientation of Musaddiq and his colleagues, but they were not entirely demoralized. Musaddiq himself indicated that he was aware of the sums of money which the British had spent to orchestrate parliamentary opposition to him, and was suspicious that the Americans were either involved in the efforts to oust him or at least aware of them in advance.[247] Efforts were concentrated on restoring order and calm and no popular appeal was made, as Musaddiq had consistently refused to appeal to the people to risk their lives in order to keep him in power.[248] Some arrests were made in connection with the coup, and the Royal Guard was disarmed; few other effective, co-ordinated measures were adopted, however, and the Cabinet apparently continued to tackle its routine tasks.[249]

When the Tudeh Party reportedly demanded arms to counter the coup[250] Musaddiq refused for two reasons. First, he was not prepared to rely on the Tudeh Party, and, secondly, he and his followers were unanimous in disapproving of violence as a means of retaining power. They knew that the military coup could not have taken place or succeeded without foreign support and were confident that when this came to light it would deprive the post-coup regime of its legitimacy. They believed in any case that overthrow by such a coup was more dignified than collapse as the result of seemingly legitimate parliamentary machinations; that if they had suffered a political defeat they had won a moral victory.

With the end of Musaddiq's active political life came the beginning of a myth. As with all such myths it was built upon actual or perceived aspects of his personality, beliefs and behaviour. The most remarkable trait of Musaddiq's personality was the intensity of his emotions, a trait fully congenial with the 'Dionysian' components of Iranian culture, that is with the unrestrained display of strong emotions.[251] Musaddiq's single-mindedness and intransigence were matched by his affectivity, compassion and sincerity, which made him the object of popular affection and esteem.

While in other political milieux statesmen normally feel it necessary to demonstrate their good health and physical vigour, the essential components of Musaddiq's political style were physical feebleness, ill health, tears, fainting fits and other melodramatic behaviour as the occasion demanded.[252] Musaddiq conducted most governmental affairs from his house, often clad in 'pyjamas', reclining on his metal bed covered with a blanket.[253] To those who regarded 'normal' behaviour as being in conformity with Eurocentric conventionalism, and 'rational' belief in accordance with stereotypical assumptions and narrow pragmatism, Musaddiq's idiosyncratic behaviour and beliefs naturally appeared abnormal and irrational, hence Shepherd's *ad nauseum* reference to Musaddiq as a 'lunatic'.[254]

One of Musaddiq's qualities which not even his enemies disputed was his incorruptibility.[255] As a deputy in the 16th Majlis and as Prime Minister he even refused to collect his salary, and donated it instead to charities.[256] This was perhaps his greatest asset in the context of a kleptocratic political structure and in a society where few were spared the charge of corruption. He had also tried fastidiously to choose his colleagues from among men of probity. Without being a moralizer, Musaddiq desired to elevate adherence to ethical values and civic standards in the Iranian political culture. His main vision was to establish a polity which would be impervious to corruption and would, therefore, enhance the credibility of the government and ultimately give substance and meaning to citizenship and political participation.

In the society which he envisaged, liberty and the dignity of the citizen as well as the true independence and political development of the country were revered far more than ostentatious material progress and 'modernization'. In his own words:

> Anyone who aims to belittle the holy struggle of our nation by assessing the achievements of the Iranian movement in economic terms and by comparing the independence of our country with a few million pounds, has undoubtedly perpetrated a blunder.[257]

The first step towards the achievement of such a polity was the realization of true national sovereignty, which would, in turn, give rise to an autonomous ruling elite in no need of the advice or support of foreign embassies. Musaddiq was the only Prime Minister in the period under study who did not take for granted the right of foreigners, particularly the British, in this respect. He dealt with all of them as the leader of a truly independent and free country, and not as a politician compensating for his lack of domestic support by reliance on foreign powers.

Musaddiq was a nationalist, but his nationalism was not used as an instrument of oppression at home in the name of achieving independence, nor for the mobilization of racial or communal prejudices against 'inferior' nations and communities. In his struggle against the AIOC and the British Government he was not inspired by dogmatism or xenophobia, but rather by the desire to use the struggle primarily as a means of instilling national pride and self-confidence into the hearts of his compatriots. In order to achieve this, however, self-sacrifice, dedication and perseverance would be required:

> If the Iranian nation, among other great nations of the world, desires to regain the status and position which it deserves, and is worthy of its proud past, it must not be afraid of deprivation, difficulties, devotion and self-sacrifice. We must not be satisfied with and tolerate life in whatever form or quality it is presented to us: life is entirely worthless if not combined with liberty and independence. In achieving such

noble aims, the history of great nations has witnessed struggles, endeavours, sacrifices and devotion.[258]

Initially Musaddiq concentrated on parliamentary means in order to achieve his goal, although his mode of political activity, particularly after his assumption of office, included a strong populist component. As a deputy he had often appealed to the people in order to put pressure on governments, and as Prime Minister he increasingly appealed to the people in order to counter his opponents. When on one occasion he faced an inquorate Majlis, he addressed the crowds in Parliament Square, asserting that 'wherever the people are, parliament is there'.[259] And when resorting to a referendum, which was the culmination of his populism, he announced that 'in democratic countries no law is above the will of the people'.[260]

Musaddiq's 'magic appeal'[261] and unrivalled power of oratory always ensured him an attentive and responsive audience; when he appealed to the people it was to inform them on issues and seek their informed judgement. He believed that the will of the people was a sufficient legitimizing source for the change of laws which contravened his ideals or could easily be manipulated by his opponents. He believed in the intrinsic goodness of ordinary Iranians,[262] in contrast to the corruption, greed and degeneration of the pro-British upper class. Although he was labelled a demagogue by his enemies, he seldom inspired the people without himself being inspired by them; it was for this reason that one of his supporters commented that a statesman must enchant the masses but not allow himself to be enchanted by them.[263] Musaddiq's populism, and in fact his assumption of power, had proved to be incongruent with the tenets of clan politics, which during his term of office had been overshadowed by nationalism and its manifestation in the movement for the nationalization of the oil industry. It had been challenged by Musaddiq's own standing, by mobilized public opinion, the effective politicization of the urban population and the politics of the street.

Musaddiq's blatant populist disposition signified his growing awareness of the defects of the prevailing parliamentary arrangements, which he believed could only be remedied by ensuring the election of 'real' representatives of the people through a reformed electoral law, a law which he devised but failed to implement. It was, however, very unlikely that such a law could have ensured the election of 'real' representatives of the people, as the conventional mechanisms and methods of franchise, not to mention numerous other structural constraints, did not facilitate the election of such deputies. Moreover, limiting the franchise to the literate section of the population, as he had envisaged, could not be easily justified, excluding as it did the 'ordinary' people whose traditional civic virtues he had so frequently admired. Musaddiq had, in fact, failed to create a viable means of establishing his desired form of parliamentarianism, or even of salvaging the existing arrangements which had virtually reached an impasse.

In order to give meaning to the elections, sustain a parliamentary majority and provide a mechanism for the mobilization of popular support *vis-à-vis* anti-Government activities, it was necessary to form a pro-Government political party. It was initially hoped that the National Front could play such a role. Unfortunately its ideology and structure made it inherently inappropriate as a basis for government; in any case Musaddiq refused to attend its sessions soon after becoming Prime Minister,[264] on the grounds that as the head of state he must be independent of any party.[265] Since he chose to stand above party politics and factional alliances he had to rely primarily on popular support.

Later in life Musaddiq attributed Iran's backwardness to the absence of political and social organizations which had caused the country to lose its freedom and independence.[266] Perhaps this was where he failed at the time, since at one level he understood the usefulness of political parties but at a deeper level he did not fully appreciate the need for proper organization. It is true that he tried to groom the Iran Party as the main Government party; however, he appeared firmly convinced that in the Iranian political culture party politics was barely distinguishable from factionalism and cliquishness, and did not regard it as a commendable form of political activity. The result was that the Government was blamed for its close relations with the Iran Party, and the Party itself either denied its close links with the Government or was apologetic about them.

There were numerous other structural obstacles to successful party formation, and, on the basis of bitter experience, Musaddiq appeared to be deeply pessimistic about its imminent possibility.[267] When the National Front was being formed, there was some discussion about the formation of a party, but nothing was achieved. Such discussions recurred, again inconclusively, at the time of the referendum. Given this background, it would be plausible to ask how Musaddiq expected the nation to achieve or deserve democracy when even its most patriotic and devoted elements were not able to form an effective party. This was one of the main unresolved contradictions of Musaddiq's political thinking and practice.

The task of holding office, in the face of overwhelming odds, had led Musaddiq to re-evaluate his previous political behaviour and his disposition, which had often been negative. As Prime Minister he had found the opportunity to adjust his ideas in the light of experience and the requirements of the task. He had recognized not only the extent of the Government's vulnerability *vis-à-vis* the Parliament and the Court, as well as the ease with which the Constitution and the parliamentary system could be manipulated, but also the need to change the situation.[268] His *ad hoc* solution, namely the demand for plenary powers, had of course provoked severe opposition, while the potential long-term solution, that is parliamentary approval of the report of the eight-man committee, was never achieved. In view of the numerous difficulties in securing the free election of the people's 'real' representatives, combined with his pessimism about party politics, he had failed both on theoretical and practical grounds to work out other solutions; he had constructed no coherent ideological framework and no organizational structure within which to operate.

For a variety of reasons, in particular the need constantly to allay the fears of the Shah, Musaddiq had pledged to respect the monarchy and not to assume the presidency should the country ever become a republic.[269] He had of course realized that monarchy in its existing form, or at least with its then incumbent, could not be successfully reconciled with a working form of parliamentary government. He had also realized that the salvation of Iranian parliamentarianism lay with the crucial strengthening of the government. Nevertheless he had not adequately considered the prospect of having to remain in power with the Shah in exile or with the monarchy abolished; he had indeed made little mental or practical preparation for such a development. Given the prevailing situation he was understandably apprehensive about facing such a prospect, but had he survived longer in power he might have initiated effective mechanisms to cope with it.

Musaddiq's efforts and achievements in reviving the spirit of constitutionalism have, however, remained unrivalled in the history of Iranian parliamentary politics. He reduced the Shah to a position of near redundancy, contained the royal family and its clientele, and deprived the Court of its pivotal position in the Iranian body politic. As a statesman, he was distinguished by adherence to democratic principles and commitment to non-violence, although there were also elements in his political thinking and behaviour which could be construed as authoritarian and were discernible in his views concerning the people's 'real' interests. He genuinely believed that he was qualified both to recognize the 'real' interests of the people, and to realize these interests with the direct help of the people. Musaddiq's qualities led the French Ambassador in Tehran to describe him as 'a cross between Gandhi and Rousseau'.[270] In addition, his consistent belief in a foreign policy based on 'negative equilibrium' made him one of the forerunners of the non-aligned movement.

Finally, although Musaddiq's fall was a setback for the Iranian democratic nationalist movement, it did not mark its defeat. Indeed, he became the movement's most inspiring myth, depicted by every group according to its own expectations and desires. Although his emergence had been largely the result of an intricate set of structural preconditions, he, for his part, had entangled himself in a struggle which, in a world dominated by *realpolitik* was more likely to end in defeat than victory. Yet fear of defeat had not dissuaded him from embarking on such a struggle. In the words of Fatimi, Musaddiq was committed to combating 'spiritual defeatism';[271] he had stepped forward to assume office motivated primarily by hope and a sense of mission. Like many men of action, Musaddiq also had – to paraphrase Gramsci – defied the pessimism of the intellect in favour of the optimism of the will.

Conclusion

The period 1941–53 has a special place in the historical consciousness of the Iranian people and many intellectuals look at it with deep
nostalgia. In this period the hampered spirit of constitutionalism
perservered in defiance of all obstacles, and the political culture of
the country showed signs of enrichment, while the political
consciousness of the urban population increased markedly. Although
martial law remained imposed on Tehran and other areas during the
greater part of this period, freedom of expression, including
criticisms and challenges directed against the ruling elite, encountered
no systematic curtailment. The religious forces in the country were in
no position seriously to threaten the essentially secular nature of the
existing political arrangements. Despite the weakness and fragility of
the state, the plurality of conflicting ideologies and beliefs and the
unrestrained possibility of political discord, violence and chaos did
not prevail and the integrity of the country was not undermined.
During the premiership of Musaddiq in particular, there was no
outbreak of serious disorder or sign of any real threat to the
territorial integrity of the country, despite the extensive destabilizing
efforts of his opponents. In short, in the eyes of many Iranians this
period constituted a potentially viable alternative to royal authoritarianism. The manner in which this period came to an end, that is
through the foreign-sponsored coup of August 1953, left many
Iranians gripped by a tragic sense of their history and they have not
ceased to contrast what happened with what could and should have
happened.

The Iranian Constitutional Revolution of 1906 had taken place in
circumstances in which many of the preconditions necessary for its
success were absent. There had been neither a centralized credible
state, nor an effective administrative apparatus; no proper system of
communications, nor a widely shared consciousness of belonging to a
distinct territorial entity called Iran. By the time of the abdication of

Reza Shah, some of these problems had been resolved and conditions were far more congenial to the emergence of a viable parliamentarianism than had been the case in the pre-Reza Shah era.

Although in the post-1941 period the power of the centralized state was eroded, its basic structure – including the organs of law enforcement, the bureaucracy, the system of communications – remained unshaken. Moreover changes in the economic and financial organization of the country, a degree of industrialization, increasing social differentiation, the growth of nationalism, expansion of the intelligentsia and the system of education, the development of civil law and other changes of this nature, were likely to contribute to the establishment of effective parliamentary government. The functioning of such a form of government in this period, however, proved to be deeply problematic.

Parliamentary government in the post-Reza Shah era was characterized by Cabinet instability. During the twelve-year course of this period, twelve prime ministers formed seventeen Cabinets which underwent twenty-three major reshuffles. The average duration of each Cabinet, irrespective of reshuffles, was eight months, and including reshuffles was only three and a half months. Cabinet instability greatly vitiated the efficacy of the government but did not significantly affect the composition of the established ruling elite. Of 150 politicians who held prime-ministerial and ministerial positions in this period, one-third assumed ministerial portfolios regularly. Of the latter, over two-thirds were royalist politicians who owed their secure positions primarily to the patronage of the Court. The existing perpetual political flux had no real bearing on the entrenched power position of this group.[1]

The experience of this period clearly demonstrated that effective parliamentary government in Iran required a strong and durable executive which would not be vulnerable to the incessant challenges of a recalcitrant Majlis, or constantly hampered by the encroachments of the Court. The complex set of structural factors which impeded the emergence and consolidation of such a government was buttressed by the inherent ambiguities of the Constitution which supplied no uncontested line of demarcation between various powers. On the one hand, the resulting situation made for a faction-ridden legislature invested with wide-ranging power but often capable of accomplishing little beyond the frequent replacement of enervated Cabinets. On the other hand, it provided for a monarch who was not constitutionally accountable and whose prerogatives were essentially ceremonial, but who was the most powerful individual in the country.

Despite his privileged power position, the dissatisfied Shah tried to enhance his prerogatives formally through the revision of the Constitution, which in the event did not produce the desired result. Yet he contrived through a variety of means to vie with the parliament, aiming to maximize royal control over the executive. Whenever he proved successful, the parliament did not hesitate to undermine Court-sponsored Cabinets, and whenever the legislature appeared to have the upper hand, the Shah stepped up his obstructive tactics against the parliament-backed government. If the Cabinet tried to assert itself *vis-à-vis* the Court and the Majlis, large numbers of deputies co-operated with the Shah against it. The picture was further complicated by the constant flux of loyalties and the fragile nature of factional relations, as well as the impact of foreign pressures and influence, ideological challenges, the sensationalism of the press and various socio-economic factors and issues. The Cabinet was, in any case, the main victim, continually subjected to exhaustive and debilitating pressures.

In the period under review, executive authority was formally invested in the Cabinet as a collective body, but in fact government by Cabinet did not exist; rather there was government by prime minister and the identity of the Cabinet was superseded by that of the prime minister. Weak prime ministers, therefore, signified weak governments and *per contra*. Strong prime ministers such as Qavam, and on a more systematic and consistent basis, Musaddiq, tried to revitalize the authority of the executive by preventing or minimizing the undue interference of the Court. The ensuing deep-seated tensions, resulting in bitter overt or covert struggles, however, resisted resolution, while the configuration of Iranian parliamentary politics generated stalemate and showed no ability to retrieve itself from the situation. The advent of Musaddiq's Government heralded a major constitutional victory, although in the event it proved to be short lived. His fall signified the beginning not only of the irresistible royal victory but also of the unbridgeable disjunction of monarchism and constitutionalism. The events of August 1953 sparked off a process of delegitimization which eroded the credibility of the government and gradually widened the gap between the elite and the rest of society. This process eventually culminated in the overthrow of the monarchy a quarter of a century later.

Yet Iranian parliamentarianism need not necessarily have met such an end. Had the Court restrained itself from aiming at the total exclusion of its effective rivals from the political process, the pluralistic nature of Iranian politics might not only have survived, but might have transformed itself into a potentially viable system. Such a system may not have proved particularly congenial with rapid socio-economic change, yet the cost of imposed royal authoritarianism was immeasurably higher. The role and behaviour of the monarchy had undeniable structural determinants, yet what took place was not entirely irrevocable. Indeed, no power can meaningfully be attributed to the Shah without holding him personally responsible for the greater part of his actions.

The Shah's evident lack of political sensitivity and foresight in his unfailing pursuit of personal rule, and his disbelief in the practicability and even desirability of genuine parliamentary government, significantly undermined the prospects for such a government. His failure to control the corruption and extravagance of his family and entourage accelerated the erosion of his personal and moral credibility. His positive dislike of independently-minded politicians and men of principle, and his self-righteous dismissal of criticism ensured that he would be surrounded by opportunists and sycophants. His paranoid fear of genuine political parties and associations meant that his style of rule would defy efforts to create any credible semblance of participatory politics. Finally, the Shah's uncritical, almost fatalistic subscription to the prevailing conventional wisdom concerning the ubiquitous influence of foreign powers over the direction of Iranian politics, coupled with the absence of any real popular power-base, prevented him from ever gaining sustained self-confidence. The cumulative effect of such factors rendered him increasingly authoritarian but also increasingly vulnerable. In view of this, and the institutional structure of the Iranian polity, it is only a truism to assert that had the idiosyncratic nature of the Pahlavi monarchy undergone a change, or had the Shah happened to possess a markedly different character, the course of Iranian history might have been significantly different.

Within the totality of existing conditions, the paths facing the prevailing non-viable mode of parliamentary politics can tentatively be outlined as follows.

The first and the most likely path was royal authoritarianism, which would have institutionalized monarchical hegemony, thereby enabling the Shah to exercise power effectively and to reduce the entire parliamentary framework to the role of performing merely ceremonial functions. This is what happened after 1953.

The second and less likely path was the emergence of a strong executive with sustained organizational support, capable of reducing the undue power both of the parliament and the Court, and delineating the exact boundaries of the authority invested in various institutions of the state. Such an executive could assert itself on the basis of a radical anti-royalist interpretation of the Constitution, or even its revision, which would also have reduced the power of the Majlis. Any such interpretation or revision had to incorporate at least those measures resorted to during the Musaddiq era, such as the abortive report of the eight-man committee concerning the ceremonial nature of royal authority, as well as some aspects of Musaddiq's acquired plenary powers.

The third and perhaps the least likely path was the holding of free elections and the emergence of a parliament in which a large majority, consistently loyal to the Musaddiq-led nationalist movement, could ensure a viable government.

The last two possibilities would have provoked strong adverse reactions. Neither the Court nor the bulk of the army would have acquiesced in such developments. The Western powers, for their part, were likely to oppose the consolidation of a Musaddiqist government, on the grounds that it neither provided a bulwark against communism nor assured the safety of strategic Western interests. Similarly, the Soviet Union would doubtless have had reservations regarding such a government. In short, the opportunity for the development of a self-sustaining parliamentary government immune to external and domestic – particularly royalist – challenges was minimal. If constitutional monarchy had been stipulated to be logically possible within the framework of the Constitution of 1906–7, it had proved to be empirically improbable.

The fourth path was, of course, the emergence of a self-confident republic with a thoughtful and well-devised constitution which invested sufficient power in the executive, and combined legality with efficiency and liberty with order. Such a form of government could originate from Musaddiqist nationalism, rely on a democratic-populist basis and organizationally sustain itself through genuine efforts at party politics. It had to be based on new political orientations and a fundamental reassessment of existing democratic perceptions. It had to transform radically the prevailing political culture and transcend the class basis of Iranian politics.

Obstacles to attaining and sustaining a republican form of

government would, most likely, have proved insurmountable. Even if such an arrangement could have been easily set up, its continuation would have been likely to provoke strong internal and external challenges. Yet it appears that there had been no serious thinking towards such an end. Indeed, there had been surprisingly little mental or practical preparation on the part of Musaddiq and his followers even to face the prospect of governing in the absence of the Shah from the political scene. On the one hand, this was an indication of the institutional strength of the monarchy within the Iranian body politic, as well as the strength of the royalist subculture; and on the other, it implied an evident lack of intellectual vigour, perceptive thinking and analysis, or any thoughtful planning on the part of the nationalist leadership, which in practice amounted to political pessimism and surrender in the face of rising royal authoritarianism.

Notes

Introduction

1. According to Poggi: 'The moral ideal that ultimately legitimizes the modern state is the taming of power through the depersonalization of its exercise'. Gianfranco Poggi, *The Development of the Modern State* (London, 1978), p. 101.
2. On the Iranian Constitution see: Mustafa Rahimi, *Qanun-i Asasi-yi Iran* (Tehran, 1968); Qasim Qasimzadih, *Huquq-i Asasi* (Tehran, 1955), pp. 360–502; Lawrence Lockhart, 'The Constitutional Laws of Persia', *MEJ*, vol. XIII (Autumn 1959); Mansur us-Saltanih Adl, *Huquq-i Asasi ya Usul-i Mashrutiyyat* (Tehran, 1948).
3. Mansoureh Ettehadieh Nezam-Mafi, 'Origins and Development of Political Parties in Persia 1906–1911' (Ph.D. thesis, University of Edinburgh, 1977, p. 236).
4. Sayyid Hasan Taqizadih, *Tarikh-i Majlis-i Milli-yi Iran* (Berlin, 1919), pp. 28–31.
5. Jean Blondel, discussing the crippling impact of the motion of interpellation on French governments before 1958, comments: 'What had started as an instrument of scrutiny of the 'general policy' of the Government had turned into a vicious technique which demoralized Ministers, reduced them to impotence and turned politics into a series of elaborate chess moves.' J. Blondel, *Contemporary France: Politics, Society and Institutions* (London, 1972), p. 55.
6. Le Rougetel to Bevin, 13 May 1948, FO371 EP68705.
7. According to Lukes, 'an *ability* is the absence of internal constraints (that is, the presence of an internal permissive condition) and an opportunity [is] the absence of an external constraint (that is, the presence of an external permissive condition)'; S. Lukes, 'Power and Structure', in *Essays in Social Theory* (London, 1977), p. 11. For a discussion of the concepts of 'power' and 'structure' as well as the notion of 'structural constraint' and its 'internal' and 'external' variants, see *ibid.*, pp. 3–29. More specifically on power see the same author's *Power: A Radical View* (London, 1974), and also 'Power and Authority', in T. Bottomore and R. Nisbet (eds), *A History of Sociological Analysis* (London, 1978), pp. 633–76. For Lukes' reply to some of the philosophical criticism levelled against his treatment of power, see: 'On the Relativity of Power', in S. C. Brown (ed.), *Philosophical Disputes in the Social Sciences* (Brighton, 1979), pp. 261–74.
8. Speech in the Majlis, *Muzakirat-i Majlis*, 4 December 1944.
9. Le Rougetel to Bevin, 18 November 1949, FO371 EP75468.
10. The first policy, that of 'positive equilibrium', was more or less followed by

Ahmad Qavam; while the second, known as 'negative equilibrium', was elaborated and championed by Dr Musaddiq.

11. For more details of the factors militating against the effective functioning of the Iranian Cabinet, see Leonard Binder, 'The Cabinet of Iran: A Study in Institutional Adaptation', *MEJ*, vol. XVI (Winter 1962).

12. Marvin Zonis, *The Political Elite of Iran* (Princeton, 1971), p. 21.

13. Mohammad Reza Pahlavi, *Mission for my Country* (London, 1960), p. 60.

14. 'Institutional salience', according to Giddens, 'can be defined as residing in the degree to which a given institution affects the life-chances of the mass of those belonging to it.' Philip Stanworth and Anthony Giddens (eds), *Elites and Power in British Society* (Cambridge, 1974), p. 8.

15. Similarly, according to Waterbury, 'The monarchy is the major distributor of spoils and patronage in Morocco, and it considers the entire elite as its clientele group. To maintain its following, to protect the faithful, to attract new recruits, and to chastise the recalcitrant, the palace manipulates the system of rewards, political, economic and spiritual, to great advantage. Every elite faction is constantly trying to anticipate the King's next move, and all of their actions are calculated with regard to his likely reaction.' John Waterbury, *The Commander of the Faithful: the Moroccan Political Elite – A Study in Segmented Politics* (London, 1970), pp. 142–3. This book provides many valuable insights, but most characteristics attributed to the 'Moroccan' and not just the Moroccan elite, might be argued to be universal. See for instance: Erving Goffman, *Strategic Interaction* (Oxford, 1970); *The Presentation of Self in Everyday Life* (Harmondsworth, 1971); *Encounters* (Harmondsworth, 1972).

16. The attribution of the continuity of Iranian monarchy to its ancient 'mystical' aura and traditionally rooted stature in Iranian culture has been popular with some orientalists. See for instance Richard Frye, 'Charisma of Kingship in Ancient Iran', *Iranica Antiqua*, IV (1964), pp. 36–54; Pio Fillippani-Ronconi, 'The Tradition of Sacred Kingship in Iran', in George Lenczowski (ed.), *Iran Under the Pahlavis* (Stanford, 1978), pp. 51–83.

17. Waterbury, *op. cit.*, p. 152.

18. An example of such officers was General Ahmadi who also played an important role in the post-1941 period as War Minister in many Cabinets. He was described, not exaggeratedly, by the British as follows: 'He accepts no master but the Shah, is fond of European society, and has on a few occasions been friendly and helpful to the British. In his early days of power he robbed shamelessly, but has learnt to rob with tact. Has accumulated great wealth and owns large property in Tehran.' Report on Personalities in Persia, 1940, FO371 EP24582. See also I. Khajih-Nuri, *Bazigaran-i Asr-i Tala'i: Sipahbud Amir Ahmadi* (Tehran, 1978).

19. According to an Iranian army publication, on the eve of the occupation, the Iranian army was 'composed of 18 divisions, organized and equipped in modern style, and numbered about 200,000 men'. *Rahnama-yi Iran, Nashriyyih-yi Dayirih-yi Jughrafia'i-yi Artish* (Tehran, 1951). Foreign sources quoted by Abrhamian, however, estimated the size of the army at 124,000 men; Ervand Abrhamian, 'Factionalism in Iran: Political Groups in the 14th Parliament (1944–46)', *MES* XIV, 1 (January 1978), p. 29.

20. Arsalan Khal'atbari, 'Vizarat-i Jang va Siyasat', *Jibhih*, 25–6 April 1946.

21. The riots of December 1942 in Tehran and the southern tribal rebellion of late summer 1946 were both utilized by the Court and the army to undermine the position of Ahmad Qavam or to compel him to modify his policies.

22. After the fall of Reza Shah the Iranian gendarmerie was separated from the army and put under the control of the Ministry of the Interior. Many deputies tried to restrict military expenditure and encouraged the strengthening of the gendarmerie and the police as countervailing powers *vis-à-vis* the army. According to a bill passed in the Majlis on 23 October 1943, the gendarmerie was put under the direct command of Colonel (later General) Schwartzkopf, the American military adviser, and it was not before 1950 that the army and the gendarmerie were reunited under one command.

23. The introduction of radio to Iran was considerably delayed, reportedly due to the opposition of Reza Shah. Ahmad Matin-Daftari, 'Majara-yi Intikhabat dar Iran', *Salnamih-yi Dunya*, XII (1955), pp. 3–11.

24. For the elaboration of this conception of power see S. Lukes, *Power: A Radical View*.

25. Some writers identify elites largely in terms of their privileged access to the command of the major institutions of a society. For C. Wright Mills it is access to such institutions which largely determines the chances of men to be in elite positions and to enjoy celebrity, wealth and power; C. Wright Mills, *The Power Elite* (New York, 1959), pp. 10–13. Similarly, according to Giddens, 'Those individuals who occupy formally defined positions of authority at the head of a social organization or institution' can be designated an elite group (Stanworth and Giddens, *op. cit.*, p. 4). In Iran, however, there were individuals who were in a position to influence politically significant policies and issues and thus, without necessarily holding formal positions of power, entered the category of the elite.

26. For discussions of patron-client relationships see: Ernest Gellner and John Waterbury (eds), *Patrons and Clients* (London, 1977); Eric Wolf, 'Kinship, Friendship and Patron–Client Relations in Complex Societies', in Michael Banton (ed.), *The Social Anthropology of Complex Societies* (London, 1966); Steffen W. Schmidt et al. (eds), *Friends, Followers and Factions: A Reader in Political Clientelism* (Berkeley, 1977); Paul Littlewood, 'Patronage, Ideology and Reproduction', *Critique of Anthropology*, 15, vol. 4 (Spring 1980), pp. 29–45; G. Poggi, 'Clientelism', *Political Studies*, XXXI (1983), pp. 662–7; S. N. Eisenstadt and René Lemarchand (eds), *Political Clientelism, Patronage and Development* (Beverly Hills, 1982).

27. Gellner and Waterbury, *op. cit.*, p. 5.

28. See further, Abner Cohen, *Two Dimensional Man: An Essay on the Anthropology of Power and Symbolism in Complex Society* (London, 1974), pp. 32ff.

29. D. Cruise O'Brien, *Saints and Politicians: Essays in the Organisation of Senegalese Peasant Society* (Cambridge, 1975), p. 192. The term 'kleptocracy was coined by S. Andreski in his study *The African Predicament* (London, 1968).

30. Cruise O'Brien, *op. cit.*, p. 149.

31. Stanworth and Giddens, *op. cit.*, p. 5.

32. For a study of the political influence of powerful families in Egypt, which could benefit anyone interested in influential families in Iran, see Robert Springborg, *Family, Power and Politics in Egypt* (Philadelphia, 1982).

33. As Waterbury puts it: 'In the poorer societies patronage helps obscure and disorient class alignments and to perpetuate the power advantage of the dominant groups by the conscious cultivation of vulnerability and dependency.' Gellner and Waterbury, *op. cit.*, p. 340.

34. Stanworth and Giddens, *op. cit.*, p. 5.

35. Dr Ahmad Matin-Daftari, himself a prime minister during the time of Reza Shah

and an influential politician thereafter, echoes many members of his generation in enumerating the practical disadvantages of adhering to civic virtues. Matin-Daftari, 'Fi'l ya Tark', *Salnamih-yi Dunya*, XI (1955), pp. 3–10.

36. See Marvin Zonis, *op. cit.*; James A. Bill, *op. cit.* and 'Modernization and Reform from Above, the Case of Iran', *Journal of Politics*, XXXII, 1 (February 1970), pp. 19–40.

37. It would perhaps be more appropriate to refer to Iran in the period under study as a 'class-divided society', which is contrasted by Giddens with 'class-society ushered in by capitalism'. A 'class-divided society', according to Giddens, is a society in which there are classes, but where class analysis does not serve as a basis for identifying the basic structural principle of organization of that society. Anthony Giddens, *A Contemporary Critique of Historical Materialism* (London, 1981), p. 108.

38. Frank Parkin, *Class Inequality and Political Order* (London, 1972), pp. 29–102.

39. See S. Lukes, *Power. A Radical View*, *op. cit.*

40. John Dunn (ed.), *West African States* (Cambridge, 1978).

1 The Government of Furughi

1. Lambton to Bullard, 1 May 1940, FO371 EP24582.

2. *Ittila'at*, 4 July 1941.

3. See further, F. Eshraghi, 'Anglo-Soviet Occupation of Iran in August 1941', *MES*, XX, 9 (January 1984), pp. 27–52. See also Abbas Quli Gulsha'iyan, 'Memoires', text in Cyrus Ghani (ed.), *Yaddashtha-yi Dr. Qasim Ghani*, vol. XI (London, 1984), pp. 522–604; Javid 'Amiri, 'Shahrivar-i 1320', *Salnamih-yi Dunya*, no. 19, (1963), pp. 23–5, 31.

4. Ibrahim Khajih-Nuri, *Bazigaran-i Asr-i Tala'i: Ali Suhaili* (Tehran, 1977), pp. 76–7.

5. *Khatirat-i Siyasi-yi Farrukh*, ed. Parviz Laushani, vol. I and II (Tehran, 1968), pp. 469–70.

6. Speech by Abdullah Intizam on the 30th anniversary of Furughi's death, Tehran University, November 1971, text in *Rahnama-yi Kitab*, XIV, nos 9–12 (December 1971–March 1972).

7. Bullard to Eden (Annual Political Report for 1941) IOR:L/P&S/12/3472A, 17 June 1942.

8. Muhsin Sadr, *Khatirat-i Sadr-ul Ashraf* (Tehran, 1985), p. 379.

9. Lambton to Bullard, 4 October 1941, FO371 EP27157.

10. Mihdi Bamdad, *Tarikh-i Rijal-i Iran dar Qurun 12,13,14* (Tehran, 1968), vol. 3, pp. 450–1, 388. Report on Personalities in Persia, 1940, FO371 EP24582. For further details see Ghani, *op. cit.* vol. IX, pp. 97–102.

11. For an assessment of Furughi's personality and learning see speech by Ali Akbar Siyasi, text in Husain Kuhi-yi Kirmani, *Az Shahrivar-i 1320 ta Faji'ih-yi Azarbaijan va Zanjan* (Tehran, n.d.).

12. See for instance Furughi, 'Farhangistan Chist' in *Namih-yi Farhangistan*, vol. 1, no. 1 (March–May 1943).

13. Mihdi Quli Hidayat, *Khatirat va Khatarat* (Tehran, 1965), p. 408; Bamdad, *op. cit.*

14. Furughi's letter, text in *Rahnama-yi Kitab*, vol. 15, nos 10–12 (January–March 1973), pp. 833–45.
15. Iraj Afshar (ed.), *Taqrirat-i Musaddiq* (recorded by Jalal Buzurgmihr) (Tehran, 1980), p. 100.
16. Bullard to Eden, 17 June 1942 (Annual Political Report for 1941) IOR:L/P&S/12/3472A.
17. Bullard to FO, 22 September 1941, FO371 EP27158.
18. Eden to Cripps, 21 October 1941, FO371 EP27155.
19. Text of Furughi's Cabinet programme in Kuhi-yi Kirmani, *op. cit.*, vol. 1, pp. 116–17.
20. For the text of the treaty see A. H. Hamzavi, *Persia and the Powers* (London, 1946), pp. 65–9.
21. No comprehensive study of the political role of the tribes in modern Iranian history is yet available. See however, P. Oberling, *The Qashqa'i Nomads of Fars* (The Hague, 1974) and Lois Beck, *The Qashqa'i of Iran* (New Haven and London, 1986). For more specifically anthropological studies, see Fredrik Barth, *Nomads of South Persia* (Oslo, 1961). Also the articles by Barth and G. Reza Fazel in C. Nelson (ed.), *The Desert and the Sown: Nomads in the Wider Society* (Berkeley, 1973); Gene Garthwaite, *Khans and Shahs: the Bakhtiari in Iran* (Cambridge, 1981).
22. Farrukh, *Khatirat*, p. 473.
23. Vaughan-Russell to Bullard, 13 October 1941, FO371 EP27155.
24. The Chief of Police of Maraghih was one official who refused to retreat and was killed by the Russians. Cook to Bullard, 27 October 1941, FO371 EP27158.
25. Cook to Bullard, 31 August 1941, FO371 EP27153.
26. Cook to Bullard, 28 September 1941, FO371 EP27156.
27. Cook to Bullard, October 1941, *ibid.*
28. Cook to Bullard, 13 October 1941, FO371 EP27157.
29. Bullard to Eden, 17 June 1942 (Annual Political Report for 1941) IOR:L/P&S/12/3472A.
30. Cook to Bullard, 21 September 1941, FO371 EP27155.
31. Vaughan-Russell to Eden, 1 November 1941, FO371 EP27159.
32. Bullard to Eden, 28 July 1942, FO371 EP31443.
33. Bullard to Eden, 17 June 1942 (Annual Political Report for 1941) IOR:L/P&S/12/3472A.
34. Speeches by Ali Dashti, Sayyid Ya'qub Anvar and Abulqasim Naraqi, *Muzakirat-i Majlis*, 16 September 1941.
35. Dashti's speech, 6 October 1941; Naraqi's speech, 8 October 1941, *ibid.*
36. Hidayat, *op. cit.*, p. 457; Farrukh, *Khatirat*, p. 341.
37. *Ittila'at*, 11 November 1941.
38. Furughi, speech in the Majlis, 14 December 1941. Text in Kuhi-yi Kirmani, *op. cit.*, vol. 1, pp. 195–202.
39. Bullard to Eden, 29 April 1943 (Report on Political Events of 1942) IOR:L/P&S/12/3472A.
40. Bullard to Eden, 10 April 1942, FO371 EP31385.
41. Furughi, radio speech, 6 October 1941; text in Kuhi-yi Kirmani, *op. cit.*, vol. 1, pp. 167–71. Furughi's speech in the Majlis, *ibid.*, pp. 195–202. Farrukh, *Khatirat*, pp. 526–7.
42. Kuhi-yi Kirmani, *op. cit.*, vol. 1, p. 172. Farrukh, *Khatirat*, pp. 538–40.

43. Speech in the Majlis, 23 September 1941, text in Kuhi-yi Kirmani, *op. cit.*, vol. 1, pp. 117–19.
44. *Muzakirat-i Majlis*, 1 February 1942.
45. A. K. S. Lambton, *The Persian Land Reform, 1962–66* (Oxford, 1966), p. 50.
46. Bullard to FO, 23 December 1941, FO371 EP27158. Bullard to FO, 29 September 1942, FO371, EP31385.
47. Bullard to Eden, 10 April 1942, *ibid.*

2 The Government of Suhaili

1. *Ittila'at*, 13 March 1942.
2. Bullard to FO, 2 March 1942, FO371 EP31385.
3. Bullard to Eden, 10 April 1942, *ibid.*
4. Bullard to FO, 7 March 1942, *ibid.*
5. Bullard to FO, 2 March 1942, *ibid.*
6. Bullard to FO, 14 March 1942, *ibid.*
7. Farrukh, *Khatirat*, p. 550; Khajih-Nuri, *op. cit.*, p. 135.
8. Bullard to Eden, 29 April 1943 (Report on Political Events of 1942) IOR:L/P&S/12/3472A.
9. Bullard to Eden, 10 April 1942, FO371 EP31385.
10. Bullard to FO, 14 March 1942, *ibid.*
11. Bullard to Eden, 29 April 1943 (Report on Political Events of 1942) IOR:L/P&S/12/3472A.
12. *Ibid.*
13. Husain Kay-Ustuvan, *Siyasat-i Muvazinih-yi Manfi dar Majlis-i Chahardahum*, vol. I (Tehran, 1950), p. 394.
14. Farrukh, *Khatirat*, pp. 633, 638; Khajih-Nuri, *op. cit.*, pp. 9ff.
15. Khajih-Nuri, *op. cit.*; see also Ibrahim Safa'i, *Rahbaran-i Mashrutih: Ali Suhaili* (Tehran, 1969), pp. 28–9.
16. Khajih-Nuri, *op. cit.*, p. 26; Farrukh, *Khatirat*, p. 550.
17. Bullard to FO, 16 March 1942, FO371 EP31390.
18. Bullard to FO, 3 April 1941, *ibid.*
19. Bullard to FO, 29 April 1942, *ibid.*
20. Report on Personalities in Persia, 1940, FO371 EP24582.
21. Bullard to FO, 29 April 1942, FO371 EP31390.
22. Fletcher to FO, 13 May 1942, FO371 EP31391.
23. Vaughan-Russell (British Consulate in Kirmanshah), 19 May 1942, *ibid.*
24. Isfahan Consular Diary, 1–15 July 1942, FO371 EP31412.
25. Isfahan Vice-Consular Diary, 16–31 March 1942, *ibid.*
26. Bullard to Eden, 28 July 1942, FO371 EP31443.
27. Bullard to Eden, 28 July 1942, *ibid.*
28. Khajih-Nuri, *op. cit.*, p. 174; Farrukh, *Khatirat*, p. 573.
29. Bullard to Eden, 28 July 1942, FO371 EP31443.
30. *Ibid.*
31. Vaughan-Russell (British Consulate in Kirmanshah), 19 May 1942, FO371 EP31391.
32. Suhaili, speech in the Majlis, *Muzakirat-i Majlis*, 19 April 1942.

33. Bullard to Eden, 28 July 1942, FO371 EP31443.
34. Minute by Pink, July 1942, FO371 EP31385.
35. Bullard to Eden, 23 August 1942, *ibid.*
36. Bullard to FO, 21 May 1942, *ibid.* The Americans had been asked by the British to help with the provision and transport of war materials to the Soviet Union and their forces had thus entered Iran without any formal agreement. See further Keyvan Tabari, 'Iran's Policies Towards the United States During the Anglo-Russian occupation 1941–1946' (Ph.D. Thesis, Columbia University, 1967), pp. 21–30 and Mark H. Lytle, *The Origins of the Iranian–American Alliance, 1941–1953* (New York, 1987).
37. Minute by Pink, May 1942, FO371 EP31385.
38. FO to Tehran, 27 May 1942, *ibid.*
39. Bullard to Eden, 29 April 1943 (Report on Political Events of 1942) IOR:L/P&S/12/3472A.
40. Bullard to Eden, 23 August 1942, FO371 EP31385.
41. Khajih-Nuri, *Ali Suhaili*, p. 157; Farrukh, *Khatirat*, pp. 550, 573.
42. Musaddiq, speech in the Majlis, text in Kay-Ustuvan, *op. cit.*, vol. I, pp. 253–8.
43. Farrukh, *Khatirat*, pp. 554, 560.
44. Bullard to Eden, 28 July 1942, FO371 EP31443.
45. Bullard to Eden, 23 August 1942, FO371 EP31385.
46. Farrukh, *Khatirat*, pp. 573–6.
47. *Ibid.*, p. 579; Khajih-Nuri, *Ali Suhaili*, p. 160.
48. Text in Kuhi-yi Kirmani, *op. cit.*, vol. 1, pp. 472–6, 478–80.

3 The Government of Qavam

1. Hasan Arsanjani, 'Yaddashtha-yi Siyasi-yi Man', *Bamshad*, 6–13 August 1956, pp. 63–6.
2. Anvar Khamih'i, *Fursat-i Buzurg-i az Dast Raftih*, (Tehran, 1983), pp. 73, 127.
3. Arsanjani, *op. cit.*, 20–7 August 1956.
4. Bullard to Eden, 22 September 1942, FO371 EP31443.
5. Arsanjani, *op. cit.*, 6–13 August 1956; Ahmad Ali Sipihr, 'Qavam us-Saltanih ba'd az Shahrivar', in *Maqalat-i Siyasi* (Tehran, 1962) pp. 18–27; Farrukh, *Khatirat*, p. 621.
6. Bullard to Eden, 10 April 1942, FO371 EP31385.
7. Bullard to FO, 29 July 1942, *ibid.*
8. Ibrahim Safa'i, *Rahbaran-i Mashrutih* (Tehran, 1965), pp. 652–710; Husain Makki, 'Aqa-yi Ahmad Qavam', *Salnamih-yi Dunya*, no. 2 (1946), pp. 81–3; Ali Vusuq, *Chahar Fasl dar Tafannun va Tarikh* (Tehran, 1982); Mihdi Quli Hidayat, *op. cit.*, pp. 329–30; Mihdi Davudi, *Qavam us-Saltanih* (Tehran, 1948).
9. Safa'i, *op. cit.*, p. 704; Khajih-Nuri, *Khandaniha*, 22 July 1952, p. 5.
10. Sadiq Rezazadih-Shafaq, 'Khatirati az Qavam us-Saltanih', *Khandaniha*, 23 January 1955; Arsanjani, *op. cit.*, 13–20 August 1956.
11. A. Mustaufi, *Tarikh-i Ijtima'i va Idari-yi Iran dar Daurih-yi Qajariyyih*, vol. 3 (Tehran, 1962), pp. 567–70.
12. Farrukh, *Khatirat*, p. 582.
13. Report on Personalities in Persia, 1940, FO371 EP4582.
14. Speech in the Majlis, *Muzakirat-i Majlis*, 9 August 1942.

15. Bullard to FO, 5 August 1942, FO371 EP31385.
16. Bullard to FO, 15 August 1942, *ibid.*; FO to Tehran, 19 August 1942, *ibid.*
17. Bullard to FO, 2 September 1942, *ibid.*
18. FO to Tehran, 11 September 1942, *ibid.*
19. Bullard to FO, 5 August 1942, *ibid.*
20. FO to Tehran, 11 September 1942, *ibid.*
21. Ali Dashti, speech in the Majlis, *Muzakirat-i Majlis*, 23 September 1942.
22. Speech in the Majlis, *Muzakirat-i Majlis*, 27 September 1942.
23. Bullard to FO, 30 September 1942, FO371 EP31386.
24. Bullard to FO, 7 October 1942, *ibid.*
25. FO to Tehran, 20 October 1942, *ibid.*
26. Bullard to FO, 22 October 1942, FO371 EP31386.
27. *Ittila'at*, 17 November 1942; Bullard to FO, 18 November 1942, FO371 EP31386.
28. Bullard to FO, 16 November 1942, *ibid.*
29. *Ibid.*
30. Memorandum to John D. Jernegan, 23 January 1943, text in Yonah Alexander and Allen Nanes (eds), *The United States and Iran, a Documentary History*, (Frederick, 1980), pp. 94–9.
31. Qavam's speech, text in Kuhi-yi Kirmani, *op. cit.*, vol. 2, pp. 256–8.
32. Bullard to FO, 18 November 1942, FO371 EP31386.
33. Dreyfus to the Secretary of State, 17 October 1942, text in Alexander and Nanes, *op. cit.*, pp. 87–8.
34. *Ibid.*
35. Kuhi-yi Kirmani, *op. cit.*, vol. 2, p. 303.
36. Bullard to FO, 18 November 1942, FO371 EP31386.
37. *Ibid.*
38. Bullard to FO, 19 November 1942, *ibid.*
39. Bullard to FO, 19 November 1942, FO371 EP31386.
40. *Dad*, 13 January 1943, *Bakhtar*, 21–5 January 1943. According to the newspaper *Iran*, the students' demands concerned educational problems and had nothing to do with the shortage of bread (20–8 January 1943).
41. Bullard to FO, 9 December 1943, FO371 EP31387; CICI Baghdad to War Office, 11 December 1942, *ibid.*; Hasan Arfa, *Under Five Shahs* (London, 1964), pp. 318–20: Farrukh, *Khatirat*, pp. 615–17.
42. *Rahbar*, 27 July 1943.
43. Senator Muhammad Tadayyun later asserted in the Senate that 54 people were killed during the events. *Muzakirat-i Sina*, 23 May 1950.
44. Arsanjani, *op. cit.*, 20–7 August 1956.
45. Bullard to FO, 9 December 1942, FO371 EP31387.
46. Kuhi-yi Kirmani, *op. cit.*, vol. 2, p. 309.
47. Bullard to Eden, 29 April 1943 (Report on Political Events of 1942), IOR:L/P&S/12/3472A.
48. Bullard to FO, 9 December 1942, FO371 EP31387.
49. Farrukh, *Khatirat*, p. 616.
50. Bullard to FO, 15 December 1942, FO371 EP31387.
51. Qavam, speech in the Majlis, *Muzakirat-i Majlis*, 20 December 1942.
52. Bullard to Eden, 27 March 1943, *ibid.*
53. Farrukh, *Khatirat*, p. 626.

54. Bullard to Eden, 27 March 1943, FO371 EP35070.
55. *Ibid.*; Farrukh, *Khatirat*, pp. 622–3.
56. Bullard to Eden, 27 March 1943, FO371 EP35070.
57. *Rahbar*, 9 February 1943.
58. Qavam, speech in the Majlis, *Muzakirat-i Majlis*, 10 February 1943.
59. Bullard to Eden, 27 March 1943, FO371 EP35070.
60. Farrukh, *Khatirat*, p. 624.
61. Bullard to FO, 13 February 1943, FO371 EP35069.
62. *Ibid.*; Bullard to Eden, 27 March 1943, FO371 EP35070.
63. Bullard to FO, 13 February 1943, FO371 EP35069.
64. Bullard to Eden, 22 September 1942, FO371 EP31443.
65. Bullard to Eden, 22 September 1942, *ibid.*
66. Khajih-Nuri, *Khandaniha*, 22 July 1952, p. 5.
67. Kuhi-yi Kirmani, *op. cit.*, vol. 2, pp. 387–8.
68. Millspaugh's first mission to Iran in 1921 had also coincided with the premiership of Qavam.
69. Bullard to Eden, 12 May 1944, FO371 EP40164.
70. Bullard to FO, 8 March 1944, FO371 EP40186.

4 The Government of Suhaili

1. Bullard to FO, 14 February 1943, FO371 EP35069.
2. Kuhi-yi Kirmani, *op. cit.*, vol. 2, p. 406.
3. Bullard to FO, 14 February 1943, FO371 EP35069.
4. Text in Kuhi-yi Kirmani, *op. cit.*, pp. 397–8.
5. Khamih'i, *Fursat*, pp. 16–24.
6. *Ibid.*, pp. 31–128.
7. *Ibid.*, pp. 75–9.
8. 'Usul-i Asasi-yi Maram-i Hizb-i Tudeh', *Rahbar*, 12, 14 February 1943.
9. Bullard to FO, 12 March 1943, FO371 EP35069.
10. Letter from the British Minister in Tehran to Prime Minister, 1 April 1943, FO371 EP35070.
11. Bullard to Eden, 23 June 1943, FO371 EP35072.
12. FO to Tehran, 25 March 1943, FO371 EP35069.
13. Minute by Pink, March 1943, *ibid.*
14. Bullard to all Consuls in Persia, 6 June 1943, FO371 EP35071, Bullard to FO, 7 September 1943, FO371 EP35075.
15. Minute by Pink, 20 April 1943, FO371 EP35070; FO to Tehran, 23 April 1943, *ibid.*
16. Bullard to Eden, 6 May 1943, FO371 EP35071.
17. Bullard to FO, 20 April 1943, FO371 EP35070.
18. Bullard to FO, 24 March 1942, *ibid.*
19. Bullard to FO, 9 April 1943, *ibid.*
20. Bullard to FO, 24 March 1943, *ibid.*
21. Bullard to FO, 17 April 1943, *ibid.*
22. Bullard to FO, 21 April 1943, *ibid.*
23. Text in Kuhi-yi Kirmani, *op. cit.*, vol. 2, pp. 425–6.
24. Bullard to FO, 31 August 1943, FO371 EP35070.

25. See p. 38 above.
26. Bullard to Eden, 21 September 1943, FO371 EP35076.
27. Bullard to FO, 9 July 1943, FO371 EP35072; *Rahbar*, 3 July 1943.
28. Bullard to FO, 9 July 1943, *op. cit.*
29. *Rahbar*, 10 November 1943.
30. Bullard to FO, 15 June 1943, FO371 EP35071.
31. Musaddiq, speech in the Majlis, 3, 4 June 1943, text in Kay-Ustuvan, *op. cit.*, vol. II, pp. 12–23.
32. Bullard to FO, 27 October 1943, FO371 EP35077.
33. Bullard to FO, 12 May 1944, FO371 EP40164.
34. *Rahbar*, 29 May, 1 June 1943.
35. 'Qat'namih-yi Nakhustin Kungrih-yi Hizb-i Tudeh-yi Iran dar maurid-i Siyasat-i Dakhili', *Rahbar*, 15 August 1944.
36. Dr. Ali Shayigan, 'Iran Bayad bih Dast-i Irani Idarih Shavad', *Kayhan*, 24 August 1943.
37. Bullard to FO, 16 April 1943, FO371 EP35070.
38. Bullard to FO, 11 March 1943, FO371 EP35069.
39. Bullard to FO, 17 April 1943, *ibid.*; Kuhi-yi Kirmani, *op. cit.*, vol. 2, pp. 455–6.
40. Bullard to FO, 31 May 1943, FO371 EP35071.
41. Bullard to FO, 21 April 1943, FO371 EP35070.
42. Kuhi-yi Kirmani, *op. cit.*, vol. 2, p. 457.
43. Text in Kuhi-yi Kirmani, *op. cit.*, vol. 2, pp. 489–94.
44. Chiefly in *Dad*, edited by Amidi-Nuri.
45. Bullard to FO, 20 July 1943, FO371 EP35072.
46. Bullard to FO, 28 July 1943, *ibid.*
47. Bullard to FO, 13 July 1943, *ibid.*
48. FO to Tehran, 1 August 1943, *ibid.*
49. Minute by Pink, 24 July 1943, FO341 EP35072.
50. Bullard to FO, 18 August 1943, FO371 EP35074.
51. Bullard to FO, 27 October 1943, FO371 EP35077.
52. Bullard to FO, 20 November 1943, *ibid.*
53. Bullard to FO, 17 December 1943, *ibid.*
54. Khamih'i, *Fursat*, pp. 80–1.
55. Bullard to Eden, 6 April 1944 (Report on Political Events of 1943), IOR:L/P&S/12/3472A.
56. *Ibid.*
57. Text in Kuhi-yi Kirmani, *op. cit.*, vol. 2, pp. 427–35.
58. Bullard to Eden, 6 April 1944 (Report on Political Events of 1943), IOR:L/P&S/12/3472A.
59. Measures approved by the 13th Majlis included bills for compulsory education, insurance for workers, the establishment of a police training college, the transfer of cases involving military personnel to the jurisdiction of civil courts, except in instances of purely military offences, and various other legislation sponsored by the Millspaugh mission.
60. Bullard to Eden, 6 April 1944 (Report on Political Events of 1943), IOR:L/P&S/12/3472A.
61. Bullard to FO, 27 February 1944, FO371 EP40186.

5 The Government of Sa'id

1. *Ra'd-i Imruz*, 19 March 1944.
2. Ibrahim Safa'i, *Sa'id ul–Vizarih* (Tehran, 1969), p. 3.
3. Abdulhusain Bihniya, *Pardibha-yi Siyasat* (Tehran, n.d.), p. 20.
4. Safa'i, *op. cit.*, p. 30.
5. Bullard to FO, 14 February 1943, FO371 EP35069.
6. Report on Personalities in Persia, 24 February 1940, FO371 EP24582.
7. Bullard to FO, 14 March 1942, FO371 EP31385.
8. Ghani, *op. cit.*, vol. XI, p. 9.
9. Ali Vusuq, *op. cit.*, pp. 75–90.
10. Safa'i, *op. cit.*, p. 30.
11. *Ra'd-i Imruz*, 20 February 1944.
12. *Rahbar*, 7 April 1944.
13. Bullard to FO, 7 April 1944, FO371 EP40186.
14. *Rahbar*, 17 April 1944.
15. Sa'id, speech in the Majlis, *Muzakirat-i Majlis*, 16 April 1944.
16. *Rahbar*, 17 April 1944.
17. 'Tarikhchih-yi Ittihadiyyih-yi Kargaran-i Isfahan', *Rahbar*, 19 June 1944.
18. F. Kishavarz, speech in the Majlis, *Rahbar*, 30 April 1944; Iraj Iskandari, speech in the Majlis, *Rahbar*, 3 May 1944.
19. See further, H. Ladjevardi, 'Politics and Labour in Iran' (D.Phil. thesis, University of Oxford, 1981), pp. 374–424. See also pp. 148–71 of the revised version of this thesis which has been published under the title *Labour Unions and Autocracy in Iran* (Syracuse, 1985); hereafter references are to the thesis.
20. Bullard to Eden, 6 July 1944, FO371 EP40187.
21. Bullard to FO, 17 May 1944, *ibid*.
22. *Rahbar*, 16, 19 May 1944.
23. Musaddiq, speech in the Majlis text in Kay-Ustuvan, *op. cit.*, vol. I, pp. 22–40.
24. Sayyid Zia, speech in the Majlis, text in *ibid.*, pp. 40–79.
25. Kay-Ustavan, *op. cit.*, vol. II, p. 82.
26. Bullard to FO, 10 May 1944, FO371 EP40186.
27. *Rahbar*, 25 May 1944.
28. 'Taktik-i Jadid-i Sayyid Zia', *Rahbar*, 23 April 1944.
29. Some of his political views were expressed in a turgid and stilted fashion in a pamphlet entitled *Sha'a'ir-i Milli* (Tehran, 1943). See also various issues of *Ra'd-i Imruz*, particularly between September 1943 and March 1944.
30. For the text of the interview see *Iqdam*, 28 January 1943.
31. Bullard to FO, 30 May 1944, FO371 EP40187.
32. Bullard to FO, 10 May 1944, FO371 EP40186.
33. Bullard to FO, 30 May 1944, FO371 EP40187.
34. *Ibid.*
35. Tehran to FO, 27 August 1944, *ibid*.
36. *Ibid.*
37. Musaddiq, speech in the Majlis, text in Kay-Ustuvan, *op. cit.*, vol. I, pp. 89–127.
38. *Rahbar*, 18 April 1944.
39. Bullard to Eden, 12 May 1944, FO371 EP40164. Among other things, Sayyid Zia subsidized the newspaper *Sitarih* to support Millspaugh (Tehran to FO, 15 August 1944, *ibid.*).

40. Sa'id's letter to Millspaugh, text in Kay-Ustuvan, *op. cit.*, vol. I, pp. 136–142.
41. *Rahbar*, 28 June 1944.
42. Tehran to FO, 3 July 1944, FO371 EP40164.
43. *Rahbar*, 1 September 1944.
44. Musaddiq, speech in the Majlis, text in Kay-Ustuvan, *op. cit.*, vol. I, pp. 130–42.
45. Bullard to Ministry of Information, 17 September 1944, FO371 EP40187.
46. F. Kishavarz, speech in the Majlis, *Rahbar*, 14 September 1944.
47. Bullard to Ministry of Information, 17 September 1944, FO371 EP40187.
48. Musaddiq, speech in the Majlis, text in Kay-Ustuvan, *op. cit.*, vol. I, pp. 130–42.
49. Bullard to Eden, 9 March 1945 (Review of events in Iran during 1944), IOR: L/P&S/12/3472A.
50. Abbas Mas'udi, speech in the Majlis, *Muzakirat-i Majlis*, 18 October 1944.
51. Bullard to FO, 23 October 1944, FO371 EP40241.
52. Bullard to Eden, 9 March 1945 (Review of events in Persia during 1944), IOR: L/P&S/12/3472A.
53. Quoted in Keyvan Tabari, *op. cit.*, p. 94.
54. Bullard to FO, 10 October 1944, FO371 EP40241.
55. Tehran to All Consuls, 1 November 1944, FO371 EP40188.
56. For critical expositions of the inconsistencies between the words and deeds of the Tudeh leadership by two prominent ex-party members, see Khalil Maliki, *Barkhurd-i Aqayid va Ara* (Tehran, 1950); Khamih'i, *Fursat*. For a less sophisticated and more emotional treatment of the same subject by a disillusioned member of the Party, see A. Tahuri, *Sarabi bih Nam-i Hizb-i Tudeh-yi Iran* (Tehran, 1979). For a detailed account of the Tudeh Party which takes into account the problems and adversities which it faced, see Ervand Abrahamian, *Iran Between Two Revolutions* (Princeton, 1982), pp. 281–415. See also Sepehr Zabih *The Communist Movement in Iran* (Berkeley and Los Angeles, 1966).
57. *Rahbar*, 12, 14 October 1944.
58. *Mardum bara-yi Raushanfikran*, 10 November 1944.
59. *Ibid.*
60. Bullard to FO, 27 October 1944, FO371 EP40241. See also Khamih'i, *Fursat*, pp. 130–7.
61. *Rahbar*, 1 November 1944.
62. The central organ of the Tudeh Party identified 'fascists' as those who 'oppose the labour movement in the country and follow a policy of hostility towards the Soviet Union' (*Rahbar*, 19 November 1944).
63. Bullard to Eden, 9 March 1945 (Review of events in Persia during 1944), IOR: L/P&S/12/3472A.
64. An example of the resentment and bitter feelings of Iranians towards the Russians can be found in an article in *Bakhtar*, 26 October 1944.
65. Bullard to FO, 24 October 1944, FO371 EP40241.
66. Bullard to FO, 30 October 1944, *ibid.*
67. Tehran to All Consuls, 6 November 1944, FO371 EP40242.
68. Cadogan to Duke, 9 December 1944, FO371 EP40243.
69. Parliamentary session, 15 November 1944; FO to Tehran, 18 November 1944, FO371 EP40242; Kirsch to Cadogan, 28 November 1944, *ibid.*
70. Minute by Young, 10 December 1944, FO371 EP40243. In essence this was, ironically, what Ihsan Tabari also advocated.
71. FO to Tehran, 21 November 1944, FO371 EP40242.
72. Bullard to FO, 10 October 1944, FO371 EP40164.

73. Lascelles to FO, 5 September 1944, FO371 EP40187.
74. Bullard to FO, 11 October 1944, FO371 EP40188.
75. Musaddiq, speech in the Majlis, *Muzakirat-i Majlis*, 17 October 1944.
76. Bullard to Eden, 11 September 1943, FO371 EP40164.
77. Lascelles to FO, 6 September 1944, *ibid.*
78. Kuhi-yi Kirmani, vol. II, p. 624.
79. Bullard to FO, 26 November 1944, FO371 EP40242; Bullard to FO, 10 November 1944, FO371 EP40188.

6 The Government of Bayat

1. Lascelles to F0, 5 September 1944, FO371 EP40187.
2. Musaddiq's letter to the Speaker of the Majlis, 13 November 1944; Musaddiq's letter to the Shah, 14 November 1944, texts in Kay-Ustuvan, *op. cit.*, vol. I, pp. 184–7; Musaddiq, speech in the Majlis, 2 December 1944, text in *ibid.*, pp. 190–201.
3. *Rahbar*, 20 November 1944.
4. Bullard to FO, 20 November 1944, FO371 EP40242.
5. *Rahbar*, 21 November 1944.
6. Report on Personalities in Persia, 24 February 1940, FO371 EP24582.
7. Bullard to FO, 20 November 1944, FO371 EP40246.
8. *Rahbar*, 20 November 1944.
9. *Ibid.*
10. Musaddiq, speech in the Majlis, 2 December 1944, text in Kay-Ustuvan, *op. cit.*, vol. I, pp. 190–201.
11. *Rahbar*, 23 November 1944.
12. FO to Tehran, 22 November 1944, FO371 EP40242; Bullard to FO, 26 November 1944, FO371 EP40189.
13. Bullard to FO, 22 November 1944, FO371 EP40242.
14. Musaddiq, speech in the Majlis, 2 December 1944, text in Kay-Ustuvan, *op. cit.*, vol. I, pp. 190–201, 207–9, 215–16.
15. Bullard to FO, 17 January 1945, FO371 EP45443.
16. Khalil Maliki, 'Sar-u-Tah-i Yik Karbas', *Rahbar*, 7, 8, 10 December 1944; *idem*, 'Ustrasism-i Rusiyyih', *Rahbar*, 18 December 1944.
17. For an elaboration and defence of his position, see Musaddiq's speech in the Majlis, 19 December 1944, text in Kay-Ustuvan, *op. cit.*, vol. I, pp. 227–37, and Musaddiq's letter to Maximov (the Soviet Ambassador), 13 March 1945, text in *ibid.*, pp. 245–9.
18. In the view of the Tudeh, however, this was not the end of the oil problem which, it claimed, 'Musaddiq and his followers' had not solved, but had merely 'removed from the jurisdiction of the Iranian government, handing it over to foreign circles' (*Rahbar*, 10 December 1944).
19. Bullard to FO, 8 December 1944, FO371 EP40189.
20. Bullard to Eden, 25 April 1945, FO371 EP45448.
21. *Ibid.*
22. MAIS, 11–17 March 1946, FO371 EP52710.
23. Bullard to Eden, 12 May 1945, FO371 EP40164.

24. Office of Strategic Services, Research and Analysis Branch, 'The present situation in Iran with regard to the Millspaugh Mission (May–October 1944)', text in Alexander and Nanes, *op. cit.*, pp. 120–1.
25. Musaddiq, speech in the Majlis, 19 December 1944, text in Kay-Ustuvan, *op. cit.*, vol. I, pp. 227–37.
26. Tehran to FO, 19 January 1945, FO371 EP45481.
27. He continued to express his strong and contemptuous disbelief in the competence of Iranians to manage their own affairs (*New York Times*, 4 April 1946); see further Arthur C. Millspaugh, *Americans in Persia* (Washington, 1946); J. Thorpe, 'The Mission of Arthur C. Millspaugh to Iran, 1943–45' (Ph.D. dissertation, University of Wisconsin, 1973).
28. *Ra'd-i Imruz*, 18 April 1945.
29. Bullard to Eden, 25 April 1945, FO371 EP45448.
30. Musaddiq, speech in the Majlis, 4 June 1945, text in Kay-Ustuvan, *op. cit.*, vol. II, pp. 12–23.
31. Musaddiq, speech in the Majlis, 4 March 1945, *ibid.*, pp.285–9.
32. For the attitude of some newspapers towards this incident, see *ibid.*, pp. 298–308.
33. Bullard to Eden, 25 April 1945, FO371 EP45448.
34. Bullard to FO, 29 March 1945, FO371 EP45447.
35. Lascelles to FO, 6 April 1945, FO371 EP45447.
36. *Ra'd-i Imruz*, 6 April 1945; Lascelles to FO, 6 April 1945, *ibid.*
37. *Ibid.*
38. *Ibid.*
39. Musaddiq, speech in the Majlis, 17 April 1945, text in Kay-Ustuvan, *op. cit.*, vol. II, p. 9. The day before the fall of the Cabinet, Sayyid Zia presented a motion of interpellation against it, but later withdrew.
40. Bayat, speech in the Majlis, *ibid.*, pp.12–23.
41. Khamih'i, *Fursat*, p. 160.
42. *Ibid*, p. 162.

7 The abortive Government of Hakimi

1. Lascelles to FO, 29 April 1945, FO371 EP45448.
2. *Ra'd-i Imruz*, 6 May 1945; Musaddiq, speech in the Majlis, text in Kay-Ustuvan, *op. cit.*, vol. II, pp. 12–23.
3. Bullard to FO, 2 May 1945, FO371 EP45448.
4. Mihdi Bamdad, *Rijal-i Iran*, vol. I, pp. 8–10.
5. Ibrahim Safa'i, *Hakim ul-Mulk* (Tehran, 1968), pp. 41, 42.
6. Musaddiq, speech in the Majlis, text in Kay-Ustuvan, *op. cit.*, vol. II, pp. 12–23.
7. Bamdad, *op. cit.*, vol. I, p. 10.
8. Le Rougetel to FO, 18 November 1949, FO371 EP75468.
9. *Ra'd-i Imruz*, 4 June 1945.
10. Bullard to FO, 21 May 1945, FO371 EP45448.
11. MAIS, 14–24 May 1945, FO371 EP45458.
12. *Ra'd-i Imruz*, 23 May 1945.

8 The Government of Sadr

1. *Ra'd-i Imruz*, 6 June 1945.

2. Musaddiq, speech in the Majlis, 30 June 1945, text in Kay-Ustuvan, *op. cit.*, vol. II, pp. 38–43; Musaddiq, speech in the Majlis, 15 September 1945, *ibid.*, pp. 68–76; 'Bayaniyyih-yi Aqalliyyat', *Ittila'at*, 17 June 1945.
3. Musaddiq, speech in the Majlis, 27 September 1945, text in Kay-Ustuvan, *op. cit.*, vol. II, pp. 96–100.
4. Dashti, speech in the Majlis, *Muzakirat-i Majlis*, 30 June 1945.
5. MAIS, 6–12 August 1945, FO371 EP45458.
6. Sadr, *Khatirat*, pp. 30–191, 288–93; Report on Personalities in Persia, 24 February 1940, FO371 EP24582.
7. Sadr, speech in the Majlis, *Muzakirat-i Majlis*, 23 September 1945.
8. MAIS, 27 August–2 September 1945, FO371 EP45458.
9. MAIS, 20–6 August 1945, FO371 EP45458; *Ra'd-i Imruz*, 20 August 1945; see further Arfa, *op. cit.*, pp. 343–5; Sipahbud Ahmad Vusuq, *Dastan-i Zindigani: Khatirati az Panjah Sal Tarikh-i Mu'asir, 1290–1340* (Tehran, n.d.), pp. 60–78. Vusuq, then a colonel, was the Mashhad Division Commander. See also Khamih'i, *Fursat*, pp. 175–87.
10. MAIS, 13–19 August 1945, FO371 EP45458.
11. MAIS, 27 August–2 September 1945, FO371 EP45458.
12. Bullard to Bevin, Report for July to September 1945, 7 November 1945, FO371 EP45452.
13. MAIS, 24–30 September 1945, FO371 EP45458.
14. Musaddiq, speech in the Majlis, 6 October 1945, text in Kay-Ustuvan, *op. cit.*, vol. II, pp. 98, 111.
15. MAIS, 24–30 September 1945, FO371 EP45458; Bullard to Bevin, 7 November 1945, FO371 EP45452.
16. MAIS, 1–7 October 1945, FO371 EP45458.
17. *Ibid.*, 12–23 September 1945.
18. Sadr, *Khatirat*, p. 517.
19. MAIS, 11–17 June 1945.
20. *Ibid.*, 1–7 October 1945.
21. *Ibid.*, 15–21 October 1945.
22. Sadr, speech in the Majlis, *Muzakirat-i Majlis*, 5 September 1945.
23. Arfa, *op. cit.*, p. 338.
24. *Ra'd-i Imruz*, 16 September 1945.
25. MAIS, 22–8 October 1945, FO371 EP45458.
26. *Ra'd-i Imruz*, 29 June, 13 September 1945.
27. Bullard to FO, 30 September 1945, FO371, EP45451.
28. MAIS, 27 August, 2 September 1945, FO371 EP45458.
29. Musaddiq, speech in the Majlis, text in Kay-Ustuvan, *op. cit.*, vol. II, p. 11.
30. In Bullard's estimate, about 90 deputies out of a total of 115 voted for the postponement (Bullard to FO, 16 October 1945, FO371 EP45451).
31. The essential components of Musaddiq's ideas on electoral reform were as follows: (1) separation of rural from urban constituencies; (2) electoral supervisory boards to be composed of senior judges, university professors and leading government officials; (3) duration of elections to be limited to one day; (4) franchise in urban areas to be confined to the literate. Musaddiq's preoccupation with electoral reform can be traced back to the 1920s. See Musaddiq, 'Intikhabat dar Urupa va Iran', *Ayandih*, II (1926), pp. 122–30, reprinted in Afshar (ed.), *Masa'il-i Huquq va Siyasat* (Tehran, 1979), pp. 73–90. During his second term of office in 1952,

Musaddiq incorporated some of these ideas into his electoral reform law which, in the event, remained unimplemented.
32. Bullard to FO, 22 October 1945, FO371 EP45451.
33. MAIS, 22–8 October 1945, FO371 EP45458.
34. Musaddiq, speech in the Majlis, Kay-Ustuvan, *op. cit.*, vol. II, pp. 117–18.
35. For example, a proposal made on 9 September 1945 by Nasir Quli Ardalan, a deputy for Sanandaj, banning the future employment of foreign nationals by the Government without the prior sanction of the Majlis was overwhelmingly approved by the deputies.
36. Bullard to FO, 8 October 1945, FO371 EP45451.

9 The Government of Hakimi

1. H. Arsanjani, 'Yaddashtha-yi Siyasi 1945–47', *Bamshad*, 13–20 August 1956; Kay-Ustuvan, *op. cit.,*, vol. II, p. 180.
2. MAIS, 29 October–11 November 1945, FO371 EP45459.
3. J. Pishihvari, 'Sarguzasht-i Man', *Azhir*, 6 December 1943.
4. Malik ush-Shu'ara Bahar, 'Hizb-i Dimukrat-i Azarbaijan', *Iran-i Ma*, 16 September 1945; see also Anvar Khamih'i's article in *Rahbar*, 18 April 1946 and Abd ur-Rahman Faramarzi, 'Payam bih Pishihvari', *Kayhan*, 16 January 1946.
5. These tensions are very clear in various editorials and articles in *Jibhih*, the newspaper of the Iran Party (an association consisting mainly of engineers and lawyers), particularly between January and December 1946.
6. The bulk of the deputies, along with Hakimi, pronounced the leaders of the Azarbaijan autonomy movement to be rebels, much to the dislike of the left (*Jibhih*, 20, 23 December 1945).
7. For an account of Iran's contribution to the Allied war effort, see Muhammad Khan-Malik Yazdi, *Arzish-i Masa'i-yi Iran dar Jang, 1939–1945* (Tehran, 1945).
8. Bullard to FO, 15 December 1945, FO371 EP45439.
9. Extract from Soviet Monitor, issued by Tass, 17 December 1945, *ibid.*
10. Bullard to FO, 15 December 1945, FO371 EP45437.
11. Bullard to FO, 13 December 1945, *ibid.*
12. Extract from Soviet Monitor, issued by Tass, 16 December 1945, *ibid.*
13. Consulate, Tabriz, to Tehran, 20 December 1945, FO371 EP45440.
14. Tehran to FO, 27 December 1945, *ibid.*
15. Soviet Embassy in Tehran to Iranian Ministry of Foreign Affairs, 26 November 1945, FO371 EP45437; *Rahbar*, 3 December 1945.
16. MAIS, 17–23 December 1945, FO371 EP52710; *Jibhih*, 28 December 1945.
17. MAIS, 26 November–3 December 1945, FO371 EP45459.
18. Bullard to FO, 10 December 1945, FO371 EP45452.
19. Bullard to FO, 1 December 1945, *ibid.*
20. Farquhar to FO, 22 December 1945, *ibid.*; Musaddiq, speech in the Majlis, text in Kay-Ustuvan, *op. cit.*, vol. II, pp. 204–12.
21. Farquhar to FO, 22 December 1945, FO371 EP45452; MAIS, 17, 23 December 1945, FO371 EP52710. Nariman had also been put in charge of the Tehran municipality after the removal of Ibtihaj.
22. Bullard to FO, 18 December 1945, FO371 EP45439.
23. Bullard to FO, 27 December 1945, FO371 EP45440.

24. Bullard to FO, 27 November 1945, FO371 EP45437; Bullard to FO, 2 December 1945, FO371 EP45452. The Shah also reiterated his regret that 'the Constitution did not permit of his dissolving the Majlis and holding fresh elections', adding that 'once foreign troops had left, constitutional problems must receive attention'.
25. Bullard to FO, 24 November 1945, FO371 EP45436.
26. FO to Tehran, 25 November 1945, FO371 EP45437.
27. Bullard to FO, 27 November 1945, *ibid.*
28. Bullard to FO, 2 December 1945, *ibid.*; Farquhar to FO, 22 December 1945, F0371 EP45440.
29. Musaddiq, speech in the Majlis, text in Kay-Ustuvan, *op. cit.*, vol. II, pp. 204–12.
30. MAIS, 31 December 1945–6 January 1946, FO371 EP52710. See further James F. Byrnes, *Speaking Frankly* (London and Toronto, 1947), pp. 110–22; Sir Reader Bullard, *The Camels Must Go* (London, 1961), pp. 266–9; Alan Bullock, *Ernest Bevin: Foreign Secretary 1945–1951* (London, 1983), pp. 217–18.
31. MAIS, 3 December 1945–6 January 1946, FO371 EP52710.
32. *Ittila'at*, 6 January 1946.
33. *Kayhan*, 16 January 1946; *Darya*, 7 January 1946; *Mardum*, 8 January 1946.
34. Musaddiq, speech in the Majlis, text in Kay-Ustuvan, *op. cit.*, vol. II, pp. 223–7; Farivar, speech in the Majlis, text in *ibid.*, pp. 227–30.
35. Hakimi, speech in the Majlis, text in Kay-Ustuvan, *op. cit.*, vol. II, pp. 232–4. Hakimi's Foreign Minister, Abulqasim Najm, also disclosed later in the Senate (19 July 1950) the circumstances in which the scheme had been presented to the Government, hinted at disagreements between the British and American representatives, and stated that he had been opposed to it from the outset. Text of speech in *ibid.*, pp. 235–8.
36. MAIS, 14–20 January 1946, FO371 EP53710.
37. Bullard to FO, 27 November 1945, FO371 EP45437.
38. FO to Tehran, 2 January 1946, FO371 EP52661.
39. FO to Washington, 5 January 1946, *ibid.*
40. Extract from Bevin's speech in the House of Commons on 21 February 1946, FO to Tehran, FO371 EP52665, See also Bullock, *op. cit.*, pp. 206–19.
41. FO to Washington, 2 January 1946, FO371 EP52661.
42. Washington to FO, 3 January 1946, *ibid.*
43. Tehran to all Consuls, 19 January 1946, FO371 EP51663.
44. Musaddiq, speech in the Majlis, 9 January 1946, Kay-Ustuvan, *op. cit.*, vol. II, pp. 223–7.
45. Prime Minister Razmara's proposals for decentralization and the establishment of local councils made a few years later provoked strong opposition and suspicion, and some of its opponents referred to the tripartite scheme of 1946 to justify their misgivings. See below Part IV, Chapter 16.
46. MAIS, 10–16 December 1945, FO371 EP45459; Hakimi, speech in the Majlis, *Muzakirat-i Majlis*, 18 December 1945. This speech contains an account of the rejectionist policy of Hakimi's Government *vis-à-vis* the regime in Azarbaijan.
47. See further, A. H. Hamzavi, *Persia and the Powers* (London, 1946).
48. Musaddiq, speech in the Majlis, text in Kay-Ustuvan, *op. cit.*, pp. 190–5.
49. Musaddiq, speech in the Majlis, *ibid.*, pp. 204–12.
50. MAIS, 14–20 January 1946, FO371 EP52710.
51. MAIS, 26 November–3 December 1945, FO371 EP45459.
52. MAIS, 17–23 December 1945, FO371 EP52710.

53. MAIS, 10–16 December 1945, FO371 EP45459.
54. FO to Moscow, 22 December 1945, FO371 EP45439.

10 The first period

1. H. Arsanjani, 'Yaddashtha-yi Siyasi', *Bamshad*, 12–19 November 1956; 'I'lamiyyih-yi Kumitih-yi Markazi-yi Hizb-i Tudeh-yi Iran', *Rahbar*, 13 June 1946.
2. Arsanjani, *op. cit.*, 17–20 September, 29 October, 5 November 1946.
3. Sipihr, *op. cit.*, pp. 18–27; Bullard to FO, 26 January 1946, FO371 EP52663.
4. For a detailed account of the trip by an ex-minister and a member of the delegation, see Hamid Sayyah, 'Qavam us-Saltanih dar Muskau', *Salnamih-yi Dunya*, no. 18 (1962), pp. 103–6. For further details, see Qasim Mas'udi, *Jarayan Musafirat-i Misiun-i I'zami-yi Iran bih Muskau* (Tehran, 1946).
5. Tehran to all Consuls, 20 March 1946, FO371 EP52668.
6. FO to Tehran, 15 March 1946, FO371 EP52667.
7. *Rahbar*, 5 April 1946.
8. Bullard to FO, 1 March 1946, FO371 EP52665.
9. Bullard to FO, 21 February 1946, FO371 EP52665.
10. Memorandum by Howe, 16 April 1946, FO371 EP52673; Minute by Butte, 20 April 1946, FO371 EP52674. Bevin refused to countenance such measures; minutes of FO meeting, 18 April 1946, FO371 EP52673.
11. *Dad*, 23 April 1946.
12. *Dad*, 14 May 1946.
13. *Azarbaijan*, 15 May 1946, Le Rougetel to FO, 17 May 1946, FO371 EP52676.
14. Farquhar to FO, 16 April 1946, FO371 EP52673.
15. From an interview with Nasir Zulfaqari, April 1983.
16. Minute by Holt, 29 April 1946, FO248 1462; Minute by Roberts, 2 May 1946, *ibid.*
17. From an interview with Firuz, April 1983. Firuz was of the opinion that the terms of the proposed Irano-Soviet oil company were infinitely superior to those of the AIOC.
18. Murray to Secretary of State, 22 March 1946, text in Alexander and Nanes, *op. cit.*, p. 167.
19. Ahmad Aramish, *Haft Sal dar Zindan-i Aryamihr*, ed. Ismail Ra'in (Tehran, 1979), p. 107.
20. See further R. W. Van Wagenen, *The United Nations Action: The Iranian Case 1946* (New York, 1952).
21. For Ala's account of these events, see 'Tarh-i Mas'alih-yi Azarbaijan dar Shaura-yi Amniyyat', *Salnamih-yi Dunya*, no. 20 (1964). On the complex deliberations of the Security Council and the arguments of the Iranian representatives Taqizadih, and later Ala, see Van Wagenen, *op. cit.* See also A. H. Hamzavi, *op. cit.*
22. *Iran-i Ma*, 16 June 1946.
23. Le Rougetel to Bevin, 25 May 1946, FO371 EP52705.
24. 'I'lamiyyih-yi Ra'is Muhtaram-i Daulat', *Jibhih*, 7 June 1946.
25. MAIS, 3–9 June 1946, FO371 EP52710.
26. *Jibhih*, 4 June 1946.

27. Le Rougetel to FO, 24 May 1946, FO371 EP52677.
28. Le Rougetel to FO, 9 June 1946, *ibid*.
29. 'Qat'namih-yi Nakhustin Kungrih-yi Hizb-i Tudeh-yi Iran dar Maurid-i Siyasat-i Dakhili', *Rahbar*, 15 August 1944.
30. Le Rougetel to FO, 4 August 1946, FO371 EP52706.
31. *Rahbar*, 23 October 1946.
32. 'Nazari bih Yaddashtha-yi Qavam', *Khandaniha*, 12 October 1946; Sipihr, *op. cit.*, p. 25.
33. MAIS, 11–17 March 1946, FO371 EP52710; Bullard to FO, 13 March 1946, FO371 EP52667.
34. Inverchapel (Washington) to FO, 24 June 1946, FO371 EP52678.
35. Ambassador to the State Department, 22 March 1946, *Foreign Relations of the United States*, 1946, VII, pp. 369–73; quoted by Abrahamian, *Iran Between Two Revolutions*, p. 229.
36. Inverchapel (Washington) to FO, 24 June 1946, FO371 EP52678.
37. The idea of forming a political party was entertained by Qavam long before his second term of office in the post-1941 era (Farrukh, *Khatirat*, p. 915).
38. *Journal de Tehran*, 1 July 1946; Le Rougetel to FO, 1 July 1946, FO371 EP52705.
39. *Jibhih*, July 1946; Ihsan Tabari, 'Nazar-i Ma dar barih-yi Hizb-i Dimukrat-i Iran', *Rahbar*, 17 July 1946.
40. Le Rougetel to FO, 2 July 1946, FO371 EP52705.
41. *Jibhih*, 2 August 1946. One newspaper described this Cabinet as 'the best Government of the democratic era' (*Shahid*, 4 August 1946), a view shared by many others.
42. MAIS, 27 May–2 July 1946, FO371 EP52710.
43. Le Rougetel to FO, 2 August 1946, FO371 EP52706.
44. Le Rougetel to FO, 6 August 1946, FO371 EP52679.
45. *Jibhih*, 5, 7, 9 August 1946.
46. 'I'lamiyyih-yi Kumitih-yi Markazi-yi Hizb-i Tudeh-yi Iran', *Rahbar*, 4 August 1946.
47. See further Mustafa Fatih, *Panjah Sal Naft-i Iran* (Tehran, 1955), pp. 439–42.
48. Ladjevardi, *op. cit.*, p. 193.
49. MAIS, 22–8 April 1946, FO371 EP52710; article by Lieutenant Colonel Pitt (Political Intelligence Officer at the British Embassy in Tehran 1943–5) in *Daily Telegraph*, 28 September 1946.
50. Le Rougetel to FO, 30 August 1946, FO371 EP52680.
51. *Ibid*.
52. FO to Tehran, 31 August 1946, *ibid*.
53. *Jibhih*, the organ of the Iran Party, asserted that 'everyone knows that events in the south took place with the backing of the British'; few Iranians would have disputed this (*Jibhih*, 30 September 1946).
54. FO to Le Rougetel, 31 October 1946, FO371 EP52682.
55. Shiraz to Tehran, 19 September 1946, *ibid*.
56. *Jibhih*, 26 September 1946.
57. *Dad*, 24 September 1946.
58. Le Rougetel to FO, 23 September 1946, FO371 EP52681.
59. Le Rougetel to Bevin, 22 January 1947, FO371 EP61969. General Ahmadi later admitted that he had been imposed on Qavam by the Shah, and that despite pressure from Tudeh ministers he had insisted that the army had no forces at the

time to send to Fars. He added that with the co-operation of the Government the army could have reoccupied Azarbaijan within two weeks. (Amir-Ahmadi, 'Vizarat dar Daulat-i Qavam us-Saltanih', *Salnamih-yi Dunya*, no. 13 (1957). pp. 80–4).

60. *Jibhih*, 8 August 1946.
61. Le Rougetel to FO, 30 August 1946, FO371 EP52680.
62. *Daily Telegraph*, 28 September 1946.
63. Minute by Baxter, 8 October 1946, FO371 EP52683.
64. Le Rougetel to FO, 2 October 1946, *ibid.*
65. Reportedly Zahidi 'had a secret understanding with Qashqa'is enabling them to capture' these towns 'almost without a fight' (Minute by Zaehner, 19 February 1952, FO248 1532).
66. Interview with Nasir Zulfaqari, April 1983. It is in any case true that Qavam had good relations with the Qashqa'i leaders, who had joined his party.
67. Le Rougetel to FO, 18 October 1946, FO371 EP52684.
68. *Rahbar*, 14 October 1946.
69. *Iran-i Ma*, 13 October 1946.
70. Le Rougetel to FO, 18 October 1946, FO371 EP52684.
71. Le Rougetel to FO, 28 October 1946, FO371 EP52685.
72. *Jibhih*, 21 October 1946.
73. Le Rougetel to FO, 18 October 1946, FO371 EP52684.
74. Quoted in Ladjevardi, *op. cit.*, p. 193.
75. Le Rougetel to FO, 23 October 1946, FO371 EP52685.
76. Le Rougetel to FO, 28 October 1946, *ibid.*
77. Le Rougetel to FO, 15 November 1946, *ibid.*
78. Le Rougetel to FO, 18 October 1946, *ibid.*
79. *Rahbar*, 13 October 1946.
80. *Jibhih*, 20 October 1946.
81. From an interview with Dr. F. Kishavarz (August 1982); see also Khamih'i, *Fursat-i*, pp. 272–324.
82. Le Rougetel to FO, 5 September 1946, FO371 EP52680.
83. Le Rougetel to FO, 14 November 1946, FO371 EP52685.
84. Le Rougetel to FO, 26 November 1946, FO371 EP52686.
85. Le Rougetel to FO, 20 November 1946, *ibid.*
86. FO to Tehran, 25 November 1946, *ibid.*
87. *Rasti*, 24 November 1946.
88. *Azarbaijan*, 7 December 1946.
89. *Rahbar*, 3 December 1946.
90. Le Rougetel to Bevin (Report for quarter ending 31 December 1946), FO371 EP61988.
91. Le Rougetel to FO, 29 November 1946, FO371 EP52687.
92. Le Rougetel to FO, 29 November 1946, FO371 EP52686. According to the British military attaché, after the defeat of the Democrats the army 'exchanged its role from that of oppressor to that of saviour. This glory was reflected in the person of the royal Commander-in-Chief and the astute General Razmara' (MAIS, 13–19 January 1947, FO371 EP61982).
93. Le Rougetel to FO, 9 December 1946, FO371 EP52687.
94. See further W. Eagleton Jr., *The Kurdish Republic of 1946* (London 1963); A. Roosevelt Jr., 'The Kurdish Republic of Mahabad', *MEJ* (July 1947), reprinted in G. Chaliand (ed.), *People Without a Country* (London, 1980), pp. 135–50.

95. British military attaché's tour of Azarbaijan, 23 December 1946–3 January 1947, FO371 EP61968. On the Azarbaijan regime see further A. Amidi-Nuri, *Firqih-yi Dimukrat* (Tehran, 1946); N. Pisyan, *Marg Bud, Bazgasht ham Bud* (Tehran, 1947); R. Rossow Jr., 'The Battle of Azarbaijan', *MEJ*, vol. 9 (Winter 1956); M. Modjtehedi, 'La question d'Azarbaidjan: La Mouvement des Democrats et les Efforts de l'ONU' (Doctoral thesis, University of Paris, 1952); P. Homayounpour, *L'Affaire d'Azarbaidjan* (Lausanne, 1967).

96. Le Rougetel to FO, 15 November 1946, FO371 EP52686.

97. Khalil Maliki, *Barkhurd-i Aqayid va Ara*, pp. 79–80.

98. *I'lamiyyih-yi Kumitih-yi Markazi-yi Hizb-i Tudeh-yi Iran*, December 1946; 'I'lamiyh-yi Hay'at-i Ijra'iyyih-yi Muvaqqat', *Namih-yi Mardum*, 5 January 1947.

99. See further Maliki, *op. cit.*; Ephrim Ishaq, *Chih Bayad Kard* (Tehran 1946); Alatur, *Hizb-i Tudeh bar Sar-i Du Rah* (Tehran 1947); K. Maliki, *Du Ravish Bara-yi Yik Hadaf* (Tehran, 1948); Homa Katouzian, *Khatirat-i Siyasi-yi Khalil Maliki* (Tehran, 1980); Jalal Al-i Ahmad, *Yik Chah va Du Chahlih* (Tehran, 1964); *idem, Dar Khidmat va Khiyanat-i Raushan-fikran* (Tehran, 1978), vol. II, pp. 161–215; Katouzian, *The Political Economy of Modern Iran* (London, 1981), pp. 141–63.

11 The second period

1. Le Rougetel to FO, 24 October 1946, FO371 EP52685.

2. *Jibhih*, 13 November 1946.

3. One such manifesto was published by a group named the 'National Front' (Jibhih-yi Milli) which consisted of pro-Sayyid Zia newspaper editors. Besides the call for fair elections, they demanded the release of Sayyid Zia, for which they also received the support of Sayyid Zia's old opponent, Musaddiq. *Bazpurs (Iqdam)*, 27 December 1947.

4. 'Namih-yi Dr. Musaddiq bih Nakhurst Vazir', 17 November 1946, *Nabard-i Imruz (Jibhih)*, 28 November 1946; 'Namih-yi Dr. Musaddiq bih Ruznamih-yi Jibhih', *ibid.*; 'Arizih-yi Sargushadih-yi Janab-i Aqa-yi Dr. Musaddiq bih A'lahazrat-i Shah, 4 January 1947', *Akhbar-i Iran (Jibhih)*, 7 January 1947; Musaddiq, speech in the Masjid-i Shah, *ibid.*

5. *Akhbar-i Iran (Jibhih)*, 13 January 1947; Le Rougetel to FO, 14 January 1947, FO371 EP61988.

6. Le Rougetel to FO, 16 January 1947, *ibid.*

7. *Ittila'at*, 20 December 1946.

8. Le Rougetel to FO, 16 January 1947, FO371 EP61988.

9. *Ibid.*

10. *Ibid.*

11. Le Rougetel to Bevin (Report for quarter ending 31 March 1947), FO371 EP61989. In Fars there was considerable bargaining over Qavam's candidates, which eventually resulted in their success. In Azarbaijan, however, 'in spite of determined efforts, Qavam was unable to impose any of his candidates', according to Le Rougetel. Le Rougetel to Bevin (Events in Persia during 1947 and 1948), 17 January 1949, FO371 EP75458. The deputies for Azarbaijan included prominent politicians such as Taqizadih and Sa'id. Most of them helped to form the nucleus

of the National Union faction *(Fraksium-i Ittihad-i Milli)* which, in its opposition to Qavam, enjoyed the support of the Court.

12. Le Rougetel to FO, 28 February 1947, FO371 EP61989.
13. *Ibid.*
14. Sargent to Le Rougetel, 30 January 1947, FO371 EP61968.
15. 'Nazari bih Yaddashtha-yi Qavam', *Khandaniha*, 28 September 1955.
16. Le Rougetel to Baxter, 19 March 1947, FO371 EP61989. Qavam later admitted that such licences had been sold but that the proceeds were paid to informers who spied in Azarbaijan on behalf of the central government. Qavam's letter to the Justice Committee of the Majlis, 18 September 1948, text in *Dimukrat-i Iran*, 12 October 1948.
17. *Ibid.*
18. Sadiq Rezazadih-Shafaq, 'Khatirati chand az Qavam us-Saltanih', *Khandaniha*, 23 January 1956. See also *idem, Khatirat-i Majlis va Dimukrasi chist* (Tehran, 1955).
19. Le Rougetel to Bevin, 21 March 1947, FO371 EP61989.
20. Le Rougetel to Bevin, 21 March 1947, *ibid.*
21. Le Rougetel to N. M. Butler, 1 May 1947, *ibid.*
22. *Ibid.*
23. Le Rougetel to FO, 27 May 1947, FO371 EP61971.
24. Le Rougetel to FO, 31 May 1947, *ibid.*
25. Le Rougetel to FO, 12 August 1947, FO371 EP61972.
26. Muhammad Taqi Bahar (Malik ush-Shu'ara), *Divan-i Ash'ar*, vol. 1 (Tehran, 1956), pp. 718–21 (Shikayat az-Dust); Sipihr, *op. cit.*
27. Le Rougetel to FO, 13 June 1947, FO371 EP61989.
28. Aramish's own account is different: he asserts that he gave up his position voluntarily because of differences with his colleagues (Aramish, *op. cit.*, p. 106). His later political career was turbulent: in the post-1953 period he took up a ministerial position and became head of the Plan Organization. He eventually broke away from the Shah, spent some years in prison and as a confessed republican was killed by SAVAK in October 1973. See further *ibid.*, pp. 175–245.
29. Le Rougetel to FO, 23 June 1947, FO371 EP61989.
30. Prime Minister's statement, *Dimukrat-i Iran*, 1 August 1947.
31. Le Rougetel to FO, 2 July 1947, FO371 EP61989.
32. Le Rougetel to FO, 8 July 1947, FO371 EP61990.
33. Le Rougetel to FO, 11 July 1947, *ibid.*
34. Le Rougetel to FO, 5 July 1947, *ibid.*
35. *Ibid.*
36. Qavam, speech in the Majlis, *Muzakirat-i Majlis*, 9 December 1947.
37. Le Rougetel to FO, 13 August 1947, FO371 EP61972.
38. Le Rougetel to FO, 2 August 1947, FO371 EP61990.
39. Le Rougetel to FO, 17 August 1947, FO371 EP61972.
40. Le Rougetel to Wright, 31 July 1947, FO371 EP61990.
41. Asadi also later conveyed to a member of the British Embassy that the emissaries of the Court openly told the deputies that they had the choice of 'antagonizing' either the Court or the Prime Minister (Embassy Minute, 6 December 1947, FO248 1462).
42. Le Rougetel to Wright, 31 July 1947, FO371 EP61990.
43. Le Rougetel to Bevin, 13 August 1947, FO371 EP61991.
44. Le Rougetel to Bevin, 27 August 1947, *ibid.*
45. Le Rougetel to FO, 30 August 1947, *ibid.*

46. *Dimukrat-i Iran*, 30 August 1947.
47. Le Rougetel to Bevin, 10 September 1947, FO371 EP61991.
48. *Dimukrat-i Iran*, 14 September 1947; Hidayat, *op. cit.*, p. 495.
49. Creswell to Bevin, 6 October 1947, FO371 EP61991.
50. Peterson (Moscow) to FO, 28 May 1947, FO371 EP61971.
51. Le Rougetel to FO, 31 July 1947, *ibid.*
52. Minute by Pyman, 1 August 1947, *ibid.*
53. Le Rougetel to FO, 13 August 1947, FO371 EP61972.
54. Le Rougetel to FO, 2 September 1947, *ibid.*
55. *Razm*, 23 October 1947; 'Ahmad Qavam, lackey of the dollar' was the title of an article which appeared on 3 December 1947 in the Russian *Literary Gazette*; Peterson (Moscow) to FO, 8 December 1947, FO371 EP61975. This article summarized the drastically revised Soviet view of Qavam which was reiterated in their various organs of propaganda and reproduced by the Tudeh Party's press.
56. Le Rougetel to FO, 10 December 1946, FO371 EP52688.
57. Le Rougetel to FO, 22 August 1947, FO371 EP61972; *Manchester Guardian*, 12 September 1947 (Text of Allen's speech to the Irano-American Society in Tehran); Allen's declaration, *Journal de Tehran*, 14 September 1946.
58. Minute by Pyman, 22 April 1947, FO371 EP61970.
59. FO to Washington, 19 August 1947, FO371 EP61972; minutes by Pyman, 10 September 1947, *ibid.*
60. Minute by Pyman, 25 August 1947, FO371 EP61973.
61. Minute by Burrows, 23 September 1947, *ibid.*
62. Peterson (Moscow) to FO, 28 May 1947, FO371 EP61971. The target of leftist newspaper attacks in the post-1946 period shifted understandably to 'American imperialism'. On British policy towards Iran in the 1945–7 period, see further Wm. Roger Louis, *The British Empire in the Middle East 1945–51* (Oxford, 1984), pp. 54–73; more specifically on Bevin's attitude, see Bullock, *op. cit.*, pp. 185–351.
63. Minute by Burrows, 23 September 1947, FO371 EP61973.
64. Le Rougetel to FO, 9 September 1947, FO371 EP61972.
65. For instance, *Ittila'at* referred to Anglo-Soviet complicity, the revival of the Anglo-Russian agreement of 1907, and the intensification of the war of nerves against Iran (*Ittila'at*, 11 September 1947).
66. FO to Tehran, 15 September 1947, FO371 EP61972.
67. Minute by Le Rougetel, 18 September 1947, FO371 EP61973.
68. Roberts (Moscow) to Creswell (Tehran), 18 October 1947, *ibid.*
69. Creswell to Burrows, 1 October 1947, FO371 EP61973. Creswell was in charge of the Embassy in Tehran at the time, as Le Rougetel stayed in London for the two sensitive months preceding the rejection of the Russian oil demand, returning well after the Majlis resolution was passed. According to *The Scotsman*, he had remained absent from Tehran in order not to find himself in the position of having openly to deny the Iranians the same assurances as the Americans had given them (*The Scotsman*, 1 November 1947).
70. Full text in *Dimukrat-i Iran*, 22 October 1947, reprinted in H. Makki, *Naft va Nutq-i Makki* (Tehran, 1978), pp. 16–86.
71. *Muzakirat-i Majlis*, 21 October 1947.
72. According to *Mardum*, the central organ of the Tudeh Party, the Majlis resolution was dictated by the American Embassy, and the reference to the AIOC was added in order to alarm America's rivals, the British.

73. Minute by Pyman, 24 October 1947, FO371 EP61974.
74. Creswell to FO, 28 October 1947, FO371 EP61991.
75. Creswell to FO, 2 November 1947, *ibid.*
76. *Ibid.*; Creswell to Burrows, 4 November 1947, *ibid.*; Le Rougetel to FO, 14 November 1947, FO371 EP61992.
77. Creswell to FO, 2 November 1947, FO371 EP61991.
78. Le Rougetel to FO, 14 November 1947, FO371 EP61992.
79. Embassy minute, 6 December 1947, FO248 1462. For a sympathetic account of Hikmat, see Safa'i, *Rahbaran-i Mashrutih* (Tehran, 1967), pp. 615–86.
80. Creswell to Bevin, 6 October 1947, FO371 EP61991.
81. Le Rougetel to Warner, 25 November 1947, FO371 EP61992.
82. Minute by Pyman, 3 December 1947, FO371 EP61975.
83. Arsanjani later became the architect of Iranian land reform but, largely as the result of his popularity with the peasantry, he was removed from the political scene by being dispatched as Ambassador to Rome. For his obituary, see I. Afshar, 'Darguzasht-i Sayyid Hasan Arsanjani', *Rahnama-yi Kitab*, vol. 12, no. 3–4 (June–July 1969), pp. 207–8.
84. 'Nazari bih Yaddashtha-yi Qavam', *Khandaniha*, 6 November 1955; Le Rougetel was 'reliably informed' that the National Union faction, 'with strong encouragement from the Court, pushed forward to a successful conclusion their efforts to detach from Qavam us-Saltaneh's party a faction of about thirty Deputies under the leadership of the president of the Majlis' (Le Rougetel to Bevin, 18 December 1947, FO371 EP61992).
85. MAIS, 2 December 1947, FO371 EP61983.
86. Le Rougetel to FO, 6 December 1947, FO371 EP61992.
87. Le Rougetel to Bevin, 18 December 1947, FO371 EP61992. For the text of a letter addressed to Qavam, in which his ministers tried to justify their action in submitting their resignation to the Shah rather than to him, see Ibrahim Safa'i, *Namihha-yi Tarikhi* (Tehran, 1969), pp. 170–1.
88. Qavam's speech in the Ministry of Foreign Affairs, *Dimukrat-i Iran*, 3 December 1947.
89. Text in *Dimukrat-i Iran*, 10 December 1947.
90. It was openly rumoured in the Majlis that to give Qavam a vote of confidence would displease the Shah (*Dimukrat-i Iran*, 12 December 1947).
91. Quoted in Ladjevardi, *op. cit.*, p. 195.
92. *Dimukrat-i Iran*, 7, 12 December 1947. The same point was raised by Abbas Iskandari in the Majlis; *Muzakirat-i Majlis*, 5 January 1948. The Tudeh Party also attributed Qavam's downfall largely to the activities of the British who wanted to dislodge a man who was 'recognized as an enforcer of American policy in Iran' (*Mardum*, 10 December 1947).
93. Subsequent events proved that Iskandari's motives were less than genuinely patriotic. When he witnessed the nationalization of AIOC by Musaddiq, a goal he had himself advocated, Iskandari turned against Musaddiq, trying to undermine his government and replace him with Qavam. Whatever his character and motives, however, Iskandari played an important part in making the southern oil question into a major issue.
94. Muhammad Muhit-Tabataba'i's less than courteous description of Qavam as 'the decrepit old man of the monastery [*khaniqah*] of reaction' epitomized the usual repertoire of anti-Qavam rhetoric (*Muhit*, no. 13, 5 December 1947, pp. 2–5).

95. Creswell to FO, 2 November 1947, FO371 EP61991.
96. In his view, Iran had little choice but to follow such a policy, which also helped to prevent the imposition on Iran of a military dictatorship by one of the great powers (Qavam's interview with *La Tribune des Nations*, translated text in *Sitarih*, 26 January 1948).
97. Le Rougetel to FO, 5 February 1947, FO371 EP61969.
98. M. Foot, 'The devious way of Mr. Ghavam', *Daily Herald*, 24 April 1946. Sipihr goes much further than this, claiming that Qavam actually intended, with the help of the Russians, to change the Iranian regime and assume the leadership of the country (Sipihr, *op. cit.*, pp. 26–7). According to Kishavarz, however, General Razmara had tried to persuade Qavam to oust the Shah and form a republic, but Qavam had considered such an idea to be premature (interview with Kishavarz, August 1982). It is not possible to ascertain whether Razmara was sincere or just trying to test Qavam.

12 The Government of Hakimi

1. Le Rougetel to Burrows, 16 December 1947, FO371 EP61992.
2. Hasan Iqbali (ed.), *Naft va Bahrain, ya Abbas Iskandari dar Khidmat-i Majlis-i Panzdahum* (Tehran 1952), p. 100.
3. Le Rougetel to Burrows, 24 December 1947, FO371 EP68704.
4. Minute by Pyman, 31 December 1947, FO371 EP61992.
5. Iskandari, speech in the Majlis, text in Iqbali, *op. cit.*, pp. 102–28; Rahimian, speech in the Majlis, *Muzakirat-i Majlis*, 1 January 1948.
6. Le Rougetel to Attlee, 12 January 1948, FO371 EP68704.
7. Taqizadih, speech in the Majlis, *Muzakirat-i Majlis*, 7 January 1948; Iskandari labelled Hakimi's Cabinet 'the Cabinet of Taqizadih' (Iqbali, *op. cit.*, p. 124).
8. Le Rougetel to Attlee, 12 January 1948, FO371 EP68704.
9. Le Rougetel to Bevin, 20 January 1948, *ibid.*
10. Le Rougetel to Bevin, 22 January 1948, *ibid.*
11. Le Rougetel to FO, 8 February 1948, FO371 EP68711.
12. For the text of Kashani's letters, declarations, etc., see Muhammad Dihnavi, *Majmu'ih'i az Maktubat, Sukhanraniha, Piamha va Fatavi-yi Ayatullah Kashani*, 3 vols (Tehran, 1982–3). See also Muhammad Hassan Faghfoory, 'The Role of the Ulama in Twentieth Century Iran, with Particular Reference to Ayatullah Haj Sayyid Abul-Qasim Kashani' (Ph.D. dissertation, University of Wisconsin – Madison, 1978); Shahrough Akhavi, *Religion and Politics in Contemporary Iran: Clergy–State Relationships in the Pahlavi Period* (Albany, 1980), pp. 68–71.
13. The assassin was released mainly due to pressure from religious circles. For an informative account of the Fida'iyan by one of its members, see Sayyid Muhammad Vahidi, 'Khatirat-i Fida'iyan-i Islam', *Khandaniha*, 23 September–14 November 1955. See further Sayyid Husain Khushniyyat, *Sayyid Mujtaba Navvab-Safavi* (Tehran, 1981); Reza Gulsurkhi, 'Fida'iyan-i Islam', *Ittila'at, 30 April 1979; Hamid Enayat, Modern Islamic Political Thought* (London, 1982), pp. 93–9. For an elaboration of the Fida'iyan's views, see *I'lamiyyih-yi Fida'iyan-i Islam* (Tehran, 1950), reprinted as *Jami'ih va Hukumat-i Islami* (Tehran, 1978).

14. Creswell to Burrows, 19 May 1948, FO371 EP68706. Sayyid Zia later told the British Oriental Counsellor that upon hearing from the Shah of his desire to revise the Constitution, he formed a 'front against dictatorship' in association with journalists and members of the Tudeh Party (Le Rougetel to Bevin, 10 November 1948, FO371 EP68709).

15. *Mard-i Imruz*, 13 February 1948.

16. F. Kishavarz, *Man Muttaham Mikunam* (Tehran, 1978), pp. 97–102; H. Lankarani's article in *Kavih*, XVIII, 2 (75) October 1982.

17. Iqbali, *op. cit.*, p. 142.

18. Five Lankarani brothers were arrested, ostensibly to show that Mas'ud's murder was being investigated, but in fact because they were suspected of working to set up a 'committee for the establishment of a republic' (Le Rougetel to Burrows, 7 April 1948, FO371 EP68705).

19. Le Rougetel to FO, 19 February 1948, FO371 EP68715.

20. Le Rougetel to Bevin, 17 March 1948, FO371 EP68705.

21. Le Rougetel to Bevin, 17 January 1949, FO371 EP75458.

22. Creswell to Bevin, 2 June 1948, FO371 EP68706.

23. Creswell to Burrows, 19 May 1948, *ibid.*

24. *Pravda*, 26 December 1947, Peterson (Moscow) to FO, 28 December 1947, FO371 EP61992.

25. For the full text of agreement, see Alexander and Nanes, *op. cit.*, pp. 155–61.

26. A French translation of the text published in Moscow appeared in the *Journal de Tehran* on 6 February 1948.

27. Le Rougetel to Bevin, 17 January 1948, FO371 EP75458.

28. For the text of the contract, see Alexander and Nanes, *op. cit.*, pp. 122–7.

29. Le Rougetel to FO, 5 February 1948, FO371 EP68715.

30. Allen to the Secretary of State, 5 January 1948, text in Alexander and Nanes, *op. cit.*, p. 192.

31. The contracts of American missions in the army and gendarmerie were thereafter regularly renewed, and remained effective well into the 1970s, when they were eventually terminated by the revolution of 1979. See further Thomas M. Ricks, 'US Military Missions to Iran', *Iranian Studies*, 3–4 (Summer–Autumn, 1979).

32. On Iran–US relations in the post-1941 period, see Barry Rubin, *Paved with Good Intentions: The American Experience in Iran* (New York and Oxford, 1980); Rouhollah K. Ramazani, *Iran's Foreign Policy, 1941–73; A Study of Foreign Policy in Modernizing Nations* (Charlottesville, 1975); Bruce R. Kuniholm, *The Origins of the Cold War in the Middle East: Great Power Conflict and Diplomacy in Iran, Turkey and Greece* (Princeton, 1980); James A. Bill, *The Eagle and the Lion: The Tragedy of American–Iranian Relations* (Yale, 1988).

33. Tehran to FO, 8 May 1948, FO371 EP68705.

34. Muhammad Sururi (Justice Minister), report to the Majlis, *Muzakirat-i Majlis*, 11 April 1948.

35. Le Rougetel to Bevin, 20 April 1948, FO371 EP68705.

36. Le Rougetel to Bevin, 21 April 1948, *ibid.*

37. *Ibid.*

38. Sixty-seven voted in favour, 2 against, and 19 abstained.

39. *Ittila'at*, 10 May 1948.

40. *Dimukrat-i Iran*, 4 May 1948.

41. Tehran to FO, 8 May 1948, FO371 EP68705.

42. Najm, speech in the Majlis, *Muzakirat-i Majlis*, 11 May 1948. Najm's attitude in this regard largely accounted for his description by Le Rougetel as 'determined and exceptionally honest' (Le Rougetel to Bevin, 17 January 1949, FO371 EP75458).
43. Hazhir, speech in the Majlis, *Muzakirat-i Majlis*, 16 May 1948.
44. Iskandari, speech in the Majlis, text in Iqbali, *op. cit.*, pp. 212–13.
45. Najm, speech in the Majlis, *Muzakirat-i Majlis*, 25 May 1948.
46. Creswell to Bevin, 2 June 1948, FO371 EP68706.
47. Iqbali, *op. cit.*, pp. 134–48.
48. Creswell to Bevin, 2 June 1948, FO371 EP68706.
49. Hakimi, speech in the Majlis, *Muzakirat-i Majlis*, 8 June 1948.
50. Creswell to Bevin, 2 June 1948, FO371 EP68706.

13 The Government of Hazhir

1. Qasim Ghani, *Khatirat-i Dr Qasim Ghani* (Tehran, 1982), p. 245.
2. Tehran to FO, 14 June 1948, FO371 EP68706.
3. Creswell to Bevin, 23 June 1948, *ibid.*
4. Bamdad, *op. cit.*, vol. 2, pp. 258–60; I. Safa'i, *Abdulhusain Hazhir* (Tehran, 1949). According to a different account his father was 'one of the Fida'is of the early days of the Constitution' (Report on Personalities in Persia, 1940, FO371 EP24582).
5. *Ibid.*
6. Bamdad, *op. cit.*; Safa'i, *op. cit.*; *Bakhtar-i Imruz*, 5 November 1949.
7. Qasim Ghani, an ex-minister who was then the Iranian Ambassador in Cairo, had many harsh words to say about Hazhir and some of his colleagues (see Ghani, *op. cit.*, pp. 245–6). In this he undoubtedly echoed the sentiments of a number of other politicians.
8. Anon., 'Yaddashtha'i az Daurih-yi Nakhustvaziri-yi Hazhir', *Khandaniha*, 23 March 1951.
9. Creswell to Bevin, 23 June 1948, FO371 EP68706.
10. Tehran to FO, 22 June 1948, *ibid.*; minute by R. A. Clinton-Thomas, 23 June 1948, *ibid.*; Jahangir Tafazzuli, interview in *Iran-i Ma*, 13 July 1948. Tafazzuli was the editor of *Iran-i Ma* and political Under-Secretary to Hazhir.
11. Hidayat, *Khatirat va Khatarat, op. cit.*, p. 462.
12. Tehran to FO, 22 June 1948, FO371 EP68706.
13. Tehran to FO, 24 June 1948, *ibid.*
14. British Embassy (Washington) to FO, 30 June 1948, *ibid.*
15. *Iran-i Ma*, 31 June 1948.
16. Creswell to Burrows, 29 June 1948, FO371 EP68706; Creswell to FO, 16 July 1948, FO371 EP68707.
17. Iskandari, speech in the Majlis, 19, 21, 23 August 1948, text in Iqbali, *op. cit.*, pp. 246–97, 305–12. It was during these speeches that Iskandari went so far as to advocate the nationalization of the oil industry. The FO and AIOC officials did not as yet appreciate the increasing significance of the oil issue.
18. Ardalan, speech in the Majlis, *Muzakirat-i Majlis*, 22 August 1948.
19. Iskandari, speech in the Majlis, 19 August 1948, text in Iqbali, *op. cit.*, pp. 246–73.

20. Minute by Pyman, 30 July 1948; Burrows to Le Rougetel, 13 August 1948, FO371 EP68729.
21. Creswell to Bevin, 24 August 1948, FO371 EP68707; Iqbali, *op. cit.*, p. 317.
22. Le Rougetel to Bevin, 31 August 1948, FO371 EP68707.
23. Ha'irizadih, speeches in the Majlis, *Muzakirat-i Majlis*, 31 August, 2 September 1948; Taqizadih, speech in the Majlis, *ibid.*, 5 September 1948.
24. Abulhasan Sadiqi, speech in the Majlis, *ibid.*, 2 September 1948; Sadiq Rezazadih-Shafaq, speech in the Majlis, *ibid.*, 7 September 1948.
25. The original 50-article labour bill had been reduced to 21 articles in order to facilitate its approval.
26. Creswell to Burrows, 28 June 1948, FO371 EP68706.
27. Le Rougetel to Bevin, 15 September 1948, FO371 EP68707.
28. *Ibid.* As Le Rougetel estimated, out of 400 newspaper permits issued, only about 40 belonged to government officials, but many were staffed and financed by them.
29. Le Rougetel to Bevin, 31 August 1948, FO371 EP68707.
30. Tehran to FO, 1 October 1948, FO371 EP68708.
31. Le Rougetel to Wright, 29 September 1948, *ibid.*
32. Le Rougetel to Wright, *ibid.*
33. Le Rougetel to Burrows, 8 September 1948, FO371 EP68713.
34. British Embassy (Washington) to FO, 30 June 1948, FO371 EP68708.
35. British Embassy (Washington) to FO, 30 June 1948, FO371 EP68706.
36. Pyman to Creswell, 6 July 1948, FO371 EP68706.
37. Le Rougetel to FO, 18 October 1948, FO371 EP68708.
38. Le Rougetel to Orme-Sargent, 27 October 1948, *ibid.*
39. *Ibid.*
40. FO to Tehran, 1 November 1948, *ibid.*
41. Frank (Washington) to FO, 30 September 1948, FO371 EP68714.
42. Gerald Dooher, the controversial Irish-born Oriental Secretary of the American Embassy who, according to Le Rougetel, attended the Majlis more regularly than many deputies, had apparently described the Shah's threat of abdication as a bluff. This assertion, which was bound to be interpreted as sabotage of the Shah's plan by the Americans, had resulted in the anger of Princess Ashraf at John Wiley, the American Ambassador, to whom it had been attributed (Le Rougetel to Wright, 1 November 1948, FO371 EP68708).
43. Le Rougetel to FO, 6 August 1948, FO371 EP68707.
44. Le Rougetel to FO, 25 October 1948, FO371 EP68708.
45. Le Rougetel to Burrows, 13 October 1948, *ibid.* Hikmat was none the less elected, but by only 53 votes to 46, the other votes being cast for Taqizadih.
46. Tehran to FO, 24 June 1948, FO371 EP68706.
47. Creswell to FO, 30 June 1948, *ibid.*
48. Hazhir, speech in the Majlis, *Muzakirat-i Majlis*, 23 August 1948.
49. Le Rougetel to Burrows, 13 October 1948, FO371 EP68708.
50. Le Rougetel to Bevin, 8 September 1948, FO371 EP68713.
51. Creswell to FO, 31 July 1948, FO371 EP68707; Tehran to FO, 9 November 1948, FO371 EP68708.
52. By late September Le Rougetel had begun to wonder whether Hazhir would 'ever be able to stand on his own legs' (Le Rougetel to Wright, 29 September 1948, FO371 EP68708).

53. Tehran to FO, 6 August 1948, FO371 EP68707.
54. Tehran to FO, 19 August 1948, *ibid.*
55. Le Rougetel to Bevin, 31 August 1948, *ibid.*
56. Iqbali, *op. cit.*, pp. 236–41. The pilgrimage had recently been resumed following a long period of interrupted diplomatic relations between Iran and Saudi Arabia resulting from the decapitation of an Iranian *hajji* in Mecca in 1944.
57. In October, three members of Kashani's clientele sent a letter on behalf of Iran's Islamic Association to the Majlis, the UN, the press and foreign embassies, condemning the Government of Hazhir and warning against the consequences of its continuation (*Ittila'at*, 22 October 1948; Tehran to FO, 27 October 1948, FO371 EP68708).
58. Le Rougetel to Wright, 3 November 1948, *ibid.*
59. FO to Tehran, 6 November 1948, *ibid.*

14 The Government of Sa'id

1. Le Rougetel to Wright, 10 November 1951, FO371 EP68709.
2. *Ruznamih-yi Zindigi (Dimukrat-i Iran)*, 9–11 November 1948.
3. *Ibid.*, 17 November 1948.
4. Tehran to FO, 23 November 1948, FO371 EP68709.
5. Le Rougetel to Bevin, 24 November 1948, *ibid.*
6. Ahmad Razavi, speech in the Majlis, *Muzakirat-i Majlis*, 23, 28 November 1948; Mihdi Batmanqilich, speech in the Majlis, *ibid.*, 28 November 1948. See further Ahmad Razavi, *Matn-i Nutq-i Namayandih-yi Kerman dar Majlis-i Shaura-yi Milli* (Tehran 1948).
7. Le Rougetel to FO, 26 December 1948, FO371 EP68709.
8. *Ruznamih-yi Zindigi (Dimukrat-i Iran)*, 29 November 1948, 3 January 1949.
9. Le Rougetel to Bevin, 2 January 1949, FO371 EP75464.
10. Le Rougetel to FO, 26 November 1948, FO371 EP68709.
11. Le Rougetel to FO, 17 December 1948, *ibid.*
12. Le Rougetel to Bevin, 2 January 1949, FO371 EP75464.
13. Le Rougetel to Bevin, 31 December 1948, *ibid.*
14. Le Rougetel to Bevin, 15 January 1949, *ibid.*
15. Le Rougetel to FO, 25 January 1949, *ibid.*; O. Franks (Washington) to FO, 31 January 1949, *ibid.*
16. Kishavarz, *op. cit.*, pp. 99–133; Lankarani, *op. cit.*; interview with Buzurg Alavi, 1983.
17. Le Rougetel to FO, 12 February 1949, FO371 EP75464.
18. FO to Tehran, 19 February 1949, *ibid.*; O. Frank (Washington) to FO, 31 February 1949, *ibid.*
19. Le Rougetel to FO, 16 February 1949, *ibid.*
20. Le Rougetel to FO, 17, 19 February 1949, *ibid.*
21. Le Rougetel to FO, 21 February 1949, *ibid.*
22. FO to Tehran, 22 February 1949, *ibid.*
23. Washington to FO, 21 February 1949, *ibid.*
24. *Ittila'at*, 12 January 1949.
25. Iskandari, speech in the Majlis (20–7 January 1949), text in Iqbali, *op. cit.*, pp. 350–423. Following the attempt on the Shah's life, Iskandari left Iran and

stayed abroad for two years, ostensibly because he was refused a visa to return.
26. Taqizadih, speech in the Majlis, 27 January 1949, text in Iqbali, *op. cit.*,
    pp. 423–31. The version given by Ala, another member of the Iranian negotiating
    team in 1933, to the British Ambassador was identical (Shepherd to Morrison, 19
    March 1951, FO371 EP91524). A. K. Rothnie of the Foreign Office confirmed
    Ala's view (Minute by Rothnie, 24 March 1951, *ibid*).
27. Le Rougetel to Bevin, 2 February 1949, FO371 EP75464.
28. Manuchihr Iqbal, The Minister of the Interior and arch-enemy of the Tudeh
    Party, who proposed the bill for its dissolution and suppression, had told Wiley,
    the American Ambassador, that such a bill had been prepared by the Government
    of Hazhir (of which he was also a member) but that the Government had not
    dared to submit it to the Majlis.
29. A move which later provoked Musaddiq to castigate them for their readiness 'to
    dig their graves with their own hands' (press conference given by Musaddiq,
    Bakhtar-i Imruz (Bakhtar), 14 September 1949).
30. Taqizadih's views were expressed in an article in *Ittila'at* published on 1 March
    1949. The approval and support of Hakimi, Sadiq, Sadr and other 'fathers of the
    Constitution' for the Shah's plan was also faithfully aired in the press (*Kayhan*, 26
    February 1949; *Kushish*, 3 March 1949). According to the approved article, the
    Majlis and the Senate, with a two-thirds majority, could independently or
    according to a government proposal vote for the convening of a Constituent
    Assembly; such an assembly would be convened with the approval and the decree
    of the Shah to revise specific articles of the Constitution.
31. Le Rougetel to Bevin, 26 April 1949, FO371 EP75464; *Ittila'at*, 8, 9 May 1949.
32. For instance, articles by Rahmat Mustafavi in *Kayhan*, 10 March 1949, and by
    Arsalan Khal'atbari in *Sitarih*, 1 August 1949.
33. For the texts of the speeches of these deputies, see H. Makki, *Istizah-i Husain
    Makki, Dr. Muzaffar Baqa'i, Abulhasan Ha'irizadih az Daulat-i Sa'id, 1328*
    (Tehran, 1978).
34. Le Rougetel to Bevin, 3 May 1949, FO371 EP75465.
35. Le Rougetel to Bevin, 17 May 1949, FO371 EP75466.
36. Le Rougetel to Bevin, 18 July 1949, *ibid.*
37. For the text of the Agreement, see Norman Kemp, *Abadan* (London, 1953),
    pp. 266–70.
38. Gulsha'iyan's report to a group of politicians, text in H. Makki, *Naft va Nutq-i
    Makki*, pp. 204–12.
39. Makki *et al.*, speeches in the Majlis, 23–6 July 1949, *ibid.*, pp. 223–4.
40. Mu'azzami, speech in the Majlis, *Muzakirat-i Majlis*, 24 July 1949.
41. See further L. P. Elwell-Sutton, *Persian Oil* (London, 1955), pp. 163–84; M.
    Fatih, *op. cit.*, pp. 388–403.
42. Le Rougetel to FO, 16 August 1949, FO371 EP75466.
43. Lawford to FO, 13 October 1949, *ibid.*
44. Lawford to Burrows, 26 September 1949, FO371 EP75500.
45. *Ibid.*; these included men such as Ali Asghar Hikmat, whom Le Rougetel had
    described as 'well disposed to us', and Gulsha'iyan, the Finance Minister, whom
    he had characterized as a man who 'can be relied on not to do anything
    precipitate in matters concerning our interests' (Le Rougetel to Wright, 17
    November 1948, FO371 EP68709).
46. Minute by G. Wheeler, 10 August 1949, FO248 1486.
47. Minute by Jackson, August 1949, *ibid.* Iqbal alluded to the responsibility of the

British and American Embassies in such a development, while professing disbelief at the possibility that the British Embassy had 'deserted' him and Hazhir for Tabataba'i and Hikmat. For Wheeler, however, the move constituted another instance of 'typical' behaviour on the Shah's part (Minute by Wheeler, 20 August 1949, FO248 1846).

48. Announcement by the army's Chief of Staff, 6 September 1949; Iqbal's press conference, *Ittila'at*, 10 September 1949; *ibid.*, 27 September 1949.

49. Musaddiq's press conference, *Shahid*, 12 October 1949; Musaddiq's proclamation, *ibid.*, 13 October 1949.

50. Lawford to FO, 13 October 1949, FO371 EP75466.

51. Of the twenty who took sanctuary, five were journalists, one was a *mullah* and the rest were primarily reformist politicians; among them Amir-Ala'i, Yusuf Mushar, Dr. Karim Sanjabi, Nariman and the journalist. Dr. Husain Fatemi later assumed ministerial portfolios in Musaddiq's Cabinet, while Makki, Baqa'i, Ha'irizadih, Azad and Shayigan were elected or re-elected as Majlis deputies.

52. 'Exchanges between the Shah and the *mutahassinin*' (those taking sanctuary), *Shahid*, 15 October 1949; Hazhir's letter to the *mutahassinin*, *ibid.*, 18 October 1949. Musaddiq's letter to Hazhir, *ibid.*, 19 October 1949; Le Rougetel to Burrows, 24 October 1949, FO371 EP75466.

53. 'Statement of the *mutahassinin* to the nation', *Bakhtar-i Imruz*, 18 October 1949.

54. 'National Front' is not an adequate translation of *Jibhih-yi Milli*, but other renderings such as 'popular' or 'democratic' advocated by Katouzian in *The Political Economy of Iran*, pp. 164–87, are less adequate. In the language of modern Persian political discourse *milli* has a wider meaning than 'national' or 'nationalist'; its meaning varies contextually and can have rightist, conservative, etatist, or leftist, liberal, populist connotations. In the case of Musaddiq and the movement which he led, *milli* distinctly denoted the latter set of meanings; yet the nationalist component was nevertheless predominant. Hence the qualified usage of the term 'National Front' in this book.

55. 'Asasnamih va A'innamih-yi Jibhih-yi Milli', *Bakhtar-i Imruz*, 1 July 1950. See further H. Makki, *Khal'-i Yad*, part 1 (Tehran, 1981), pp. 36–46; Ahmad Maliki, *Tarikhchih-yi Jibhih-yi Milli* (Tehran, 1953).

56. Strong objections to such a move were raised by *Mardum*, the clandestine organ of the banned Tudeh Party; (*Mardum*, 22 October 1949).

57. 'The statement of the *mutahassinin* to the nation', *Bakhtar-i Imruz*, 18 October 1949.

58. The bloodiest of these clashes occurred in the southern city of Lar in which, according to the British consul, about fourteen people were killed (Le Rougetel to FO, 25 October 1949, FO371 EP75466).

59. In Tehran only 15,280 ballots were cast during the Senate elections (*Bakhtar* (*Bakhtar-i Imruz*), 31 August 1949).

60. Le Rougetel to Wright, 15 November 1949, FO371 EP75467. Imami and Tahiri were two of the most influential *mutavallis* who had been prevented by Qavam from resuming their seats in the 15th Majlis, but who had retained their ability to influence factional manoeuvres in the Majlis; hence their inclusion in the Sa'id Government. They resigned their respective positions in late September 1949, being candidates for the 16th Majlis.

61. Minute by L.A., 29 December 1949, FO248 EP1486.

62. For a list of Ashraf's entourage, see Ghani, *Khatirat* (Tehran), p. 244.

63. Le Rougetel to Wright, 18 July 1949, FO371 EP75466. Jam was sent to Rome as Ambassador.
64. *Bakhtar (Bakhtar-i Imruz)*, 5 November 1949. A report in this newspaper reveals the strikingly incompetent medical treatment which Hazhir received during the afternoon of 4 November, when he was shot, and the morning of the next day, when he died. Le Rougetel provided a similar account (Le Rougetel to Bevin, 17 November 1949, FO371 EP75467).
65. Le Rougetel to FO, 7 November 1949, *ibid.*
66. Le Rougetel to FO, 18 November 1949, FO371 EP75468. In a meeting with Le Rougetel the Shah had also described Hazhir as 'a kind of dervish'.
67. Le Rougetel to FO, 7 November 1949, FO371 EP75467.
68. Le Rougetel to FO, 11 November 1949, *ibid.*; *Bakhtar (Bakhtar-i Imruz)*, 9 November 1949.
69. *Bakhtar-i Imruz*, 13 November 1949. In all likelihood Zahidi's putative sympathy for the National Front was inspired more by the Front's hostility to Razmara than by any genuine attachment to its ideals.
70. *Bakhtar-i Imruz*, 8 December 1949.
71. Le Rougetel to Strang, 12 November 1949, FO371 EP75468.
72. Le Rougetel to FO, 1 November 1949, FO371 EP75467; Minute by Leavett, 16 November 1949, FO371 EP75468.
73. Such assumptions had formed part of the Tudeh Party's scheme for the explanation of most events in Iran. *Mardum* even regarded the death of Hazhir as a by-product of Anglo-American imperialist rivalries, and an event arranged by the British to prevent the Shah's journey to the United States (*Mardum*, 13 November 1949).
74. Le Rougetel to FO, 12 November 1949, FO371 EP75468.
75. For an interesting account of the Shah's trip to the United States, see Ghani, *op. cit.*, vol. XI, pp. 6ff.
76. Minute by Leavett, 16 November 1949, FO371 EP75468.
77. Le Rougetel to FO, 18 November 1949, *ibid.*
78. Le Rougetel to Strang, 18 November 1949, *ibid.*
79. FO to Le Rougetel, 17 December 1949, *ibid.*
80. Minute by Leavett, 22 December 1949, *ibid.*
81. Le Rougetel to Wright, 16 December 1949, *ibid.*
82. Minute by Clinton-Thomas, 27 April 1948, FO371 EP68705; Le Rougetel to Bevin, 10 November 1948, FO371 EP68709.
83. Le Rougetel to Bevin, 1 November 1949, FO371 EP75467. The incompatible views of the Shah and Sayyid Zia with regard to the function of royal authority, however, had led Le Rougetel to remark that, despite all his qualities, Sayyid Zia 'may prove to be a bull in a china shop' (Le Rougetel to Wright, 16 December 1949, FO371 EP75468).
84. It had 'already been agreed', wrote a Foreign Office official, that 'the American Ambassador should oppose any suggestion to appoint Qavam' (Minute by Leavett, 22 December 1949, FO371 EP75468).
85. Le Rougetel to Attlee, 1 January 1950, FO371 EP82310.
86. Le Rougetel to FO, 6 January 1950 (monthly report for December 1949), FO371 EP82307.
87. Le Rougetel to FO, 9 January 1950, FO371 EP82310.

88. *Ibid.*
89. Lawford to Bevin, 21 February 1950, *ibid.*
90. Lawford to Bevin, 3 March 1950, *ibid.*
91. In the Senate, more than twelve senators registered their names to speak against the Government and none to speak in its favour (*Bakhtar-i Imruz*, 2 March 1950). Similarly, in the Majlis twelve deputies registered their names in the opposition column (*Bakhtar-i Imruz*, 6 March 1950).
92. Le Rougetel to Wright, 16 December 1949, FO371 EP75468.
93. Le Rougetel to Bevin, 18 February 1950, FO371 EP82310.
94. Minute by Leavett, 17 March 1950, *ibid.* This was a view which few Foreign Office officials could dispute, although it did not persuade them to reconsider their 'firm' position before it was too late.
95. Minute by Rudgeon, 27 March 1950, *ibid..*
96. Le Rougetel to Bevin, 27 January 1949, FO371 EP75464.
97. Le Rougetel to Bevin, 18 November 1949, FO371 EP75468.

15 The Government of Mansur

1. Le Rougetel to Wright, 10 November 1948, FO371 EP68709.
2. Le Rougetel to FO, 26 November 1948, *ibid.*
3. Le Rougetel to Wright, 15 December 1949, FO371 EP75468.
4. Minute by Leavett, 22 December 1949, FO371, *ibid.*
5. Shepherd to FO, 23 April 1950, FO371 EP82310.
6. *Bakhtar-i Imruz*, 13 April 1950.
7. *Ibid.*, 15 April 1950.
8. *Salnamih-yi Dunya*, no. 2 (1946).
9. Report on Personalities in Persia, 1940, FO371 EP24582.
10. *Ibid.*; see also Hidayat, *op. cit.*, p. 416.
11. An editorial written by Baqa'i for his newspaper *Shahid*, had resulted in his arrest (see *Shahid*, 29 December 1949).
12. For Baqa'i's defence, see *Shahid* and *Bakhtar-i Imruz*, 14 January–13 April 1950.
13. *Bakhtar-i Imruz*, 11 April 1950.
14. Shepherd to Younger, 30 May 1950, FO371 EP82311.
15. *Bakhtar-i Imruz*, 19, 22 April 1950.
16. Shepherd to Younger, 22 April 1950, FO371 EP82311.
17. *Bakhtar-i Imruz*, 25 April 1950.
18. *Ibid.*, 25 April 1950.
19. *Ibid.*, 26 April 1950.
20. *Ibid.*, 17 May 1950.
21. Musaddiq, speech in the Majlis, *Muzakirat-i Majlis*, 25 May 1950. On 13 June Musaddiq submitted a bill to the Majlis which demanded that the decisions taken by the Constituent Assembly be declared null and void. Musaddiq's bill was not adopted but his persistent efforts helped to prevent any serious discussion in the Majlis concerning a further increase of royal prerogatives.
22. The speech also received a favourable response in the Senate, where his advice to the Shah was repeated by Senator Khajih-Nuri (*Muzakirat-i Majlis-i Sina*, 31 May 1950).

23. Mansur's reply to Musaddiq, *Muzakirat-i Majlis*, 25 May 1950.
24. Shepherd to Younger, 28 April 1950, FO371 EP82311.
25. Minute by Furlonge, 23 May 1950, FO371 EP82330.
26. For the texts of Qavam's letter and Hakimi's reply, see *Bakhtar-i Imruz*, 8 April 1950. Qavam responded to Hakimi's reply with a further letter, text in *ibid.*, 3 July 1950. He thus proved that his spirit had not been weakened by the threats of royal protégés who vowed to press for the renewal of indictment charges brought against him in the 15th Majlis (speech by Mihdi Pirastih, *Muzakirat-i Majlis*, 9 April 1950).
27. Shepherd to Bevin, 8 April 1950, FO371 EP82310.
28. Shepherd to Younger, 9 June 1950, FO371 EP82330.
29. Shepherd to Younger, 12 June 1950, FO371 EP82311.
30. For instance, while the Shah criticized the existing principles of land ownership, Mansur regarded them as 'very favourable' to the peasantry 'who received 70–75% of the products' (Shepherd to Bevin, 8 April 1950, FO371 EP82311). The Shah's own claims to favour land distribution among the peasants were not sufficiently backed by action: he had told Shepherd that he had transferred 'all the crown lands' to a charitable organization (Shepherd to Bevin, 8 April 1950, FO371 EP82310). Alan Leavett of the Foreign Office, however, noted that 'only a small proportion of the 15% of Persian agricultural land which is the property of the Crown (namely, lands confiscated from private owners by the late Reza Shah) had been transferred to the Imperial Social Services Organisation' (Minute by Leavett, 27 April 1950, FO371 EP82310).
31. Shepherd to Younger, 9 June 1950, FO371 EP82330.
32. Minute by Shepherd, 26 May 1950, FO248 EP1493.
33. Shepherd to Younger, 23 June 1950, FO371 EP82311.
34. Musaddiq, speech in the Majlis, *Muzakirat-i Majlis*, 25 May 1950.
35. Shepherd to Bevin, 8 April 1950, FO371 EP82311.
36. Shepherd to Bevin, 8 April 1950, FO371 EP82310; see also Minute by Furlonge, 23 May 1950, FO371 EP82330.
37. Shepherd to Furlonge, 5 June 1950, FO371 EP82311.
38. *Bakhtar-i Imruz*, 21 June 1950.
39. Minute by Leavett, 15 June 1950, FO371 EP82311.
40. Shepherd to FO, 19 June 1950, *ibid.*
41. Minute by Pyman, 16 June 1950, FO248 EP1493.
42. Précis of message sent to Mr. Northcroft by the Prime Minister through Dr. Jalali, 20 June 1950, text in Isma'il Ra'in (ed.), *Asnad-i Khanih-yi Sidan* (Seddon) (Tehran, 1979), p. 170.
43. Shepherd to Wright, 5 June 1950, FO248 EP1493.
44. Shepherd to FO, 23 March 1950, FO371 EP82310; memorandum by Lawford, *ibid.*
45. Minute by Leavett, 27 April 1950, FO371 EP82311.
46. Besides being a deputy, Dihqan also published the weekly journal *Tehran Musavvar*, as well as managing a playhouse in Tehran; his murder was initially attributed to the Tudeh Party on the basis of 'evidence' given by the assailant. The Chief of the Army's 2nd Bureau, however, told a Reuters correspondent that they 'had not yet finished fabricating the documents' (Shepherd to Furlonge, 5 June 1950, FO371 EP82311).
47. Shepherd to FO, 10 June 1950, *ibid.*

48. *Bakhtar-i Imruz*, 21 June 1950.
49. *Ibid.*, 5 June 1950.
50. Musaddiq, speech in the Majlis, *Muzakirat-i Majlis*, 27 June 1950.
51. Musaddiq contended that the Shah had forced Mansur out of office without even agreeing to offer him the ambassadorship in Rome (*Muzakirat-i Majlis*, 29 June 1950). However, Mansur was eventually sent to Rome as Ambassador.
52. Shepherd to Furlonge, 5 June 1950, FO371 EP82311.
53. Mansur was not deterred by this experience and did not refrain from contesting the premiership later.

16 The Government of Razmara

1. Minute by Lawford, 17 June 1950, FO248 EP1493; Minute by Pyman, 10 June 1950, *ibid.*
2. Frank (Washington) to FO, 19 May 1950, FO371 EP82311.
3. Shepherd to FO, 2 June 1950, *ibid.*
4. Minute by Leavett, 5 June 1950, *ibid.*
5. FO to Washington, 7 June 1950, *ibid.*
6. Minute by Pyman, 5 June, 1950, FO248 1493; Minute by Pyman, 26 June 1950, *ibid.* Shahrukh, along with Dooher of the American Embassy, actively liaised on Razmara's behalf.
7. Shepherd to FO, 19 June 1950, FO371 EP82311.
8. *Ibid.*
9. In a meeting with Lawford of the British Embassy, the Shah 'remarked somewhat petulantly that the people are known to complain that he [the Shah] was a weak man incapable of taking decisions. This time he was going to show them what he could do' (Minute by Lawford, 22 June 1950, FO248 EP1493).
10. Safa'i, *Razmara* (Tehran, 1969), pp. 1–8. Razmara was married to the sister of the prominent writer Sadiq Hidayat. He was called Hajji Ali because he had been born on the eve of Id-i Qurban (Feast of the Sacrifice).
11. Bamdad, *op. cit.*, vol. 1, pp. 302–3.
12. Arfa, *op. cit.*, p. 205.
13. *Ibid.*, p. 327.
14. *Ibid.*, p. 330.
15. Arfa, *op. cit.*, pp. 369–75; interview with Firuz, April 1983.
16. In Arfa's words, 'Razmara was a shrewd and intelligent man who seldom acted on impulse . . . he had . . . much more to gain by showing himself loyal to the monarchy' (Arfa, *op. cit.*, p. 375).
17. MAIS, 13–19 January 1947, FO371 EP61982.
18. Minute by Wheeler, 11 May 1949, FO248 EP1486.
19. Arfa, *op. cit.*, p. 393.
20. Ja'far Sharif-Imami, 'Daulat-i Sipahbud Razmara', *Salnamih-yi Dunya*, no. 19 (1963), pp. 72–5.
21. Minute by Pyman, 20 June 1950, FO248 EP1493; Sipihr, *Maqalat-i Siyasi*, p. 13. In compliance with American wishes, Razmara included in his Cabinet Taqi Nasr, whom the Americans apparently regarded as 'the economic hope of Iran'. This was done at the cost of the removal of Ibtihaj, whose dismissal Nasr

had made a condition of accepting office (John Murray to Logan, August 1951, FO371 EP91462).

22. On the internal organization of Razmara's Cabinet, see further Bihnia, *op. cit.*, pp. 28–37.
23. Shepherd to FO, 27 June 1950, FO371 EP82312.
24. *Bakhtar-i Imruz*, 27 June 1950.
25. Interview with Ha'irizadih, *Khandaniha*, 30 January 1956; Husain Makki, *Khal'-i Yad*, vol. 2, p. 58. He also tried, directly and indirectly, to reach an understanding with Musaddiq, but to no avail (Musaddiq, speech in the Majlis, *Muzakirat-i Majlis*, 20 July 1950).
26. *Bakhtar-i Imruz*, 27 June 1950.
27. Musaddiq, speech in the Majlis, *Muzakirat-i Majlis*, 27 June 1950.
28. Musaddiq, speech in the Majlis, *ibid.*, 4 July 1950.
29. Baqa'i, speech in the Majlis, *ibid.*, 27 June 1950.
30. Senator Nasir Qashqa'i had tried to persuade Kashani not to create any trouble in the event of Razmara's premiership; Dooher had also reportedly arranged a meeting between Kashani and Razmara (Minute by Pyman, 23 June 1950, FO248 EP1493; Minute by Lawford, 17 June 1950, *ibid*).
31. Text in *Bakhtar-i Imruz*, 27 June 1950.
32. *Bakhtar-i Imruz*, 8 July 1950.
33. See further Makki, *Khal'i-Yad*, vol. 2, pp. 73–113.
34. *Bakhtar-i Imruz*, 4 July 1950.
35. *Ibid.*, 10 July 1950.
36. Shepherd to FO, 14 July 1950, FO371 EP82312.
37. Musaddiq, speech in the Majlis, *Muzakirat-i Majlis*, 13, 16 July 1950; Kashani's message, *Bakhtar-i Imruz*, 8 July 1950.
38. Kashani's press conference, *ibid.*, 6 August 1950.
39. Razmara, speech in the Majlis, *Muzakirat-i Majlis*, 7 August 1950.
40. Minute by Barnett, 18 August 1950, FO371 EP82312.
41. The idea of decentralization had other exponents which did not help to make it more acceptable. Sayyid Muhammad Baqir Hijazi, a protégé of Sayyid Zia and editor of the newspaper *Vazifih*, was one example; he had gone so far as to advocate the establishment of a 'federation' with 'autonomous cities' (S. M. B. Hijazi, *Ayandih-yi Iran* (Tehran, 1947), p. 76).
42. *Bakhtar-i Imruz*, 19 August 1950.
43. Shepherd to Bevin, 1 September 1950, FO371 EP82312.
44. Exchanges between Musaddiq and Razmara in the Majlis, *Bakhtar-i Imruz*, 7 September 1950.
45. Text in *Bakhtar-i Imruz*, 7 September 1950. Razmara's bill pointed out that not only had the purge committee limited itself to the investigation of 1000 out of 158,000 government employees, but also that even in these cases the investigations had been conducted improperly, since any dealings with officials such as deputies, senators, senior judges and ministers were subject to specific and special regulations.
46. Hasan Sadr, 'Qanun-i Tasfiyih', *Bakhtar-i Imruz*, 13 August 1950.
47. The Shah told Lawford, the Counsellor of the British Embassy, that if the report of the purge committee resulted in 'unjustifiable expulsions' the victims might join the Tudeh Party (Shepherd to Attlee, 16 September 1950, FO371 EP82312).
48. Imami, speech in the Majlis, *Muzakirat-i Majlis*, 28 September 1950.
49. Razmara, speech in the Majlis, *op. cit.*, 30 September 1950.

50. Influenced by some of his entourage, the Shah also seemed to favour its 'postponement' or abandonment in favour of municipal councils (Shepherd to Bevin, 4 December 1950, FO371 EP82313). However, Razmara pledged not to abandon the idea as long as he lived (press conference, *Bakhtar-i Imruz*, 9 November 1950).

51. Minute by Pyman, 14 February 1951, FO248 EP1514.

52. Minute by Pyman, 9 February 1951; Minute by Pyman, 25 January 1951, *ibid.*

53. Minute by Pyman, 25 January 1951, *ibid.*

54. Embassy minute, 9 August 1950, FO248 EP1493.

55. Minute by Pyman, 10 June 1950, *ibid.*; Minute by Pyman, 26 June 1950, *ibid.*

56. Matin-Daftari, speech in the Senate, *Muzakirat-i Sina*, 8 July 1950; Hidayati, speech in the Majlis, *Muzakirat-i Majlis*, 17 October 1950.

57. *Bakhtar-i Imruz*, 9 January 1951.

58. Shepherd to Bevin, 16 October 1950, FO371 EP82313.

59. Jamal Imami, speech in the Majlis, *Muzakirat-i Majlis*, 26 November 1950.

60. Shepherd to Morrison, 2 May 1951, FO371 EP91467.

61. *Bakhtar-i Imruz*, 4 March 1951.

62. Najm, speech in the Senate, *Muzakirat-i Sina*, 3 March 1951.

63. Shepherd to Bevin, 17 December 1950, FO371 EP82313.

64. The article added that his term of office was 'a period unfortunate for American imperialist ascendency in Iran' ('Mysterious doings in Iran', *Pravda*, 18 March 1951); Chancery (Moscow) to FO, 20 March 1951, FO371 EP91454. For a translation of this article see *Ittila'at*, 19 March 1951.

65. *Bakhtar-i Imruz*, 7 November 1950.

66. Minute by Furlonge, 5 January 1951, FO371 EP82313. Shepherd confessed to having met him six times during the last weeks of his life (Shepherd to Bowker, 12 March 1951, FO371 EP91454).

67. Minute by Barnett, 31 August 1950, FO371 EP82312.

68. Minute by Furlonge, 11 August 1950, FO371 EP82375.

69. Musaddiq had been elected Chairman of this committee on 26 June 1950, soon after it had been formed and on the same day as Razmara had assumed office.

70. *Bakhtar-i Imruz*, 2–19 October 1950.

71. *Ibid.*, 18 October 1950.

72. Razmara, speech in the Majlis, *Muzakirat-i Majlis*, 19 October 1950.

73. *Bakhtar-i Imruz*, 25 November 1950.

74. *Ibid.*; Kashani's proclamation, text in *Bakhtar-i Imruz*, 13 December 1950. Several other *ayatullahs*, including Sayyid Muhammad Taqi Khansari, issued *fatvas* in favour of nationalization, texts in *Bakhtar-i Imruz*, 27, 28 January, 15 February 1951.

75. Furuhar, speech in the Majlis, *Muzakirat-i Majlis*, 26 December 1950. See also *Kayhan*, 26, 28 December 1950.

76. *Bakhtar-i Imruz*, 31 December 1950.

77. Safa'i, *op. cit.*, p. 26.

78. *Bakhtar-i Imruz*, 18 January 1951. Jazayiri himself resigned on 23 January.

79. Gass argued that the Agreement had a chance of approval if the Government 'defended it collectively', and Northcroft blamed Razmara for not having 'taken a stronger line with the Majlis', as well as for not having 'properly organized his majority' (meeting at the Foreign Office, 16 January 1951, FO371 EP91524).

80. Minute by Furlonge, 5 January 1951, FO371 EP91452.

81. Minute by Furlonge, 5 January 1951, *ibid.*

82. Shepherd to Bevin, 31 December 1950, *ibid.*
83. Minute by Logan, 29 January 1951, FO371 EP91452.
84. Minute by Fry, 30 January 1951, *ibid.*
85. Minute by Pyman, 14 February 1951, FO248 EP1514.
86. Shepherd to FO, 19 February 1951, FO371 EP91452
87. The advocacy of some form of 50:50 arrangement in Iran well preceded the Aramco–Saudi agreement. See, for instance, Kazim Hasibi, 'Muqayisih-yi Qarardad-i Naft-i Iran ba Qarardadha-yi Khavar-i Miyanih', *Shahid*, 2, 3 September 1950.
88. Shepherd to FO, 11 February 1951, FO371 EP91522.
89. The short-sighted rigidity of the AIOC had been rigorously criticized by its labour adviser, Sir Frederick Legget, who advocated a 50:50 profit-sharing arrangement based on the equal partnership of both parties (Minute by Fry, 6 February 1951, *ibid.*). Such voices, however, were rarely heard.
90. Shepherd to FO, 21 February 1951, FO371 EP91522.
91. For Iranian objections to the 1933 and the Supplemental Oil Agreements, see K. Hasibi, 'Chira Millat-i Iran Qarardad-i 1933 ra bih Rasmiyyat Nimishinasad', *Shahid*, 7 November, 13, 17, 22, 28 December 1949. See also Fatih, *op. cit.*, pp. 413–56.
92. Shepherd to FO, 21 February 1951, FO371 EP91522.
93. FO to Tehran, 23 February 1951, *ibid.*
94. Minute by Fry, 30 January 1951, FO371 EP82313.
95. As Middleton later observed, Razmara 'was manoeuvring himself into a position in which to make best use of the fifty–fifty offer when he was murdered' (Middleton to Eden, 22 February 1952, FO371 EP98596).
96. Minute by Logan, 7 March 1951, FO371 EP82313.
97. The extent of Razmara's unpopularity can be gauged by the fact that, although at least two prominent *mullahs* were among the circle of his close friends (Sipihr, *op. cit.*, p. 13), apparently no *mullah* agreed to deliver a sermon at his funeral (*Asr*, 11 March 1951).
98. A. Khal'atbari, 'Agar Razmara An Namih-ra Ifsha Mikard, Kushtih Nimishud', *Khandaniha*, 22 April 1955. See also Sipihr, *op. cit.*, pp. 9–17; Fatih, *op. cit.*, pp. 404–8.
99. Minute by Pyman, 28 July 1950, FO248 EP1493.
100. Minute by Pyman, 20 June 1950, *ibid.*
101. Minute by Pyman, 15 March 1950, *ibid.*
102. Embassy minute, 25 October 1950, *ibid.*
103. Minute by Pyman, 30 June 1950, *ibid.*
104. Minute by Pyman, 30 September 1950, *ibid.*
105. Minute by Pyman, 3 July 1950, *ibid.* Among his collaborators were Saham ud-Din Ghaffari (Muhandis ul-Mamalik), a Minister in Qavam's last Cabinet, Jamshid Mufakhkham, a senior official of the Finance Ministry, and Nur ud-Din Alamuti, a judge and ex-member of the Tudeh Party.
106. *Ibid.*
107. Minute by Pyman, 7 July 1950, *ibid.*
108. Minute by Pyman, 3 July 1950, *ibid.*
109. Minute by Pyman, 12 October 1950, *ibid.*
110. Minute by Shepherd, 26 May 1950, and 11 December 1950, FO248 EP1493.
111. Minute by Shepherd, 6 February 1951, *ibid.*

112. The Shah's speech on the occasion of convening the Senate, text in *Bakhtar-i Imruz*, 7 October 1950; Makki, speech in the Majlis, *ibid.*, 19 October 1950.
113. Shepherd to Bevin, 19 January 1951, FO371 EP82313.
114. Minute by Pyman, 24 January 1951, FO248 EP1514.
115. Minute by Pyman, 27 March 1950, FO248 EP1493.
116. Minute by Pyman, 25 August 1950, *ibid.*
117. Minute by Pyman, 24 January 1951, EP1514. Following disorder during the wedding of the Shah and his second wife on 13 February 1951, Hakimi (the Court Minister) resigned and was replaced by Ala (*Bakhtar-i Imruz*, 13, 20, 24 February 1951). Ala, who had long been expected to replace Hakimi, was believed not to favour Razmara. However, Razmara did not remain in office long enough to be affected by this.
118. Minute by Shepherd, 11 December 1950, FO248 EP1493. Sayyid Zia asserted, for instance, that almost all members of Sa'id's Cabinet had been nominated by the Shah, who had thus weakened the Cabinet from 'its inception'.
119. Minute by Pyman, 5 August 1950, *ibid.*
120. Minute by Pyman, 17 August 1950, *ibid.*
121. Minute by Pyman, 25 August 1950, *ibid.*
122. *Sitarih*, 30 June 1950.
123. Baqa'i, speech in the Majlis, *Muzakirat-i Majlis*, 27 June 1950.
124. Minute by Pyman, 3 October 1950, FO248 EP1493.
125. Minute by Pyman, 16 January 1951, FO248 EP1514.
126. Minute by Pyman, 17 August 1950, FO248 EP1493.
127. Minute by Pyman, 25 August 1950, *ibid.*
128. Minute by Jackson, 30 August 1951, FO248 EP1514.
129. Minute by Pyman, 17 August 1950, FO248 EP1493.
130. Minute by Pyman, 9 January 1951, FO248 EP1514.
131. Minute by Pyman, 1 March 1951, *ibid.*
132. H. Katouzian, *The Political Economy of Iran*, p. 163, n.23.
133. Minute by Jackson, 14 June 1951, FO248 EP1514. A number of Razmara's associates were arrested on the grounds of complicity in the intended coup (*Bakhtar-i Imruz*, 18 September 1951).
134. On the eve of his assumption of office Razmara had asked the British and American representatives to express their support for his Government publicly. They confined themselves to giving guidance to the press in its coverage of the new Prime Minister but refused to make any formal statement, wishing to avoid openly creating an image of Razmara as an Anglo-American candidate (FO to Washington, 27 June 1950, FO371 EP82312).

17 The Government of Ala

1. Shepherd to FO, 7 March 1951, FO371 EP91453.
2. FO to Tehran, 9 March 1951, *ibid.*
3. FO to Washington, 8 March 1951, *ibid.*
4. Steel (Washington) to FO, 9 March 1951, *ibid.*
5. Shepherd to Bowker, 12 March 1951, FO371 EP91454.

6. *Ibid.*
7. *Bakhtar-i Imruz*, 12 March 1951.
8. In 1931 the British were unwilling to accept him 'on the grounds that his attitude in reporting a libel on His Majesty King George V rendered it difficult to suppose that he was then animated by friendly sentiments' (Report on Personalities in Persia, 1940, FO371 EP24582).
9. *Ibid.*
10. *Ibid.*
11. Ala's letter to Ghani, 12 February 1949, text in Ghani, *op. cit.*, vol. IX, pp. 563–6.
12. Musaddiq, speech in the Majlis, *Muzakirat-i Majlis*, 12 April 1951; Ghani, who knew Ala intimately, did not dispute his integrity but regarded him as gullible, unsophisticated, naive and even stupid. See, for instance, Ghani, *op. cit.* vol. XI, p. 28.
13. *Bakhtar-i Imruz*, 18 March 1951.
14. Shepherd handed Ala a note which deprecated nationalization and expressed the Company's readiness to negotiate 'a still more generous basis of payments to the Persian Government'. Ala had apparently promised, but failed, to deliver this note to the Majlis prior to its adoption of the nationalization principle (Shepherd to FO, 28 March 1951, FO371 EP91454).
15. Shepherd to FO, 14 March 1951, FO371 EP91524; Shepherd to FO, 16 March 1951, FO371 EP91453.
16. Shepherd to FO, 28 March 1951, FO371 EP91454.
17. Minute by Furlonge, 20 March 1951, FO371 EP91524.
18. *Ibid.*
19. Shepherd to FO, 18 March 1951, FO371 EP91542.
20. Shepherd to Morrison, 3 April 1951, FO371 EP91455.
21. Shepherd to Morrison, 19 March 1951, FO371 EP91524; Embassy minute, 21 March 1951, FO248 EP1514.
22. National Front's proclamation, *Bakhtar-i Imruz*, 29 March 1951; the Persian solar year 1329 was a leap year; therefore, the year after (1 Farvardin–28 Isfand 1330) corresponds to 22 March 1951–20 March 1952. In converting dates in this particular year (1330) this must be borne in mind.
23. Shepherd to FO, 27 March 1951, FO371 EP91454.
24. *Bakhtar-i Imruz*, 16, 17 April 1951.
25. Shepherd to FO, 5 April 1951, FO371 EP91455.
26. Musaddiq, speech in the Majlis, *Muzakirat-i Majlis*, 12 April 1951; there were, however, dissenting voices in the National Front, notably Mahmud Nariman and Ali Shayigan, who were inclined to oppose Ala.
27. See further Elwell-Sutton, *op. cit.*, pp. 209–13; Fatih, *op. cit.*, p. 409.
28. Shepherd to FO, 15 April 1951, FO371 EP91455; Furlonge to Burrows, 25 April 1951, FO371 EP91456.
29. Shepherd to FO, 16 April 1951, FO371 EP91455.
30. Shepherd to FO, 15 April 1951, *ibid.*
31. *Bakhtar-i Imruz*, 15 April 1951; Bagley to Shepherd, 17 April 1951, FO371 EP91458.
32. Elwell-Sutton, *op. cit.*, pp. 213–14.
33. Frank (Washington) to FO, 12 April 1951, FO371 EP91455.
34. Shepherd to FO, 13 April 1951, 35. Shepherd to FO, 19 April 1951, FO371 EP91456.

35. Shepherd to FO, 19 April 1951, FO371 EP91456.
36. Ala to Shepherd, 22 April 1951, *ibid.*
37. Shepherd to FO, 7 March 1951, FO371 EP91453.
38. Shepherd to FO, 9 March 1951, *ibid.*
39. Minute by Pyman, 19 March 1951, FO248 EP1514. The sum of £5 million had presumably been paid to Razmara's Government.
40. Minute by Pyman, 19 March 1951, *ibid.*
41. *Ibid.*
42. Minute by Pyman, 28 December 1950, FO248 EP1493; Minute by Pyman, 19 February 1951, FO248 EP1514.
43. Minute by Jackson, 10 January 1951, *ibid.*
44. Minute by Logan, 2 April 1951, *ibid.*
45. Shepherd to FO, 7 March 1951, FO371 EP91453; Shepherd to FO, 21 March 1951, FO371 EP91454.
46. Musaddiq, speech in the Majlis, *Muzakirat-i Majlis*, 12 April 1951.
47. A charge levelled against him by Farrukh in the Senate publicly signified that the Court had as yet not extended its favour to Qavam (*Bakhtar-i Imruz*, 21 April 1951).
48. Washington to FO, 16 April 1951, FO371 EP91453.
49. FO to Washington, 18 March 1951, *ibid.*
50. Frank (Washington) to FO, 16 April 1951, FO371 EP91455; Frank to FO, 17 April 1951, FO371 EP91456.
51. Frank (Washington) to FO, 16 April 1951, FO371 EP91455.
52. FO to Washington, 17 April 1951, *ibid.*
53. Minute by Logan, *ibid.*
54. For instance, in response to Ashtianizadih's frequent requests for 'instructions' from the Embassy, he was told that he could oppose Ala, who, in any event, was not expected to last long (Minute by Hillier-Fry, 6 April 1951, FO248 EP1514). Ashtianizadih launched his attack against Ala the next day (*Muzakirat-i Majlis*, 7 April 1951).
55. Shepherd to FO, 21 April 1951, FO371 EP91456.
56. Shepherd to FO, 28 April 1951, *ibid.*
57. Shepherd to FO, 16 April 1951, FO371 EP91453.

18 The first Government of Musaddiq

1. Shepherd to FO, 28 April 1951, FO371 EP91456; Musaddiq, speech in the Majlis, *Muzakirat-i Majlis*, 12 May 1951.
2. Musaddiq, speech in the Majlis, *Muzakirat-i Majlis* 11 April 1951. Prior to Razmara's death, Imami had, on behalf of the Shah, invited Musaddiq to form a Cabinet; Musaddiq had proved unfavourable and Imami scarcely expected him to have undergone a total change of heart. See Musaddiq, *Khatirat va Ta'allumat-i Duktur Muhammad Musaddiq* (Tehran, 1986), p. 178.
3. Iraj Afshar (ed.), *Taqrirat-i Musaddiq dar Zindan*, recorded by J. Buzurgmihr (Tehran, 1980), pp. 120–1.
4. *Bakhtar-i Imruz*, 28 April 1951.
5. Shepherd to FO, 29 April 1951, FO371 EP91456.
6. Shepherd to FO, 1 May 1951, *ibid.*

7. Minute by Hillier-Fry, 3 May 1951, FO248 1514.
8. *Bakhtar-i Imruz*, 29 April 1951.
9. Shepherd to FO, 28 April 1951, FO371 EP91456; Shepherd to FO, 29 April 1951, *ibid.*
10. See further Bahram Afrasiabi, *Musaddiq va Tarikh* (Tehran, 1981); Ali Janzadih, *Musaddiq* (Tehran, 1979); Anon, *Musaddiq va Nahzat-i Milli-yi Iran* (n.p., 1978).
11. For a crude attempt to show the contrary, however, see Dr. Bahman Isma'ili, *Zindiginamih-yi Musaddiq us-Saltanih* (n.p., n.d.); see also Sayyid Hasan Ayat, *Chihrih-yi Haqiqi-yi Musaddiq us-Saltanih* (Qum, 1981), pp. 26–78.
12. Editorial, *Bakhtar-i Imruz*, 3 May 1951. This newspaper had become the organ of the National Front and its editor, Dr. Husain Fatimi, soon became Musaddiq's political and parliamentary Under-Secretary.
13. *Bakhtar-i Imruz*, 6 May 1951; *ibid.*, 8 May 1951.
14. Azad, speech in the Majlis, *Muzakirat-i Majlis*, 10 June 1951; see also *Khandaniha*, 18 January 1956. Azad's increasingly hostile attitude not only resulted in his own expulsion from the National Front, but even provoked Musaddiq to state that he himself could no longer belong to it. This was not then taken seriously (Makki, *Khal'-i Yad*, vol. II, pp. 230–1). It revealed Musaddiq's pessimism about the possibility of relying on the National Front as an adequate source of support.
15. Musaddiq, 'Message to the nation', text in *Bakhtar-i Imruz*, 30 April 1951.
16. Musaddiq, speech in the Majlis, *Muzakirat-i Majlis*, 13 May 1951.
17. Ashtianizadih, speech in the Majlis, *ibid.*, 14 May 1951.
18. Tahir Ahmadzadih, 'Tahlili az Nahzat-i Milli', text in Afrasiabi, *op. cit.*, p. 313. See further Khushniyyat, *op. cit.*, p. 83; Muhammad Turkaman, *Tashannujat, Dargiriha-yi Khiyabani va Tauti'ihha* (Tehran, 1980), pp. 90–108.
19. Gandy to Logan, 11 June 1951, FO371 EP91460.
20. See, for instance, Fatih, *op. cit.*, p. 523.
21. Fergusson to Stokes, 3 October 1951, FO371 EP19607.
22. These views were also widely propagated in the British press. See further Hamid Enayat, 'The British Public Opinion and the Persian Oil Crisis' (M.Sc. dissertation, London University, 1958).
23. See further Elwell-Sutton, *op. cit.*, pp. 228–32; Fatih, *op. cit.*, pp. 528–34. The former work provides a passionate account and a moral indictment of British policy.
24. Shepherd to FO, 22 June 1951, FO371 EP91460.
25. *Bakhtar-i Imruz*, 21–3 June 1951.
26. *Ibid.*, 17 July 1951.
27. *Mardum*, 21 July 1951.
28. See further Turkaman, *op. cit.*, pp. 111–58; see also F. M. Javanshir, *Tajribbih-yi 28 Murdad* (Tehran, 1980), pp. 132–44. This latter book provides not only a typical Tudeh Party post-eventum apologia but, omitting inconvenient facts, claims that the Tudeh Party was truly on Musaddiq's side. For a further apologetic account on behalf of the Tudeh Party, see Rasul Mihrban, *Gushihha'i az Tarikh-i Mu'asir-i Iran* (n.p., 1982). For an interesting and informative account of Musaddiq–Tudeh relations in particular and the Musaddiq era in general, see Arsalan Puria, *Karnamih-yi Musaddiq va Hizb-i Tudeh*, 2 vols (Florence, n.d.). See also Zabih, *op. cit.*, pp. 166–207.
29. Musaddiq, speech in the Majlis, *Muzakirat-i Majlis*, 9 September 1951.

30. Speeches by Jamal Imami, Imad Turbati and Azad, *Muzakirat-i Majlis*, 17 July 1951.
31. Memorandum by Ramsbotham, 30 July 1951, FO371 EP91575.
32. Musaddiq, report to the Majlis, *Muzakirat-i Majlis*, 22 August 1951; Musaddiq, speech in the Majlis, *ibid.*, 9 September 1951.
33. Stokes to Morrison, 6 September 1951, FO371 EP91591.
34. Stokes to Younger, 24 September 1951, *ibid.*; Stokes to Morrison, 8 October 1951, FO371 EP91590.
35. Musaddiq, report to the Majlis, *Muzakirat-i Majlis*, 22 August 1951.
36. *Bakhtar-i Imruz*, 22 August 1951.
37. Shepherd to FO, 29 August 1951, FO371 EP91462.
38. FO to Tehran, 30 August 1951, *ibid.*
39. Musaddiq, speech in the Senate, *Muzakirat-i Sina*, 5 September 1951.
40. FO Minute (undated), FO371 EP91464.
41. Shepherd to FO, 18 September 1951, FO371 EP91433.
42. Elwell-Sutton, *op. cit.*, p. 256.
43. Shepherd to FO, 19 September 1951, FO371 EP91433.
44. See further Makki, *Khal'-i Yad*, Part II; Fatih, *op. cit.*, pp. 561–8: Elwell-Sutton, *op. cit.*, p. 255–7.
45. See further Wm. Roger Louis, *op. cit.*, pp. 657–78.
46. Minute by Logan, 9 July 1951, FO371 EP91461.
47. Minute by Berthoud, 15 June 1951, FO371 EP91548.
48. *Ibid.*
49. See further C. M. Woodhouse, *Something Ventured* (London, 1982), pp. 105–35.
50. Minute by Hillier-Fry, 6 July 1951, FO248 1514.
51. A. Maliki, *op. cit.*, pp. 6–8.
52. Minute by Zaehner, 3 May 1952, FO248 1531.
53. Minute by Pyman, 19 December 1951, FO248 1514; Minute by Jackson, 21 December 1951, *ibid.*
54. Jamal Imami, speeches in the Majlis, *Muzakirat-i Majlis*, 22, 25 September 1951. For Musaddiq's own account of the activities of his parliamentary opponents, see Musaddiq, *Khatirat*, pp. 246–50.
55. Minute by Pyman, 11 July 1951, FO248 1514; Minute by Pyman, 13 September 1951, *ibid.*
56. Minute by Pyman, 20 September 1951, *ibid.*
57. Minute by Hillier-Fry, 12 July 1951, *ibid.*; Minute by Pyman, 13 September 1951, *ibid.*; Minute by Pyman, 28 August 1951, *ibid.*; Minute by Pyman, 30 August 1951, *ibid.*
58. FO Minute, 29 August 1951, FO371 EP91462.
59. Minute by Pyman, 29 August 1951, *ibid.*; Minute by Pyman, 5 September 1951, *ibid.*; Minute by Pyman, 30 August 1951, *ibid.*; Minute by Pyman, 19 December 1951, *ibid.*
60. Minute by Pyman, 8 September 1951, *ibid.*; Minute by Jackson, 13 December 1951, *ibid.*
61. Makki, *Si-yi Tir* (Tehran, 1981), p. 73 n.
62. Shepherd to Morrison, 16 July 1951, FO371 EP91462; Shepherd to FO, 15 September 1951, FO371 EP91463. For Sayyid Zia's inaugural speech on the occasion of relaunching his party, see *Nahzat*, 14 September 1951.
63. Minute by Pyman, 8 September 1951, FO248 1415.

64. Minute by Pyman, 27 August 1951, *ibid.*
65. Minute by Pyman, 11 July 1951, *ibid.*
66. Minute by Pyman, 15 September 1951, *ibid.*; Minute by Pyman, 17 September 1951, *ibid.*
67. Minute by Pyman, 18 December 1951, *ibid.*
68. Minute by Pyman, 17 September 1951, *ibid.*
69. Minute by Middleton, 18 September 1951, *ibid.*
70. Minute by Rothnie, 5 September 1951, FO371 EP91462.
71. Shepherd to FO, 4 September 1951, FO371 EP91463. See further Shepherd, 'A comparison between Persian and Asian nationalism', 11 October 1951, FO371 EP91464.
72. Wheeler's letter, 29 October 1951, *ibid.*
73. Minute by Sarell, 13 February 1952, FO371 EP98596.
74. Minute by Pyman, 22 September 1951, FO248 1514.
75. The Shah later told Nikpay that 'the British know that Sayyid Zia is unpopular; they want to make me champion his cause so that I shall be unpopular too, and then they will be able to get rid of me' (Minute by Pyman, 21 January 1952, FO248 1532).
76. Bowker to Attlee, 2 September 1951, FO371 EP91463.
77. Prime Minister to Strang, 3 September 1951, *ibid.*
78. Frank (Washington) to FO, 4 September 1951, FO371 EP91462.
79. Shepherd to FO, 12 September 1951, FO371 EP91463.
80. Shepherd to Morrison, 16 July 1951, FO371 EP91462. Minute by Zaehner, 12 November 1951, FO248 1914.
81. Minute by Hillier-Fry, 30 March 1951, *ibid.*
82. Minute by Zaehner, 21 September 1951, *ibid.*
83. Minute by Pyman, 19 December 1951, FO248 1514.
84. Minute by Zaehner, 27 August 1951, *ibid.*
85. Shepherd to Morrison, 2 July 1951, FO371 EP91461.
86. Minute by Pyman, 25 September 1951, FO248 1514.
87. A committee composed of Hikmat, Tahiri, Nikpur and Abkar had been established to 'handle such funds' (Minute by Jackson, 21 December 1951, *ibid.*).
88. Minute by Pyman, 20 September 1951, *ibid.*; Minute by Pyman, 22 September 1951, *ibid.*; Minute by Pyman, 26 September 1951, *ibid.*
89. Such activities did not go unnoticed by the National Front; see, for instance, *Shahid*, 18, 19 November 1951.
90. Minute by Jackson, 22 October 1951, FO248 1514. Burujirdi had earlier sent a message to the Shah saying that Musaddiq's Government had 'his entire support' (Minute by Pyman, 1 October 1951, *ibid.*).
91. Referring to Qavam, the Shah told Sayyid Zia: 'There is no harm in his trying and letting himself in for a bit of abuse into the bargain.' The Shah, however, had also instructed Perron 'to assure' Qavam of his 'appui' (Minute by Zaehner, 12 November 1951, *ibid.*).
92. Minute by Zaehner, 12 November 1951, *ibid.*
93. Minute by Pyman, 5 November 1951, *ibid.*
94. Middleton to FO, 16 November 1951, FO371 EP91465. According to Middleton the figure 25:75 was submitted for bargaining purposes and what Qavam actually had in mind was a 50:50 arrangement.

95. Middleton to Furlonge, 19 November 1951, FO248 1514.
96. Musaddiq, *Taqrirat*, p. 133.
97. Minute by Shepherd, 6 July 1951, FO248 1514.
98. Minute by Jackson, 1 October 1951, *ibid.*
99. Minute by Zaehner, 3 May 1952, FO248 1531.
100. The statement of the opposition, text in *Bakhtar-i Imruz*, 30 September 1951.
101. Ha'irizadih, speech in the Majlis, *Muzakirat-i Majlis*, 2 August 1951.
102. Matin-Daftari, speeches in the Senate, *Muzakirat-i Sina*, 4, 8 August 1951.
103. Makki, interview in *Bakhtar-i Imruz*, 17 October 1951. Speech in the Majlis, *Muzakirat-i Majlis*, 1 November 1951. Farhudi informed Pyman that Makki was 'extremely discontented' and that he would support Kazimi; he (Makki) also had 'excellent' relations with Sayyid Zia, and had expressed his willingness, through Farhudi, to re-establish contact with Pyman (Minute by Pyman, 15 October 1951, FO248 1514).
104. Minute by Pyman, 29 October 1951, *ibid.*
105. Jamal Imami, speech in the Majlis, *Muzakirat-i Majlis*, 11 November 1951.
106. See, for example, Shushtari, speech in the Majlis, *Muzakirat-i Majlis*, 2 October 1951. The opposition had also not hesitated to raise hopes about Musaddiq's achievement at the UN, so that his failure could then become more exploitable on his return. For an illuminating account of Musaddiq's negotiations with the American officials in the course of this trip, see George McGhee, *Envoy to the Middle World: Adventures in Diplomacy* (New York, 1983), pp. 388–404.
107. Musaddiq's report to the Majlis, *Muzakirat-i Majlis*, 25 November 1951; Musaddiq's speech, *ibid.*
108. *Bakhtar-i Imruz*, 25 November 1951. Jamal Imami strongly attacked Musaddiq and expressed his repentence and regret at having suggested him for office and denied his success at the UN (speech in the Majlis, *Muzakirat-i Majlis*, 25 November 1951).
109. *Bakhtar-i Imruz*, 26 November 1951.
110. Minute by Hillier-Fry, 31 October 1951, FO248 1514.
111. Minute by Pyman, 20 September 1951, *ibid.*; Minute by Pyman, 25 September 1951, *ibid.*; Minute by Pyman, 21 October 1951, *ibid.*
112. *Bakhtar-i Imruz*, 26 November 1951.
113. Minute by Shepherd, 22 September 1951, FO248 1514. Taqizadih's position led Sipihr, for instance, to describe him as not being a friend of Britain and to assert that 'Taqizadih recognized that he had burned his boats by his untruthful and pusillanimous statements at the inception of the agitation against the 1933 Oil Agreement, and he therefore felt that he had nothing further to hope for in the way of British assistance in his political career' (Minute by Jackson, 13 December 1951, FO248 1514).
114. Text in *Bakhtar-i Imruz*, 28 September 1951.
115. Middleton to FO, 28 November 1951, FO371 EP91465.
116. Minute by Zaehner, 1 October 1951, FO248 1514.
117. Gass to Bowker, 3 December 1951, FO371 EP91464.
118. Minute by Zaehner, 28 November 1951, FO248 1514.
119. Middleton to FO, 28 November 1951, FO371 EP91465.
120. FO to Tehran, 4 December 1951, *ibid.*
121. Middleton to Eden, 10 December 1951, FO371 EP91466. Report of the Special

Governmental Committee of Inquiry: text in *Bakhtar-i Imruz*, 31 December 1951.

122. *Kayhan*, 6 December 1951.
123. According to the British Embassy, from early July to mid-December 1951, out of seventeen anti-Government demonstrations, at least fourteen were organized by the Tudeh Party (Embassy Minute, December 1951, FO248 1531).
124. 'Hukumat-i Dr. Musaddiq', *Mardum*, 5 May 1951.
125. These events were referred to by the Tudeh Party as 'the most shameful fascist stain' in Iranian history ('I'lamiyyih-yi Kumitih-yi Markazi-yi Hizb-i Tudeh-yi Iran', *Arzish-i Kar*, December 25 1951).
126. *Dad*, 9 December 1951.
127. Speeches by Jamal Imami, Azad, Ashtianizadih, *Muzakirat-i Majlis*, 9 December 1951.
128. Musaddiq, speech in the Majlis, *ibid.*, 11 December 1951.
129. *Bakhtar-i Imruz*, 12, 13 December 1951.
130. Middleton to FO, 13 December 1951, FO371 EP91466; Middleton to Bowker, 17 December 1951, FO371 EP98595.
131. Middleton to Bowker, 17 December 1951, *ibid.*
132. *Iran-i Ma*, 21 December 1951.
133. Deputies such as Ashtianizadih and Azad also tried to dissociate themselves from the right-wing, anti-Musaddiq opposition. Ashtianizadih, interview, *Bakhtar-i Imruz*, 22 December 1951; Azad, interview, *ibid.*, 8 January 1952. Deputy Malik-Madani, however, who was unjustifiably regarded as a British tool, had continued to support Musaddiq.
134. Minute by Pyman, 2 January 1952, FO248 1531; Minute by Pyman, 27 January 1952, *ibid.*; Minute by Pyman, 22 April 1952, *ibid.*
135. *Bakhtar-i Imruz*, 19 December 1951; the insulting of Kashani by a few deputies was given as the reason.
136. See further Makki, *Si-yi Tir*, p. 61.
137. Shepherd, who was recalled from Iran in late January 1952, predicted that Musaddiq would stay in power and thus the Tudeh Party's 'prospect of bringing about a successful coup some months after the opening of the 17th Majlis would appear to be considerable' (Shepherd to Strang, 21 January 1952, FO371 EP98596).
138. Musaddiq, *Taqrirat*, pp. 122–5.
139. *Tulu'*, 23 January 1953.
140. Minute by Pyman, 7 February 1952, FO248 1531. Pyman had even heard from Ali Dashti that Jamal Imami was 'patching up some sort of truce with Musaddiq'.
141. Against royal resistance he successfully dismissed Iqbal, who had been Governor-General of Azarbaijan since August 1950. This, in Shepherd's view, was another victory over the Shah, while the British lost 'not only a personal friend but also a bulwark against the growth of communism' (Shepherd to Younger, 24 September 1951, FO371 EP91464).
142. Musaddiq, letter to the deputies, text in *Bakhtar-i Imruz*, 30 April 1952.
143. General Vusuq, who was then Commander of the gendarmerie, asserted that on his own personal initiative he had ordered the prevention by 'whatever means' of the election of anti-regime and leftist candidates, among others (Vusuq, *op. cit.*, p. 97).
144. A. Maliki, *op. cit.*, pp. 118–19; Minute by Falle, 4 May 1952, FO242 1531.

Ha'irizadih demanded that the Government aid the election of his protégés from Yazd by preventing the election of Tahiri and his friends.

145. Minute by Jackson, 19 May 1952, FO248 1531.
146. A. Maliki, *op. cit.*, pp. 46–7; Fatimi 'Khatirat' text in Afrasiabi, *op. cit.*, pp. 352–71.
147. *Bakhtar-i Imruz*, 14 January 1952.
148. For instance, Ibrahim Karimabadi, leader of the teahouse owners' guild who lost the Gulpayigan elections to Mu'azzami, reportedly deserted Musaddiq and joined Qavam's camp (Minute by Jackson, 20 February 1952, FO248 1531).
149. *Bih Su-yi Ayandih*, 12 February 1952.
150. Minute by Pyman, 27 January 1952, FO248 1531.
151. Minute by Pyman, 17 January 1952, *ibid.*
152. Minute by Pyman, 7 January 1952, *ibid.*
153. Minute by Pyman, 7 January 1952, *ibid.*
154. Minute by Pyman, 17 January 1952, *ibid.*
155. Pyman to Ross, 3 March 1952, FO371 EP98596.
156. Press interview by Bushihri (the Government spokesman), *Bakhtar-i Imruz*, 20 March 1952.
157. Middleton to Ross, 18 April 1952, FO371 EP98599.
158. Minute by Zaehner, 16 February 1952, FO248 1531; Turkaman, *op. cit.*, pp. 90–108.
159. Maliki, *op. cit.*, p. 72.
160. Khushniyyat, *op. cit.*, pp. 83–8.
161. Reported instances of the activities of the Bihbahanis include: in order to undermine the moderating influences in the Court, Ja'far Bihbahani reportedly told Ala, causing him great fear, that the Fida'iyan were bent on assassinating him because he had told the Shah that 'vox populi' was fully behind Musaddiq (Minute by Jackson, 5 March 1952, FO248 1531); Sayyid Muhammad Reza Bihbahani emphatically asked the British Embassy to make him the 'head of the religious bequests' so that he could use that position to fight Musaddiq and communism (Minute by Jackson, 19 May 1952, *ibid.*); Sayyid Muhammad Reza's son reportedly confirmed that his father had received 2000 tuman from the Shah's mother to organize anti-Musaddiq meetings or *bast* in mosques (Minute by Jackson, 21 May 1952, *ibid.*); and Mir Sayyid Ali Bihbahani tried to postpone the opening of the 17th Majlis in the hope that the plans of Musaddiq's opponents would mature (Minute by Jackson, 24 April 1952, *ibid.*).
162. Middleton to Eden, 28 April 1952, FO371 EP98599. For the text of Kharrazi's speech, see *Journal de Tehran*, 24 April 1952.
163. Minute by Middleton, 22 September 1951, FO248 1531.
164. Middleton learned from a 'confidential and reliable' source that the Shah had recently reproached Tafazzuli, the editor of *Iran-i Ma*, in view of his attack on Baqa'i and his party (Middleton to Ross, 28 January 1952, FO371 EP98595).
165. Minute by Zaehner, 15 May 1952, FO248 1531.
166. The scheme had been approved by the Council of Ministers in early July 1951 (*Bakhtar-i Imruz*, 9 July 1951). Musaddiq's public appeal was made on 22 December 1951, backed by Kashani's appeal the next day (*Bakhtar-i Imruz*, 23–4 December 1951). One of the rich who did support it was Kaziruni, the Isfahani merchant (*Bakhtar-i Imruz*, 16 January 1952); the Tudeh Party

boycotted the scheme and agitated against it (*Bih Su-yi Ayandih*, 30 December 1951).

167. Musaddiq, report to the Senate, *Muzakirat-i Sina*, 21 May 1952. See further Elwell-Sutton, *op. cit.*, pp. 273–80; Fatih, *op. cit.*, pp. 384–92.

168. The Shah's speech on the occasion of opening the 17th Majlis, text in *Bakhtar-i Imruz*, 27 April 1952.

169. Walker to Ross, 19 May 1952, FO371 EP98599.

170. FO371 EP98597.

171. *Muzakirat-i Majlis*, 25 November 1951.

172. Minute by Ross, 28 April 1952, FO371 EP98599.

173. Makki, *Si-yi Tir*, pp. 62–8.

174. Musaddiq's letter, text in *Bakhtar-i Imruz*, 30 April 1952.

175. Middleton to Eden, 5 May 1952, FO371 EP98599.

176. Minute by Zaehner, 15 May 1952, FO248 1531. Sayyed Zia wrote a speech for Mihdi Mir-Ashrafi, the staunchly anti-Musaddiq deputy, for the purpose of attacking the credentials of the National Front deputies.

177. *Ibid.*

178. Minute by Middleton, 9 June 1952, *ibid.*; Minute by Falle, 20 June 1952, *ibid.*

179. *Bakhtar-i Imruz*, 29 June 1952.

180. *Bakhtar-i Imruz*, 1 July 1952.

181. Musaddiq, *Taqrirat*, pp. 148–51.

182. Minute by Falle, 14 June 1952, FO248 1531; Minute by Falle, 21 June 1952, *ibid.*

183. Minute by Pyman, 2 January 1952, *ibid.*

184. Minute by Pyman, 3 January 1952, *ibid.*

185. Minute by Pyman, 23 January 1952, *ibid.*

186. Minute by Jackson, 14 March 1952, *ibid.*

187. Minute by Zaehner, 18 March 1952, FO248 1531.

188. Minute by Zaehner, 20 March 1952, *ibid.*

189. Minute by Pyman, 17 April 1952, *ibid.* Pyman rejected this saying that 'we have made it abundantly clear that we desire the fall of Musaddiq as soon as possible'.

190. Minute by Zaehner, 17 May 1952, *ibid.*

191. Minute by Zaehner, 15 May 1952, *ibid.*

192. Minute by Pyman, 3 April 1952, *ibid.*; Minute by Jackson, 5 April 1952, *ibid.*; Minute by Falle, 29 April 1952, *ibid.*; Minute by Pyman, 22 April 1952, *ibid.*

193. Henderson had found the Shah to be 'as indecisive as ever' (Minute by Middleton, 16 April, 1952, FO248 1531). On a further occasion Henderson referred to the Shah as the 'Persian Hamlet' (Minute by Middleton, 18 April 1952, *ibid.*). Similarly, in Tahiri's view, the Shah was 'as irresolute as ever' (Minute by Pyman, 24 April 1952, *ibid.*

194. Minute by Zaehner, 4 June 1952, *ibid.*).

195. Ala told Middleton that Musaddiq 'must go honourably' and the Shah himself wanted Musaddiq 'to go without fuss' (Minute by Falle, 28 June, 1952, *ibid.*; Minute by Middleton, 4 July 1952, *ibid.*).

196. Makki, *Si-yi Tir*, pp. 86–93. For Musaddiq's activities at The Hague, see *Mudafi'at-i Musaddiq va Rulan (Rollin) dar Divan-i Bainulmilali-yi lahih* (Tehran, 1978).

197. Minute by Falle, 18 June 1952, FO248 1531; Minute by Falle, 25 June 1952, *ibid.*; Minute by Middleton 29 May 1952, *ibid.*; Minute by Middleton, 9 June

1952, *ibid.* Following a secret meeting with Bushihri, Middleton found him to be as 'unrealistic as his master [Musaddiq]' (Minute by Middleton, 10 June 1952, *ibid.*). Salih, on the other hand, in addition to his own lack of willingness, was, in Henderson's view, regarded by the State Department as 'totally unfavourable' (Minute by Middleton, 11 June 1952, *ibid.*).

198. Minute by Zaehner, 21 April 1952, *ibid.*
199. Minute by Middleton, 1 May 1952, *ibid.*
200. Ali Asghar Amirani, 'Asrar-i Muhimmi az Vaqayi'-i Si-um-i Tirmah 1331', text in Makki, *Si-yi Tir*, pp. 94–144.
201. Minute by Jackson, 24 May 1952, FO248 1531.
202. Minute by Middleton, 11 June 1952, *ibid.*
203. Minute by Middleton, 14 June 1952, *ibid.*
204. Minute by Zaehner, 23 June 1952, FO248 1531.
205. Minute by Falle, 21 June 1952, *ibid.*
206. *Ibid.*
207. Minute by Zaehner, 11 June 1952, *ibid.*
208. Minute by Zaehner, 15 June 1952, *ibid.*
209. *Bakhtar-i Imruz*, 3 July 1952. It had also been announced that the election for the remaining seats of the 17th Majlis (only 79 seats were filled) would not start until after the revision of the electoral law (*Bakhtar-i Imruz*, 26 June 1952).
210. Message to the nation in *Bakhtar-i Imruz*, 5 July 1952.
211. Middleton to FO, 6 July 1952, FO371 EP98600.
212. *Bakhtar-i Imruz*, 6 July 1952.
213. Middleton to FO, 7 July 1952, FO371 EP98600; *Bakhtar-i Imruz*, 7 July 1952.
214. Middleton to FO, 11 July 1952, FO371 EP98600.
215. *Bakhtar-i Imruz*, 9 July 1952.
216. Minute by Falle, 9 July 1952, FO248 1531.
217. *Bakhtar-i Imruz*, 9 July 1952.
218. Minute by Falle (conversation with Imam Jum'ih), 12 July 1952, FO248 1513; Minute by Falle (conversation with Hikmat), 12 July 1952.
219. Minute by Falle, 13 July 1952, *ibid.*
220. Minute by Middleton, 10 July 1952, *ibid.*
221. *Bakhtar-i Imruz*, 13 July 1952.
222. Middleton to FO, 17 July 1952, FO371 EP98600.
223. *Bakhtar-i Imruz*, 17 July 1952. Musaddiq later confessed in his memoirs to have made a grave error in resigning on that occasion; an error that could have irretrievably jeopardized the achievements of the nationalist movement (Musaddiq, *Khatirat*, p. 259).

19 Qavam's débâcle and the July Uprising

1. Minute by Falle, 28 April 1952, FO248 1531.
2. Minute by Falle, 12 July 1952, *ibid.*
3. Minute by Falle, 14 May 1952, *ibid.*
4. H. Arsanjani, *Yaddashtha-yi Siyasi: '30 Tir 1331'* (Tehran, 1956), p. 25. Arsanjani's account is apologetic, but interesting and informative particularly as it vividly portrays the uncertain atmosphere of Qavam's camp during the uneasy

days ending on 21 July 1952. Although unconvincing, it aims to acquit Qavam not only by emphasizing his old age but also his manipulation by his own putative followers. Not surprisingly it makes no mention of the background to Qavam's convoluted activities, particularly in enlisting British support in order to regain power.

5. Arsanjani, *op. cit.*; Amirani, *op. cit.*, pp. 110–11.
6. Text in Makki, *Si-yi Tir*, pp. 178–81. This declaration had apparently been written by Sipihr; it was countered by a moving response and a defiant press conference by Kashani. Texts in Dihnavi, *op. cit.*, vol. 2, pp. 205–14.
7. Arsanjani, *op. cit.*, p. 30.
8. Middleton to Eden, 28 July 1952, FO371 EP98602.
9. *Ibid.*
10. Arsanjani, *op. cit.*, p. 52.
11. This was done by Arsanjani, acting on behalf of Qavam. Text in Guruhi az Havadaran-i Nahzat-i Islami-yi Iran va Urupa (ed.) *Ruhaniyyat va Asrar-i Fash Nashudih az Nahzat-i Milli Shudan-i Naft* (Qum, 1979), p. 155.
12. Arsanjani, *op. cit.*, pp. 45–6.
13. Middleton to Ross, 21 July 1952, FO371 EP98601.
14. Text in Dihnavi, *op. cit.*, pp. 216–17.
15. *Bakhtar-i Imruz*, 20 July 1952.
16. Minute by Middleton, 22 July 1952, FO248 1531.
17. 'Qat'namih-yi Pilinum-i Vasi'-i Kumitih-yi Markazi-yi Hizb-i Tudeh-yi Iran', text in *Asnad-i Tarikhi: Junbish-i Kargari, Susyal-Dimukrasi va Kumunisti-yi Iran* vol. I (Florence, 1974), pp. 366–84. See also Puria, *op. cit.*, vol. I, pp. 269–78.
18. Arsanjani, *op. cit.*, p. 68.
19. Middleton to Eden, 28 July 1952, FO371 EP98602.
20. According to Middleton this was on the Shah's orders, *ibid.*
21. Middleton to Eden, 28 July 1952, *ibid.*.
22. The extent of Qavam's anger at the Shah's behaviour can be deduced from a statement he is alleged to have made to Alam. See Katouzian, *The Political Economy of Iran*, p. 176.

20 The second Government of Musaddiq

1. Makki, *Si-yi Tir, op. cit.*, p. 122n.
2. *Ibid.*
3. *Bakhtar-i Imruz*, 27 July 1952.
4. Text in Hasan Tavana'iyan-i Fard, *Musaddiq va Iqtisad* (Tehran, 1981), pp. 203–16; see also Lambton, *Persian Land Reform*, pp. 37–60.
5. Even before the promulgation of the decrees, Farrukh accused Musaddiq of pursuing a land policy more radical than that of Pishihvari (*Bakhtar-i-Imruz*, 21 April 1952). Later Zahidi declared that Musaddiq had 'weakened the principle of ownership, in"ontravention of holy Islamic precepts' and created 'discord among the people in the form of class warfare' (*Dad*, 15 October 1952). Lambton, however, ignores the difficulties and casts doubts on Musaddiq's genuine desire to improve the conditions of the peasants (*op. cit.*, p. 40). See also Puria, *op. cit.*, vol. 2, pp. 301–27.
6. For the text of much of this legislation, see Tavana'iyan-i Fard, *op. cit.*,

pp. 218–320. See also Afrasiabi, *op. cit.*, pp. 235–46.

7. *Bakhtar-i Imruz*, 2 October 1952.

8. Puria, *op. cit.*, vol. 2, pp. 292–3.

9. *Bakhtar-i Imruz*, 17, 20 November 1952.

10. In the Ministry of Foreign Affairs, the traditional bastion of the ruling elite, some reforms were initiated by Fatimi, who had become Minister for Foreign Affairs and Government spokesman on 11 October 1952. This was shortly after his return from Europe where he had been receiving medical treatment for injuries received in the assassination attempt against him.

11. Text in *Bakhtar-i Imruz*, 27 September 1952.

12. *Ibid.*, 2 December 1952.

13. Puria, *op. cit.*, vol. 2, p. 300.

14. Some of Musaddiq's followers, notably Nariman, advocated female franchise, but many deputies were opposed to it, producing letters from Ayatullah Burujirdi and others to this effect (*Bakhtar-i Imruz*, 4 January 1953). Deputy Qanatabadi expressed opposition on behalf of the merchants (*ibid.*), and Kashani did not respond favourably to the appeals made by a number of women (Dihnavi, *op. cit.*, vol. 3, pp. 192, 448).

15. See, for instance, Musaddiq, *Taqrirat*, p. 134.

16. Minute by Falle, 4 August 1952, FO248 1531.

17. Middleton to Bowker, 9 August 1952, FO371 EP98602.

18. Minute by Bowker, 3 July 1951, FO371 EP91461. Amir-Kayvan elaborated his plan during talks between himself and Fredrick Lee, the British Minister of Labour, while they were both attending a labour conference in Geneva (Bowker to Shepherd, 5 July, *ibid.*).

19. Shepherd to Strang, 11 September 1951, FO371, EP91463.

20. Minute by Middleton, 10 January 1952, FO248 EP91463.

21. Minute by Falle, 24 May 1952, *ibid.*

22. Woodhouse, *op. cit.*, p. 116.

23. Minute by Falle, 30 June 1952, FO248 1531.

24. Middleton to FO, 7 August 1952, FO371 EP98602.

25. Embassy Minute, 26 July 1952, FO248 1531.

26. Minute by Falle, 7 August 1952, FO 248 1531.

27. Minute by Falle, 28 July 1952, *ibid.*

28. Minute by Ross, 29 July 1952, FO371 EP98603.

29. Minute by Falle, 7 August 1952, FO248 1513.

30. War Office to Military Attaché, Tehran, 29 July 1952 FO371 EP98602. He added that, as Musaddiq's plans for the army became clearer, 'most of the senior officers would favour a coup d'état' but that it could only be launched 'in the name of the Shah' (Middleton to FO, 6 August 1952, *ibid.*).

31. Minute by Falle, 28 July 1952, FO248 1513.

32. Burrows to Bowker, 30 July 1952, FO371 EP98603.

33. Foreign Office Secret and Whitehall Secret Distribution (August 1952), *ibid.*

34. 6 August 1952, FO371 EP98602. See also David Carlton, *Anthony Eden: A Biography* (London, 1981), pp. 289ff; Anthony Eden, *Memoirs: Full Circle* (London, 1960).

35. Minute by Falle, 7 August 1952, FO248 1513; Minute by Falle, 28 July 1952, *ibid.*

36. Middleton to Ross, 13 August 1952, FO371 EP98604; Middleton to Eden, 30 August 1952, *ibid.*

37. *Dad*, 15 October 1952. Zahidi was one of thirty Senators appointed by the Shah.
38. The original bill demanded his acquittal, but on the appeal of Lutfi, the Minister of Justice, acquittal was replaced with amnesty (*Bakhtar-i Imruz*, 7 August 1952).
39. *Ibid.*, 21 August 1952.
40. Speeches by Qanatabadi and Karimi, *Muzakirat-i Majlis*, 19 October 1952.
41. Speeches by Nariman, Shayigan and Sanjabi, *Muzakirat-i Majlis*, 21, 23 October 1952. As early as 18 August that year there had been an editorial in *Bakhtar-i Imruz* demanding the dissolution of the Senate.
42. Musaddiq, *Khatirat*, p. 373.
43. Middleton to FO, 22 October 1952, FO371 EP98605.
44. *Ibid.*
45. *Bakhtar-i Imruz*, 23 October 1952.
46. *Ibid.*, 30 July 1952.
47. Dean Acheson, *Present at the Creation* (New York, 1969), p. 504.
48. Middleton to Ross, 4 August 1952, FO371 EP98603.
49. Outward telegram from Commonwealth Office, 30 July 1952, FO371 EP98602.
50. Text in Alexander and Nanes, *op. cit.*, pp. 227–8; see also Elwell-Sutton, *op. cit.*, pp. 286–9; Fatih, *op. cit.*, pp. 609–29.
51. Musaddiq's report to the Majlis, *Muzakirat-i Majlis*, 16 September 1952.
52. *Bakhtar-i Imruz* 16 October 1952; Fatih, *op. cit.*, pp. 629–34.
53. Middleton to Eden, 23 September 1952, FO371 EP98604.
54. Middleton to Eden, 30 August 1952, *ibid.*
55. Acheson, *op. cit.*, p. 511.
56. *Bakhtar-i Imruz*, 18 September, 1952.
57. Middleton to Ross, 20 October 1952, FO371 EP98605.
58. *Dad*, 15 October 1952.
59. Minute by Logan, 30 October 1952, FO371 EP98605.
60. A. Khal'atbari, 'Dr. Musaddiq va Mas'alih-yi Naft', *Khandaniha*, 8 June 1954.
61. Rumbold (Paris) to Ross, n.d. (March 1953?), FO371 EP104564.
62. 'Jarayan-i Muhakimih-yi Dr. Musaddiq', text in *Khandaniha*, 14 November 1953–9 January 1954; see particularly the issue of 21 November 1953; see also Elwell-Sutton, *op. cit.*, p. 307.
63. Middleton to Eden, 30 September 1952, FO371 EP98604.
64. Middleton to FO, 22 October 1952, FO371 EP98605.
65. Middleton to FO, 28 August 1952, FO371 EP98603.
66. British Embassy (Washington) to FO, 24 December 1952, FO371 EP98606.
67. For instance, on the occasion of convening the third term of the Senate; *Bakhtar-i Imruz*, 6 October 1952.
68. Minute by Ross, 16 November 1952, FO371 EP98605.
69. Middleton to Eden, 30 September 1952, FO371 EP98604.
70. Middleton to Bowker, 28 July 1952, FO371 EP98602.
71. Makki, *Si-yi Tir*, pp. 304–18.
72. *Ibid.*, pp. 309–10.
73. See Vusuq, *op. cit.*, pp. 97–100; Minute by Logan, 20 August 1952, FO371 EP98603.
74. Musaddiq's message to the nation, *Bakhtar-i Imruz*, 6 April 1953; reprinted in *Nutqha va Maktubat-i Dr. Musaddiq*, vol. 2 (n.p., 1971). The Government was

sensitive on the issue announced that it had no intention of retiring more officers, and that the cases of those retired would be carefully investigated (*Bakhtar-i Imruz*, 6 April 1953).

75. Formed in 1948 by Zahidi and other officers in order to protect those officers retired by Razmara, the Association initially had some sympathy for the anti-Razmara National Front. It had 400 active members, but its affiliated membership reached approximately 2000. See further *Ittila'at*, 6 March 1953.

76. FO to New York, 19 November 1952, FO371 EP98606.

77. Note of informal meeting between Mr. Middleton and representatives of four 'old' Commonwealth Governments on 25 November 1952, FO371 EP98606.

78. Minute by Falle, 4 August 1952, FO371 EP98606.

79. Draft note by Rothnie for Director of Military Intelligence, January 1953, FO371 EP104561.

80. Middleton to Ross, 4 August 1952, FO371 EP98603. On Musaddiq–Kashani relations see also Faghfoory, *op. cit.*, pp. 227–91; Yann Richard, 'Ayatollah Kashani; Precursor of the Islamic Republic?', in Nikkie Keddie (ed.), *Religion and Politics in Iran* (New Haven and London, 1983), pp. 101–24; Richard Cottam, *Nationalism in Iran* (Pittsburgh, 1964), pp. 150–7, 264–76; Farhang Rayman, 'Kashani va Musaddiq' *Jibhih-yi Azadi*, 5–25 May 1953.

81. Middleton to Eden, 11 August 1952, FO371 EP98603.

82. In a session held in his summer residence, Kashani dismissed all of Musaddiq's entourage as 'incompetent', while Karimi and Qanatabadi severely criticised the Cabinet ministers (*Bakhtar-i Imruz*, 23 September 1952).

83. Minute by Rothnie, 22 December 1952, FO371 EP98606.

84. Minute by Rothnie, 2 December 1952, *ibid.* During these demonstrations slogans were chanted against the British and the Americans, but also against certain aspects of government policy.

85. Interview with Professor Mihdi Ha'iri, September 1985; Ha'iri then liased with Musaddiq on Burujirdi's behalf.

86. Fatih's diary, 22 December 1952, FO371 EP104561.

87. See further Kashani, *op. cit.*, pp. 165–87.

88. *Bakhtar-i Imruz*, 6, 15 January 1953. See also the open letter of the Toilers' Party Executive Committee to Musaddiq, *Shahid*, 20 December 1952.

89. Washington to FO, 2 January 1953, FO371 EP104561.

90. See further, Puria, *op. cit.*, vol. 2, pp. 392–9.

91. Middleton to FO, 7 August 1952, FO371 EP98602.

92. Maliki, *op. cit.*, pp. 121–2; Fatimi, 'Khatirat', text in Afrasiabi, *op. cit.*, p. 370.

93. See *Bakhtar-i Imruz*, 28 October–5 November 1952.

94. For the list of their names see *Bakhtar-i Imruz*, 28 July, 2 August 1952.

95. Musaddiq's letter to the Majlis, *Bakhtar-i Imruz*, 11 August 1952.

96. Middleton to FO, 20 August 1952, FO371 EP98603.

97. Middleton to Ross, 13 October 1952, FO371 98605.

98. Text in *Bakhtar-i Imruz*, 23 October 1952.

99. Text in *Shahid*, 5 November 1952.

100. Musaddiq's letter to the Majlis, text in *Bakhtar-i Imruz*, 11 November 1952.

101. Text in *Shahid*, 27, 29, 30 November 1952. This was not the first time he had made such a speech; in the Majlis session of 19 October he had pledged to incite the people to rebel and destroy the Government, which had not allowed the punishment of Qavam to take place (*Bakhtar-i Imruz*, 19 October 1952).

102. *Ibid.*, 29 November 1952.
103. Musaddiq's letter to the Majlis, text in *ibid.*, 7 December 1952.
104. Text in *Ittila'at*, 7 December 1952.
105. Exchanges between Shayigan and Makki, *Bakhtar-i Imruz*, 25 December 1952.
106. American Embassy Tehran, 'Iranian political trends from the Departure of the British Embassy in 1952 to the end of the Iranian year March 20 1953', 24 April 1953, FO371 EP104567.
107. *Bakhtar-i Imruz*, 5 January 1953.
108. Kashani's statement, text in *Kayhan*, 5 January 1953.
109. *Bakhtar-i Imruz*, 4 January 1953.
110. Text in *Bakhtar-i Imruz*, 6 January 1953.
111. *Ibid.*
112. Text in *Shahid*, 10 January 1953.
113. *Bakhtar-i Imruz*, 15 January 1953.
114. Speech in the Majlis, text in *Shahid*, 18 January 1953.
115. *Bakhtar-i Imruz*, 15 January 1953.
116. *Bakhtar-i Imruz*, 17 January 1953.
117. *Bakhtar-i Imruz*, 18 January 1953.
118. Speech in the Majlis, *Muzakirat-i Majlis*, 18 January 1953.
119. Kashani's letter, text in Dihnavi, *op. cit.*, vol. 3, pp. 206–8.
120. *Bakhtar-i Imruz*, 18 January 1953.
121. *Ibid.*, 19, 20 January 1953.
122. Text in Dihnavi, *op. cit.*, vol. 3, pp. 205 and 213; see also Kashani's letter to Musaddiq, text in *ibid.*, pp. 210–12.
123. Musaddiq's radio broadcast, text in *Bakhtar-i Imruz*, 24 January 1953.
124. Text in *ibid.*, 28 January 1953, also in Dihnavi, *op. cit.* vol. 3, p. 221. Deputy Khusrau Qashqa'i, himself a member of the reconciliation committee, told a member of the US Embassy that the committee 'concluded nothing' (Minute by Rothnie, 3 February 1953, FO371 EP104561).
125. In the view of the French Ambassador in Tehran, however, the opponents of Musaddiq could not employ religious extremism in undermining his Government since: 'The Persians were not religious fanatics, and were not likely to be swept away by this kind of extremism; just as the French were Voltairian Christians, so the Persians were Voltairian Mohammedans' (Hardy (Paris) to Dixon, 14 January 1953, FO371 EP104561).
126. *Bakhtar-i Imruz*, 8 February 1953.
127. *Mard-i Asia*, 21 January 1953.
128. Khushniyyat, *op. cit.*, pp. 83–8.
129. American Embassy report, 10 June 1953, FO371 EP104568; see also Khushniyyat, *op. cit.*, pp. 83–126. Having only reluctantly condoned the exoneration of Razmara's assassin, the Government considered him as still being guilty on the grounds of illegal possession of firearms.
130. Minute by Logan, 26 February 1953, FO371, EP104562; see also *Bih Su-yi Ayandih*, 20 February 1953.
131. In early January 1953, the NMF proceeded to elect its officers and drafted a provision of its statute which was to be endorsed by all its members within about a month. By refusing to give their endorsements, Makki, Baqa'i, Ha'irizadih and a few others formally left the NMF.
132. Minute by Rothnie, 7 February 1953, FO371 EP104562.

133. US Embassy Telegram, 22 February 1953, FO371 EP104563.
134. US Embassy, 'Iranian Political Trends', 24 April 1953, FO371 EP104567.
135. U.S. Embassy Telegram, 22 February 1953, FO371 EP104563. See also Musaddiq, *Taqrirat*, pp. 127–31.
136. Minute by Rothnie, 27 February 1953, FO371 EP104562.
137. *Ibid.*; see also *Dad*, 23 February 1953.
138. Minute by Rothnie, 27 February 1953, FO371 EP104562.
139. Musaddiq's message to the nation, *Bakhtar-Imruz*, 6 April 1953; see also Musaddiq, *Taqrirat*, pp. 127–31.
140. Texts in Dihnavi, *op. cit.*, vol. 3, pp. 261–6.
141. Musaddiq's message to the nation, *Bakhtar-i Imruz*, 6 April 1953. See further Musaddiq, *Khatirat*, pp. 262–7.
142. Minute by Rothnie, 3 March 1953, FO371 EP104563.
143. Minute by Rothnie, 2 March 1953, *ibid.*
144. FO to Secretary of State, 3 March 1953, FO371 EP104562. See also Puria, *op. cit.*, vol. 2, pp. 415–40.
145. Minute by Rothnie, 2 March 1953, FO371 EP104563.
146. Minute by Rothnie, 24 February 1953, FO371 EP104562.
147. It is worth noting that Bakhtiari had a long history of friendship with Zahidi and had collaborated with him and Kashani during the Second World War in the pro-German 'Siyah Pushan' organization (Bennett's memorandum on political parties in Persia, 7 August 1943, FO371 EP35074). The present rebellion was quelled by the Government and, much to the dismay of the opposition, it did not spread to other tribes. See further 'Mas'alih-yi Bakhtiariha', *Kayhan*, 1 March 1953.
148. *Bakhtar-i Imruz*, 1 March 1953; Minute by Rothnie, 3 March 1953, FO371 EP104563.
149. *Bakhtar-i Imruz*, 3 March 1953.
150. Even actively anti-Government retired officers appealed to Kashani for protection (*Ittila'at* 2 March 1953).
151. *Kayhan*, 1 March 1953; *Ittila'at*, 4 March 1953; Dihnavi, *op. cit.*, vol. 3, p. 272.
152. *Bakhtar-i Imruz*, 1–3 March 1953.
153. *Bakhtar-i Imruz*, 2–4 March 1953; Kashani's letter to Musaddiq, text in *ibid.*; Kashani's letter to Zulfaqari, text in *ibid.*
154. Musaddiq's letter to Kashani, text in *ibid.*, 5 March 1953.
155. This committee included the following deputies: Mu'azzami, Sanjabi and Majdzadih – who were appointed by the NMF – as well as Makki, Baqa'i, Ha'irizadih, Ganjih'i and Rafi', who were selected by other deputies.
156. *Ittila'at*, 8 March 1953.
157. Text in *Bakhtar-i Imruz*, 12 March 1953.
158. See, for instance, speech by A. Faramarzi, *Muzakirat-i Majlis*, 12 March 1953.
159. Mu'azzami, speech in the Majlis, *op. cit.*, 28 May 1953.
160. *Bakhtar-i Imruz*, 12 March 1953.
161. Deputies such as Faqihi-yi Shirazi, Hamidiyyih, Afshar-i Sadiqi, Bahaduri, Huda and others (*Bakhtar-i Imruz*, 14 March 1953).
162. Minute by Rothnie, 12 March 1953, FO371 EP104563.
163. Minute by Rothnie, 19 March 1953, FO371 EP104564.
164. Top Secret Memorandum, 7 April 1953, *ibid.* According to this report, 'Ala said that Kashani supported Zahidi, but, as with Makki, he hesitated to go all out.

While giving lip-service, both appear to maintain a position which would allow them to plead non-involvement should the attempt to overthrow Musaddiq by peaceful or other means fail.'

165. *Bakhtar-i Imruz*, 17 March 1953.
166. *Ibid.*, 30 March 1953; see also Anon., 'Razha-yi Fash Nashudih az Vaqi'ih-yi 28 Murdad', *Ashuftih*, nos 1–13, 1954; in fact, following the events of February, Musaddiq declined any audience with the Shah and rejected mediation efforts to bring the two together (Musaddiq, *Khatirat*, p. 267).
167. Musaddiq's message to the nation, text in *Bakhtar-i Imruz*, 6 April 1953.
168. In March 1953 Ha'irizadih intended to visit a number of neighbouring countries. Apparently intending to lure him and keep him preoccupied, the Government is reported to have offered him the task of inspecting the Iranian diplomatic missions in such countries; he was, however, pressed by Ayatullah Bihbahani to refuse (Minute by Rothnie, 2 April 1953, FO371 EP104564). Ha'irizadih was in close contact with people such as Bihbahani and Imam Jum'ih.
169. *Jibhih-yi Azadi*, 21 May 1953; (Roy M.) Melbourne, 'Most Recent Factional Alignment in the 17th Majlis', 6 May 1953, FO371 EP104566.
170. *Bakhtar-i Imruz*, 16–22 April 1953.
171. From an interview with a British diplomat; it is of course difficult to imagine that the murder of Afshartus was not a logical conclusion of the kidnapping and particularly of the brutal treatment which he received.
172. *Bakhtar-i Imruz*, 5 May 1953; also Dihnavi, *op. cit.*, vol. 3, pp. 356–7. Zahidi left his refuge in the Majlis on 16 July and went into hiding.
173. *I'lamiyyih-yi Farmandari-yi Nizami*, text in *Bakhtar-i Imruz*, 2 May 1953.
174. Reports in *Bakhtar-i Imruz*, 7 May 1953; and corroborated by the newsreels of the period; Newsreel collection, Granada Television Company, London.
175. *Bakhtar-i Imruz*, 27–8 April 1953. see further Baqa'i *Man Namayandih-yi Kerman Hastam* (Tehran, May–June 1953). For a collection of Baqa'i's speeches, letters etc., see *idem, Shinakht-i Haqiqat: Duktur Muzaffar Baqa'i-yi Kermani dar Pishgah-i Tarikh* (Tehran, 1979).
176. *Bakhtar-i Imruz*, 10 May 1953.
177. *Ibid.*, 20 May 1953.
178. *Ibid.*, 17 May 1953.
179. *Ibid.*, 19 May 1953.
180. *Muzakirat-i Majlis*, 21 May 1953.
181. *Bakhtar-i Imruz*, 23–6 May 1953.
182. Interview with Baqa'i, September 1979; *idem*, speech in the Majlis, 26 May 1953, text in *Shahid*, 27 May 1953; various issues of *Shahid*, particularly from April 1953 onwards.
183. *Muzakirat-i Majlis*, 28 May 1953.
184. *Bakhtar-i Imruz*, 7 June 1953.
185. *Ibid.*, 9–18 June 1953.
186. *Ibid.*, 17 June 1953.
187. Text in *ibid.*, 20 June 1953.
188. One Foreign Office official, however, stated that 'Neither we nor the Americans see any hope in Kashani as a successor to Musaddiq, nor, *a fortiori*, do we see any sense in assisting him to power' (Minute by Rothnie, 11 May 1953, FO371 EP104565).
189. *Bakhtar-i Imruz*, 23 June 1953.
190. *Ibid.*, 27 June 1953.

191. 'I'lamiyyih-yi Aqalliyyat', text in *Bakhtar-i Imruz*, 28 June 1953.
192. *Bakhtar-i Imruz*, 1 July 1953. Adhering to the ethos of clan politics, some deputies claimed that it would be wise to re-elect Kashani to ensure the balance between the legislature and the executive; *ibid.*, 28 June 1953.
193. Text in *Shahid*, 2 July 1953.
194. *Bakhtar-i Imruz*, 8 July 1953.
195. *Ibid.*, 9–11 July 1953.
196. *Ibid.*, 23 November 1952; see also Elwell-Sutton, *op. cit.*, pp. 290–1.
197. 'Jarayan-i Muhakimih-yi Dr. Musaddiq', *op. cit.*, particularly the issue of 21 November 1953. Musaddiq asserted that votes cast for Makki were intended to bring down the Government. See also Musaddiq, reply to the students affiliated to the National Front, 17 April 1969, text in *Mukatibat-i Musaddiq: Talash Bara-yi Tashkil-i Jibhih-yi Milli-yi Sivvum* (n.p., 1975), pp. 15–19.
198. *Bakhtar-i Imruz*, 8, 9 April 1953.
199. *Iran-i Ma*, 23 April 1953.
200. *Bakhtar-i Imruz*, 30 March, 5 April 1953. The name of Makki had also been mentioned as a possible candidate.
201. *Ibid.*, 11 May 1953.
202. US Embassy Telegram, 10 April 1953, FO371 EP104565.
203. Musaddiq's New Year speech of 20 March 1953, text in *Bakhtar-i Imruz*, 28, 30 March 1953. See further Fatih, *op. cit.*, pp. 637–64; Elwell-Sutton, *op. cit.*, pp. 286–308.
204. Interview with Kashani, *Ittila'at*, 28 March 1953, text in Dihnavi, *op. cit.*, vol. 3, pp. 317–19; Ha'irizadih, speeches in the Majlis, *Muzakirat-i Majlis*, 19, 21 May 1953.
205. *Bakhtar-i Imruz*, 11 March, 17 May 1953.
206. *Ibid.*, 20 May 1953; *Shahid*, 25 May 1953.
207. Texts of the Musaddiq–Eisenhower exchanges in Alexander and Nanes (eds), *op. cit.*, pp. 230–5. For more on US–Iranian relations in this period, see Rubin, *op. cit.*; Bill, *op. cit.*
208. Commonwealth Relations Office to Rothnie, 13 March 1953, FO371 EP104563.
209. *Bakhtar-i Imruz*, 24 June 1953.
210. M. Agah, 'Some Aspects of Economic Development of Modern Iran' (D.Phil. Thesis, Oxford, 1958), p. 212, quoted in H. Mahdavi, 'The Patterns and Problems of Economic Development in Rentier States: the case of Iran', in M. A. Cook (ed.), *Studies in the Economic History of the Middle East* (London, 1970), p. 442. See also Katouzian, *The Political Economy of Iran*, pp. 184–5.
211. *Bakhtar-i Imruz*, 3 June 1953.
212. See further, Puria, *op. cit.*, vol. 2, pp. 329–36; Zabih, *The Mossadegh Era* (Chicago, 1982), pp. 90–3.
213. US Embassy Report, 14 August 1953, FO371 EP104569.
214. *Ittila'at*, 2 February 1953; Minute by Rothnie, 11 February 1953, FO371 EP104562.
215. US Embassy Report, 10 April 1953, FO371 EP104565; US Embassy Report, 24 April 1953, *ibid.*
216. Kashani also put pressure for the release of Shaikh Muhammad Tehrani, the head of the 'Qa'imiyyih Society', who had been arrested in late May 1953 because of his strong anti-Government sermons, which were partly reproduced in the opposition newspaper (Kashani, letters to Mussadiq, texts in

Dihnavi, *op. cit.*, vol. 3, pp. 378–80); US Embassy Telegram, 3 June 1953, FO371 EP104567.

217. The charge of dictatorship has also been reiterated by some foreign writers. See, for instance, Marbury Efimenco, 'An Experience with Civilian Dictatorship in Iran: The Case of Mohammad Mossadegh', *Journal of Politics*, XVII, no.3 (August 1955), pp. 390–406.

218. In an interview with the *Daily Worker*, prominent Tudeh leaders, Dr. Reza Radmanish, Ihsan Tabari, Mahmud Buqrati, Ahmad Qasimi and Dr. Ghulam Husain Furutan asserted that the Government of Musaddiq was not based on the Iranian people and was the representative of 'another section' of the 'Iranian ruling class' (*Daily Worker*, 2 March 1953).

219. Such as the strikes in Tehran's tobacco factory in early May 1953; see further Puria, *op. cit.*, vol. 2, pp. 462–5.

220. Ledwedge (Kabul) to FO, 12 June 1953, FO371 EP104567. In the assessment of the French military attaché in Tehran, the Tudeh Party had no chance of an imminent assumption of power.

221. *Kayhan*, 16 May 1953; *Bakhtar-i Imruz*, 18, 23 May 1953.

222. See for instance, A. Khal'atbari, 'Dr. Musaddiq ra ki bih Zamin Zad', *Khandaniha*, 2 January 1953; *idem*, 'Dakhil-i Dastgah-i Dr. Musaddiq chih Khabar Bud', *op. cit.*, 7 October 1955. Similarly, Khalil Maliki argues that if Musaddiq's Government had firmly controlled the Tudeh Party, the Americans would not have turned against Iran (Khalil Maliki, 'Tahlil-i Mukhtasari az Guzashtih bara-yi Tarsim-i Rah-i Ayandih', *Nabard-i Zindigi* (April–May 1956), pp. 32–7).

223. Estimates varied. The US Embassy estimated Tudeh at 4000 and non-Tudeh at 2500 (Minute by Gandy, 27 July 1953, FO371 EP104569) while the Pakistani Embassy estimated non-Tudeh demonstrators to number 4000–5000 (Commonwealth Relations Office to FO, 10 September 1953, FO371 EP104571). Other sources give much larger estimates for Tudeh demonstrators; see, for instance, S. Zabih, *The Communist Movement in Iran*, p. 199.

224. See further Farhad Kazemi, 'The Military and Politics in Iran: The Uneasy Symbiosis', in E. Kedourie and S. Haim (eds), *Towards a Modern Iran* (London, 1980), pp. 217–40.

225. The French military attaché in Tehran asserted that 'the widespread belief that the Persian Army was finished as a political force was mistaken' (Ledwedge (Kabul) to FO, 12 June 1953, FO371 EP104567).

226. Musaddiq, *Taqrirat*, pp. 132–5.

227. For Musaddiq's explanation of the need for the referendum, see Musaddiq, *Khatirat*, pp. 253–5.

228. Minute by Rothnie, 24 February 1953, FO371 EP104562.

229. The Union faction's letter to Musaddiq; text in *Bakhtar-i Imruz*, 4 July 1953; the Country faction's letter to Musaddiq, text in *ibid.*, 6 July 1953; see also *ibid.*, 16, 18 July 1953.

230. *Ibid.*, 13, 14 July 1953.

231. *Ibid.*, 28 July 1953.

232. *Dad*, 16 April 1953; *Mard-i Asia*, 22 April 1953.

233. *Bakhtar-i Imruz*, 1 August 1953.

234. Text in Dihnavi, *op. cit.*, vol. 3, pp. 407–21; see also Majma'-i Musalmanan-i Mujahid, *Chira ba Rifrandum Mukhalifim?*, 2 August 1953.

235. Text in *Shahid*, 3 August 1953.

236. Text in *ibid.*, 2 August 1953.

237. FO Minute, 15 August 1953, FO371 EP104569.

238. For further details of the background to the coup see Kermit Roosevelt, *Countercoup: The Struggle for the Control of Iran* (New York, 1979); see also Ali Atabaki and Ahmad Bani-Ahmad, *Panj Ruz-i Rastakhiz-i Millat* (Tehran 1958); Ghulamreza Nijati, *Junbish-i Milli Shudan-i San'at-i Naft-i Iran va Kudita-yi 28 Murdad 1332* (Tehran, 1985), pp. 297ff.

239. Washington to FO, 17 August 1953, FO371 EP104569. The Defense and State Departments deferred a full discussion of these matters until the meeting of the National Security Council on 27 August 1953.

240. Draft Telegram to Washington, *ibid.*

241. From an interview with a British diplomat.

242. *Shuja'at (Bih Su-yi Ayandih)*, 9 August 1953; Nur ud-din Kianuri, *Hizb-i Tudeh-yi Iran va Duktur Muhammad Musaddiq* (Tehran, 1980), pp. 34–6.

243. 'Jarayan-i Muhakimih-yi Dr. Musaddiq', *Khandaniha*; especially the issue of 21 November 1953.

244. For the text of Kashani's letter and Musaddiq's reply, see Guruhi az Havadaran-i Nahzat-i Islami-yi Iran va Urupa, *op. cit.*, pp. 185–7.

245. Mark Gasiorowski, 'US Foreign Policy and the Client State: Implications for Domestic Politics and Long-Term US Interests in Iran' (Ph.D. dissertation, University of North Carolina at Chapel Hill, 1984), pp. 135–42; see also idem, 'The 1953 *Coup d'Etat* in Iran', *IJMES*, 19 (August 1987), pp. 261–86.

246. His own nephew, Brigadier Daftari, whom he appointed the Chief of Police after 16 August 1953, was perhaps the most obvious example.

247. Minute by Bowker 19 August 1953, FO371 EP104570.

248. Compare with his behaviour during the events leading to 21 July 1952.

249. Saifullah Mu'azzami's testimony in the court. *Dadgah-i Tarikhi* (Tehran, n.d.), p. 145.

250. Javanshir, *op. cit.*, p. 312.

251. For a discussion of the Dionysian pattern of culture in contrast to the Apollonian, see Ruth Benedict, *Patterns of Culture* (London, 1968), pp. 56ff.

252. During his trip to New York to attend the UN, for instance, Musaddiq pleaded illness, and hospitalized himself so that he would conveniently be able to meet many American politicians. Musaddiq, *Taqrirat*, pp. 146–7.

253. Musaddiq's behaviour in this regard also enabled him to hold Cabinet sessions in his own house and thereby exclude the Shah from attending them. In the past, Cabinet sessions had often been held in the Shah's presence.

254. Such views were also widely reiterated by the British press: in an *Observer* 'profile' of Musaddiq written only three weeks after his assumption of office, he was called an 'old Robespierre' who 'is likely to prove an involuntary Kerenski' and whose regime would be a 'threshold' for communism. He was described as a man 'wholly impervious to commonsense arguments of expediency', surrounded by 'crooks, adventurers and madmen . . . truly a Frankenstein . . . pathetic . . . [and] desperately short-sighted' (*Observer*, 20 May 1951).

255. Abdulhusain Bihnia, a prominent official who as the head of the 'Foreign Exchange Committee' had himself been prosecuted by Musaddiq's Government on charges of corruption, emphatically asserted that Musaddiq was 'beyond any kind of financial corruption and in principle avoided co-operation with

opportunists and men of ill repute' (Bihnia, *op. cit.*, p. 105).

256. Makki, speech in the Majlis, *Muzakirat-i Majlis*, 4 January 1951, 'Jarayan-i Muhakimih-yi Dr. Musaddiq', *Khandaniha*, see especially the issue of 21 November 1953.

257. Musaddiq, Report to the Majlis, *Muzakirat-i Majlis*, 14 December 1952.

258. Musaddiq's message to the nation, text in *Bakhtar-i Imruz*, 22 July 1953.

259. *Bakhtar-i Imruz*, 28 September 1953.

260. Musaddiq's message to the nation, *ibid.*, 27 July 1953.

261. Richard Cottam, 'Political Party Development in Iran', *Iranian Studies*, vol. 1, no. 3 (Summer 1968), pp. 82–94.

262. Musaddiq, *Taqrirat*, pp. 161–4; *idem*, speech in the Majlis, 11 November 1945, text in Kay-Ustuvan, *op. cit.*, vol. II, pp. 179–82.

263. Maliki, 'Tahlil-i Mukhtasari az Guzashtih', pp. 54–6.

264. A. Maliki, *op. cit.*, pp. 21–3; according to this account, Musaddiq attended the National Front sessions only once as Prime Minister.

265. Khal'atbari, 'Dr Musaddiq ra ki bih Zamin Zad', *op. cit.*

266. Letter to Shayigan, 3 September 1962, text in *Mukatibat-i Musaddiq*, *op. cit.*, p. 103.

267. Musaddiq, *Taqrirat*, pp. 136–7.

268. Musaddiq's message to the nation, *Bakhtar-i Imruz*, 27 July 1953.

269. See, for instance, Musaddiq, *Khatirat*, pp. 259, 273.

270. Hardy (Paris) to Dixon, 14 January 1953, FO371 EP104561.

271. Fatimi's radio broadcast, text in *Bakhtar-i Imruz*, 12 August 1953.

Conclusion

1. No study of the social background of Iranian prime ministers and ministers is yet available. The only volume of Zahra Shaji'i's work *Vizarat va Vaziran dar Iran* (Tehran, 1976) which has so far appeared deals mainly with the formal organizational structure and functions of various ministries. In contrast to Shaji'i's book on the deputies, namely *Namayandigan-i Majlis-i Shaura-yi Milli dar bist-u-yik Daurih-yi Qanun-guzari* (Tehran, 1965), this volume provides little information of sociological value. Such information is, however, expected to be provided in the forthcoming volumes.

Bibliography

A. Archives

Public Record Office documents: FO371, 1941–53; FO248, 1946–53.
India Office documents: L/P&S/12/3472A, 1941–7.

B. Published documents, compilations and special publications

Alexander, Yonah and Nanes, Allan (eds). *The United States and Iran: a Documentary History*. Frederick, MD: University Pbls of America, 1980.
Anon. *Dah Guzarish az Duktur Musaddiq bih Daulat va Majlis*. N.p.: Zibarjad Pbls, n.d.
Anon. *Mukatibat-i Musaddiq: Talash barayi Tashkil-i Jibhih-yi Milli-yi Sivvum*. N.p.: Musaddiq Pbls, 1975.
Asnad-i Tarikhi-yi Junbish-i Kargari, Susyal-Dimukrasi va Kumunisti-yi Iran. 5 vols. Florence, Mazdak Pbls, 1974– .
Buzurgmihr, Jalil (ed.) *Musaddiq dar Mahkamih-yi Nizami*. Book One. Vols 1 & 2. Tehran: Nashr-i Tarikh-i Iran, 1984.
Buzurgmihr, Jalil (ed.) *Musaddiq dar Dadgah-i Tajdid-i Nazar-i Nizami*. Tehran: Intishar Pbls, 1986.
Dadgah-i Tarikhi; Muhakimih-yi Aqa-yi Duktur Muhammad Musaddiq dar Dadgah-i Nizami. Tehran: Raushanfikr Pbls, n.d.
Dihnavi, Muhammad. *Majmu'ih'i az Maktubat, Sukhanraniha, Piyamha va Fatavi-yi Ayatullah Kashani*. 3 vols. Tehran: Chapakhsh Pbls, 1982, 1983.
JAMI. *Guzashtih Chiragh-i Rah-i Ayandih Ast*. N.p., 1978.
'Jarayan-i Muhakimih-yi Duktur Musaddiq', *Khandaniha*, 14 November 1953–9 January 1954.
Guruhi az Havadaran-i Nahzat-i Islami-yi Iran va Urupa. *Ruhaniyyat va Asrar-i Fash Nashudih az Nahzat-i Milli Shudan-i Naft*. Qum: Dar ul-Fikr Pbls, 1979.
Iran dar rah-i Islahat-i Dimukratik dar Taht-i Rahbari-yi Janab-i Aqa-yi Qavam us-Saltanih, Bilan-i Amaliyyat-i Daulat dar Sih-Mahih-yi 1325.
Iran Party. *Tahlili az Mubarizat-i Millat-i Iran bih Rahbari-yi Duktur*

Musaddiq. Tehran: Iran Party Pbls, 1978.

Iqbali, Hasan (ed.) *Naft va Bahrain ya Abbas Iskandari dar Khidmat-i Majlis-i Panzdahum.* Tehran, 1952.

Kay-Ustuvan, Husain. *Siyasat-i Muvazinih-yi Manfi dar Majlis-i Chahardahum.* 2 vols. Tehran: Taban Pbls, 1950.

Kuhi-yi Kirmani, Husain. *Az Shahrivar-i 1320 ta Faji'ih-yi Azarbaijan va Zanjan.* 2 vols. Tehran: Mazahiri Pbls, n.d.

Majma'-i Musalmanan-i Mujahid. *Chira ba Rifrandum Mukhalifim?* Tehran, August 1953.

Makki, Husain. *Istizah-i Husain Makki, Dr Muzaffar Baqa'i, Abulhasan Ha'irizadih az Daulat-i Sa'id 1328.* Tehran: Amir Kabir Pbls, 1978.

——. *Naft va Nutq-i Makki; Jarayan-i Muzakirat-i Naft dar Majlis-i Panzdahum.* 1st edn 1949. Tehran: Amir Kabir Pbls, 1978.

——. *Khal'i Yad.* Parts I & II. Tehran: Bungah-i Tarjumih va Nashr-i Kitab, 1981.

——. *Vaqayi'-i Si-yi Tir 1331.* Tehran: Bungah-i Tarjumih va Nashr-i Kitab, 1981.

Majmu'ih-yi Maqalat-i Duktur Sayyid Husain Fatimi. N.p.: Mudarris Pbls, 1978.

Matn-i Kamil-i Difa'-i Aqayan-i Duktur Musaddiq va Sartip Riyahi dar barih-yi Radd-i Salahiyyat-i Dadgah-i Nizami. Tehran, n.d.

Mudafi'at-i Musaddiq va Raulan (Rollin) dar Divan Bainulmilali-yi Lahih. Tehran: Zibarjad Publications, 1978.

Musaddiq va Masa'il-i Huquq va Siyasat. Ed. Iraj Afshar. Tehran: Zaminih Pbls, 1979.

Musaddiq, Muhammad. *Khatirat va Ta'allumat-i Musaddiq.* Ed. Iraj Afshar. Tehran: Ilmi Pbls, 1986.

Muzakirat-i Majlis-i Shaura-yi Milli. *Ruznamih-yi Rasmi-yi Kishvar-i Shahanshahi,* 1941–53.

Muzakirat-i Majlis-i Sina, *Ruznamih-yi Rasmi-yi Kishvar-i Shahanshahi,* 1950–2.

Nutqha va Maktubat-i Duktur Musaddiq. N.p.: Musaddiq Pbls, 1971.

Nutqha va Maktubat-i Duktur Musaddiq dar Daurihha-yi Panjum va Shishum-i Majlis-i Shaura-yi Milli. N.p.: Musaddiq Pbls, 1971.

Nutqha-yi Duktur Musaddiq dar Daurih-yi Shanzdahum-i Majlis-i Shaura-yi Milli. Vol. 1. N.p.: Musaddiq Pbls, 1967.

'Qat'namih-yi Pilinum-i Vasi'i-i Kumitih-yi Markazi-yi Hizb-i Tudeh-yi Iran', in *Asnad-i Tarikhi-yi Junbish-i Kargari, Susyal-Dimukrasi va Kumunisti-yi Iran.* Vol. I. Florence, 1974, 366–84.

Rahnama-yi Iran Nashriyyih-yi Dayirih-yi Jughrafiya'i-yi Artish. Tehran: Taban Pbls, 1951.

Razavi, Ahmad. *Matn-i Nutq-i Namayandih-yi Kerman dar Majlis-i Shaura-yi Milli.* Tehran: Yaghma, 1948.

Sadr-i Hashimi, Muhammad. *Tarikh-i Jarayid va Majallat-i Iran.* 4 vols. Isfahan: Kamal Pbls, 1984.

Sazman-i Mujahidin-i Inqilab-i Islami. *Nigarishi Kutah bar Nahzat-i Milli-yi Iran*. Tehran, 1979.

Shinakht-i Haqiqat: Duktur Muzaffar Baqa'i-yi Kirmani dar Pishgah-i Tarikh. Kerman, 1979.

Taqrirat-i Musaddiq dar Zindan. Recorded by Jalil Buzurgmihr, ed. Iraj Afshar. Tehran: Farhang-i Iranzamin Pbls, 1980.

US Department of State, *Foreign Relations of the United States*. Washington, DC: Government Printing Office, 1941–53.

C. Other books and articles in Persian

Adl, Mustafa (Mansur us-Saltanih). *Huquq-i Asasi ya Usul-i Mashrutiyyat*. Tehran, 1948.

Afrasiabi, Bahram. *Musaddiq va Tarikh*. Tehran: Nilufar Pbls, 1981.

——. *Khatirat va Mubarizat-i Duktur Husain Fatimi*. Tehran: Sukhan Pbls, 1987.

Afshar, Iraj. 'Darguzasht-i Sayyid Hasan Arsanjani', *Rahnama-yi Kitab* XII, 3–4 (June–July 1969), 207–8.

——. 'Yadbud-i Furughi', *Rahnama-yi Kitab* XIV, 9–12 (November 1971–March 1972).

—— (ed.) *Maqalat-i Taqizadih*. 5 vols. Tehran, 1970–5.

Ala, Husain. 'Tarh-i Mas'alih-yi Iran dar Shaura-yi Amniyyat, *Salnamih-yi Dunya* XX (1964), 110–13.

Alatur. *Hizb-i Tudeh bar sar-i Du Rah*. Tehran, 1946.

Alavi, Buzurg. *Panjah-u-Sih Nafar*. Tehran, 1944.

Al-i Ahmad, Jalal. *Yik Chah va Du Chalih va Masalan Sharh-i Ahvalat*. Tehran: Ravaq Pbls, 1964.

——. *Dar Khidmat va Khianat-i Raushanfikran*. 2 vols. Tehran: Kharazmi Pbls, 1978.

Amidi-Nuri, Abulhasan. *Firqih-yi Dimukrat*. Tehran, 1946.

Amir-Ahmadi, Sipahbud Ahmad. 'Vizarat dar Daulat-i Qavam us-Sultanih', *Salnamih-yi Dunya* XIII (1957), 80–4.

Amir-Ibrahimi, Abdulhusain. *Mardan-i Nami-yi Iran*. Tehran, 1953.

Amir-Ala'i, Dr Shams ud-Din. *Khal'-i Yad az Shirkat-i Naft-i Iran va Inglis*. Tehran: Dihkhuda Pbls, 1978.

'Amiri, Javad. 'Shahrivar-i 1320', *Salnamih-yi Dunya* XIX (1963), 23–5, 31.

Anon. *Chand Pardih az Zindigani-yi Rijal-i Ma'ruf-i Iran*. Tehran: Umid Pbls, 1945.

Anon. 'Yaddashtha-i az Dauran-i Nakhust Vaziri-yi Hazhir', *Khandaniha*, 12–30 March 1951.

Anon. 'Chira Razmara ra Kushtand?', *Khandaniha*, 1 February 1952.

Anon. *Musaddiq va Nahzat-i Milli-yi Iran*. N.p., n.d.

Anon. 'Razha-yi Fash Nashudih az Vaqi'ih-yi 28 Murdad', *Ashuftih* IX,

1–13 (1954–5).

Anon. 'Nazari bih Yaddashtha-yi Qavam', *Khandaniha*, 23 September–6 November 1955.

Anon. *Musaddiq va Muvazinih-yi Manfi*. N.p.: Zibarjad Pbls, 1972.

Arsanjani, Hasan. 'Yaddashtha-yi Siyasiyi-Man', *Bamshad*, 11 June–26 November 1956.

———. *Yaddashtha-yi Siyasi, Si-um Tir 1331*. Tehran: Bamshad Pbls, 1956.

Atabaki, Mansur Ali and Bani-Ahmad, Ahmad. *Panj Ruz Rastakhiz-i Millat-i Iran*. Tehran, 1958.

Ayat, Sayyid Hasan. *Chihrih-yi Haqiqi-yi Musaddiq us-Saltanih*. Qum: Daftar-i Intisharat-i Islami, 1981.

Bahar, Muhammad Taqi (Malik ush-Shu'ara). 'Hizb-i Dimukrat-i Azarbaijan', *Iran-i Ma*, 16 September 1945.

———. *Divan-i Ash'ar*. 2 vols. Tehran: Amir Kabir, 1956.

———. *Tarikh-i Mukhtasar-i Ahzab-i Siyasi: Inqiraz-i Qajariyyih*. 1st edn 1944. Tehran, 1978.

———. *Tarikh-i Mukhtasar-i Ahzab-i Siyasi*. Vol. 2. Tehran: Amirkabir Pbls, 1984.

Bamdad, Mihdi. *Sharh-i hal-i rijal-i Iran dar qarn-i 12 va 13 va 14 Hijri*. 6 vols. Tehran, Zavvar Pbls, 1968.

Baqa'i-yi Kirmani, Muzaffar. *Man Namayandih-yi Kirman Hastam*. Tehran, May–June 1953.

Bihbudi, Sulayman. *Khatirat-i Sulayman Bihbudi*. Tehran, n.d.

Bihnia, Abdulhusain. *Pardihha-yi Siyasat*. Tehran, n.d.

Buzurg-Umid, Abulhasan. *Az Mast kih Bar Mast*. Tehran: 1957.

Davudi, Mihdi. *Qavam us-Saltanih*. Tehran, 1948.

Faramarzi, Abd ur-Rahman. 'Payam bih Pishihvari', *Kayhan*, 16 January 1946.

Farrukh, Sayyid Mihdi. *Khatirat-i Siyasi-yi Farrukh*. Ed. Parviz Laushani. Tehran: Sipihr Pbls, 1969.

Fatih, Mustafa. *Panjah Sal Naft-i Iran*. 1st edn 1956. Tehran: Kavush Pbls, n.d.

Furughi, Muhammad Ali. Text of a letter. *Rahnama-yi Kitab* XV, 10–12 (January–March 1973), 832–45.

———. 'Farhangistan Chist'. *Namih-yi Farhangistan* I, 1. (March–April 1943), 20–39.

Ghani, Cyrus (ed.) *Yaddashtha-yi Duktur Qasim-i Ghani*. 12 vols. London: Ithaca Press, 1980–4.

Gulsurkhi, Reza. 'Fida'iyan-i Islam', *Ittila'at*, 30 April 1979.

Hakimi, Ibrahim. 'Pasukh bih Namih-yi Qavam', *Bakhtar-i Imruz*, 8 April 1950.

Hasibi, Kazim. 'Chira Millat-i Iran Qararadad-i 1933 ra bih Rasmiyyat Nimishinasad', *Shahid*, 7 November, 13, 17, 22, 28 December 1949.

———. 'Muqayisih-yi Qarardad-i Naft-i Iran ba Qarardadha-yi Khavar-i

Miyanih', *Shahid*, 2, 3 September 1950.

Hidayat, Mihdi Quli. *Khatirat va Khatarat*. Tehran: Zavvar Pbls, 1965.

Hijazi, Sayyid Muhammad Baqir. *Ayandih-yi Iran*. Tehran: Vazifih Pbls, 1947.

Ihtishami, Abulhasan. *Bazigaran-i Siyasat*. Tehran: Imruz Pbls, 1949.

Intizam, Abdullah. 'Gushih'i az Vaqayi'-i Shahrivar', *Salnamih-yi Dunya* XIX

(1963), 155–8.

Ishaq, Eprim. *Chih Bayad Kard*. Tehran, 1946.

Isma'ili, Bahman. *Zindiginamih-yi Musaddiq us-Saltanih*. N.p., n.d.

Ja'fari-Alizadih, Ahmad. *Shuhada-yi Si-um-i Tirmah-i 1331*. Isfahan, 1952.

Janzadih, Ali. *Musaddiq*. Tehran: Hamgam Pbls, 1979.

Javanshir, F. M. *Tajribih-yi 28 Murdad*. Tehran: Tudeh Party Pbls, 1980.

Kambakhsh, Abd us-Samad. *Nazari bih Junbish-i Kargari va Kumunisti dar Iran*. 2 vols. Stockholm: Tudeh Party Pbls, 1972–4.

Kashani, Sayyid Mahmud. *Qiyam-i Millat-i Musalman-i Iran 30 Tir 1331*. Tehran: Khushih Pbls, 1980.

Katouzian, Muhammad Ali Humayun. *Khatirat-i Siyasi-yi Khalil-i Maliki*. Tehran: Ravaq Pbls, 1981.

Khajih-Nuri, Ibrahim. *Bazigaran-i Asr-i Tala'i: Davar, Taymurtash, Ayrum, Amir-Tahmasibi, Dashti*. Tehran, 1961.

——. *Bazigaran-i Asr-i Tala'i: Ali Suhaili*. Tehran: Javidan Pbls, 1977.

——. *Bazigaran-i Asr-i Tala'i: Sipahbud Amir-Ahmadi*. Tehran: Javidan Pbls, 1978.

Khal'atbari, Arsalan. 'Mas'ulin-i Daurih-yi Diktaturi', *Ra'd-i Imruz*, 19 February–2 March 1944.

——. 'Vizarat-i Jang va Siyasat', *Jibhih*, 5, 6 April 1946.

——. 'Duktur Musaddiq ra ki bih Zamin Zad', *Khandaniha*, 2 January 1954.

——. 'Duktur Musaddiq va Mas'alih-yi Naft', *Khandaniha*, 8 June 1954.

——. 'Asrari kih Ba'd az Chahar Sal Fash Shudih Ast', *Khandaniha*, 10 May 1955.

——. 'Agar Razmara An Namih ra Ifsha Mikard Kushtih Nimishud', *Khandaniha*, 22 May 1955.

——. 'Dakhil-i Dastgah-i Duktur Musaddiq chih Khabar Bud', *Khandaniha*, 7 October 1955.

Khamih'i, Anvar. *Panjah Nafar va Sih Nafar*. Tehran: Haftih Pbls, 1983.

——. *Fursat-i Buzurg-i az Dast Raftih*. Tehran: Haftih Pbls, 1983.

——. *Az Inshi'ab ta Kudita*. Tehran: Haftih Pbls, 1984.

Khan-Malik-i Yazdi, Muhammad. *Arzish-i Masa'i-yi Iran dar Jang 1939–1945*. Tehran, 1945.

Khushniyyat, Sayyid Husain. *Sayyid Mujtaba Navvab-Safavi, Andishihha, Mubarizat va Shahadat-i u*. Tehran: Manshur-i Baradari Pbls, 1981.

Kianuri, Nur ud-Din. *Hizb-i Tudeh-yi Iran va Duktur Muhammad Musaddiq*. Tehran: Tudeh Party Pbls, 1980.

Kishavarz, Firaydun. *Man Muttaham Mikunam*. Tehran: Ravaq Pbls, 1978.

Makki, Husain. 'Aqa-yi Ahmad Qavam', *Salnamih-yi Dunya* II (1948), 81–3.

——. 'Jibhih-yi Milli Chihgunih Tashkil Shud', *Khandaniha*, 2 October 1953.

Maliki, Ahmad. *Tarikhchih-yi Jibhih-yi Milli*. Tehran: Taban Pbls, 1953.

Maliki, Khalil. 'Sar-u-Tah-i Yik Karbas', *Rahbar*, 7, 8, 10 December 1944.

——. 'Ustrasism-i Rusiyyih', *Rahbar*, 18 December 1944.

——. *Du Ravish bara-yi Yik Hadaf*. Tehran, 1948.

——. 'Sarnivisht-i Tarikhi-yi Libiralism dar Du Qarn-i Akhir', *Ilm u Zindigi* I, 7 (August–September 1952).

——. 'Sharayit-i Idamih-yi Piruzmandanih-yi Nahzat-i Milli', *Ilm u Zindigi* I, 8 (September–October 1952).

——. 'Alami az Nau Bibayad Sakht', *Ilm u Zindigi* I, 9 (January–February 1953).

——. 'Mubarizih ba Buzurgtarin Khatari kih Nahzat-i Milli ra Tahdid Mikunad', *Ilm u Zindigi* II, 3 (May–June 1953).

——. 'Tahlil Mukhtasari az Guzashtih bara-yi Tarsim-i Rah-i Ayandih', *Nabard-i Zindigi* I, 10 (April–May 1956).

——. *Du Namih*. Tehran: Murvarid Pbls, 1979.

——. *Barkhurd-i Aqayid va Ara: Hizb-i Tudeh Chih Miguft va Chih Mikard?* Tehran: Taban Pbls, n.d.

Matin-Daftari, Ahmad. 'Fi'l ya Tark', *Salnamih-yi Dunya* XI (1955).

——. 'Khatirati az Intikhabat dar Iran', *Khandaniha*, 5 April 1956.

——. 'Majara-yi Intikhabat dar Iran', *Salnamih-yi Dunya* XII (1956).

Mas'udi, Qasim. *Jarayan-i Musafirat-i Misiun-i I'zami-yi Iran bi Muskau*. Tehran: Chap pbls, 1946.

Mihdiniya, Ja'far. *Zindigi-yi Siyasi-yi Razmara*. Tehran: Pasargad Pbls, 1984.

Mihrban, Rasul. *Gushihha'i az Tarikh-i Mu'asir-i Iran*. N.p.: Atarud Pbls, 1982.

Muhit-i Tabataba'i Muhammad. 'In ham Qavam us-Saltanih', *,Muhit* XIII, 5 December 1947.

Musaddiq, Muhammad. *Madarik-i Huquq-i Islami va Vasiyyat dar Mazhab-i Shi'ih*. Trans. from the French by Matin-Daftari et al. Tehran: Kalimiyan Pbls, 1923.

——. 'Intikhabat dar Iran va Urupa', 1 & 2, *Ayandih* III, 2–3 (1926).

——. 'Tarh-i Jadid bara-yi Islah-i Qanun-i Intikhabat', *Ayandih* III, 2 (September–October 1944).

Mushir, Murtiza (ed.) *Khatirat-i Allahyar Salih*. Tehran: Vahid Pbls, 1985.

Nafisi, Hasan (Musharraf). *Pasukh bih Izharat-i Aqa-yi Duktur Musaddiq*. Tehran: Taban Pbls, 1953.

Navab-Safavi, Sayyid Mujtaba. *Jami'ih va Hukumat-i Islami*. Tehran, 1978. 1st edn titled 'I'lamayyih-yi Fida'iyan-i Islam' was published in 1950.

Nijati, Ghulamreza. *Junbish-i Milli Shudan-i San'at-i Naft va Kudita-yi 28*

Murdad 1332. Tehran: Intishar Pbls, 1986.

Pishdad, Amir and Katouzian, M. A. H. *Milli Kist va Nahzat-i Milli Chist?* N.p., 1981.

Pishihvari, Ja'far. 'Sarguzasht-i Man', *Azhir*, 6 December 1943.

Pisiyan, Najaf Quli. *Marg bud Bazgasht ham bud.* Tehran, 1947.

Puria, Arsalan. *Karnamih-yi Musaddiq va Hizb-i Tudeh.* 2 vols. Florence: Mazdak Pbls, n.d.

Qadimi, Zabihullah. *Tarikh-i Bist-u Panj Salih-yi Artish-i Shahanshahi.* Tehran, 1947.

Qasimi, Abulfazl. *Tarikhchih-yi Jibhih-yi Milli.* Tehran: Iran Party Pbls, 1978.

———. *Uligarshi ya Khandanha-yi Hukumatgar dar Iran.* 4 vols. Tehran: Ruz Pbls, 1974–78.

Qasimzadih, Qasim. *Huquq-i Asasi.* 7th edn. Tehran: Ibn-i Sina Pbls, 1961.

Qavam, Ahmad. 'Arizih-yi Sargushadih', *Bakhtar-i Imruz*, 8 April 1950.

———. 'Pasukh bih Namih-yi Hakim ul-Mulk', *Bakhtar-i Imruz*, 3 July 1950.

Qurayshi, Hasan (ed.) *Chihrihha-yi Ashna.* Tehran: Kayhan Pbls, 1966.

Rahimi, Mustafa. *Qanun-i Asasi-yi Iran va Usul-i Dimukrasi.* Tehran, 1968.

Ra'in, Isma'il. *Asnad-i Khanih-yi Sidan.* Tehran: Bungah-i Tarjumih va Nashr-i Kitab, 1979.

——— (ed.). *Haft Sal dar Zindan-i Aryamihr: Yaddashtha-yi Shadravan Ahmad Aramish.* Tehran: Bungah-i Tarjumih va Nashr-i Kitab, 1979.

Ravandi, Murtiza. *Tafsir-i Qanun-i Asasi-yi Iran.* Tehran: Mubashshiri Pbls, 1978.

Rezazadih-Shafaq, Sadiq. *Khatirat-i Majlis va Dimukrasi Chist.* Tehran: Kayhan Pbls, 1955.

———. 'Khatirat-i Chand az Qavam us-Saltanih', *Khandaniha*, 23 January 1956.

Ruhani, Fuad. *Tarikhchih-yi Milli Shudan-i San'at-i Naft-i Iran.* Tehran, 1974.

———. *Zindigi-yi Siyasi-yi Musaddiq dar Matn-i Nahzat-i Milli-yi Iran.* London, 1985.

Sadr, Hasan. 'Qanun-i Tasfiyih', *Bakhtar-i Imruz*, 30 August 1950.

Sadr, Muhsin. 'Dastan-i Nakhust Vaziri-yi Man', *Salnamih-yi Dunya* XIV (1958).

———. *Khatirat-i Sadr ul-Ashraf.* Tehran: Vahid Pbls, 1985.

Safa'i, Abd us-Sahib. *Tarikh-i Mukhtasar-i Ahzab-i Siyasi pas az Shahrivar 1320.* N.p.: Iran Pbls, 1949.

Safa'i, Ibrahim. *Rahbaran-i Mashrutih.* Tehran: Javidan-i Ilmi Pbls, 1965.

———. *Rahbaran-i Mashrutih: Hakim ul-Mulk.* Tehran: Sharq Pbls, 1968.

———. *Namihha-yi Tarikhi.* Tehran, 1969.

———. *Rahbaran-i Mashrutih: Sa'id ul-Vizarih.* Tehran: Sharq Pbls, 1969.

———. *Rahbaran-i Mashrutih: Abdulhusain Hazhir.* Tehran: Sharq Pbls, 1969.

——. *Rahbaran-i Mashrutih: Sipahbud Razmara*. Tehran: Sharq Pbls, 1969.

Saulat-i Qashqa'i, Muhammad Nasir. *Salha-yi Buhran: Khatirat-i Ruzanihaz Farvardin 1329 ta Azar 1332*. Tehran: Rasa Pbls, 1987.

Sauti, Muhammad Ali (ed.) *Khatirat-i Duktur Qasim Ghani*. With an introduction by Bastani-Parizi. Tehran: Kavush Pbls, 1982.

Sayyah, Hamid. 'Qavam us-Saltanih dar Muskau', *Salnamih-yi Dunya* XVIII (1962), 103–6.

Shafa'i, Ahmad. *Qiyam-i Afsaran-i Khurasan, ya Si-yu-haft Sal Zindigi dar Shauravi*. Tehran: Kitabsara Pbls, 1986.

Shaji'i, Zahra. *Namayandigan-i Majlis-i Shaura-yi Milli dar bist-u-yik Daurih-yi Qanunguzari*. Tehran: Mu'assisih-yi Mutali'at va Tahqiqat-i Ijtima'i Pbls, 1965.

——. *Vizarat va Vaziran dar Iran*. Vol. 1. Tehran: Mu'assisih-yi Mutali'at va Tahqiqat-i Ijtima'i's Pbls, 1976.

Sharif, Ali Asghar. 'Sabiqih-yi Tarikhi-yi Hukumat-i Nizami', *Kanun-i Vukala* XI–XIII, 69–73, 76 (January 1959–July 1961).

Sharif-Imami, Ja'far. 'Daulat-i Sipahbud Razmara', *Salnamih-yi Dunya* XIX (1963), 72–5.

Sipihr, Ahmad Ali (Muvarrikh ud-Daulih). 'Qiyam-i Pishihvari', *Salnamih-yi Dunya* XIV (1958), 124–7.

——. *Maqalat-i Siyasi*. Tehran: Ata'i Pbls, 1962.

Tabari, Ihsan. 'Nazar-i Ma dar barih-yi Hizb-i Dimukrat-i Iran', *Rahbar*, 17 July 1946.

——. *Kazhrahih: Khatirati az Hizb-i, Tudeh*. Tehran: Amir Kabir Pbls, 1987.

Tabataba'i, Sayyid Zia ud-Din. 'Interview', *Iqdam*, 28 January 1943.

——. *Sha'a'ir-i Milli*. Tehran, 1943.

Tafazzuli, Mahmud. *Musaddiq, Naft, Kudita*. Tehran: Amir Kabir Pbls, 1978.

Tafrishiyan, Abulhasan. *Qiyam-i Afsaran-i Khurasan*. Sweden: Kanun-i Kitab, n.d.

Tahuri, Abd ur-Rahim. *Sarabi bih Nam-i Hizb-i Tudeh-yi Iran*. Tehran: 1979.

Taqizadih, Sayyid Hasan. *Mukhtasar-i Tarikh-i Majlis-i Milli-yi Iran*. Berlin: Kavih Pbls, 1919.

Tavana'iyan-i Fard, Hasan. *Musaddiq va Iqtisad*. Tehran: Agah Pbls, 1981.

Turkaman, Muhammad. *Tashannujat, Dargiriha-yi Khiyabani va Taut'ihha dar Dauran-i Hukumat-i Duktur Muhammad Musaddiq*. Tehran: Rasa Pbls, 1980.

——. (ed.) *Qiyam-i Milli si-um-i Tir bih Ravayat-i Asnad va Tasavir*. Tehran, 1983.

——. *Asnadi Piramun-i Tauti'ih-yi Rubudan va Qatl-i Sarlashkar Afshartus*. Tehran: Rasa Pbls, 1984.

Vahidi, Sayyid Muhammad. 'Khatirat-i Fida'iyan-i Islam', *Khandaniha*, 23 September–14 November 1955.

Vusuq, Sipahbud Ahmad. *Dastan-i Zindigani: Khatirati az Panjah Sal Tarikh-i Mu'asir, 1290–1340 (1911–1961)*. Tehran, n.d.
Vusuq, Ali. *Chahar Fasl dar Tafannun va Tarikh*. Tehran, 1982.
Zargham-Burujini, Jamshid. *Daulatha-yi Asr-i Mashrutiyyat*. Tehran, 1971.

D. Books and articles in other languages

Abrahamian, Ervand. 'The crowd in Iranian politics 1905–1953', *Past and Present* XLI (December 1968), 184–210.
——. 'Communism and communalism in Iran: the Tudeh and the Firqah-i Dimukrat', *International Journal of Middle Eastern Studies*, I, 4 (October 1970), 291–316.
——. 'Factionalism in Iran: political groups in the 14th Parliament (1944–6)', *Middle Eastern Studies* XIV, 1 (January 1978), 22–55.
——. 'The strength and weaknesses of the labour movement in Iran in 1941–53', in *Continuity and Change in Modern Iran*. Ed. Michael Bonine and Nikkie Keddie. Albany, NY: State Univ. of New York Press, 1981.
——. *Iran Between Two Revolutions*. Princeton: Princeton Univ. Press, 1982.
Acheson, Dean. *Present at the Creation: My Years in the State Department*. New York: W. W. Norton, 1969.
Akhavi, Shahrough. *Religion and Politics in Contemporary Iran: Clergy–State Relations in the Pahlavi Period*. Albany, NY: SUNY Press, 1980.
Amirsadeghi, Hossein and Ferrier, R. W. (eds). *Twentieth Century Iran*. London: Heinemann, 1977.
Andreski, Stanislav. *The African Predicament*. London: Michael Joseph, 1968. Arfa, General Hassan. *Under Five Shahs*. London: John Murray, 1964.
Atyeo, H. C. 'Political developments in Iran 1951–1954', *Middle Eastern Affairs* V, 8–9 (August–September 1954), 249–59.
Bialer, Uri. 'The Iranian connection in Israel's foreign policy, 1948–1951', *Middle East Journal* XXXIX, (Spring 1985), 292–315.
Banani, Amin. *The Modernization of Iran, 1921–1941*. Stanford, CA: Stanford Univ. Press, 1961.
Banton, Michael (ed.) *Political Systems and the Distribution of Power*. London: Tavistock Pbls, 1965.
Banuazizi, Ali. 'Iranian "national character": a critique of some Western perspectives', in L. Carl Brown and Norman Istkovitz (eds), *Psychological Dimensions of Near Eastern Studies*. Princeton: Darwin Press, 1977, pp. 210–39.
Barth, Fredrik. *Nomads of South Persia: the Basseri Tribe of the Khamsah Confederation*. Oslo: Univ. Press. London: Allen and Unwin, 1961.
Bayne, Edward A. *Persian Kingship in Transition: Conversations with a*

Monarch Whose Office is Traditional and Whose Goal is Modernization. New York: American Universities Field Staff, 1968.

Beck, Lois. *The Qashqa'i of Iran.* New Haven and London: Yale Univ. Press, 1986.

Benedict, Ruth. *Patterns of Culture.* 1st edn 1935. London: Routledge and Kegan Paul, 1968.

Bharier, Julian. *Economic Development in Iran, 1900–1978.* London and New York: Oxford Univ. Press, 1971.

——. 'The growth of towns and villages in Iran, 1900–66', *Middle Eastern Studies* VIII, 1 (January 1972), 51–61.

Bill, James Alban. 'The social and economic foundations of power in contemporary Iran', *The Middle East Journal* XVII, 4 (Autumn 1963), 400–18.

——. 'Modernization and reform from above: the case of Iran', *Journal of Politics* XXXII, 1 (1970), 19–40.

——. 'The politics of legislative monarchy: the Iranian Majlis', in *Comparative Legislative Systems: a Reader in Theory and Research.* Ed. Herbert Hirsch and M. Donald Hancock. New York: Free Press, 1971, 360–9.

——. *The Politics of Iran. Groups, Classes and Modernization.* Columbus, Ohio: Charles E. Merrill, 1972.

——. *The Eagle and the Lion: the Tragedy of American–Iranian Relations.* New York and London: Yale Univ. Press, 1988.

Binder, Leonard. *Iran: Political Development in a Changing Society.* Berkeley and Los Angeles: Univ. of California Press, 1962.

——. 'The Cabinet of Iran: a case study in institutional adaptation', *The Middle East Journal* XVI, 1 (Winter 1962), 29–47.

Birch, A. H. *Representation.* London: Macmillan, 1971.

Blondel, Jean. *Contemporary France: Politics, Society and Institutions.* London: Methuen, 1972.

Bonine, Michael and Keddie, Nikki R. (eds). *Modern Iran: the Dialectics of Continuity and Change.* Paperback edn: *Continuity and Change in Modern Iran.* Albany, NY: SUNY Press, 1981.

Bullard, Sir Reader. *The Camels Must Go: an Autobiography.* London: Faber and Faber, 1961.

——. 'Persia in the Two World Wars', *Journal of the Royal Central Asian Society* L (1963). 6–20.

Bullock, Alan. *Ernest Bevin: Foreign Secretary 1945–1951.* London: Heinemann, 1983.

Byrnes, James F. *Speaking Frankly.* London and Toronto: William Heinemann, 1947.

Carlton, David. *Anthony Eden: a Biography.* London: Allen Lane, 1981.

Chaliand, Gerard (ed.) *People Without a Country: the Kurds and Kurdistan.* London: Zed Press, 1980.

Cohen, Abner. *Two Dimensional Man: an Essay on the Anthropology of*

Power and Symbolism in Complex Society. London: Routledge and Kegan Paul, 1974.

Cottam, Richard W. 'Political party development in Iran', *Iranian Studies* I, 3 (Summer 1968), 82–95.

———. 'The United States, Iran and the cold war', *Iranian Studies* III, 1 (Winter 1970), 2–22.

———. *Nationalism in Iran; Updated through 1978*. 2nd edn. Pittsburgh: Univ. of Pittsburgh Press, 1979.

Cruise O'Brien, Donal. *Saints and Politicians: Essays in the Organisation of Senegalese Peasant Society*. Cambridge: Cambridge Univ. Press, 1975.

D'Erme, G. 'I Partici politici in Persia del 1941–1944', *Oriente Moderno* L, 3 (March 1971), 213–35.

Diba, Farhad. *Mohammed Mosadegh: a Political Biography*. London and Dover: Croom Helm, 1986.

Doenecke, Justus D. 'Revisionists, oil and cold war diplomacy', *Iranian Studies* III, 1 (Winter 1970), 23–33.

Douglas, William Orville. *Strange Lands and Friendly People*. New York: Harper and Row, 1951.

Dunn, John (ed.) *West African States: Failure and Promise*. Cambridge: Cambridge Univ. Press, 1978.

Eagleton, William Jr. *The Kurdish Republic of 1946*. London and New York: Oxford Univ. Press, 1963.

Eden, Anthony. *Memoirs: Full Circle*. London: Cassell, 1960.

Efimenco, N. Marbury. 'An experiment with civilian dictatorship in Iran: the case of Muhammad Mussadegh', *Journal of Politics* XVII, 3 (August 1955), 390–406.

Eisenstadt, S. N. and Lemarchand, René (eds). *Political Clientelism, Patronage and Development*. Beverly Hills, CA: Sage, 1982.

Elwell-Sutton, P. 'Political parties in Iran: 1941–1948', *The Middle East Journal* III, 1 (January 1949), 45–62.

———. 'Nationalism and neutralism in Iran', *The Middle East Journal* XII, 1 (Winter 1958), 20–32.

———. 'The Iranian press, 1941–1947', *Iran* VI (1968), 65–104.

———. *Persian Oil: a Study in Power Politics*. London: Lawrence and Wishart, 1955.

Enayat, Hamid. *Modern Islamic Political Thought*. London: Macmillan, 1982.

Eshraqi, F. 'Anglo-Soviet occupation of Iran in August 1941', *Middle Eastern Studies* XX, 1 (January 1984), 27–52.

Fatemi, Nasrullah. *Diplomatic History of Persia, 1917–1923*. New York: Russell F. Moore, 1952.

Ferrier, R. W. *The History of the British Petroleum Company: the Developing Years, 1901–1932*. Vol. I. Cambridge: Cambridge Univ. Press, 1982.

Fillippani-Ronconi, Pio. 'The tradition of sacred kingship in Iran', in *Iran Under the Pahlavis*. Ed. George Lenczowski. Stanford, CA: The Hoover Institution, 1978.

Floor, Willem, M. 'The revolutionary character of the ulama: wishful thinking or reality?', in Nikki, R. Keddie (ed.), *Religion and Politics in Iran*. New Haven and London: Yale Univ. Press, 1983, 73–97.

Foot, Michael. 'The devious way of Mr Ghavam', *Daily Herald*, 24 April 1946.

Frye, Richard. 'Charisma of kingship in ancient Iran', *Iranica Antiqua* IV (1964), 36–54.

Garrod, Oliver. 'The nomadic tribes of Persia today', *Journal of the Royal Central Asian Society* XXXIII, 1 (January 1946), 32–46.

———. 'The Qashqai tribe of Fars', *Journal of the Royal Central Asian Society* XXXIII, 3–4 (July–October 1946), 293–306.

Garthwaite, Gene. *Khans and Shahs: the Bakhtiari in Iran*. Cambridge: Cambridge Univ. Press, 1984.

Gasiorowski, Mark. 'The 1953 *coup d'etat* in Iran', *International Journal of Middle East Studies*, XIX (August 1987), 261–86.

Ghani, Cyrus. *Iran and the West: a Critical Bibliography*. London and New York: Kegan Paul International, 1987.

Giannini, A. 'La Costituzione persiana', *Oriente Moderno* II, 7 (July 1931), 317–34.

Gellner, Ernest. *Nations and Nationalism*. Oxford: Basil Blackwell, 1983.

Gellner, E. and Ionescu, G. (eds). *Populism, its Meanings and National Characteristics*. London: Weidenfeld and Nicolson, 1969.

Gellner, E. and Waterbury, J. *Patrons and Clients in Mediterranean Societies*. London: Duckworth, 1977.

Giddens, Anthony. *A Contemporary Critique of Historical Materialism*. London: Macmillan, 1981.

Goffman, Erving. *The Presentation of Self in Everyday Life*. Harmondsworth: Penguin, 1971.

———. *Encounters*. Harmondsworth: Penguin, 1972.

———. *Strategic Interaction*. Oxford: Basil Blackwell, 1972.

Goodell, Grace E. *The Elementary Structure of Political Life: Rural Development in Pahlavi Iran*. New York and Oxford: Oxford Univ. Press, 1986.

Gramsci, Antonio. *Selections from the Prison Notebooks*. London: Lawrence and Wishart, 1971.

Grué, B. 'Le Rôle social de l'armée en Iran', *Orient* XXIV (1962), 49–54.

Hamzavi, A. H. 'Iran and the Tehran Conference', *International Affairs* XX, 2 (April 1944), 192–203.

———. *Persia and the Powers*. London: Hutchinson, 1946.

Harris, Franklin S. 'The beginnings of Point IV work in Iran', *The Middle East Journal* VII, 2 (Spring 1953), 222–8.

Homayounpour, Parviz. *L'Affaire d'Azarbaïdjan*. Lausanne, 1967.

Jeffries, Richard. 'Revolution in Black Africa', in Noel O'Sullivan (ed.), *Revolutionary Theory and Political Reality*. Brighton: Wheatsheaf Books, 1983.

Jones, Geoffrey. *Banking and Empire in Iran: the History of the British Bank of the Middle East*. Vol. I, Cambridge and New York: Cambridge Univ. Press, 1986.

Katouzian, Homa. *The Political Economy of Modern Iran*. London: Macmillan, 1981.

Kazemi, Farhad. 'The military and politics in Iran: the uneasy symbiosis', in Elie Kedourie and Sylvia Haim (eds), *Towards a Modern Iran*. London: Frank Cass, 1980.

Keddie, Nikki (ed.) *Scholars, Saints and Sufis: Muslim Religious Institutions Since 1500*. Berkeley and Los Angeles: Univ. of California Press, 1972.

——. *Iran: Religion, Politics and Society*. London and Ottowa, NJ: Frank Cass, 1980.

——. *Roots of Revolution*. New Haven and London: Yale Univ. Press, 1981.

—— (ed.) *Religion and Politics in Iran: Shi'ism from Quietism to Revolution*. New Haven and London: Yale Univ. Press, 1983.

Kemp, Norman. *Abadan: a First-hand Account of the Persian Oil Crisis*. London: Allan Wingate, 1953.

Kuniholm, Bruce R. *The Origins of the Cold War in the Middle East: Great Power Conflict and Diplomacy in Iran, Turkey and Greece*. Princeton: Princeton Univ. Press, 1980.

Ladjevardi, Habib. 'The origins of U.S. support for an autocratic Iran', *International Journal of Middle East Studies* XV (May 1983), 225–39.

——. *Labor Unions and Autocracy in Iran*. Syracuse, NY: Syracuse Univ. Press, 1985.

Lambton, A. K. S. 'Some of the problems facing Persia', *International Affairs* XXII, 2 (April 1946), 254–72.

——. 'The impact of the West on Persia', *International Affairs* 33, 1 (January 1957), 12–25.

——. *The Persian Land Reform, 1962–1966*. Oxford: Clarendon Press, 1969.

Lapping, Brian. *End of Empire*. London: Granada, 1985.

Lenczowski, George. 'The communist movement in Iran', *The Middle East Journal* I, 1 (January 1949), 29–45.

——. *Russia and the West in Iran, 1918–1948: a Study in Big-Power Rivalry*. Ithaca, NY: Cornell Univ. Press, 1949.

——. 'Iran: nationalism erupts', *Current History* 21 (July 1953).

Littlewood, Paul. 'Patronage, ideology and reproduction', in *Critique of Anthropology* 15, 4 (Spring 1980), 29–45.

Lockhart, Laurence. 'The causes of the Anglo-Persian oil dispute', *Journal of the Royal Central Asian Society* XL, 2 (April 1953), 134–50.

——. 'The constitutional laws of Persia: an outline of their origin and development', *The Middle East Journal* XIII, 4 (Autumn 1958), 372–88.

Louis, Wm Roger. *The British Empire in the Middle East 1945–1951.* Oxford: Oxford Univ. Press, 1984.

Louis, Wm Roger, and Bill, James A. (eds). *Musaddiq, Iranian Nationalism, and Oil.* London: I. B. Tauris, 1988.

Lukes, Steven. *Essays in Social Theory.* London: Macmillan, 1977.

——. 'Power and authority', in Tom Bottomore and Robert Nisbet (eds), *A History of Sociological Analysis.* London: Heinemann, 1978.

——. *Power: a Radical View.* London: Macmillan, 1979.

——. 'On the relativity of power', in S. C. Brown (ed.), *Philosophical Disputes in the Social Sciences.* Brighton: Harvester, 1979.

Lytle, Mark H. *The Origins of the Iranian–American Alliance.* New York: Holmes and Meier, 1987.

Machalski, Francis. 'Political parties in Iran in the years 1941–1946', *Folia Orientalia* III, 1–2 (1961), 135–70.

Mahdavi, H. 'The patterns and problems of economic development in rentier states: the case of Iran'. In M. A. Cook (ed.), *Studies in the Economic History of the Middle East.* London: Oxford Univ. Press, 1970.

McGhee, George. *Envoy to the Middle World: Adventures in Diplomacy.* New York: Harper & Row, 1983.

Mehdevi, Anne Sinclair. *Persian Adventure.* London: Victor Gollancz, 1953.

Miller, William Green. 'Political organization in Iran: from Dowreh to political party – I', *The Middle East Journal* XXIII, 2 (Spring 1969), 159–67; Part II, XXIII, 3 (Summer 1969), 343–50.

Millspaugh, Arthur Chester. *Americans in Persia.* Washington: Brookings Institution, 1946; repr. edn. New York: Da Capo Press, 1976.

Mills, C. Wright. *The Power Elite.* New York: Oxford Univ. Press, 1959.

Misri, B. A. 'The Kurdish struggle for autonomous existence', *The Islamic Review* LIII, 4 (April 1965), 8–11; 5 (May 1965), 29–32.

Miyata, Osmau. 'The Tudeh military network during the oil nationalization period', *Middle Eastern Studies* XXIII, 3 (July 1987), 313–28.

Moore, Barrington Jr. *Social Origins of Dictatorship and Democracy: Lord and Peasant in the Making of the Modern World.* Harmondsworth: Penguin, 1973.

Nairn, Tom. *The Break-up of Britain: Crisis and Neo-Nationalism.* London: New Left Books, 1977.

Naraghi, Ehsan. 'Elite ancienne et élite nouvelle dans l'Iran actuel, avec une note sur le système d'éducation', *Revue des Etudes Islamiques* XXV (1957), 69–80.

Oberling, Pierre. *The Qashqa'i Nomads of Fars.* The Hague: Mouton, 1974.

Olson, Wm J. *Anglo-Iranian Relations During World War I.* London: Frank Cass, 1984.

Pahlavi, Ashraf. *Faces in a Mirror: Memoirs from Exile.* Englewood Cliff,

NJ: Prentice-Hall, 1980.

Pahlavi, Mohammad Reza. *Mission for My Country*. New York: McGraw-Hill, 1961.

——. *Answer to History*. Briarcliffe Manor, NY: Stein and Day, 1980.

Parkin, Frank. *Class, Inequality and Political Order*. London: Paladin, 1972.

Poggi, Gianfranco. *The Development of the Modern State*. London: Hutchinson, 1978.

——. 'Clientelism', *Political Studies* XXXI (1983), 662–7.

Ramazani, Rouhollah K. *Iran's Foreign Policy 1941–1973: a Study of Foreign Policy in Modernizing Nations*. Charlottesville, VA: Univ. Press of Virgina, 1975.

Rezun, Miron. *The Soviet Union and Iran*. Geneva: Institut Universitaire des Hautes Etudes Internationales, 1981.

Richard, Yann. 'Ayatollah Kashani: precursor of the Islamic Republic?' in Nikki R. Keddie (ed.), *Religion and Politics in Iran*. New Haven and London, 1983, 101–24.

Ricks, Thomas M. 'U.S. Military Missions to Iran', *Iranian Studies* 3–4 (Summer–Autumn 1979), 163–94.

Roosevelt, Archie Jr. 'The Kurdish republic of Mahabad', *The Middle East Journal* I, 3 (July 1947), 247–69.

Roosevelt, Kermit. *Countercoup: the Struggle for Control of Iran*. New York: McGraw-Hill, 1979, 1980.

Rossow, Robert Jr. 'The battle of Azarbaijan, 1946', *The Middle East Journal* X, 1 (Winter 1956), 17–32.

Rubin, Barry. *Paved with Good Intentions: the American Experience in Iran*. New York and Oxford: Oxford Univ. Press, 1980.

Samii, Kuross A. 'Truman against Stalin in Iran: a tale of three messages', *Middle Eastern Studies* XXIII, 1 (January 1987), 95–107.

Savory, Roger M. 'The principle of homeostasis considered in relation to political events in Iran in the 1960's', *International Journal of Middle East Studies* III, 3 (July 1972), 282–302.

Scarcia, Gianroberto. 'La Persia durante la seconda guerra mondiale: materiali e documenti', *Oriente Moderno* XLVI, 5–12 (May–December 1966), 269–343.

Schmidt, Steffen W. et al. (eds). *Friends, Followers, and Factions: a Reader in Political Clientelism*. Berkeley: Univ. of California Press, 1977.

Shwadran, B. 'The Anglo-Iranian oil dispute 1948–1953', *Middle East Affairs* V, 6–7 (June–July 1954), 193–231.

Sinclair, Angus. 'Iranian oil', *Middle East Affairs* II, 6–7 (June–July 1951), 213–24.

Skrine, Sir Clarmont. 'Iran revisited', *Journal of the Royal Central Asian Society* XLV, 3–4 (July–October 1958), 218–32.

——. *World War in Iran*. London: Constable, 1962.

Springborg, Robert. *Family, Power and Politics in Egypt*. Philadelphia: Univ. of Pennsylvania Press, 1982.

Stanworth, Philip and Giddens, Anthony (eds). *Elites and Power in British Society*. Cambridge: Cambridge Univ. Press, 1974.

Thorpe, James A. 'Truman's ultimatum on the 1946 Azarbaijan crisis: the making of a myth', *Journal of Politics*, 4, (February 1978).

Truman, Harry S. *Memoirs: Years of Trial and Hope, 1946–1952*. New York: Garden City, 1956.

Van Wagenen, Richard W. *United Nations Action: the Iranian Case 1946*. New York: Carnegie Endowment for International Peace, 1952.

Walters, Vernon A. *Silent Missions*. New York: Doubleday, 1978.

Waterbury, John. *The Commander of the Faithful, the Moroccan Political Elite – a Study in Segmented Politics*. London: Weidenfeld and Nicolson, 1970.

Wilber, Donald N. *Riza Shah Pahlavi: the Resurrection and Reconstruction of Iran: 1878–1944*. Hicksville, NY: Exposition Press, 1975.

Wolf, Eric. 'Kinship, friendship and patron–client relations in complex societies', in Michael Banton (ed.), *The Social Anthropology of Complex Societies*. London, 1966.

Woodhouse, C. M. *Something Ventured*. London, Toronto, Sydney, New York: Granada, 1982.

Young, T. Cuyler. 'The problem of Westernization in modern Iran', *The Middle East Journal* II, 1 (January 1948), 47–59.

——. 'The social support of current Iranian policy', *The Middle East Journal* VI, 2 (Spring 1952), 125–43.

Zabih, Sepehr. *The Communist Movement in Iran*. Berkeley and Los Angeles: Univ. of California Press, 1966.

——. *The Mossadegh Era: Roots of the Iranian Revolution*. Chicago, Ill.: Lake View Press, 1982.

Zonis, Marvin. 'Political elites and political cynicism in Iran', *Comparative Political Studies* I, 3 (October 1968), 351–72.

——. *The Political Elite of Iran*. Princeton: Princeton Univ. Press, 1971.

——. 'The political elite of Iran: a second stratum?', in Frank Tauchau (ed.), *Political Elites and Political Development in the Middle East*. New York: Schenkman, 1975, 193–216.

E. Theses and dissertations

Abrahamian, Ervand. 'Social Basis of Iranian Politics: the Tudeh Party 1941–53'. Ph.D. thesis, Columbia University, 1969.

Agah, M. 'Some Aspects of Economic Development of Modern Iran'. D.Phil. thesis, University of Oxford, 1965.

Ettehadieh Nezam-Mafi, Mansoureh. 'Origin and Development of Political Parties in Persia 1906–1911'. Ph.D. thesis, University of Edinburgh, 1979.

Enayat, Hamid. 'The British Public Opinion and the Persian Oil Crisis'.

M.Sc. dissertation, University of London, 1958

Faghfoory, Mohammad Hassan. 'The Role of the Ulama in Twentieth Century Iran with Particular Reference to Ayatullah Haj Sayyid Abul-Qasim Kashani'. Ph.D. dissertation, University of Wisconsin, Madison, 1978.

Gasiorowsky, Mark. 'U.S. Foreign Policy and the Client State: Implications for Domestic Politics and Long-Term U.S. Interests in Iran'. Ph.D. dissertation, University of North Carolina at Chapel Hill, 1984.

Ghoreishi, Ahmad. 'Soviet Foreign Policy in Iran 1917–1966'. Ph.D. thesis, University of Colorado, 1965.

Hekmat. H. 'Iran's Response to Soviet–American Rivalry, 1951–1961: a Comparative Study'. Ph.D. thesis, University of Columbia, 1974.

Khodayar–Mohebbi, Manoutchehr. L'Influence religieuse sur le droit constitutionnel de l'Iran. Thèse, Université de Paris, 1957. Imprimerie Taban, Tehran, 1958.

Ladjevardi, Habib. 'Politics and Labour in Iran'. D.Phil. thesis, University of Oxford, 1981.

Malik-Mahdavi, Ahmad. 'Le Parlement Iranien'. Thèse, Université de Neuchâtel, 1954.

Modjtehedi, M. 'La Question d'Azarbaidjan: la Mouvement des Democrats et les efforts de l'O.N.U.' Doctoral thesis, University of Paris, 1952.

Mohammadi-Nejad, Hassan. 'Elite-Counterelite Conflict and the Development of a Revolutionary Movement: the Case of the Iranian National Front'. Ph.D. thesis, Southern Illinois University, 1970.

Mojdehi, Hassan. 'Arthur C. Millspaugh's Two Missions to Iran and Their Impact on American–Iranian Relations'. Ph.D. thesis, Ball State University, 1975.

Tabari, Keyvan. 'Iran's Policies towards the United States During The Anglo-Russian Occupation 1941–46'. Ph.D. thesis, Columbia University, 1967.

Tavallali, Djamchid. 'Le Parlement Iranien'. Thèse, Université de Lausanne, 1954.

Thorpe, J. 'The Mission of Arthur C. Millspaugh to Iran 1943–1945'. Ph.D. thesis, University of Wisconsin, 1973.

F. Newspapers

Iranian

The following newspapers are daily, published in Tehran and available for the entire period 1941–53 unless otherwise indicated.

Asr 1949–52.

Azarbaijan (in Turkish) bi-weekly, Tabriz, 1941–6.

Azhir thrice weekly, 1943–4.

Bakhtar-i Imruz 1949–53.
Bi su-yi Ayandih 1950–3.
Dad 1942–60.
Dimukrat-i Iran 1946–8.
Iran-i Ma 1943–53.
Iqdam 1941–3.
Ittila'at.
Jibhih 1945–8.
Jibhih-yi Azadi 1950–3.
Journal de Tehran (in French).
Kayhan 1942– .
Mard-i Asia 1952–3.
Mard-i Imruz weekly, 1942–52.
Mardum daily, later irregular, 1944–53.
Rahbar 1943–6.
Ra'd-i Imruz 1943–5.
Rasti thrice weekly, Mashhad, 1943–5.
Razm daily, later irregular, 1943–8.
Shahid weekly, later daily, 1946–54.
Sitarih.
Tulu' 1949–52.
Vazifih 1944–62.

Non-Iranian

Daily Herald.
Daily Telegraph.
Daily Worker.
Le Monde.
Manchester Guardian.
New York Times.
Observer.
Scotsman.
The Times.

Supplementary Bibliography

Due to constraints of space I have confined myself to selected items in English and Persian.

In English

Azimi, Fakhreddin. *The Quest for Democracy in Iran: A Century of Struggle Against Authoritarian Rule*. Cambridge, Mass & London: Harvard University Press, 2008.
——. 'Unseating Mosaddeq: the Configuration and Role of Domestic Forces', in Gasiorowski, Mark & Malcolm Byrne (eds). *The Coup of August 1953 In Iran*. New York: Syracuse University Press, 2004.
——. 'On Shaky Ground: Concerning the Absence or Weakness of Political Parties in Iran', *Iranian Studies*, vol. 30, nos. 1–2 (Winter–Spring 1997–8), pp. 53–75.
——. 'British Influence in Persia: 1941–79', *Encyclopaedia Iranica*, vol. XI, Fascicle 3, pp. 234–46.
——. 'Elections under the Qajar and Pahlavi monarchies', *Encyclopaedia Iranica*, vol. VIII, Fascicle 4, pp. 345–50.
Bamburg, J. H. *The History of the British Petroleum Company*, vol. 2, *The Anglo-Iranian Years, 1928–1954*. Cambridge: Cambridge University Press, 1994.
Behrooz, Maziar. *Rebels with a Cause: the Failure of the Left in Iran*. London: I.B.Tauris, 1999.
Brands, H. W. *Inside the Cold War: Loy Henderson and the Rise of the American Empire, 1918–1961*. New York: Oxford University Press, 1991.
Bullard, Reader. *Letters from Tehran*, ed. E. C. Hodgkin. London and New York: I.B.Tauris, 1991.
Elm, Mustafa. *Oil, Power and Principle: Iran's Oil Nationalization and its Aftermath*. New York: Syracuse University Press, 1992.
Fawcett, Louise L'Estrange. *Iran and the Cold War: The Azarbaijan Crisis of 1946*. Cambridge: Cambridge University Press, 1992.
Foreign Relations of the United States, 1952–54, vol. X., Washington DC, 1989.
Gasiorowski, Mark & Malcolm Byrne (eds). *Mohammad Mosaddeq and The Coup of August 1953 in Iran*. New York: Syracuse University Press, 2004.
Goode, James F. *The United States and Iran: In the Shadow of Musaddiq*. New York: St. Martin's Press, 1997.

Heiss, Mary Ann. *Empire and Nationhood: The United States, Great Britain and Iranian Oil, 1950–54.* New York: Columbia University Press, 1997.

Jarman, R. L. (ed.). *Iran: Political Diaries, 1881–1965,* 14 vols. Slough, UK: Archive Editions Limited, 1997.

Katouzian, Homa. *Musaddiq and the Struggle for Power in Iran.* London: I.B.Tauris, 1990.

Meier, Daniela. 'Between Court Jester and Spy: The Career of a Swiss Gardener at the Royal Court in Iran. A footnote to Modern Iranian History', *Critique,* Spring 2000, no. 16, pp. 75–88.

Siavoshi, Sussan. *Liberal Nationalism in Iran: The Failure of A Movement.* Boulder, CO: Westview Press, 1990.

Wilber, Donald. *Candestine Service History: Overthrow of Premier Mossadeq of Iran, November 1952–August 1953,* (1954).

Zahidi, Ardishir. 'Five Decisive Days, August 14–18, 1953', mimeograph, n.d.

In Persian

Abadian, Husain. *Zindiginamih-yi Siasi-yi Duktur Muzaffar Baqa'i.* Tehran: Mu'assisih-yi Mutali'at va Pazhuhish-ha-yi Siasi, 1998.

Abbasi, Muhammad Reza, and Bihruz Tayarani (eds). *Khatirat-i Nasrullah Intizam.* Tehran: Sazman-i Asnad-i Milli-yi Iran Pbls., 1992.

Afshar, Iraj (ed.). *Parvandih-yi Salih.* Tehran: Ketab-i Raushan Pbls., 2005.

——. (ed.). *Zindigi-yi Tufani: Khatirat-i Sayyid Hasan Taqizadih.* Tehran: Ilmi Pbls., 1993.

——. *Namihha-yi Landan: Az Dawran-i Sifarat-i Taqizadih dar Ingilistan.* Tehran: Farzan Pbls., 1996.

——. *Namihha-yi Tehran.* Tehran: Farzan Pbls., 2000.

——. 'Namih-yi Kashani bih Musaddiq az Nigah-i Sanadshinasi', in Mahdavi, Yahya and Iraj Afshar. *Haftad Maqalih,* vol. 1., Tehran: Asatir Pbls., 1990.

'Ala, Husain, Daily reports to the Shah, text in *Tarikh-i Mu'asir-i Iran,* vol. I, no. 2, summer 1997, pp. 130–74.

Amu'i, Muhammad Ali. *Durd-i Zamanih.* Tehran: Anzan Pbls., 1998.

Azimi, Fakhreddin. *Hakimiyat milli va dushmanan-i an: pazhuhishi dar karnamih-yi mokhalifan-i bumi va biganih-yi Musaddiq.* Tehran: Nigarih-yi Aftab Pbls. 2004.

——. 'Intikhabat bidun-i Haqq-i Intikhab? Intikhabat-i Parlimani va Tadavum-i Farhang-i Siasi dar Iran', *Negah-e Nau,* no. 42, Fall 1999, pp. 13–47.

——. *Ta'ammuli dar Nigarish-i Siasi-yi Musaddiq.* Tehran: Khojastih Pbls. forthcoming.

Bihzadi, Ali. *Shibh-i Khatirat.* 2 vols., Tehran: Zarrin Pbls., 1996, 1998.

Burhan, Abdullah. *Nahzat-i Milli-yi Iran va Idalat-i Ijtima'i.* Tehran: Markaz Pbls., 1999.

——. *Karnamih-yi Hizb-i Tudeh va Raz-i Suqut-i Musaddiq.* Tehran: Ilm Pbls., 2000.

——. 'Aya Qatilan-i Afshartus shikanjih shudand?', *Negah-i Nau,* vol. 25, August–September 1995, pp. 48–87.

Markaz-i Barrasi-yi Asnad-i Tarikhi-yi Vizarat-i Ittila'at. *Azad Mard: Shahid Tayyib Haj Riza'i bih Rivayat-i Asnad-i Savak*. Tehran: 1999.

——. *Sayri dar Nahzat-i Milli Shudan-i Naft: Khatirat-i Shams Qanatabadi*. Tehran, 1998.

——. *Rauhani-yi Mubariz: Ayatullah Sayyid Abulqasim Kashani bih Ravayat-i Asnad*. Tehran, 2000.

Davani, Ali, et. al. (eds). *Khatirat va Mubarizat-i Hujjat al-Islam Falsafi*. Tehran: Markaz-i Asnad-i Inqilab-i Islami Pbls., 1997.

Dihbashi, Ali. (ed.). *Namihha-yi Jalal Al-i Ahmad*. Tehran: Buzurgmihr Pbls., 1988.

Gul-Muhammadi, Ahmad. *Jam'iyat-i Fida'iyan-i Islam bih Ravayat-i Asnad*, 2 vols., Tehran: Markaz-i Asnad-i Inqilab-i Islami Pbls, 2004.

Gulsha'iyan, Abbas Quli. *Guzashtihha va Andishihha-yi Zindigi, ya Khatirat-i Man*, 2 vols., Tehran: Einstein Pbls., 1998.

Ibtihaj, Abulhasan. *Khatirat-i Abulhasan Ibtihaj*, 2 vols. London: 1991.

Iraqi, Mihdi, *Naguftihha: Khatirat-i Shahid Haj Mihdi Iraqi*. Tehran: Rasa Pbls., 1991.

Ja'farian, Rasul (ed.). *Buhran-i Azarbaijan (Salha-yi 1324-1325): Khatirat-i Mirza Abdullah Mujtahidi*. Tehran: Muassisih-yi Mutali'at-i Tarikh-i Mu'asir Pbls., 2002.

Kianuri, Nur ud-Din. *Khatirat-i Nur ud-Din Kianuri*. Tehran: Ittila'at Pbls., 1992.

Kishavarz-Sadr, Hushang, and Hamid Akbari (eds). *Tajribih-yi Musaddiq dar Chishmandaz-i Ayandih-yi Iran*. Bethesda, MD: Ibex Pbls., 2005.

Kuhistani-Nizhad, Mas'ud. *Hizb-i Iran*. Tehran: Shirazih Pbls., 2000.

Ladjevardi, Habib (ed.). *Khatirat-i Shapur Bakhtiar*. Iranian Oral History Project, Bethesda, MD, 1996.

——. (ed.). *Khatirat-i Ali Amini*. Iranian Oral History Project, Bethesda, MD, 1995.

Makki, Husain. *Khatirat-i Siasi-yi Husain Makki*. Tehran: Ilmi Pbls., 1989.

——. *Kudita-yi 28 Murdad-i 1332*. Tehran: Ilmi Pbls., 1999.

[Matin-Daftari, Hedayat (ed.)]. *Vizhih-yi Musaddiq: Yadvarih-yi Panjahumin [Sal-i] Milli Shudan-i Naft: Tashkil-i Daulat-i Musaddiq*, Azadi, vol. 2, nos. 26–7, 2001.

Musaddiq, Ghulam Husain. *Dar Kinar-i Pidaram*. Tehran: Rasa Pbls., 1990.

Musavvar-Rahmani, Ghulam Reza. *Kuhnih Sarbaz: Khatirat-i Siasi va Nizami*. Tehran: Rasa Pbls., 1988.

Muvahhid, Muhammad Ali. *Khab-i Ashuftih-yi Naft: Duktur Musaddiq va Nahzat-i Milli-yi Iran*, 2 vols. Tehran: Karnamih Pbls., 1999.

Nijati, Ghulam Reza (ed.). *Shast Sal Khidmat va Muqavimat: Khatirat-i Muhandis Mihdi Bazargan*, 2 vols. Tehran: Rasa Pbls., 1998.

——. *Musaddiq: Salha-yi Mubarizih va Muqavimat*, 2 vols. Tehran: Rasa Pbls., 1997.

Pakdaman, Nasir. *Qatl-i Kasravi*. Germany: Foruq Pbls., 2001.

Pichdad, Amir and Homa Katouzian. *Namihha-yi Khalil Maliki*. Tehran: Nashr-i Markazi, 2002.

Rahimi, Mustafa. 'Musaddiq va Hizb-i Tudeh', *Ittila'at-e Siasi va Iqtisadi*. vol. 13, nos. 7–8, 1999, pp. 9–82.

Rahnima, Ali. *Niruha-yi Mazhabi bar Bastar-i Harakat-i Nahzat-i Milli*. Tehran. Gam-e Nau Pbls., 2005.

Rasulipur, Murtiza (ed.). *Nagoftihha'i az Daulat-i Duktur Musaddiq*, Tehran, Nazar Pbls., 2001.

Riahi, Manuchihr. *Sharab-i Zindigi*. Tehran: Tehran Pbls., 1992.

Sadiqi, Ghulam Husain. 'Ruz-i Kudita', *Dunya-yi Sukhan*, 13, no. 75 (August–September 1997).

Safari, Muhammad Ali. *Qalam va Siasat*, vol. I. Tehran: Namak Pbls., 1992.

Sahabi, Izzatullah. *Musaddiq, Daulat-i Milli va Kudita*. Tehran: Tarh-i Nau, 2001.

Sanjabi, Karim. *Umidha va Na-umidiha*. London: Jibhih Pbls., 1989.

Sarrishtih, (Col.) Husainquli. *Khatirat-i Man*. Tehran, 1988.

Sarshar, Homa (ed.). *Sha'ban Ja'fari*. Los Angeles: Nab Pbls., 2002.

Shayigan, Ahmad (ed.). *Sayyid Ali Shayigan: Zindiginamih-yi Siasi: Nivishtihha va Sukhanraniha*. 2 vols., Tehran: Agah Pbls., 2005.

Tafrishi, Majid, and Mahmud Tahir Ahmadi (eds). *Guzarishha-yi Mahramanih-yi Shahrbani*. 2 vols., Tehran: Sazman-i Asnad-i Milli-yi Iran Pbls., 1992.

Tayarani, Bihruz (ed.). *Asnad-i Ahzab-i Siasi-yi Iran*, 2 vols. Tehran: Sazman-i Asnad-i Milli-yi Iran Pbls., 1997.

Turbati-Sanjabi, Mahmud. *Kuditasazan*. Tehran: Farhang-i Kavush Pbls., 1997.

Turkaman, Muhammad. *Bih Yad-i Shahid Duktur Husain Fatimi*. Tehran: Hazaran Pbls., 1995.

——. *Namihha-yi Duktur Musaddiq*, 2 vols. Tehran: Hazaran Pbls., 1995–8.

Varqa, Mashallah, *Nagoftihha'i piramun-i forurizi-yi hukumat-i Musaddiq, va naqsh-i hizb-i Tudeh-yi Iran*. Tehran: Baztab Nigar Pbls., 2005.

Zargari-Nizhad, Ghulam Husain. *Khatirat-i Nakhustin Sipahbud-i Iran: Ahmad Amir-Ahmadi*, 2 vols. Tehran: Mu'assasih-yi Pazhuhish va Mutali'at-i Farhangi, 1994.

Zirakzadih, Ahmad. *Pursishha-yi bi Pasukh dar Salha-ye Istisna'i: Khatirat-i Muhandis Ahmad Zirakzadih*. Tehran: Nilufar Pbls., 1997.

Index

427